ALLIES AGAINST
TWO EVILS

Georgian P.O.W.s in World War II's "Bergmann" Units
and the Quest to Liberate the Caucasus from
Russian Imperialism

ALLIES AGAINST TWO EVILS

Georgian P.O.W.s in World War II's "Bergmann" Units
and the Quest to Liberate the Caucasus from
Russian Imperialism

By Dr. Givi Gabliani, MD

DoppelHouse Press | Los Angeles

Editing: Carrie Paterson and Gregory Gabliani
Book design: Alexandre Venancio
Typesetting: Carrie Paterson

Publisher's Cataloging-in-Publication data

Names: Gabliani, Givi, author.
Title: Allies against two evils : Georgian P.O.W.s in World War II's "Bergmann" units and the quest to liberate the Caucasus from Russian imperialism / By Dr. Givi Gabliani, MD.
Description: Includes bibliographical references and index. | Los Angeles, CA: DoppelHouse Press, 2023.
Identifiers: LCCN: 2023940998 | ISBN: 9781954600249 (hardcover) | 9781954600911 (paperback) | 9781954600232 (ebook)
Subjects: LCSH Germany. Heer. Sonderverband Bergmann. | World War, 1939-1945--Regimental histories--Germany. | World War, 1939-1945--Caucasus. | World War, 1939-1945--Campaigns--Eastern Front. | Caucasus--History--20th century. | Georgia (Republic)--History--20th century. | BISAC BIOGRAPHY & AUTOBIOGRAPHY / Military | BIOGRAPHY & AUTOBIOGRAPHY / Personal Memoirs | HISTORY / Wars & Conflicts / World War II / Eastern Front | POLITICAL SCIENCE / World / Russian & Former Soviet Union
Classification: LCC D757.4 .G33 2023 | DDC 940.54/21--dc23

 DoppelHouse Press | Los Angeles, California

Contents

Contents continued

Preface to the Memoirs of Givi Gabliani

Until shortly before the end of the last century, when the Iron Curtain divided the world into two "camps," one could have heard countless incredible stories about Givi Gabliani in Georgia. They were told with a mysterious mien and in whispers. In the listener, his name did not evoke the idea of a real, but rather of a mythical person, so that one was not sure whether there really was a Givi Gabliani or whether the collective imagination had invented him as a hero in order to take revenge on the imposed communist order and the hated political police; that is, the KGB.

For example, it was said that Givi Gabliani, overcome by homesickness, sneaked into the Soviet Union under an invented name and with a false passport without any difficulty, traveled through Georgia, spent a few days in his native village, and only then quietly left the country for America. It was also said that the KGB was doing its best to trap and kidnap him, that it was recruiting killers to take him out, but that it was always unlucky and never reached its goal. Thus, even as a schoolboy, I heard an exciting story that my cousin, five years my senior, had told me in confidence: Givi Gabliani owned a Caucasian shepherd dog that would lie quietly beside his master's desk in his doctor's office and guard it faithfully. It would be enough if the KGB agent disguised as a patient entered the room even with one step—the clever animal would recognize the enemy in an instant and neutralize him with one jump.

It is probably not surprising that in my younger years I hardly believed in the existence of a real Givi Gabliani.

On the other hand, I knew very well that there were other people who had the name Gabliani and who really existed. Two of them, both no longer alive, enjoyed a particularly high reputation among the young people of my generation.

The famous mountaineer Iliko Gabliani had suffered a fatal accident in August 1961 while descending a few hours after climbing the highest peak of the *Heaven Mountain* range, the 7,439-meter *Tomur Peak*. The northernmost seven-thousand-meter peak in the world, called *Iron Peak* in China, bore the name given to it in 1946 in Kyrgyzstan, which was then part of the Soviet Union, in reference to its victory in World War II: *Victory Peak*. In addition to Iliko Gabliani, the summit had claimed the lives of two other Georgian climbers, both of whom were buried in Tbilisi's Didube Pantheon—in the cemetery where the nation's most distinguished representatives rest. The respect for youthful bravery and boldness expressed by this gesture evoked in us a romantic enthusiasm for the selflessness of the deceased, especially since the whole story was accompanied by a certain mystery: Iliko Gabliani's friends failed to bring him down, so he rested in the highest of all tombs, in a place closest to heaven, on a peak whose name at the same time commemorated the victims of the war. It was only much later that I learned that Iliko Gabliani was Givi Gabliani's cousin, son of Givi's father's brother.

For the other Gabliani, the ethnologist and archaeologist Egnate Gabliani (1881–1937), we young people had a deep admiration mainly because, as it was said, he was one of the leaders of the anti-Bolshevik uprising in 1924. However, this was only talked about at home or among close friends, because talking about Egnate Gabliani in the "open" was dangerous, not because the Soviet government had declared him an "enemy of the people" and sentenced him to death (almost all those executed in the Soviet Union during the "Great Purge" of 1937–1938 were rehabilitated after Stalin's death, so that their names were no longer taboo), but because his son... was a certain Givi Gabliani, a doctor living in the USA.

> "During Adenauer's first trip to America I was secretary-general of his delegation. We stopped briefly in Chicago on 14 and 15 April, 1953, where we stayed, incongruously, at the Bismarck Hotel. While there, I received an unexpected telephone call from Givi, now a doctor in the United States. He told me that he wanted to see me, and also wanted to meet Chancellor Adenauer, whom he considered to be a great man. When I mentioned this to Adenauer, the Chancellor seemed delighted and within the day these two figures from such different phases of Germany's recent history shook hands."

This is an excerpt from the book *Between Hitler and Stalin* by Hans-Heinrich von Herwarth (1904–1999). The quotation is revealing, because here three persons are depicted together, who were driven all their lives by one goal, the welfare of their homelands, even if at first sight they were destined to go opposite ways.

H.-H. Herwarth, a well-known diplomat who after the war represented the Federal Republic of Germany first in the United Kingdom and then in Italy as Ambassador, served as Attaché as well as the Second Secretary of the German Embassy in Moscow from 1931–1939. For Herwarth, who had a close friendship with the Moscow-based American diplomats George F. Kennan, Charles E. Bohlen, and Charles W. Thayer, Bolshevism and Nazism were equally hateful. This was the reason why in August 1939 he leaked the secret protocol on the partition of Poland, signed by the Soviet Union and Germany, to his American friends in order to prevent with the help of the United States the realization of said plan, which in his opinion would lead Germany to ruin. In 1939 Herwarth was promoted to the Abwehr, from where he sent the Wehrmacht plan of attack on the Soviet Union to the Allies in the fall of 1940. According to Herwarth, the failure of the Nazis was the only chance of survival for Germany. That is why he tried to shake the principles of the regime from within. In the words of Sir Fitzroy Maclean, Herwarth was a "patriotic German, strong and truly anti-national socialist."

The chancellor mentioned in the quote, the first head of the government of the Federal Republic of Germany, Konrad Adenauer (1876–1967), is one of the most important politicians in the recent history of Europe. In 1933, Adenauer was mayor of Cologne and has remained unforgettable not only for this city, but for the whole of Germany, after he demonstratively refused to receive the newly crowned Chancellor of the Reich, Adolf Hitler, at the airfield. Even more, as if this were not hard enough: he refused the request to decorate the bridges with swastika flags. Four weeks later he was removed from the mayor's office and was no longer allowed to hold an official post. After Hitler's assassination attempt in July 1944, Adenauer, who was one of the active politicians of the Weimar Republic and thus a suspect for the new regime, was arrested by the Gestapo. Today, he is still thanked in Germany for the efforts he made to free German prisoners of war from Bolshevik camps.

As for the third member of the trio, Givi Gabliani, it is remarkable that the Chancellor took time to meet with him, when every minute of his state visit to America was strictly regulated by protocol.

Givi Gabliani, already a doctor in America at the time of Adenauer's visit, is, to use Herwarth's phrase, considered a figure of recent German history. Throughout the war, he was a kindred spirit and comrade-in-arms of those German officers who opposed the National Socialist ideology and Hitler's inhuman policies. However, he, who in the summer of 1941 was none other than a prisoner of war and a little later a former Soviet soldier who had defected to the enemy side, together with his compatriots who came from faraway Georgia, also—and actually above all—fought against Bolshevism and Stalinist terror.

"During World War II, an unofficial alliance came about between a group of influential anti-Hitler Germans and anti-Stalin Georgians and other Easteners. They were caught between those two evils. A world without oppression became their common quest," writes Givi Gabliani in the Foreword to his "Memoirs." There could have been no better description of the atmosphere that prevailed in the Caucasian Legion of the Wehrmacht, the "Bergmann" Company, where Germans and Georgians in German uniforms fought shoulder to shoulder.

The "Memoirs" of Givi Gabliani is a unique historical document that sheds light on many aspects of World War II that have remained unknown or under-examined by researchers. Moreover, it is an honest and masterfully narrated adventure of a multi-talented personality as well as of an entire generation that had to experience the calamity of war firsthand.

* * *

Georgia, whose population is barely four million, is comparable in area to the state of West Virginia. It became visible on the political map of the modern world only thirty years ago, after the disintegration of the Soviet Union. Until then, however, for the whole seventy years, Georgia, belonging to the Soviet Union, was nothing other than Russia in the imagination of foreigners, so that it was hardly known outside a narrow circle of experts that, for example, Georgian is a completely different language from Russian, that Georgian has its own alphabet, which is neither Cyrillic nor Greek nor Latin nor Arabic nor anything else, that the literature written in this language with these letters looks back on a sixteen-century-old history, and that, finally, already in the first third of the 4th century, Christianity was declared the state religion of Georgians.

The easternmost country bordering the Black Sea lies on the threshold between Europe and Asia. It borders on the Russian Federation, Turkey, Armenia and Azerbaijan. In the north, the country is framed by the Caucasian mountain range. In one of the most famous ancient Greek myths these mountains appear in a big way. It is the Caucasus to which, by Zeus's order, *Prometheus* is chained because he stole fire from the gods to bring it to mankind. Prometheus is condemned to eternal suffering: Every day an eagle seeks out the captive Prometheus and eats from his liver, which is always renewed.

The setting of another no less popular myth, the saga of the *Argonauts*, is the South Caucasian coastal country of *Colchis*, i.e. the western part of Georgia. The legend is about the voyage of *Jason* and his companions from Greece to Colchis. The travel companions are called Argonauts after their ship, the *Argo*. The aim of the Argonauts is to steal the *Golden Fleece*, which the Colchian king *Aeëtes* has chosen the ever-watchful and never-sleeping dragon to protect. With the help of the king's daughter *Medea*, who falls in love with Jason, the Argonauts succeed in capturing the Golden Fleece. Jason marries Medea and takes her to Greece. From ancient authors such as Apollonius of Rhodes and Euripides to modern writers and artists, Medea remains an inexhaustible source of inspiration.

Western Georgian *Colchis* and Eastern Georgian *Iberia*, both geostrategically important and both surrounded by powerful states, represented the target of incessant attacks and raids, which led them to be under the influence of quite different empires in different eras: Rome, Sassanid Empire, Caliphate, Byzantium.

At the end of the 10th century the united Georgian Kingdom was formed, whose "Golden Age" arrived at the beginning of the 12th century and lasted until the first quarter of the 13th century.

During this period, a comprehensive church reform was carried out and a regular army was created. Academies, precursors of Western European universities, were founded, one of which, the *Gelati* Monastic Academy, was called "the second Jerusalem and the other Athens" by a medieval chronicler. *King David IV* (1089–1125), known as "the Builder," could be considered as the true symbol of Georgia at that time. This extraordinarily clever and brave strategist, who fought as an army commander against Seljuks and Arabs shoulder to shoulder with his soldiers on the battlefield, is said, according to the chroniclers' descriptions, to have always gone to war accompanied by a part of his extensive library carried by camels and mules. He, an Orthodox Christian, ensured that not only Georgians and other diophysite Christians, but also Muslims, Jews and monophysite Armenians enjoyed equal rights in his empire.

During the reign of David, as well as of his successors, especially the female "king of kings and queen of queens" *Tamar* (1184–1213), unique examples of church architecture, mural painting, polyphonic chant and court poetry were created. In the 12th century, the epic "The Knight in Tiger's Skin" by *Shota Rustaveli*, the poetic work belonging to the treasures of the world literature, was created.

The conquest and sacking of the Georgian capital Tbilisi in 1226 by the army of Jalal ad-Din, Shah of Khwarazm, a once powerful empire on the territory of today's Uzbekistan and Turkmenistan, who had fled from Mongols, marked the beginning of the disintegration of the Georgian kingdom. However, the inhabitants

Tetnuldi peak towering over the Gabliani's village of
Mulakhi in Svaneti, Georgia. Photo by Jim Irwin.

of the country could not come to terms with the foreign rule. It is known from the
history of the country that there were, for example, a total of eight uprisings against
Timur Leng (Tamerlane), who was known for his proverbial brutality, although the
suppression of each uprising brought immense destruction and looting.

In the early 17th century, in 1616, the Persian Shah Abbas I deported 200,000
people from eastern Georgia to Persia. In the 18th century, Georgia fragmented into
several small kingdoms and principalities.

In 1783, when the British Empire signed the *Treaty of Paris*, thus recognizing
the United States, a "Treaty of Friendship" was signed in the North Caucasian
fortress of *Georgievsk*, according to which the East Georgian kingship of *Kartli-
Kakheti* placed itself under the protection of the Russian Empire. Although the treaty
envisaged not the weakening but the strengthening of the Georgian kingship, in
1801 the Russian Empire declared it one of its governorates. The gradual appropri-
ation of remaining Georgian lands, thus set in motion, was successfully completed
by the Russian Empire in the second half of the 19th century. In 1853, *Svaneti*, the
most mountainous of all Georgian provinces, was also annexed.

In Svaneti, in a picturesque village called *Mulakhi* passed the childhood of
Givi Gabliani.

Mulakhi is located at the foot of *Tetnuldi*, one of the most spectacular mountains of the Caucasus. According to a Svan legend, the mountain peak Tetnuldi,
covered with eternal snow, is a virgin, and the gloomy mountain *Ushba*, rising in the
distance opposite her, is a young man. They are, of course, in love with each other.

From year to year the number of tourists who come to Georgia from different
parts of the world is increasing. To a great extent, Svaneti is "to blame" for this. As

if attracted by a magnet, visitors are attracted both by the "creations" of nature, such as mountains of rare beauty, and by the centuries-old creations of man, such as extended family towers, which cannot be found in this form anywhere else [see pages 428–429]. In addition, there are churches from the 10th–12th centuries with ancient frescoes and icons. But if the traveler also hears the polyphonic Svanian songs and gets to know some legends from the inexhaustible Svanian folklore treasure chest, he is overcome by a feeling of being in a fairy tale world.

Givi Gabliani's father devoted all his knowledge and skills to the study of the history and folklore of Svaneti, which a hundred years ago was difficult to reach and cut off from the outside world, to the meticulous description of the customs and habits of the people living here, to the scientific study of Svanian, a script-less language related to Georgian (not a dialect!) and, above all, to the effort to improve the living conditions of the people of Svaneti.

Egnate Gabliani graduated from one of the most prestigious universities of the Russian Empire, the Saint-Petersburg University, from the Faculty of Oriental Studies. Remarkably, his mentor, Professor *Nikolai Marr* (1865–1934), was also from Georgia. Incidentally, the Georgian Professor Marr was appointed Dean of the mentioned Faculty in 1911 and a full member of the Russian Academy of Sciences the following year. In 1914, Professor Marr even received the rank of Real State Councilor and thus the right to be addressed as "Your Excellency." Although the professor's native language was Georgian, teaching at the university was conducted only in Russian. This means that Egnate Gabliani was also fluent in written and spoken Russian, which was not at all a matter of course at that time.

After graduation, he returned to Svaneti to serve as a provincial commissioner for over ten years. His wife Vera, née Tevzadze, also came from Svaneti and worked there, though later in Tbilisi, as a primary school teacher.

On December 19, 1915, their son Givi was born.

This period is a particularly dramatic period in the recent history of Georgia.

The war that broke out on the European continent in 1914 and soon became a world war led to great upheavals in the Russian Empire. In 1917, the Tsar abdicated, the monarchy was dissolved, and in October of that year, the Bolsheviks led by *Vladimir Ilyich Lenin (Ulyanov)* (1870–1924) seized political power in Russia.

Georgia, no longer part of the Russian Empire, celebrated the regaining of long-awaited freedom. On February 8, 1918, the first Georgian university was founded in Tbilisi. On May 26, the Democratic Republic of Georgia was proclaimed and the elections of the Constituent Assembly of Georgia were held. The Social Democratic Party won the elections with a large majority. Thus, Georgia became the first social-democratically governed state. Five women were elected to the legislative body, which was something unimaginable in international politics at that time. On May 7, 1920, a treaty was signed between the Georgian Democratic Republic and the Russian Soviet Federative Socialist Republic (RSFSR). Russia recognized the sovereignty of Georgia. This was a real celebration. The centuries-long dream of the Georgian people became a reality. Georgia was filled with great hope for the future and enormous creative energy.

All of a sudden, the hustle and bustle city of Tbilisi turned into a place of attraction for artists. During the First World War, and especially after the Bolshevik coup d'etat, which was called the *Great October Socialist Revolution*, many inhabitants of Moscow and St. Petersburg, especially artists, were forced to leave their home-towns and homeland to find a more peaceful place to live. Many rushed to Georgia. Apart from them, artists who came from other cultural backgrounds—Polish, Ukrainian, German, Armenian—gathered in Tbilisi. However, they were all received with sincere hospitality by Georgian writers, painters, musicians and actors.

Amazingly quickly, an extremely dynamic and diverse multilingual cultural scene emerged. Quite naturally, as if by itself, the new "nickname" of Tbilisi also emerged: *The Fantastic City*.

"Tbilisi is imbued with an aesthetic perception of the world. That's how the city was in the past, that's how it is today. ... One can mention many names. They are all united by art. People of different nations and different cultures are brothers in art. We believe in this new 'International'. Here in Tbilisi the foundation for its construction is to be laid," wrote in 1919 the mentor of the Georgian symbolists, members of the poetic order "Blue Drinking Horns," *Grigol Robakidze* (1882–1962), who, however, counted himself among the representatives of "mythical realism."

"We are united in hostile friendship," wrote the Russian Futurist *Igor Terentiev* (1892–1937) half-jokingly in the same year, when he reported on the competition between artists belonging to different currents and competing with each other.

Even the provinces far away from the capital, which did not really suffer from the absence during their membership in the Russian Empire—and instead were grateful for being cut off from the outside world, i.e. the hated administration—now felt a sincere desire to integrate. The Svans once again elected Egnate Gabliani as speaker for Svaneti. On February 12, 1919, together with a group of Svanetian representatives, he visited Georgian Prime Minister *Noe Jordania* (1868–1953) and presented him with a report on the situation and concerns of Svaneti. The most important request that Egnate Gabliani submitted to the Georgian head of govern-ment on behalf of all Svanetians was to arrange for the construction of roads to Svaneti.

The whole country was as if reborn and full of desire for growth.

One can easily imagine the grief and disappointment of the people that would have been caused by another loss of political independence: on February 25, 1921, the Red Army of Soviet Russia invaded Georgia and occupied the capital Tbilisi.

The Georgian Bolsheviks seized power. The entire government, as well as the majority of the members of anti-Bolshevik political parties, left the country for France, Germany or Switzerland. No one would have been surprised if Egnate Gabliani, a member of the Socialist-Federalist Party, was among the emigrants: his political sympathies belonged to those who went into exile and not to those who had taken the lead.

However, Egnate Gabliani decided to stay.

Already in 1921, even before they came to Georgia, the Red Army occupied Armenia and Azerbaijan. In March 1922, the Transcaucasian Federation was established, uniting Armenian, Azerbaijani and Georgian Soviet Socialist Republics.

After the seizure of power, the main concern of the Bolsheviks was the restoration of the disintegrated empire, not with emperors, of course, but under the dictatorship of the proletariat (the last Tsar Nicholas II was shot together with his wife, three daughters and minor son on July 17, 1918).

On December 30, 1922, the Union of Soviet Socialist Republics was founded. This now had to include, in addition to the Russian Federation (RSFSR), the Ukrainian Soviet Socialist Republic and the Belarusian Soviet Socialist Republic, the Transcaucasian Federation.

If one were to think of Georgian history, one might assume that the country would have begun to prepare for an uprising. That is what happened. Together with some younger comrades-in-arms, Egnate Gabliani, already over forty, took on the task of organizing the resistance in Svaneti.

The protest movement started in Svaneti as early as 1921, but a real uprising did not occur until 1924, when the Committee for the Independence of Georgia called for an armed uprising against the Bolsheviks on August 29.

The uprising failed. The insurgents were severely punished. Egnate Gabliani faced the death penalty. However, since the execution of the man who enjoyed the highest confidence of the Svans could lead to new unrest, the government decided to reconcile with him: In the summer of 1925 he was sentenced to three years' imprisonment "under extraordinary isolation," but in view of a decision of the

Central Executive Committee of the Soviet Union, taken later that March, he was exempted from punishment.

In contrast to Egnate Gabliani, some Georgians were even decorated in 1924—for their contribution to the suppression of the uprising. One young man in particular stood out, a twenty-five-year-old Chekist—that's what the members of the Soviet secret police were called—Lavrentiy Beria, who was awarded the Order of the Red Banner, the government's highest honor at the time. This is the *Lavrentiy Pavlovich Beria* who, barely fifteen years later, at the end of 1938, would be brought to Moscow by his older compatriot, the Georgian *Joseph Stalin (Dzhugashvili)*. Stalin would appoint him as Minister of the Interior of the Soviet Union, but after the course of another barely fifteen years, in June 1953 very soon after Stalin's death, Beria would be overthrown, arrested and executed by the rest of the elite of the Communist Party of the Soviet Union.

Looking at Bolshevik nationalities policy from the mid-1920s to the mid-1930s, one is inclined to note a certain paradox of the period, namely, that colonization initiated and stimulated the very process of decolonization.

This phase of the Soviet Union's existence is referred to in historical research as the stage of Nation building (rus. *nacionaljnoe stroiteljstvo*). Soviet nationality policy of the 1920s headed toward having the national i.e. non-Russian parts of the Soviet Union led by the national cadres, "since the newly formed Russian leaders were insufficient to direct the newly formed vast empire" (Hélène Carrère d'Encausse). By the mid-1930s, the push-back against the Russian language, Russian cadres, and Russian culture was the official party line. The goal was set to create nations. Thus, Anastas Mikoyan, a high-ranking party official, in June 1925 stated: "The most original thing is that Soviet power, the most internationalist of all governments, is indeed forming and organizing new nations."

In the opinion of Stalin, who was the People's Commissar for Nationalities Affairs of the RSFSR until 1923 and who was considered the main expert on the national problem, having one's own language was one of the (four) main characteristics of a nation. It followed that the policy of national construction had to take care of national languages. This naturally included promotion of the printed word as well as theater and film in the national language.

The other main characteristic of a nation, according to Stalin's theory, is the possession of its own territory. And so he gained a support for the new 'Union'. The borders of republics, federations, subjects of federations—in short, of *nations*—were deliberately designed in such a way that there was enough fuel for conflicts of all against all. Thus, each nation had to enlist the support of its "elder brother," i.e. the

Russian nation, in case things got serious. The older brother, on the other hand, made sure that things never got serious. The classical formula "Devide et impera" served as a basic principle in the new empire.

All political parties in Georgia, in spite of their opponents and, in part, their mutual enmity, were characterized by one common feature: The goal of each of them was the sustainability of actual Georgian culture. This meant the establishment of an educational system and the promotion of culture and science in Georgia that would be based not on the foreign, Russian, but on their own, Georgian, language. Georgian language had been successively displaced from all spheres of life throughout the 19th century, and for its rescue, *Ilia Chavchavadze* (1837–1907), the leader of the national liberation movement, initiated the establishment in 1879 of a society for the dissemination of literacy among Georgians.

In addition to the nationalities policy of the Soviet government, there was another factor assisting the shaping of national culture, namely Soviet literary and cultural policy. If the nationalities policy was the work of Stalin, behind the literary policy were party greats such as *Leon Trotsky* (1879–1940) and *Anatoly Lunacharsky* (1875–1933). If one wanted to characterize Soviet literary policy in the 1920s in one word, *liberal* would probably be the most appropriate. "Since the party did not want a cultural revolution, it allowed censorship to be generous and to apply only to 'counterrevolutionary' material, and freedom was preserved in the artistic sphere" (Karl Eimermacher).

So it happened that the writers, artists and scientists who had not emigrated, regardless of their political sympathies and antipathies, seized the existing opportunity and began to use it with great enthusiasm. In the first third of the 20th century, an extremely diverse literary, artistic, theatrical and film production was created in Georgia, as well as a complete terminology for all fields of science was elaborated. Studies in all higher education institutions were now conducted in Georgian for all disciplines in all faculties of humanities, natural sciences and engineering.

Egnate Gabliani was one of the most significant participants and supporters of this process. During this period, the highly talented ethnologist published several famous books: *The Old and New Svaneti* (1925), *Free Svaneti* (1927), and *Ibex in the Mountains of Svaneti* (1930). At his request, the Ethnographic-Historical Museum of Svaneti was founded in 1936, and he was entrusted with its management by the Soviet government. On his initiative the first passable road to *Mestia*, the district center of Svaneti, was built. All the important personalities, politicians, businessmen, journalists, artists, and scientists who visited Svaneti found a gracious host and advisor in the person of Egnate Gabliani and his family. Egnate's son Givi, who knew the emigrated Georgians very well from his father's stories, maintained personal and sometimes very cordial relations with the VIPs living in Soviet Georgia since his school days.

The cultural and nationality policy was accompanied and in a certain sense supported by the liberal *New Economic Policy*, abbreviated *NEP*, which included a partial restoration of the capitalist market economy and a legalization of different forms of ownership. On the one hand, peasants were allowed to freely sell the products they had left after fulfilling the levy—thirty percent of the harvest belonged to the state—and, on the other hand, foreign entrepreneurs were offered to invest in the Soviet Union, so that the numerous concessions thus created greatly improved living conditions for the workers.

The originator of this policy was Lenin himself, although after his death *Nikolay Bukharin* (1888–1938) emerged as the most ardent advocate of the NEP. His appeal to the peasants became almost an aphorism: "Enrich yourselves, accumulate, develop your economy!"

And it was precisely the NEP that was affected by restrictions before all other policies. In 1929 an all-encompassing collectivization was announced in the Soviet Union, which meant the unification of individual farms and economies into collective and Soviet economies (abbreviated *kolkhoz* and *sovkhoz*), i.e. the abolition of private property by collective property. This *Great Turning Point* (J. Stalin) could be achieved only with the help of an extremely painful and sometimes bloody process of so-called decollectivization: Peasants who resisted the transfer of their property to collective farms were subjected to brutal repressive measures, including the death penalty.

In 1931, free trade was banned by law, officially sealing the end of New Economic Policy. One more family joined the Georgian emigration in Germany that year. The above-mentioned author Grigol Robakidze, whose novel was published in Germany in 1928 with a preface by Stefan Zweig and who was invited to Germany with his wife and daughter in 1931, did not return to the Soviet Union. (Incidentally, Grigol Robakidze had a close friendship with Egnate Gabliani—this is also reported in the present memoirs—and it was Egnate Gabliani from whom the writer received the valuable information about the customs and traditions of Svaneti when he was working on one of his Caucasian novellas). For Grigol Robakidze, the end of the NEP was an indication that the liberal cultural policy would soon come to an end.

In 1932 *Maxim Gorky* (1868–1936), a friend of Lenin and Stalin, returned to Soviet Russia from many years of exile. Gorky, who had been nominated for the Nobel Prize three times between 1918 and 1928, received the Order of Lenin in Moscow and a request from Stalin to prepare a meeting of Soviet writers. A few months before Gorky's arrival, the term Socialist Realism appeared in the Soviet press. But the 1st Writers' Congress, held in the late summer of 1934 under Maxim Gorky's chairmanship, declared Socialist Realism the only approved form of Soviet literature and united the writers "scattered" in various associations under the umbrella of a *Writers' Union*, which from now on functioned as the only officially recognized and approved association for writers. "This is nothing but a kolkhoz," wrote the famous Russian author Mikhail Prishvin in his diary. Shortly thereafter, a witticism began to circulate: *litkolkhos* ("literary collective economy"), which, however, was superseded by an even more sarcastic pun, *elitkolkhos*.

On December 5, 1936, the 7th Extraordinary Congress of Soviets in Moscow adopted the new Constitution of the Soviet Union. This event acquired the significance of a symbol. The so-called liberal phase was now finally over and the period of terror, the *Great Purge* of 1937–1938, was ushered in, replacing the liberal policy of nationalities with a policy of extermination of the national elites. A single example should suffice to illustrate this: Two members from Georgia were elected to the board of the aforementioned Writers' Union of the USSR, both of whom were executed in 1937.

On July 1, 1937, Egnate Gabliani was arrested. Like tens of thousands of his contemporaries in Georgia and throughout the Soviet Union, charges were brought against Egnate Gabliani for alleged anti-Soviet activity and he was declared an enemy of the people. The day of his execution remains unknown to this day.

In the army of this bloody state run by criminals, the son of the enemy of the people, Givi Gabliani, at twenty-three years of age, was called up in September 1939; the Second World War had already broken out. Only a few months before, he had graduated from the College of Medicine with plans to become a doctor.

* * *

On June 22, 1941, the German Army invaded the Soviet Union. That same summer, the military doctor of the 82nd Regiment of the 55th Division, Givi Gabliani became a prisoner of war. For a while the prisoner was allowed to work as a doctor in a hospital in Krestitelevo, in the Cherkasy region of occupied Ukraine. But soon the circumstances changed and the young doctor ended up in Steinau prison camp in Germany.

At the end of April 1942, Givi Gabliani was accepted into "Bergmann," a special unit that was composed of prisoners of war coming from Caucasus, and was sent to Mittenwald in Upper Bavaria. "Bergmann" was under the leadership of *Professor Theodor Oberländer*, who is notable in the recent history of Germany not only because after the war, from 1953 to1960, he was Minister for Displaced Persons,

Refugees and Victims of War in the Adenauer Cabinet, but more so for the reason that from the fall of 1941 to the summer of 1943 he wrote six extensive memoranda for submission to Hitler, in which he insisted more and more emphatically on more respectful treatment of the inhabitants of the occupied countries in the East, as well as on the creation of independent states under German protectorate in the occupied territories, whose governments would include representatives of Ukrainian, Belarusian and Caucasian populations respectively. The result was that in August 1943, Professor Oberländer was taken "into city arrest" in Prague and was ordered to prepare severely wounded SS officers for exams at the University of Prague.

On May 26, 1942, "Bergmann" celebrated the Georgian national holiday, Day of Achieving Independence. Georgians in exile who had emigrated to Europe after the Russian occupation, as well as Georgians who had recently belonged to the Soviet army—now they all wore German military uniforms—celebrated the Feast of Free Georgia together with German officers. The honor of giving a ceremonial speech was given to Givi Gabliani. Here is a quote from his speech:

> "The only reason we are in 'Bergmann' is that we stand for the 26th of May and the three-colored Georgian flag, the symbols of a sovereign Georgian State, which must be resurrected again as Phoenix from the ashes. We have pledged alliance to the German Armed Forces because we believe they will help us toward the realization of this goal now as they had before, during our independence of 1918–1921." [p. 120]

Together with "Bergmann," Givi Gabliani went through the war in the Caucasus and Crimea. On October 5, 1943, he was appointed head of the Military Department of the Georgian Liaison Staff and he had this task until the end of the war.

In 1950, he and his wife Rusudan, née Alshibaja, moved to the United States, where he ran a medical practice in Quincy, Illinois as a surgeon until his retirement. The daughters of Givi and Rusudan Gabliani, Vera and Eteri, as well as their son Gregory, are American citizens, and since the disintegration of the Soviet Union they have maintained increasingly broad contact with independent Georgia.

Givi Gabliani died on April 27, 2001.

* * *

Givi Gabliani's memoirs provide the reader with a wide range of information both about individual episodes of the war and about German military personnel, diplomats and politicians from the anti-Hitler movement, as well as about people from the anti-Stalin movement who were citizens of the Soviet Union or the Tsarist Empire in the prewar period.

Under the most diverse circumstances, historical figures of German history appear in the memoirs, some of whom were executed after the attempt to assassinate Hitler on July 20, 1944. The author manages to create impressive pictures of them.

Many unknown facts can be found in the memoirs of Givi Gabliani both by readers interested in the history of Georgian emigration and by those interested in the history of political parties in Georgia. The list of the acting persons is very long. It includes not only the members of the government in exile or the well-known politicians, officers, scientists, writers, artists and journalists, but also less known highly interesting and deserving personalities, whose portraits enormously enrich the overall picture of Georgian history.

Even though the present memoirs are an example of documentary prose and not a scientific treatise, some events and circumstances are described with truly scientific accuracy by the author. Thus, to cite just one example, the reader will find a clear and pertinent account of Caucasus projects that had been developed both in the Foreign Office and separately in the Ministry for Occupied Eastern Territories. Valuable from the historical perspective is the accurate description of the antagonisms, even enmities, that existed between the Wehrmacht and the so-called civil administration as well as between various branches of the political leadership in the Third Reich. Against this background, it is impressive to learn about the deeds of officers and officials who—regardless of their institutional affiliation—tried (and succeeded) to remain true to the principles of humanity in every situation.

As for the history of Georgian-German relations, the memoirs contain references not only to the fact that in the 19th century, from 1817 to 1830, some settlements of "colonists" who emigrated from South Germany were established in Georgia and that the coexistence of the local population with the colonists was based on sincere mutual respect for several decades, but also to lesser known historical facts, such as the establishment of a Georgian Legion during the First World War by the German Armed Forces and the role and importance of the German Army for the first Democratic Republic of Georgia in 1918.

Finally, the greatest discovery for the reader—at least for me—is the main character of this book, its author Givi Gabliani.

Doctor Givi Gabliani.

After reading his memoirs, I, who in my younger years, as I mentioned before, had difficulty believing in the real existence of Givi Gabliani, was convinced that my cousin was right when he claimed that Givi Gabliani was a doctor.

Being a doctor seems to have been Givi Gabliani's true vocation, his deepest actual nature. He was a doctor in Georgia and he was a doctor in the United States, his second home. Givi Gabliani was a doctor even when he was outside of his homeland(s), wearing a military uniform of whatever color instead of a white coat.

More than that, Givi Gabliani tried to follow his vocation even when he was not allowed to practice medicine. Being a doctor is a daily concern for people's lives, for their salvation. From October 1943 until the last day of the war, the daily concern of the head of the Military Department of the Georgian Liaison Staff, Givi Gabliani, was the rescue of people, the transfer of Georgian legionnaires scattered over a vast territory to safe places. Writes Givi Gabliani, "The general position of the Georgians abroad during W.W. II was to save all Georgian lives regardless of their political belief or party affiliation." [p. 118]

However, this concern was not only directed at the Georgians. To the same extent, it concerned, for example, the Russian prisoners of war. "We were not and are not haters of the Russian people, indeed discrimination against other people is alien to Georgians," writes Givi Gabliani with a certain pride.

In this regard, one more passage of the memoirs should be particularly noted. Addressing the political colorfulness of the Georgian emigration, Givi Gabliani remarks that the *Tetri Giorgi* (White George) movement "had a resemblance to Mussolini's Fascist Party." However, he continues, "It is important to emphasize that the 'Tetri Giorgi' organization and its members were free of any anti-Semitism, which is due to a deep-rooted Georgian tradition. […] I personally have not met a Georgian who was anti-Semitic, and racism has not been observed in our country." [p. 104]

That the rejection of racism united all members of "Bergmann" is also proven by the following recollection of Professor Johannes Semmler, at that time a young non-commissioned officer in "Bergmann":

"There were also three Jews in 'Bergmann' who had been captured by 'Bergmann' together with other Georgians in 1942. […] Explainably, coming from the other side of the front, they could not have known about the 'measures' to which the Jews, whom the Einsatzkommandos of the SS had got hold of, were subjected: Arrest, transfer to concentration camps or ghettos, and, it was rumored, perhaps murder. So it was not a desire to hide in a Wehrmacht unit when they agreed to join the 'Bergmann' unit, as most of their fellow prisoners did. Rather, they did so as Georgian patriots and victims of Stalin. Their Georgian comrades agreed. To escape Jews from the grasp of the SS was punishable by law. The Georgian sergeant Bagrat Tschanturia, one of the interpreters at

'Bergmann,' reported this tricky situation to the commander, Captain Oberländer, with the proposal to accept these three Jews into the unit 'Bergmann.' Oberländer agreed on the condition that this 'incident' should not become known beyond the small circle of people who had already been involved with it." (Semmler 2003, 324)

It remains only to add that Givi Gabliani belonged to the "small circle" of the German-Georgian working group of Professor Oberländer from the first day of his arrival in "Bergmann."

And finally, another quote, this time again from Givi Gabliani's memoirs, which shows how far removed from Nazi racism and anti-Semitism were even those high-ranking German officials who were among Bergmann's most important protectors and supporters:

"The Jews still had to endure unspeakable suffering in the Caucasus since SS Security Service was under the direct orders of Himmler. But Köstring, 'Bergmann's' Oberländer and Bräutigam, with support from Kleist were able at least to save the Jewish mountaineers—Tats, who had already been marked for extermination by the SS. Since all three above-named persons were recognized specialists of the Soviet Union, their argument that the Tats were of a Jewish religious faith, but ethnically just ordinary Caucasus Mountaineers, was finally accepted. Incidentally, there was strong grassroots support for helping the Jews among the Caucasian population. In gratitude, the Tats presented Oberländer and some other officers of 'Bergmann' sheep skin coats, hand made by them as a gift. I not only proudly wore mine but especially appreciated it while traveling on horseback after the onset of cold weather." [p. 141]

The doctor's task is to heal lacerations and fractures. "The amalgamation of the Georgian emigres and the newcomers from Soviet Georgia was vital for our success. I like to think that, perhaps in a small way, I too, made some contribution toward this end," writes Givi Gabliani [p. 125]. When reading these lines, the famous saying of Willy Brandt comes to mind, coined by the famous German politician on the day of the fall of the Berlin Wall on November 9, 1989: "What belongs together grows together."

"I personally never emphasized anyone's party affiliation […] in order not to weaken the national unity. For us, in 'Bergmann,' […] the Georgian question was not one of political parties but a non-partisan national question," writes Givi Gabliani [p. 100]. To restore the broken bridge (in the words of Ilia Chavchavadze, the "father of the Georgian nation," whom Givi Gabliani holds in the highest esteem) between the Georgians who emigrated to Europe years ago and those who remained in the Soviet Union—between the Westerners and the Easterners—was a task of the most difficult kind. It was Givi Gabliani who took on this task as a very young man and who served it conscientiously all his life.

Givi Gabliani as a young man. Tbilisi, Georgia.
Circa mid 1930s.
Courtesy Gabliani Family Archive.

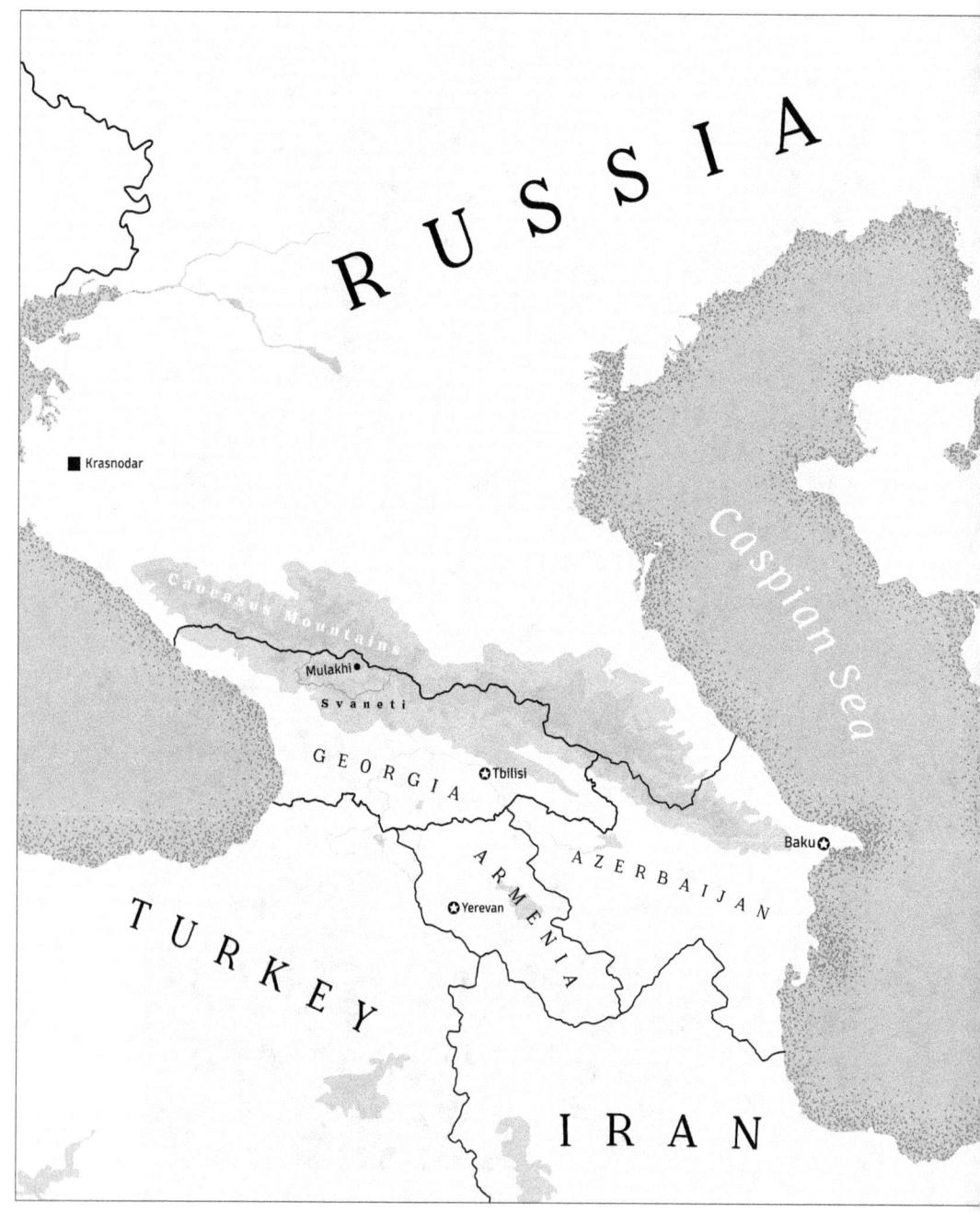

Map: Dennis Nishi

Georgia and its neighbors in the Caucasus, Azerbaijan and Armenia, are surrounded by would-be conquering nations and empires.
Also see the larger neighborhood map, pp. 412–413.

FOREWORD

Relatively few people in the Western World appreciate the fact that the October 1917 Bolshevik Revolution was solely a Russian phenomenon—it never took place in Georgia and other countries of the Caucasus region. Instead, the Caucasians used this opportunity to declare themselves sovereign democratic states, and as such were recognized by many countries, among them Bolshevik Russia. For instance, a treaty was signed on May 7, 1920, between the Democratic Republic of Georgia and the Russian Socialist Soviet Federative Republic. Article I of this document states, "Russia recognizes without reservation the independence and sovereignty of the Georgian State and voluntarily renounces all sovereign rights which belonged to Russia with respect to the Georgian people and their territory." However, on February 11, 1921, without the slightest provocation by Georgia and without any warning by Russia, the Red Army invaded Georgia. The Georgians fought as best they could but were surprised, outnumbered and out-gunned. The occupied Georgian nation was subjected to the deprivation of elementary human rights. Empowered by the Constitutional Assembly, the Georgian government traveled to Western Europe in order to appeal to the civilized world for help, "and to continue the fight against the invaders from Moscow until final victory."

Some members of the Constitutional Assembly and of political parties also went into exile. There was considerable understanding and sympathy for Georgia in the League of Nations and among politicians of the Western World but during the years that followed, Bolshevik Russia gained gradual recognition in the world community of nations. France was the last major power who held out and continued recognizing the Georgian Embassy for thirteen years. The Georgian Emigration never abandoned its quest for freedom and although a strong divisiveness along party lines was present, it remained the torch bearer for the defense of the Georgian national interests. It was never the representative of any privileged class of the elite—it was a national emigration. It may be fitting to quote here the British Scholar, W.E.D. Allen, who noted, "We find throughout the history of Georgia, as of Spain and Ireland, that it is the nation that is held sacred and not this or that principle."[1]

Some Georgians felt that it was a failure of democracy that Bolshevik Russia was allowed to swallow Georgia and other Caucasian democratic states. In spite of this, the overwhelming majority of emigres continued to be members of the traditional democratic political parties. (Concerning the Georgian political parties see chapters "In the Bergmann Unit and Caucasus" and "Leaving Crimea for Germany.") The majority of Georgians in exile were taken by surprise when Hitler invaded his former ally, Stalin's Empire. The German Army's progress created a real possibility for entering the Caucasus. Therefore, the emigres put forth considerable effort to learn about the German plans toward Georgia and other parts of the Caucasus and, if need be, to influence them in a positive direction. It was a popular thought that Germany would now pursue the same Caucasus policy as it had during World War I, when Georgian independence from 1918–1921 thrived due to German help. Such hope was further strengthened due to the fact that during World War II in the German occupied North Caucasus, the German policy was quite different as compared to other occupied Eastern territories where the indigenous population had suffered due to Hitler's inhuman decrees. The reason for such difference was the fact that Hitler did not have territorial claims toward the Caucasus. This situation was adroitly taken advantage of by some German military leaders and persons from the civilian sector who were convinced that Hitler was leading Germany toward its destruction. They tried to alter his course.

One of the important members of this circle was a general staff officer in the Organization Division of the Army, Major later Colonel Count Claus von Stauffenberg, who in 1944 attempted to kill Hitler and therefore was executed. He was able to arrange that General Ernst Köstring was appointed as "General in charge of Caucasian Affairs."[2] In this capacity, Köstring was an important advisor to his old friend Field Marshal E. von Kleist—the commanding general of the Army Group South (Caucasus). Köstring's adjutant was Captain Hans von Herwarth, also a diplomat, specialist on the U.S.S.R., a close co-worker of Stauffenberg and a long time member of the resistance movement against Hitler. Other advisors and contributors to the Caucasus Policy were Otto Schiller, the former agricultural

1- W. E. D. Allen, *A History of the Georgian People*, introduced by Sir Denison Ross, London: Kegan Paul, Trench, Trubner and Co., 1932.

2- Köstring was the former German military attache in Moscow and one of the great experts on the U.S.S.R. He was born in Imperial Russia and genuinely loved the Russian and non-Russian Soviet people, whose trust he enjoyed. He loathed the Nazi regime.

attache of the German Embassy in Moscow, Otto Bräutigam formerly from the foreign Ministry now working for the Ostministerium and Professor G. von Mende the Chief of Caucasian and Turkish Section of the Ostministerium.

Thanks to the concerted efforts of such well-intentioned, high caliber experts and their co-workers, the Caucasus Policy was a success as a result of humane treatment of the people. Field Marshal von Kleist ordered his troops to behave in the Caucasus as they would have if they were on maneuvers in their own country—Germany. Among other positive measures were the agrarian reforms, good treatment of the civilian population as well as P.O.W.s. As a result, the Caucasian population was very friendly to the German soldiers, the economic situation was satisfactory and therefore there was no significant partisan movement among the indigenous population. Stauffenberg and his friends wanted to use a successful Caucasian experiment for bringing about similar changes in all other German occupied Eastern territories. The Caucasian Policy was further strengthened by the presence of the volunteer Caucasian military units, among them the Caucasian "Bergmann," a mountain unit which had been created on orders of Admiral Canaris, the chief of the military intelligence (Abwehr), who appointed Captain Professor T. Oberländer as its commanding officer.[3] There were other Caucasian military units—the battalions of the Caucasian Legions as well which were formed by the efforts of Stauffenberg, assisted by Herwarth. Another good friend of the Caucasians, Count Friedrich Werner von Schulenburg had also been an essential force to bring about formation of the Caucasian Legions.[4] Oberländer, due to his criticism of the Nazi policy in occupied Eastern territories in his memoranda, was dismissed from the army and the party during the summer of 1943. He was interrogated by the Gestapo. The SS wanted to court-martial him, but this was prevented by efforts of the Army General Staff.

From the above, it emerges that during World War II, an unofficial alliance came about between a group of influential anti-Hitler Germans and anti-Stalin Georgians and other Easteners. They were caught between those two evils. A world without oppression became their common quest.

My memoir is about this drama.

3- Admiral Canaris was one of the most important members of the conspiracy against Hitler. He was executed during 1945.
4- Schulenburg was executed during 1944 because of his part in the conspiracy against Hitler.

1

LEAVING GEORGIA FOR RUSSIA

A farewell at a railroad station is usually an emotional experience, therefore, I pleaded with my mother and sister to stay home so I could say goodbye to them there. In return, I promised to write often, behave myself and come back home as healthy as ever after my two years in Russia. I was headed west of the Urals, so they had no need to fear my rock climbing.

Sister Eteri was convinced but not my mother. Her beautiful expressive eyes, with the dark circles around them were full of tears. She had gone through so much and had only the two of us left from her immediate family. Two of her children died of some common childhood disease and her husband, our father, had perished during the 1937 "purges" (only two years previous), not to mention many other turbulences in her life.

A number of years later she, too, would be arrested and deported to Kazakhstan, because of me. She was a dedicated teacher, loved by her pupils and their parents alike and was affectionately referred to as "Vera Maszavlebeli." (Teacher Vera). Sister Eteri was almost seventeen years old then, an adorable person, studying languages at the University of Tbilisi and had many good friends. Having graduated from Tbilisi Medical School, I had been a Fellow in Surgery and Endocrinology in one of the University hospitals.[1]

In September 1939, I was ordered to start two years of obligatory military duty in Kursk, Russia. The chair of the Endocrinology Department respectfully requested that my military conscription be deferred since I was "essential" for the work of the department but in vain.

Now a friend of mine, a marvelous person, Dr. Othar Rcheulishvili and I were

---

1- I worked under the Chairmanship of Prof. Aleko Tsulukidze but directly under his instructors Joseph Aslanishvili and Giorgi Hitchinashvili.

leaving for Russia. The railroad station in Tbilisi, Georgia was full with all kinds of people. Many of our friends and a lot of well wishers came to bid us farewell and wish us "God's Speed." Of course, everyone brought presents for us, such as Georgian cognac, wine, "Hachapuri" (a special Georgian cheesecake), fruit, etc. Among the many friends who came was my teacher, Dr. Joseph (Soso) Aslanishvili, the famous alpinist's sister and brother Alexandra and Aliosha Djaparidze, our classmates and relatives. It was a beautiful fall afternoon, warm and pleasant, and as the train began to roll out of the station, we were glued to the window to keep the familiar images in view as long as possible.

Those images were, indeed, remembered for a long time while "lost" abroad, when things weren't as well as we thought they should be. We shared our presents with the other passengers and the conductors regardless of their ethnic origin, creed, or gender. The conductor, in turn, was serving delicious tea with sugar cubes.

Speaking of gender, among the passengers were some Russian and Ukrainian girls—mostly tourists. They were very complimentary about the Caucasus and the hospitality there. Their presence added to the cheer of this trip. The cheer was needed because as the train reached the endless and monotonous Russian steppes (the prairies) with the gray skies and colder weather, our mood and our faces became less than happy.

Finally the train arrived at our destination, Kursk, the university city of Central Russia, which also housed the headquarters of the 55th Infantry Division and the Heavy Artillery Regiment, number 772 of the Army Corps.

As we learned to appreciate later on, we were privileged to have been assigned to the Heavy Artillery Regiment 772 and not to one of the infantry regiments of the 55th Division since the living conditions were better in the Artillery. Coming from sunny Tbilisi, Georgia, we did not realize at first that there were a great many less agreeable places than Kursk.

It was the end of September 1939, and the regiment had just returned from a military invasion of Poland, about which no one would say much. It was certain that it was the result of a pact between Bolshevik Russia and Hitler's Germany.

My friend, Dr. Othar Rcheulishvili and I were assigned to a six month obligatory regular soldiers' training ignoring the fact that we were M.D.s. The regiment had recently been mechanized but still kept some horses, just in case. Grooming the horses was also part of our training which is not as easy as it sounds. The lieutenant often supervised such an endeavor, and when we thought it was over and his final criteria for the "job well done" had been met, he stroked the hair of the animal with a white cloth. If the cloth did not remain just as pristine as before, the procedure had to be repeated again and again. I have owned and loved horses since my early childhood, but I began to wonder if they really deserved my original affection after all. In any case, it was most difficult to meet the lieutenant's standards of horse grooming.

The gray sky and what seemed to be unseasonably cold temperatures became a permanent feature. Our lifestyle, including our lodging, physical exposure to the climate and food(or lack thereof) was spartan. No one in Georgia would ever expect a fish soup to be served for breakfast, and here we had it three times a week. The regimental campus was surrounded with a tall, barbed-wire fence. Next to the military drills, considerable time was devoted to political indoctrination. Besides the Marxist-Leninist dogmas, an eternal vigilance was impressed on us since "we were surrounded by the imperialist-capitalistic forces from outside and deceived by their agents from inside." According to such paranoia, the enemies were everywhere, but no derogatory reference was made against Germany at that time.

One day when everything went wrong and we even missed our supper, Othar turned to me and said, "You are a Svan (a highlander) always loving weapons, horses and wandering in the wilderness—I am sure you are happy now."

"Very happy," I quipped, "and on top of it all there is a chance that they will make a real soldier out of the sedentary doctor that you are." Our Georgian humor (which, incidentally is seldom understood by "outsiders") kept us going. When we mailed our first letters home that included "soldier boy's" photos, the reply came, "Can't you smile a little? Surely doomsday is not here yet!"

Only two things made our life somewhat brighter. The student girls' dormitory was located a short distance from our backyard fence and we were able to see them, and at times the wind even carried their giggles in our direction. Secondly, on some weekends one could get a pass to the city if our performance on duty had been good. Then one could stroll and observe the people, what the Russians referred to as "Guliat" and even make acquaintances. One could go to the movies and also eat somewhat better food—if one had money, which for us, was not easy to come by.

But suddenly things got better than expected. Because of the obvious shortage of doctors, our military course was cut short and at the onset of the winter, we were transferred to the "Sanitary Department of the Regiment" to work there as doctors. The chief of this department was a cadre officer and a graduate of the Military Medical Academy with the rank of captain.

He treated us well and introduced us to his wife, who was an attractive and well-educated lady. Every so often they invited us for tea and a lively discussion usually would follow. My Georgian friend Othar was somewhat older than me, already married, obviously a diplomat, good natured, patient and practical and usually kept a low profile. I am afraid I could not claim all those virtues and had a tendency to be outspoken and a hothead. Therefore, when the conversation at times got "vivacious." Othar had to observe me so I did not go too far.

Those were the days after Stalin's bloody purges and one had to watch one's words more than ever. Many leading officers were "liquidated" and their positions had to be filled by less qualified ones from the lower ranks. The Red Army had obviously suffered a major loss of military leadership, the results of which was soon to be seen during the embarrassing Soviet offensive in Finland.

I was much impressed by the genuine warmth, consideration and kindness shown to Othar and me by the majority of our Russian doctor colleagues. They also were capable practitioners and scientists and dedicated to their patients all in the tradition of Hippocrates and of old, good Russian medical education. This was contrary to the Bolshevik teaching that the interests of the State are more important than the welfare of an individual person. It was clear to me that the prevailing system of central bureaucratic "planning" and absence of any positive reinforcement for the doctors, as well as inadequate allocation of the resources, resulted in the poor quality of medical care for the average Soviet citizen today. Certainly it is not the fault of the medical profession there.

Kursk had a good-sized, decent hospital staffed by experienced doctors and we, the military M.D.s, had the privilege of referring seriously ill soldiers there from the entire garrison. We were also happily assigned on a rotation basis for night duty and participated in the morning rounds with the attending men. I was looking forward to my turn since, in addition to gaining experience, there was an additional bonus of a wonderful hot bathtub and a good supper served in a pleasant environment. This, after things had quieted down for the night.

The entire medical community of Kursk—civilian as well as military—had a series of well organized periodical scientific meetings. The lectures were followed by informal "round table" discussions, which were of educational and practical value as well as pleasant. It was there I first met the Chief Medical Officer of the 55th Division and of the garrison, Dr. Major Ivan Kniazev. As it turned out, he was married to a charming Cirecassian lady, Aisha Ahmedovna, therefore, he well understood our Caucasian customs, spirit and manners.

The Kniazevs invited Othar and me to an evening party on some festive occasion. I got there somewhat late, hungry and frozen because of the unusually heavy duty that day. To "warm" and "cheer me up," the host proposed a toast with a generous sized glass of vodka and it served its purpose very well. Until then I had not had much experience with this famous Russian beverage. After the initial stunning effect, I took a few more drinks and felt pleasantly warm. My hunger and unhappiness had disappeared and now I began a series of toasts. First, a toast to our hostess, then to our host, then to our friends that were present and those who were not. I wished that they were and so on. Othar pulled my sleeve several times whispering, "You have had enough," but what did he know? He was a "lowlander" and I was a "highlander."

I reassured him—I had never felt better and asked him to stop worrying and invited him to help me with a Georgian song I started. Next thing I remembered was the following morning when I woke up lying on the couch in the home of our big boss. He had gone to work but Othar gave me the account of all the nonsense that I had said while under the influence of Russian vodka. It was a humbling experience for the "highlander," to say the least. Our hostess hurried up to reassure us that everything was all right. As a North Caucasian Muslim, she did not drink at all, but she wished I would have eaten some food before I did so.

Later on while walking the streets of some Russian cities, including Moscow, I observed (not infrequently) men in a crowd uncorking a vodka bottle and letting the cork fly away as a useless commodity and emptying the whole thing. I followed them, being curious about what would happen next. After a while, one would slow down and with a happy smile on his face eventually would fall asleep on some stranger's staircase. The gray skies, unfriendly weather and many other problems no longer bothered him now.

For my part, I decided never again to indulge in vodka to such an extent. This incident apparently did not bother our boss, Dr. Major Kniazev, and after a month or two he transferred me to the Infantry Regiment No. 111, where they were badly in need of a medical doctor, and then three months later he further appointed me in the headquarters of the 55th Division as his "aide-de-camp" to fill the position of the "senior physician at his disposal" ("starshi vrach dlia poruchenee"). I was sorry to part from Othar, who was to remain in the Artillery Regiment 772, which later on was transferred to the Southeast Krasnodar Area.

In Infantry Regiment No. 111, things were worse than I expected. First of all, most of the new conscripts were still clad in summer uniforms and it was a cold December. This was particularly difficult for the recruits from the Soviet Turkestan, such as the Uzbeks, Turkmens, Kazakhs, Kirghiz and Tadshiks, as they were not adapted to the severe Russian winter nor to Russian food.

Pneumonia, other respiratory disorders and digestive problems prevailed in epidemic proportions. Body parasites were common among native Russian recruits from the villages. Due to the severe cold, people had to huddle together. The community bathing houses were not available in adequate numbers and many individual families, not equipped with private bathing facilities, were unable to bathe.

This would change in the spring since people would then take advantage of not only the village bathing houses but also of the rivers and lakes. However, as of now, it posed a considerable problem. Daily morning checks done by the non commissioned officers were necessary. The groups of soldiers were lined up in dormitories, they had to pull their shirts over their heads and all crevices were inspected. The physician usually moved from one unit to another for overall supervision. One day I was suspicious of a non-commissioned officer himself harboring the offenders. When the inspection was over, I had a "man-to-man" talk with him about it. Needless to say he was displeased and wanted to know how I arrived at such a conclusion. My response was that this was a "professional secret" that distinguishes doctors from non-commissioned officers and secondly, I observed some suspicious motions of his hands and body ever so often, and last but not least, he had never been checked.

As it turned out, the "master sergeant" did indeed have parasites but that secret was kept between the two of us. I was amused to note the same day during an odd hour, several non-commissioned officers, led by the master sergeant, were marching to the special bathing facility. Some time later on I ran into this master sergeant and he made a remark, "Doctor, one day you will make a real good physician." On my question as to how I deserved such a high mark, he smiled and responded, "because your brain works" (bashki rabotaiut). This was one of the greatest compliments I received during my service in the Regiment of No. 111.

Military doctors of the garrison were also assigned on a rotating basis to the sanitary screening establishment located at the Kursk Railroad Station. Here passing trains loaded with new military conscripts, still in civilian clothing had to stop. Sanitary inspections took place by the military doctor in charge and his assistant medics after which the conscripts had to shower in a well organized facility while their clothing was processed through the steam chambers for disinfection and elimination of parasites that might possibly be present. This often continued throughout the entire night and the first half of the next day. Thanks to such vigorous preventive methods, contagious diseases, especially the dreaded typhus, were practically eliminated.

Less exhausting was the inspection of the military kitchens and the obligatory probing and approval of the food by a doctor "before the soldiers were allowed to eat it." Food samples were also stored for twenty-four hours. This was a curious rule and amounted to using a doctor as a lab animal.

A couple of months later, four additional military doctors joined the medico-sanitary department of the 111 Regiment and very soon after this, I was transferred, as I already mentioned, to the headquarters of the 55th Division. The chief medical officer, Dr. Major Ivan Kniazev, after briefing me about my duties, made clear that I was expected to inspect every unit of the Division on an ongoing basis and to asses the quality of the medical care as well as the sanitary conditions there and keep abreast of the situation.

The prewar Soviet Infantry Division was a huge military force. In addition to three infantry regiments, it possessed a medium range artillery regiment and many special units. Their quarters were scattered in the vicinity of Kursk, and to inspect them I had to travel by train, motor vehicles or horseback. The medical officers of those units had to work hard but their efforts at times were frustrated by the lack of cooperation from the superintendents, commanding officers and the political commissars, who were ignorant of medico-sanitary matters. Rather than write a big report on the deficiencies of the system, our efforts were directed to eliminate the misunderstanding on the spot and to strengthen the position of the local doctor and promote cooperation between all concerned on an ongoing basis.

Soon my chief was promoted to a higher position and was replaced by Dr. Major Shcheglov. He was a good natured elderly gentleman, easy to work with but who lacked Dr. Kniazev's energy and charisma. He introduced me to his niece, a very nice young lady, a teacher in Kursk and after encouragement by Dr. Shcheglov, I began to date her. She was shy but intelligent and she helped me to understand civilian life in a Russian city.

I remember well one embarrassing episode as she, my boss Shcheglov and I were strolling in the streets of Kursk. A Russian peasant (probably on business in the city and who obviously had a few drinks) in a loud and hostile voice addressed the Dr. Major, "Look at you!" he said, "splendidly dressed like a barin (a squire), well paid, well fed, having a good time and look at the wretched peasant, me. Parasites like you are sucking our blood."

Shcheglov, embarrassed shouted back, "How dare you, we are your defenders."

"Our defenders?" bitterly laughed the peasant, "from whom? We need defense from people like you!"

Finally we walked away from this unpleasant encounter. It is to Dr. Shcheglov's credit that he did not report the poor devil to the police; perhaps he understood the problems of the peasants in the "collective farms." During military maneuvers that brought us in closer contact to the villagers, this became painfully clear to me also. Lenin considered peasants with their strong sense of private property, not only unreliable but a hostile force against the communist society. Peasants had participated in the revolution in order to gain land that previously belonged to the land owners. Thus their goal had been already achieved, and from then on peasants, especially "the rich" ones or so-called "kulaks" had to be eliminated in due time as the enemy class. But, this was not done because the Bolshevik takeover, with their decrees and the civil war that followed, had virtually destroyed the economy.

Lenin had no choice but to proclaim the New Economic Policy (NEP) in March 1921. The NEP permitted some private initiative and private property, including a small land ownership for the peasants, small manufactures, shop keepers, etc. with the profit making motive. Decentralization and the regional economic autonomy was emphasized and the market forces permitted to operate. Lenin called this reform a "temporary retreat" imposed by the necessity of "one step back" to be "followed by a two step forward leap," as soon as conditions would permit.

Travel restrictions abroad were also eased, a certain "democratization" within the communist party was tolerated. Exports and imports were promoted. "The capitalists will sell the rope to us with which they are going to be hanged," said Lenin. The economic improvement due to NEP was spectacular and if the Bolshevik leadership had cared for the welfare of the people, they would have let things develop in that direction. Apparently they cared more to prove their dogma and above all for maintaining the unlimited control in their hands of virtually every aspect of life, including the economy.[2]

In the early 1930's, faithful to his master Lenin's teachings, Stalin felt that the time had come to "leap forward" and he introduced a most rapid and brutal collectivization. Thus NEP was terminated and the merciless requisition of private property from the peasants included even their grain earmarked for seed. A severe famine broke out and many millions of peasants were deported to forced labor camps, others starved to death or were shot. An appreciable number moved to the cities to become factory workers, so rapid urbanization began to take place.

In the years to follow, one could see gangs of homeless and parent-less children, "Besprisorniki," as a result of the destroyed families, roaming the streets and railroad stations or cities, surviving on handouts and/or stolen food.

Would this have happened had Lenin remained at the helm and not Stalin? According to the Soviet historian Robert Conquest, Lenin was vacillating about the proper duration of the NEP. In a letter to Kamenev on March 3, 1922, (not printed until 1959) Lenin stated, "It is a great mistake to think that NEP put an end to

---

2- After Lenin's death in January 1924, during the power struggle for his succession, Stalin revealed a superb Machiavellian skill. He defeated Trotsky (who was considered to be Lenin's successor) with the help of Trotsky's own "fellow left wingers," Zinoviev and Kamenev. The "left wingers" were advocating a policy of struggle against the "kulaks" now and the rapid industrialization of the country. Having weakened the "left," Stalin now turned around and sided with the party's "right wingers" led by Bukharin, Tomsky and Rykov. They were opposed to persecution of the kulaks and regarded rapid industrialization with great skepticism. Together with them in 1925 at the 14th party congress, Stalin defeated and expelled from the communist party the weakened left. In due time, Stalin also eliminated the "right wingers" and established his own firm command over the party.

terror, we shall again have recourse to terror and to economic terror." Mr. Conquest also quotes Adam Ulms's classic work on Lenin who concludes that if he had lived, Lenin would have ended NEP earlier than Stalin.[3]

I have heard remarks by certain people that Georgia had been affected less because Stalin himself was a Georgian and therefore less excesses occurred there. This, of course, is nonsense. Stalin was not a Georgian patriot but a ruthless dictator of Russia, who was obsessed with creating a powerful Great Russia under his total control.

Lenin himself made a remark about Stalin, a Georgian, and Feliks Dzerzhinsky, a Pole, "that they were more Russian chauvinists than the Russians themselves." Brutality and executions committed by the secret police and the military occupation forces in Georgia already during 1923 were incredibly harsh, overseen by Ordzhonikidze under Stalin's order. Apparently, it was too excessive even for the chief of the secret police, Dzerzhinsky himself, who reported it to Lenin. As far as the bloody purges of 1936–37 are concerned, although I do not have accurate statistics, I was an eyewitness to this horror. Almost all "old" Georgian Communists were "liquidated." Numerically, of course, the Ukrainians lost more people, being a nation of forty to forty-five million as compared to three and one-half to four million of ethnic Georgians.

Now back to Kursk.

While Major Dr. Kniazev was still at the helm of the medico-sanitary service, the 55th Division was sent to Finland during the middle of February 1940. Already, on November the 30th, 1939, Finland had been attacked by Soviet Armed Forces, as Soviet propaganda would have like us to believe, "In order to repeal the Finnish Aggression." The Finns fought with great courage and skill under the leadership of their hero (also my hero) Field Marshal Carl Gustaf Mannerheim. Soviet casualties were staggering, and it was necessary to throw in the battle several Soviet military districts, outnumbering the Finns in every respect.

The Red Army at that time revealed its poor preparation and inability for a coordinated offensive war. For instance, according to the reports, the Soviet artillery, not infrequently would erroneously bombard its own infantry positions rather than the Finns. Purges of the best Red Army officers by Stalin and his associates during 1936 and 1937 were perhaps a contributory factory to such situations. However, in no way should one underestimate the great courage, military ability and patriotism of the Finnish soldiers.

3- Robert Conquest, *The Harvest of Sorrow: Soviet Collectivization and the Terror-Famine*, New York: Oxford University Press, 1986, p. 60.

I have listened to the stories told by the wounded Georgian and Russian soldiers about "The Mannerheim Line," a defense line across Finland's southeastern frontier. They also reported how the Finns would appear out of nowhere, camouflaged in white garb and on skis. The Finns would separate the Soviet military units into smaller groups. The front was cut off from the rear; from the supplies and from the communications. The Finnish slang for such a tactic was to divide them in the "mottis" (wood piles) and then "chop them up."

Many Soviet soldiers had frozen feet and hands. The poor performance of the Red Army in Finland may have contributed later on to Hitler's erroneous underestimation of its ability in defensive war. The Finnish spirit is well seen in one of their many jokes. After having observed an overwhelming number of the opposing Soviet troops, they had exclaimed, "So many Russians, where are we going to bury them?" In spite of an enormous manpower and material superiority, the Soviets had to resort to the air force bombing of Helsinki.

Embarrassed, Molotov had to offer an official "explanation" to the foreigners, that those were not the bombs over Helsinki but the "food packages" thrown down for the "starving Finns." In return, as a strange coincidence, the Finns made Molotov's name immortal by inventing what became known worldwide as a "Molotov Cocktail," a kerosene-filled bottle with a wick, with which Finns destroyed many Soviet tanks.

The final outcome could not have been victory for Finland, fighting alone against the Superpower. This was revealed by the Soviet advances at the Karelian Isthmus.

Nevertheless, due to the heavy losses and deeply impressed by the Finnish undiminished fighting spirit and stubbornness, Stalin agreed to enter into peace negotiations with Finland during the first half of March 1940. The Finns ceded part of their Southeast territory and leased Hanko Naval Base to the enemy but in return kept their statehood.

This should have been a lesson for the larger and stronger democratic nations, about the value of courage and determination in fighting a totalitarian aggressor, even if it happens to be a superpower. As a Georgian, my heart was and is with the Finns and would be with any other small democratic nation in a similar situation.

The 55th Division arrived at the border of Finland in early March but never was engaged in active combat as the peace treaty was signed about this time. Subsequently, the 55th Division was transferred back to Kursk. The newly appointed Dr. Major Shcheglov left on spring vacation and I had to "cover for him" all the functions of the chief medical officer of the division. I did not feel adequately prepared for such a task in spite of his assurances to the contrary. With Dr. Shcheglov still on vacation, the 55th Division was loaded on several trains and transported to

Lithuania, a small Baltic country, which we invaded in June 1940, and "liberated from the Capitalistic Yoke" to use the Soviet term for such a venture. Simultaneously, Latvia and Estonia also had been taken over by different Red Army units.

This turned out to be an unforgettable and an eye-opening experience for many of us. Lithuania was a beautiful, peaceful and compared to our standards, incredibly prosperous free country. The shops were full of all kinds of goods and food was plentiful for all. Nothing like that existed anywhere in the Soviet Union. The Red Army officers descended upon those shops like locusts on fields to be harvested. The Lithuanian shopkeepers were amazed when one officer after another purchased several wrist watches at once as well as a disproportionate amount of other consumer goods.

A question in my mind was what the shop owners could do with all this Soviet money in the future? Were there any wholesale houses or industries left in Lithuania to resupply them? It was striking how well fed and dressed the Lithuanians were. They appeared by far happier and less subdued in spite of the recent occupation by the enemy than the "free" Soviet citizens.

This also applied to the farmers, who instead of the Soviet collective farms had very well organized cooperatives and individual private properties, producing plenty of food for everyone. Farm animals were well fed and cared for. I was involved in inspecting the food supplies for the Division, which exclusively came from the Lithuanian land, to see that they were of the highest quality. One could not help but be impressed by the well-dressed Lithuanian officers promenading with a dignified manner and courtly saluting us. (They were allowed to be free at first.)

Near the city of Ukmerge, there was a beautiful hill with a forest where the "Medico-Sanitary Battalion" was stationed. From there I could see the river Villia, where people were sailing their boats. While in this forest, I was deeply impressed by a religious procession, led by priests moving from one holy shrine to another with hymns and prayers. There was a great ecstasy and peace on their faces.

Why were we here, interfering in the happy lives of the Lithuanians? "Liberating" them? From what? Clearly the only reason was to satisfy the ferocious, imperialistic appetite of the Soviet leaders. I have witnessed a fake "spontaneous" demonstration of about one hundred people in the city of Ukmerge. It was staged by the two Soviet agitators of Lithuanian origin, whom we "exported" on the 55th Division train to Lithuania for this special purpose.

The demonstrators carried posters where one could read, "The Lithuanian People wish their country to become a part of the Soviet Union." This was, indeed, corresponding to Moscow's plans. The army troops soon were followed by the N.K.V.D. commandos (the Soviet Secret Police). Their mission was to "clean up" the country of politically "dangerous" people. Why they were considered as such remained a secret for everyone. Soon I observed that day after day, the freight trains packed with Lithuanians, guarded by N.K.V.D., were transported eastward. Their destiny obviously was forced labor camps or "gulags." I could only see the prisoners' hands through small steel braced windows of the railroad cars.

The same took place in the remaining two Baltic States. I was upset and depressed by all of this human tragedy. The memory of arrests during 1921, 1924, insurrections and Stalin's purges in Georgia in 1937 and 1938, vividly resurfaced. Among them were my father, together with many neighbors, acquaintances, cherished professors and others, who perished for no valid reason at all. There was hardly one family in Georgia unharmed.

The happiness of three, small, beautiful and peaceful countries were being sacrificed, without provocation, by aggressive tyranny. Surely there must be some just force under the sun to stop this evil. Germany had a "friendship pact" with the Soviets but perhaps England and her allies could do something about it one day. Those were the thoughts of one unexperienced and angry young doctor those days, while in Lithuania.

A number of desertions had occurred from our division. This was amazing, given the hopeless outlook for such a venture to succeed. Soon they were all captured and summarily executed, among them three Georgians. I remember when this was announced. I was visiting in one of the regiments, when the first lieutenant of artillery, a Georgian Simon Lagidze, said in a choked voice that three million Georgians had been reduced by another three young lives today.

The exposure to the Baltic States demonstrated to all of us the superiority of the "capitalistic system" with free enterprise and a western democracy as compared to the reality of Soviet "paradise." It was an eye opener for even some convinced communists and in my opinion had an impact on the Soviet soldiers' behavior during the outbreak of the German-Russian War in 1941.

The 55th Division was gradually removed from the Baltic area and set on a march toward Brest-Litovsk, the former city of East Poland which the Soviets acquired during the 1939 invasion of this country.

We arrived there during September of 1940. The military quarters at our disposal were originally built by Poles for their own garrison. The facilities appeared to be of the highest quality and we had seen nothing like it before.

Unfortunately, due to the lack of "know-how" of the system, the toilets were soon out of order. Because of prevailing paranoia, "the enemies and spies are everywhere," it was frowned on to solicit the help of the civilian expert plumbers in Brest-Litovsk who were readily available.

I just had enough of carrying out the duties in the medico-sanitary depart-ment at the headquarters of the 55th Division. I much preferred to care for the sick and injured as their doctor. Finally my plea was satisfied and I was transferred to the Infantry Regiment 228 of the 55th Division, where there was a vacancy. At this time the Division was distributed around Brest-Litovsk and alongside the river. Our immediate goal was to build a defense line consisting of the hidden "bunkers" for artillery, heavy machine guns and trenches for the infantry. On the opposite shore of the river, the German Cavalry Unit could be observed; I admired their good horses.

Many years later, during a conversation with my famous German friend "Johnnie" von Herwarth, we did establish that across the river, (which became a new border between Germany and the Soviet Union) actually our regiments were facing each other. I also told "Johnnie" that I had some thoughts at that time to escape Bolshevik tyranny and cross the line to the west without knowing what to expect there but assuming that anything would be better than what we were stuck with at home. I did not do so because of concern for my mother and sister. "It was fortunate that you did not run over," he said, "for given German-Soviet relationship at that time, there is little doubt that our side would have handed you back to the Soviets."[4]

Brest-Litovsk is a historical city and had considerable meaning for me. During World War I, the Brest-Litovsk Peace Treaty had been signed by Germany and her allies with Russia's new rulers—the Bolsheviks—during early March of 1918. Shortly before that, Germany had already signed a separate peace treaty with the Ukrainian "Rada," which outraged the Russians. According to this treaty, the new Russian rulers (the Bolsheviks) made many other concessions. For instance, they ceded an important Georgian territory, the city of Batumi and also Ardahan to Turkey, which was then a German ally. They also ceded Karsi (Kars) to Turkey, the area inhabited mostly by the Armenians. Russian Bolsheviks ceded part of Georgian territory to Turkey. The independence of Ukraine and Finland had to be recognized. Russia also renounced control over the Baltic States, Russian "Poland" and a large part of Belorussia.[5]

Bolsheviks had no significant influence in the Caucasus, as the Caucasians did not think much of the Bolshevik Revolution and their rule in Russia. They hoped that Lenin's rule would be defeated by other Russian forces and democracy would again prevail. Therefore, the three Transcaucasian states; Georgia, Armenia and Azerbaijan declared a Transcaucasian Federation. However, collapse of the Russian southern front against Turkey created a dangerous situation in the Transcaucasus

---

4- Hans von Herwarth's "Introduction to Dr. Givi Gabliani's Memoirs" and Affidavit is in the Appendix.
5- For more about this, see the Appendix "Brest-Litovsk Treaty."

because of Turkish aggressive territorial designs against her. Turkey invaded the Caucasus and achieved considerable territorial gain and there was no one to stop their further advances, since the Transcaucasian Federation did not have a strong enough military force available. Moreover, the Transcaucasian Muslims clearly would not resist Turkey. There were many other overwhelming problems as well. The Federative Republic lasted only one month.

Turkey now occupied an important Georgian city, Batumi, the Black Sea harbor through which the Baku oil (in Azerbaijan) could have been exported. The "peace" conference at Batumi took place between the Transcaucasus representative and the Turks on May 11, 1918. Here the Turkish representative, Vehip Pasha, demanded further territorial and railroad concessions from the Transcaucasians, who had no choice. But here, paradoxically, help came from Imperial Germany, then a Turkish ally. Germans, at that time, dominated the Black Sea and were moved by a great need of Caucasian oil. The German representative also attended the above said Batumi conference.

In spite of German efforts to mediate, the Turks remained adamant about their demands. But in a coordinated move between the Transcaucasians and the Germans, this is what took place:

1. On the twenty-sixth of May 1918, the Transcaucasian representatives received a Turkish ultimatum that had to be accepted within seventy-two hours, with cessation to Turkey of vast territorial concessions.

2. Since the Transcaucasian Federative Republic was no longer a viable option, it was dissolved at once and each of her member nations had to look out for their own interest and declare statehoods. On May 26, 1918, (the day of Turkish ultimatum) Georgia declared her own independent republic.

3. The German Representative, General Kress von Kressenstein and F.W. von der Schulenburg announced in Tbilisi the establishment of a German Protectorate over the Georgian Republic. A provisional agreement was signed between Imperial Germany and the Georgian Republic in the city of Poti, two days later, May 28, 1918.

4. The head of the German delegation, General von Lossow, was sent to Tbilisi. Colonel (later General) Kress von Kressenstein put together a special military force from the German P.O.W.s, the farmers from the German settlements in Georgia and used them as a barrier to halt Turkish advance.[6] Once the

6- Marshall Lang, *A Modern History of Soviet Georgia*, New York: Grove Press, 1962, chapters IX–X. Hans von Herwarth with S. Frederick Starr, *Against Two Evils*, New York: Rawson Wade, 1981.

German representatives such as Lossow, Kressenstein, Schulenburg, Arthur Leist (a scholar of Georgian literature), O. von Wesendok (later Consul General in Tbilisi) became acquainted with Caucasians, a great deal of lasting friendships and mutual trust were established between the two sides. Without a doubt, this had a great influence on the Caucasian friendly attitude shown to the Germans during W.W II. It probably left a feeling of good will toward the Caucasian people as well. Especially with some of the Germans who, during World War II, were opposed to Hitler's policies.[7]

In Brest-Litovsk during the fall of 1940, the 228 Regiment was commanded by Lieutenant Colonel Gregory Chaganava, a Georgian. He was a well-respected and capable professional. He was decent, elegant and a real gentleman. He was not a fanatic, but I have no doubt that he would fight until the last for the Red Army to which he had a commitment on a voluntary basis. He was convinced that sooner or later a war in "Europe" (as he chose to call it) was imminent. Less than one year since he had made such a statement, I met him in the Belorussian swamps. I met him the last time during general retreat when the 55th Division tried to get out of the German "pincer maneuver." His horse had been lost and his personal regimental auto had to be abandoned. Bravely, he was limping and retreating on foot. At that time, I was no longer in his unit but in the 82 Artillery Regiment.

As two Irishmen or Georgians would do, we had a long chat ignoring general chaos and haste. He told me that he could not see how the Germans could be stopped under the present circumstances, neither in Belorussia or Ukraine. But he said there will be a great battle for Moscow which will be defended at any cost. He was determined to somehow break through and reach Moscow to participate in this grand stand. We shook hands and parted. I only hoped that he would reach Moscow and remain alive throughout the war. His military analysis turned out to be entirely correct.

Another Georgian officer in Regiment 228, Captain Mikhail Kartvelishvili, was a capable commander of a battalion and the best shot in the 55th Division. He was also the instructor in charge of officers' training in competitive shooting. Captain Kartvelishvili took certain pride in my accomplishment in this endeavor. Being from the Georgian mountains, I was not exactly a newcomer to firearms (I had been exposed to them at age nine) but under his tutorship, I improved and consistently scored second best after him. This apparently also impressed the participating high ranking officers more than my medical degree. So whenever I was introduced by

---

7- See copy of an article published in Germany by one of the members of the German Delegation in the Caucasus 1918–1921 confirming this view. See copies and photographs in author's archives.

them to a newcomer or a visitor, instead of saying, "This is our doctor," they would say enthusiastically, this is our best shot. I did not know how to react to this, whether to take it as a compliment or not.

Captain M. Kartvelishvili and I became friends and often we rode together to inspect the troops. Ever so often, he would ask me to substitute for him and take the officers for practice on the shooting range. It must have looked funny to strangers to see the combat officers being led by a doctor for target shooting rather than to the medical facility. I know that Captain Kartvelishvili was chuckling and joking about it.

When Mrs. Kartvelishvili arrived from Georgia to visit her husband in Brest-Litovsk, there was a dinner party in their apartment where Georgian dishes "à la maison" were served. Some Georgian officers of the garrison were invited, including Lieutenants Simon Lagidze, Dimitri Nuzubidze and Lieutenant Colonel Chaganava. Late in the night we talked and toasted each other with "Kakhetian" wine and shared unusual delicacies.

During December of 1939 and early January, 1940, the 55th Division was ordered again to march, this time in the direction of the Belorussian city, Slutzk, which would become our "home base." It was bitterly cold, the horses were covered with ice and snow, and all we horseback riders had the appearance of Santa Claus. Fortunately, Mrs. Kartvelishvili had been wisely sent back to Georgia on the train.

Finally, when we arrived at our destiny, I received mail from Mother. It was, as usual, an optimistic description of things but mentioned that my sister Eteri had been ailing. "Nothing serious, of course," but while on the campus of the university, she sustained a head injury due to a fall. She and her friends were chasing each other in the hall and she fell, hitting the back part of her head. She was hospitalized at first but now she was resting at home more comfortably, even though she continued having headaches.

I did not like the sound of it, so I requested and received permission from my medical superior as well as from the commanding officer of the regiment to visit my family. Lieutenant Colonel Chaganava also ordered me to purchase Georgian costumes and musical instruments while I was in Tbilisi. He was sponsoring a Georgian singing and dancing group in his regiment (and possibly in the division).

At last my train approached the city of Ordzhonikidze, (the name given to it by the Bolshevik conquerors). An old Russian name for it was "Vladi Kavkaz" which means "Conquer the Caucasus," leaving no doubt about the Russian czars' intentions. The real old name of the city had been Dzaujikau or Dzaugi. At last I could see "my" beautiful Caucasus Mountains in the distance. Further south. I had actually climbed some of them. It now seemed a century ago. At the north Caucasian railroad stations, the women and children were selling delicious roasted chickens, meat pies, cheese, bread and yogurt. The train proceeded to follow the north side of the Caucasian mountain chain, direction east, and after reaching Baku, on the Caspian Sea, it would turn around and continue to the west (opposite direction) and then follow the south side of the same mountains in the direction of Tbilisi, Georgia.

This is a long hairpin-shaped tract considering a much shorter "straight" north to south line between Ordzhonikidze and Tbilisi. Indeed, the "Georgian Military Highway" utilizes this line, crossing over the "Dshvari Pass" and the continental divide and to Tbilisi. It also passes near Mount Kazbek, which is one of the tallest "giants" of Europe. Here, nature is breathtaking and beautiful and the historical landmarks are very interesting. The road is temporarily closed during winter. The north part of the highway follows the river Tergi (Terek) and the south part follows the Aragavi River. Mt. Kazbek and the surrounding area, including the city of Kazbek, had been my stomping ground serving my alpinist activities, as I shall discuss later on.

As our train headed in the direction of the Caspian Sea and to the city of Derbent and Baku, I shared a compartment with two North Caucasian gentlemen, a father and son from Dagestan. They were headed back home from Moscow, where they had staged an exhibition in the circus of the Caucasian horsemanship—the art of "Jigit." The father was distinguished looking and had a "hawkish" face. He appeared to be a true descendant of his ancestors, who under the leadership of the great Imam Shamil fought against the Russian czar for over thirty years to defend the freedom of his country. We two Caucasians had much to tell each other and felt close, even though I was a Christian and he was a Muslim. His son was a handsome man in his twenties.

The son, as a Muslim, should not have, but nevertheless did indulge in alcohol. Frequently visiting the diner car and on his way back, the young "Jigit" decided to demonstrate his art of horsemanship on the banisters and the buffers between the railroad cars. This would be a dangerous exercise especially when the train is moving, even if one is sober, which he was not. Father was napping in the compartment, so I took it upon myself to prevent him from having an accident. While he appreciated my efforts and politely thanked me for them, with a happy smile, he continued the acrobatics. I badly needed help and suddenly got it.

He was a young, giant Dagestani man in Caucasian attire. His chest was adorned with a "Lenin Order," the highest reward in the Soviet Union. He reached over the rails, grabbed his countryman and together we hoisted and carried him inside the wagon. The giant's first name was Giorgi, as he introduced himself; it happens to be a Georgian name but I thought it to be an unusual name for a

Dagestani. As we both started gently coaxing our "protege" in the right direction to his father's compartment, we noticed ahead of us a good looking Russian couple enjoying the scenery out of the window from the passageway. As our young "horseman" was passing them and not being steady on his feet, he unintentionally bumped into the couple.

The Russian pushed him away with an angry, nasty remark such as "the primitive, savage drunkard." We did notice that the Russian was also wearing on his chest the same order as Giorgi, a sign of some significant accomplishment for the Soviet State. This did not deter Giorgi, however and infuriated by the Russian's insulting words toward his countryman, he grabbed the Russian, shook him and shouted, "I bet you and your lady are drunk and worse more often than my friend here." "Incidentally," he added, "this is not the only bad habit you Russians have."

The Russian was at a loss for an answer and obviously was not prepared for such a confrontation. I pleaded with Giorgi to get over his anger, reminding him that it was the Caucasian tradition to do so since a lady was present and she was begging with her eyes for peace. This seemed to have convinced Giorgi and he took his hands off the Russian fellow, the carrier of the Lenin Order. Then he turned to me and said, "You went to a lot of trouble to protect the young Dagestani man from hurting himself because you are a Georgian and your heart is in the right place. I am sure that it would not even have occurred to this Russian to do so." In disgust he turned his back on them. As the train reached Derbent Station, the father and son and Giorgi got off the train after exchanging with me the usual Caucasian pleasantries.

It was interesting for me to observe the two Soviet V.I.P.s displaying their nationalist bias in Stalin's streamline monolithic society. Giorgi was furious because he recognized in the Russian's remarks, "primitive and savage" directed toward his neighbor Caucasian, the continuation of the Russian Czar's chauvinistic colonial attitude toward the conquered non-Russian people. It was well remembered that the Czar and his people often tried to justify such a conquest by claiming that those non-Russians were "wild, primitive savages, less cultured, cruel, asians, etc." How fortunate for them, at last, to be included in the civilized Russian Empire where they now had the prospect of being educated and enlightened. No mention was made about the fact that some of the annexed non-Russians had a history of a much older civilization and statehood than the Russians themselves.

The Russification policy had begun: teaching in the schools had to be in the Russian language, local universities were forbidden. Those who could afford it had to enter the Russian universities except there were some who choose to go to Western Europe. As if the loss of national independence, coupled with the social injustice prevailing in imperial Russia was not bad enough, such a forced Russification policy further fomented the anti-Russian sentiment among the indigenous people. One did not take into consideration that there were also such Russians who were opposed to their own czar's wrong policies.

Unfortunately, the remnants of such an ugly, chauvinistic attitude still could have been observed in my time and even more now in the Red Army, among the "half-educated," unsophisticated, non-commissioned and commissioned officers. It was not uncommon to hear derogatory names and sarcastic references to non-Russian soldiers especially of Turkestani origin. To be sure, those soldiers were different than Russians, but being different does not necessarily mean worse. It did not occur to the chauvinists that due to their Soviet government's policy, non-Russians were forced to serve in Russia rather than in their native land, which posed linguistic and other hardships on them.

All of these thoughts helped me to take my mind off my sister's illness. The following morning, as we were approaching Tbilisi, my heart began to pound from joy and anticipation. I could hardly control it. There it was, the city built in the fifth century that has seen so many good and bad times, glory and defeat but mostly the struggle for survival. Maybe this is why Georgian songs are, at times, very sad and again vivacious and cheerful, as our visiting American friends have noticed. They have written this to us from there.

I don't quite know how I got home; I remember telling the carriage driver to hurry up if he wanted a good tip. The large red brick house at the foot of the hill, our apartment on the top floor looked unchanged.

As I ran up the stairs, there she was, my sister Eteri, lying in bed surrounded by her university classmates. "Mother will soon be back," they cheerfully shouted. Eteri was a beautiful eighteen-year-old, with large expressive brown eyes. Long eyelashes moved up and down like small butterflies. Her face was somewhat pale and delicate, a pleasant smile as always. As I embraced her, I noticed that she had lost weight. Eteri explained that she had difficulty with her balance and still had considerable headaches and a loss of appetite so she stayed in bed most of the time. "Since you are here, I will be all right," she said and clasped her hands.

Doctors were not sure what was causing her symptoms. She had an appointment with the ear, throat and nose professor (a specialist in this field) the following day.

"Still no news from Father," said Eteri.

Mother seemed to have aged considerably, it was a small wonder—loss of her husband four years ago, now Eteri's illness, and me stationed in remote, vast Russia. As I have said, Mother was a recognized teacher with tenure; her salary was very modest, probably one hundred-fifty to two hundred rubles, as this was the going rate in the Soviet Union for the majority of teachers. My Red Army salary was some thirty-two rubles plus shelter, uniforms and food. Even though I was doing the job of a medical officer, I was not given an officer's salary because I was serving two years of obligatory duty.

Mother had written many times after Father's arrest to influential persons, including Beria and Stalin. She pleaded to know of his fate and also what charges were made against him. She assured them that Father had intended no harm. Several times a day, I walked around the compounds where N.K.V.D. was housed in the hope of glimpsing Father by some sheer luck.

Mother was allowed to hand over fifty rubles through the "pigeon hole" to the N.K.V.D. guard for Father's use. During October 1937, the money was no longer accepted and she was told that her husband had been sentenced to an undetermined location for an "undetermined number of years" and "without the privilege of communication." Unofficial information, however, spread the news that prisoners of such a category had already been executed.

Father's arrest and disappearance during July of 1937 devastated each of us. Eteri, being the youngest, visibly wilted after that and could not comprehend the reason for Father's punishment. We all adored Father but it was a special delight to see him with Eteri horseback riding or discussing things. It appeared as if the King of the Mountains—the Caucasian Eagle, had spread his wings and was hovering over his little eaglet, Eteri.

After Father's arrest, when a car stopped near our house during the night, we would wake up shivering with fear since we expected that our mother also would be arrested. This, in fact, was the fate of many wives of political prisoners. Somehow this did not take place during the four years that followed, the reason for which was not entirely clear to us. Perhaps, the bureaucratic accounting during such massive arrests were not infallible after all. One possible explanation may have been that Father's arrest was registered and took place in our province, Svaneti, and Mother at that time was in Tbilisi.

She did not, however, escape such fate in the long run. She was deported during 1950 to Kazakhstan, this time because of my disappearance to the West, which was an act of opposition to the regime. She was released only after Khrushchev's denunciation of Stalin's crimes in 1956. After her return to Georgia from exile, she was no longer able to walk because of severe crippling rheumatism.

Eteri was a good student at the university and did qualify for a very modest stipend as long as she continued to have good grades. In the government stores, prices were very reasonable but the lines were long and goods in short supply. Teaching long hours in school, Mother's chance of getting anything from such stores (even after standing in line a long time) was remote. Prices were much higher at the private market, but it was tolerated by the system because there was no other way to supply the consumers.

Fortunately, during the last three years of medical school, I held night jobs at the university hospital earning a small income. Moreover, during the last two summers, I had two occupations in the high Alpine camp "Devdoraki," near Kazbek. One, a position for physician and secondly, that for a certified, junior instructor of alpine sport. My combined salary there was probably higher than a full time professor anywhere in the Soviet Union. The reason for such a disproportionate reimbursement was because alpine sport is considered potential military preparation for young people and that made the difference. In fact, twice during the season, an army major paid a visit to our "civilian camp." Good food, equipment, lodging, transportation and some of the clothing were supplied to me at no cost. I simply transferred all my earnings to Mother and Eteri. This helped maintain the minimum standard of living, given to mother's thriftiness.

I took Eteri to the professor of ear, nose and throat the next day. After the examination, it was unfortunately clear that the reason for her symptoms did not originate in her inner ear. This, of course, left the back part of the brain, or as the doctors call it, the posterior fossa region where the cerebellum is located, as the source of her ailment. Was it a blood clot, as the result of the fall she sustained in school or a brain tumor?

We went back to my former teacher, Professor Simon Kipshidse, the chairman of the Department of Neurology at Tbilisi Medical School. He was an excellent teacher, had great knowledge in his specialty and was an astute diagnostician. In those days—before CT scans, M. R. I. and isotope scans—this was an accomplishment. Years later, I was still grateful to him for the benefits of his teaching. Yet I was not impressed by him as a compassionate physician concerned on an ongoing basis for his patients. If he had this quality, it did not show on the surface and he came across as a somewhat cold and detached person. (Opposite to this were many of his senior associates, notably, Dr. Gregory Grigolashvili, who revealed a great deal of personal human concern and compassion.) After a thorough examination, the professor expressed his opinion of "some kind of cerebellar brain lesion." There were no suggestions made by him regarding further treatment. "Eteri," he said, "just as well go back home." At that time, there was not a single neurosurgeon in the large city of Tbilisi capable of such surgical exploration.

The final results of such a condition are poor in the majority of cases even after the operation. This was well known to us, but there were exceptions and the patient is entitled to the benefit of the doubt. A neurosurgeon of great reputation in the U.S.S.R. was Professor Burdenko in Kiev. The wheels had to be set in rapid motion so I could take Eteri there myself.

In the Georgian Ministry of Health, there were some of my former medical school teachers holding positions and were capable of understanding the medical situation. They issued permission for such an absolutely justified referral of the patient. The patient was accepted by Professor R. Burdenko and an appointment was made in Kiev. A compartment in the train was arranged for Eteri's comfort. The commanding officer of my regiment granted me a longer leave of absence.

While this was going on, Eteri was surrounded by much love and attention from relatives and school friends. Among them Liziko Bagrationi, Mania Kobulashvili, Natela Chachba, and our cousins the Tevzadses, Wachtang, Nina, Kolia and Aunt Nina. They all hovered over her.

Mother was encouraged by all this action, but I was terribly worried and restless. I tried not to give outward signs of this.

One night, Eteri had a more severe episode of headaches than usual. She got very little sleep. Mother's cousin Wachtang Tevzadze (a last year medical school student), and I were taking turns to sit at her bedside. Finally, I went to bed since in the early morning I had to arrange papers and attend to final preparations for the trip to Kiev. When I returned home at noon, Eteri was no more.

Our neighbors all gathered in her room. Mother's appearance defied description, but the old veteran of disastrous experiences, as always, thought first of others. She rushed to me with the reminder of our ancestors who endured even more tragedies but were strong during such times. There was nothing more to say.

Eteri's funeral turned out to be a demonstration of sympathy and solidarity with our family because it was a tragedy of one of the many repressed Georgian families and this touched many hearts. The powerless people obviously wanted to express not only their compassion but also to protest against unheard of mental cruelty. Cruelty of forcing shivering and scared children of "purged" parents to denounce their own parents in open meetings of the universities, while saying that they now were severing bonds with them. As the funeral procession reached Rustaveli Avenue, all traffic was paralyzed for many blocks. The procession was led by students carrying garlands arranged around the horns of the Caucasian Ibex, a symbol of our province.

As we reached Eteri's final resting place, the chorus of Svans (men from Svaneti) moved forward and began to sing the ancient mourning hymn "Zari." The public was stunned and frozen by this sad and majestic song performed by the mountain men who descended over snow-covered passes to be with us and express their deep grief.

I glanced at Mother. I felt so terribly sorry for her; she and her husband had spent their best years in Svaneti to guide and serve these legendary peoples. They did earn their trust and affection. Suddenly and spontaneously, with a choked voice, I let out what was inside of me in the tune of "Zari, where are you Father Egnatius during this time of our despair?" As I said this, our Abkhaz relatives, the Gablias from the town of Tamush knelt in complete silence next to us trying to comfort us. One could hear only the subdued sobs. When we left Eteri's grave, I felt as if part of me had died with her.

Close friends and relatives came to our home that evening for much needed togetherness. The mountain people of "Free Svaneti" (part of upper Svaneti) for many centuries lived by their own unwritten rules and traditions and have never tolerated the oppression and have remained free. The ultimate Judge was God Himself. For instance, a person accused of a serious wrongdoing had to appear in the sacred monastery of the Saints, Kvirike and Ivlita and swear there on the Icon of Shallian that he was not guilty of the crime or else God should strike him down. If he swore so, he was pronounced free. People served on a voluntary basis during the war only to the few favorite Georgian Kings, e.g. Queen Thamar in the twelfth century who gained their trust and affection by treating them with great respect. Their life was structured around the church and the family clan. Common serious matters such as war were decided by the Council of Wise Men elected by the voters and the "Makhvshi," sort of a president, likewise elected. Vendetta was prevalent—a paradox in this deeply religious, old Christian country. My cousins, Vasili, Alfez, Seraphion, Iliko and Mamuli, expressed their satisfaction and pride because of the great respect and compassion shown to "our clan" by the overwhelming number of people during those difficult days. Our Abkhaz relatives, the Gablias from Tamush also remained with us for a few days. Their presence added to our comfort, especially Akaki Gablia and his gracious wife, whose maiden name was Emukhvari. Two legendary brothers Emukhvari were especially distinguished because of their resistance of the Bolshevik rulers. "Abkhazeti" is in the Northwest part of Georgia.

Our name Gablia and Gabliani is the same. A feud had developed between us and another influential family. As was told to me by my father, bloodshed had occurred between us and therefore one part of the Gablias moved to the adjacent mountainous "Free Svaneti" and settled there. There were no "rulers" and no "ruled." Every clan had its own tower "Murkvam" and each clan had equally massive stone houses. Such a defense complex was surrounded by a fortress fashioned by nature—the mountains, which were difficult for the enemy to overcome. This, combined with courage, a fierce fighting spirit and a love of freedom made it possible for the Free Svans to survive with dignity.

* * *

I remained in Tbilisi for two and one-half or three weeks, trying to comfort Mother. There was a general mood of gloom among many friends, for now it had become certain that a large part of our leading intelligentsia had been murdered due to fabricated charges by N.K.V.D. (M.V.D.) on orders of Stalin and Beria. Characteristic was the accusation against Professor Dr. Giorgi Eliava, a leading bacteriologist; as if he wanted to poison the city water supply system in Tbilisi. The official information given to relatives of those who were put to death was, "sentenced to undetermined place for an undetermined number of years and without the privilege of communication." It was a lie; they were already dead.

As if this were not bad enough, many young Georgians, including the university graduates, were removed from their home country and sent to Russia for military service or to remote areas for civilian duty as engineers, architects, M.D.s, etc. Some of them, very likely, would get situated and married there and not return to their country—a painful loss for a nation of three-and-a-half million.

While still in Tbilisi, I received an incredible message to see Ilia Phaliani at his residence. I did not realize that he was alive since he had been arrested during the summer of 1937 with my father and with other innumerable Georgians. He was an old and trusted friend of our family. We called him "Uncle Ilia." He was married to Aza Kebadze; the Kebadzes were famous for commercialization of a popular Georgian mineral water "Borjomi." Uncle Ilia Phaliani was one of a few who recently were released by the secret police (N. K. V. D.) When I arrived at his apartment in a fashionable district, he was alone since Mrs. Phaliani was visiting her relatives. Uncle Ilia appeared much older than his actual age. He was pale, weak and remained in bed most of the time. I could hardly recognize him. For the next several hours, I listened to the horror story of his incarceration.

He was kept in dungeons, tortured and barely survived. "The men of N.K.V.D.," he said, "behaved worse than predator beasts. They will torture you until you are near death in order to get a false confession, then they will allow time for you to come to life and the whole thing will be repeated over and over again." After a long silence, he added, "I am afraid that due to your pride and upbringing you will fight well as a soldier. I am pleading with you now not to do that, and I am going to tell the same to my nephew who is in the Air Force. For ours is a criminal government, it deserves to be destroyed and the sooner, the better. The Czar's tyranny which was by far better than what we have now, was brought down by the First World War.

"The Bolshevik tyranny may also come to an end if Russia gets involved further in the general war. It has already begun to move in this direction, by signing a pact with Hitler and invading Poland, Finland and the Baltic States. Stalin expects Germany and other western powers will fight each other to death and after that he will take the world over by their default. Criminals like him usually make a fatal mistake somewhere."

I sat there without uttering a word.

The unbearable thought was going through my head—what tortures my father must have endured before they put him to death. This encounter with Ilia Phaliani had the most profound effect and influence on me. His words sounded to me as if they were my father's last will before they killed him. It was not the first time I felt that we had a criminal government. I did so, for instance, after the 1936–37 purges, and having witnessed the Soviet invasion of the Baltic States, but this was the "last straw." There was no way to stop this injustice from inside and peacefully since the lawless dictator and his associates were permitted, by the prevailing system, the total control of everything. They were not accountable to people and not even to their own party; how else would they eliminate so many ranking Bolsheviks?

"Justice," with special courts, secret police, the army, M.V.D. troops and the party itself were only the tools of unlimited Kremlin power. Even the universities and the factories had a party and a secret police cell for constant supervision by virtue of the informers. The only possibility of bringing down this totalitarian tyranny was a major event such as the war—as Uncle Ilia had indicated. During my farewell, I told him that we were in agreement and that I would not kill myself to defend the present system.

I did not engage in such a discussion with my other friends in order not to endanger them since M.V.D. had its "ears" everywhere. The days I had left in Tbilisi were passing fast and a number of friends were visiting me. After my departure to Russia, they wrote me; I carried their letters as precious cargo and still have them in my possession. Among them are ones from Aliosha Djaparidze, his sister Alexandra, Mother Lyda and Dr. Vadim Tchenkeli. Brother and sister Djaparidzes have contributed enormously to the progress of Georgian alpinism throughout the country along with other dedicated members of the Georgian Alpine Club. I had the privilege of belonging to this club and through their guidance, I was able to establish the Alpine Sport Organization in Tbilisi Medical School, in 1938.

Discounting politics on our side, we simply believed this sport to be a good one for the education of the body and ethics for the youth. Such had also been the belief of the Georgian sports group, "Shevardeni" (The Hawk) created during the Georgian independence that shortly after Soviet occupation had been forbidden by the Bolshevik authorities. Now the interested youth of the medical school were also given the opportunity to climb to the summit of such a majestic mountain as

Kazbek during the summer of 1938 and Mt. Khabarjina during late October or early November of 1938.

Preceding such an endeavor, they had to undergo a vigorous training in mountain climbing theory and technical practice in the surrounding terrain. In order to gain official support, the October expedition had to be dedicated to the anniversary of the October Revolution in Russia. The weather in high mountains during this time of year is short of being good, therefore, we chose the somewhat less high Khabarjina for our expedition this time. We were joined by another group from a sports organization, "Spartacus" under the leadership of no one else but my famous friend Aliosha Djaparidze. The weather was beastly and unfortunately two men from his group, Dunaevski and Kveniashvili died of exposure and cardiac failure.

Our greatest concern had been Lamara Kecharadze, the only lady participant from the doctors' group. She did better than anyone else, proving one more time the wisdom of Shota Rustaveli who said, "The lion's cubs are equal be it male or female." Aliosha Djaparidze was also very successful in planning the hydroelectric power plants. His sister was an excellent alpinist in her own right and was also a specialist in meteorology. Their Mother, Lida, a remarkable lady and a true Georgian mother, was totally dedicated to her family and friends.

There is also a letter and a poem by Dr. Vadim Chkhenkeli, a trusted friend and a gifted poet. He, too, had been mobilized in the Soviet Army and sent to Kishinev "Moldavian Republic," one of the newly "liberated" and occupied territory of the Red Army. In his last letter to me, Vadim correctly predicted the outbreak of the war and his own demise as a result of it.

An eyewitness reported later that he was gravely wounded during the German attack and since his condition was hopeless, he put an end to his unbearable suffering by his own bullet. Among Vadim's many writings there is an allegoric poem, "The Mad Gardner"—the villain, walking in the garden, instead of taking care and nurturing beautiful flowers, chopped them down. Vadim Chkhenkeli, of course, was referring to Joseph Stalin, "The Great Father and Teacher of the Soviet People."

The time finally came to say goodbye. Everyone assured me that Mother would not be left alone. I was anticipating returning to Tbilisi during September 1941, just seven months away, since this would be the end of my two years of obligatory military service. As it turned out, this was the last time I ever saw Georgia and loved ones there.

I arrived back in Slutzk to resume my usual duties in Regiment 228. Two weeks later I was transferred to the Artillery Regiment 82, since the chief medical officer there had to leave for post graduate studies and I was needed to replace him. I bid farewell to my friends in Regiment 228. Among them were Lt. Colonel, Gregory

Chaganava and Capt. Misha Kartvelishvili. The Captain was known not only as the best shot but also for his humor and jokes. Georgian jokes don't always translate well in Russian or other languages.

He told me how, during my absence, his humor almost got him in trouble. One of his pupils, a Russian officer, was not scoring well in the Captain's shooting class. This went on for a while and finally the Captain told his pupil, "Maybe I am a poor teacher and it's my fault; but on the other hand," he jokingly added, "probably not because I am a smart Georgian." Next thing he knew, he was summoned by the Regimental Commissar (the political officer) for an explanation. Apparently the pupil had complained that the Captain, by insinuation, meant that Russians were stupid. Capt. Kartvelishvili simply told the commissar, "Comrade Commissar, such an accusation just does not make any sense at all. It is common knowledge that the smartest man in the whole world was our leader Comrade Lenin and he was a Russian, wasn't he?" The commissar apparently was pleased and lost for an answer after such an explanation, and the final outcome was good.

I found the majority of officers in the Artillery Regiment 82 to be friendly and easy to work with. I was the only M.D. there and gradually had to assume the role of a family physician for the officers' families. Major Voropaev was an impressive officer who had participated in the Spanish Civil War and was decorated with the highest honor for it. The regiment had the intermediate range artillery guns which were pulled by horses and consisted of three divisions. It proved to be a formidable force in the marshlands and forests of Belorussia during the war with its ability to maneuver camouflage with ease and the accuracy of fire. I particularly befriended the commander of one of the divisions, Capt. Lubianski. He was a cultured, bright, gentleman who kept a low profile but was a man of courage. He demonstrated tremendous ability to command on the battlefield. Capt. Lubianski acted during the war as if this were a war game. His cool-headedness, disregard for personal danger and his military skill had a great effect on his soldiers.

Another friend of mine was the chief of the Veterinary Service, Major Dr. Israel Aaronovitch Poljakov. While riding often together, we had essentially uninhibited discussions about art, history and even politics. One day, he told me that things would have been different if Lenin were alive and at the helm. He remembered his "N.E.P.," the New Economic Policy with more "freedom." The doctor also deplored "liquidation" of so many good officers of the Red Army. "Look at the chaos in our infantry regiments," he said, "Germans call us the Russian Pigs." I did not disagree with him but asked him a question about what he thought of a system that allows one person to govern without any control or accountability to anyone? He appeared startled and rode next to me but refrained from answering my question.

During April or at the beginning of May, the regiment was ordered to move into the spring and summer quarters, outside of Slutzk in the forest. Having completed the regimental vaccination program and the general physical examinations, I treated myself to the cavalry games which temporarily helped me to overcome the terrible sadness. The regiment had very good horses, but two were outstanding. One belonged to Major Voropaevs and another to Lieutenant Mussey. They allowed me to ride their horses when I desired. It was rather a rainy spring but there were some good days in between for outdoor activities.

2

ENTRANCE INTO WORLD WAR II

On June 22, 1941, a great alarm was sounded—it was announced that Germany invaded the Soviet Union [Operation Barbarossa] and now World War II began also for her. Lieutenant Colonel Grisha Chaganava's prediction was correct, it was incredible that the greatest Machiavellian Kremlin politicians apparently were caught unprepared and surprised by such an attack. One would hardly expect that the innocent victims of previous brutal Soviet aggression such as Poland, the Baltic States and Finland felt any particular sympathy for a predator in trouble now. Certainly this was also true for persons with a long memory in non-Russian Soviet Republics, the "older" victims of the Bolshevik Russian aggression.

Artillery Regiment 82, with other components of the 55th Division was set on march, direction northwest. Commissar of the regiment in a special "pep speech" declared that we shall "destroy the enemy and take no prisoners." That meant that any enemy soldier who surrenders should be shot on the spot. My first thought was about the international agreements concerning the P.O.W.s and what about the wounded soldiers? I did not dare to question the angry commissar, but I knew I would not follow his advice. After a few days, we got our first look at the German soldiers. Two of them on a motorcycle, probably on a scouting mission and simply were lost. They were shot and wounded by our advanced scouts. I immediately gave them medical aid. One of them clearly would not make it; the other one was in better shape and was referred to the Division Staff by the M.V.D. representative of our regiment for investigative purposes. So, the commissar's declaration "we shall take no prisoners" did not materialize after all.

Our medics showed me the papers found on the mortally injured German. There was a picture of his young wife and baby along with a letter expressing her love and hope for their reunion in the near future. "This is only the beginning; such tragedies will occur on a larger scale," I thought.

Soon we encountered an air attack by low flying German fighter planes; they were strafing us while making several passes back and forth over our heads. The retreating troops we encountered were in a panic but not our artillery regiment. Especially Captain Lubianski and Lieutenant Mussey who at first spread their batteries away from the road and under the trees. Without cover for themselves, they gave orders to take direct aim at the attackers and fire. It was fascinating to watch professional officers in action. Such a "duel" continued for a while until the German aircraft left, perhaps low on ammunition or fuel.

Our regiment's artillery was not meant for air defense and their ability to shoot down an airplane was very low. But this action gave a psychological boost to Lubianski's soldiers and could have impressed the attacker. Capt. Lubianski and I walked a considerable distance to see if we had any human or animal casualties and happily we found none. What we saw, however, was a panic stricken man hugging a tree with one hand and protecting his head with another and trembling. Captain Lubianski decided to administer the "shock treatment" without consulting me. He grabbed him around the waistline and in an ungodly voice shouted, "straighten up soldier." As the soldier did so, it became clear that he was a commissar in captain's rank, fortunately not from our regiment. It was difficult to tell who was more embarrassed, Captain Lubianski of the commissar. The "therapy" did work, however, and the "patient" departed in haste following his "sheep"—equally scared and retreating in the direction east while we continued in the opposite direction to meet the Germans. Captain Lubianski was mindful of the deleterious effect of a scared officer on the troops Therefore, he never failed to demonstrate his courage whenever the situation arose.

With our advancement further west, it became obvious that the skies were totally dominated by the German Air Force. This had an enormous psychological impact on the troops, especially the diving bombers—so called "Stukas" (Ju 87s). We only occasionally noted the Soviet bombers, two of them shot down by one German fighter plane over our heads. Fortunately, the pilots parachuted to safety. Our horse-driven artillery was able to move on the side roads, in the forests and swamps of Belorussia, well camouflaged. Therefore, initial casualties were light although it often fought off the German attacks without the support of the infantry. I made several trips to Smolensk Military Hospital to accompany the wounded. We usually started off during early morning or late evening to avoid the low flying German fighter planes.

In Smolensk there was a feeling of uncertainty but no panic. I was impressed by the general absence of concern among the Belorussian and Ukrainian population in the face of advancing German troops.

One day our regiment crossed the river Berezina and advanced further west. However, soon the order from the division staff reached us to retreat—direction east. The reason was obvious. The Germans were rapidly advancing on the flanks and encircling us. Crossing back across the river was dangerous especially due to the dominating hostile air force. This was the historical river, Berezina, which Napoleon with "The Great Army" also crossed twice (in the reverse, as compared to us) during his unsuccessful Russian campaign. For my own part, while moving from one shore to another, I thought that if I ever have children they shall all be good swimmers, which was more than I could say about myself.

Finally, our division did establish a defensive front line for a while and the Artillery Regiment 82 distinguished itself with a great performance. At this time, I was able to locate a post office in the small Belorussian town, Propoisk and mailed a letter to Mother. I assured her that I was doing alright and that I would survive this war (inasmuch as I was a doctor). Should she not receive letters for a long time, she should believe that I am alive. In this, somehow I was convinced myself. And yet, only a few days later Captain Lubianski's artillery division (while I was working there) suddenly came under a most severe concentrated German artillery barrage of a long duration. The casualties were heavy and the Captain and I considered ourselves lucky to have survived inasmuch as we had to go on carrying out our duties even without the simple protection of open trenches.

I was able to write Mother again seventeen years later, after she was allowed to return to Georgia (due to the Khrushchev reforms) from her exile in Kazakhstan. In this letter, I did not ask if my previous letter had been received but it was confirmed by her distant relative, visiting in the U.S.A., that she had indeed received my previous letter from Propoisk, Belorussia during the summer of 1941.

3

A GERMAN P.O.W. OUTSIDE THE PRISON CAMP

After several days, our artillery regiment had to start retreating again and continued maneuvering frequently in order to get out of the next German encirclement. Once the German tanks broke through they continued advancing forward, taking full advantage of the initial success. The Soviet tanks, however, after gaining some territory invariably would stop, waiting for further orders—what to do. This usually lead to being outflanked again by the Germans. Yet it was soon appreciated that the Soviet tank, notably T-34, at that time was the best in the field.

The Soviet artillery was very good in combat. I could personally observe the performance of the infantry on a small scale, but according to many reports, it was rather poor. To be fair, one had to consider, of course, the element of surprise due to German "blitzkrieg" ("lightning," a sudden attack) in addition to their better training and experience. Here again, purges of the best Red Army officers during 1936–37 most likely weakened the performance of the troops. But in my opinion every bit as important, if not more so, was the apathy of the soldiers who were offspring of the enslaved people with broken spirits and dissatisfaction in their hearts. And the "Soviet Fatherland"? What kind of fatherland was it, without human rights and the right to private property? The farmers were coerced into the hated collective farms and purged with fabricated charges of being "kulaks" ("rich" farmers"), as already noted. The workers were forbidden to have independent trade unions, religion was persecuted, etc.[8] It was reported that the advancing German troops were received

---

8- One day a coal miner named Stakhanow dug an enormous amount of coal, pushing himself to the limit. Having established an incredibly high "norm," he never had to work again. He received a high decoration and under the sponsorship of the Soviet government toured other coal mines lecturing them as to how to consistently produce as much coal as he had done. Instead of protesting such inhuman exploitation of the workers, "their" trade unions applauded such a policy by the government.

as the liberators by the local populace. Rumor also had it that the Germans were distributing goods among the population not otherwise available. (This, of course, was nonsense, they did not.)

The majority of the people felt that the Germans would surely improve the conditions as compared to what they had under the Kremlin rule. All of the said above were the common grievances of the Soviet people in general. In addition to that, the inhabitants of non-Russian ethnic republics felt unhappy, also due to the loss of national sovereignty by Bolshevik Russian occupation and domination. Furthermore, the Soviet people felt that the Germans were part of the civilized west and considered them to be strict but just, thrifty, orderly and inventive. "The Germans invented even the monkey," was a Russian saying (nemtsi "abezianu vidumali"). The Russian P.O.W.s in Germany returning home after W.W. I had many good things to report, which were still remembered, about Germany. The German settlers on imperial Russian territory were models of good citizens. What about vigorous Kremlin propaganda against Germany? Well, it was too "vigorous" at first, and then following the Soviet-German Pact of 1939, Germans became the "good guys."

Not only that, but as late as May 1941, the fight of Great Britain against Hitler was denounced by the Soviet news media as "the second imperialistic war," stating that Great Britain and France were to blame for it. Molotov congratulated Germany for the successful "Blitz" war against the western Allies. German Communist Walter Ulbricht, as ordered by Stalin, declared that during an important war such as this, any attempt to change the political regime in Germany would be foolish and villainous. So much for Soviet propaganda.

Speaking of propaganda, the German aircraft often dropped propaganda leaflets over our heads. On one hand, leaflets encouraged the Soviet Army soldiers to defect to the German side, promising them good treatment. On the other hand, some leaflets called on Soviet soldiers to "beat up the Commissars and Jews." I was bewildered due to such propaganda, which appealed to the most primitive and criminal human instinct by a civilized country. I had no explanation for it, but suspected that perhaps some deranged, old, "white" Russian emigre from the "Black One Hundred's Group" [of patriotic vigilantes] had been employed by the Germans because of his linguistic ability and now he was airing his old obsessive antisemitic feelings again. I resolved that should I meet the Germans face to face one day, this would be one of my first grievances presented to them. I did not realize then that this would actually take place in the near future.

On July 3, 1941, we listened to the broadcast of Stalin's speech—his first since the war started. He was addressing, "Comrades, Brothers and Sisters," appealing for total war effort and a policy of "scorched earth" before German occupation and guerrilla warfare in the rear.

During the retreat of our regiment (and being followed by the Germans rather closely), we did not notice the peasants obeying Stalin's orders. Contrary to his orders, they kept their grain reserves, their harvest and their farm animals. This friendly attitude toward Germans gradually changed after the army left and the Ukrainians and Russians had been exposed to and disillusioned by Hitler's civilian Nazi administrations in the occupied territories. We shall say more about it later on.

We did hear in our regiment about a large number of Soviet soldiers taken as P.O.W.s by the Germans. Much later on, I learned from German sources about the extent of it. The figures were:

> End of June to early July, "pockets" of Bialystok
>   and Minsk, 320,000 prisoners
>
> July, battle of Smolensk, 300,000 prisoners
>
> August, battle of Uman, 103,000 prisoners
>
> September, battle of Kiev, 665,000 prisoners
>
> October, battles of Bryansk and Vyazma, 665,000 prisoners

It totaled more than a stunning two and one-half million P.O.W.s in German hands.[9] Casualties in our regiment increased especially after the German reconnaissance airplanes began to direct artillery fire against us. Soon our regiment had to be split in three component divisions, and each division had to be separately attached to the different infantry units for more flexible support. I had to cover considerable distances while making rounds to see them, and medical care became logistically more difficult.

The professional officers in artillery, as already noted, were so good that often the spirit of the team caught up with me; although, I was not a combat officer but just a doctor. I like to think that I was doing my very best to serve and help them as a "healer" and would continue to do so until the bitter end—as long as my services were needed. But I was not ready to change to a combat soldier and fight to defend Stalin and his henchmen, as I had discussed this with Uncle Ilia in Tbilisi.

One day, while making rounds and trying to locate the divisions of our regiment with a small group of people from our 82 Artillery Regiment, we found ourselves mixed up with some large infantry unit—in retreat, direction Southeast. The Germans were on our tail and also outflanking us from the right side and trying

---

9- See Wallace Carroll, "It Takes a Russian to Beat a Russian," *Life*, December 19, 1949, and *The World Almanac of World War II*. edited by Brigadier Peter Young, New York: Pharos Books, 1981.

now to do the same from the left. This battle raged for two days, and we had enormous casualties. On the third morning before sunrise, the group from our regiment had a meeting. We took advantage of the temporary pause of German artillery and Granatwerfer (mortar) fire. My good friend, Major Dr. Isac Aaronovitch Poljakov, the chief of Veterinary Service; first lieutenant of artillery (whose name I can't recall); one of our female doctors' assistants; my ambulance driver and others were present. The first lieutenant briefed us on the map; it became clear that there was only one way of retreat left, through the wooded marshland. Only the able bodied persons could do so. The wounded people had to be left behind. Also all our vehicles, equipment and medical material had to be abandoned.

The entire group of twenty to twenty-five was eager to retreat, and there was no time to lose. The first lieutenant was reasonably sure that beyond the marshland some five to ten miles further southeast, one of our artillery divisions may have "dug in" and were holding the position. I told them to go ahead; I wanted to see several wounded people and would catch up with them eventually. I also said that in case some of them needed first aid in my absence, there was a lady doctor's assistant with them and without equipment, I could do no more than she. So they went, but at the edge of the wooded area Dr. Poljakov turned around and shouted. "Gabliani, hurry up, there is no time to lose." I was terribly sad to part from them especially from Isac Aaronovitch Poljakov. It was a very painful and difficult decision. I did visit several injured; they were in stable condition but in need of surgical care. It amazed me how little pain medication was required during the war, compared to civilian practice. It was lighter now; I bypassed one side of the hill with dug-out trenches and with further utilization of the terrain, trying not to be in the path of previous artillery fire but to the left of it. When the sun finally came out, I could see the rooftops of the village houses, and that's where the Germans appeared to be. When the artillery and mortar fire resumed, it was centered over the first hill where trenches with dug-in soldiers were barely returning fire. I did observe that the German infantrymen took the hill, so in fact now I was already behind the German lines.

I was very tired, physically as well as emotionally, with practically no sleep for three nights. I sat down on a rock to collect my thoughts. On previous pages, I told how Imperial Germany during 1918–1921 helped the independent Georgian Republic. Years later, the Germans still enjoyed a considerable measure of popularity with the Georgians as opposed to the Bolshevik Russians who had used brutal force to occupy Georgia. Now there was a possibility that quickly advancing German troops could reach the Caucasus, what then? Will Germany take the same position now as before? I suspected that perhaps our political emigrants and the government in exile had already revived the old friendship with certain influential Germans. I wanted to know about it and felt ready to help with efforts for my country's better future. I could not find out about it without first of all meeting the Germans, and this was what I intended to do.

I got myself in trouble at once. I noticed three or four German soldiers passing by, and they also saw me. They quickly approached and demanded, at gunpoint, my revolver and hands up. They also took my briefcase with maps. I had already been told in Georgia that my face often appeared serious, unsmiling and even "fierce." This was probably my ancestral heritage from the mountains. This, together with my fatigue, worries and being dirty and unshaven convinced one of my young captors that I was a "political commissar," whose hatred for the Germans could clearly be seen on my face and what was I doing in this place anyway?

He was surprised when I spoke in German and tried to explain that I was just a tired doctor and had no evil intentions toward them. I was taking care of the wounded and wanted to talk with the Germans. I even produced my military identification booklet, but he could not read Russian and in any case probably did not care. He ordered me to start walking in the direction of the village and after a while we approached a shed where a German officer was sitting on a box or stool. He probably was the commanding officer of the battalion and appeared to be relaxed and in a good mood.

My captor clicked his heels and reported to the commander about the "catch of the day," me, a possible commissar. The officer did not get excited; he summoned the interpreter who checked my identification papers and reported loud and clear that I was no one else but an "oberarzt," a senior medical physician. (My I.D. card read "Starshi Wratch dlia Poruchenia" in Russian.) The officer appeared friendlier, even smiled a bit and wondered how it was that I spoke "such a good German?" In answer to that question, I explained that many schools in Georgia taught German and we even had a German "Gimnasium"[10] in Tbilisi. Besides as a child I had a private German tutor for a number of years.

"So you are a Georgian from the Caucasus, where there are such beautiful ladies.[11] I thought you were a Russian Jew because of your good German," said the officer. (He did not mention my Mediterranean looks being contributory to his impression.) I explained to the officer that I was hoping to get in touch with Georgian emigrants in Germany to get oriented, and to see if anything was being done on behalf of Georgia.

10- Gimnasium is the equivalent of high school and two years of college.

11- As I learned later on, there had been an almanac of a dictionary published in Germany many years ago, probably by Mayer, that praised the beauty of Georgian ladies and to which incidentally, I completely agree.

The officer said, "Maybe you will in due time," but he could not help me then since he was too busy on the front line. Our conversation was coming to an end and I thought I probably had to join other P.O.W.s who were gathered some distance from us, pending their march, direction West, probably to some P.O.W. camp. Suddenly the situation took an unexpected turn. A big sized gentleman in a white gown and limping approached us. I thought he was a German medical officer from some hospital since he looked and spoke like a German. He introduced himself to the German officer, with whom I had been conversing, as Leonid Sillin, the former administrator of the Soviet field military hospital, which had recently been overrun by the German troops. He said he was acting on the high German officer's order to organize a hospital and take care of the wounded Red Army soldiers that lay everywhere in large numbers around this area. He asked the German officer for help in securing as many P.O.W. doctors, doctor's assistants, nurses, pharmacists and medics as he could possibly get. When the officer agreed, they both looked at me and Mr. Sillin asked if I would be willing to join and help him care for the wounded. Of course, I agreed. So instead of marching further west to some P.O.W. camp, the Germans in charge left me to stay near the front line at the town of Krestitelevo, Ukraine.

Under the leadership of Mr. Leonard Sillin, two nearby school buildings were converted into hospitals. As far as medical supplies, surgical instruments, transportation and gasoline were concerned, we were self-sufficient since the remnants of the Soviet field military hospital, ambulances and other vehicles had fallen into German hands. They stood idle and were at our disposal. We started collecting the wounded from farmland and marshes; some of our patients were gravely ill, due to gas gangrene and other wound infections. The life saving amputations, as a last resort, had to be carried out at times. A congenial, dedicated and capable medical-surgical team was well organized by Leonid Sillin and we worked hard, at times around the clock.

Now, as before, I was impressed by the high ethical standards, ingenuity and ability of the Russian and Ukrainian physicians. After the outbreak of the war, at times, I felt poorly prepared and painfully inadequate to care for the complex problems of mass casualties. In addition to the high number of casualties, any part of the body could have been damaged, and some patients had suffered multiple serious injuries. A quick and correct decision of the diagnosis and treatment could make the difference between life and death. Therefore, it now was a welcomed opportunity for me to work with experienced, senior surgeons, some of them trauma experts. They were more than willing to share their knowledge with me, in a kind and encouraging manner. I did not mind the hard work at all. The artillery and air raid noises were gradually becoming more distinct, a sure sign the front was moving further east, due to further German advances. All wounded soldiers in captivity, as well as those who cared for them and generally all P.O.W.s in German hands, were automatically declared by Stalin's government as traitors, regardless of the circumstances that led to their capture.

The Soviet government adamantly refused to sign the Geneva Accord. Even the Nazi government was ready to sign a treaty with the Kremlin concerning the treatment of their prisoners of war, but in vain. The Kremlin took the position that there were no Soviet P.O.W.s there, only those who were captured by the Germans alive who were traitors.[12]

In the modern history of the civilized world, to the best of my knowledge, there is no record of any government except the one in the Kremlin, that completely abandoned its own imprisoned soldiers to the hands of the enemy.

Our leader, Leonid Sillin was a very positive, bright, energetic and good-natured gentleman. He owed his German looks and the perfect command of the German language to his German mother. He was also a great Russian patriot at heart, combining this virtue with courage and humanism. He was a professional lawyer from Moscow whose hobbies included gourmet cooking. His aversion for the repressive, inhuman regime was all too obvious although he chose not to talk about it. He had impressed the German military commandants so much that not a single German soldier guarded the premises of our hospital. We had freedom of movement within a reasonable distance of a few miles around our compound; therefore, we were the P.O.W.s in German hands but outside the P.O.W. camps. In return, Sillin gave his word of honor to the Germans that everyone working with him would remain on the job and would not run away. He made this clear to everyone on his crew and also the possible consequences of the broken promise.

Sillin's wife was of Armenian descent and probably because of that, he held the Caucasian people in high esteem. He obviously had read the history of Caucasus, as well as the old legends, romantic tales and literature, some of them written by Tolstoy and Lermontov. "We Russians," he once told me, "did not treat you Caucasians well, you came to us as friends and in return we occupied you." Now you must go there and tell your mountaineers that the time has come to raise up and gain freedom. Such a statement coming from a great Russian patriot amazed me. The contrast to it was his general attitude in such matters that I experienced a short time later.

12- See Alexander Dallin, *German Rule in Russia, 1941-1945: A Study in Occupation Policies*, New York: MacMillan, 1957, p. 42. ("The official Soviet position, that any soldier who fell into enemy hands was ipso facto a traitor and deserved no protection from his government, made its contribution to the mistreatment of prisoners in the Reich.")

One day, we decided to visit a civilian hospital in a nearby small Ukrainian city (for which we had to get a special permit by the German commandant). There, we obtained some medical supplies from their pharmacy. The group of civilian Ukrainian doctors there invited us for a "high tea." During our conversation, it was clear that our Ukrainian colleagues expected to become an independent state after the German victory.

Leonid Sillin had no comments there, but I could sense that he was upset. On our way home he broke the silence and said, "See, that's what they want, to dismember Russia in pieces, until nothing is left."

"But Russia is an enormous country," I argued, "from Petrograd to Vladivostok, from Arkhangelsk to Astrakhan and much beyond that. Besides these people are just talking and who knows what is going to happen. Incidentally, did you not tell me that we, the Caucasians, should rise and free ourselves to become independent again?"

"Givi Egnatievich," answered Sillin, "you don't understand, this is an entirely different matter. Ukraine is Russia, very much like Bavaria and Saxony are part of Germany. In the Caucasus, however, we Russians behaved badly against the non-Russian independent people. Some of them had their own history; language; splendid, old culture and statehood even before the Russians did." Sillin was depressed because he suddenly became cognizant of the danger that the Ukraine may be lost for Russia as a result of the war.

Of course, to begin with, should Hitler win the war none of us knew then what his design for the Soviet Union would be. One assumed that he was just fighting against Bolshevism and not against the people (like one fights sickness and not the people who are sick), and other matters would be settled after the war in close consultation with the Soviet populace.

One day, while strolling, Sillin told me in confidence that the encounter with the Ukrainian doctors had been an eye opener for him, therefore, he decided to go back to "his people"—meaning to escape from here and rejoin the Red Army. Sillin also said that although he was opposed to Stalin's rule, the political systems come and go but the nation remains. It was more important to keep the Great Russian Nation intact and not to weaken her.

It was an important early lesson for me and helpful to better understand the nationality problems of the Soviet Union. It also made clear to me why Stalin, who treated the Soviet people in the most cruel way, was eventually able to convert the war into the war for the "Russian Fatherland" (not for the Bolshevik system) and won it. He succeeded in this because of help from Hitler, who treated the people of the occupied territories and P.O.W.s even worse than Stalin. Hitler's intention for the colonization of Russia, Ukraine and some other Soviet territories had now become clear; he no longer was considered a liberator but a cruel conqueror. From the two cruel dictators, the Russian people chose their own "Modern Ivan the Terrible," Stalin, to be the winner.

During our work in Krestitelevo, however, it was purely a military zone and as noted before, none of us knew what lay ahead of us: we did not see the German Nazi civilian administration yet. I told Sillin that his running away would in no way influence the outcome of the war, and it surely would be a disaster for our patients and also for medical and paramedical people here who had worked so hard. I suggested that he at least postpone his defection, and he agreed.

In our hospital, we often had visitors, usually German military doctors. Some of them had the official duty to supervise our work, others were simply curious. Almost all of them appeared supportive and friendly, engaging in conversation with us and observing our work. One of them approached me because he had found out that I was a Georgian. He wanted to know if I ever heard of a lady doctor, also a Georgian, Badu Tsulukidze. He had worked with her in the charity hospital in Berlin. I said I was sorry that I did not know her but perhaps she was related to professor Aleko Tsulukidze, my former teacher in Tbilisi, where I had been assigned as a fellow in endocrinology and surgery.

The German doctor was very polite and appeared to be concerned about me and said that he was going to write about our encounter to Dr. Badu Tsulukidze. When he visited me again, approximately two and one-half weeks later, he read her reply to me. She had asked her German doctor friend to do all he could to help me as needed. She also expressed hope that we meet in the near future. I was sure that her friend went to the local military commandant and spoke to him on my behalf, since later I found the commandant unusually friendly and helpful to me.

All was going reasonably well in our "field hospital" and then suddenly disaster struck; one night two orderlies disappeared. We exhausted all possibilities of finding them but, in vain. They had given their word as had the rest of us to remain on the job, and Leonid Sillin vouched for us. Now it was his duty to report the incident to the commandant. He did so, and then informed the entire hospital staff about the results, which had been catastrophic.

The commandant was furious and told Sillin that according to military protocol he, Leonid Sillin, should be shot unless the escapees were found. As a special favor, he gave him twenty-four hours for this task. Moreover, as an incentive for those disappeared, no harm was to come to them if they reported back voluntarily, except that they would be sent to a P.O.W. camp further west. Some of the hospital staff hoped that the nearby village girls may have attracted them but all efforts to find them failed.

Sillin was not only a voucher but also the spokesman for us. I told him to inform "Herr Commandant" that I would voluntarily stand next to Sillin, during his execution, in order to share the punishment because I felt that Sillin could not have helped the disappearance of the two men any more than the rest of us could. I further thought that under Sillin's leadership, an excellent medical group had been formed that took care of many wounded and worked very hard. After all, execution of our leader would signify disapproval for all of us and for our work. Sillin was apparently moved by my words and exclaimed that "only the Caucasians are capable of such friendship and courage."

I told him that he was obviously partial to the Caucasians since he was married to an Armenian beauty. My attitude in reality had not much to do with courage but rather with logical calculation. First of all, the Commandant did need our services, otherwise what would he do with so many wounded, even if there was a hospital designated for the Russian wounded somewhat further west. The transportation alone had to be difficult and costly, not to mention further care for so many. He obviously did not have enough German manpower to guard us, so he had to depend on our cooperation and show mutual trust. He had to take some risks with us. Leonid Sillin was a half German, an excellent organizer, leader and communicator and enjoyed the confidence of the Germans. Therefore, he was much needed for the job. Shooting him would be unreasonable and the Germans have the reputation of being calculators. In other words, I thought that "Herr Commandant" was bluffing just to scare us. As it turned out, I was correct but unfortunately only partly.

The Commandant did not execute Leonid Sillin but instead two orderlies who shared a room with the two who had escaped. Obviously he decided to prevent such further incidents by demonstrating the consequences such an escape would have. This he did in a very businesslike way. First, he rode a motorcycle around the background of the shooting range in the conformity of safety regulations. Then, the two innocent men to be sacrificed were blindfolded and lined up facing the firing squad. Some distance from the firing line, most of the hospital personnel were ordered to witness it all. After the shooting was over, one of our doctors had to pronounce the unfortunate ones dead.

We were all depressed. I was in a terrible mood. It was the first time, and fortunately the last time in my life, that I witnessed the execution of human beings and innocent ones at that. According to my observation, the majority of Russians somehow get over such tragedies sooner than the more emotional Caucasian people do, or so it would appear. So while walking on our way back home, a couple of young nurses were already giggling, for which I scolded them and called them idiots. Of course, I should not have, maybe this is the only way they were able to face the tragedy or perhaps this was a matter of upbringing, family background, philosophy of life of the national trait. Maybe theirs is the better way.

Activities in our hospital after this horrible experience continued at the usual pace. The patient I admired most was a lady, a military doctor in her late twenties. She was badly wounded in both lower extremities, unable to walk and must have had considerable pain. She was very well poised, never complained or asked for special attention. Not only was she brave and intelligent but also beautiful. She was from the Petersburg area and possibly had some Scandinavian ancestors. We were concerned about her long term outlook although she was improving reasonably well. It became a custom for all of us to visit her at least a couple of times a day; her visitors included many German doctors as well. We all did this to encourage her, but I also suspected that another reason was that observing her did boost our own courage. I no longer remember her name, but years later I often thought about her and wondered what became of her.

4

TRANSFER TO GERMANY

The front line was advancing further, and the news was that the Germans had great military success against the Soviet armed forces. I gave much thought to what lay ahead for my homeland, Georgia should the Germans occupy her. Being cut off from the rest of the world as usual, the Soviet people did not have any reliable information about Germany; however, (as I have already alluded to) during our independence from 1918 to 1921, Germany had actively helped the Georgian Republic in many ways. It was a curious phenomenon that the German and the Georgian soldiers fought and died together against the Turks (then the German allies) to protect the Georgian border from the invading Turkish Army.

I note on one old photo in my archive of a funeral procession in Tbilisi for Georgian and German soldiers for Georgia, that the German and Georgian dignitaries are solemnly walking together on this sad occasion; among them Count Werner von der Schulenburg—the German diplomatic representative at that time in the Georgian Republic will be recognized.

When the Germans lost World War I, the British entered the Caucasus and demanded that the Germans be handed over as prisoners of war or else. The Georgian government refused this flatly, explaining to the victorious British that according to the Georgian tradition, guests are considered sacred and the Germans were our guests. In the end, the British chose not to carry out their threats. From the German report concerning this matter by one of the German delegation members:

> . . . Such chivalry cannot and will not be forgotten in Germany; it is a comforting realization that even in these difficult times there can still be true friendship between peoples, and every German whose heart is in the right place will always be faithful to the brave Georgians who have

remained loyal to their friends in times of need. Georgians will also never forget that Germany brought them national freedom, and this great deed of Germans is engraved in Georgian history with golden letters...[13]

The Georgians then organized several banquets in honor of the Germans, after which they were escorted to the railroad station and a safe passage was made for them up to the Georgian Black Sea coast. Of course, I did not have such photos or reports from the publication at that time but only a general knowledge of what had taken place. I was hoping that there were still some Germans alive who remembered the past. This could even offer us some chance of reestablishment of the independent Georgia. My plan was to somehow get to Berlin where an old friend of my father, Grigol Robakidze, the well-known writer in Georgia, as well as in Germany, was living.

I had long been fascinated by his writings but especially by a play, "Lamara," which had been performed for a number of years in the Rustaveli Theatre in Tbilisi. It was known that many of his works had also been published in Germany and were much appreciated there. Should I succeed in seeing Robakidze, I was hoping he would help me to contact other Georgian emigrants, especially the Georgian government in exile.

When I shared my plan with Leonid Sillin, he was ready to help at once. First he "dropped in" to talk about it with the German commandant, to "feel him out" and "prepare ground." He came back with a beaming face and informed me that Herr Commandant would see me the next day. From his account of the meeting, it was clear to me that Sillin blew me and my "importance" entirely out of proportion. I told him that he probably was reciting passages out of the book written about Shamil, the great North Caucasian leader of the thirty-year-long heroic war against Imperial Russia for the freedom of the country rather than presenting the "real me."

"Givi Egnatievich," answered Sillin, "I just summarized your extraordinary past and background for the Commandant as I know it from many conversations you and I have had. I conveyed your plea to be permitted to travel to Berlin. I also informed him about the high esteem we all hold for you here in our hospital." The history of my past that Sillin was referring to was that my father was the administrator for our mountainous province Svaneti during the Czar's rule as well as during the Georgian Independent Republic 1918–1921.

My father was much admired and loved by the mountaineers who also considered him their leader. As noted before, he had written books after long ethnological

---

13- See Appendix p. 359 for a continuation of this testimony in German and with an English translation.

and historical research and was a corresponding member of the Petersburg Academy of Science. He also was a pupil of the well known Prof. N. Marr; after the Bolshevik occupation of Georgia, he was arrested in the city of Kutaisi but miraculously broke out of jail. He then went home over the snow covered passes and after many close calls, to relative safety during the winter.

During August of 1924, the Georgian insurrection broke out against the Russian Bolsheviks, and he was the chief of staff of the insurgent force in his province, "Free Svaneti." The mountaineers quickly overthrew the local Bolshevik administration and advanced further south where they captured the city of Tsageri of the adjoining province Lechkhumi but the news arrived that the insurrection in the Georgian heartland and everywhere else had been crushed by the much stronger regular Red Army troops. The expected help from the West was never received. Father's forces had to retreat back to their mountains, but eventually the Red Army also occupied the most important parts of our territory.

Mother, little sister Eteri and I, together with father and his group of faithful, armed men, took refuge in the forest covered hills. From there, with field glasses, we could observe movement of the troops and how they dynamited our home but did not succeed to blow up our tower, as it turned out to be too tough for their explosives. Our cattle, horses and etc. were also taken away.

My father and his group remained at large and this obviously worried the Bolshevik government in Tbilisi. At first they tried an appeal to the population by dropping leaflets from biplanes to capture Father and hand him over to the authorities—but in vain. After having executed many leaders and partakers of the insurrection the Bolsheviks apparently felt in control of the situation but wanted even more security. They began sending negotiators to Father, guaranteeing him freedom and complete amnesty. All he had to do was to appear voluntarily in the capital city, Tbilisi, register with the "law officers of Cheka"[14] and renounce further fight. After considerable deliberation. Father recognized the hopelessness of further struggle.

This was further confirmed by a letter from Bidzina Pirvely, the main leader of the uprising in Svaneti. He had been captured by the government earlier and apparently without bargaining and promises. Father was much disappointed, bewildered and bitter that the expected help from the west never materialized. He did not wish to leave the country and escape to the west, so he accepted the negotiated terms. The Bolsheviks kept their part of the bargain and accordingly, just as a formality, the court sentenced Father to ten years. This was, at the time, a maximum jail term. The next

14- Later known as the K.G.B.

step would have been capital punishment. The sentence was totally suspended and for a one or two year term, he was not allowed to leave the capital city, Tbilisi, and had to appear ever so often at the "special commissions" (the Cheka) for verification of his presence. He also kept his word and devoted his enormous energy exclusively to his previous research.

His three books were published, and he had the fourth one ready. This was the period in the U.S.S.R. of the famous New Economic Policy (N.E.P.) introduced by Lenin to prevent an economic disaster. A degree of free enterprise in the economy and some "liberalization" within the communist party and in general were permitted. The Georgian Bolsheviks, clearly not having the majority of the population on their side, embarked on the policy of reconciliation, especially with the stubborn mountaineers.

Taking advantage of Father's popularity there, he was eventually appointed an assistant administrator of the Upper Svaneti. (The chief, of course, was a Bolshevik Party Member.) Later on, they made Father the director of an all important project—the first highway to be built through the fierce mountains of Svaneti. After that, he was entrusted with organizing and directing the ethnographic historical museum of considerable scientific importance for Georgian scholars.

It had been Father's life work to establish an inventory and to protect the priceless icons and other historical monuments of Svaneti. During turbulent times, the Svans were made, by Georgian kings, custodians of these treasures. Father's incentive in pursuing such projects was based on his belief that this was for the good of the country. The Bolshevik government, on the other hand, was using him, since by his presence there and his ability to organize would almost guarantee the confidence and cooperation of the local populace. One of the most curious and seemingly paradoxical tasks given to Father by the Georgian Bolshevik government was to lead the delegation of Svans to the Kremlin in order to obtain necessary funds for the highway.

As the giants from the mountains, in national attire and with straight two-edged short swords dangling from their belts, walked the streets of Moscow, the crowds followed them everywhere. It probably had the effect of legendary figures from the past history of Caucasus suddenly coming alive.

The delegation was introduced in the Kremlin to Mikhail Kalinin (the President of the Central Executive Committee of the Soviet Government) by Avel Yenukidze, himself an old Georgian Bolshevik. Yenukidze had a big position in the Kremlin, next to Kalinin and was considered a decent and benevolent man. Kalinin wondered why one should spend so many resources for building the highway in difficult terrain. Would it not be better to resettle the mountaineers—Svans—in the easier accessible and better flat farming land somewhere else, for instance in Russia? Here, Yenukidze came with the explanation that the Svans had lived in their ancestral land for centuries and they would not be removed from there alive. Then he pointed to my father and said, not without pride, "Comrade Kalinin do you know that this man is the same Egnatius Gabliani who was one of the leaders of the uprising against us?" Kalinin briskly turned to my father and wanted to know if this were true and if so, why? Yenukidze intervened again and explained, "You see, Mikhail Ivanovitch, there were some mistakes made, resulting in further misunderstandings," etc.

After they left the Kremlin, Father turned on Yenukidze, whom he knew well since the time of their youth and reproachfully said, "Abel, if you wanted my execution, why did you bring me all the way to Moscow for that?" Yenukidze exploded with laughter and replied, "Nonsense, you gentlemen actually made a great impression on Comrade Kalinin; it was good for him to know what kind of people you are. I bet you will get funds for your highway."

Father told me this story one day when our surefooted mounts carried us through the difficult terrain of the magnificent canyon of the River Inguri in Svaneti. Some distance ahead of us, we could hear the explosion of the dynamite well, since the work on the Svaneti Highway was in progress. Father had been appointed the director of this project; Yenukidze was correct, Kalinin had allocated the necessary funds. This encounter took place during the late twenties but during the 1937 "purges," two Georgian personalities of such a different background; old Bolshevik, Yenukidze and my father, the "Federalist" Party member of Georgia, were murdered by Stalin with many others. Stalin could do this because of the system Lenin had created which made possible such a dictatorship without checks and balances or accountability to anyone.

As soon as my father was arrested in 1937, some mountaineers were ready to ambush the local jail and free him before the M.V.D. would fly him to Tbilisi. I made this plan known to Father, but he absolutely declined such a solution and called this "madness." He was certain that there was some mistake and he soon would be cleared and freed by the central authorities.

For my own part, especially in retrospect, I have often regretted this. I felt that the two of us had a good chance in the given environment to go into hiding locally, at first and later on crossing the passes to the North Caucasus. He had several old friends there and we would find a secret refuge. From there if need be, we could "submerge" in some big city in Ukraine or Russia. This was the story I told Leonid Sillin about my past.

"But the story I told you," I said to Sillin, "was about my father, and there was not much there about me except perhaps about my passion for mountain climbing."

Sillin objected. "Like father, like son," he said, "besides none of us had such an unusual experience and background as you and, he added, "we all who work with you think that you are a 'hawk' and the 'prince' of the Caucasus Mountains, capable of many good things. I made our feelings about you known to the commandant and he made some notes. If he thinks that a person like you may be of some asset for his country, he may help you. Otherwise, tell me Givi Egnatievich, how many P.O.W.s are going to be sent from here to Berlin?"

The next day the commandant received us very well. Apparently Leonid Sillin's previous visit had "prepared the ground" and perhaps the benevolent doctor from Berlin, who had worked with Dr. Badu Tsulukidze, also helped. I told the commandant about the friendship of our two countries that had developed during W.W. I and that I was interested in traveling to Berlin, hoping to find out from a friend of my Father, Mr. Robakidze, if the participating personalities from that past history were still around. Perhaps, they even intended to revive the old friendship. I also said that I felt it to be my duty for the good of my country to contribute to it as guided by my elders in exile.

The commandant said he would phone an officer in the army headquarters in Alexandria (Ukraine) and if the response were positive, I could leave soon with a convoy of trucks in that direction. We were notified the next day to be ready to leave the following morning. It was with heartfelt sorrow that I bade farewell to Leonid Sillin and other friends from his group. I could never forget these warm, dedicated and courageous people who were good to me and taught me much. It has remained my unfulfilled wish to meet them again or at least to find out about their fate.

I learned later that the Soviet Army soldiers had a very poor survival record. A fifty per cent death rate was awaiting them during the winter of 1941–42 in the P.O.W. camps, and if they lived through it and were again captured by the Red Army they were executed or sentenced to the gulags as "traitors." I do hope that my friends from Krestitelevo P.O.W. hospital fared better than that.

As the convoy of the German Army trucks were making their way to Alexandria, I noticed and worried about some fields still unharvested. It was October now, and I hoped the Germans would see to it that the harvest would be brought in to prevent famine. Why not use the prisoners of war, if need be, I thought. They would be all too happy to work on the farms as we were to work in the field hospital.

In Alexandria, I was brought to a house where Major Ernst zu Eikern had his working as well as his living quarters. He was also given a letter on my behalf from the commandant of Krestitelevo. The Major was a pleasant, considerate gentleman, probably in his forties. He shook my hand and ordered his helpers to have a bedroom arranged for me, next to his own, and invited me for a walk. He wanted to hear about my past and also my views about the war. After our walk, the Major informed me that following supper he wanted me to meet some of his friends, a group of officers and said this should be mutually interesting.

The meeting took place in a room which was possibly part of the officers' club. I was properly introduced, some drinks were served and then the servants left. The Major made some introductory remarks about my general background and also my work in the field hospital for the wounded P.O.W.s (prisoners). He said that while my "forte" was medicine, I also had other strong, definite views, especially about the present situation. Then he suggested that I tell them about my general experiences in the Soviet Union including the war and I did so. This was a group of excellent listeners. Some of them spoke good Russian, so at times when my German floundered, they would ask me to say it in Russian which was then translated for the others.

Then the questions followed. For instance, one of them wanted to know how I thought the war was going. I responded that I thought it was going very well for the Germans, but if decisive military victory was not achieved before the onset of the Russian winter, things may be slowed down. One of them commented, "Why should we worry about the winter when we have very well organized rear zones with good supplies and communication lines?" In answering him, I observed that what he said was very important and I had no knowledge of it. I had been moving as a soldier from central Russia to Finland and the Leningrad regions, then to "Russian Poland," Belorussia and Ukraine during the winter. I also made trips from the Caucasus to Russia, back and forth, and found the weather to be incredibly severe, the distances overwhelming and the roads difficult at best. Besides, if the Germans are stopped, they are going to lose the momentum of success and the psychological edge. The Russians can retreat and will have time to recuperate and prepare themselves.

Another officer stated that the population had been receiving the Germans very well and at times even as liberators. Such a remark led me to elaborate further. I said that this in itself was of great importance since the Soviet soldiers, after all, were the "children" of the same population and they were bound to be influenced by "grassroots" feelings. I noticed a number of unharvested fields on my way to Alexandria [Oleksandriya]; why not use the prisoners of war to bring in the harvest before it's too late? Everyone would be happy.

I also said that I was bewildered to have read some of the German propaganda leaflets, dropped from airplanes. They called on the Soviet soldiers "to beat up the Commissars and the Jews," and to defect to the German side. Imperial Russia was capable of such discriminatory expressions and deeds. Bolshevik Russia had been taking a similar stance against the so called "class enemies" and the real or imaginary political opponents.

On the other hand, the population in general regards the Germans to be cultured and civilized people, strict, thrifty and just and also to be representative of Western Europe. The people here may appear to be simple but they understand the difference between good and bad. They overthrew the Czar, but then found themselves betrayed by the Bolsheviks usurpers of power. They were stuck with a new, much more brutal regime than the Czar's ever was. During the revolution, land, freedom and peace was promised to them but in fact, all of it was taken away and millions of people were destroyed. This was true for the Soviet non-Russian nationalities as well but they, in addition, have suffered the loss of national independence that they had temporarily regained after the overthrow of the Czar. It follows then that they have an additional grievance against their rulers. Because they have a good name in Russia, the population believes, as I do, that the Germans will bring about changes for the best.

"In my opinion," I said, "your propaganda leaflets should clearly and sincerely promise that and not appeal to primitive, bad human and outmoded instincts and talk about 'beating up the Commissars and Jews.'" Not once was I interrupted but I did notice that the listeners exchanged glances. I felt at ease while expressing my views, no doubt because of the encouragement given to me by Major Ernst zu Eikern.

After I was finished, some officers spoke up; one made an observation that the Soviet People knew, after all, this was war and in due time they would, no doubt, get what they hoped for. Another said that as far as the propaganda leaflets were concerned, the officers present here had nothing to do with this. In answer, I said that I was sure of good German intentions, but in my view it was very important that the people hear about it from the very outset. When our meeting was over, I had the feeling that my host, as well as the other officers understood me and appreciated my frankness. We shook hands and wished each other well—"alles gute."

Later I learned that Major zu Eikern had been assigned to this army staff as a representative of the Admiral Canaris Organization (the military intelligence). A few years later, I could no longer recall his name but during the early fifties, while I was residing in the U.S.A. much to my surprise, a letter signed by Ernst zu Eikern, arrived. He had heard from a mutual acquaintance about me and obtained my address from him. He expressed his happiness that I had survived the war and wanted me to know that he remembered well our encounter in Alexandria during the fall of 1941. I was pleased and touched and wrote him a warm letter. Above all, I thanked him for his friendliness, encouragement, confidence in me and help during a time when I was a P.O.W. without protection or rights.

His attitude toward me, during 1941, was no longer a puzzle to me since I had become well aware of the great effort of his chief, Admiral Canaris, directed toward improvement of conditions for the Soviet P.O.W.s and civilian populations in the occupied Eastern territories. I already knew of Canaris's opposition to Hitler and his policy. I think my experience in Alexandria was among one of my most unusual early lessons. It became more and more obvious to me how little, if any, insight I had about the real state of affairs in Germany. There was no choice but to go through the tough school of learning by trial and error. I still was luckier than many of my peers in large P.O.W. camps, as I found out later.

I remained in Alexandria two or three more days and was free to walk around without apparent supervision. During this time, I tried to collect my thoughts and visualize the future.

The Major also introduced me to a Ukrainian gentleman who came to see him. His name was Tchaikovsky, a name which is easy to remember because of an identical name of the great Russian composer. As he left, I decided to take a walk with him and we shared some of our experiences. He was from Galicia, the western part of Ukraine; the inhabitants there have a reputation of being especially conscious of their national heritage and independence. I could not help but feel that he was somewhat disappointed by the Germans, who had occupied his homeland for three months and so far did not recognize their hoped-for independence. I also thought that had he completely trusted me, he possibly would have said more. "There is still a war going on, and when it is over the Germans are likely to meet the desire of the Ukrainian people," I said. I tried to comfort Tchaikovsky with this borrowed remark made by a German officer during a recent encounter with him. "It is probably true," he agreed.

I thought of him and his people when I learned later how they were subjected to brutal treatment, not by the German Army but by Hitler's commissar for the Ukraine, one Erich Koch and other henchmen, such as Sauckel and Himmler. The Major soon informed me that he would be able to arrange my trip to Berlin to meet the friend of my father, Grigol Robakidze and perhaps some other Georgians as well. With a characteristic German talent for organization, he killed two flies at the same time.

He permitted one of his master sergeants to take a vacation ahead of time and while on his way home, to be my military escort to Berlin. This worked very well. My companion turned out to be a pleasant young man, who also felt somewhat grateful to me since his vacation had been realized earlier than expected. Not all German officers turned out to be as well disposed as Major Ernst zu Eikern, as I soon found out.

At first, we traveled on a rather luxurious bus where almost all the passengers were officers. One of them, a captain, was angry apparently because my escort dared to bring me, a Soviet P.O.W., aboard such an excellent "motor club." In the loud barking voice of a Prussian officer, he went on and on while my escort stood at attention and appeared pale and embarrassed. When at last the captain allowed him to explain how all this came about, my escort quietly produced a document which the captain read. Now he appeared somewhat embarrassed. He grumbled a bit, saluted us, turned around and left us alone. My companion and I sat silently until the time came to change to a train. Then he apologized to me on behalf of the German captain. He also observed that in the bus only one officer had disapproved of our presence there; one has to be ready for meeting prejudiced and arrogant people everywhere, he said.

I was curious to know what was in the "magic" paper which had such a calming effect on the outraged captain. It was a certificate from the army headquarters, signed by "our" Major of the General Staff, that gave us the privilege to literally use any transport passing by at anytime. It also stated that any courtesy and help given to us would be appreciated. Looking at "us" first, the Captain did not expect that, chuckled my escort. We traveled by train passing the cities of Lviv, Krakow, Breslau and got to Berlin at the onset of dark.

In Berlin, we stayed overnight in the "soldiers' home," a part of the chain of such organizations in Germany during the war providing shelter and food for the military in transit. Berlin was darkened because of danger of bombing by the Royal Air Force at night. While in the dining room, I noticed a curious group of people in German military uniforms who did not appear to be Germans. It was explained to me that they were members of the Spanish volunteer "Blue Division," which was participating in the fight against the Soviet Army.

Having read, at the age of twelve, *Don Quixote* by Cervantes, I have been fascinated by Spain. The Spanish Civil War further increased my interest inasmuch as it received its share of coverage by the Soviet news media and was even reflected in art. Dolores Ibárruri, a leading Spanish woman Communist, appeared in the Soviet Union, receiving a heroine's welcome and a group of Spanish children came to Georgia as guests. One would presume that basking in the Georgian sun, the Georgian traditions and customs and in general the Mediterranean features of the country made them feel more at home than they would in central Russia. I wanted to ask many questions of those Spaniards in Georgia then as well as now in Berlin, but it was not feasible.

The following morning, my escort and I took a brief stroll and then took the subway to get to an impressive building on Kurfürstenstrasse. To me, Berlin was a very interesting city. Although it was kept dark during the night in anticipation of air raids, there were no noticeable damages so far. The buildings were clean, the people appeared well dressed, busy, reserved, orderly and polite. Commercial advertising was visible all over; this was a strange sight for me. The consumers in the Soviet Union were ready to devour any items as soon as they appeared in a store, without advertisement. Subways and trains commuted right on schedule.

We walked up the steps to the first or second floor, where a gentleman received us in the waiting area. My escort and I bade each other farewell and as he left, I noticed a strikingly good-looking young lady running upstairs to the next floor. I had a "gut feeling" that she was a Georgian. Somehow, I was too inhibited to ask my new guide about her. I actually met this mysterious and lovely person less than two years later. She was indeed a Georgian and her name was Marina von Moltke-Kazbek and I will have more to say about her and her adorable mother, Nina Dadiani Kazbek, later on.

My new host led me to a large room that appeared to be a combination of a meeting as well as a dining facility. There, I met the old friend of my father, the famous writer Grigol Robakidze and another Georgian, Misha (Mikhail) Kedia and several Germans—two of them in military uniform. Robakidze greeted me cordially and wanted to know how some of his friends were doing back home. Kedia also expressed his happiness to see me; he said that he had known my family as a young man in Georgia. He also indicated that he represented Georgians in Paris. The Germans in military uniform were Dr. Werner Markert, of a captain's rank, and Lieutenant Lange. I fail to remember the names of the other Germans present.

Lunch was served, and I told them about my past and my wartime observations. My discussion was, more or less, a repetition of the one held for the group of officers in Alexandria. The response I got also indicated (perhaps even more so) that some of my views were well understood by the listeners. Now, in turn I wanted to know if there had been any liaison established between the Georgians and the Germans in the spirit of 1917–1921. Kedia asked me if this were so, was I prepared to contribute to it? I said, "Yes, I would." Kedia requested permission from the Germans to meet me the following day so the two of us could discuss matters privately and this request was granted to him.

Grigol Robakidze addressed the group with fascinating general philosophical remarks about literature, culture and the history of Georgia and Russia, etc. He frequently quoted appropriate passages from his books. This turned out to be a long luncheon. It was decided that I should be driven to Luckenwalde, near Berlin, where I would get shelter and the following day I would meet M. Kedia. I was anxious to have such an opportunity, inasmuch as he said he represented the Georgian emigration in France, where I also knew our government in exile resided.

The whole purpose of my trip here was to establish a liaison with them and now my dream had come true. Kedia also requested that instead of Luckenwalde, I should remain with him, but this was flatly refused by the military since it would have been against regulations.

In Luckenwalde, there was a small P.O.W. camp—clean, orderly and the inmates were treated well. They took my picture there and filled out a questionnaire. My Soviet military uniform was changed to French, presumably because it was readily available since France had been occupied by the Germans. A middle-aged German who was in charge of all such formalities was friendly and communicative. He told me that he had seen Georgians before and it had been a pleasure to meet them. "They were true gentlemen," he continued, "dignified with excellent manners and had served in the Polish Army and had defended their host country, Poland, during the 1939 German-Soviet invasion."

I vaguely remember two names he specially mentioned, Colonels Vatchnadze and Kutateladze. I was pleased to hear my countrymen mentioned with such admiration and therefore had no choice but to be on my best behavior. In Luckenwalde, I also met briefly a few Soviet P.O.W.s of Georgian origin, but I don't remember their names nor their background.

Next morning the army sergeant drove me to Berlin and left me alone with M. Kedia in a splendid restaurant which I believe was a part of the Hotel Adlon. It was a good opportunity for two countrymen to have a talk, and I was hungry for any information I could get. Kedia said that the contact indeed had been established between the leaders of Georgian emigres and the friendly Germans who already had been of considerable help to the Georgians in occupied territories. Some steps were also under consideration to help P.O.W.s in prison camps.

Kedia reaffirmed that he had come here representing the Georgians in France in order to negotiate and also to learn about the German plans toward our land. Some of our friends in Germany were hoping to be able to influence the policy for our benefit. Later on, I learned that Kedia was referring to Count von Schulenburg's efforts and his famous plan and about certain actions [of the German Resistance] taken by Admiral Canaris and others [against Hitler]. Kedia indicated that, at this point, the Georgians were rather concerned but hopeful. I wondered if our government in exile was aware of all this? And how President Noe Jordania was doing? "Yes they are aware of it," said Kedia, and "the President is doing very well."

I handed a letter to Kedia that I had written the night before and asked if he would be kind enough to deliver this to our president and he said he would. I told Kedia that I did so as a faithful citizen in order to express my respect to our president in exile and also to report to him about the situation in our country and some of my other views. I also told Kedia that many Georgians felt Jordania was the only lawful Georgian head of state in recent history elected by an overwhelming majority of the people in a free election where all other parties including the communists had also been allowed to participate on equal terms but lost. Also that restoration of the independent Georgian state during 1918 for us was a momentous landmark and not to be forgotten.

"I do not consider myself to be a social democrat," (the party of President Jordania), I said, "but it does not matter, since in my view, the Georgian question was not one of political parties but a national question" ("Erovnuli Sakithi"). I was sure that even for many Georgian Communists, it must have been an eye opener, to see what a destructive monster the Kremlin dictatorship turned out to be. I would expect that at least some of them would love their country more than their party. I was also convinced that the large nations would survive a cataclysm such as W.W. II, but it may not be the same for small nations like us, inasmuch as we, the Georgians, were buffeted between hostile forces.

One has to recall the situation that occurred in Georgia and Transcaucasia at the end of W.W. I. At that time, fortunately Germans recognized the Georgian Independent Republic and helped to protect it from the Turks. One should hope that the Germans would take the same attitude now. I had heard that the Germans helped to organize the Georgian Legion then. Perhaps, they will allow the Georgians to form the Georgian military again. In which case, our national political cause may gain more respect and this may also offer us an opportunity to get our military men to the Georgian homeland.

Kedia appeared pleased, excited and as he said, surprised since he did not quite expect to hear all this from one who just got here from the Soviet Union. Then he jubilantly added, "What you said to me now is what we are telling our German friends. Looks like you are giving us important help in this effort since some Germans think that such views are no longer alive in the land but only among us, the old emigres. Well, you proved them incorrect—you just now came here from Georgia. We shall tell all our friends about it. The letter you wrote to our president in exile, on your own initiative, is further proof of it."

Finally the time had come to thank and say goodbye to Misha Kedia; it was an emotional event as we embraced in the Georgian tradition. All of this must have been rather confusing for the other guests of the Adlon—if one imagines a strange looking man in a French P.O.W. uniform being embraced by a well dressed Western

European gentleman from Paris and both of them speaking a language that certainly was not French and no one understood.

I was transferred back to the Luckenwalde P.O.W. camp, and soon it became clear to me that Kedia's request was not accepted by the German military, at least for the time being. I did not see Kedia again until early summer of 1943, but he kept his promise to deliver my letter to President Noe Jordania. He also tried to establish contact with me.

It was the late fall of 1943 when at last I had the honor and great pleasure to see our president in exile at his home near Paris. He shook my hand and said, "Young man, I have had many good reports about you." I thought he just said this to encourage me, but nevertheless it was a great thrill to be praised by him. After all, he was chosen and installed in the office of the President by the "will of the Georgian People" and therefore by "the will of God," as they say in Georgia. ("Khma erisa da khma Khvtisa.") President Jordania was a distinguished looking and handsome gentleman with a long gray beard and mustache; wise eyes, full of life; a warm voice and dignified manners. He had the appearance of a patriarch. He was a good speaker and an equally good listener and impressed me to be a man of courage and optimism. I thought he was born just to be a president. We shared a great deal of concern for the fate of the Georgian P.O.W.s and although we knew that conditions had been considerably improved for them, there still was room for further improvement. Indeed there was good reason to be concerned about the future. The same applied to the legionnaires but the situation there was much more complex. I told the President that we had just received permission to visit them and also assess the prevailing conditions there to see what could be done for their benefit. I will have much more to say about this later on. We parted cordially, and I have never forgotten about this meeting with my President.

Soon after, from the Luckenwalde P.O.W. camp I was transferred to Berdikow, a small camp east of Berlin. There I was interviewed by Lieutenant Lange, who had been present during my first meeting with Kedia, Robakidze and Dr. Markert.

Lieutenant Lange was well aware of my anti Kremlin views. Now he suggested that I join his group in Berdikow which was housed in the barracks for the "Working German Youth" (Reichsarbeitsdienst). His group consisted of Baltic Germans, North Caucasians, one Georgian and one Russian.

They had a mission to fulfill in the Caucasus. The exact nature of this mission and my part in it was not defined by Lieutenant Lange, probably because it had to be a "secret." However, after a short time, it was clear that at some point he intended to land his group in the Caucasus, most likely behind the front line. Daily training was geared toward guerrilla warfare, including the use of explosives. I thought that perhaps Lange was interested in me as a doctor for his group. During one such training exercise, in a wooded area of Berdikow, we were surprised by a large herd of deer running across the field. An ancestral instinct must have moved me as I took aim at a buck and shot it. I thought it would be a good opportunity to enrich our kitchen where the meat supply appeared to be rather short, at least, by Caucasian standards. The Germans as well as the Caucasians present congratulated me for being a "good shot" but later on, one non-commissioned officer had second thoughts about it. This forest belongs to Herr Reichsmarschall Göring he told us, and there is a severe penalty for hunting here. Needless to say, I expressed my sincere regrets for such a misunderstanding and lack of beforehand knowledge of the regulation.

It was a pleasant late fall afternoon with the leaves in all kinds of colors. We all decided to camouflage our prey until the onset of darkness and then move it to our quarters. Our Caucasians were expert in this as well as how to skin and clean the deer and prepare the Caucasian delicacy, "shashlik," sort of a shish kebab, in Georgian referred to as "mzvadi." It had been a long time since we had last eaten it.

Of course, this had to be reported to Lieutenant Lange and I was to appear in his office alone for an explanation. Lange, and understandably so, was less than happy about it all. I repeated my apology and said that I had no idea that the forest where we were being trained was private property, not to mention the deer. I explained that where I was from such conditions did not exist and to put him in a better mood, I also told him about some of the hunting rituals, ethics and the restrictions they impose, while hunting ibex in the Svanetin mountains.

According to Svan mythology there is the goddess of hunting—beautiful Dali, much like the Greek goddess of hunting, Artemida or the Roman Diana. Since Dali is jealous of women, they are not allowed to take part in high mountain hunting. According to the legend, Dali had fallen in love with a handsome hunter with disastrous consequences for him when he became unfaithful. From such a union, a baby boy was born whose name was Amirani or Prometheus. He was a Titan and challenged even the Gods, and for this he was chained to the Caucasus Mountains. I enumerated a few other ritualistic restrictions on the hunters.

Lieutenant Lange seemed to have mellowed a bit during this conversation and he even accepted our invitation to the "Caucasian Evening," where the deer meat was served and heartily eaten by the Germans and Caucasians alike. Beer was also available and Caucasian songs and dances followed late into the night. We all promised each other never to mention to anyone what kind of meat we had eaten. I heard later that our Baltic Germans had turned this whole thing around and privately told others, including Lieutenant Lange, that the deer hunting had been good field experience in securing food during the pending military mission.

Baltic Germans in our unit all spoke Russian and were a courageous, individualistically minded people and not robots or they would not be part of such an undertaking. They knew that more risk than hunting deer in the Reichsmarschall's forest lay ahead of us all. Lieutenant Lange's group was transferred, (I believe it was the end of November) by train to Bärnsee in the Bavarian mountains in order to pursue further training in terrain similar to Caucasus.

The Caucasians were "glued" to the wagon windows since this trip, from near Berlin to the Bavarian Alps, offered us an unusual opportunity of sightseeing in Germany. The villages, towns and cities we passed through revealed uniformly well-kept, nice houses. Everything was clean, orderly and pleasing to the eye. So was the farmland that had already been harvested. Nowhere was there to be seen a broken down tractor or other machinery. The farm animals appeared well fed. Farmers' houses and surrounding property were testimonial of their prosperity. Well kept churches were frequently seen.

One also noticed a number of hotels ("Gasthauses") adorned with paintings on the wall and flower boxes on the balconies and underneath the windows. One could appreciate how much prettier they would have looked during springtime. In the railroad stations one observed well dressed people with good manners. The factories were numerous and impressive. All this was a far cry from the Soviet realities and twenty-three years of "Socialist paradise." After all, Germany had lost World War I and heavy reparations were imposed on her. Envious thoughts were crossing our minds; why were we unable to have something in the U.S.S.R. approaching such a standard of living? Showing all of this to us was the best unintentional propaganda one could imagine.

Experience after the Soviet invasion of the Baltic States further confirmed the belief that everyone in Europe had better living conditions than the Soviet People. Hitler did not take away the private property of the German farmers, factory owners or the people in general. Therefore they were, from the German point of view, more free even under one party hegemony than their counterparts were in the Soviet Union. Of course, Hitler's attitude was confined to the Germans only, as it became more and more clear to us as time passed.

On a few occasions, I had the opportunity to exchange greetings and have a brief conversation with civilian passengers. We had strict instruction not to reveal our true identity but pretend to be Croatians (from Yugoslavia). Being in Bavaria lifted my spirits since it reminded me of my ancestral land.

We arrived and settled in the small town of Bärnsee. In spite of my elation from being in mountainous Bavaria, my deep concern continued just the same. First, I still had not heard from M. Kedia, who wanted me to stay with him and said he would initiate some steps in this direction. Second, I did not understand the meaning of Lieutenant Lange's military undertaking for my country. If I would ever involve myself in such a thing, there had to be, at least, a clear message for the Georgian people, such as what to expect if the Germans arrived in Georgia. Contact with political Georgian emigration and coordination of our activities therefore appeared imperative but not forthcoming.

I shared my concerns with Lieutenant Lange in the most polite and diplomatic manner that I was capable of. He listened to me with a certain sympathy but his response was that, as he saw it for now, we should all fight against communism and defeat it first. Other matters of a political nature would no doubt be settled later. He was not a politician but a soldier, he said, who needs to accomplish a certain objective. Although I politely listened to Lange's statements and tried not to argue with him, I was not at all satisfied. I was sure he felt it. I thought that perhaps he had some good will toward me and probably personally toward the Caucasians but could offer no solution.

Therefore, a person such as I may well have caused certain difficulties for his military objective. It was becoming clearer for both of us that in the long run, we probably would not be compatible. Two well-educated North Caucasians, Beshtokov and Nagoev, during a confidential discussion with me, expressed the same concerns on their part as I had. Generally speaking, the North Caucasian people in Lange's group were remarkably polite, trusting and we often advised each other on matters of mutual concern.

The younger ones always treated their elders with great respect and they were very similar to the Georgians, especially those from Abkhazia. We felt a definite affinity for each other. Geographically we all occupied the foothills of the Caucasus Mountains, they from the north side and we from the south side, with the distance between some of our respective towns being only one day's horseback ride over the passes. Only two North Caucasians of Ossetian decent, Tsogolov and Dzotsoev, appeared cool and reserved toward me. Tsogolov, who had joined the group some time ago was considered by the Lieutenant sort of a spokesman for the North Caucasians. After my arrival, things probably got somewhat confusing for him. I, a newcomer, had several private meetings with his chief, without an interpreter and frequent associations with the instructor—Baltic German—and also with the North Caucasians. Unintentionally I must have hurt his feelings and I was not aware of it until later.

The Baltic Germans were inquisitive about my views as well as the past history of Georgia and we became friends. Especially one of them, Nikolai Lilienthal, opened his heart to me. He was, by age, the oldest among the Baltic Germans and also very sincere, decent, free of prejudices toward the other people and at the same time a patriot of his country. He helped my general orientation greatly by giving to me German journals and newspapers to read and also certain tips and comments. For instance, one day having read a newspaper article about Hitler's "elite troops," the "Waffen-SS," I told Nikolai that I was impressed by the write up, as well as the photographs, showing how uniformly tall and handsome all appeared. And as the paper reported, they also distinguished themselves as brave soldiers in the field.

We were alone and Nikolai told me, "you are mistaken, Doctor, they are not real soldiers like us; we have to train just as hard but have to wait for our promotion much longer and are paid less. They are picked not only for their body size but also for special political purposes and therefore are given preferential treatment. I personally don't care for them," he said, then added, "but it is better to keep this statement to ourselves." Perhaps they are more like the praetorian guards, like the ones used for the Roman emperors, I thought.

Three unexpected and unpleasant incidents took place involving me approximately during late November and early December. One was that during a rather vigorous soccer game played on a cold day and without a previous "warm up," I dislocated my left knee joint. This is considered a serious injury and should be taken care of promptly. It was done so and put back in place by one of my teammates, the North Caucasian from Dagestan, with instant relief of pain. Needless to say, I was very grateful and wanted to know how he could do it since the best orthopedic surgeon would have been proud of such an accomplishment, especially without the aid of anesthesia. He explained that his father was the doctor in the mountainous Dagestan and while "Papa" traveled on horseback and took care of his villagers, his son accompanied and helped him. "One picks up a few little tricks here and there," he added with a modest smile, "and we were fortunate we did so before muscle spasms set in."

Following the knee reduction, I had to be examined, including X-rays, and treated by the military doctors in a nearby town, Mittenwald. The left leg was placed in a cast from the toes up to the groin. The doctors thought that the cartilages as well as several ligaments of the left knee joint were injured. The long term outlook for my climbing mountains or engaging in sports was very unfavorable. But after four weeks, when the cast was changed and after a thorough examination, they said that it was almost unbelievable how well the knee was progressing. The only possible explanation was the prompt reduction on the scene of the accident.

The doctors said that the cast would be removed again in three weeks, and I was encouraged by the good progress. Nevertheless I felt very clumsy with the cast, more so because even partial weight bearing was not permitted on the injured side while on crutches. The people around me were very helpful and nice especially my neighbor, Mamulashvili, who occupied a "bunk" above me and another Georgian, Katsitadze, who just joined the unit. He was a man of great physical strength who literally carried me "piggy back" to the nearby practice field. There, I could observe activities of other fellows and was even able to practice target shooting, which was much easier on me than if I had been completely confined to the barracks all day long. This helped my spirits, but then another unpleasant and uncalled for incident took place.

One night, my neighbor, Mamulashvili, on his upper "bunk" and I on the lower one, were conversing as usual. This apparently bothered one Ossetian, Dzotsoev, two bunks away from us who was trying to sleep. He, for some reason, always appeared reserved and unfriendly to me but still I treated him with polite consideration. This time, instead of telling us about his sleeping problem, in an angry voice in Ossetian language, said something very insulting about me. My neighbor, Mamulashvili, understood Ossetian and interpreted this to me. He had referred to my mother in a most obscene way.

Some people from different countries may not understand it, but for the Caucasians, such behavior is against elementary tradition and is considered to be one of the greatest insults. I was stunned and did not know how to react to it but react one must, unless one wishes to lose respect of fellow Caucasians. I hardly slept that night and in the morning, standing on one leg and leaning against the "bunk," I informed Dzotsoev that I was aware of his despicable insult and if he had a good reason for doing so, to let me know, otherwise apologize to a fellow man who happened to be physically disabled as I was. Several Caucasians present urged him to do so. He adamantly refused and rudely grumbled under his breath. I shouted at him then that I would teach him the lesson of his life and reached for my automatic gun, hanging next to my "bunk." My neighbor Mamulashvili and other Caucasians got between us pleading with me not to do this. Dzotsoev became visibly scared, pale and shaking and did not appear to want to use his gun which was readily accessible to him. Obviously, he did not expect such a reaction especially from a physically disabled man. They soon whisked him from the room.

His friend, Tsogolov reported his version of the incident to the lieutenant. The Baltic Germans, however, hurried up to explain to the lieutenant that Dzotsoev had it coming because of his uncalled for rudeness and insult according to the Caucasian code of ethics. I assured Lieutenant Lange that in no way did I really intend to shoot Dzotsoev but wanted only to teach him a lesson. Especially how to respect the dignity of another person and not to try to walk over him when he is physically disabled. I was reasonably sure that under normal circumstances, Dzotsoev would not dare to behave like that and he had taken advantage of my disability. The Lieutenant appeared to be satisfied with my explanation.

After my cast was removed, it was amazing how fast I was rehabilitated. The doctors declared that my cast could be left off. The usual muscle exercise, hot packs were prescribed and this all helped but still no one expected such good results. After an additional ten to fourteen days, I was gradually able to resume almost all the "usual" activities with certain common sense restrictions.

Around this time, another Georgian, Cholokava, a former Red Army political officer ("politruk") joined Lange's group which increased the number of Georgians to four men. Paradoxically, I was very happy to see the "politruk"; not only did he survive but was even accepted in Lange's group. It will be remembered from previous pages that at the onset of the war, the German propaganda leaflets called on the Red Army soldiers "to beat up the commissars," (same as politruk) "and the Jews." To me, the arrival of Cholokava was a sign of amending an insane and cruel policy by the Germans and such a reversal, I expected, would also apply to the Jews. Cholokava was not a typical Georgian as he was a man of few words, cautious and an introvert but during a private conversation with me he complained about the miserable life in the Soviet Union in general and the Red Army in particular.

My main problem while being in Lieutenant Lange's group remained unsolved. I did not see any logical connection between his narrow military objective and my goal to serve the Georgian interests. Nothing had improved in this respect, and there was no indication that this would change in the future. I remained isolated from the Georgian exiles and could not help but feel that it was not a mutually beneficial association with Lieutenant Lange but it mainly served his purpose.

This led to the growing conflict between us, and under such circumstances, even minor differences of opinion appeared more significant than they really were. For instance, a draft of some propaganda leaflet to be dropped (probably over Caucasus) was referred to Lange for his comments. He, in turn, wanted to have our input about it. As it happened, my views did differ from his and of some of the others; especially of the "speaker," Tsogolov. This seemed to have irritated the Lieutenant somewhat out of proportion, even though I did not pretend that my opinion was the only one. Another apparent idiosyncrasy of his was that I did not jump to my feet and at attention whenever he passed by while we were in our quarters and off duty. I felt that such was uncalled for since we both were of comparable age and while he was a lieutenant, I was a doctor. The fact that he was a German did not constitute a reason for me to do so—it may have been interpreted as a symbol of undue submission by a Georgian.

Still another reason, as I was told later, it had been his suspicion that I had more "influence" on the majority of the Caucasians under his command than he did. I very much doubt that this was the case although I enjoyed a good mutual relationship with them.

As if things were not already bad enough, during the second part of January 1942, I was hospitalized in Garmisch-Partenkirchen. The surgeon, Dr. Major Meltreter removed a ruptured appendix and established drainage. Those were the days before antibiotics and intravenous replacement or fluids and electrolytes were well developed. I was sick but by the Lord's grace and the efforts of the surgeon and matching good nursing care, I made it. Especially-contributing to my recovery was "Schwester" (Sister) Gretel from Vienna.

This experience did much in furthering my understanding and compassion for my patients. As soon as permitted, I got out of bed and started to walk in the halls and recreation room of the hospital. Looking out of windows to snow covered mountains and trees of beautiful Garmisch, it was difficult to imagine that somewhere the ruthless war was raging and people were dying by the thousands. I observed the gloomy-faced wounded German soldiers, out of acute care and now being treated by rehabilitative procedures. For some of them, the war had ended because of severe disability.

Often, I was awakened in the early morning by a Bavarian worker in colorful national attire and a big pipe in his mouth. With a knock on the glass door of my room, he would greet me, "Grüss Got" (God bless you) and then he would go on scraping the snow off the porch. Sister Gretel volunteered to walk with me outside on the well-groomed streets of Garmisch. She even bought me a giant glass of Bavarian beer (without my doctor's permission)—"I needed liquids," in the gasthaus of the "Three Hussars."[15] There I had an opportunity to observe the Bavarian townsfolk having a good time. They were all drinking their famous beer, smoking big pipes and talking incredibly loudly. I almost felt at home, since they reminded me of our mountaineers, to a point that some of them even had large goiters as we did. Such outings in the fresh air and away from the hospital environment did wonders for my recovery and sooner than expected.

I was able to go back to the Bärnsee barracks of Lieutenant Lange's domain. While remembering the old days, some forty-six years later when I was visiting a very good friend of mine, Shota Margwelashvili, in Los Angeles, he mentioned to me that during late spring of 1942, he also had his appendix removed in Garmisch

---

15- A European light-armed cavalry man.

Hospital. He clearly remembered that a Viennese nurse, because of his manners, looks and accent, thought that he had to be my countryman. She was concerned and wondering what happened to Dr. Gabliani who suddenly disappeared as soon as he left the hospital and no one had heard about him since. There was not even a customary follow up with the operating surgeon. Sister Gretel was correct with her concern. Shortly after my arrival in the Bärnsee quarters, Lieutenant Lange summoned me to his office and in the presence of non-commissioned officers, "Grish" Johansen and Moritz, this is approximately what he told me: I had never recognized nor accepted the German leadership and often had been too critical. Therefore, I had to be transferred to the punitive camp. In vain, I tried to explain that I did not see the problem like that and pleaded with him to make it possible for me to pursue the plan that I came to Germany with in the first place. His response was that he had already wasted too much time on me and I should be leaving soon—today.

So I bid farewell to my new friends, who were all speechless. One of them, the Georgian Mamulashvili, pledged that if he survived and returned to Caucasus, he would do his utmost to somehow notify my mother that I was alive. I knew that he really meant it, and I was deeply grateful for that. During our trip on the train, my military escort, a Baltic German, told me that I was rather fortunate since the Lieutenant had decided to transfer me to the infamous Dachau concentration camp near Munich. But, he said, the Baltic Germans of the unit who had all become my friends had persuaded him to send me somewhere else instead. Therefore, we arrived in the small city of Steinau, not far from the city of Hanau, in a "milder" camp where I worked daily, unloading coal for factories. Due to conditions existing there and my recent surgery, I lost a lot of weight. I have never again met Lieutenant Lange, but on three occasions I had an opportunity to hear about him. Such occurred first while I was in North Caucasus with the military unit "Bergmann." The 1st Company of this unit was holding the front line south of the North Ossetian city Mozdok. Here, during the fall of 1942, two men from Lieutenant Lange's group made their way back to our side, coming from behind the Soviet side of the front. I knew both of them: Aliev and Ismailov from Dagestan. I had met them in Bavaria (Bärnsee) while we were in Lieutenant Lange's group together. Aliev was the one who reduced my dislocated knee as has been already noted.

We were happy to see each other again and had a lot to talk about. According to them, Lange's group had been parachuted deep in the Soviet North Caucasus. The only Russian member of the unit fractured his leg during the landing and had to be left with some friendly villagers. Contact was easily established with the Soviet North Caucasians and many of them volunteered to join them in the fight against the Kremlin regime.

However, Lieutenant Lange could not take advantage of it since he had no weapons to arm them. Moreover, the German advances in North Caucasus came to a halt and the front line was stabilized since the German armored division was not able to take the city, Ordzhonikidze. There was nothing else left for Lieutenant Lange and his group but to make their way back to German lines. They were separated somehow, and Lieutenant Lange did not make it back with the group.

Therefore, the non-commissioned officer "Grish" Johansen went back to find the Lieutenant and assist him. During this effort Johansen was severely wounded and he opted to detonate his hand grenade, killing himself, rather than falling into enemy hands. "Grish" was a brave Baltic German, much admired by all of us. As far as I know, Lange's mission achieved only one thing, it established the already well known fact that the many North Caucasians hated the Kremlin rule over them. Upon his return, Lange apparently had a talk with Professor Oberländer, the chief of "Bergmann," who confirmed all I had heard from Ismailov and Aliev.

During 1948, my wife and I were visiting in Stuttgart, West Germany; a friend of mine, a Georgian officer, Zurab Abdushelishvili, who at that time was seriously ill and had been hospitalized. There we also met another Georgian, Giorgi Kipiani. Kipiani was wondering if I knew a Baltic German, Nikolai Lilienthal, who often spoke of me and was looking forward to seeing me. I told him that I knew him well and I would very much like to see him. It was another joyous reunion when we visited Nikolai in his apartment. He presented me with a Caucasian short sword "Hanjali,"[16] which was given to him while with Lange in North Caucasus during 1942. To this day, I still have the sword in my possession.

Nikolai told me how upset the Baltic Germans of the unit were when Lange sentenced me to the punitive camp. They thought that the real reason for his action was a fear that I had gained more influence and authority among the Caucasians in his unit than Lange himself. (This differs from my own interpretation of the reason.) According to Nikolai, following the Caucasian adventure, Lange got another job in Albania and while hunting there, in a company of "very important people," was accidentally shot in his head and after protracted illness barely recovered. Although, in all honesty, Lange has never been on my list of favorite people, I never wished him to get in such trouble.

I considered Lange to be a courageous and intelligent officer but a bit too ambitious, self-centered and cold. In retrospect, I am sure that I gave him a difficult time and his decision for us to part was a correct one and best for both of us. However, his intention to send me to Dachau does not exactly make him a humanitarian, and

---

16- Also known as "Kinjal."

if the Baltic German soldiers had not talked him out of it, I may never have survived W.W. II. This was the third and last time I ever heard about Lieutenant Lange.

Steinau P.O.W. punitive camp was a relatively small one; the inmates were all of Soviet origin and mostly non Russians. They were housed in a huge hall of some old building surrounded by a series of barbed wire. There were no bathroom facilities available there but instead a large kettle had been placed in the center of the hall. Since our lunch and supper consisted mostly of thin soup the inmates frequently got up during the night to relieve themselves and the hall was not heated. After a while, one did get used to the disagreeable smell and also to the cold temperature.

Early morning we would get out of our bunks, the guards arrived shortly after and marched us through the streets of Steinau to the outskirts of the city where the soap factory complex was located. There in a small, old building that apparently once had been used by German factory workers, was our first station with bathrooms and washing facilities, what a relief.

We breakfasted on some kind of coffee substitute, a piece of bread and a teaspoon of marmalade. Then the work began, unloading coal for the factory from railroad cars, interrupted only for lunch and supper. After work, we were marched back again to our quarters with the big kettle in the center. Most of us were weak and life appeared unattractive, but one should not complain since one could survive under such conditions. As I found out later, this was not the case for thousands of Soviet P.O.W.s who had not been transferred to Germany due to Hitler's refusal. They remained in occupied Eastern territories during the terrible winter of 1941-42.

As I learned during the spring of 1942, additional tragic problems had been the execution of the Jewish P.O.W.s when discovered by Himmler's commandos. Such was the fate of many Caucasian Muslims also. Their problem, not looking like a Russian, was compounded by the fact that in a true Muslim tradition they had also been circumcised, as have the Jews. As far as Christian Georgians were concerned, in several instances, they were also singled out for punishment. This was not only for their Mediterranean looks with the aquiline noses but because they were denounced as "Stalin's Hawks" to the German SS guards by some Russian fellow P.O.W.s in order to gain badly needed favor for themselves. When this became clear to the Germans later (after already having "liquidated" scores of people), such practices stopped, (except for the Jews).

Now the Georgians and other Caucasians P.O.W.s in camps were able to protect their Jewish compatriots by declaring them to be Georgian Muslims or simply Caucasian Muslims. Later, when things had improved, the Jews were simply declared by us as Georgians or other Caucasian nationals.

Our guards, in Steinau, were army soldiers and they treated us correctly. The exception was the interpreter, a Baltic German, Latz, who apparently demonstrated his "power" by threatening and abusing the prisoners verbally and at times physically, such as pulling their ears. I tried my best to stay out of his way which was easier for me than for some other fellow inmates, since I spoke German and therefore hardly ever needed his "help" as an interpreter.

But one day, for some reason, Latz was especially mean to one debilitated prisoner who picked up a cigarette butt from the street while we were led to work. I became so infuriated that I told "Herr" Latz to leave the poor man alone. At first he was startled but then shouted at me, "How dare you, I will show you, you communist." His words did not do much to lessen my anger. Suddenly I stepped in his direction and shouted back that he should not dare to talk to me that way again or come what may, I would get even with him. He obviously was startled and stepped back. I had the feeling that our guards, who were all simple, decent, military soldiers did not especially care for Latz, but nevertheless they had to report this incident to the prison camp commandant.

When I received the notification to see him, a thought went through my mind: "This is all you need, on top of already (not so long ago) being punished by Lange for 'not recognizing the German leadership and being critical of it'." Now another conflict, with a different German official. At best, I could be transferred to Dachau this time. Fortunately the commandant, a non-commissioned officer, Dr. Fick (this may not be correctly spelled) turned out to be a decent man. As I learned later, he was a doctor of archeology from Silesia and assigned to present non-combat duty because of his age and possibly some physical handicap.

The commandant knew that I spoke German, therefore the "service" of Mr. Latz was not necessary this time. He wanted to know what happened and why I was so upset with the interpreter Latz (who also was a private in the army). I started with the statement that "in my opinion Herr Latz's harshness and abusiveness toward the prisoners was uncalled for. Most of them were weak, some of them sick but nevertheless working every day. A person who humbles himself so much as to pick up cigarette butts on the street should be pitied and does not deserve to have his ears pulled inasmuch as they are already frightened and had lost self esteem. As far as calling me a communist was concerned, Herr Latz assumes that I am one and does not know my background. While I do not feel especially hostile toward a 'simple-ordinary' communist as an individual, nevertheless, it was the communist rule that brought disaster upon my country and my family. I am opposed to it and therefore I resent Mr. Latz's addressing me as such." The commandant apparently was satisfied with my explanation, and no further punitive measures were ordered against me.

In fact, he wanted to see me the next day and asked if I would be willing to check my fellow inmates periodically and report to him who was in need of medical attention. Then the guardsman would take us to the French P.O.W. hospital which was within walking distance. We did that and found the P.O.W. French doctors to be very helpful and cordial. Our sick people received good care.

They also invited me into the doctor's room and hosted me with coffee, chocolate and other sweets. They apparently received these regularly in the mail from their homes along with letters from loved ones. They did not look frightened, undernourished and forsaken by all as did the Soviet P.O.W.s. I chose not to discuss things such as this with our French colleagues but our appearance revealed the situation. French P.O.W. doctors in this hospital worked with the German Red Cross nurses (sisters) and under a civilian administrator, who curious enough was an Italian.

Steinau was not far from the larger city of Hanau, which had been considered an important center of aluminum production. In this factory, the French and other Western European P.O.W.s were working; their living conditions were considerably better than ours in Steinau, as I was told by one of the French doctors. This information turned out to be of some importance to us as we shall see later on.

It goes to Commandant Fick's credit that he was able to somewhat improve our food probably as a result of negotiations with the factory management and also our health care. He also stopped the interpreter Latz's abuses. I also discovered that Dr. Fick was interested in Georgian archeology. I told him all I could remember about it and also mentioned the archaeological exploration my father had carried out in Svaneti.

While building the road in the mighty River Inguri canyon, my father noticed that several hills were covered by pieces of old clay pipes, one end of which were burned due to exposure to heat and discarded as useless. This led Father to do excavations near the summits of the hills and it revealed the ancient factories or workshops, where metal was melted and beautiful enamel was produced. Another interesting thing was that while plowing the fields, the farmers would at times find golden coins and figurines in the ground. Furthermore, one local hunter had also discovered an old building in the forest when the ground caved in under his feet. It apparently was an old roof and he fell in. The building was full of golden coins and figurines. The hunter kept this secret to himself but he would trade coins with peddlers for necessary utilities.

After some time, one disaster after another began to occur in his family. This was interpreted by him as a curse of an angered god, since the discovered "treasure" must have been divine property. So he returned all the items still in his possession to the secret place, camouflaged it even better and died without revealing this secret to anyone. A couple of such coins were obtained by my father and donated to some museum. One coin had written on it, "Alexander" which obviously meant Alexander the Great. On the other side of the coin, there was an image of a horse's head with an arrow through its neck.

In my father's opinion, there was no question about it, the Colchians (the west Georgians), of which Svaneti was a part, had been engaged in prospecting gold and converting it into coins and other precious commodities on a large scale. I also spoke about the ancient method of obtaining gold from the Inguri River and its tributaries where it is still found mixed with sand. A sheep skin was placed in the water, the gold being heavier, would get trapped in the wool and thus harvested. The sand would be washed away. This probably gave origin to the legend of the "Golden Fleece" which was stolen by Jason and his Argonauts from the King of Colchis with the help of the King's daughter, a sorceress, Medea, who followed Jason to Greece.

The German archaeologist, of course, knew about this Greek legend but not necessarily about the setup surrounding it and showed a great deal of interest in the details. Other conversations took place between us frequently.

One day, Dr. Fick said that there must have been a mistake or misunderstanding that I had been sent to this camp. He suggested that I write my side of the story and he would see to it that the letter be forwarded to the appropriate place. I frankly thought that it was useless but felt inhibited to turn down such a well intentioned proposition and therefore complied with it. Dr. Fick also informed me that he was scheduled to leave shortly, on vacation, for his home city of Liegnitz in Silesia. Much to my surprise, I was invited to be their family guest and of course, I accepted. So we traveled by train, during which time my host delivered splendid lectures on Silesia for my benefit.

Silesia had a turbulent history and one which was not unlike the Caucasian past including the Mongol invasion in the thirteenth century which was finally stopped during the battle of Liegnitz. We finally arrived there, and Mrs. Fick was a gracious hostess. I especially enjoyed playing with their small children. It had been a long time since I had the pleasure of doing so and therefore I gladly "babysat" while my hosts went out. Dr. Fick warned me not to leave the house without his company because I was in French P.O.W. attire. The police may have questioned me and of course, I had no documents of any kind. This was fine with me—what better place would I go to under the given situation?

Dr. Fick also took me on a tour of Liegnitz so I could satisfy my curiosity about this old city. The vacation was soon over, and on our way back to the prison camp, my host decided to stop in Vienna for some business. There in the "soldiers home," he somehow learned that the number of Georgian soldiers were located in one of the military quarters of Vienna. Dr. Fick thought it would be of interest for me to see my countrymen so we visited them. I met a very nice, well-educated, soft-spoken gentleman. Mr. Mathe Kereselidze, an old emigrant from Paris, also a number of former Georgian P.O.W.s and their superior, a non-commissioned officer, Mr. Hermann.

Dr. Fick left me alone with them for a few hours. They all kept a "tight lip" about their business and only a few months later, I learned that they were part of the "Thamar I" unit, being trained for parachuting in Georgia during the war. I was instantly drawn to Mathe Kereselidze, and we had a cordial conversation as one Georgian to another without any witnesses.

He said that he already knew about my existence and then greatly surprised me with the statement that the Germans "respected" me, they would "never send me back to the unit (Lange) where I had been before." Until this day, I do not know how Mathe Kereselidze could get such information except perhaps through his "boss," Mr. Hermann. In any case, I was grateful to him for tipping me off to the possibility that something was going on behind the scenes on my behalf. Furthermore, the way Kereselidze said it, I had the feeling that Lange may even have been reproached by his superiors for the way I was treated by him.

Mathe Kereselidze's group (from "Thamar I") did indeed land in the northwest part of Georgia during late spring or early summer 1942; some of them died or were wounded in the shootout with the Soviet forces, others were captured. Mathe was one of the few, who contrary to general expectations, was freed by the Soviets after fourteen to fifteen years in prison and allowed to return to the West. Perhaps, due to the fact that he never had been a Soviet citizen and also due to Khrushchev's decrees after Stalin's death and Chancellor Adenauer's efforts on behalf of the German P.O.W.s during his Moscow trip.

It was sometime during the late fifties or early sixties when I met Mathe Kereselidze again, this time in the city of Dusseldorf, West Germany, He had just returned from captivity and was working now with Professor Gerhard von Mende in the Institute for "Research of East Europe." We shall say much more about Professor Gerhard von Mende, who was a friend and protector of the Caucasian and Turkestani people. He was an outstanding personality to whom the Georgians affectionately referred to by the Georgian name "Gogii."

My wife and I visited von Mendes in Dusseldorf, and for this occasion they also invited Mathe Kereselidze. Mrs. Karo von Mendes served lunch, and we stayed there until late. There, Mathe told me about some of the most interesting episodes of "Thamar I's" landing in Georgia and its consequences. Mathe was a Georgian patriot which was a tradition for his family. What he and some others did during

W.W. II was in defense of Georgian national interest, for which they were ready to sacrifice their lives, but never got any credit.

Shortly after Dr. Fick's and my return to Steinau, two North Caucasians, Beshtokov and Nagoev, were brought to the prisoners' camp of Steinau. They were also from the Lange group. The reason for such punishment was probably "noncompliance and criticism," just as in my case. They were both educated and intelligent persons and at times perhaps "uncomfortable" for Lange. We were happy to see each other again. Conditions in our camp had already improved considerably. In addition to better food, some time was allowed for recreational activities for the prisoners and the guards had more smiles for us.

But the real paradox and the sign of change was when I was asked one evening to see the interpreter, Latz, professionally as he had developed some medical problem. I was surprised to see the non-commissioned officer, Moritz, from Lange's group in his room. Apparently he was passing by Steinau and decided to stop and visit Mr. Latz, whom he knew from Balticum. Obviously, it was he who suggested they call me for help, and Latz agreed. Happily, I was able to assure the patient that he was going to be all right.

Then one day at work, during lunch hour, a general staff officer entered the room. All the German guards sprung to their feet and stood at attention while the commandant made a report to him as is customary in the military service. The officer sat at the head table and through the interpreter briefly conversed with each prisoner, asking name, background and etc.

I was the only one whom he chose to ignore but when this was all over and the prisoners were leaving for work, the officer inconspicuously approached and asked if he could have a word with me. Then he went on to say that they heard about me and regrettably some mistakes had been made in my treatment. He shook my hand, asked me to keep this conversation confidential and departed, leaving me to wonder what would happen next. A few months later, I learned that he was executed for a reason not entirely clear to me. It was the beginning of April 1942, and the weather was on our side, lifting up our spirits.

To the number of unpleasant encounters one more was added in Steinau. As we were led from work to our living quarters through the street, the school children were grimacing and casting small stones at us. One had the definite feeling that they actually hated us. Children normally are champions of the wretched and the weak and that we certainly were, so someone was teaching these little people to hate us. I could not help but remember German journals shown to me by Nikolai Lilienthal while in Lange's unit.

In those journals photographs of hundreds of the Red Army soldier P.O.W.s were printed—unshaved, clad in rags, starved and with depressed faces. With such "subhuman" hordes, "die Untermenschen," Stalin wanted to "conquer Europe," stated the editor in "explaining" the appearance of these poor people by the inherent inferiority of their race and not mentioning the real cause of it—the inhuman conditions in the P.O.W. camps.

But who in Germany was doing it? I remembered well how Major Ernst zu Eikern and his friends, the army officers in Alexandria, had made it clear to me that they had nothing to do with the preparation of some obnoxious German propaganda leaflets. So I assumed that it must have been a propaganda policy of the ruling government. I had witnessed a similar situation in the Soviet Union where even after the victorious Civil War in Russia and having "liquidated" the classes, the Bolsheviks still engaged in propaganda of class hatred and struggle, even brainwashing the school children in this direction up to the point of denouncing their own parents for some "misdeeds."

One young poet wrote. "I shall kill my parents, if the revolution orders me to do so." Now again, as during the Red Army invasion of the Baltic States, I thought that if there was no chance of removing a ruthless ruler from inside, surely there must be just forces somewhere in the world, perhaps led by England, to defeat any form of tyranny and establish human rights for everyone.

Youth has a tendency to dream and believe of just and straight-forward solutions, even for the most complex problems. Perhaps this is just as well, otherwise they would never act.

But one also has to be ready for disappointments on the road of the quest.

5

IN THE "BERGMANN" UNIT AND CAUCASUS

One Sunday morning during the middle of April 1942, an officer entered our living quarters. His appearance was very impressive; dressed in a splendid uniform, wearing a monocle, his chest adorned with a huge medal and carrying himself with great dignity. I thought that he was probably a general at the very least. Therefore, I was surprised when he announced that he was looking for me. After I identified myself, he in turn introduced himself as Baron Walter von Kutzschenbach, an associate of Professor Oberländer, on whose behalf he wanted to talk to me privately.

Then in very good Russian he politely told me, "potrudites poshalusta" which means "please make an effort to follow me." After my daily "efforts" of loading coal, I thought this one more "effort" should not be too difficult. Herr Baron led me to a nearby inn and invited me to a delicious lunch in a secluded area of the restaurant. The innkeeper apparently felt honored with such a guest and acted accordingly. Von Kutzschenbach preferred to converse with me in Russian for "security" reasons (as he explained). At times he also threw in some Georgian expressions, such as "my dear fellow," or "how are you doing" etc., which at once warmed my heart.

It was a very interesting conversation where I did more listening than talking. Von Kutzschenbach said that he was born and raised in Georgia in a family of German immigrant parents. Their family estate and well known cheese factory was located in the town of Mamutli, Borchalo a southeast province of Georgia, which has a large number of Muslim or so called "Tatar" inhabitants. During the Georgian independence 1918-21, young Walter von Kutzschenbach had performed services for the independent Georgian Republic, while also in the corps of Colonel (later, General) Kress von Kressenstein as the officer's aspirant. For this, he was decorated with a beautiful Georgian Medal of Queen Thamar, which he proudly wore until the present day. It was the one that caught my eye at once and frankly, I envied him for this. During the turbulent situation of those years, unfortunately the "Tatars" killed Walter's father. He chose to emigrate to Germany; basically considering himself to be a German. Von Kutzschenbach also felt himself to be a Georgian. This feeling was shared by his cousins, whom I met after World War II in West Germany. Von Kutzschenbach was called to duty by the army and because of his unusual background and linguistic ability, was found to be well suited for special duty; and with the rank of a non-combat lieutenant (so called "sonderführer"—"a special guide"), he joined Professor Theodor Oberländer in his "Bergmann."[17]

Von Kutzschenbach said that Oberländer was considered an expert of the Soviet Union. He also said that the Germans were making many "mistakes" in occupied zones and Oberländer and some other Germans were determined to alter the situation. It is not the military who is responsible for such a "blunder," he said, but civilian bureaucrats who take over the administration as soon as the military moves forward with the advancing front. Von Kutzschenbach also said that this should not be allowed to be repeated in the Caucasus, which may well come under German occupation after the resumption of the spring offensive.

Oberländer believed that the presence of the Caucasian military unit, "Bergmann," in the Caucasus would go a long way to help toward this goal. This special military unit consisted of former Caucasian P.O.W.s and Georgian emigre volunteers from France, the number of which would increase shortly. "All the Georgians put together will be in a majority as compared to any other single Caucasian group in 'Bergmann,'" he said. The strongest point von Kutzschenbach made was when he said that "'Bergmann' is dedicated to the reestablishment of the free Caucasian people and their states."

According to him, among other officers in "Bergmann" there was also Lieutenant von Kressenstein, as a symbol of Caucasian and German friendship, since his ancestor, General Kress von Kressenstein had lent great support to the independent Caucasian States during 1918, as we all knew. Now his young descendant was keeping up that tradition. How did von Kutzschenbach's visit to me come about?

As Professor Oberländer recalled later, Misha Kedia, at that time residing in Berlin, was unhappy about my disappearance and he informed Count Frederich Werner von Schulenburg[18] about it. Schulenburg, in turn contacted Hans von

---

17- A Soviet propaganda publication, during the defamation attempt, had "interpreted" von Kutzschenbach's rank "sonderführer" as one belonging to the infamous SS. Not only was it complete nonsense, but also von Kutzschenbach had always had great dislike for the party organizations in general, and the SS in particular.

18- Schulenburg was a former German Representative in Georgia, during 1918-21 and was considered to be our friend. Later, he was the German Ambassador in the Soviet Union. Schulenburg was executed by Hitler in 1944, after the 20th of July failed putsch.

Herwarth, who was his as well as Lieutenant Colonel Claus von Stauffenberg's associate[19] in the organization department of the Army General Staff, who had been put in charge of the formation of the volunteer units. Herwarth then informed Oberländer about it, who undertook steps, identified my location and sent von Kutzschenbach to Steinau. I am not clear if the letter I wrote on Commandant's Dr. Fick's suggestion had anything to do with it. Von Kutzschenbach proposed to me that I see Oberländer and join his Caucasian unit "Bergmann."

I was invited to breakfast the following morning by von Kutzschenbach. Here again he made another strong point, namely: given my Georgian patriotism, what could I achieve by staying in Steinau, or for that matter some where else in Germany, even if a more comfortable place could have been arranged for me? (He probably could have arranged this.) An important action is pending in the Caucasus and assuredly many problems will have to be solved there, some of them probably vital for Georgia and I could be of help. I replied that I would like to ponder about it a bit. Von Kutzschenbach then informed me that we both were invited for dinner by the factory owner for whom I had been loading coal. "He is my old acquaintance," he said.

This whole thing had the twist of a fairytale such as the "Arabian Nights," rather than reality. Our guards were also confused and no longer sure of their expected behavior toward me. Instead of the prisoners' quarters, behind barbed wires, that evening I went with von Kutzschenbach to the factory owner's mansion near the wooded hill. It was a moving experience for me when von Kutzschenbach introduced me to the factory owner's family with a certain warmth and pride in his voice as "my Georgian friend and doctor...." Then the factory owner, in turn, introduced both of us to their other guests.

The ladies looked beautiful to me and the gentlemen distinguished. I felt somewhat uncomfortable, but as I followed Baron von Kutzschenbach's lead and kissed the hand of the hostess and other married ladies, my self confidence returned to me gradually. The handsome Baron had soon captivated the audience, not only by his appearance but also by telling them about his experiences and other stories. He eventually pulled me into the conversation. From the two us, they heard about a few things—probably not found in the newspapers. At times the Baron would whisper to me in Russian, "Vsio ne govorite," (don't say everything) suggesting a certain precaution was still in order.

At the dinner table there was a young lady present, a relative of our hosts. She was especially attentive to me and proudly mentioned that she was from Czechoslovakia. I had very superficial and limited information then about her

---

19- Stauffenberg was one of the main organizers of the failed putsch against Hitler; he also was executed during 1944.

country and only from Soviet and German sources. I made a stupid observation that the name Czechoslovakia had been changed now to "Protectorate," hoping to hear what it really meant. Some guests responded with an uncomfortable smile, but the Czech lady appeared unhappy.

After dinner, I approached her and on a one-to-one basis, she explained to me about the tragedy of her cultured and civilized country and about the brave people. Later, I was able to gather more information about it. The Czechs had a respectable, well trained military force. They were armed with modern weapons and also had a well prepared terrain for defensive war. They were resolved to fight the invader, who would have had a very costly war on his hands. (This was demonstrated by four and one-half million Finns later on.) Unfortunately, the Western Allies weren't prepared to back them up if need be. In fact, they even discouraged their thought of resisting; they would rather sacrifice them on the altar of "Peace in our time."

It should have remained a permanent lesson for the world, that the military weakness of the major democratic powers would always be taken advantage of by totalitarian states. The former will agree at first to certain concessions in the name of "peace," but this only wets the aggressor's appetite. The agreements will be broken and the stage will be set for a major catastrophe—the all out war. The military unpreparedness, in the face of possible danger, points to either a complacent, naive government or one that hides its head in the sand. They are unable to communicate the unpopular truth to their constituents and prepare them for the defense of national interests.

During the 1938 crisis, apparently the French and English were not ready to take a firm stand on behalf of the Czechs. Hitler was wrongly convinced that the democracies had neither the will nor the ability to resist his further aggression. Therefore, after "The Molotov-Ribbentrop Pact," he invaded Poland, and W.W. II was now on. As far as the Kremlin was concerned, it had no intention of demonstrating the readiness of helping Czechoslovakia.[20] It has recently been found from the Romanian Archives that Moscow rejected the option of sending military force across Romania to help the Czechs, in case it would be invaded. Not only that, but the Soviets recognized the legality of abolishment of the Czech statehood in 1939 and urged the western powers to do the same.[21]

My conversation partner, the Czech lady, was hoping that the Soviet Union and her allies, in the case of victory, would restore the independence of Czechoslovakia as it was before and all would be well. I did not want to disappoint

---

20- Hans von Herwarth, *Against Two Evils*.
21- Gerhard L. Weinberg. "Munich After 50 Years." *Foreign Affairs*. Fall 1988.

her, and all my sympathy and best wishes were with her. I wanted to be honest and shared some of my experiences in the Soviet Union with her. She simply could not believe it, and I did not press the issue. On the other hand, in retrospect, it is possible that in the long run her country fared better, even under the "Brezhnev Doctrine" than it would have under Hitler's "Protectorate."

The next day, von Kutzschenbach discussed with me the aluminum factory in nearby Hanau, to which I have referred before. He wondered how much I knew about it. I told him that according to the French P.O.W. doctors, conditions were much better there than here in Steinau, especially the living quarters. He asked if I would accompany him, to get first hand knowledge about the place. We did so and it confirmed our positive expectations.

Kutzschenbach said that he would be able to arrange a transfer of the remaining P.O.W.s from our camp in Steinau to the Hanau factory. This should have improved their situation somewhat. All this time I was thinking of Kutzschenbach's suggestion to see Professor Oberländer and join his Caucasian mountain military unit.

I decided to do it, and there were several reasons for my decision.

1. Von Kutzschenbach made a good impression on me; I had the feeling that he, too, was part of Georgia's recent history 1917–1921.

2. The Caucasian military unit was declared to be dedicated to the cause of the Caucasian people, even though it also served German military objectives.

3. An equally important single factor for me was the presence of a large number of Georgian emigres from France who represented the political parties in exile. After all, the original reason for my journey to Germany was to get in touch with them and find out what could be done for Georgia, since I considered them to be our well informed "ambassadors" in the west. This opportunity, which Lieutenant Lange did not or could not do, was offered to me now by von Kutzschenbach.

4. It also appeared now that there were some people in Germany who displayed sensitivity to our problems and were willing to help.

Von Kutzschenbach was pleased by my decision and informed me that the two North Caucasian officers, Beshtokov and Nagoev would also join us. One Georgian, Valiko Maglakelidze would be transferred to "Bergmann" later on or to another appropriate place; permission also had been received to transfer all remaining Steinau inmates to Hanau, for which we all thanked him. Among the inmates in Steinau, there were also two Georgian Jews and I think with assumed names. In our conversations, we were careful not to inadvertently reveal this to the Germans, although as it appeared, the Germans in our camp did not harbor any hostility toward the Jews. One of the Georgian Jews was a convinced Stalinist. I pointed out to him the ruthlessness and the bloody deeds as a result of which many Georgian and non Georgian families were destroyed. I also added that Stalin was just Lenin's pupil and Lenin started all this, to make it clear to him that without Lenin and his system, Stalin would not exist.

His answer was, "I like and respect you, Doctor. You are a good man but what you are telling me is a different matter. You will see that Stalin will win the war, there is no world leader like him. He has done nothing wrong, it's the people around him who are making those 'mistakes'. He is not aware of it; he has so many other things to do, you know. Moreover, the Russian people can be governed with a firm hand only." I have often thought about the psychology of such a blind, undeserved faith in some leaders by their subjects. Such a conviction has not been uncommon during the twentieth century, even after the dictator's demise.[22]

It was now the second part of April 1942 and a few of us from "Steinau Camp" with Baron von Kutzschenbach took the train to the Bavarian city Mittenwald; then a short, uphill car ride on the meandering road to Luttensee. There, in the military quarters of the Bavarian mountain troops, the Caucasian unit "Bergmann" ("Mountain Man") was located. The beauty of the surrounding mountains and nature in general was overwhelming. Spring revealed herself in all her splendor but on the mountain slopes, especially those facing north, the snow was still present. I felt an irresistible urge to climb the summits and then slide down on the snow. The houses in military quarters were built according to Bavarian architecture, keeping in harmony with the environment.

On the central gathering place and between the buildings, the Caucasian and German soldiers were seen in mountain troop uniforms. Beside the usual emblem of the edelweiss flower, there was a Caucasian short sword, "Handzali" (or Kinjal), which adorned the hats of the instructors. This was a symbol of friendship between the Caucasian and the German mountain soldiers. The "Handzali" sign was designed by von Kutzschenbach. As we arrived, a Georgian company was just returning from

---

22- Among the inmates of Steinau there were two very interesting intellectuals from Turkestan. In retrospect, one of them resembled Mao Tse-Tung and the other Chou En-lai. This applied not only to their physical appearance but also to their political beliefs. They were convinced communists but also had strong nationalistic feelings opposing the Russian domination of their country. Such observations time and time again confirmed to me that serious nationality problems existed in the Soviet Union but on the surface, due to suppression, all appeared to be well.

field exercise. It was an impressive looking formation and they were also singing well the old Georgian song, "It's me and my Nabadi (woolen Georgian overcoat) that helps see me through the night." The effect of this song and the environment was undeniably strong on me.

Von Kutzschenbach first introduced me to the former Red Army captain Simon Tsiklauri, who was to be my future roommate. He next made an appointment for me to meet with Professor Oberländer in a couple of hours, then von Kutzschenbach left us alone. Captain Tsiklauri welcomed me in a very friendly way. He was a tall and rather handsome man, probably in his thirties and had been born in the eastern Georgian mountain foothills. Since I was from the western mountains, we shared some common traditions and features characteristic for the mountaineers in Georgia and to a certain extent everywhere in the world. These were, for instance, to be somewhat of a quixotic disposition, stubborn and an exaggerated sense of pride and honor. I liked him and felt privileged to be his roommate.

Captain Tsiklauri explained a few things about the unit and gave me some useful, practical tips. We also briefly told each other about our past which, as time went by, was more detailed. He had been a professional officer in the Red Army and prevailing conditions there got under his skin. Particularly the "politruk" (commissar) was making his life miserable, so he said. The military unit should have only one commander and not two, he also commented. Following the last argument between the Captain and the politruk, Captain Tsiklauri shot him and crossed the front line with some of his soldiers to become a P.O.W. in German hands.

In the P.O.W. camp in (or near) Poltava, a German professor interviewed him and Tsiklauri volunteered to serve in the Caucasian military unit. On answering my question if he had a close relationship with Georgian emigrants, he said that he had met those already in the unit and had also made a trip to visit a group of forty or fifty of them formerly from "Thamar II" who were just about to join the "Bergmann" unit.

Much to my surprise, Tsiklauri went on to say that the emigrants were "useless" since they had lost touch with the home country. They became "degenerates" under the influence of Western Europe and they should have no voice concerning Georgian matters. I learned later that Tsiklauri quite bluntly made these views clear to the group of emigrants during his visit. Predictably the emigrants were stunned at first and then a heated argument had followed, especially between Tsiklauri and Victor Nozadze, a former social democrat and a man of letters from Paris. Some emigrants wanted to beat up Tsiklauri, but the others prevented this.

I could not understand the Captain's opinion about our emigrants, the majority of whom had dedicated their lives to the Georgian cause and one recent example being their presence in "Bergmann." Politely but firmly, I at once made it clear to Tsiklauri that I did not share his views about the Georgian emigres. "Quite the contrary." I said. "We need them, if for nothing else, for their knowledge of the western world where we now reside and about which we know so little. We are not well oriented to many things and are prone to making mistakes. They also need us as grassroot representatives from today's Georgia. Our country needs all of us together." I was hoping to "convert" the captain gradually and win him over to my view.

We had to interrupt our conversation since the time had come for my appointment with Professor Oberländer. I was led to see him in a comfortable small conference room adjoining the officers' mess. Probably in his mid thirties, he appeared to be a pleasant, polite and cordial gentleman, a positive thinker and full of energy which was contagious. He was a university professor with two doctoral degrees, one in economics and the second one in political science. A short time after my arrival here, he was promoted from an army first lieutenant to a captain.[23]

The professor astounded me by his frankness, delivering a blistering attack against the German policy in occupied Eastern territories. I already had heard something about it from von Kutzschenbach a few days ago, but it was Oberländer who fully explained its disastrous nature. No such news ever reached me before during my isolated existence in Germany from October 1941 until now, April 1942. Therefore, it was a "shocker." Oberländer underlined how the overwhelming majority of the military men were for decent and humane treatment of the indigenous population and P.O.W.s but they were followed by a second wave of civilian bureaucrats.

For instance, the commissar for the Ukraine, Gauleiter [Nazi regional administrator] Koch (whom Oberländer despised), adhered to the policy of total exploitation of the Ukrainians, treating the population as sub-human. Koch denied to them any form of self-government or other human rights, their leaders were thrown into jails and many persons were herded and forced into labor camps in Germany. Oberländer said that things were just as dismal in the camps for the prisoners of war. Higher ups in the government, at first, forbade transporting them to Germany

23- As part of the defamation propaganda in the sixties and seventies, in some of the Soviet Georgian publications, Oberländer had falsely been depicted as an SS officer. [Not to be confused with the Nazi war criminal Helmut Oberlander, Theodore Oberländer had been a member of the *Ostforschung,* a scientific organization that believed in Aryan superiority and whose ideology was used to justify ethnic cleansing of Jews and Poles from the East, though Oberländer himself did not endorse those views or the genocide, but rather advocated for a softer form of colonial administration of Slavic peoples. Givi Gabliani's memoir conforms to this latter view of Oberländer. For more about Oberländer, see Victor Silling, *Die Hintergründe des Falles Oberländer,* Germany: Grenzland Verlag, 1960, pp. 60–61 and biographer of Oberländer's supporter, Konrad Adenauer, Hans Peter-Schwarz, *Konrad Adenauer: A German Politician and Statesman in a Period of War, Revolution and Reconstruction — The Statesman: 1952–1967,* New York: Berghahn Books, 1997, pp. 91, 432. In context of Russia's 21st century wars of agression against Ukraine, Ukrainian nationalism and claims of "Nazis" in Ukraine, see Kai Struve, "Theodor Oberländer and the Nachtigall Battalion in 1959/60—an Entangled History of Propaganda, Politics, and Memory in East and West," *Slavic Review* 81 (3), February 2023: 677–700. —Ed.]

and an overwhelming number of P.O.W.s remained in occupied territories without adequate shelter, food or sanitary conditions—the death rate was staggering.

As I heard later, some influential man among them, Oberländer's Chief Admiral Canaris, had tried energetically to intervene on behalf of the Soviet P.O.W.s with the appropriate authorities.[24] The results were not clear yet but improvement was hoped for. It was Oberländer's expectation that "Bergmann's" military presence in the Caucasus would be a factor in preventing a repetition of the Ukrainian tragedy. While his unit had a definite military assignment, parallel to it there was an even more important objective to be demonstrated by the German military, that good treatment of the Caucasian soldiers, of P.O.W.s as well as of the civilian population would make them reliable allies for the Germans against Stalin's Bolshevik regime. This, of course, should include positive agrarian and political reforms as well. If this proved to be successful, then such an example could be used as an argument to bring about the change of the present "East Policy" in other occupied territories as well.

To help him in formulating and bringing his concepts into focus, Oberländer enlisted in "Bergmann" several capable broadminded experts on East Europe (including the Soviet Union). With a twinkle in his eyes, he baptized them as the "brain trust of Bergmann." It included such impressive personalities as Dr. Hermann Raschhofer, Dr. Ted (Ehrenfried) Schütte, Dr. Friedrich Richter and a couple other men. They were all "puritans" as was our chief, Professor Oberländer, himself. Being not quite as intellectual and puritan, Walter von Kutzschenbach and I considered ourselves only ex officio, non voting members of the "brain trust." I shared, however, the passion for discussion and hiking with them and those went hand in hand. Von Kutzschenbach was somewhat less enthusiastic about hiking since his monocle and his beautiful officers' riding boots did not go well with it.

Oberländer enjoyed walking and so did I, so we took a walk in the nearby hills before supper and continued our conversation. I was pleased to hear him say that von Kutzschenbach and he had great confidence in me. This was based, he said, not only on their instinct and Kedia's excellent recommendation but also on how I stood up for my principals and beliefs openly while I was somewhere else, (obviously referring to Lieutenant Lange's group). He suggested that I be just as open with him and voice my opinion, and I said of course, I would.

I was much impressed by Professor Oberländer during our very first encounter. He appeared genuinely concerned about the people of Caucasus and the Soviet Union in general. He had a deep knowledge of their socio-economic, political and nationality problems; he was equally concerned by the bad relationship, rapidly

---

24- Alexander Dallin, *German Rule in Russia 1941–45*. Concerning this matter and Canaris, see Oberländer's memoranda.

developing between them and his own country—Germany, due to the criminal "East Policy," of the German leaders. Oberländer had courage, not only to make his controversial views known in the series of reports ("die Denkschriften"), but also to propose an alternate plan and to pursue it.

We were back just in time for dinner and in the officers' mess, Oberländer introduced me to other officers. They were a group of cordial people. I was particularly pleased to meet Lieutenant von Kressenstein, the descendant of General Kress von Kressenstein, as already mentioned, an old friend of the Georgians during our independence. The young von Kressenstein was a small sized gentleman with mild manners, modest and pleasant. The mountain troops generally had the reputation of being elegant and gallant and "Bergmann" was no exception. But the German officers, non-commissioned officers and others in "Bergmann" had to have an additional quality; namely, to be free of prejudice against the "foreigners from the east" and sympathetic to their cause. Oberländer was especially sensitive about this issue; he carefully selected the Germans for his unit and lectured them about the Caucasian people but a number of them still did not meet his criteria and had to be transferred somewhere else. They clearly were victims of Nazi propaganda against the "Easterners."

After the war, Oberländer allowed me to make notes from his diary; it was clear how early and persistently he opposed the policy of the Nazi higher ups. For instance, during the beginning of September 1941, accompanied by von Kutzschenbach, he visited the headquarters of the "South Army Group." Oberländer bitterly complained to Colonel Winter, an influential person in the General Staff, about the poor treatment of the people in the Ukraine. Oberländer recorded that the overwhelming majority of the army officers were for good treatment of the indigenous population, among them the Jews. Unfortunately the civilian Nazi commissars and Himmler's people, being in charge of such matters were adamantly opposed to such views. During the middle of October 1941, the South Army Staff initiated a meeting where the agrarian questions were brought up, hoping to bring about positive changes.

Oberländer and the former German agrarian attache in the U.S.S.R., Otto Schiller participated and both suggested abolishing the collective farms and returning the land to the farmers. This did not pass because Himmler wanted to keep the collective farms, since this enabled him to have better control and ruthless exploitation of production. Such a "policy" often led to destruction and inability for the farms to produce further. For instance, in order to obtain a large quantity of meat, all sows were slaughtered, with predictable results—there were no more pigs on the farms.

In the beginning of January 1942, Oberländer had a meeting in the Foreign Service with Leibrant, Bräutigam and the Ambassadorial Council Hilger, the Soviet specialists. They all agreed that there was need for the different "East Policy." Following the meeting, Hilger distributed Oberländer's memorandum devoted to this subject. Following this, Oberländer visited the Ministry of Eastern Affairs to gain their support for his views. Professor G. von Mende, representing the Ministry completely agreed with Oberländer. To no one's surprise, during the special January 1942 meeting between Admiral Canaris and Oberländer, the Admiral expressed his appreciation and total support of Oberländer's efforts and analyzed the latest situation in the east as he conceived it.

During the end of January 1942, Oberländer delivered a lecture in Berlin for the "Central Office for Eastern Europe," in the presence of Professor Gerhard von Mende; Professor Werner Markert from the Canaris Organization and Otto Schiller, the Soviet agrarian expert from the Foreign Office, as already mentioned. The participants once more were in total agreement as to what had to be done in the occupied east territories. Therefore, pursuant to this goal two memoranda were prepared again by Oberländer, specifically about the Ukraine and the Caucasus.

One could not help but be impressed by Oberländer's initiative and dedication to the cause; therefore, it was surprising to me when I learned that Professor Oberländer actually had been a member of the "National Socialist German Workers Party." But then I remembered about some "old" Bolsheviks who were also disillusioned by their party's crimes which they had not anticipated when it all started.

Hans von Herwarth, a staunch anti Nazi and a member of the German resistance since 1938[25] in his book *Against Two Evils,* writes about Oberländer in a very positive way. He remarks that "Oberländer was himself a curious phenomenon in the history of National Socialism," and goes on to say, "When I first met him in Moscow in the mid 1930's, when he came in his capacity of Professor and head of the East European Institute at the University of Königsberg, Wilhelm Baum, our press attache and a staunch anti Nazi, knew Oberländer and thought well of him."

Knowing that he was a Nazi Party member though, I handled him rather carefully. When I next met him in 1942, I saw an entirely different side of the man and we got along extremely well. Herwarth also notes that "Oberländer got more and more upset by the crimes being committed in the occupied territories by the civilian administration." Herwarth then discusses Oberländer's memoranda where he denounces the Nazi administration methods and "called for radical changes." —"Oberländer's action in writing this tract was most courageous and predictably it

25- Charles Bohlen, *Witness to History 1929–1969,* New York: W.W. Norton & Company, 1973.

gave rise to an effort to court martial him. Köstring and the General Staff swung into action in his defense but their success was only partial. In the end, he was dismissed from the army."[26] He was also dismissed from the party, and the Gestapo had him under house arrest during November 1943. My own observations about Oberländer have been very positive and completely in line with Herwarth's opinion.

There were several Georgians Jews in "Bergmann," concealed by the Georgians as soldiers. Oberländer knew about it but kept it secret; he also knew that should this somehow become known to the Nazi higher ups (already unhappy because of Oberländer's criticism of their policy) he would be in trouble. There already were a number of Georgian emigrants in "Bergmann" when I got there but as expected, one week later, a large group of them from "Thamar II" joined us. As with its "sister" group, "Thamar I," "Thamar II" had also been formed on orders of Admiral Canaris. This obviously was against the official Nazi policy that had been made known to all German organizations, according to which no "Eastern emigres" could be employed, but the Canaris organization still enjoyed a considerable measure of autonomy.

As already mentioned, "Thamar I" was parachuted into the northwest part of Georgia. "Thamar II," however, after military training in Romania, became part of "Bergmann." While in Romania, the Georgians from "Thamar II" learned that the Soviet P.O.W. camps were located nearby and conditions there were wretched. Clad in German Army uniforms, the emigres invaded P.O.W. camps as locust would in fields to be harvested. They undertook great efforts to improve conditions in the camps and many lives were saved including the Georgian Jews, who simply were freed as other Georgians.

Here some clarification is in order to understand why this all took place and how. After the forcible Soviet Russian occupation of Georgia, the majority of Georgian political emigres settled in three European countries: France, Poland and Germany. The legal Georgian Government in exile settled in France, headed by the internationally known social democrat, President Noe Jordania and representatives of various political parties. This was the largest group of all and Paris became the center of political activity for restoration of the Georgian sovereignty and defense of her people's human rights. This has been well documented in many publications.[27] Several cadets from the Georgian military school also left the country and were accepted in French military school. Upon completion, they served in the French Foreign Legion with distinction.[28]

26- Hans von Herwarth, *Against Two Evils*, pp. 232-233.

27- Constantin Kandelaki, *The Georgian Question Before the Free World* (Acts – Documents – Evidence) Paris: Impr. de Navarre, 1953.

28- In Poland, the majority of Georgian cadets were enrolled in the military school and after graduation they became the contract officers and were appointed in various regiments. There were also approximately six Georgian generals, nine colonels, eleven majors and nine captains who were also

In Paris, after the outbreak of W.W. II, President Jordania on February 4, 1940, made an announcement in the name of his government at the convention of the Georgia Constituent Assembly in exile.

The following are excerpts from his address.

"In the present armed conflict, we took our stand right from the beginning. We are on the side of the Franco-British bloc. We are the children of an oppressed people. The force of a foreign power has deprived us of our national liberty. Our people and nation are bearing a foreign yoke. Who can better understand our suffering than those who believe in these two liberties, who have inscribed on their banner the rights of man and the rights of peoples and proclaimed those rights for the whole world and for all of humanity? It is France who always was and will always remain the defender of the oppressed.

"International banditism has destroyed all the rights of man, under any conceivable form. The Georgian People are suffering under the domination of Soviet Russia. They have never accepted this state of affairs and have never ceased to fight its oppressors in Moscow, and with them, against all those who are their allies, no matter who they may be.[29] We have never been and can never be on the side of Stalin and those who defend him either ideologically, politically or nationally. The bridges have long since been burnt between us and war declared. The Allies have now placed themselves in the same position we are in. The denunciation of Bolshevism by us, being the revival of 'ancient Russo-Asiatic barbarism!' has now become evident and is shared by the entire civilized world.

"Our protest in 1934 to the League of Nations against the admission of the U.S.S.R. has now been approved by the League of Nations itself by the expulsion of the U.S.S.R. from the international institution.

---

accepted. It was made possible for them to bring their knowledge up to date by participating in specially arranged courses. The total number of Georgian officers in Poland's army was estimated around eighty persons. In Germany, there were fewer Georgians but among them were recognized professors such as Mikhako Tsereteli, brothers Nikuradze Zurab Avalishvili and Mikheil Akhmeteli. Also in Germany were the Doctors Gogi Magalashvili and, as noted before, Badu Tsulukidze, as well as Former Ambassador Lado Akhmeteli. Because of the Soviet Russian occupation of Georgia, the Ambassador designate to Berlin, Dr. Grigol Alshibaja as well as his family had to move to Poland, where he commenced the practice of medicine. The well known writer Grigol Robakidze also resided in Berlin, as already noted.

29- Jordania is referring to the Hitler-Stalin pact of 1939.

> "The National Government of Georgia, which left its native land after the decision of the constituent assembly with the special mission to continue the fight against the Moscow invaders until final victory, now invites all Georgian emigrants to join on the side of the Allies wishing them victory and uniting to work with all their might for the liberation of the Georgian People."[30]

The Georgians in France and Poland fought against the invading Germans and Russians respectively, in defense of their host country; the Georgian officers in the French Foreign Legion went on fighting in Africa with distinction. After the Soviet Union had attacked a small country, Finland, during late November 1939, Colonel Soliko Zaldastanishvili pleaded with the responsible French government representative to form a volunteer Georgian military brigade to assist Finland in her battle against the Soviet aggressor. He was not able to obtain permission but the noble Georgian desire to assist a small brave nation in her self-defense was clearly demonstrated.

When Hitler occupied France during late June 1940 and then invaded his former friend Stalin's empire one year later, the situation changed for the Georgian emigres in France and Poland; they could no longer militarily help their occupied host countries. Many Georgians now felt that while the two villains, Hitler and Stalin, were at war with each other, there may be a chance to free Georgia. (After all, wasn't it as a result of W.W. I that the Georgians gained back their lost independence?) But how? At that time, only Admiral Canaris's organization was giving them a practical opportunity to get in position, establish connections, learn about the German plans toward the Caucasus and Georgia and perhaps influence them in a positive direction. Some Georgian P.O.W.s who volunteered were freed and adopted by "Thamar II" as fellow soldiers. Of course, the Georgians could not have done all this without the help of their German officers.[31] The emigres, as well as former P.O.W.s in "Thamar II" and "Bergmann," from the very beginning were very much concerned about the future of their country. Such feelings deepened even more with the passing of time and there were reasons for it. To begin with, the German government had not yet officially declared its intention of reestablishing our sovereign state. It was hoped that our influential German friends would help us to achieve our quest.

30- Constantin Kandelaki, *The Georgian Question Before the Free World*, pp. 145–147.

31- Among other dedicated emigres there was also a great patriot, already mentioned above—Colonel Soliko Zaldastanishvili, who unfortunately became infected with encephalitis while caring for his P.O.W. countrymen, which led to his demise. It was a natural feature for the Colonel to be a humble servant of his country and sacrifice himself for her cause.

An easy "political explanation" for the delay was offered by some Germans from the lower echelon—the political decision by the German government had been "postponed" until after the end of the war. For most of us, this was not a satisfactory clarification, inasmuch as the conditions in the German occupied Eastern territories were worrisome, as already noted. The question was asked and had to be answered, "What about us if the Germans occupied Caucasus? Will they be any different?" Moreover, by now the news was arriving about racial discrimination and persecution especially of the Jews by arrogant and inhuman Himmler commandos.

The Georgians in France right after the German occupation already had to face the dangerous problem of potential persecution of the Georgian Jews. All Georgians, regardless of their political views, made the unanimous decision to save them at any cost. As we shall see on the following pages, the Georgians took early precaution in this direction and were quite successful.

Another problem was also to protect other Georgians endangered because of their political beliefs and affiliations which were not acceptable to certain German authorities. Of special concern were the former Red Army soldiers, now P.O.W.s in German camps. Helping them in local and isolated instances was not enough to solve this great problem. It was difficult to establish an exact number of them, but a preliminary figure was at least fifty thousand men after only a few months of fighting. It has already been noted that early reports about most of the P.O.W. camps indicated terrible conditions there and urgent help was clearly needed.

It was mandatory to have a body of Georgian representation in Germany approved by the Georgians as well as by the Germans. The organization would then negotiate with responsible German institutions on behalf of Georgian interests. As we shall see later on, this turned out to be a difficult task to achieve because of Hitler's belligerent opposition to it. Nevertheless, during the spring of 1942, the German Army began to form the Georgian Legion, from which several battalions were born. This in itself was a salutary achievement but again existence of the recognized Georgian national representation was now, more than ever, necessary in order to give political goal to the legionnaires.

How such representation should have been established is another matter and will be discussed later on. Here I shall only mention very briefly my own view. It was my feeling that the Georgian government in exile should have formed its backbone. Probably it should have been enlarged by adding others from the opposition parties and also those without party affiliation, including the legionnaires. The organization of the national alliance should also have included the members of the constituent assembly in exile. All of the above was meant to be a temporary caretaker organization until Georgia was liberated; after such time, of course, the Georgian people would elect their representative government.

During the early stage of war, the Georgian Emigration could not even hope to tackle such problems. Then, unexpected help came. After the occupation of France in 1940, during the fall of 1940 in Paris, a close contact had developed between Canaris's Military Intelligence, the "Abwehr II" organization in France (Dr. Werner Markert and later Dr. Hans Raupach) and the Georgian emigration circles, especially with Spiridon Kedia, Mikheil (Misha) Kedia, the former Secretary of State, Evgeni Gegechkori and Vachnadze.[32]

The German connections existed to all Georgian circles and at the beginning, among others, to the Georgian Nationalists (Professor Nikuradze in Berlin, Salia in Paris). But from the political and intelligence point of view, only connections with the close circle around Mikheil Kedia (Tsomaia, Korkia, Kobakhidze) and with the social democrats (Jordania, Gegechkori, Menagarashvili) proved to be valuable. The German liaison person (on whose report I am basing my statements here) concerned himself at first with general assistance to the emigres "from the east." But soon this developed into a close and mutually trusting personal relationship between him and the leaders of the Georgian group.

This friendship was further enforced as a result of successful action taken for the protection of the Georgian Jews in France; who during 1941 were facing grave danger of being deported. Mikheil Kedia, along with the German liaison person, succeeded with the support of the appropriate department of high military command in France, to have the responsible service of S.D. (security service) amend the registration and deportation ordinance for the Georgian Jews. Briefly stated, Mikheil Kedia made a point that the Georgian Jews were Georgians but they were of a "minority confession, as were the Georgian Catholics and the Muslims. By their language, their character traits and shared national interests they belonged to the Georgian Nation."

The Georgian Christians in France set up a committee to determine who was Jewish Georgian and so entitled to be reclassified and obtain exemption to this effect:

> "The committee was also authorized to issue identification cards, which the French police accepted. Sasha Korkia, a prominent member of the Christian Georgian community was appointed head of the committee. A list of two hundred and forty-three Jewish Georgian families was drawn up (approximately one thousand individuals.). This was substantially more than the actual number

---

32- The above and following contains reporting and, at times, excerpts from the German document, *The Undertaking Mainz (Unternehmen Mainz)* and *The Fate of Oriental Jews in Vichy France* by Warren Green. The Georgians helped a number of Georgian Jews as well as French and Russian Jews.

of Georgian Jews in France. Family names were changed, birth certificates and other documents were forged in order to save as many lives as possible."[33]

We shall have more to say about this problem later on, especially about an increase of danger for our Jewish compatriots again during 1943 and 1944.

I have already mentioned concerns about the Georgians in "Thamar II," due to circumstances created by German policy in the Eastern occupied territories. Therefore, the idea was born to establish direct contact with the Georgians in the land, including some of the influential circles. The message to them would be that if the German Army secures our land, the Georgians should at once declare reestablishment of an independent state and form a temporary government, elections to follow later. Thus, the Germans would face the accomplished fact, and in the opinion of those patriots, would not abolish the independent Georgian state. After all, did not Germany protect the Georgian Independence in 1918–1921? The presence of the Georgian volunteer military units, who fought for and would enter their homeland with the German troops should further boost the cause.

Help from our supporters in the German Army and of some civilian personalities was heavily counted on. It also made sense for Germany to be on friendly terms with the Caucasians and have access to minerals and oil with the Baku-Batumi line rather than risk hostilities with them in this also strategically important land with a rather difficult terrain.

This thought was deeply rooted in "Thamar II" and during the later part of 1941, under the leadership of Colonel Soliko Zaldastanishvili, a plan was submitted through the proper channels to the German high command in Bucharest. According to this plan, a selected group of Georgians would have been smuggled into the country with submarines "To prepare the country for proper and frictionless reception of the Germans." Such a suggestion was not accepted by the German High Command. After "Thamar II" joined "Bergmann," this idea was presented to Mikheil Kedia who at that time was in Berlin. Since such action would be purely of the political nature. Kedia thought it necessary to inform the responsible leaders of the political emigration for evaluation of the plan and for this he wanted to share the responsibility with them.

First of all, Kedia approached the President of the Georgian Republic in exile, Noe Jordania. He accepted the idea without hesitation and agreed to activate

---

33- Warren Green, *The Fate of Oriental Jews in Vichy France*, Wiener Library Bulletin (Great Britain) vol. 32, no. 49, 1979: 49-50. Note: based mostly on archives of the Centre de Documentation Juive Contemporaine in Paris; 45 notes.

an already existing suitable group under the leadership of Sandro Menagarashvili. Menagarashvili and his men were located in Turkey and through their connections were capable of getting into Georgia and crossing back into Turkey when needed.

The second route was developed from North Caucasus after the German occupation there. Alexandre Asatiani, Alexandre Tsomaia and Dimitri Sindikashvili, all representing the National Democrat Party, were appointed as a task force. Both groups had significant success. In the instructions sent to Georgia, it was strongly emphasized that any hasty action may be fraught by disaster and no declaration should be made unless the German occupation appeared certain and solid.

Kedia could establish such connections with Georgia only with the help of the German intelligence service and that's why he accepted such a compromise; each side pursued its own goal. History has known a number of such examples, one of the most striking being the father of the Russian Bolshevik revolution, Lenin, who "allied" himself with the Imperial German Intelligence Service during W.W. I. He was smuggled by the Germans from Switzerland via Finland into St. Petersburg, having also obtained from them a considerable sum in gold. (This was previously referred to during the discussion of the Brest-Litovsk Treaty.)

Lenin used such support to further the cause of revolution and to take over total power in Russia. The bonus for Germany was that after this successful coup d'etat, Lenin at once started unilateral peace negotiations with her, without consulting England and France, then Russian allies. He thus eliminated the second front for the Germans and strengthened their position against the western powers. Ignoring such historical facts and setting a double standard as usual, Soviet propaganda for many years described political emigres as nothing better than "the agents of capitalist imperialistic countries."

I was thrilled to see so many Georgian emigres arrive in "Bergmann" and felt as if a reunion was taking place between me and long separated brothers. Mindful of a very unpleasant encounter they had with Captain Tsiklauri, I made a special effort to show them that not all "newcomers" from Soviet Georgia shared the captain's views. I visited the emigres often and soon we had a two way communication established, telling each other some of our experiences and talking about the future. We got along very well and as time went by, I felt that I profited by their knowledge of the west.

One of our Georgian traits is to quote our poets, and one day this nearly got me in trouble and taught me one more lesson. During a small gathering, differences of opinion among certain groups were discussed. I spoke and quoted from Akaki Tsereteli's poetry, where he describes the shepherd's dogs—how they fight each other, but at the sight of a wolf-pack, infighting stops and they turn on the wolves together. The poet finishes with a sad exclamation. "O Lord, grant to the Georgians the wisdom of the shepherd dogs."

I thought the audience surely must have been impressed by these words of wisdom from our beloved poet. The next morning, I got feedback indicating an adverse effect on some of my listeners, who were rather vocal about it. They felt and were telling others not present during the discussions that I had compared them to the dogs—surely an insult. Such a reaction was the last thing I would want from the people who already had been sensitized by a previous encounter with Captain Tsiklauri. Fortunately the majority of the emigres understood me and the initially somewhat hostile, vocal minority also joined them and again we got along very well.

We the "newcomers" had been living under the totalitarian political system for a long time and most of us sincerely disliked that ruthless domination and wanted to change it. Yet, not infrequently, arguments of a political nature among our emigres along the party lines were difficult for us to understand and at times bewildering. We blamed this on their exposure to French politics and jokingly called such state of affairs "a French disease." It is obvious that we did not know much about democracy at that time.

As far as my efforts to bring about a change of Captain Tsiklauri's attitude toward the emigres was concerned, it was a failure so far. He always had some derogatory remarks about them, they just could not do anything right. A simple and perhaps amusing example of this was when we caught sight from a window one day of an emigrant carrying a small pet dog in his arms. "Look at this degenerate," said the Captain, "embracing this miserable little creature. What kind of Georgian is he?" Politely but definitely, I would usually disagree with the Captain and in this instance, I simply reminded him that "a dog is man's best friend"—also in Georgia.

I was not the only one who tried to bring a change of heart between Captain Tsiklauri and the emigrants. One of them who probably tried the hardest was Victor Homeriki, an energetic, likable young emigre from Paris. He was a social democrat and a born diplomat. For instance, when he came back after Easter vacation in Paris, he brought for the Captain, from the Georgian Colony, some presents and cards with warm greetings that included the names of some of the loveliest ladies in Paris. Surely this should have warmed Tsiklauri's heart. At least, the personal relationship between the Captain and Victor appeared to be good.

Victor's father, the late Noe Homeriki, was a prominent social democrat and the Minister of Agriculture during the independent Georgian Republic. After the Soviet occupation of Georgia, Victor followed his father into exile in France and remained there while his father returned to Georgia, illegally, in order to organize the 1924 insurrection against the Russian Bolshevik occupants. The insurrection was ruthlessly crushed in blood by the Russian troops in overwhelming numbers. Expected help from the western democratic countries never arrived. Victor's father was arrested and executed.

Victor, who had already lost his mother, was now left without any parental support, and yet he overcame this devastating experience and became well-educated, brave and a patriotic person. He kept up with his father's legacy and was always a great helper for those in need and a troubleshooter. He joined "Bergmann" with several other fellow social democrats to protect the interests of his country during this perilous time. It did not mean that while so doing, Victor and other social democrats of the overwhelming majority of other Georgians in "Bergmann" approved of the political system ruling Germany at that time. No more than the Finns approved of Hitler's political system while fighting against Soviet Russia, nor more than the English and Americans had approved of the Bolshevik regime while allying themselves with the Soviet Union to fight against Hitler's Germany during W.W. II.

I knew about the fate of Noe Homeriki and had a special solidarity feeling toward his son Victor, since my father, too, had been executed by the same regime. When we shook hands the first time, I expressed to Victor a hope that we both serve our country as well as our fathers had. He must have been moved by those words since he reminded me of them twenty years later in Paris.

In "Bergmann," Homeriki had an official position as an interpreter of the 1st Company. But in fact, his services were indispensable as an adviser not only to the company chief but also to many Georgians and Germans as well. He was able to prevent many small and major misunderstandings between them and kept morale up when things were not going so well.

Probably the following incidence characterizes Victor best. It took place during the retreat of the German Southern Army in 1944. The Georgian battalion "Bergmann I"[34] found itself in Greece and remained there until further orders. Victor had an audience with the commanding General Felmi. Homeriki related to the General his feeling, shared by other Georgians, that Georgia and Greece enjoyed mutual friendly and close relationships since ancient times. Therefore, the Georgians could not fight the Greeks even if ordered to do so. During war, such behavior is a clear reason for soldiers to be court martialed; however, the General took a broader view of it and displayed a great deal of understanding for the Georgians in "Bergmann" who had in the past distinguished themselves as good soldiers.

Other social democrats who were more noticeable for me in "Bergmann

---

34- During 1943, the battalion "Bergmann" reached the strength of three battalions: one Georgian, one North Caucasian and one Azerbaijani ("Bergmann I," "II" and "III").

II" were Bagrat Chanturia, Gigo Jordania, Akaki Kvitaishvili,[35] Mathe Bolkvadze[36] and Varden Chikashua.[37] Bagrat Chanturia was the nephew of the former Georgian Ambassador (minister plenipotentiary) to France—Akaki Chkhenkeli. Bagrat appeared to be a serious, intelligent introvert and a man of few words. He was the interpreter of the 4th Georgian Company and not only the adviser to the company chief but also directly to Professor Oberländer.

Oberländer had a great deal of confidence in him and vice versa. For instance, it was Bagrat who informed Professor Oberländer that we had a number of Georgian Jews in "Bergmann," which was totally in line with the Georgian tradition and their way of thinking. Bagrat had correctly judged that this would also be acceptable for Oberländer. Bagrat, when we first met, was polite but appeared reserved—it did not change in the long run, since this turned out to be his nature. I shall have more to say about him shortly in conjunction with a painful incident for all of us that took place in "Bergmann" shortly after my arrival there.

Gigo Jordania was related to our President in exile, Noe Jordania. I knew his younger brother, Simonika, from Tbilisi school days. Gigo was an analytically minded person and also a man of few words. He was pleased to be able to talk to me about his brother and other things. During the fall of 1943, with the help of some benevolent Germans, the Georgians were allowed to establish a caretaker organization, a mission, "The Liaison Staff" ("Der Verbindungsstab"), to defend Georgian interests in Germany and occupied territories. The name "staff" was a compromise and had to be substituted by Professor von Mende for "committee," since the later name may have had some political meaning and therefore was not permitted by the Nazi "higher ups." This was characteristic of their unyielding nature, even during the time when winning the war did not appear likely.

I had been nominated to be a member of this Liaison Staff by the "Georgian National Alliance" and others to represent and be a speaker for the Georgians

35- Akaki Kvitaishvili, a graying, hawk-faced, tough gentleman was a former major of the Georgian "Social Democrat Peoples Guard" ("Erovnuli Gvardia"). He had much to say about his interesting experience during the battle against the invading Red Army troops. In addition to Akaki Kvitaishvili, there were other emigre Georgian officers in "Bergmann" but not affiliated with the Social Democrat Party. They were Mikhail ("Misha") Dadiani, Giorgi ("Goglik") Vachnadze and David ("Dodik") Chavchavadze. Dadiani, originally a cadet of the Georgian military school, had served in the Polish Army. Vachnadze served in the French Navy and Chavchavadze already in the Imperial Russian Army, if my memory serves me right. Their senior officer, Soliko Zaldastanishvili, parted with his life in "Thamar II" before he could join "Bergmann."

36- Mathe Bolkvadze was also a Social Democrat and an old fighter with a touch of Robin Hood. Holding his chest out, chin up, the graying mustache and beard (always properly groomed), with sparks in his eyes and always an optimist, he often encouraged the younger generation and was very popular with them.

37- Varden Chikashua was a quiet man of considerable size, whose dream was to establish contact with his fellow man in Georgia via the Turkish border. I think, therefore, that he felt somewhat out of place in "Bergmann" and kept a low profile.

serving in the army. During this meeting, apparently only one person voted against me, Gigo Jordania, himself a soldier. He informed me about it and went on to say approximately as follows, "The Germans are going to lose this war mainly because of the criminal Nazi leadership. They may kill those few Germans who are our supporters and possibly some of us as well, certainly you are not excluded. But the Georgian question will still remain. Those of us who survive will have to talk to the Englishmen and their western allies about it. We will need people like you then and therefore I want to save you for such time and not waste you now," he concluded.

Gigo also reasoned that both the Russians and the Germans could lose the war, as was the case in W.W. I, thus creating an opportunity for reestablishment of Georgian sovereignty with all the joy of it, but which also could create associated dangerous problems. For instance, the danger of anarchy and of our historically aggressive southern neighbors whose only interest has been to "grab" our territory. Therefore, every Georgian soldier should be saved and brought back to Georgian soil for her protection. Good relationships should be established with all our neighbors.

This took place during the fall of 1943. I listened to Gigo with great interest. His thoughts did not differ significantly from my own and the majority of the Georgians around us. I felt, however, that I personally would have limited importance in the possible set up described and hoped for by Gigo. His thought pattern reminded me of my fellow mountaineers who believed in saving the little ammunition they had for the big game only. I thanked Gigo for being a sincere and thoughtful friend and for having so much confidence in me. In the years to come, I remembered his words.

Victor Nozadze had been a Social Democrat but during the process of the "political experimentation," changed his affiliation to the "Tetri Giorgi" party; we shall touch upon this matter again. We got along well. I liked him and we had plenty to talk about. During his younger days back in Georgia, he knew my parents and also Ilia Phaliani, a close friend of our family.[38] Nozadze was very talented and he had made major and original contribution to research of Shota Rustaveli, a twelfth century Georgian giant, the poet and philosopher and whose influence, like the Georgian Church, has been immense on the Georgian people. I have even met some old timers in the mountains, without any formal education, who could beautifully recite the verses from Rustaveli.

Nozadze was also a great Georgian patriot, faithful to his friends, and a much

---

38- It so happened that Uncle Ilia was married to Nozadze's relative Aza Kebadze. Victor and I both knew and admired Ioseb Imedashvili, the editor of a journal, *The Theatre and the Life* in Tbilisi. I believe my father had occasionally contributed an article to this publication and invited Imedashvili to our home. While discussing the books published abroad about Georgia, Nozadze especially recommended *A History of the Georgian People* by W. E. D. Allen of Great Britain, which he himself did not possess. Years later, remembering his recommendation, I was able to obtain this book from Canada.

respected person. But in the opinion of some, because of naivete and insufficient political acumen, his political performance did not always keep in step with his achievement as a scholar. Victor himself realized it and on occasion would admit this to some friends. It was also felt that some shrewd persons took advantage of his trusting nature and while posing as his friends, were using him for their own purpose. Well, the Lord rarely bestows all virtues on one person and Victor already had many of them.

Having mentioned the Georgian Social Democrats in "Bergmann," it is appropriate to mention their political background. The founder and leader of the Georgian Social Democrats, Noe Jordania, had traveled and studied Western Europe extensively. This was long before he was elected President of Georgia. As a result of these studies and observations he was convinced that the European type of Social Democracy was much more suitable for Georgia that Lenin's so called "Democratic Dictatorship" of one party, another name for it being "Communism" or "Bolshevism," the system introduced by Lenin in Russia and the Soviet Union.

Jordania believed that it is the workers' right to form their organization themselves and to elect their own leadership "from below" by democratic methods. He believed in dialogue between the party leaders and the rank and file and decision making by mutual agreement. It is only fair to compare the Georgian Social Democrats with their counterparts everywhere in Western Europe.

Opposed to it were the Leninists (Bolsheviks) who believed that they, the professional revolutionaries, should form the organizations "from above" and impose them on the workers by dictatorship. They, the professional elite, knew what was best for the workers. Such dogma projected a basic mistrust in workers and ignored their rights of organizing their own movement. The result of it was seventy years of political isolation, economic stagnation, substandard living conditions, absence of human rights and terror.

In Georgia, the Social Democrats had overwhelming control of the workers' organization and the Bolsheviks, including Stalin, were humbled there.[39] As it happens, the author of this work is a follower of two economists, Adam Smith and Milton Friedman. But if I were a Georgian worker in the early twentieth century, I would surely vote for Noe Jordania rather than Lenin's Party.

I also had frequent contacts in "Bergmann" with the National Democrats.[40]

39- Noe Jordania, *My Past*, Paris, 1953.

40- Aliosha Abashidze, Giorgi ("Goglik") Vachnadze, Mikhail ("Misha") Kavtaradze, Grigol ("Grisha") Lordkipanidze, Giorgi ("Gogi") Beridze, Irakli Djaparidze, Giorgi ("Jora") Indjia, Dimitri ("Dutuli") Akhvlediani, Archil Dadiani, David ("Dodik") Chavchavadze, Shota Gedevanishvili, Grigol Abuladze, Themo Taktakishvili, Aleksandre Tarasashvili, Kote Washadze. Others that the line of duty did not as often bring me face to face with were Nikoloz Amirejibi, Giorgi Shakiashvili, Bidzina Eristavi, Vano Gigauri, Shalva Indjia, Elizbar Makashvili, Giorgi Chkheidze, Zurab Tsitsishvili and others.

They were all men of courage and dedication, and patriotism moved them to abandon relative personal safety. They had joined a very risky undertaking in being part of "Thamar II" and "Bergmann." A couple of days after my arrival in "Bergmann," three of them—Aliosha Abashidze, Jora Indjia, and Dutuli Akhvlediani—visited me to make me feel welcome; during the friendly and warm conversation, it became clear that we had many common views. As time went by, I had similar conversations with other National Democrats. Misha Kavtaradze impressed me as a quiet man, often deep in thought. But once stimulated during discussion, a solid knowledge especially of Georgian history and literature was revealed.

At times I also met with the Georgian emigre officers, especially "Dodik" Chavchavadze, "Goglik" Vachnadze and "Misha" Dadiani, together with some German officers, especially Lieutenant Martin Schütte and 1st Lieutenant Weyh. The German officers would usually invite us during "off" time to join them in nearby Mittenwald coffee houses. There, over coffee and "kuchen" (cake), in a relaxed atmosphere we exchanged views with each other. The topics varied from music, poetry and philosophy to our past, our countries and military matters. Our concentration was occasionally deflected only by the waiter or a Bavarian beauty passerby. I found out that "Dodik" and "Goglik" were National Democrats while "Misha" belonged to "Tetri Giorgi"—the "White George," a relatively newly established party or movement.

I personally never emphasized anyone's party affiliation during the war, especially in "Bergmann," in order not to weaken the national unity. For us, in "Bergmann," but also for the majority of emigres generally, the Georgian question was not one of political parties but a non-partisan national question. Indeed, in "Bergmann" there were some Georgian Communists. While this was not advertised, they served faithfully for the good of the national interest. (We experienced only one exception to it, as we shall see later on.)

Members of the National Democrat Party of Georgia were some of the followers of Ilia Chavchavadze (1837–1907). He was a poet, a patriot, a political figure and one of the greatest Georgians of all time. He dedicated his life to the cause of unification of all Georgians, regardless of their social status, in a coherent society that one day would succeed in gaining freedom and independence from the Russian conqueror. "We should belong to ourself," was his motto. At the same time, he was by no means insensitive to the existing social injustices which he severely denounced.

It followed that Ilia, himself an aristocrat, devoted one of his moving and mourning poems to the defeat of the Paris Commune 1871, as a sign of the defeat of Justice. (With all due respect, I must confess that I am not favorably impressed by all the bloodshed it caused.) Chavchavadze believed in sound economical principles, such as the right of private property, importance of market forces and necessity of banks. His ideas found powerful support among the Georgian intellectuals. Ilia Chavchavadze's peaceful crusade was interrupted by assassins' bullets during 1907. According to recently discovered documents, most likely two Georgian Bolsheviks had organized such a horrible crime. Recently the Georgian Church canonized him, to the joy of the Georgian people.

Ilia Chavchavadze had established a remarkable newspaper, *Iveria*,[41] in 1877, which, of course, was not permitted to continue during Bolshevik rule. In 1947, the Georgian National Democrat Party, having emigrated to Paris, resumed *Iveria*. This was possible under the leadership and thanks to the dedicated work of Elise Pataridze, who was a capable journalist and a great patriot. After his painful demise, *Iveria* was continued by Pataridze's close family friend, "Misha" Kavtaradze, also a great patriot and talented journalist.[42]

The National Democratic Party of Georgia abroad had many distinguished members. The leader was a great gentleman and an experienced politician, Spiridon Kedia. Second in command was Alexandre Asatiani, a tough and fearless fighter. Next to him, Elise Pataridze, who as already noted, had established the journal *Iveria* in Paris. With them in leadership was Colonel Soliko Zaldastanishvili, whom, as I said above, I had never met because of his untimely demise in the service the Georgian Cause; however, I knew much about the Colonel from our mutual friends and I was fortunate to have met his outstanding family after the war in the U.S.A. They were his wife, Mariam and two sons, Givi and Othar. Our families formed a lasting and deep friendship.

The younger generation of emigre National Democrats counted among themselves such gifted, energetic, dedicated and already experienced freedom fighters as Alexander Tsomaia, Dimitri Sindikashvili and Mikhail Kavtaradze. Incidentally all of them were journalists and writers. Their prewar political activities were extended during the war by participating in it according to their ability and where they were needed the most. Such activities continued after the war. Alexander Tsomaia, in New York, became the editor in chief of the English language journal-bulletin *Voice*

41- David Marshall Lang, *A Modern History of Soviet Georgia*.
42- Kavtaradze, who was among the National Democrats in "Bergmann," served with distinction as a soldier and was wounded during the battle in Crimea. After his recuperation, he was appointed as a coworker in the Military Department of the Georgian Mission Staff in Berlin (Der Verbindungsstab). Here Kavtaradze's assignment was to observe conditions in the Georgian field battalions on an ongoing basis and to keep the military department up to date about it. Thanks to his services, a number of shortcomings were eliminated. It is heart warming to note that M. Kavtaradze had been assisted in editing *Iveria* by Elise Pataridze's son and daughter and after so many years, on the final page of *Iveria* one still reads Editor in Chief, Mikhail Kavtaradze; The Director, Othar Pataridze; The Editorial Board, (among others) Mrs. Gulnara Pataridze-Uratadze.

of Free Georgia, filled with high quality information about Georgia. Before that, Tsomaia spent many years of research on his main work devoted to the history of the relations between Georgia and Russia. Dimitri Sindikashvili was the editor in chief of the newspaper *Georgian Opinion* (*Kartuli Azri*) published in New York in the Georgian language. It was also rated as an excellent paper by the majority of its readers. It depicted current and past problems of Georgia.

There were also a number of other National Democrats whom I had met only a few times or never had an opportunity to meet. From the senior members, I recall David (Datha) Vachnadze and Razo Gabashvili, whom I met a couple of times in Berlin during 1943. They both played an active and an important role during the Georgian Independence. This continued during the 1924 insurrection and also while in emigration. Although my father was a recognized member of the Georgian Federalist Party, I considered myself a National Democrat and "officially" joined it after the war. What influenced me was that, in spite of the Federalist Party affiliation, Father's final views were close to those of Ilia Chavchavadze. Another factor was that in our summer vacation home in Svaneti, one day I discovered many original publications of *Iveria* by Chavchavadze, bound together. I could not stop reading them. There they were, a treasury of thoughts and aspirations of the Chavchavadzes's contemporary "golden" Georgian intelligentsia, during the second half of the nineteenth and early twentieth century.

These great minds were clearly reflected in the polemics, reporting and other educational articles. One could learn from them the true history of the world around us, which was no longer accessible to the students in the Soviet State, where the history books were changed and written only to justify the Marxist-Leninist dogma, that "the history of mankind was only the history of the struggle between the classes."

As if nothing else had taken place anywhere.

Many students, sensing this falsification, were bored during such instructions and felt that it was an insult to their intelligence. A few pleasing remnants of the past teaching still were to be seen, in the teachers' conference room. Such were the pictures on the walls and of the statues, representing ancient Greco-Roman culture—the part of history no longer officially taught. Having said that, I must emphasize that the Georgian youth of my generation is in deep debt to teachers, many of whom under most difficult circumstances somehow still managed to convey a high quality of knowledge, including some of Georgian history and literature in a classic sense.

As already noted, the relatively new political party "Tetri Giorgi"—"The

White George"—had been formed by some emigres.[43] The name was derived from St. George, our patron saint. The term "White George" had first been introduced during the formation of the independent Georgian Republic; it was an essential part of her emblem. In deference to St. George, the emblem presented the knight jumping his white "Pegasus" (without the wings) over the mountain top. The knight is also holding a spear, but there is no dragon to be seen. Seven stars also adorned the emblem, representing the seven provinces of Georgia. If my memory serves me right, this was done in order to separate the state and religion, and the "White George" had been a compromise substitute for St. George, while the founding fathers were shaping things.

The "Tetri Giorgi" movement had a resemblance to Mussolini's Fascist Party. One may explain the creation of such a political movement only if the general situation in post W.W. I Europe is appreciated. Democracy then appeared to be in retreat, impotent and unable to solve the mounting socio-economic, political and international problems. Therefore, seeds of radicalism were falling on fertile soil. One of the most curious phenomenons, probably of all time, was when Benito Mussolini, once a leading Social Democrat of Italy became a founding father of Italian Fascism.

These were also trying times for the Georgian emigres, when Red Russia in 1921, without provocation from Georgia, broke the 1920 peace treaty and invaded and occupied her against international law. The the western democracies, most of whom had recognized Georgian sovereignty, stood idle, unable to help the victim. In 1924, the Georgian people rose up in a great insurrection to rid herself of the occupants, but again no help arrived from the West. Not only that, but the aggressor was admitted to the League of Nations. Only France, in a charming and sympathetic gesture, allowed the Georgian Embassy to remain open until after the recognition of the U.S.S.R. in 1933.

Three virulent, younger political movements were on the horizon around this time: an imperialistic messianic Communism with its mecca in Moscow; Fascism in Italy; and its German version, Nazism. Both of the last were opposed to the former. When democracy just "hung back," some disappointed emigres decided to experiment with Fascism.

An emigre poet, Simonika Berejiani, probably expressed such emotions in the following verse: "I shall try one more path by pleading with the devil himself, perhaps he is the only one who will realize my despair." For some "joiners" such affiliation was very short-lived and they left the party soon (like M. Kedia), others

---

43- It was also called "The Movement of National Unity." Not to be mistaken for "The Georgian National Alliance" in Paris, which was a temporary, non partisan coalition of different parties during the war.

kept a low profile about it. The leaders and more active members, however, had set their mistaken expectation that they would be treated with special consideration by the German Nazi higher-ups after the eventual outbreak of the German-Soviet conflict.

It is important to emphasize that the "Tetri Giorgi" organization and its members were free of any anti-Semitism, which is due to a deep-rooted Georgian tradition. It is no exaggeration to say that I personally have not met a Georgian who was anti-Semitic, and racism has not been observed in our country.

A Modern History of Soviet Georgia by D.M. Lang quotes Latin patriarch of Jerusalem, Jacques de Vitry, who describes Georgian knights and pilgrims who used to visit the Holy City at the time of crusaders, "... with banners displayed, without paying tribute to anyone, these men especially revere and worship Saint George whom they make their patron and standard-bearer in their fight with the infidels." Lang then adds, "...yet Georgian Christianity has never been exclusive or intolerant, it has not been a persecuting faith. Narrow fanaticism is alien to this easy going people, who found it no strain to tolerate in their midst Muslims, Jews, Catholics and members of other persuasions." Several stories are told, illustrating the kindness of the Georgian kings to their Muslim subjects.

To the best of my knowledge, in "Bergmann" there were three followers of "Tetri Giorgi." Two of them already mentioned, Mikhail ("Misha") Dadiani and Victor Nozadze. The third one was David ("Datha") Vachnadze, a former member of the Georgian Federalist Party. During the early twenties, he had studied in Germany and remained abroad. He was an eloquent speaker (also in German), a man of a restless nature, great energy, dedication and somewhat impulsive. I did not know him as well as some others. The founders and leaders of "Tetri Giorgi" were Professor Mikhako Tsereteli and General Leo Kereselidze.

During his youth, Mikhako Tsereteli joined the anarchist movement of the Russian prince Peter Kropotkin, because it promised emancipation of the individual and the small nations as well—which would include his beloved Georgia. During World War I, Mikhako Tsereteli gave up anarchism and joined "The Committee of Independent Georgia." The committee also included Leo Kereselidze and others, Petre Surguladze being a chairman and the Imperial German government being the sponsor of the committee. The Georgian Legion was formed and stationed in Turkey.

For the love of his country, again, Mikhako Tsereteli took on the dangerous task of landing in Georgia from a German submarine. His mission was to meet secretly with political leaders of Georgia, notably the Social Democrats, who were in the majority and proposed certain joint actions. Mikhako Tsereteli met with Noe Jordania in Kutaisi (the second largest city of Georgia). According to Jordania's memories, the meeting took place in an atmosphere of mutual understanding and respect, but he felt that no joint action was desirable. He thought it was safer for the Georgian people that each group pursue their own path and that one way or another, they would succeed in the end for the good of the country. In other words, Jordania did not want to risk putting all the eggs in one basket.

With Georgian independence killed by the Bolshevik Russian troops in 1921, broken hearted Mikhako Tsereteli settled in Germany. He studied and became a much respected university professor; his line of expertise being Sumerian and Hittite languages. He continued activities for a free Georgia whenever he could. He believed that, for Georgia to be sovereign and survive, she had to have at least one major power as a friend. Based on past experience, Tsereteli saw no one else on the horizon but Germany as a potential and practical helper. Professor Tsereteli had worked toward this end for a long time.[44]

I first met him in Berlin during the summer of 1943. We had both been invited for dinner at Mr. Kale and Mrs. Nino Salias's apartment. Mikhako had experienced a personal tragedy; his only son Othar, who had been mobilized in the German Army, was killed at the front. In addition to his father, Othar was survived by his wife and baby daughter.

The professor wanted me to tell him all I knew about the current Georgia, the situation on the front, "Bergmann" and about my parents. We met one more time in Berlin and again after the war in Munich. In Berlin, during the summer of 1943, he told me that Germany would not be able to win the war. He said that the American airplanes were flying higher than the German anti-aircraft artillery could reach. Therefore, the German cities and other targets would be destroyed. I can never forget the depressed face of an old gentleman who had lived through so much and most of it for his unvanishing love for his Georgia. I would have definitely disagreed with him about the political concepts of his party, but it would be impossible for me not to consider him a great Georgian patriot and not to sympathize with his dedication to the cause. I always felt that a person should be judged on his individual merit and not only on this or that party affiliation. General Leo Kereselidze [the other Tetri Giorgi co-founder] also had been living in the west for a long time and continued his fight with other emigres for restoration of the Georgian State. I only vaguely remember him from our brief encounter. He was killed during one of the many air raids in Berlin.

It is only fair to make an explanatory note about the Georgian Federalist

---

44- It is telling to see his presentation to the German Reichstag concerning Georgia. Mikhako von Tsereteli, *Das Neue Georgien. Eine Denkschrift, Nebsteinem Anhang,* Auszuge aus den Reichstagssitzungen, June 24–25, 1918. (It stresses the mutual benefit of cooperation between two countries.)

Party (same as the Socialist Federalist Party), which was formed approximately 1902–1904. Its founding fathers were Archil Djordjadze, Giorgi Laskhishvili, Giorgi Dekanozishvili, Vladimer Lordkipanidze and others. They were men of great integrity, vision and dedication. The Federalists acknowledged existence of the classes and polarization between them in Georgia but at the same time felt that class interests ought to be subordinated to the common national interests. They pledged to fight against the Czar's centralistic, national as well as social, subjugating regimen. They also believed in a free association of commonwealth or federation with the idea of the Caucasian Federation considered as a possible option. It is interesting to note that Mikhako Tsereteli, (at that time also a member of the Federalist Party) and Giorgi Matchabelli,[45] (a member of the National Democrat Party) during 1917 in Stockholm presented a memo to the International Socialist Commission together. This was a move for gaining support for Georgian independence.

Much earlier (1902), some leaders of the Federalists had traveled to West Europe to establish connections with progressive circles there and win their support for the Georgian cause. In close cooperation with those Georgians already in the west, they published in 1903 the first free Georgian journal, the information bulletin *Georgia*, abroad in Georgian as well as in French. It was devoted to the restoration of Georgian independent statehood. It was to inform the Western Europeans of the Czarist Russian occupational policy, characterized by coercion and terror. Needless to say, such publications were strictly forbidden inside of the Russian Empire.[46]

During my arrival in Mittenwald, there were ongoing military courses for the Caucasian officers and also many field exercises of various companies. Von Kutzschenbach recommended that I, too, should take advantage of it. I especially enjoyed the outings where my heart always belongs—in the mountains. One of our favored terrains was to go up and over the Karwendel Mountains and then descend to the other side of it to the Scharnitz river valley. There, we invariably stopped in the Austrian town of Scharnitz and tasted the wine there. Then we would turn around to follow the highway back to Mittenwald and Luttensee.

During this relaxed march the Georgians and the Germans sang together. The favored songs were "Nino had a pet blackbird in a cage and one day it flew away. Do not be sad, Nino, it will fly back to you again," or "There was a beautiful lady

---

45- Later known in the U.S.A. for his cosmetics.

46- During the reestablished Georgian sovereignty, 1918–1921, several leading members of the Federalist Party participated in the coalition government, including Giorgi Laskhishvili and Shalva Maskhi. The vice chairman of the Georgian Constitutional Assembly and also the Georgian Representative in Angora, Turkey was Svimon Mdivani and Grigol Rtskhiladze was the Georgian Ambassador to Turkey. See the Georgian journal *Mamull*, no. 6, January 1953, edited in Buenos Aires, pp. 167–171.

waving her hand to me from the balcony." From the German side, a Tyrolean song, "One Tyrolean man wanted to hunt a silver and gray chamois. Indeed he wanted it but could not succeed because the little animal was too smart." The echo of those rhythmic songs were finally swallowed by the evergreen treetops.

All the "Bergmann" Caucasians had received instructions not to reveal their true national identity for military security reasons. As it turned out, such secrets are difficult to keep. At least on one occasion, I was inadvertently guilty of not observing such regulation. This is what happened: At times our field exercise would coincide with the Bavarian mountain troops stationed in Mittenwald. For transportation of supplies and light artillery they used mules and small horses. It was fun for me to watch and remember some of my earlier experiences, since in my native Svaneti, we also at times utilized mules. This was done due to steep terrain on which mules perform even better than the surefooted mountain horse. A mule's disposition, however, is something else.

Sure enough, during one such outing, I could see a mule refusing any further handling from one young Bavarian corporal. This went on for awhile and I decided to help. I talked to it gently while patting it at the same time. Then I had a bright idea, to offer the mule a sugar coated vitamin C tablet that the Master Sergeant, Fritz Hiebsch, from "the Sudetenland" had shared with me. The animal loved it and moved uphill in tandem with his master and me, catching up with the rest. The corporal wanted to know just what language I had spoken to his animal. I had no choice but to deliver a brief "lecture" about the Georgian tongue, not realizing at first, that I was breaking the "Bergmann" ordinance. Then I added that the language had nothing to do with the mule's response but the sugar probably did it. I also said that the mule's hearing is better than that of a human being, as is its strength, therefore, shouting and pulling will serve no purpose. The corporal was not convinced and continued uphill while muttering, "the Georgian, the Georgian." I worried about revealing the secret but found out later that the natives of Mittenwald already knew without my help that we in Luttensee were Caucasians but pretended not to be.

On the sixth of May 1942, Admiral Canaris visited "Bergmann." This coincided with the oath taking ceremony for the Caucasians. The special status had been arranged by the Admiral and Professor Oberländer, so that the Caucasians in "Bergmann" took an oath to the German Armed Forces and not to Hitler.

I quote Dr. Raschhofer here. "It was essential for the military and political morale of the Caucasian unit, that its members take a military oath of fealty, which definitely did not contain an oath binding them to the person of Adolf Hitler. The formula had been worked out and agreed upon with Admiral Canaris; the omission of the passage obliging the soldiers to keep faith with Hitler proves that 'Bergmann' was politically autonomous."[47]

After the oath taking ceremony was over, Professor Oberländer informed me that Admiral Canaris wanted to meet me. I was sure that the Admiral was a very important person although the extent of his position, duties and the degree of his influence was not clear to me then but I assumed that they were substantial. The meeting was on a one-to-one basis and took place in the same room where I first met Professor Oberländer—next to the officers' dining room. After a warm handshake, the Admiral motioned me to sit down and wanted to know how I liked "Bergmann" and about my thoughts in general.

There he was, the great Admiral, willing to listen to me and he did so with obvious sympathy for me—a man who less than one month ago was locked up in a prison camp. But I decided to be myself and organize my thoughts because this soft spoken gentleman of few words, with good-natured eyes could, perhaps, influence German policy toward my country.

Briefly, I told the Admiral that I was very much impressed with the quality of people in "Bergmann," that they had excellent equipment and were getting matched training in the mountains. All this, however, I said, would have been useless without Professor Oberländer's declaration of commitment to dedicate "Bergmann" to the better future of the Caucasian people. We can be reliable allies only if we believe in that, and needless to say, this is equally true of all other Soviet nationalities. I did most of the talking, but when the audience was over, there was no doubt in my mind that the Admiral did not only know the problem but completely agreed with me. What more could have been asked for? The Admiral also met some other Caucasian officers. Professor Oberländer later commented that his chief was pleased with such direct communication with us and impressed by us.

Gradually over the next few years, I learned more about Admiral Canaris, not only as the head of the German Military Intelligence ("Abwehr") but also as a decent and non violent person. He and his associate General Oster did all they could to reverse or prevent the criminal actions committed by Hitler and his henchmen. For instance, they intervened as early as September 1941 on behalf of the Soviet P.O.W.s in German hands who, especially during the winter of 1941–1942, were treated in an inhuman way and against accepted international laws.

They took the same attitude in defense of the population of the occupied territories. He wanted, together with some other personalities, to free people of the

---

47- Hermann Raschhofer, *Political Assassination: The Legal Background of the Oberländer and Stashinsky Cases*, Tubingen, West Germany: F. Schlichtenmayer, 1964, pp. 75–76; Hans von Herwarth, *Against Two Evils*, p. 232.

Soviet State from the Bolshevik and Stalinist oppressive regime and make them partners of Germany that also would be free of Hitler's Nazi regime. "Bergmann" was also a tool toward realization of this goal. Canaris was a central figure in resistance, and with General Oster, they protected the people who were conspirators against Hitler. "Abwehr" gave warning in advance to the victims of Nazi aggression as in the case of Denmark and Norway, Belgium and the Netherlands. Professor John Wheeler-Bennett calls him "the Hamlet of conservative Germany" and together with Oster, they were "the intellect and the sword arm of the conspiracy in its early stages."[48]

Some time after the Canaris inspection, we had another visitor in "Bergmann." He was Hans Herwarth von Bittenfeld, a cavalry officer and a diplomat. Oberländer wanted me to meet von Herwarth and was sure that it would be interesting for me, and it was. From Herwarth I learned that outside "Bergmann," other Caucasian military units were being formed by the German Army. This was taking place in occupied Poland and Ukraine. In fact, there also were formations of other Soviet nationalities there. Herwarth had been appointed to help and advise the Army General Staff to carry out such a complex project.[49] He had come to us to see how Oberländer's parallel experiment with "Bergmann" was going. Herwarth spoke fluent Russian and obviously was a gentleman of outstanding background and qualities. He was eminently qualified for his Army General Staff assignment. Two important names came up during our conversation, one of Ambassador Count Friedrich Werner von Schulenburg and another of Major in General Staff, Count Claus von Stauffenberg. I knew the name Schulenburg, since for many Georgians he was closely identified with the Georgian Independence 1918–1921. He was considered to be our reliable friend and representative of the best in Germany. I was soon drawn to Herwarth, and his association with Schulenburg probably was a contributing factor.

I heard the name Stauffenberg for the first time but it was not to be the last. It was he who, from the position in the Organizational Division of the Army General Staff, with the help of Herwarth and the contribution of Schulenburg and other personalities, engineered a Herculean task of formation of the above mentioned units. This also included preparation of Military Administration of the North Caucasus in case of German military occupation of it. Canaris and Oberländer's "Bergmann" and other indigenous military units had to contribute toward the same goal. As it has been noted, this was to prevent repetition of the inhumanity that had occurred

---

48- John Wheeler-Bennett, *The Nemesis of Power: The German Army in Politics 1918–1945*, New York: St. Martin's Press, 1954, pp. 597–599; Hans von Herwarth, *Against Two Evils*, pp. 268–269; Alexander Dallin, *German Rule in Russia*, pp. 416–417.

49- Joachim Hoffmann, *Die Ostlegionen. 1941–1943*, Freiburg, West Germany: Verlag Rombach, 1986, p.82.

in other German-occupied Soviet territories. The difficulties Stauffenberg and his group were to overcome while pursuing his goal is well described in Herwarth's book and elsewhere.[50] If successful, the Caucasus experiment could have been used by its proponents as an argument for the change in other occupied territories as well. Later on, I shall have some comments borne out of my personal observations while in North Caucasus during 1942.

I also met the general in charge of Caucasian Affairs, Ernst Köstring, a remarkable person who was accompanied by von Herwarth. Much to my surprise and pleasure, Hans von Herwarth in the Caucasus was "wearing the hat" of the General's adjutant but it was more than that—they were also close personal friends. Stauffenberg is well depicted in Herwarth's already mentioned book; it is a small wonder, since they were associates not only in their work but eventually also in the German Resistance against Hitler.[51]

I think that Professor John Wheeler-Bennett in his book, *The Nemesis of Power*, summarized Stauffenberg's ideas well. "Certain it is that he rejected absolutely every form of rule by force and all manifestations of totalitarianism. He dreamed and had actually taken some steps toward the practical realization of his dream that the overthrow of authoritarian tyranny in Germany should coincide with or at least closely precede a similar liberation of thought and civil liberty in Russia."[52] Alexander Dallin, while quoting Professor Bennett, adds his own remarks about Stauffenberg: "It was in this spirit that he paired his anti-Hitler activities with what little practical help he could give the budding, indigenous anti-Stalin movement in the East."[53]

As far as Herwarth is concerned, Charles E. Bohlen, U.S. Ambassador to Moscow in his book, *Witness to History 1929–1969*, devoted Chapter V entirely to him, then the Second Secretary of the German Embassy. Herwarth was a staunch anti-Nazi, who in despair, risked his life by leaking to Bohlen his conviction that Hitler intended to attack Poland after the conclusion of the 1939 pact between Germany and the Soviet Union (which was pending). To Herwarth, this meant that Germany would be drawn into the war against France and England with disastrous consequences. He had information according to which Hitler acted on an erroneous assumption, based on the Czechoslovakian and other examples that England and France would not enter the war on behalf of Poland.

50- Hans von Herwarth, *Against Two Evils*, Chapters 15 and 16; Joachim Hoffmann, *Die Ostlegionen. 1941–1943,* especially p. 50.

51- Joachim Kramarz. *Stauffenberg, the Architect of the Famous July 20ᵗʰ Conspiracy to Assassinate Hitler*, translated from German by R.H. Barry, New York: MacMillan, 1967.

52- John Wheeler-Bennett, *The Nemesis of Power,* p. 601.

53- Alexander Dallin, *German Rule in Russia,* p. 544.

Therefore, since he could not thwart a German-Soviet agreement, Herwarth's effort was designed to move the Western powers to a firm preventive declaration to convince Hitler that the invasion of Poland meant an all out war.[54]

Of course, I did not know all this when I first met Herwarth but I already felt that he was an unusual personality. During the years to follow, I had many opportunities to meet him and General Köstring in the Caucasus, Crimea and Germany. We understood each other well and became friends.

During his first visit, Herwarth was already impressed by "Bergmann" and he comments, "It was an unusual formation in every sense, even to the point of taking its oath not to Hitler but to the German Wehrmacht. While 'Bergmann' included Armenians and other Caucasian peoples, the bulk of its members were Georgians, among them a number of former officers in the Red Army. During my visit, I was fascinated by the way in which Georgian emigres and former officers of the Red Army amalgamated to form a new and cohesive unit. It was also instructive to see how well organized the Georgian emigres were. This was no doubt helped by the fact that a short-lived Georgian Republic had flourished briefly under German protection at the end of World War I."[55]

Herwarth's observations were correct but during the interim between Admiral Canaris and Herwarth's visit, the "Bergmann" soldiers had to face a very unpleasant problem that left lifelong scars in our memories.

54- Charles E. Bohlen, *Witness to History 1921–1969*, pp. 71-91.
55- Hans von Herwarth, *Against Two Evils*, p. 232.

6

PLOT IN BERGMANN

One day, when I had barely been in "Bergmann" for five weeks, I received a message from Professor Oberländer to meet him behind the building that housed our business office. This in itself was not unusual, since the two of us had taken a stroll together at times in the surrounding terrain. This time, however, it turned out to be an unofficial meeting between Oberländer and two other Georgians. One of them was Bagrat Chanturia, the interpreter of the 4th Company, whom I have mentioned already, and another was unknown to me as yet, Georgian Sergeant Vano Zurgashvili.

As Oberländer told me afterwards, he wanted me to witness this important meeting since I was under consideration for appointment as a liaison "Ordonnanz-offizier" on the "Bergmann" staff, between the Georgians and the Germans. Chanturia appeared somewhat startled by my presence there but greeted me and told me later that he was glad to see the Professor had such confidence in me.

Zurgashvili unveiled the story which was translated for Oberländer by Chanturia from Georgian to German. According to Zurgashvili, there was a communist plot in "Bergmann" headed by Captain Simon Tsiklauri and First Lieutenant Shalva Tabidze and it involved fifty or sixty Georgians. The plot had already existed in Neuhammer-Silesia where "Bergmann" had been formed before its transfer here. In fact, the plotters somehow were able to listen to Soviet radio and had meetings there with the minutes of these meetings also kept and hidden there. The reason for this was that one day when the victorious Red Army occupied Silesia, as they were convinced it would, the minutes would be found and would serve as proof for the conspirators' activities for the Soviet cause already that early.

Such meetings were continued and were disguised as "card playing" outings in nearby hills—the main purpose being to recruit more members. Zurgashvili then went on to reveal some details of the conspirators' intended plan. According to him, as soon as "Bergmann" moved to the front line, all Germans and also nonconforming Georgians would be killed and the entire unit would go over to join the Red Army.

Oberländer obviously had some beforehand warning from Chanturia about the nature of the pending meeting, therefore, he appeared collected. I was the only one taken by complete surprise. Oberländer suggested we keep all this to ourselves and then the two of us took a walk—as usual. I could only utter that I could not believe what we had just heard; he nodded that he understood how I felt.

Needless to say, it was a grave matter, inasmuch as "Bergmann" was being prepared to be transferred to the front in the near future. What would cause the least possible harm to the people and at the same time save the unit? It was to be expected that the question of the reliability of the entire unit was, after all, to be raised by the superiors.

Oberländer felt that it would be best to follow the German Army judicial system, already in existence and applicable to such situations, and which was autonomous from civilian authorities. The Georgians in "Bergmann" had taken the oath of loyalty to the German Armed Forces, therefore, it was appropriate to treat them as German soldiers. An alternate plan would be just to send all fifty to sixty persons, named by Zurgashvili as the alleged participants, to P.O.W. camps. Choosing this alternate path, even if Oberländer would be permitted to do so by his superiors, was fraught by the danger of punishing some innocent people.

For instance, some of them may have attended "the card party" but did not necessarily participate in the plot. It also may undermine the self esteem and morale of the rest of the Caucasian soldiers. The thought would be, "Today a soldier and tomorrow a P.O.W.—what then is the value of being a 'Bergmann' soldier?" Furthermore, although Zurgashvili appeared very convincing, it was still one man's presentation and further investigation was clearly necessary. Oberländer felt that the alleged conspirators only represented a small group of the convinced communists and dissatisfied volunteers. Such were Professor Oberländer's thoughts, and I had no better suggestions to make during the given situation.

The Professor also availed himself of a few other persons to help; for instance, the before-mentioned interpreter, Victor Homeriki and former Second Lieutenant of the Soviet Army, Shalva Okropiridze, of the 1st Company. He was well liked by the Georgians as well as the Germans and spoke German in a satisfactory manner. A special associate of Oberländer, Walter von Kutzschenbach, also arrived back to "Bergmann" from his vacation and of course was of great help to him during this difficult time.

And difficult it was; also personally for me. Captain Tsiklauri had been (and still was) my roommate since my arrival in "Bergmann" some four and one-half to five weeks ago. I became fond or him and now had to pretend that things were as usual and as if I had no knowledge about his alleged participation in the plot. I had an almost irresistible urge to confront him and ask if this were true and if so, why? I barely slept during the following seemingly endless nights.

"You appear to be unusually restless in your sleep," Tsiklauri observed one morning. Then he said, "You know I, myself, had a strange dream last night. I dreamed of my favorite grandfather—he was waving and telling me to go to him and he would take good care of me." Tsiklauri then told me about his grandpa's influence and how close they had been during his childhood. I developed goose pimples while listening to Tsiklauri. This revealed a warm, human side of him as did some stories and jokes he told me from time to time.

Tsiklauri appeared disturbed about this unusual dream during the entire day, as if it were a premonition of some pending trouble. On the preceding pages, I discussed Tsiklauri's almost morbid hate of the old emigres and all our attempts to change this were in vain. We also had other differences of opinion. For instance, although we agreed that the Germans had not as yet won the war against Russia, I felt that this was mainly due to the Russian winter for which they apparently were not prepared. With the onset of spring, there would be another German offensive and they had a good chance to win, especially if the Germans would make their good intentions known at once to the Soviet people. They also needed to prove it by humane treatment of the population, P.O.W.s and by far-reaching agrarian as well as political reforms.

The Bolsheviks' rule had been cruel to their own people who, therefore, would be glad to get rid of their oppressors provided some better option was given to them. Tsiklauri, on the other hand, felt that the Red Army would win the war in the long run and the Battle of Moscow had been the turning point of the war, in favor of Russia.

I considered Stalin a great tyrant and the Bolshevik oligarchy around him to be responsible for the bloody purges and forced collectivization and the famine and continued inhumane treatment of the people.

Tsiklauri shared none of the above views. I was told that Tsiklauri not only verbally but perhaps also physically abused a "Bergmann" Georgian soldier who had composed a funny and disrespectful song about Stalin. In spite of all this, I respected the captain because of his straight-forward character and the dignity with which he conducted himself. Perhaps both of us felt that we were entitled to our own opinion and treated each other with great respect and tolerance. I did not think that he was totally convinced of the Red Army victory. If so, what was he doing in "Bergmann" and why was he proposing an airborne landing?

Captain Tsiklauri had come to "Bergmann" long before me and not directly from the P.O.W. camp but a subordinate section of O.K.W.—Abwehr (The Military Counter Intelligence) had detailed him for service with the "Bergmann" unit.[56] He had been highly recommended by the German professor Hans Raupach, who recruited him earlier in the P.O.W. camp in or near Poltava-Ukraine.[57] According to Tsiklauri, he himself had shot the political commissar who was supervising Tsiklauri's unit and defected to the Germans with his soldiers from the battalion. He related the same information to me when we first met with the explanation that the commissar had made their life miserable. Killing a man, even if he happens to be a difficult commissar, bothered me, although such could occur during heated arguments, under stress.

But now, according to Zurgashvili, the part of Tsiklauri-Tabidze's alleged plot was to kill again. This time, the "Bergmann" Germans and some Georgians in cold blood, preceding his second defection. If Zurgashvili's allegations were true and Tsiklauri-Tabidze really intended the premeditated murders, the only explanation I could find was the Bolshevist-Lenin-Stalinist education—that a human being was easily expendable, if it served a useful purpose. Our morality based on Christian heritage apparently had been effectively eliminated by the new "religion."

I remembered my father's words, that he never knowingly had killed a man, that it was most awful to shed blood and would use weapons only if the life of his loved ones or his own was clearly in jeopardy. He was considered to be one of the tough "mountaineers," yet he applied his principle even during the Georgian insurrection of 1924 when he was Chief of Staff of the insurgents in the "Free Upper Svaneti." For instance, during the battle of Tsageri, in the Province of Lechkhumi, his men had captured a number of Red Army Russian soldiers. The insurgents on the move had neither the manpower nor the prison camps to keep and guard the prisoners. Father ordered his men to set the Russians free once they had been interrogated. There was no one among his associates—all of them Svans—who had

---

56- Dr. Hermann Raschhofer, *Political Assassination*, pp. 82–83; Joachim Hoffmann, *Die Ostlegionen. 1941–1943*, p. 150.

57- After the war. Professor Dr. Hans Raupach was Professor for the "Economy and Social Science of East Europe" at Munich University. He was also the Director of the "Ost-Europe Institute" in Munich. In addition to many publications in German, I am also aware of his contribution to the *Journal of Contemporary History*, London, 1963: "The Impact of the Great Depression on Eastern Europe." I had an unusual opportunity to discuss Captain S. Tsiklauri with him during the summer of 1949 in Augsburg-Bavaria. Professor Raupach stated that he still could not believe that Captain Tsiklauri was a communist or even a communist sympathizer. Furthermore, he could not have been more surprised when informed about the Tsiklauri-Tabidze plot.

objected to such an order, even though they knew the freed men would most likely take up weapons against them again some day. The freed Russians could not believe it and while walking away, turned around every so often, obviously scared that the "wild" Svans would shoot them. If the roles had been reversed, the Svans probably would have not fared so well. I was told that it was not an uncommon practice to shoot the captured Georgians in the back and then, as an excuse, declare that "the prisoner wanted to run away."[58]

Earlier, Tsiklauri had proposed a plan to the Germans concerning the military operation in the Caucasus. According to this plan, the airborne unit would land behind the front line, south of the continental divide, in northwest Georgia near an area called Oshki. This was considerably further west of the Georgian military highway. The Germans, at that time, felt the plan to have considerable merit. Shortly after my arrival in Luttensee, Oberländer, von Kutzschenbach and Tsiklauri informed me about it. I was also asked to study the maps of the Caucasus and express my opinion. I felt in principle that it may well be a viable option but not the only one. This all points to the confidence which the German leadership at "Bergmann" had in Tsiklauri—until now.

A number of other Georgians also thought about the landing possibility in Georgia one way or another and I was no exception. The motivation for it has been noted already. However, making such a plan is easier that putting it into practice. According to Zurgashvili, First Lieutenant Shalva Tabidze was allegedly a co-leader of the plot. I had met Tabidze a few times, including during field exercise. He impressed me as an unpleasant person and perhaps of the type created during the Stalinist-Bolshevik terror. They were ready to denounce their own coworkers during party or other meetings, as ordered from above. Repeating parrot-like accusations against a person without any proof of guilt, they called from the podium to purge them without a sign of mercy and late repentance. Stalin, Beria and the like were promoting cadres from such young and usually mediocre Bolsheviks, who quickly replaced those purged and were faithful followers of the leaders. Some chairman of the collective farms, party secretaries, censors, newspapermen, political commissars and M.V.D. workers were recruited from such men.

I don't know how Tabidze had joined "Bergmann." He apparently brought

---

58- While writing on such a somber subject, somehow I remember a small humorous but not necessarily socially acceptable incident that also took place in Tsageri. Svans, who were quite victorious regionally against the Red Russian soldiers, nevertheless received an order to retreat back to their own mountains. The reason was that the military operations were not as successful in some other parts of Georgia. They were terribly frustrated to have to retreat from the enemy already on the run but the orders had to be obeyed. So in a rare display of displeasure and contempt, the otherwise modest soldiers of Svaneti displayed their bared posteriors to the fleeing Bolsheviks while watching them from the hills of Tsageri.

several men from his group to "Bergmann." Some of the men had remained somewhere else in Germany. The two groups, however, communicated with each other.
In fact, around this time, Oberländer had dispatched Tabidze and made known his
pending trip to the men from the Tabidze group in Luttensee. He also told them
that if they had any letters, he would gladly deliver them to their comrades out of
town. In response, a letter was given to him by a person who was suspected of being
one of the conspirators. Lieutenant Okropiridze stole the letter and read it in secret,
finding it rather informative concerning the suspected plot. He approached me and
suggested I interpret this letter to Oberländer or von Kutzschenbach, since I was
the liaison officer and spoke better German than he did. I did not particularly like
his method of opening someone else's letter, but I also realized the difficult situation
we all were in. I translated it either to Oberländer or von Kutzschenbach the same
day. The best I remember of this letter, one person was complaining and expressing
his fear to another that "the men were impatient and hurrying too much and that
may spoil everything."

Although not providing definite proof, this letter in conjunction with
Zurgashvili's allegations was possibly pointing to an existing conspiracy. The investigation had to proceed, and at this point, Oberländer, in cooperation with his
superiors, organized a trip to Berlin for all "Bergmann" officers and some others.
Officially, this was an excursion for us to see the capital of Germany. However, this
did not turn out to be so.

While in Berlin, we were led into a reception hall or a tall building. There, each
of us was introduced to some military dignitaries, following which we were split in
two groups. The group I was a part of was led through a different exit and directed
back to the hotel. We were told that the other group, which included Captain
Tsiklauri, was arrested for investigation. The invitation to Berlin for sightseeing
apparently had been arranged in order to avoid any sensational incident.[59] This whole
thing was depressing, and I wanted to take a long walk alone.

While passing in front of the hotel, I noticed Lieutenant Okropiridze talking
to a number of Georgians. I could not help but hear part of what he was saying, and I
could hardly believe my ears. He was simply boasting that he had solved the "puzzle"
of the Tsiklauri-Tabidze group and my help had been essential to this end: "One
could say that the two of us had uncovered a plot." He sounded like Mr. Sherlock
Holmes himself, telling one of his recent mysteries.

I was far from being amused and motioned Okropiridze to follow me. I told
him that he was distorting the truth—he only handed me a letter written by one of

---

59- Dr. Hermann Raschhofer, *Political Assassination*, p. 82.

the alleged plotters. I had only passed that letter according to the chain of command, and I never suspected the plot until after Professor Oberländer invited me to witness Zurgashvili's report about it. So it was not Okropiridze but Zurgashvili who discovered and reported the conspiracy, and Zurgashvili was not bragging about it.

It was not a bragging matter, I pointed out, but a sad situation for all of us in "Bergmann." And incidentally, those were allegations only and no final judgment had been passed as yet. Okropiridze appeared embarrassed, and I hoped that my "lecture" may have done him some good. I thought, at that time, that as a former young Soviet officer, Okropiridze's behavior was due to the environment of the totalitarian state. The methods such as spying and reporting others were encouraged and even rewarded by the State. Therefore, I was hoping that such features would gradually disappear in Okropiridze. Regretfully, over a period or time, I came to the conclusion that he also had somewhat of an irresponsible personality.

While the majority of us participating in the Berlin tour returned to Luttensee, Tsiklauri and others arrested in Berlin were transported to Garmisch-Partenkirchen also in Bavaria, not all that far from us. There in the garrison quarters of the Gebirgsjäger Division (the Mountaineers Division), the accused would be kept in detention, pending further investigation and possible court trial.

Victor Homeriki, mentioned on preceding pages, was also one of the participants of the Berlin "excursion." After the arrest of Tsiklauri, Homeriki phoned Misha Kedia, informing him about the arrest. The two of them discussed what could be done to save the accused from a severe form of punishment. Homeriki also informed me about his action. Misha Kedia happened to be, at that time, in Berlin to represent the Georgian emigrants in France and had important connections, as noted before, with Admiral Canaris's organization, with Count von Schulenburg of the Foreign Ministry, and Professor von Mende from "The Ministry of Eastern Affairs."

The general position of the Georgians abroad during W.W. II was to save all Georgian lives regardless of their political belief or party affiliation, except for the criminals. Tsiklauri's group had not murdered anyone so far, although such action allegedly had been considered by them at some point in the future. But there is a difference between talking about and actually committing the crime. But during wartime, usually more severe sentences apply, and there was real danger for the accused.[60]

Before we proceed discussing further developments, two observations are of interest. The first is that Homeriki accompanied Captain Tsiklauri on the train trip from Berlin to Garmisch-Partenkirchen Military Prison, as an interpreter. During

---

60- One year or so later, when I met Kedia, he had a perfect recollection or it. He also confirmed his intervention on behalf of the accused with authorities in Berlin, but in vain.

this trip, Tsiklauri assured Homeriki and insisted that he, Tsiklauri, "would never commit treason toward us—the other Georgians in 'Bergmann.'" This statement remained a puzzle to Homeriki and myself in the years to come. The second is how Misha Kedia misconceived "The Tsiklauri Plot" when he first heard about it. He thought it was nothing more than minor intrigue, due to existing hostility between old emigres and Tsiklauri.

This, however, did not turn out to have been so. Soon a special investigator-adviser to the military court arrived in "Bergmann" for further investigation. After conferring with Professor Oberländer, he met other men who included von Kutzschenbach, Chanturia, Zurgashvili, Okropiridze, Homeriki, me and many others at first, then again at the conclusion of his investigation. He also met and questioned those Georgians who were on Zurgashvili's list of suspects but not really involved, totaling approximately sixty men.

During our second meeting, it was clearer that only approximately one-third of the suspects possibly had some kind of affiliation with the alleged plotters (already in custody). Walter von Kutzschenbach felt that the Georgians, in general, tend to talk excessively and are prone to exaggerate things a bit, which he should have known as he was born in Georgia and grew up there. Moreover, Oberländer and von Kutzschenbach knew more about the soldiers in "Bergmann" than some of us, especially myself, a newcomer. They were the co-founders of this unit, along with the "father" of it, Admiral Canaris, and they had recruited the men for "Bergmann" since the very beginning. They felt that the plotters in reality represented only a small group.

The special investigator appeared to be an astute person with common sense and excellent rapport with all of us but especially with Homeriki, who did some translations for him. Homeriki played a very useful moderating role in this situation which saved some people from being punished, and we did our best to help him. Together we soon realized we must be mindful of the dangers of paranoid reaction and blowing things out of proportion.

After sentences had been passed on the Tsiklauri-Tabidze group, the question was raised in Berlin as to the reliability of the remainder of the unit. Oberländer and Kutzschenbach discussed this with each other and decided to discharge from "Bergmann" approximately twenty who were not believed to be absolutely reliable Georgian volunteers. During July 1942, they were transferred to a factory in Hanau for foreign workers, where conditions were believed to be satisfactory.[61]

61- Dr. Hermann Raschhofer, *Political Assassination*, p. 83. As already mentioned before arriving in "Bergmann." I had been lodged in punitive P.O.W. camp in Steinau and von Kutzschenbach visited

Surprising enough, Lieutenant Okropiridze was also suspected as having had a degree of knowledge about the existing plot but there was no evidence of his participation in it. Von Kutzschenbach, who had personally recruited Okropiridze for "Bergmann," told me that he was somewhat disappointed by Okropiridze's imperfect conduct and felt let down by his protege.

It became known in "Bergmann" that the alleged conspirators would have a court trial the latter part of June 1942. We also were told that some of us with whom the special investigator had a meeting would also have to appear there as witnesses—not a very pleasant prospect. I was to appear in court on a witness stand (as I was told) for two reasons One, because with Professor Oberländer, I had witnessed Zurgashvili's initial report about the plot in "Bergmann" and second, since I was Tsiklauri's roommate.

The question in von Kutzschenbach's mind (at least at that time) was: Did Okropiridze present the letter written from one of the accused men to another to save himself or to help the cause of justice? Okropiridze was difficult to evaluate. He had a number of good qualities. For instance, he was a well-trained officer and had the ability to organize, and also had military bearing and looks that were admired even by the Prussian soldiers. But in order for him to be a functional and useful team member, it was indispensable to have at all times an alert and strict supervisor above him.

Meanwhile, on the 26th of May, the Georgian Independence Day Celebration was due. But not many of us were in a mood to celebrate just now and understandably so. Nevertheless, the important tradition had to be kept alive. The persons in charge of planing the celebration had decided that a special 26th of May address speech to the battalion was needed and I was elected to deliver it. Apparently, they thought that coming from me, it would be well received by all the "Bergmann" soldiers regardless of their background. I considered it an honor, inasmuch as I was a newcomer here and with those very words, I began the introduction to my speech.

All Georgian companies were lined up around the podium in total silence with the beautiful mountains in the background. This is approximately what I said:

> "The only reason we are in 'Bergmann' is that we stand for the 26th
> of May and the three-colored Georgian flag, the symbols of a sovereign
> Georgian State, which must be resurrected again as Phoenix from the
> ashes. We have pledged alliance to the German Armed Forces because

---

me there with the mission to free me. We both heard that conditions in Hanau were much better than in Steinau. We then both visited Hanau and established that our information about it had been correct. Therefore, von Kutzschenbach arranged a transfer of several P.O.W.s from Steinau to Hanau in order to improve their living and working conditions.

we believe they will help us toward the realization of this goal now as they had before, during our independence of 1918–1921, and our new German friends indicate that they will do so again.

"But Germany did lose World War I and had to withdraw from Caucasus. Without a friend and alone, the Georgian Democratic Republic could not survive the simultaneous military onslaught by the vastly outnumbering Bolshevik Russian troops from the north and east and the Turkish Army from the south. Georgia had lost her statehood twice in relatively recent history due to the treachery of the czars and of the Bolsheviks.

"The Bolsheviks usurped the power not only in the Caucasus and other non Russian Republics but in Russia also. The 1924 Georgian uprising demonstrated to the whole world her dedication to freedom and dignity. Today, one more time, some of us have stood up for the same reason. This is the continuation of the 1924 uprising—that is why we are in Luttensee, and someday this too may be recorded in the annals of Georgia.

"We were not and are not haters of the Russian people, indeed discrimination against other people is alien to Georgians. It is a historical fact that Georgian kings extended the hand of friendship to the Russian czars and also asked for help in the later part of the eighteenth century. The government of the Democratic Republic of Georgia also extended a hand to post-revolution Russia as a gesture of friendship during 1920. The hand was accepted each time, the treaties were signed each time and they were broken each time; not by the Georgians but by the Russian rulers without any provocation from our side. Obviously our agreements had not been signed in good faith by them.

"Before there is a 'next time,' the Russians have to accept and declare in good faith the right of self-determination of Georgians and other Caucasian people. In the first place, this will be a most fortunate sign for the much abused Russian people themselves. It is overdue for their rulers to think more about the welfare of their own people than to go on with the conquest of their neighbors and thus increase the list of the abused."

I also mentioned the "sadness" due to the unpleasant occurrence in "Bergmann," the clarification of which was pending. I could not have said more about it, even if I wanted to, before the anticipated trial. I ended then with a typical Georgian call, "May God grant victory to Georgia, to her three-colored flag and to the 26th of May."

The address appeared to have been well received, if loud applause is an indication of this. Also many "old" emigres, as well as the "new" ones shook my hand and expressed their appreciation after it was over. One of my old friends from the time of our youth in Tbilisi, Dr. Rezo Gogitidze was among the listeners. (How could I have missed him—a tall basketball and volleyball player, he had competed for our team in Georgia.)

Rezo approached me with his hands characteristically spread widely while gesticulating and shouted, "Katso" (which means a man in Georgian), "how much can you talk and how do you remember all that, especially the dates?"

"I just keep reading books and then climb mountains pondering about it," I quipped, "while some people, including you, would rather hang around here and stare at the Major's beautiful daughter." There was some truth in that joke, the commandant in charge of military quarters of Luttensee, Major Zabuesnig, indeed had a captivating daughter. It was an inspiring experience to see her on a bike, "schussing" from the hill of Luttensee down to the city of Mittenwald. Dr. Rezo, who was working in the medical department of "Bergmann" and being a neighbor to the Major's family, was one of the many admirers of the young lady. The list also included a popular Bavarian Lieutenant Kress von Kressenstein. Shortly after my conversation with Rezo, an engagement was announced between that young lady and the Lieutenant von Kressenstein. Being a good sport, Dr. Rezo did not lose sleep after that "defeat" and with other gentlemen accepted this fact of life.

Many years after the war it was a joyous experience for me to see my old friend, Rezo, this time in Paris. He was fortunate and happy because not only did he survive the war without a scratch but also became a member of the French national volleyball team. A much more important reason for his happiness, however, was that he had married a wonderful, young Georgian emigre, Nelli Mdivani.[62] They had equally adorable children, Liia and Michel, both in law school. Dr. Rezo had just retired from his work in the chemical laboratory of a prestigious French firm. My wife and I enjoyed the Gogitidzes' hospitality as Rezo taxied us every day all over Paris, her suburbs and surrounding areas. We walked and talked endlessly about a wide variety of subjects, mostly about our past. We did this so loudly and with so much laughter and gesticulation that even the French students passing by, who have a reputation of being loud themselves, turned their heads in amazement.

62- One of the daughters of Simon Mdivani: the former Georgian Representative in Angora, Turkey and the Vice Chairman of the Georgian Constituent Assembly.

On the preceding pages, I have attempted to present sketches of a few Georgian "Bergmann" soldiers, whom I had met more often. Those were mostly emigres from France. This was because, as a newcomer to the West, I was fascinated by them and as a result of frequent get-togethers, I received considerable information of great interest to me. This was, in the first place, about the lives and activities of the emigrants themselves, who were proven fighters for the Georgian cause. Secondly, I was learning the truth about the world beyond the "Iron Curtain." Thirdly, how they visualized our future in Georgia, given our cooperation with the German military. I realized that while they knew more than I did, none of us had all the answers. Still, I had profited a great deal due to the close contact with the emigrants. (I also had continued frank discussions with Professor Oberländer and von Kutzschenbach, which also helped to widen my horizon as time went by.)

Therefore, during the first few weeks after my arrival, I did not have much time for personal meetings with other "Bergmann" Georgians of recent Soviet origin although we often were together on field exercise outings. I have already described a few of the "new refugees" such as Tsiklauri, Okropiridze and Gogitidze but there was also a Georgian lieutenant in "Bergmann," Irakli Alimbarashvili from Tbilisi. He was not only a good officer but also one could hardly imagine anyone more good-natured, decent and willing to help and share with others what little he had. He appeared rather easy going with a good sense of humor, was an excellent dancer and also artistically inclined. This last virtue could have been to some measure due to the influence of his relative, Lado Godziashvili, one of the well known stage actors of the Rustaveli Theatre in Tbilisi. Lieutenant Alimbarashvili's short acting performances in "Bergmann" brought tears of laughter from many—including Admiral Canaris. Lieutenant Alimbarashvili and V. Homeriki were the main organizers of Georgian singing and dancing activities in "Bergmann." They popularized a famous Georgian Love Song, "Suliko" (Sweetheart), which became the song for all the "Bergmann" soldiers, not only on the front line but it even endured to the postwar era.

Two persons from the 1st Company made a special impression on me. Both were also "newcomers" to the west and certainly set an example for all of us to follow, although neither of them were commissioned officers. They conducted themselves as medieval knights at all times and during any situation. They were there whenever and wherever needed, as the Georgian poet and philosopher Shota Rustaveli would have wanted them to be.[63] Their names were Shota Margwelashvili and Gabriel (Gabo) Gogelashvili. I will have more to say about them later on. But there were others similar to them in "Bergmann," where generally speaking, the soldiers of

---

63- The author of a famous poem of the twelfth century, "The Knight in Tiger's Skin," Shota Rustaveli had a profound influence upon the Georgian code of ethics.

Soviet Georgian origin were men of outstanding quality including their political attitude. They were motivated because of family influence and had a sober, critical view of the Bolshevik system.

One of the characteristics of such a system was abolishment of the national army for Georgia and other non Russian republics, a deeply resented state of affairs in Georgia and to the best of my knowledge also in other non Russian Republics for a number of reasons. Another one of the characteristics was the inability of self defense should some crisis occur. For example at the end of W.W. I, the Russian government collapsed; so did the Russian Army. This resulted in a disorderly withdrawal of Russian troops from the Transcaucasian front, as the Russian soldiers used all means of transportation to get back home to Russia in a hurry. Now Georgia and other Transcaucasian nations were left facing the armed forces of Turkey across the border without armies of their own. In other words, Russia had abandoned them. Certain disaster was averted, at least for the time being, by unexpected help from Imperial Germany.

Georgian youth would have served proudly in their own army, on familiar terrain and environment. Historically, the Georgians had fiercely fought for the defense of their own land against the outnumbering invading forces. Moreover, the way it was now, the young conscripts were taken away from their country and dispersed all over the vast Soviet territory for two years of obligatory military service. The conditions were frequently demoralizing, including the great Russian chauvinistic discriminations. It is not to say that all Russians were chauvinists, but often even an ugly minority is able to spoil the atmosphere on a large scale. Lenin himself had well recognized and commented about the existence of such chauvinism. This revealed itself even in the P.O.W. camps, where frequently the Russian P.O.W.s denounced the P.O.W. Georgians to the Germans as Stalin's Hawks, since Stalin happened to be of Georgian decent. At the same time, another group of Russian soldiers, while in Tbilisi, behaved as hoodlums on the streets and railroad cars. Their slogan was, "The Georgians are traitors, beat them up."

During World War II, however, obviously the Kremlin itself encouraged such an attitude, calling it "Russian Patriotism,"[64] since the people simply would not fight for communism during the war. But since the rulers generally did not treat the ruled ones in good faith, this trust could not go far, even toward ethnic Russian soldiers. Therefore, every Red Army unit in addition to the military commander had a political commissar and also a secret police cell for constant supervision. The above is only a partial sketch attempting to explain grievances of the former Soviet Georgians now in "Bergmann" against the Bolshevik Kremlin rulers. Other, even

---

64- Alexander Werth, *Russia at War 1941–1946*, New York: E.P. Dutton, 1964.

more serious ones have already been referred to. Radical changes would have to take place in the Soviet Empire before Georgia and other non Russians would be allowed to have their own army.

The "Bergmann" soldiers knew what they were opposed to but not necessarily how they wanted to replace it and here without a doubt in my mind the Georgian emigrants helped to bring about political maturity in the newcomers. They directed and focused their view on the experience of the Independent Democratic Georgian Republic—a truly pluralistic, multi-party democracy. "The Act of Independence of Georgia" declared social justice and universal human rights for every citizen regardless of their sex, ethnic origin, religious and political beliefs.[65]

Thus we already had political experience to follow for the future. It was not a theory but a reality from our past. Even so, our Republic that lasted only three years had some remarkable achievements to be proud of and the Georgian emigres from France were eyewitness to all of this.[66] No German instructors or leaders even of such outstanding quality as Canaris, Oberländer and von Kutzschenbach could have been substituted for the emigres in this respect. The above-named Germans realized this and despite the initial conflict between such newcomers as Captain Tsiklauri and the emigrants, the amalgamation of the Georgian emigres and the newcomers from Soviet Georgia was vital for our success. I like to think that, perhaps in a small way, I too, made some contribution toward this end.

During the later part of June, the military court went into session in Garmisch-Partenkirchen. The court availed itself of services of "Bergmann" interpreters. Among those I remember were Victor Nozadze, Bagrat Chanturia and two Germans, but there may have been some others. I received more information as to what actually took place during the court sessions from our interpreters (who were briefing us) than I did as a result of my own one-time appearance in court.

According to the interpreters, the military court was in session for many days and it followed the customary code to the letter. Furthermore, Captain Simon Tsiklauri conducted himself with great dignity. He admitted neither his nor anyone else's participation in the alleged plot to the end. Then things took a surprising turn when First Lieutenant "Commissar," Shalva Tabidze, the suspected co-leader of the conspiracy, soon confirmed existence of the plot. But as he said, he joined it in order to familiarize himself with the plotter's plans and to report them to Oberländer, all in due time. Moreover, he offered his faithful service in the future to the Germans. It

---

65- The Georgian Act of Independence, Sakartvelos Damoukideblobis Akti; Constantin Kandelaki, *The Georgian Question Before the Free World*, pp. 180–181, also the Constitution of Georgia, pp. 192–209. [*Also see http://www.library.court.ge/upload/Georgian_Constitution_1921.pdf (in Georgian) —Ed.*]
66- Of course, the "loyal opposition" to the government made its criticism known from time to time.

is clear that Tabidze's declaration convinced the court that the deposition of a main witness, Zurgashvili, was more than just one man's allegations. It also increased the value of a letter which Lieutenant Okropiridze had presented before as additional incriminating evidence. I knew that many other witnesses were requested to appear, but I had not been informed about their depositions.

I was summoned to appear in court for one morning session. Professor Oberländer, von Kutzschenbach and a few others were there, all as witnesses. Captain Tsiklauri and Tabidze sat in the front row and other defendants behind them. After customary identification of myself etc., the court counselor questioned me as to whether I knew Captain Tsiklauri. I said that indeed I knew him since we were roommates. What was our relationship and how did we get along? I replied that it was very good and we got along well. Did I suspect him of anything? My answer was that I did not. Was I familiar with Zurgashvili's allegations? Yes, I was. Was I familiar with a military plan that Tsiklauri had proposed to Professor Oberländer and what did I think of it. I stated that I was familiar with the plan and in my opinion it was a good one.

Now the presiding general or colonel wanted to know about the plan. Here von Kutzschenbach asked and received permission for a comment. He suggested the plan not be revealed in court since it was a military secret and still considered to be a viable option. The court agreed with that request. Did I have any disagreements with Tsiklauri? I said we had some differences of opinion. What were these? The main difference, I replied, concerned the Georgian emigrants from France, now volunteers in "Bergmann." I consider them to be important for our mutual cause and would welcome the amalgamation between them and us (the newcomers) in the west. Much to my regret, Captain Tsiklauri considered them more or less useless because he felt that they were out of touch with present reality in the country. What more? Another difference was, I answered, that I had been more optimistic about the final outcome of the war. Provided, however, that the civilian administration in the occupied Eastern territories would discontinue their present "erroneous" practices and treat the natives in a much better way. I had not seen this myself, but I had been told about it by many. Captain Tsiklauri spent some time there and such observation may have fed his pessimistic attitude. We must win over people there on our side and not help the Soviet propaganda against us.

Here, again the presiding officer wanted to know what I meant by that. Professor Oberländer (or von Kutzschenbach—I believe the former) again intervened and offered his personal explanation about this, which the General accepted. In retrospect, I think Oberländer felt that recording of criticism about the German civilian government's policy, in the military court proceedings, had a potential for dangerous repercussions. Off the record, he could have discussed such matters as one officer to another. (I did not realize then that I was sticking my neck out so far and also perhaps endangering Oberländer.)

I completed my answer to the last question with a remark that probably Tsiklauri was not as pessimistic as he appeared on the surface. Otherwise, what would he be doing in "Bergmann" and why would he submit a military plan of operation? After my statement, there was a recess. I walked to Captain Tsiklauri and after a warm handshake I told him that it was heart-breaking for me to see him in a situation such as this. As I shook hands with Tsiklauri again, to say goodbye, he in a loud and clear voice told me, "Givi, do you remember when once I told you about dreaming of my grandfather, who told me to go to him and he would take care of me?" I answered that of course I did, and again I developed goose pimples and my legs barely carried me out of the courtroom.

I was depressed again thinking about a little boy following his grandpa somewhere in the Georgian mountain foothills. Who would imagine then that grown up, Simon Tsiklauri would be in a predicament like this, thousands of miles from his home. Outside the courtroom, other witnesses were waiting at the entrance door for their turn to testify. Among them I recognized Zurgashvili. He appeared unhappy and torn between feelings of pity for the accused on one hand and doing what he thought was the right thing to do on the other hand, when he reported the pending danger to his superior. Now Zurgashvili had to face the accused and testify against them in court. He was talking to others and helplessly looking around, presumably for some counseling. He was due to enter the courtroom any time but noticing me turned around and asked me what he should do. I wished I had a magic formula for a perfect solution for this terrible problem. All I could tell him was that there was no way he could back out of the truth in the given situation even if he wanted to. Perhaps, this was the third time I had ever seen Zurgashvili, and we did not know each other well.

Under normal circumstances, I probably would not be his first choice for asking advice; he was a very unhappy man that day. I was somewhat unhappy also with my own performance on the witness stand in answering—especially the last question. Not that it would have made much difference in the final outcome of the court decision but still I should have prepared my answers more deliberately and simply. The problem was that I had no prior experience with any kind of court. In retrospect, this case probably was the most unusual experience for the military court also. While trying the accused as German soldiers and following the existing regulations, the court probably would not be able to evaluate and consider the cause and relationship between the behavior of the accused and the Nazi policy in occupied Eastern territories and conditions in the P.O.W. camps there. Nor could they appreciate the vulnerability of the accused to Soviet propaganda.[67] Therefore, my hint in this direction probably confused rather than helped the court.

One of the basic foundations for "Bergmann" was to treat the Caucasian volunteers as having rights and duties equal to the German soldiers after they had taken the oath. The oath was also on a volunteer basis. In the long run, this principle was proved essential for creation of a high quality and trustworthy military unit. Consequently, Oberländer, while facing the crisis of an alleged plot decided to remain on the same foundation; hence the military investigation and the court.

Once the military court entered the picture, neither Oberländer nor anyone else in "Bergmann" had anything to do with the verdict of the type of punishment imposed by the court. After one of the main plotters, Tabidze, had turned into a witness against the other defendants, paired with the first main witness, Zurgashvili, it was clear that the "guilty" verdict would be passed against some of the defendants. We learned this to be the case and the majority of the accused were condemned to death.[68] Needless to say, neither the Georgians nor the Germans in "Bergmann" wanted to have the plotters shot. We had hoped that those found guilty would get jail sentences to be served in labor camps for whatever length of time was designated and their lives would be spared.

It is informative to quote Dr. Joachim Hoffmann, a noted contemporary West German military historian, about the nature and action of the court:

> "As members of the armed force, who had taken oath, they were accused because of military betrayal during wartime and they had started it by disintegrating military power and by mutiny. The sixteen accused Georgian soldiers, nevertheless, were given an opportunity to defend themselves before a senate of the Reich Court Martial, during the many days of negotiations. Senate of the Reich Court Martial consisted of a chairman of the Reich Court Martial[,] Biron, one major general, two colonels and one Supreme Court Martial counsel.
>
> "Twelve of the accused Georgians had to be condemned to death by shooting, according to the existing regulations and so would have all the ethnic German soldiers under identical circumstances. Objectivity of the court may be seen from the fact that the remaining four Georgian soldiers, who also were accused of identical conduct,

---

67- We were told by some Georgians that the alleged conspirators were able somehow to listen to Soviet radio.

68- There are two different data available concerning the number of condemned Georgians executed. Dr. Raschhofer sets the number at seven (p. 82 in his book) and Dr. Hoffmann refers to twelve out of sixteen accused condemned to death (p. 150 in his publication). It appears that Dr. Hoffmann is correct concerning this matter.

were set free because of inadequate proof. Moreover, the court martial decision given the legionnaires was not binding and could not have been carried out unless approved by the special general at large—or the Supreme Command of the Army. Such a general had the status of Supreme Commanding General of the Army."[69]

"Bergmann" interpreters who served the military court told us about an unusual occurrence following the final session. One of the ranking members of the court, (a general or colonel) approached Captain Simon Tsiklauri, shook his hand and expressed his appreciation for the captain's dignified conduct during the entire trial.

All we could hope now was that the supreme instance of the military judiciary would amend the death sentence after appeal by the condemned. It would probably be several weeks before we would hear of it.

Around this time another danger arose for "Bergmann" from a different direction, which threatened its existence. During early spring of 1942, the German Army had appointed Major General Oskar Ritter von Niedermayer as a commander of 162 Turkic Infantry Division. His headquarters was located in the city of Myrhorod of the occupied Ukraine. The goal of this division was to form Muslim volunteer battalions from Turkestan and the Caucasus, as soon as possible.

One of the difficulties for such a task was a critical shortage of German and indigenous instructors for training and supervision of the new legionnaires. This moved someone in the "Army Group South" to propose that "Bergmann" be used for such a purpose since it was a superbly trained unit. When Oberländer was notified of it in an official order he made a trip to Myrhorod to see the 162nd Division and found there "a totally unorganized collection of Mahomedan P.O.W.s." Oberländer could not accept "Bergmann's" dissolution in this amorphous mass. Therefore, after a discussion with General von Niedermayer, he flew back to the Army headquarters in Lötzen [now Giżycko, Poland]. There, Oberländer had a conference with Lieutenant Colonel Herre, of the Army General Staff and gained his support to keep "Bergmann" for its original mission in the Caucasus. Oberländer simultaneously had notified Admiral Canaris in O.K.W. (Supreme Command of the Armed Forces) who in turn authorized his close associate colonel in the General Staff, Lahausen, to undertake

69- Joachim Hoffmann, *Die Ostlegionen. 1941–1943*, p. 150.

appropriate steps. The final outcome was positive which was made known to us on July 11th. Thus Oberländer, thanks to his energetic interference, saved his unit.[70][71][72]

70- Professor Theodore Oberländer, *History of the "Bergmann" Unit, Geschichte der Einheit "Bergmann,"* (report). Munich: Josef M. Greska.1983. p. 10; Joachim Hoffmann, *Die Ostlegionen. 1941–1943*, p. 67.

71- In his book, *Against Two Evils*, Hans von Herwarth characterizes General von Niedermayer as "a kind of German Lawrence of Arabia, at once a soldier, scholar and adventurer." During his formative years, Niedermayer had studied several Muslim languages and during W.W. I was sent to Afghanistan to further anti British feelings there, without success. He converted to the Muslim religion and made a pilgrimage to Mecca. At one time, he had directed the Institute of Strategic Studies in Berlin and had been the Reichswehr's unofficial representative to the Red Army in the early thirties. With such credentials, it was a small wonder that General von Niedermayer was appointed Commander of the 162 Turkic infantry division. Hans von Herwarth, *Against Two Evils*, p. 226.

72- My observations about the court martial had been written when, at last, I received a copy of *The Slavonic and East European Review*, Band XL 52 #109, 1969, pp. 483–509. I learned about author Professor F.L. Carsten's essay, titled "Bolshevik Conspiracy in the Wehrmacht," from a military historian. This is a document from the files of the highest military court in Germany from the years 1937 to 1944, as explained by Professor Carsten in his introductory note. All sixteen pages are exclusively about the plot in "Bergmann." I have decided not to alter my memoirs concerning this conspiracy in "Bergmann," but rather separately supplement it with some information (until now, unknown to me), obtained from this document. See Appendix "The Plot in 'Bergmann,'" p. 378.

7

TO THE UKRAINE AND CAUCASUS
Treatment of P.O.W.s

My last alpine climb from the Bavarian home base took place in Tyrol, located in west Austria and north Italy. It was proposed by Lieutenant Pöhlmann and turned out to be more dangerous than usual—as well as memorable. The young Bavarian officer was the son of a well-known professor of pediatrics at Munich University. Lieutenant Pöhlmann and I both liked high-alpine sport but he also was a faithful student and follower of Friedrich Nietzsche—the nineteenth century German philosopher. We traveled by train, bus, bicycle and foot. Nietzsche was the favorite topic for discussion during our rather long trip. It was a lesson for me since where I came from, Nietzsche and all other philosophers had been replaced by Marx, Engels, Lenin and Stalin. Stimulated by Pöhlmann's lecture, I read later about Nietzsche and it helped me to better understand my partner and perhaps a partial understanding of the "western world." Nietzsche advanced the concept of a nonconformist self-overcoming man, that is to say, overcoming his many weaknesses and perfecting himself. He wanted to recreate himself, to become a creator rather than a mere creature. He called such a man the "Übermensch."

Our goal, this time, was to climb the summit of the Similaun North Face, which was graded "difficult" even for an experienced alpinist. We spent our first night in an alpine hut and skied from there over a snow-covered glacier to the foot of our targeted mountain. We bivouacked there on the glacier in the tent, got up somewhat stiff and cold and started our ascent on the north wall long before sunrise. For all practical purposes, it was a very steep solid mass of ice; the summit had overhanging, frozen snow in our direction, which had the potential for an avalanche if exposed to the sun for an undetermined length of time. This is why we spent the night at the base, to commence our ascent early and beat the sun to the summit. Our plan was to descend from the summit, not the same way but over the west side which was less steep and had no potential for an avalanche. We would then go around to reach our bivouac, pick up our belongings and ski back to the alpine hut. For such an ascent, one had to carry the heavy alpine hardware and ropes and cut seemingly endless steps in the ice with an ice axe.

Lieutenant Pöhlmann led and I thought that after one hour or so, he would ask me to take over and so at reasonable intervals, we would continue taking turns. This is hard work, especially in high altitudes and one can become exhausted which may then create a dangerous situation. The Lieutenant labored hard, I am sure due to politeness to me but perhaps at the subconscious level, he was also pleasing Nietzsche. Almost half way up, he finally had to stop and told me that he was very, very tired. With an ice axe, I cut a big ice platform for him so he could turn around, face the down hill and rest; in the depth below us, we could observe some birds flying.

After a while, the Lieutenant improved and was breathing better. I thought that we could continue our ascent. I told him that even though I did not count the number of steps in the ice, he had already filled his quota and I would be the commander now. He smiled but did not argue. While cutting the steps, I found that I apparently had been keeping myself in good shape, and we needed it. We made our way through the overhanging snow mass near the summit before the sun warmed it and therefore without causing an avalanche. We congratulated each other for the successful conclusion of a very difficult climb. We decided that Nietzsche probably would have been pleased. I felt, however, that we were fortunate that the weather remained good otherwise we may not have made it to the summit. And if so, turning around and going back and down to where we had started from on a gigantic ice wall could also have been terribly difficult.

As tired as he was, Lieutenant Pöhlmann still took a few photo snapshots, and I still have them. By some miracle, those survived the war. Lieutenant Pöhlmann, unfortunately did not, and it was with great sadness that I received the bad news during September 1942, in the Caucasus. His small detachment of "Bergmann" soldiers had been ambushed by the larger Soviet military unit. Only one or two soldiers survived from his group and reported what had really happened. The ambush took place near the foothills of Europe's highest mountain, Elbrus, in North Caucasus (18,510 feet).

Lieutenant Pöhlmann had wanted to climb Elbrus with his group of soldiers, however, he did not have clearance from Professor Captain Oberländer or any other superior for this. I often thought about him and his grieving parents in Munich and also the parents of others who perished during his undertaking. I could not help but think about Nietzsche's glorification of a "self-overcoming non-conforming man" and his influence on Lieutenant Pöhlmann. How else could one explain such behavior from an otherwise well disciplined and educated German officer?

While all this was going on in "Bergmann," on the southeastern front, west of Donetsk, as a result of a successful encircling maneuver, the Germans took 250,000 Red Army soldiers as P.O.W.s during the end of May 1942. The battle for Sevastopol (Crimea) started in early June, and it fell to the Germans in four weeks' time. Both sides had heavy casualties, but the Germans took 90,000 P.O.W.s. In the beginning and middle of July, the Germans took Voronezh and Voroshilovgrad [present-day Luhansk], respectively. They reached the river Don and were menacing Rostov.[73]

The Germans were now poised for Caucasian invasion, and the time was nearing for "Bergmann" to be transferred to Caucasus. Admiral Canaris visited us again on July 7th, in Luttensee. He inspected the battalion and delivered a special speech. He stressed the high quality of "Bergmann" not only as a military unit but especially its importance for the better future of Caucasus.

One week later Professor Oberländer was promoted from first lieutenant to captain and we were all happy about it, inasmuch as it also meant recognition for "Bergmann." On July 26th, Oberländer visited the headquarters of the 17th Army, which was part of the Army Group South, in order to discuss "Bergmann's" front line participation and also to discuss the military administration for North Caucasus in case of expected German occupation of it. Participants of this discussion were, in addition to Oberländer, Admiral Canaris, Colonel Freytag von Loringhoven and Colonel Hansen. We shall have much more to say about the military administration of North Caucasus later on.

During early August 1942, "Bergmann" was transported back to its original place of formation, Neuhammer-Silesia. On the 15th of August, an order for the transfer of "Bergmann" to the Caucasus front was received and during the following days the companies of "Bergmann" were loaded, one after another, on railroad cars and set in motion to Caucasus over Ukraine. In the beginning of August in 1942, the Southern German Army had reached the Kuban river, continued attacks southeast toward Stavropol and Maykop and by the middle of August were closing in on Georgievsk in the Caucasus.

I was traveling toward the front in the company of Lieutenant Mikheil Dadiani and non-commissioned officer, Fritz Hummel. Hummel was born in Azerbaijan of German parents from Swabia. His ancestors were settlers in South Caucasus (Transcaucasus) since the early part of the nineteenth century (1817–1818).

73- *The World Almanac of World War II.*

This was possible because of Catherine the Great's (of Russia) manifesto of 1764, which encouraged German emigrants to settle in the Russian Empire. The German settlers in South Caucasus were different from other German groups, for instance, such as the Mennonites. The difference was that they were followers of the old Lutheran Church Rite, which after the 1609 reform in Württemberg-Swabia had been persecuted.

Therefore, their original goal was Jerusalem; however, under the influence of their leader, it was changed to Georgia and South Caucasus in general.[74] Thus it would appear fitting to call them the puritan pilgrims of Transcaucasia. Fritz Hummel spent many of his formative years in Azerbaijan before he emigrated to Germany. Therefore, he had not only mastered the Turkish language of the indigenous people but knew their characteristics and also spoke good Russian. This was the reason for his assignment to "Bergmann" as an interpreter liaison man to the Azerbaijan company (the third) and also an advisor to the company chief and Captain Oberländer. Hummel was a cheerful extrovert arid loved to entertain his friends with his accordion. He was married to a good-looking young German lady, whom he affectionately referred to as "moi vorobey" (my sparrow) in Russian and whose photos he treasured and carried. Professor Captain Oberländer interrupted Hummel's and my trip to the front line. He caught up with us somewhere in Ukraine and explained that "Air Force #4" had requested help in interpreting and composing propaganda leaflets in Georgian and Turkish languages. These were to be dropped over the respective lands. Oberländer wanted Hummel and me to carry out this task.

I personally did not particularly care for such work but nevertheless considered this to be a challenge, especially given my previous criticism of the German leaflets. Moreover, I had many discussions in "Bergmann" with the "old" as well as "new" emigres and we had a consensus of opinion about many Georgian problems. Therefore, I did not anticipate much difficulty in expressing the non partisan majority views in the leaflets for the Georgian people.

So Hummel and I arrived in Mariupol on the Sea of Azov and were immediately directed to the headquarters of "Air Force #4." We were introduced to a German colonel and two Baltic German non-commissioned officers, with whom we had to work on the propaganda leaflets. The atmosphere was congenial, sleeping quarters and food were good, and working hours long. Mariupol apparently did not suffer any serious destruction due to the war, and the local populace communicated with the German military authorities freely and appeared at ease. The German Air

---

74- A. Sanders (pseudonym for Alexander Nikuradze), *Kaukasien: Nordkaukasien, Aserbeidschan, Armenien, Georgien — Geschichtlicher Umriss*, München: Hoheneichen-Verlag, 1944.

Force soldiers were dating local women as if they were in Germany, and quite a few swimmers enjoyed the Sea of Azov. Looking at all of this, it was hard to believe that not all that far from here, the war was going in full swing.

Our working group met every morning, discussing and revising samples of the proposed propaganda leaflets for Caucasus. Not infrequently, we completely replaced them with ones we had composed ourselves. After reading his leaflet out-loud to me, Fritz Hummel's favorite question was, what do you think the commissars would say about my leaflet? If my answer was that the commissars would be upset, Fritz would comment, then it must be a good one. The fact was that most leaflet samples we had received were satisfactory even before revision. They were much different from the ones I had read and criticized while on the Ukrainian front about one year ago.

Instead of a hate campaign against the commissars and Jews, the positive German intentions toward a better future of all Caucasian people was emphasized and also German respect for them. As Hummel and I learned somewhat later, the reason was that, unlike the Ukraine, the German Army was running the show in the Caucasus and not the so called "Golden Pheasants."[75] We shall have more to say about this later.

I composed a special leaflet to be dropped over Georgia, which addressed questions about the Georgian communists. I actually expressed, in this leaflet, the view of the majority in "Bergmann"; that should we occupy Georgia, no one would be in jeopardy just because they belonged to the Communist Party, unless they had the blood of innocent people on their hands. I thought it important to convey this information to the Georgian people as soon as possible so they knew where they stood. This may have prevented a panic reaction among the communists as well as a possible vendetta by the embittered anticommunists, against the communists instead of unifying all Georgians. Such leaflets bore no personal signature but were issued by the German Army and as such, it was reasonable to assume that they would carry considerable weight among the Georgian people. After approximately two weeks, Hummel and I left Mariupol for "Bergmann" which was already fighting on the Caucasus front line.

On our way there we had to stop in some city (possibly Donetsk?) in order to change airplanes and were invited to the officers' casino for lunch in army headquarters. There I was introduced to a countryman of mine, Niko (Nikoloz) Nakashidze, an emigre from Berlin, who now worked as an important interpreter in some army headquarters. He greeted me with genuine warmth and told me that he had been

---

75- Nickname for the Nazi civilian bureaucrats who administered the occupied Eastern territories, except for the Caucasus. They were notorious for mistreating the population.

a close friend of my uncle, Grisha (Grigol) Tevzadze during the good old days in Kutaisi.[76] This friendship continued after Uncle Grisha had returned from Russia where he had graduated (St. Petersburg or Moscow) from law as well as a military school of Pavlov.

"We had a marvelous time in Kutaisi," said Niko, "as young students. Your father invited us to good restaurants and always paid the bill. You know why?" he asked. I had to confess that I did not know. "Well," he said, "that's because he wanted to marry your mother, Vera—Grisha's sister—and needed Grisha's 'vote' in this matter. And now," he said, "you are declaring amnesty for the Georgian communists—just like that," and he threw his hands up; we both broke out in genuine loud laughter.

Obviously Nakashidze had read the leaflet I had composed in Mariupol. "This is the view of the majority in 'Bergmann,'" I responded, "which includes representatives of all political parties and also those without party affiliation. Now, we should like to know, Sir, where do you stand concerning this matter?" Still laughing, he gently nodded his head in a sign that he was with us.[77]

It was rather difficult for me to part from Niko Nakashidze after such a short visit. He brought back to my memory many dear names from the past and displayed so much warmth toward me. It was, however, not the last time I saw Niko, neither during nor after the war.

The headquarters of "Bergmann" was located in Russkaia II, somewhat north of the city Mozdok, in North Caucasus and this is where Hummel and I landed on a nearby dirt road, flown in by a Fieseler Fi 156 Storch (Stork) kindly provided for us by "Air Force #4." This was an amazing light transport aircraft capable of landing and taking off on a very short runway. For a moment, we both felt like V.I.P.s to have been shown such courtesy by "Air Force #4." Russkaia II was a small settlement on a prairie with a few peasant houses, each of them had small private lots, growing vegetables, sunflowers and corn. They were strategically arranged alongside a long irrigation canal (or perhaps a natural stream), a real lifeline in the prairie. The soil appeared reasonably fertile and the kolkhoz (the collective farm) or sovkhoz (the soviet farm) was a short driving distance from us. In the far south during good weather, the Caucasus Mountains were visible. The city of Mozdok and the river Terek were between us and the foothills of those magnificent giants.

The headquarters of "Bergmann" was housed in a typical building seen in Ukraine because our hosts were the Ukrainian settlers in North Caucasus. We

---

76- Second largest city in Georgia, considered an old cultural center.
77- Incidentally, many years after the war. a visitor from Georgia told me that such leaflets had been dropped over Tbilisi, probably during September or October 1942.

reported to Oberländer and von Kutzschenbach about our experience in Mariupol and in turn were briefed about the current state of affairs: Oberländer had visited our "neighbors," the 13th Panzer Division and the Panzer Corps. He also had open, ongoing communication with the headquarters of the Army Group South and also with General Köstring, the "General in charge of Caucasian Affairs," and his adjutant von Herwarth, whom I remembered very well from our meeting in Luttensee, Bavaria, not so long ago. The "Bergmann" companies had been assigned to the different areas of the long Caucasus front. For instance, the 1st and 5th Companies (Georgian), south of Mozdok; 3rd Company (Azerbaijan) in Kurskaia; 2nd Company (North Caucasian) in Malka; 4th Company (Georgian) in Baksan. We already had war casualties.

Oberländer obviously had to travel a great deal and von Kutzschenbach and I also found ourselves constantly on the move. This included not only visiting "Bergmann" companies (I personally spent several days with most of them) but also visiting P.O.W. camps within the territory of the Army Group South and more often the camps in the Mozdok and Georgievsk areas because of their size and strategically important location where most of the P.O.W.s would congregate. We were checking living conditions, nutrition and possible abuses of the P.O.W.s. Oberländer and I were firm believers in physical fitness; so when our busy schedule permitted, we jogged along the stream, usually early in the morning. At times we would run into a flock of sheep—moving slowly and grazing. The shepherd would watch us in confusion, unable to figure out whom we were chasing. I loved such a rustic scene and during the night while thinking about various problems and if I had trouble falling asleep, I would visualize the shepherd and his flock. The owner of the house we had occupied, contrary to my expectation, was pleased to have us because he liked Oberländer, who loved to talk Russian with the country folks as his equals. He would discuss their problems and solutions with them, and indeed was helpful whenever possible. He was immensely popular with indigenous people, be it in the Caucasus or Crimea. He was a vocal advocate for abolishment of the collective farms and restoration of the right for private property and was a believer of the market oriented economy and full human rights for the indigenous population.

I think Oberländer was a farmer at heart; he welcomed any opportunity to chop wood, work in the garden or carry out other similar chores. This is probably why he also affectionately referred to one of his sons, Dieter, as "das Bäuerchen"—"the little farmer." Indeed, after the war, the Oberländers settled in Augsburg for a number of years. Next to their house a respectable sized garden was immediately arranged. The professor and his three sons all worked there and grew enough potatoes and vegetables, not only for their family of seven but also enough to share with their neighbors.

German Army policy in occupied North Caucasus was much different from the inhuman behavior the Nazis displayed in other occupied Eastern territories, to which we already have referred. The reason was that Hitler apparently did not have any territorial design on the Caucasus as he did toward other occupied territories. He was only interested in the Caucasian oil and the geostrategic position of the Caucasus for further expansion to the near and middle east. Moreover, according to their paranoid delusion of grandeur, the Nazis accepted the Caucasian people better since they were non Slavic and also considered by them to be Aryans. (Whatever that meant, especially after looking at the picture of Goebbels.)[78]

The situation was adroitly used by the German military as well as some civilians involved in Caucasus affairs, who were in resistance to Hitler's disastrous policies and who desperately tried to bring about change. The most effective and organizing member of this group, among the military, was Colonel Claus von Stauffenberg. He was Head of the Organization Section of the Army High Command (O.K.H.) to whom, as mentioned earlier, Hans von Herwarth had been seconded as a special associate. The others were the Commander in Chief of the Southern Army (Group A), Field Marshal von Kleist, (who had replaced Field Marshal von List); the Quartermaster General of the Army, General Wagner; Lieutenant Colonel Hans von Altenstadt (who under General Wagner was nominally responsible for the military administration of the occupied Soviet territories).

Taking advantage of Hitler's plans toward the Caucasus (or in a way the absence thereof), General Wagner urged Hitler to make "public declaration about political intentions in the Caucasus, guarantee of full political independence, in close military and economic co-operation with the Great German Reich."[79] Hitler agreed and issued a directive authorizing the Army Group A commander to be in complete charge of Caucasus, (subject to co-ordination with Göring and Rosenberg). He also authorized the furtherance of indigenous puppet regimes among the Caucasian nationalities. Now it was left to Stauffenberg, Altenstadt and Bräutigam to work out a detailed agreement.[80]

Among the civilians the most important contributors were: the representatives of the Ostministerium Professor Gerhard von Mende, ("protector of the Caucasian People"), Otto Bräutigam, and Dr. Otto Schiller, a specialist in Soviet agriculture and former member of the German Embassy in the Soviet Union.[81] This

---

78- The German consideration for pleasing Turkey, who had been an advocate of the Muslim people of the Caucasus, may also have been a factor.

79- Alexander Dallin, *German Rule in Russia*, quoting Wagner "Notizen fur Führer–Vortrag, September 1942," and Hitler directive, September 8, 1942. DW/AA-CRS.

80- Alexander Dallin, *German Rule in Russia*, p. 240.

81- Alexander Dallin, *German Rule in Russia*; Hans von Herwarth, *Against Two Evils*; Alexander

group was further fortified by two great experts on the U.S.S.R., General Köstring and his adjutant, Captain and diplomat von Herwarth.

Stauffenberg was able to get General Köstring to agree to serve and to have him assigned to the Caucasus as the General in Charge of Caucasian Affairs. In this capacity, Köstring also became the Inspector of the indigenous volunteer military troops in the Caucasus. In order to do this, Stauffenberg sent Herwarth to see General Köstring, who in his retirement resided in Berlin.

At first, the General refused to participate in such a venture because of his disappointment and aversion toward Hitler and the Nazi leadership in general. For many years Köstring had tried to improve relations between his country and the Soviet Union and had been counseling Hitler against the war, in vain. The following is an excerpt from Herwarth's account.

"I spoke of the brutality with which the Nazis were treating the former Soviet troops and the necessity of his intervention to alleviate further suffering. I also told him about the widespread feeling on the front that Germany could not expect to defeat the Soviet Union alone, but would have to make use of the strong desire of the people of the U.S.S.R. to overthrow Stalin. I argued as forcefully as I could that Köstring alone was in a position to alleviate the suffering of many millions of people, not only those Red Army soldiers who had come over to the German side but also the civilian population of the occupied territories. If he did not help, he would be personally responsible for the loss of thousands of lives. At length, Köstring changed his mind and consented to join Stauffenberg in his endeavor. Leaving Köstring, I went at once to Schulenburg, who was delighted at the prospect of his old friend being reactivated for so worthy an effort. He is absolutely the right man in the right place, Schulenburg exclaimed and promised to do whatever he could to assist us."[82]

Thus the three friends from the German Embassy in Moscow; ex Ambassador Schulenburg; his military attaché Köstring and the Ambassador's secretary Herwarth were again united in a new challenging cause little more than a year after the closure of their Embassy in Moscow. According to Herwarth, when Köstring and Stauffenberg first met, there was instant "chemistry" and mutual admiration established between these two splendid officers.

Alexsiev, *Soviet Nationalities in German Wartime Strategy, 1941–1946*, Santa Monica, Calif.: Rand Corporation, 1982.

82- Hans von Herwarth, *Against Two Evils*, pp. 221–224.

Preceding the Caucasus offensive the German troops of the Southern Army (The Army Group A) were ordered as follows;

1. The population of Caucasus should be treated as friends.
2. Mountaineers desiring to abolish the collective farms should not be interfered with.
3. Reopening of houses of worship should be allowed.
4. Private property to be respected and should it be necessary to requisition goods, they should be paid for.
5. The confidence of the indigenous population should be won by excellent conduct and behavior.
6. All necessary measures causing hardship to the population should be justified and explained to them.
7. The honor of the Caucasus women to be especially respected.[83]

Accordingly, the guidelines issued for the Armed Forces propaganda and the military administration clearly reflected this different German attitude toward the people of the Caucasus. Hummel and I also unmistakably felt this positive direction while helping with the propaganda leaflets in Mariupol on the Sea of Azov, as has already been noted.

The presence of General Köstring and his adjutant Herwarth in the Caucasus was of great importance for a more effective application of this new German policy on an ongoing basis. Field Marshal von Kleist could not have wished for better advisers and helpers for implementing his Caucasus Policy than Köstring and Herwarth. They both kept a low profile, were all over the territory, well informed and had appropriate suggestions to make at the right time. Besides being specialists of the Soviet Union, they also cared for the people there; a very happy combination in such business, indeed. Kleist also shared such feelings and being further stimulated by Köstring, he issued an order for the German soldiers in his Army Group A. It called for behaving toward the indigenous population as if they were on maneuvers in their own country—Germany. Kleist also insisted on equal treatment of non ethnic inhabitants of the Caucasus, such as Russians, Ukrainians, Cossacks, etc. Forced recruiting of the people by Sauckel[84] was not permitted, local self-government was promoted, the land was returned to the people, many collective farms were abolished and others replaced by co-operatives—according to the plan of Otto Schiller, an agrarian expert.

83- Alexander Dallin, *German Rule in Russia*, pp. 240–241, quoting (Heeresgruppe A) Befel an allen im Kaukasus eingesetzten Truppen July 1942; Alexander Alexsiev, *Soviet Nationalities in German Wartime Strategy, 1941–1946*.

84- He was in charge of securing labor from the Soviet populace, using most inhuman methods.

Thanks to all the above measures, the population of North Caucasus remained friendly toward the Germans and the partisan movement never flourished there. They encountered only small, isolated partisan groups composed of party and N.K.V.D. officials, which never enjoyed the support of the population.[85] A distinctive quality in Kleist's character was revealed in his attitude toward the SS. To quote from Dallin,

> "The role which the SS was permitted to play in the Caucasus was narrowly circumscribed. The Security Service had its 'action teams' on the spot and they were responsible for brutality and abuse. Yet withal the military command managed to keep them more successfully reined-in than had either civilian or army authorities farther north. Even the SS combat units, such as the Wiking Division, were quickly slapped down by Kleist when they sought to obey orders from SS Headquarters in Berlin."[86]

The Jews still had to endure unspeakable suffering in the Caucasus since SS Security Service was under the direct orders of Himmler. But Köstring, "Bergmann's" Oberländer and Bräutigam, with support from Kleist were able at least to save the Jewish mountaineers—Tats, who had already been marked for extermination by the SS. Since all three above-named persons were recognized specialists of the Soviet Union, their argument that the Tats were of a Jewish religious faith but ethnically just ordinary Caucasus mountaineers was finally accepted. Incidentally, there was strong grassroot support for helping the Jews among the Caucasian population.

In gratitude, the Tats presented Oberländer and some other officers of "Bergmann" sheep skin coats, handmade by them as a gift. I not only proudly wore mine but especially appreciated it while traveling on horseback after the onset of cold weather.

In spite of a decree by Kleist urging humane treatment of the population and P.O.W.s, considerable violations of the order did occur. Therefore, Köstring, Herwarth, Oberländer and all of us in "Bergmann" had to be alert and intervene at once. More serious matters were reported to Kleist by these three. I shall mention only three examples out of many, each of them of a somewhat different nature.

First, in the P.O.W. camp Georgievsk, in addition to inadequate food and unacceptable sanitary conditions, the guards were "keeping order" by letting the police dogs chase the hungry and weak P.O.W.s, who could not even get decent rest. There were incidences of dysentery which could have spread to many other P.O.W.s. The commandant was an elderly army officer (I believe a major) who had no idea what was going on in his domain and frankly did not care to know.

85- Alexander Alexsiev, *Soviet Nationalities in German Wartime Strategy, 1941–1946*, p. 24.
86- Alexander Dallin, *German Rule in Russia*, p. 243.

He delegated this difficult task to the guards and perhaps one or two non-commissioned officers.

Von Kutzschenbach and I did not conceal our bewilderment from the Major, but we could not move him in a positive direction. He would have rather not let us see the P.O.W.s to begin with, but we had been authorized to do so. I then spoke to many of them, especially of Caucasian origin among them a number of Georgians, whose faces lit up when they heard encouraging words in Georgian. We obtained some food in the city and left it with them. We also told them that we would be back very soon and conditions would improve in their camp.

Next Kutzschenbach and I spoke to the German guards, informing them that the countrymen of the P.O.W.s were fighting at that very moment on Terek, Malgobek, Baksan and nearby Nalchik. When they hear about how their countrymen are being treated in Georgievsk, there will be big trouble; we shall come back to verify positive changes. After hearing our report, Oberländer visited the camp himself. He also got nowhere with the major, whereupon Oberländer initiated steps for the major's removal with success.

In the P.O.W. camp of Mozdok, I observed how a Ukrainian auxiliary guard took the boots of a P.O.W. who was sitting on the ground, too scared to object. As we found out, it was common practice, and the guardsmen sold the boots at a good profit on the market. It was hard to imagine that a human being would do this to a fellowman. The guards knew that the P.O.W. had no chance of surviving without his boots because of the pending long march northwest and especially during the approaching winter.

I could not refrain from grabbing that "guardian" and shaking him until his hat fell off his head. I ordered him loud and clear to return the boots to the rightful owner at once, which he did. Then I took both of them to the camp commandant—a captain. I introduced myself as a liaison officer from "Bergmann" and briefed him about the odious incident that had just taken place. The captain turned out to be a decent man; he also knew about "Bergmann's" two companies which were "dug in" at the front, not so far from the city of Mozdok, establishing the bridgehead on the river Terek. The commandant appreciated our making him aware of the existing situation and at once promised to fire the guilty auxiliary guardsman, setting an example for others, and investigate in depth for possible similar or other misdeeds. I enjoyed observing the P.O.W.'s face now. With his boots on again, he must have felt ten feet tall.

Oberländer had requested and received the order from Kleist to assign one Caucasian "Bergmann" soldier to each P.O.W. camp in the Caucasus in an advisory capacity to the camp commandant. This "Bergmann" observer on behalf of P.O.W.s was actually stationed on the camp territory and usually was a Georgian emigre from France. The presence of such a multi-lingual liaison man pleased almost all German commandants since they were of real help to them in the proper running of the P.O.W. camp. Moreover, one elderly Prussian officer, now a commandant, enjoyed practicing French with his new helper. This was in the true tradition of "der Alte Fritz,"[87] who actually spoke better French than German. As far as the P.O.W.s were concerned, they felt much more secure being able to communicate in their native languages (Russian or Georgian) through the liaison person to the German commandant. Abused P.O.W.s were rare in such camps and the living conditions much more tolerable. This experiment was entirely successful, and thanks to it many lives were saved.

Some years after the war, I received a number of letters of appreciation from former P.O.W.s for the help rendered to them. Two letters among them were from the former inmates of the Georgievsk camp, Iason Iordanishvili, writing from Paris and Ilusha Amshikashvili from Israel. I was very pleased since the letters appeared to be a sincere and spontaneous expression of their feelings. (They are interesting enough to be included in the author's archive.) I am afraid they gave me more credit than I really deserve but if we did achieve success, it was thanks to the atmosphere created by outstanding Germans such as Stauffenberg, Kleist, Köstring, Oberländer and Herwarth.

A terrible and criminal violation against Kleist's order about the P.O.W.s occurred during the retreat of the Army Group A from the Caucasus in January–February 1943.[88] "Bergmann" was part of the 17th Army. Early in February 1943, the unit was getting close to Taman, at the western end of the Kuban Peninsula. With an Azerbaijani lieutenant (probably Kerim Aleskirov), we were trailing one of "Bergmann's" retreating companies on horseback. We noticed a number of dead P.O.W.s laying on the side of the road. As we increased our speed, we could hear sporadic shots. We finally caught up with a group of P.O.W.s barely retreating on foot, direction west. A smaller group of prisoners could not even keep up with them and a couple of them were sitting on the frozen ground. A German sergeant was shouting at the top of his voice to get up and start walking but they were not able to. The sergeant then took aim with his rifle at one of the two, but our ungodly loud shout, "Halt!" stopped him

---

87- Frederick the Great, King of Prussia in the eighteenth century, adored by the officers and soldiers.

88- Kleist's Army, Group A, consisted of the 1st Panzer Army and the 17th Army. Retreat was unavoidable after the defeat of General Paulus's 6th Army by the Soviets in Stalingrad and the Soviets were menacing Rostov on the river Don. Kleist managed to withdraw the 1st Panzer Army through Rostov before the Soviets could cut it off. But the 17th Army was cut off in Kuban from the other German forces. The Red Army threw eight armies against Kleist but he repelled them and held the Kuban line. He was able to evacuate the 17th Army to Crimea in good order and time. (*The World Almanac of World War II.*)

from shooting. He explained that he had his orders to do so in such instances from his commandant—"What else could one do with such P.O.W.s on retreat?"

We told him that we were officers from "Bergmann" and authorized to visit the P.O.W.s and we were amending his previous orders and going to help find a solution for those who could no longer walk. The sergeant was hesitant inasmuch as he easily detected our foreign accent but we jammed him with our horses and were so furious that he, at least for now, abandoned further killing of those unfortunate P.O.W.s who could no longer walk.

Then I told the Azerbaijani officer that I would remain on the spot and he should ride and catch up with our company and ask the German company chief to come at once to our assistance.

This, indeed, took place and the shooting did not resume.[89] We were all terribly upset in "Bergmann" because of the shooting of the P.O.W.s. I could not sleep that night and I thought of Leo Tolstoy's *War and Peace*, where he also depicts the retreat of Napoleon's "Grand Army" from Russia. The Russian prisoners who fell behind were also shot by French guards. There was a prisoner's howling dog who stayed on the spot with his dead master.

Herwarth was informed of "Bergmann's" observation of shooting the exhausted P.O.W.s by their guards. He reported this directly to Field Marshal von Kleist. Kleist was infuriated and gave immediate orders to stop such crimes.[90] A considerable number of P.O.W.s in the camps volunteered to join "Bergmann," especially before the Red Army victory in Stalingrad and the German retreat. But one had to be careful because there were advantages and disadvantages in it for both sides—P.O.W.s and "Bergmann." Yes, "Bergmann" could use the men because of some combat losses and also the plan to expand "Bergmann" to the size of a full regiment. But a new recruit had to be properly motivated and fit for it. The Georgian visitors from "Bergmann" in the P.O.W. camps had great advantage in being able to address their countrymen P.O.W.s in their native tongue, which practically no one else but the Georgians understood.

Therefore, a frank two-way exchange of views was possible, given the feature

---

89- I have consulted Professor Oberländer's diary and his manuscript concerning this matter. According to them, on February 8, 1943, shortly before reaching Taman, in the village of Korshevski, one part of "Bergmann" had made temporary quarters. One large group of the P.O.W.s was passing by and fifty to seventy of them were not strong enough to go on. A sergeant wanted to shoot them with the help of the Ukrainian Commando Detachment, but this was prevented by "Bergmann's" First Lieutenant Zag, who was stationed there. He ordered the village elder (Starosta) to distribute the exhausted P.O.W.s among the villagers, to feed and care for them. After five days, exactly on the hour, to have them gather at the commandant's quarters. This is exactly what they did and they were able to walk again, and each P.O.W. carried a small food package with him for "on the road."

90- Hans von Herwarth, *Against Two Evils*, p. 237.

of confidentiality. For instance, after introducing myself to the P.O.W.s, I would explain to them about "Bergmann" and what it stood for. It was followed by a brief review of Georgian past history including her sovereignty, how she lost it and our prospect for regaining it. Then our present relationship with the German Army and with "our" "Bergmann" Germans was explained. No derogatory reference was ever made to the Russian people but Bolshevism and its imperialism was criticized. The point was also made about the Jews, who had been a part of Georgia for centuries and always loyal to Georgia and we consider them to be our brothers. Some Germans do not feel the same way about the Jews as we do, but we Georgians should never abandon or betray the Jews.

It was also emphasized that "Bergmann" was dedicated to improving conditions in the P.O.W. camps and the Commander in Chief, the Field Marshal himself was also committed to this. Therefore, do not hurry in deciding to join "Bergmann" because of a desire to get out of the P.O.W. camp. We are a tough combat unit and most likely will have to fight in difficult terrain where one may easily get killed. Moreover, "Bergmann" wants only such men who are motivated and believe in what it stands for. With such an approach, I intended to dampen their first felt enthusiasm and have them better realize the real situation.[91]

91- See author's archive. Iason Iordanishvili's (from Paris) and Ilusha Amshikashvili's (from Israel) letters reflect the features of my address to the P.O.W.s in P.O.W. camps.

8

PATRIOTS AND DEFECTORS

We did not hesitate to accept volunteers such as Artillery First Lieutenant Irakli Macharashvili in the Mozdok P.O.W. camp. It was a curious situation since he defected to our side not only with his artillery battery but also with his wife, Eva. The first lieutenant appeared to be a good artillery officer but in my opinion he also had to be a sorcerer; how else could he have "smuggled" his wife here?

Kutzschenbach was as curious as I and we both went to see them. Irakli was a Georgian, well educated, a bright young man from Tbilisi. Eva was of Russian descent, also from Tbilisi and very attractive. The P.O.W. camp Mozdok had never seen anything like this before and the reaction to it was visible. For instance, the commandant now paid more attention to the details in his camp. I suddenly noticed my boots to be muddy and von Kutzschenbach, with his monocle in place, obviously enjoyed a long conversation with Eva and Irakli. (In beautiful Russian, I might add, since neither Eva nor the Baron, spoke Georgian, to speak of.)

Our opinion about this remarkable P.O.W. couple was favorable, therefore, Oberländer accepted Irakli in "Bergmann" with Eva at his side. This may have created some logistic problems but with Oberländer's and Kutzschenbach's good will and resourcefulness, things were arranged.

We decided to keep them near the "Bergmann" headquarters and gradually introduce Irakli to our particulars. He accompanied me on the trips which helped him to meet the other officers on the front line, and he made friends easily. Irakli had the unique ability to "organize things." For instance, with our German occupation money, in remote places, he somehow manged to get fresh food for us; I could never have done it.

Unexpectedly, we soon got another young volunteer Georgian lady in "Bergmann," Miss Nadia (Nazibrola) Pataraia. The best I can recall, she apparently had been in a Soviet auxiliary paramilitary unit of some sort. In the process of war, her unit somehow had disintegrated. She was making her way alone, on foot, through the dusty prairie north of Nalchik (or Mozdok) without the faintest idea of what to expect next. The German troops were passing by her in order to take positions, and then she heard some of those soldiers speaking Georgian. She thought that she was hallucinating like a lost traveler in the desert of the Sahara. Nevertheless, she ran after them shouting, "Are you really Georgians?" She soon found herself surrounded and was cheered and greeted by the "Bergmann" soldiers in Georgian. She was adopted on the spot by "Bergmann," and all those tough warriors pledged to her that she could count on them as on her own brothers.

The newly found brothers, however, soon found out about their own logistical limitations in caring for their newly found sister. So, of course, they referred her to "Bergmann" headquarters with the "highest possible recommendation." What to do? We were still too long a distance away from Georgia to return Nadia to her family. So we left her with us to do some work around the "house." Nadia was a cute young lady in her early twenties surrounded by men, and she was treated with utmost respect and consideration. One unfortunate German officer of a lower rank and somewhat silly disposition had tried to step out of this established protocol. His amorous advance was brought to a screechy stop by a slap in his face from "a cute little girl." We tried to hide this incident from Oberländer, knowing that he would not be amused by such conduct by an officer, who, incidentally, had already been punished by Nadia.

Meanwhile, the military situation on the Caucasus front was not totally clear and by no means uniform. For instance, on the west flank, German attack had met with stiff resistance, around Maykop[92] and along the Black Sea coast, direction toward Tuapse and Sukhumi.[93] The Germans took Maykop but suffered heavy losses, and General Konrad's mountain units could not take the city of Sukhumi.

The German 1st Panzer and the 17th Army were more successful further east in the basin of the river Terek and its tributaries such as the rivers Malka, Baksan, Cherek, Urukh and Ardon. For instance, in spite of heavy fighting by the end of August, the city of Mozdok[94] was taken. The Germans crossed the river Terek south of Mozdok and established a bridgehead there. The town of Terek was captured

---

92- City in the Adige Autonomous Region surrounded by important oil fields.

93- Sukhumi is the Capital of the Abkhaz Autonomous Soviet Socialist Republic within the Georgian Soviet Socialist Republic, and a part of it.

94- Mozdok is a small town of the North Ossetian Autonomous Soviet Socialist Republic.

during that second part of September, then Malgobek[95] in early October, Nalchik[96] in the later part of October, and the four Soviet divisions were put in jeopardy.

The headquarters of "Bergmann" was now moved to Nalchik. In the beginning of November, the Germans secured Alagir on the river Ardon, only thirty miles west of Ordzhonikidze,[97] which was threatened because of that. But the Soviet resistance around Ordzhonikidze stiffened and the German 3rd Panzer Corps were slowed down and brought under considerable pressure.

The elements from the 11th and 17th Army advanced not far from Novorossiysk and the 1st Panzer Army came near Grozny, but no further progress was made. By the middle of October, offensive actions had been suspended in the Caucasus except for the mid-reaches of the Terek basin because of the raging of crucial battle for Stalingrad.[98] For now, the essentially stable front positions had been established by "Bergmann" and its neighboring German troops, within the area of the river Terek basin.

There were well organized trenches everywhere, with heavy machine gun "nests," and excellent artillery support was also provided from the rear. Combat activities now consisted mainly of artillery duels, patrolling, scouting and brief skirmishes between the opposing forces. Rather heavily mined zones were often prepared and utilized by the Soviet forces, in order to protect the potential approach to their trenches.

It was one of my routines to visit the Georgian companies and time permitting, spend a few days with each of them. We had much to talk about with the soldiers, non-commissioned officers, as well as officers, Germans or Georgians, and some of it I had to discuss later with Oberländer and von Kutzschenbach. One of the officers of the 5th Company, German First Lieutenant Kurt Holy had been killed in action. He was an excellent officer, much respected and popular, and his soldiers were understandably depressed. Therefore, I decided to stay with them for a couple of days.

At that time, a German officers aspirant was temporarily in charge. (The best I can spell his name is Pahlen, or Paalen.) He was a courteous soft-spoken gentleman and we had a long "broad spectrum" conversation. He suddenly asked me if I would like to go with a small detachment of his soldiers on a scouting mission as he felt my presence there would lift their spirits. I said, of course I would. The objective was to get as close as possible to the enemy trenches and perhaps capture

---

95- A town south of oil producing Mozdok, located in North Ossetian Autonomous Republic.

96- Nalchik was the capital of Kabardino-Balkar Autonomous Soviet Socialist Republic, located between the Rivers Baksan and Cherek.

97- The Capital of North Ossetian Autonomous Soviet Socialist Republic, located further south on the river Terek. The Georgian Military Highway, which begins in Tbilisi, Georgia, terminates there.

98- *The World Almanac of World War II.* For chronology and other data, this has been very helpful.

an enemy soldier to obtain necessary information from him. To get there one had to maneuver between the mined zones after dark. Pahlen and his sergeant had been carefully observing the enemy's mining process through field glasses and were aware of where the mine-free areas were. This was also confirmed by observing the Soviet soldiers crossing these places without inhibition. Accordingly, a diagram was made showing the dangerous and the free areas.

The sergeant with a small group of soldiers had already scouted out close to the enemy positions a couple of times but were unable to capture any prisoners so far. The sergeant in question was a Georgian, Andro, from the province of Chiatura.[99] (I am unable to recall his last name.) He and his soldiers from the scouting group were introduced to me, we had some discussions and I was impressed by them. But I also thought, without saying it, that for such an undertaking one has to have the eyes of a cat and the nose of a shepherd dog.

We left shortly after midnight, the estimated distance to the enemy trenches was one kilometer and the mine fields were commencing probably at one-half kilometer. A clear sky and the moon were of some help in finding our way. Andro was leading us, and I followed him after a short distance. He was really good and hardly needed a compass or better light. He motioned us to stop, came toward us and whispered, "Those are the mines to the right and left of us." We proceeded slowly for another fifteen or twenty minutes and probably were not more than one hundred or so yards from the enemy trenches when Andro stopped again and went down on his knees. What happened? He noted that the ground became soft under his feet all of a sudden, and he was now gently exploring it.

After a while, he approached me again and reported, "Sir, the area ahead is also mined now; it was not so when we were here a week ago. There may be some other changes as well that we are not aware of. The only safe way would be to turn around and go back to our own base; but we will do whatever you want us to do." I would never disagree with a reasonable man like Andro, who was also a specialist of scouting and obviously had incredible sensory perception, thanks to which we all returned to our trenches in one piece.[100] Pahlen thought that probably the

---

99- An important manganese mining center.
100- During February or March of 1945, Andro visited me in Berlin (a grossly destroyed city at that time) and just a couple of months before the German surrender. He had recuperated from his wound in a military hospital in Thuringia (middle part of Germany). There he met and fell in love with a young German lady. "Get married, Andro, and add some German ending to your last name and live happy thereafter," I said. Andro was blond with blue eyes—he looked "Nordic Germanic," he had also acquired German military manners. No doubt his German girlfriend would help him to further polish his German and he could easily pass for a German sergeant. "That way you may escape Stalin's persecution. But one day, Andro," I added, "things may change in Russia and you may see Georgia again." I do hope that he survived this last phase of the war and what happened thereafter.

hostile side had noticed our previous scouting activities and therefore enlarged the mining zone.

German First Lieutenant Weyh, from the newly formed "Bergmann" cavalry squadron was less fortunate. While riding his mount near the previous battle zone left by the Soviets, near the river Cherek, a mine exploded under the horse, killing it but Weyh survived without significant injuries. "Bergmann" had lost two hundred people on the Caucasus front—dead, wounded and sick—thus our number was reduced to nine hundred men.

Many Soviet P.O.W.s of Caucasian origin had been taken on the front within the river Terek basin. A number of them volunteered to join "Bergmann" and were accepted after careful screening. Presence of the "Bergmann" soldier-observer, stationed in each P.O.W. camp as an adviser to the commandant was crucial for the recruiting process. Due to the influx of volunteers, the number of "Bergmann" soldiers tripled—up to 2,883 men. A total of twelve companies and two cavalry squadrons were formed.[101]

Increased requirement of the leaders and instructors had to be overcome. Out of the two cavalry squadrons, one was purely Georgian. The commander was First Lieutenant Mikheil Dadiani, assisted by his relative, Master Sergeant Archil Dadiani and many other Georgian emigres.[102] This squadron consisted of the North Caucasians, such as Kabardino-Balkars, Karachays and Circassians. We were proud of these new squadrons and felt that after adequate cadre of the indigenous officers had been prepared, the other "Bergmann" units would also be organized on the same principle.

"Bergmann" had now reached the strength of a regiment, not a small accomplishment, for which mainly two personalities were responsible—Admiral Canaris and Captain Professor Dr. Oberländer, with encouragement from the General in charge of Caucasian Affairs, Köstring and his associate, Captain Hans von Herwarth. General Köstring and Captain von Herwarth visited us frequently in "Bergmann" and on such occasions, we exchanged views and information of mutual interest. They recognized "Bergmann" as a successful experiment not only on the battlefield but also as contributing toward the realization of other goals. These were improving conditions for the P.O.W.s, gaining friendship of the local populace and exercising

---

101- *Bergmann Memoirs*. Put together, edited and published by the authors from the fellowship under the literary guidance of Heinz Beher, Margaretenstrasse. 44-8033 Krailling near Munich, July 1, 1983. Printed by Josef M. Greska GMCH, Munich. B.R.G.

102- For instance, David (Dodik) Chavchavadze, Giorgi (Goglik) Vachnadze, Aliosha Abashidze, Shota Gedevanishvili, Irakli Kalandarishvili, Bidzina Eristavi, Elizbar Makashvili. First Lieutenant Weyh supervised this squadron for a brief period only. The second cavalry squadron was formed shortly after the first one, under the command of First Lieutenant Weyh; Lieutenant Dodik Chavchavadze was second—to be an alternate chief.

considerable psychological impact across the front line. When the Red Army soldiers of Caucasian origin learned about our presence, many of them deserted to us; but none of us from "Bergmann" fled to the Soviet side.

During one of their visits. Köstring and Herwarth told us about the arrival in the Caucasus of the Armenian, Azerbaijan, Georgian and North Caucasian field battalions, belonging to their respective legions.[103] One of them, the Georgian Battalion 795 was now in Krupskaia-Ulyanovsk, a village northwest of Nalchik, and was being considered for transfer to the front lines.

Köstring, for some reason, was concerned about this battalion and requested help from "Bergmann." He asked Oberländer to send a team of "Bergmann" Georgians for evaluation of Battalion 795—if it was fit for combat duty. Oberländer, in turn proposed that I put such a team together, head it and visit the battalion; von Kutzschenbach would also go along with us.

Our entire team was excited and curious since never before had we encountered a battalion of the Georgian Legion. The news of our pending visit had traveled faster than us, and when we arrived there the next day (the early part of October), they all expected us and were as curious as we were. Being curious about each other and having common ethnic roots made it simple for us to get acquainted. First of all, von Kutzschenbach and I visited and introduced ourselves to the German commanding officer, First Lt. Schirr.[104] He offered us assistance if needed and extended an invitation for meals with him in the "casino." The commander also introduced us to his Georgian adviser, Shalva Maglakelidze.

Maglakelidze was a middle-aged emigre, tall, impressively handsome with good manners and of great charm. He wore a modified German uniform with non-German epaulets. They were narrow and of silver color. They were obviously designed for the legion; resembling ones that some German interpreters wore. He agreed to meet Kutzschenbach and me that evening. Kutzschenbach wanted to rest a bit, so I proposed to Maglakelidze we stretch our limbs and walk around. He agreed and eventually we stopped at a small riverbank where we sat on large stones.

I told him how rewarding an experience it had been for me to meet the Georgian emigres and make friends among them. With an ironic smile, Maglakelidze

---

103- As noted before, the Caucasian Legions and their field battalions had been organized with herculean efforts by Claus von Stauffenberg, then head of Section II of the Organizational Division of the Army's General Staff O.K.H. Stauffenberg was assisted in this by von Herwarth, in his capacity as an expert on Soviet affairs. "Bergmann," on the other hand, was created by Admiral Canaris's Abwehr section II, part of the High Command of the German Armed Forces O.K.W. Therefore, during the early stage, the Caucasian Legions and "Bergmann" did not have much in common except for ethnic origin and their goal to reestablish sovereignty of the Caucasian nations.

104- At first, I was not able to remember his name but I established it later from Dr. Hoffmann's publication.

started talking at first in parables, then gradually "warmed up" and delivered a blistering "expose" against emigration. Ever so often, he would single out certain individuals for a more detailed attack. Among them were (as I learned later on) some of his old benefactors. In conclusion, according to Maglakelidze, emigration was a group of greedy people without principles or morals who would sell their own country for personal gain. I was stunned and could only say to him that what I just heard from him was a most discouraging thing.

It was time for lunch; I parted from Maglakelidze and went to see the "Bergmann" team. On my way there, I wondered why Maglakelidze told me all of this, who was he really? and what was his game? He hardly knew me. I had more questions than answers about him, which in time I hoped to clarify with the help of our emigres in "Bergmann." Of one thing I was sure, he did not shake my confidence in our emigration. I thought there was something wrong with Maglakelidze.

The members of the "Bergmann" team visiting Battalion 795, in addition to Kutzschenbach and I, included "old" emigres as well as "newcomers," officers, non-commissioned officers and privates.[105] I divided them into smaller groups and assigned each of them to the battalion companies. They were to mingle with their hosts as much as possible and have exposure on a one-to-one basis, as well as with small discussion groups. Our team would meet at the end of each day and again after completion of our intended third or fourth day stay with Battalion 795. Von Kutzschenbach and I visited each company, spoke with as many Germans as possible as well as Georgian officers, sergeants and soldiers including a Georgian doctor who remembered me from Tbilisi.[106]

As was agreed before, Kutzschenbach and I visited Shalva Maglakelidze, the aforementioned Georgian adviser to the battalion's commander, in his apartment. As a host, he was pleasant and charming, not a derogatory word about anyone this time. He told some jokes and interesting stories. One which impressed me most was a touching and sad love story between Iason Gelovani, a married man and once a leader of nobility in Kutaisi,[107] and a young teacher, Nino, from a modest

---

105- They were Akaki Kvitaishvili, Victor Homeriki, Mikheil Kavtaradze, Vaso Shalamberidze, Pavla Vashadze, Shalva Okropiridze, Irakli Macharashvili, Shota Margwelashvili and a few others.

106- An old friend from my school days, Vane Nozadze, worked in a horse-driven supply detachment. Vane wanted to spend as much time with me as possible so I took him along during some of my visits. I was saddened by news of the tragic death of another childhood friend from Tbilisi, Amiran Shalamberidze. He had heard about our pending visit here and was looking forward to seeing me. But that day Amiran had to go on patrolling duty and was killed by what appeared to have been a stray bullet. And speaking of a stray bullet, I almost lost my life a couple of days after Amiran's death. Lieutenant Okropiridze accidentally fired his gun while cleaning it, inside the officers' quarters of our visiting team in Krupskaia-Ulyanovsk. The bullet just nicked the top of my "Bergmann" hat. The entire room froze, Okropiridze was pale as a ghost and I felt that my mother's prayers had saved me once more.

107- The capital city of West Georgia.

background.[108] Looking at our host, I had a feeling he was a master of switching from one personality to another. He did not tell us much about Battalion 795 and if he were aware of any problems there, he obviously chose not to reveal them to Kutzschenbach and me.

However, during the days to follow, our "research" team members, including myself, who mingled with the soldiers and officers, did discover many serious problems. When our work was completed, von Kutzschenbach and I, much to our regret, had to report to Oberländer that Battalion 795 was not fit for combat duty and the reasons for this. Oberländer agreed with us and reported this at once to General Köstring—that the 795 should not, under any circumstances, be taken to the front line for fear of massive defections. Köstring further reported this to the higher military authority at once. Oberländer himself had visited us in Krupskaia-Ulyanovsk during our closing days; he was well informed about the serious situation, and the final report did not surprise him a bit. The "wise old man," General Köstring, had also been briefed by Oberländer right along.

We were all pondering about the best approach in solving the problems of the 795. Meanwhile as incredible as it may seem, on orders of the local front commander, the battalion was taken to the combat line on the river Baksan. Approximately eighty legionnaires defected to the Red Army. Probably not all of them reached their goal, and some of them could have been killed by the Germans, who when noticed defection, opened fire.

The entire Battalion 795 was now surrounded by German tanks, disarmed, and the infuriated military commander of the division wanted to shoot every other man, but then "mellowed" and decided instead to shoot every tenth soldier as a punishment for the desertion of their comrades. General Köstring, who was immediately notified, obtained a substitute order at once from the higher military staff to postpone shooting and informed us in "Bergmann" about it. The entire Battalion 795 had been disarmed, arrested, lodged in tents and some soldiers who were considered most suspicious were locked up in the farmers' underground storage houses. Others had been kept in tents under guard. After the defection of eighty men, the battalion still counted approximately nine hundred soldiers, in other words, only a relatively small minority had changed sides. But, the question of punishment for the remaining "heavy suspects," "lesser suspects" and just how reliable the rest in the battalion were, had to be determined by the Germans.

108- I learned later that Maglakelidze, himself a father of a grown son, had fallen in love with a young Georgian physician, Maro Tsotadze. (His first marriage with a Baltic German lady fell apart.) Perhaps Maglakelidze was identifying his love with the one between Iason and Nino in Kutaisi and that is why he spoke about it with such deep feeling.

The above-mentioned "categories" had already been established by the German crew of 795. Maglakelidze's participation in their effort was never made clear to us. "Sorting out" the battalion that way was indeed helpful but it did not solve the problem—what to do with them? General Köstring wanted the "Bergmann" team to go there again and help him to answer that question. Our mission clearly presumed to save lives and restore the credibility of Battalion 795, if at all possible.

On our arrival in Krupskaia-Ulyanovsk, von Kutzschenbach and I found Shalva Maglakelidze amazingly well composed, considering the major shock he must have sustained during the recent drama that took place in his battalion. Besides the usual pleasantries, he offered us no suggestions of help for our difficult task; nor did he express any appreciation for our desire to help them. The only liaison he had with the legionnaires that we could discern was through Shota Kurtsikidze, a non-commissioned officer, who as I remember, was a secretary and interpreter in the battalion's staff. The German commander had directed his German personnel efficiently but he appeared to be out of touch with the Georgian legionnaires and at a loss to understand why this all took place. He certainly was "no Oberländer," nor was his German crew a match for the one in "Bergmann."

The legionnaires now appeared scared and tired, probably due to inadequate sleep. They were poorly fed, depressed and totally unclear about their future. This was more obvious for the heavy suspects who were lodged in improvised dungeons. I went down there accompanied by several "Bergmann" team members but could hardly see them in the darkness without a flashlight. I received permission from the German officer in charge of the guards to get the inmates outside. As they emerged on the surface, the effect was as if dead men were rising from their graves. Not being able to see at first, they were at a loss. I greeted them after a while and all of a sudden I had a crazy idea as to how to address this group of fifty to sixty people. This is approximately what I said:

> As we all know, the situation is very dangerous especially for you but also for your other comrades. The legionnaires who had defected probably realized very little of the predicament they created for those who did not follow them. We, the Georgians from "Bergmann," came here to help and not to point an accusing finger at anyone. If we succeed in helping you, it will be due to our good reputation and trust we earned in the eyes of the German military, including the Army High Command. They are on our side. This is because we stayed true to our given word and commitment.

Now our "Bergmann" team will be ready to risk its reputation and perhaps even a severe punishment to individual members who will be vouching for you. But for this, you have to first give your word of honor to us that you will not betray us. Then we shall ask our "Bergmann" commander and the Inspector General of the Volunteer Units that they in turn support our suggestion on your behalf at the Army High Staff level. If all goes well, then the Georgians in "Bergmann" have to adopt you gentlemen and be accountable on your behalf. Once you have joined us, you have also joined the cause of defending interests of Georgia, our way—the "Bergmann" way—where the Caucasians and Germans are dedicated together to establish sovereign Caucasian states.

The German Army is supporting our quest, and therefore we have taken an oath of allegiance to the German Armed Forces, and you will have to do the same if you join our unit. What other option do you have? Most likely a military court with an uncertain outcome.

There was a deep silence but I noticed that their eyes were watching my face now and the heads were no longer hanging down—what an improvement. I thought that I shocked them when they finally realized what I had just told them, with somewhat subdued but firm voices, one after another. Then they responded with, "Yes, sir, you can count on us, we promise," just like in a drama of a western movie.

I discussed at once this development with the "Bergmann" team and asked them if they backed me on this decision or not. They all responded with, "yes." I thought, "Dear Lord, I am not only crazy but also have crazy associates, please protect us." Then I went to see von Kutzschenbach who also approved of our decision and both of us discussed this with Professor Oberländer. The Professor was wondering if we, the "Bergmann" Georgians, would be able to handle this one. I said that I felt confident we could if he was willing to take some chance with us—of course he would.

Our team made two additional suggestions pertaining to other legionnaires of 795. First, that those who had been categorized (by their own German personal) as "somewhat suspicious" be converted to the road repair and construction unit with their activity limited to the rear region of the front but otherwise be treated as non combat soldiers. Second, the much larger group of the legionnaires who had not been categorized as "suspects" but were compromised because some of their comrades had defected, should be rehabilitated, retain the name of Battalion 795 and be proud of it. There were excellent people among them, for instance the company chief, Captain Lomtatidze, this is the best I can remember his name. The

Captain, indeed, distinguished himself as a good leader and a brave soldier later on.[109] Professor Oberländer accepted all our suggestions, General Köstring approved of them and obtained permission from Field Marshal von Kleist's Army Group A.

While all of this was going on, the rumor started among the legionnaires that the entire Battalion 795 was to be "adopted" by "Bergmann." We immediately issued the statement that this was not true but our desire was to help those who had been jailed and therefore were proposing to take only them to "Bergmann."

Now that things were clarified and the situation had improved, Maglakelidze made his presence known. Allegedly, he suspected that "Bergmann" intended to "swallow" a "small fish," 795. This strange, paranoid reaction was uncalled for inasmuch as we had explained to him and the German commander beforehand what really was happening. Apparently, Maglakelidze was incredulous and sent his secretary and interpreter, Shota Kurtsikidze to get signatures of the legionnaires expressing their desire to stay in the battalion. The legionnaires Shota had access to for signatures were not in jail in the first place and had already been proposed by Oberländer and Köstring (based on "Bergmann" team recommendation as already noted) to remain as 795. So this unnecessary commotion was difficult to understand for us as well as for the German personnel of 795.[110]

Not with one word had Maglakelidze expressed his gratitude to the "Bergmann" team for its efforts to help "his" Battalion 795. Our team members were furious, especially the old emigres. One of them, Akaki Kvitaishvili, a former major of the Georgian National Guard said that Maglakelidze was an irresponsible adventurer with a king sized ego but without a matching brain. He thought that after what happened in the battalion, Maglakelidze himself, one way or another, was also guilty at least of negligence and deserved to be "shot." (This was Akaki's way of expressing anger, he did not really want him shot.) Some in "Bergmann" especially Victor Nozadze, who was a faithful friend of Maglakelidze, had great admiration for him. Nozadze felt Maglakelidze to be a great Georgian patriot and capable of achieving a great deal for his country. I reserved my final judgment about Maglakelidze while in the Caucasus, since I did not know him adequately. Nevertheless, my impression of him was not favorable during the time of the crisis in Battalion 795.[111]

109- I met the Captain again, a bit longer then one year later. At that time, I was a speaker for the Georgians soldiers including the legionnaires and also a captain myself. Two Georgian captains had much to talk about.

110- One of the "Bergmann" team members had a theory that Maglakelidze did this in order to make it appear that he "saved the Battalion 795."

111- Dr. Joachim Hoffmann discusses the Georgian Colonel S. Maglakelidze in his book *Kaukasien 1942/43: Das deutsche Heer und die Orientvölker der Sowjetunion* (Freiburg: Rombach Verlag, 1991) and notes, "S. Maglakelidze moved to the Soviet Union after the war where he became an unpleasant

Within a week, "Bergmann" incorporated into one of its two newly formed companies stationed in Nalchik a group of men from the Legion Battalion 795. Without an exception they had all had been freed from jail and probably from military court martial for alleged conspiracy or intended mutiny and defection while in a combat zone. I no longer remember their exact number but I estimate about fifty to seventy men. What I remember exactly is waking up every morning wondering if they were still with us or not. But they kept their word and did not betray us when we had to retreat from Caucasus, which were difficult circumstances for all of us.

What went wrong in the Georgian Legion Battalion 795? Mainly, the blame should be laid at the doorstep of the Nazi leadership of Germany. Some other reasons, however, had no direct relationship with the Nazis. For instance, it was very difficult for the high military command to get a sufficient number of suitable German personnel due to an all-out war and heavy losses. The language barrier was serious (in spite of organizing courses for the interpreters). Such a situation opened the door for misunderstandings and animosity during the training of the indigenous soldier and also later. There was a shortage of top-notch quality weapons which also had an adverse effect on the legionnaires' self esteem.

The Battalion's companies had two chiefs, one German officer (or non-commissioned officer) and one indigenous officer. This was not a "healthy" situation, especially if it exceeded a certain time limit such as a period of training. One chief would have been preferable and ideally he had to be an indigenous officer.[112] Again, there was a severe shortage of suitable Caucasian officers. General Köstring, after his initial appointment as inspector general of the Caucasian and Turkish units, was

---

speaker for foreign propaganda of the MGB/KGB in Georgian matters" (Freiburg im Breisgan: Rombach GmbH + Co. Verlagshaus KG in German, 1991, p. 262). As an example of this, Dr. Hoffmann points to Maglakelidze's letter to the editor of *Zaria Vostoka*, a communist newspaper in Tbilisi (December 9, 1954).

S. Maglakelidze's journey from Munich to Soviet land was rather sudden and unexpected— some Georgians from Munich explained to me. He apparently approached Dr. Gogi (Giorgi) Vepkhvadze, trying to recruit him for the Soviet side. Vepkhvadze was not receptive of such a suggestion and he shared this with Datha Vachnadze, a senior emigrant in Munich, who also had a friendly relationship with S. Maglakelidze originating from the times of sovereign Georgia. D. Vachnadze confronted Maglakelidze and wanted an explanation. Maglakelidze disappeared from Munich and resurfaced in East Germany and later in Georgia. He was probably fearful that the American Security Service would find out about his "recruiting" efforts toward Vepkhvadze.

The Soviet government allowed the Georgian Colonel Maglakelidze (who stated that he had even been a German general) to open a law practice and he also received a pension. His wife obtained a position as a physician. This was by far better treatment than was accorded to the rank and file legionnaires who had fallen in Soviet hands, not to mention the treatment of the officers. The former would get many years in the gulag and the latter would most likely be executed.

It was rather amusing that Maglakelidze even managed to circulate the story among the emigres in the west that he had actually been kidnapped by the Soviets.

112- Even if the Germany chief happened to be a non-commissioned officer and the Caucasian chief of the same company was a first lieutenant, the German had the right to override him.

pushing hard to train as many indigenous officers as possible in German military schools. His plan was to replace the German officers by them. As important as those above noted were, still the main culprit of our difficulties was Hitler's cannibalistic Nazi ideology and policy, relentlessly pursued by him and his henchmen, some of which has already been discussed in conjunction with the "Plot in Bergmann" and elsewhere. Important differences between "Bergmann" and the Legion Battalions were:

1. Oberländer had recruited his soldiers during the middle of October 1941, from the P.O.W. camp in Poltava, before the onset of severe winter and because of that his recruits had suffered less. The legionnaires, on the other hand, generally speaking were recruited during the Spring of 1942, after having endured incredible hardships as P.O.W.s during the winter of 1941–1942. Therefore, many of them had a change of heart and felt a great deal of hostility and lack of confidence toward the Germans. Although the conditions for the P.O.W.s began to improve during early 1942, probably some of them joined the Legion to improve their living conditions, especially those convinced "Stalinists" who joined in order "to get even" with the Germans.

2. "Bergmann" was formed on German territory, housed in military quarters. Optimal training facilities and excellent weapons were available to them. The Legion battalions were formed and trained in the German occupied Poland and Ukraine. Observing the inhuman Nazi occupation policy, there had to be an obvious demoralizing effect on the legionnaires, the thought being, "This may also happen in our country should the Germans get there." In addition, the Polish and Ukrainian patriots naturally had tried their best to influence the legionnaires against the Germans; defections did occur and they joined the partisans.

3. The German personnel in "Bergmann" had been thoroughly picked up and nurtured by Oberländer and his associates. They were lectured about the Caucasus and its people and indoctrinated concerning treatment of the Caucasian soldiers on equal terms. This was especially necessary in order to counteract the usual brainwashing of the younger German generation by the Nazis—about supremacy of the "Nordic Germanic race and the inferiority of the people from the east." Unsuitable Germans had been transferred somewhere else by Oberländer, as already noted. The Caucasian Legions could ill afford the "weeding out" process of the "not suitable for

the job" Germans, due to an acute shortage of German personnel.[113]

4. "Bergmann" was blessed by being able to count a disproportionately large number of emigres from France among its soldiers. The importance of them for "Bergmann" was crucial and has already been emphasized. The entire Georgian Legion and the battalions it had created (approximately a total of 14,000 men) could count six emigres, one of them being Maglakelidze.[114] Admiral Canaris, Oberländer, von Kutzschenbach and a number of other Germans, such as Köstring and von Herwarth were able to convey a strong message to the "Bergmann" Caucasians that there existed "Other Germany,"[115] who cared for us and wanted to help our cause. Oberländer and Kutzschenbach kept close personal contact with Caucasian soldiers which was greatly facilitated by their knowledge of the Russian language.[116] Not many Caucasian Legions were able to supply their battalions with such unique personalities. The organizers of Legions had tried very hard to succeed against almost impossible odds and hurdles placed in front of them. The most difficult being Hitler's resistance against the formation of the Legions and his East Policy in general. For a legion to succeed, it is mandatory to have political representation that is recognized by the sponsoring government,[117] but Hitler did not allow them to have this.

The national Georgian flag was hoisted on May 26, 1942,[118] over the Legion's quarters, and the Army order was proclaimed that "From now on the Georgians are going to fight for the freedom of their county." (Excellent but hardly a substitute for political representation.) What helped considerably in reversing the hostile attitude of the Caucasian legionnaires toward the Germans was to witness the German Army's military administration in North Caucasus engineered by von Stauffenberg with humane policy toward the population, P.O.W.s, the agrarian and political reforms. This, for the legionnaires, was a new beginning, almost like conversion to a

---

113- During the fall of 1941, it was easier to secure more suitable Germans than later on. Moreover, initially, "Bergmann" was 1,100 man strong only, as compared to the Caucasian Legions and its battalions with an approximate number of 48,700 Caucasians, requiring more personnel as well as equipment.

114- Others were former officers from the Polish Army, Ivane (Vano) Bakradze, Vassili (Vaso) Indjia, Simon (Siko) Kobiashvili, David (Datha) Lagidze and Dimitri Shalikashvili. As few as they were, their impact on betterment of the Legions' battalions was very significant.

115- This expression was used by one of the leading members of the German resistance, Ulrich von Hassel, in his memoirs.

116- They were not afraid to criticize Nazi policy in the occupied Eastern territories with Caucasian leaders in "Bergmann."

117- For instance, Pilsudski's Legion of Poland during W.W. I.

118- Georgian Independence Day.

new faith demonstrating that, at least, the German Army was on our side.

For the soldiers of "Bergmann," however, it strongly reinforced what we already knew, that helping us there was essentially an army-based "Other Germany." The German Army could not possibly have sent better representatives to the Caucasus than Field Marshal von Kleist, General Köstring with his associate von Herwarth, Professor Captain Oberländer and von Kutzschenbach and "Bergmann" itself—as arranged by Admiral Canaris. Their work had been greatly enhanced by the team of experts from the Ministry of Eastern Affairs: Otto Bräutigam, Professor Gerhard von Mende and Otto Schiller, as has already been noted.

There were some other Georgian Legion Battalions in North Caucasus and the battalions of other Caucasian nationalities as well. At that time, I could not have close enough contact with them to be able to report my observations. This changed considerably as we shall see later. Köstring and Herwarth had an ongoing liaison with all indigenous volunteer units in the Caucasus. Herwarth states that he had witnessed formation of those units while on the staff of General von Gienanth in Poland. It was a feeling of persons involved in the organizing of native Caucasian troops that by having them stationed in the Caucasus they "would speed up the establishment of good relations between the civilian population and those in uniform and give to the inhabitants confidence that we had indeed come with good intentions."[119] He also notes that Köstring soon learned that "many German officers and non-commissioned officers had only scant knowledge of the people they commanded." They, at once, contacted Stauffenberg about this situation, who issued orders that whenever possible to replace German personnel by native leaders. "This took many months to implement but the decision was a sound one and beneficial results almost immediate."[120] Herwarth then goes on to say that their main problem was "poor quality of much of the German personnel and often unsatisfactory performance of the volunteer officers." Herwarth also notes of the Legion battalions, that while Köstring was in the Caucasus, those volunteer units saw action and they "did not discredit themselves" even though "naturally there were some deserters." He then elaborates about the excellent performance of "Bergmann"—that many Red Army soldiers defected to our side but practically none from us.[121]

119- Hans von Herwarth, *Against Two Evils*. Chapter "Caucasus."

120- Hans von Herwarth, *Against Two Evils*. Chapter "Caucasus."

121- Other Caucasian Battalions in North Caucasus in addition to the already mentioned "Bergmann" and the Legion Battalion 795 who saw action were: Azerbaijan Legion Battalions 804 in Kuban; 905, 906 and I/III near Malgobek and Ordzhonikidze; Armenian Legion Battalions 809 and 810 in the Valleys of the North Caucasian Rivers; Georgian Legion Battalions I/9, II/4, 796 and I/I in Kuban; North Caucasian Legion Battalions 842, 843, 803, 836 and 835 in Kuban, Nalchik, Malgobek and Cherek. Already mentioned Georgian Legions Battalion 795 in Baksan and Urukh. And as noted before "Bergmann," in Terek, Mozdok, Staro Fedorovskaia, Baksan and Nalchik.

Professor Captain Oberländer was a puritan, including in his eating habits and could happily feast on pumpernickel, onion and garlic. He also believed in preventive and remedial qualities of such food against certain ailments, such as infectious hepatitis. Having had many meals with Oberländer, von Kutzschenbach and I were ready for a change of our menu to Caucasian shashlik, sort of a shish kebab, and other delicacies. After an introduction of rights for private property and a market oriented economy in the Caucasus, the various shops and restaurants sprang up like mushrooms after rain in towns and cities. So whenever our duty took us to Pyatigorsk, the historic springs (Kislovodsk), Georgievsk[122] or Stavropol, we used free time to sample the Caucasian, Ukrainian and Russian dishes.

While in a Stavropol dining place (or soon after we had left there) we met a group of distinguished looking Caucasian emigres. Among them were three Georgians, Alexandre Asatiani, Alexandre Tsomaia and Dimitri Sindikashvili. They were in the company of an Armenian representative, General Drastamat Kanayan ("DRO"), the former War Minister of Independent Armenia (during the early 1920s) and the North Caucasian representative, Ahmet Nabi Magoma. They had come from Berlin in order to gain first hand experience about the state of affairs in German-occupied North Caucasus and appeared to be pleased so far.

I saw the three above-mentioned Georgians later in Nalchik, where, as has been noted, the staff of "Bergmann" was located. I had an interesting conversation with them there, which was not all that far from Svaneti. In fact, under normal circumstances and on horseback, one could cross one of the many passes and be home in less than two days. Asatiani, himself a Svan on his mother's side, as a child loved to spend as much time as possible in his maternal grandparent's home. There, in Svaneti, legends about heroes and mythology blend with reality. This captured the imagination and fascinated the boy. He grew up to be not only a courageous Georgian patriot but also a highly educated politician, at times even a merciless critic of the social democrats whom he opposed.[123] He became one of the leaders of the Georgian National Democrat Party and after the Bolshevik occupation of Georgia, had to emigrate to France. From there he continued an uphill battle for reestablishment of Georgian sovereignty. A. Tsomaia and D. Sindikashvili were his younger associates but already experienced fighters. None of these people had lost

---

122- A city of historical importance for Georgians, where a treaty of friendship was signed in 1783 between the Empress Catherine II of Russia and the King of Eastern Georgia, Irakli II. In 1801, the Emperor of Russia, Alexander I, unilaterally broke the treaty and annexed Eastern Georgia. Western Georgia was also annexed by force in the years to follow—facts never to be forgotten by the majority of Georgians and leading to serious repercussions. (As some of the Russian Emperor's advisers were warning him that annexation would.)

123- An example of this is his book—Alexandre Asatiani, *The Old and New Inheritance*, printed in France 1928, in Georgian.

contact with the reality and needs of Georgia. As I learned later, they were in North Caucasus to establish liaison with a certain circle inside of Georgia for a coordinated action in case the Germans captured the Transcaucasus as well. Asatiani, as he said, knew my parents from Georgia and was very warm and cordial to me, as were Tsomaia and Sindikashvili. Later we all became close friends.

In Nalchik, there was a small Georgian colony, most of them from the province of Racha. When they heard my name from other "Bergmann" soldiers, some of them invited me to their homes and served delicious national dishes and we toasted each other with the Racha wine "Kipiani." I was greatly pleased when they made known to me how much they had respected my parents. Nalchik had another and a different sort of surprise for us, as I found out upon returning to "Bergmann" headquarters during the later part of a December afternoon.

A frightened young Georgian man was sitting in the kitchen, and our housekeeper, Nadia Pataraia, was comforting him. A small group of former legionnaires from Battalion 795, who had been "adopted" a number of weeks ago by "Bergmann," met this young man wandering on the streets of Nalchik. He had been listed as one of those legionnaires who defected to the Soviets while on the front line of the river Baksan, as was discussed earlier. His account to his former comrades and us about what followed his defection was rather interesting. After a good reception by the Soviet Georgian officials, the defectors were assigned to a certain department of the Red Army. A special detachment was formed from them, members of which were periodically parachuted to the German Army rear areas, with spy and partisan missions. The young man in our kitchen, in his early twenties, whose name I do not remember, was one of three persons who had been recently parachuted north of Nalchik. Two older partisans were still sheltered by a family in a nearby village, but he was sent to Nalchik probably on a scouting mission.

As the former comrade legionnaires recognized him, they all agreed that it was best for all of them to go to "Bergmann" headquarters. "The 'Bergmann' Georgians helped us before and they will help you too," the young partisan was assured by his former comrades. But this was not a small task, since the SS had overall responsibility for the conduct of anti-partisan warfare in the Army Group rear area.[124] Therefore, the German officer on duty of the "Bergmann" staff had to report such a case to the security service in Nalchik at once. However, Oberländer, von Kutzschenbach and I discussed the situation and the SS officer in charge received the message that the young defector had voluntarily surrendered to "Bergmann," he sincerely told us his story and therefore our unit would like to keep him, at least in temporary custody.

124- Alexander Dallin, *German Rule in Russia*, p. 99.

The security service chief wanted to know if our quasi "protege" was willing to guide them to where the other two partisans were hiding and he said he would.

Meanwhile, it was getting dark, and of course, the police chief wanted to arrest and question the two other partisans still at large. He requested von Kutzschenbach's presence as an interpreter. Von Kutzschenbach, in turn, asked me to accompany him since he spoke very good Russian but hardly any Georgian, and conversely some Georgians had difficulty with the Russian language. I was glad he asked because it gave me at least some chance to try to help the three former Georgian legionnaires now in real trouble. Oberländer, Kutzschenbach and I all agreed to plead on their behalf, as victims of unusually difficult circumstances they were exposed to, which led to their defection. (This was previously discussed in connection with the defection from Battalion 795.) We would also argue that the defectors had no choice but to comply with whatever they were ordered to do by the new masters, even if it meant to parachute as partisans—hardly a pleasant task. We would suggest that they be treated as ordinary P.O.W.s and after investigation to transfer them to the camp.

The next morning, the young partisan sat in a truck with the Security Service chief and his men, directing them to their hideout place. Von Kutzschenbach and I followed the truck in our small car. The security men searched the house in question; there were no partisans there but only a middle-aged woman, her daughter (probably aged twenty or so) and a son in his early teens. The mother and daughter denied knowledge of the partisans' whereabouts, but the little boy was scared of the armed men searching their home. He pointed to a small barn across the yard. The policemen shouted for them to come out, and both of them did so with hands up. They had dropped their handguns inside the barn—no other weapons were found by the police.

Both partisans appeared to be hardened and firm men in their late twenties but polite and with good manners. They introduced themselves to von Kutzschenbach and me after we were allowed by the police to approach them. I cannot remember their names. To von Kutzschenbach's and my great disappointment, the police also arrested the mother and her daughter who had sheltered the partisans. How could they have refused even if they did not want to? Moreover, the villagers were not required to pledge allegiance to the Germans. Von Kutzschenbach and I were impressed by both women because of their dignity, poise and courage.

The chief of security police decided to question the two newly arrested partisans as soon as possible. Von Kutzschenbach and I were both present. I was to interpret the questions directed to the partisans in Georgian and their answers in German. Their story coincided with the one told before by the younger parachutist to us at the "Bergmann" headquarters. In the process of this conversation, I made it known to the prisoners that we in "Bergmann" wanted to help them, and we advised them to dwell on the poor treatment and the conditions they were exposed to while in the P.O.W. camps and later at the hands of some German personnel while in Battalion 795. I told them that von Kutzschenbach and I knew all about it since we had visited Battalion 795 after their defection; please, to trust us and follow our advice.

I was surprised by their response, "No sir, the Germans treated us well." The police chief wanted to know what kind of conversation was going on between us, instead of prisoners answering his questions? I explained that I was encouraging them to tell the truth. Before the questioning session was over, I reminded them one more time to emphasize the poor treatment they were subjected to; the answer was the same, "No, sir, the Germans treated us well." I told them to stop being silly, that Kutzschenbach and I knew only too well of the poor conditions in the P.O.W. camps and the low quality of German personnel in the legion battalions and the police officer should be told about it. I got nowhere with them. Von Kutzschenbach and I were at a loss to explain such paradoxical response. The best answer we could come up with later was their mistrust toward us and for that matter toward the whole world around them. Not only their P.O.W. experience but also the Soviet system and every phase of life led to this. The two parachutists probably thought that we were laying a trap for them.

We did not know for sure if their emphasis on poor treatment as a motive for becoming a partisan would help to reduce the degree of punishment. It certainly would help "Bergmann" to more effectively plead on their behalf, which Kutzschenbach did as soon as the prisoners were led out of the room. He spoke on behalf of Captain Professor Oberländer and the "Bergmann" soldiers, who not only distinguished themselves on the Caucasus front but were also considered to be experts in Caucasus matters. Therefore, we had been asked before by the high command to investigate the situation in Battalion 795, from where the defection took place. Among the defectors were today's three partisans under investigation.

Herr Baron von Kutzschenbach was firm but also a diplomat realizing that the fate of three former legionnaires now depended on this brutal SS officer; therefore, he did not flatly state that the main reason of the defections was Nazi inhumane policy toward the "Eastern People." He rather went on to say that according to our investigation, the main reason for defections were wretched conditions in the P.O.W. camps and other "environmental factors," including poor quality of German personnel. Once in the Soviet hands, the defectors had no choice but to obey orders. In the case of these three prisoners, it was to parachute behind the German front line as partisans and informers. He also stated that it was the feeling of Professor

Oberländer and the "Bergmann" soldiers that the younger partisan who turned himself in should be freed. The two older ones should be considered in the light of unusual circumstances which surrounds their past and be treated as "simple" P.O.W.s and should be transferred to one of the P.O.W. camps in the Caucasus.

Von Kutzschenbach also spoke on behalf of the Russian (or Ukrainian?) mother and daughter who had sheltered two partisans now in security service custody. He asked how they could have refused the armed man even if they wanted to. Also, he noted, no harm had been done. With his eloquent arguments, distinguished look and aristocratic manners, Kutzschenbach obviously impressed the SS officer, who said he needed to look into all of this and would have to follow the guidelines from above; however, he would not bring charges against the younger partisan and may even put in a good word for his employment by the indigenous auxiliary police force of Nalchik. We left the Security Service Chief's office in an optimistic mood, inasmuch as to our surprise, he even invited us to some pending holy day season's party. We both considered our acceptance of his invitation in the spirit of further helping the prisoners.

Around Christmas time but especially a few days after, more enemy activities had been noted and reported especially east of Nalchik. I had visited some companies on the front line around that time and returned to our headquarters in Nalchik just before dark. I found von Kutzschenbach sitting alone in the dining room with a gloomy face and sipping a drink. "Things are not so good in Stalingrad, are they?" I said, "but we are in much better shape here." I tried to start a conversation.

Kutzschenbach gave me a long look and said, "This is supposed to be the happy holy day time and two innocent people, mother and daughter, have been executed along with the two former legionnaires, probably just last night," he added. Obviously our plea to save their lives had been totally ignored. "That SS officer is a beast of the worst kind," said Kutzschenbach; I had nothing to add to that. We sat in total silence, each of us in deep thought. I needed fresh air and took a long walk in a nearby park.

When we discussed this with Oberländer, his face flushed in anger. The only comment he had was, "What a pity and this is how such men as this SS officer are losing respect and friends for all Germans." He was entirely correct.[125]

In a day or two (on December 30, 1942), "Bergmann" received orders to retreat from the Caucasus.[126] Retreat of any army poses specific and complex military

---

125- The security service chief in Nalchik was "Sturmbannführer" Persterer from Austria. After the war, Oberländer informed me that he had been killed in Italy where he had been transferred after Caucasus—far too late, I thought.

126- See the Appendix for more on the Red Army offensive during November 1942.

as well as psychological problems. This was even more true for "Bergmann" since retreating German soldiers were headed toward home but not the Caucasians. As far as the immediate, purely military end of it was concerned, the German as well as Caucasian soldiers were at ease. There was absolutely no panic, it was a well planned and masterfully organized retreat by Kleist and his associates. Complete confidence toward their commanding field marshal was felt. The available parallel communication routes had been cleverly and efficiently allocated to the elements on retreat. There were no bottlenecks on the roads nor shortage of lodging or forage. It also made it easier to survive a possible enemy attack from the air. Roads were improved on the move to make it easier for others and here also "Bergmann" contributed its share.

The psychological impact of retreat, on the other hand, was almost devastating for the Caucasians. The normally gregarious Georgians became almost silent at first. We did not admit it, even to ourselves but the unbearable thought was there, "If we are going to see our home country at all, it is not going to be for a very, very long time."

The general direction of our retreat was northwest first, leading us to the city of Pyatigorsk and near the city of Stavropol and then almost straight west toward the city of Krasnodar first and then the Taman Peninsula with cities of Taman and Temryuk.[127] Once there and if orders called for further retreat, then we would have to cross the channel, the Kerch Straight into Crimea. The "Bergmann" companies remained separated from each other during retreat by the German units. To keep liaison with them became rather difficult at times. While looking for our companies, Oberländer and I found each other near the city of Stavropol on January 11, 1943. We met Herwarth there and got some briefing from him. We were all concerned about the safety and the morale of our Caucasian soldiers.[128]

Given this situation, Oberländer and I had more frequent personal meetings than usual. During one of such meetings in Grigoripolnskaia on January 12, 1943, we discovered that our 1st Georgian Company could not be accounted for. It apparently had to change the direction of retreat because of the outflanking Soviet Panzers. It was decided that I find the company and take one German sergeant with me as an

---

127- Temryuk occupies the north part of the peninsula where the river Kuban joins the Sea of Azov (also called Kuban Peninsula).

128- The main military objective of "Bergmann" had been to secure the "Cross" pass on the Georgian Military Highway and if successful then proceed to Tbilisi. Due to the retreat from Caucasus, of course, this did not materialize. It had been a top secret between the colonel in the General Staff (Army Group A), Colonel Winter, and Oberländer. I learned about it from Oberländer only after retreat. Earlier Oberländer had been flown with a fighter plane over the "Cross" pass and was able to observe the Soviet preparedness for such a military eventuality. Two weeks after retreat from Nalchik, "Bergmann" was officially transferred from the jurisdiction of the High Command of the Armed Forces to the Army High Command. This would indicate that the High Command did not stipulate a return to the Caucasus, at least, in the near future.

assistant. In Grigoripolnskaia, I also met some other members of the "Bergmann" staff, among them Lieutenant Süss—an aide to Oberländer (who had joined us in Nalchik) and our housekeeper, Nadia Pataraia.

It was also a pleasant surprise to see my friend, Victor Homeriki, who paradoxically was from the "lost" 1st Company. He had temporarily been assigned to some other task and therefore was separated from his unit. He appeared frustrated and worried about the situation; usually very pleasant and just, Victor now made me a scapegoat for this possible mishap. "How come you lost them?" he wanted to know. "They did it without my permission," I quipped, to cheer him up. But Victor did not seem to be amused. "What took you people so long to react and look for them?" he insisted. I told Victor that we had just been informed about it and were going to make an effort in that direction.

A few days later, I returned with good news and cheered my friend; he wanted to know some details of it. After that, Victor turned around and reproached me again, "It was uncalled for you to take such a risk in finding the company," he said. I thought that one simply could not please Victor during that time. In fact, it was not difficult to find the company after good advice and a little bit of luck. Before I embarked on this little "scouting" trip, I saw von Herwarth again to get freshly oriented about the German and Soviet troop movements about which he knew as he was associated with the Army Group "A" staff. He pointed out to me how to find his friend, Panzer officer von Twardovski, whose unit was engaged in combat with Soviet troops east or northeast from us. Herwarth said that von Twardovski could be of some help to me and gave me a personal letter to deliver to him.

Finally, I located von Twardovoki's Panzer unit and the officer himself on the outskirts of a small village. After he read von Herwarth's letter, I told him what I was after. Von Twardovski said, "Right now there is a temporary pause in the Soviet attack and this will make our 'expedition' much easier." He also said that some German troops had dug in southeast of where we were. They had recently stopped a Soviet attack and there was a good chance that "Bergmann" was part of it. Then he suggested that we use an ammunition supply truck leaving shortly in this direction.

After the truck stopped at a certain point of the forward position, we continued on foot for a half hour until we stood above "Bergmann" 1st Company's trenches. I commanded the group of 1st Company soldiers, "Hands up, you are our prisoners now." Among them were Shota Margwelashvili, Tariel Kutateladze and "Kriste." We got three different reactions from them. Our medieval knight, Shota said, "Why did you come here, Batono,[129] there are enough well-trained Georgian

---

129- "Baton" means "Sir" in Georgian.

soldiers here, the situation is unstable now and why should we, on top of this, put your life in jeopardy?"[130] Tariel, the youngest among them, flushed his innocent smile. He was simply glad to see me. (He had been a childhood friend of my sister Eteri.) "Kriste" (I remember his nickname only—he lived in my neighborhood in Tbilisi) said, "I will be honest. I lost confidence in everyone including you. I thought you just abandoned us." I understood "Kriste" well; during such a retreat, the front is often unstable. By now the Russian generals had learned modern tank warfare, including pincer maneuvers from the Germans. Consequently, at times, our soldiers were surprised by Russian tanks, outflanking or even pushing ahead of us. Although our soldiers were getting used to such a situation, they could afford even less than the Germans to become P.O.W.s in Russian hands.[131]

Meanwhile evening was approaching, a low flying Soviet reconnaissance plane passed over our heads. From our trenches, we could easily see the enemy positions and suddenly what we saw was unbelievable. A Soviet airplane similar to the German "Stork" landed in the field between our and the Soviet positions. A Soviet general got out, had a look at our positions and without haste or cover walked to his soldiers and stood there, obviously having a conversation with them.

I thought it an unusual display of courage or confusion since he was within the reach of the sniper's shot and heavy weapons. It was a fighting lull and neither the Georgians nor the Germans wanted to take a shot at the general, and I was proud of them because of that. Otherwise, it would almost be equal to a cold blooded murder of a human being. I had a short meeting with the officers aspirant in charge (First Lieutenant Brand, the chief of the 1st Company had been temporarily substituted.) He felt that for now the 1st Company's flanks were protected by the German units, with whom he had a good liaison. He was also aware of the nearby Panzer unit, where I had just visited von Twardovski.[132]

130- The second medieval knight, Gabriel (Gabo) Gogelashvili, was not with this group at that time. He had sustained a severe head wound before retreat and was being treated in the hospital. He recovered, and I had the pleasure of seeing him again.

131- Something like this happened to three of us from the "Bergman" staff. Lieutenant Süss, our chauffeur and I were looking for still another "Bergmann" company on the move. It got dark, and it was decided to spend the night on a somewhat elevated and sheltered area next to a dirt road (now frozen and with only a small amount of snow covering it). We settled for the night as best we could. I was known as an "early bird" and a light sleeper. When I woke up, it was still somewhat dark, but I could see a small group of tanks probably less than one hundred yards in the distance from our rear side. I thought they were German tanks from the 1st Panzer Army but as I got closer to them it became clear that they were Soviet tanks. The men inside must have been in a deep sleep, as were Lieutenant Süss and our driver. Quietly I awakened my friends, then we pushed our car without starting the motor at first. Fortunately we had a slight downhill ahead of us making it possible for us to do so. Many years after the war, Lieutenant Süss reminded me of this episode during a "Bergman" reunion in Mittenwald. He also very generously said that I had saved his life. I corrected him—I had not done such a thing but woke up earlier than he and the Russian "tankists" that particular morning.

132- This was part of the 1st Panzer Army which was gradually making its way to Rostov on the river Don, to join the forces of Field Marshal von Manstein.

The 1st Georgian Company chief expected to receive an order for retreat, direction west, during late evening. It appeared that the Soviets did not have very strong units on our sector now. Therefore, they probably would wait for reinforcements before resumption of a forward push. My companion and I retreated with the 1st Company for one day or so. They did not appear to be in immediate danger. Therefore, we took advantage of a military vehicle passing by, which gave us a lift, and we finally caught up with our staff on the move. At that time, the headquarters of the 17th Army was located in the city of Krasnodar and of the Army Group A in Slavyanskaya.

Oberländer visited Herwarth on January 26, 1943, at the Army Group A for mutual briefing in connection with continued retreat and associated problems. Thus, Köstring and Herwarth had frequent feedback from "grassroot" origin and were better able to react to the problems of the Caucasian soldiers, P.O.W.s and the civilian population. Speaking of problems, on January 27th, "Bergmann" soldiers were dug in and defending the town of Novoleninsk. For some unexplained reason, the German General Steinbauer withdrew his troops without giving us due warning. Our flanks were soon occupied by Soviet troops, creating grave danger of our being encircled and we had to retreat in haste.

By February 4th, the 17th Army was cut off in the Kuban [Bridgehead on the Taman Peninsula, Russia]. We could get supplies only by sea or air from Crimea. The 1st Panzer Army was able to retreat toward Rostov on the river Don before it was cut off.[133] Oberländer and I discussed the newly formed Georgian 10th Company, about 250 or more man strong. They were not well trained yet and we were wondering how fit they were for retreat on foot during the given circumstances.

The chief of the 10th Company, Lieutenant Martin Schütte, was a capable Prussian officer and a sincere friend of the Georgians—fair minded and humble. For instance, he once told me that he would feel honored to be a platoon leader in the company where the Georgian First Lieutenant Mikheil Dadiani was the company chief. He did not have to say that. Schütte was well liked by his Georgian soldiers and yet Oberländer and Schütte both felt that I should temporarily stay with the 10th Company to help keep things going in the right direction. Of course, I agreed.

There were two Georgians, Mikheil (Misha) Kavtaradze and Grigol (Grisha) Lordkipanidze also present in this company; the former as an interpreter and adviser to Lieutenant Schütte, the latter as special help. When it was time for the company to stay overnight in some village, Kavtaradze, Lordkipanidze and I would share quarters. Kavtaradze was (and still is) a gentleman of few words but Lordkipanidze,

---

133- *The World Almanac of World War II.*

in addition to being a gentleman, loved to tell stories. He was a former chief of police during the Georgian independence and had a remarkable memory. I learned many interesting facts from our Georgian past especially pertaining to law and order. Our former police chief loved to wrestle, and that is usually how our morning started. Here, I could give him some pointers, having had exposure to this sport in the past.[134] Kavtaradze, watching us in amusement, compared us to Caucasian brown bears. (This is how we overcame our sadness due to the retreat.)[135]

I had frequent contacts with the Georgian soldiers of the 10th Company, and it was always a two way communication. I formed a good opinion of them and Lieutenant Schütte had no significant problems with them. In fact, he told me that he had more difficulties with some Bavarian sergeants. The Lieutenant told me, "Herr Gabliani, after this war is over, there is going to be another war." "What kind of war?" I asked in amazement. "Between the Prussians and the Bavarians," he mused; but after a while he had a smile on his face and added, "they are terribly stubborn."

We learned about capitulation by General von Paulus and his 6th Army in Stalingrad during the beginning of February 1943.[136] We also listened to the broadcast of Hitler's speech in connection with the lost battle of Stalingrad. He actually devoted more time to enumerate his past achievements, now already history. Dissatisfaction with Hitler's leadership was felt among the German officers and such intellectuals as Dr. Ehrenfried Schütte in "Bergmann."[137] After Hitler's speech, Dr. Schütte made a fitting remark, "We knew this already, what is new?"

On February 12th, Oberländer ordered our two cavalry squadrons to cross part of the Sea of Azov from the Taman Peninsula to Crimea. Fortunately, this part of the sea was solidly frozen. The ice broke only once or twice under the horse driven wagon. Two horses perished, but the driver was rescued.[138]

On February 22nd, the entirety of "Bergmann" was evacuated from the Kuban bridgehead to Crimea; partly in assault boats, others in gliders towed by small airplanes. Von Kutzschenbach and I shared a glider; it was disconnected from its tow-plane above the airport in Crimea, and we landed safely. Somehow only then it became painfully obvious to me that one of the most important chapters of my life since I had left Georgia had been closed.

134- I had the privilege of being a member of the Tbilisi Medical School wrestling team and was tutored by a professional wrestler, Lionka Dzekonski.

135- Lordkipanidze was also the father-in-law to Niko Nakashidze. I met Niko Nakashidze while on my way from Mariupol on the Sea of Azov to the Caucasus front, as already mentioned.

136- Actual capitulation took place January 31, 1943.

137- Brother of Lieutenant Martin Schütte.

138- The cavalry squadrons were led by Lieutenants M. Dadiani, Chavchavadze, G. Vachnadze and Weyh.

9

IN CRIMEA

Retreating from home and landing in Crimea was not an especially inspiring experience for the Caucasians. Our German friends, including von Kutzschenbach, Oberländer, von Herwarth and Köstring were well aware of this and were concerned. While there was no magic remedy for curing the low mood, life went on and our friends had to focus on the positive sides that Crimea offered. For instance, after a long month's retreat on foot, the soldiers of "Bergmann" needed physical and psychological rest. Moreover, "Bergmann's" size had increased threefold and it was now a regiment, due to an influx of Caucasian recruits, so now we had an opportunity to train them. During combat, we lost several excellent officers and had a serious shortage of them. It was time for us to send some of our non-commissioned officers to military schools, and after graduation they would fill in the existing vacancies. Crimea appeared to be a good spot for all these undertakings; it also was beautiful in the southern alpine part chosen for our stay.[139]

Field Marshal von Kleist's headquarters of the Army Group A was now in the Crimean city of Simferopol.[140] Based on his experience in the Caucasus, von Kleist issued a multi-part order for Crimea:

139- Crimea is a peninsula between the Black Sea and the Sea of Azov. The two seas are connected by the narrow Strait of Kerch which is located at the eastern end and separates Crimea from the Caucasus. On its northern end, Crimea is connected to the mainland of Ukraine by about the ten-mile-wide Perekop Isthmus. East of Perekop lies the Sivash or "lazy sea," which is a salty marshland. The southern part of Crimea features mountains that are higher and steeper on the south and progressively lower and gentler on the north side. The alpine region makes up one fourth of Crimea, and it is blessed by a mild climate, higher precipitation, sunshine, beautiful forests and plants. There are many resorts in this area. North Crimea is a prairie crossed by a number of rivers; albeit some of them dry out during the hot season.

140- Simferopol was the administrative center of the "Crimean Autonomous Soviet Socialist Republic." Before conquest by Imperial Russia (latter part of the eighteenth century), it had been a Crimean Tatar settlement. The railroad links Sevastopol (an important military Black Sea port), Bakhchysarai and Simferopol with Melitopol, a city in Ukraine, the general direction being from southwest to northeast and passing through the Crimean isthmus of Perekop.

1. The inhabitants of the occupied Eastern territories in his Army group were to be treated as allies. Treatment as inferiors only strengthens the enemy and costs German blood.

2. The supply of the civilian population's food, especially bread but also clothes, fuel, and consumer goods is to be improved within the limits imposed by the war.

3. Social services is to be expanded, e.g. supply of hospitals with medicines and milk for women and children . . . .

. . . 6. In principle, twenty percent of all consumer goods produced is to be distributed among the civilian population.

7. The agrarian reform is to be carried out with great dispatch. In 1943, at least fifty percent of the collectives are to be transformed into communes. In the remaining collectives, the individual plots are to be given to the peasants as tax-free property. In appropriate cases, individual farms are to be established.

8. As a rule . . . the delivery quota for agricultural produce shall not exceed that under the Bolsheviks. . . .

. . . 12. The school system is to be promoted widely.

. . . 14. Religious practice is free and is not to be impeded in any way. . .[141]

Oberländer did this and more in the region that had been assigned to our regiment, which was divided between different towns of Southern Crimea, including the Belbek Valley. Often, one would see Oberländer hosting meetings with the indigenous town representatives in the regimental headquarters which was located in the beautiful village of Kokosi on the former estate of Prince Yusupov.[142] Oberländer carefully listened to the Crimean people about their problems, treated them with respect and was always ready to help. The field military kitchens of "Bergmann" donated hot meals to needy civilians. When called on, the "Bergmann" soldiers gave a helping hand to the farmers in the fields, including our horses. Oberländer dispatched trucks to Ukraine and obtained necessary seed for future harvest. The collective farms were dissolved and the land given back to the people. All these measures, in combination with good precipitation of 1943, produced a most

141- Alexander Dallin, *German Rule in Russia*, p. 263. Dallin quotes from the document: Von Kleist, "Behandlung der Zivilbevölkerung im Operationsgebiet" February 17, 1943, EAP 99/1145, CRS.

142- Prince Yusupov took part in a successful plot to assassinate Rasputin in St. Petersburg during 1916. The reason was the alleged evil influence Rasputin exercised on Empress Alexandra and thereby endangered the Russian throne.

satisfactory harvest and the food shortage was no longer a problem for the civilian population in our sector.[143]

Oberländer permitted the communities on "Bergmann" territory to organize their own police, correctly assuming that the local people were better able to staff it with capable and trustworthy persons. How effective they were, was soon demonstrated. A house further down in the valley had been robbed, and the lone grandmother and her grandchild both brutally murdered. Within hours the local police had the suspect, a Russian handyman and drifter. He was arrested and later handed over to the central police station in Simferopol. (I knew the aunt of the murdered child, a fine young lady, now the only surviving member of the family. I had been introduced to her by a German officer in Simferopol some time before this tragedy took place.)

"Bergmann" was assigned to the 153rd German Infantry Division which had headquarters in Bakhchysarai.[144] We did not see much of them, and for the time being each pursued their own goals. But during the end of March 1943, Oberländer was ordered to attend a meeting of all the commanding officers of the Crimean troops in Simferopol. The discussion was focused on the second Romanian Mountain Division which was located in a valley next to "Bergmann." The Romanians had suffered considerable losses because of the partisans, while "Bergmann's" Belbek Valley remained free of them. Now many questions were directed to the "Bergmann" officers for a possible explanation for this. After considerable discussion, it was agreed that "Bergmann's" general policy toward the indigenous population was the main reason for such a difference.[145]

Until the above-mentioned meeting, "Bergmann" had been criticized in certain quarters for exceeding the allocated gasoline quota because of transporting seed for the Crimean farmers from Ukraine through the Perekop Isthmus. Criticism was also voiced because we allowed the populace to form their own police. Now this criticism was replaced by recognition of Oberländer's policies as a step in the right direction and an example for others to follow.

Some of the "high authorities" in Berlin also protested Field Marshal von Kleist's programs in Crimea, but Kleist "would not be budged"[146] since he was sure that his policies were correct. Kleist's confidence in "Bergmann" is also illustrated by the following example. Kleist wanted to drive from Kokosi to Yalta, over the

---

143- Professor Theodore Oberländer's report, *History of the "Bergmann" Unit, Geschichte der Einheit "Bergmann."*

144- The name means "The Garden Palace." It was the capital of the Crimean Khans, before 1784.

145- In fact, it also turned into mutual affection between the townspeople and the soldiers. For my own part to this day, I still harbor warm feelings toward the Crimean people.

146- Alexander Dallin, *German Rule in Russia*, p. 263.

Crimean Mountains [Yayla Mountains; "yaylas" are alpine meadows] and inquired at "Bergmann" headquarters if it would be safe for him to do so. In the past, this region had been known to harbor partisans. Oberländer's answer was, yes, it was no problem for the Field Marshal to do so, and "Bergmann" would assume full responsibility for safety; the trip went very well.

But things don't always turn out perfectly in this world, and "Bergmann" was no exception. Conflict of interests developed between some "Bergmann" Georgians and a local mullah. Kleist and Oberländer declared support for religious expression of the local people. The mosques were opened, and the mullahs conducted services for the faithful. The Georgian soldiers of the 1st Company soon learned that one of the local mullahs preached to the worshiping girls not to date the Georgians since they were Christians.

The Georgian soldiers were infuriated. A group of them had a conference, and the discussion went approximately like this, "Were we not nice to the local towns people? Yes, we were," they thought. "Did we not conduct ourselves as true gentlemen toward the ladies? Yes," they were sure of it. "Does love know ethnic or religious barriers? Of course not," they decided. "After all this, don't you think we are discriminated against? It's too obvious," they concluded. What to do? First they approached the mullah in question and shared their thoughts with him. The mullah agreed with the first and second points but politely disagreed with the last two. They got nowhere with him, so the Georgian soldiers placed the mullah under house arrest—"very politely, of course."

Before this news reached "Bergmann" headquarters in Kokosi, the conflict had already been resolved by the company chief and Victor Homeriki. The mullah had been freed with all possible apologies and assurances. He was told that the whole thing had been "one great misunderstanding." Discussion with the soldiers, who firmly stood on their "four point platform" was a bit more difficult. Finally, Homeriki convinced them that although they may have been right in a way, on the other hand and in the final score they were wrong. There are moments like this in life, philosophically remarked Victor, facing the disappointed soldiers.

The route the Field Marshal chose over Kokosi to Yalta was a beautiful one. The meandering road led to the Crimean Mountains over a pass from where one would face the breathtaking beauty of nature. It was a combination of the partly snow-covered green mountains, the blue sky above and the blue water of the Black Sea in the distance. The town of Yalta was located deep below on the sea coast and was adorned by gardens and trees.

Some of our other visitors in Kokosi also wanted to see this magnificent panorama, including von Herwarth. One day Herwarth, Oberländer and I decided to make a limited traverse of the mountain range overlooking Yalta. This coincided with a field exercise of one of the "Bergmann" companies in this area. The three of us walked together for a while but at some point Oberländer went over to see the company, leaving Herwarth and I to continue our walk, admiring the scenery and discussing a variety of subjects.

I remembered that shortly after Christmas of 1942, while retreating from the Caucasus, a German broadcast informed us about the former Red Army General Vlasov, who had been captured earlier by the Germans. Now under German patronage, he formed the Smolensk Committee. His goal was to organize Russian opposition to Stalin and get rid of the oppressive regime. I wanted to know Herwarth's opinion about this development since I hoped this to be a step in the right direction. Herwarth agreed with this but was rather skeptical and said that even if the German "higher ups" (meaning the top Nazis) would now allow any serious development of the Vlasov initiative, it was too late. He said that some other personalities had proposed similar and further reaching programs much earlier and at a time when the German Army was moving forward and the population welcomed them as liberators. But all such moves had been rejected and forbidden by the "German leadership," (the Nazis).

One can be certain, said Herwarth, that the Vlasov initiative was started by some Army personalities and not by the ruling party higher ups. He then stunned me with a flat statement that he did not see how Germany could possibly win the war.[147] It was now the spring of 1943, and I thought that after the lost battle of Stalingrad, perhaps the German Armed Forces would recuperate, replace losses, regroup and try the 1943 summer counter offensive; coupled with positive political moves toward the Soviet people. Coming from Herwarth, such an assessment of the military and political situation was ominous. It had to be taken very seriously because he had direct access to Field Marshal von Kleist, Ambassador von Schulenburg and Colonel von Stauffenberg.

It also had to be a warning from a good friend, who was now more than ever concerned about the future of the indigenous volunteers in the German Army. Since we obviously could not go back home, we were now the responsibility of our German friends whom we had trusted and followed. It also was a sign of our mutual confidence and friendship that Herwarth shared such dangerously sensitive information with me. How did such a relationship develop between certain Germans and indigenous officers? In Chapter 18 ("Volunteers, Generals and Conspirators") of his book, Herwarth offers a general explanation for it:

147- Hans von Herwarth, *Against Two Evils*, p. 239 (conversation with Givi Gabliani).

"They could not help but understand what people like Gauleiter Koch and Sauckel were up to when they witnessed the forced emigration of their people to work in Germany. [*This did not apply to the Caucasian, Turkic or Cossack people. –G.G.*] Had they been mere mercenaries, their disillusionment would have been less. They were idealists, however, and hence their disenchantment was more profound. In spite of this, they retained their faith in the German officers, whom they understood were opposed to this colonial policy. In fact, their trust in the German military authorities grew as their faith in the civilian, eg. Nazi authorities eroded. It was this that accounts for the peculiar intimacy that existed between volunteer officers and those German officers who tried to win concessions for the volunteers. In hundreds of cases this friendship remained intact until the end of the war."[148]

I may add that Herwarth's and my friendship continues for over forty-eight years.

The correctness of Herwarth's assessment of the unyielding Nazi politics and that it did not change even after the Stalingrad defeat was soon to be demonstrated. This also revealed the sharpening of disagreement between the German Armed Forces on one side against the SS and the Nazi Party on the other side. It was clearly felt in Berlin as well as in Crimea, as the case of Oberländer would soon reveal. For instance, on June 10th, there was a high level meeting in Bakhchysarai between Field Marshal von Kleist and his officers with Nazi Party representatives such as Alfred Rosenberg and Erich Koch.[149] Kleist's headquarters also invited Oberländer to attend the meeting.

The Field Marshal spoke as a human being and as a soldier who applied humanistic principles to the treatment of the indigenous population of Caucasus and Crimea and to the war effort itself. He advocated such a policy to be carried out everywhere. This was the position of the Armed Forces (Wehrmacht) and it envisaged to fight against Bolshevism with the people of the Soviet Union for freedom and a better future.

Rosenberg's speech was both not clear, and noncommittal. "Everything should be postponed until after the end of the war"; but basically he agreed with Kleist's good treatment of the populace. He also reminded the listeners that Crimea

---

148- Hans von Herwarth. *Against Two Evils*, p. 264.

149- Alfred Rosenberg, as noted before, was the Reich's Minister for the Eastern Territories; however very ineffectual, as we shall see later. Erich Koch, as noted already, was a tyrannical Nazi Commissar of Ukraine.

had been inhabited earlier by the Goths,[150] therefore historically it was the region of the Germanic settlers, etc.

Then Erich Koch, the tyrant of Ukraine, spoke with fury. He recited too well known "principles" of inhuman colonization of the occupied Eastern territories. Rosenberg was in disagreement with Koch's methods but unable to prevail since Koch had Hitler on his side.

Oberländer, in his diary, records that it was depressing and clear to the listeners that Eric Koch's suggestions would lead to a total loss in the east. Oberländer did not tell us about it at first, in order not to dishearten us, but later he shared this experience with me; however, this did not stop Oberländer from continuing his crusade against the Nazi higher ups' criminal policies. He (with some help of the before mentioned "Bergmann" 'think tank') composed his sixth and last World War II memorandum, "Alliance or Exploitation?" (Bündnis oder Ausbeutung?) One more time, he suggested the alliance with indigenous Eastern people instead of their exploitation and alienation.[151] On the second anniversary of the German-Soviet War (June 22, 1943), Oberländer submitted thirty copies of this memorandum, according to the proper chain of command to his superiors. It was copied and further distributed around by others interested as well as by service connected institutions. Himmler, as soon as he found out about it, demanded Oberländer's arrest and court martial. The General Staff was able to avert it, but the Army had to dismiss him.[152]

Oberländer bade farewell to "Bergmann" on August 22, 1943, never to see it again; this was followed by political difficulties for him.

In the interval between my memorable conversation with Herwarth in the Crimean Mountains and Oberländer's dismissal, General Köstring and Captain von Herwarth visited us in Kokosi on April 11th, on the occasion of oath-taking by newly formed "Bergmann" companies. Afterwards, there was some celebration and the guests were entertained with Caucasian songs and dances. It was during this get-together that Köstring, Herwarth and Oberländer decided to send some Caucasian officers to Dresden Military School. The goal was to put them on equal

---

150- A Germanic people who during the early Christian era invaded the Roman Empire. The Gothic settlers in Crimea left the remnants of their fortress, Chufut-Kale. (I visited there during the spring of 1943, with other officers.) According to Hitler's plans, the indigenous Crimean population should have been forcibly evacuated and resettled somewhere else in Russia. Crimea was then to be settled by the South Tyroleans and it would become a "German Gibraltar."

151- Thus he was in line with von Schulenburg's plan.

152- Alexander Dallin, *German Rule in Russia*, p. 514; Hans von Herwarth, *Against Two Evils*, p. 233; Author's notes from Oberländer's diaries; Theodore Oberländer, *Denkschriften aus dem Zweiten Weltkrieg: über die Behandlung der Sowjetvolkes* (*Memories of the Second World War: on the Treatment of the Soviet Peoples*), Quellenstudien Der Zeitgeschichtlichen Forschungsstelle Ingolstadt, volume 2.

footing with German counterparts, which was one of Köstring's important projects, especially after the retreat from Caucasus. This took about three months to implement, but finally in July it was announced that four Caucasian officers would be able to enter the prestigious institution. The officers were Karim Aleskirov (Azerbaijan), Irakli Alimbarashvili, Givi Gabliani and Shalva Okropiridze (the Georgians). This was only the beginning of an experiment. After retreat from Caucasus, Köstring's position as the General in charge of Caucasian Affairs had come to an end. On the other hand, by now the number of "Eastern" volunteers in the German Army was estimated to be 800,000[153] and they were needed. In January 1943, the creation of the office of the General of "Osttruppen" (the Eastern Troops) was achieved by the Organization Division of the General Staff.

Obviously Köstring was the best qualified person for the job but opposition to him "from certain influential circles" was great. Therefore, Lieutenant General Heinz Hellmich was appointed to this position. He visited us in Kokosi; he appeared to be a cordial and pleasant man although he had no knowledge of the Russian language and could not match Köstring's expertise of the Soviet Union. Herwarth thought him to be "a decent man of strong feelings, which guided him in his work, and he shared Köstring's views on the volunteers and on the proper treatment of the occupied territories and was particularly successful in choosing excellent staff officers who approached their work with enthusiasm and energy."[154]

Since Köstring was indispensable during June of 1943, Organizations Divisions managed to appoint him Inspector General for Turkic and Caucasian Units, apparently a compromise solution for the time being since he would have been eminently qualified to be a general of all the volunteer units. According to my "mini diary" notes, in Kokosi on June 28th, I was invited to a coffee by Oberländer and was seated between he and General Hellmich. Another Georgian, a non-commissioned officer, Giorgi Indjia was also present. I brought up the question of Lieutenant

153- Hans von Herwarth, *Against Two Evils*, p. 262.

154- Hans von Herwarth, *Against Two Evils*, p. 262. However, Alexander Dallin in his *German Rule in Russia*, p. 536, quotes from Hellmich's "Vortragsnotiz betr. Osttruppen," "Presentation Notes re: Eastern Troops," March 22, 1943, Document NG–3534: "The population's readiness to help, had to be exploited as much as possible....The creation of Osttruppen is a means to free German troops." Then Dallin states, "How far Hellmich was from the 'politicals' is well illustrated by his belief that the Eastern Troops had but one thing to give, their lives—which the Wehrmacht must ruthlessly exploit to the last." Dallin also adds, "He was not concerned about their political demands," (and he quotes Hellmich again), "Which are not determined by their accomplishments but above all by the proportion of their forces to ours. The stronger we are (and) the more the Eastern Peoples are bled white, the smaller will be the practical effect of their demands." After having read this, my first thought was how could this General have looked me straight in the eye in Kokosi? And later on in Lötzen headquarters, when I had lost my winter gloves, he presented me with his own—I still have them. I would hope that General Hellmich, whose two sons and himself were war casualties, wrote such terrible notes for Hitler's consumption in order to wrestle from him some concessions for his "sheep's" benefit and not to "bleed them white."

General Vlasov and his "Liberation Army." I wanted to know if Georgians were serving there. The General stated, "not to the best of my knowledge." I also wanted to know why it would not be possible to form a "Caucasian Liberation Army" to put together the Caucasian units already in existence but now scattered all over and difficult to care for. His answer was that this was currently under consideration.

I got a real answer to this question in Simferopol two weeks later from a newly acquired friend, Lieutenant Dr. Wilhelm Reissmüller. He was a special aid to General Freitag, who represented the regional organization of the General of the Eastern Volunteer Units by the Army Group A. Lieutenant Reissmüller informed me that the Regiment "Bergmann" was to be split in three separate battalions: Georgian, Azerbaijani and North Caucasian. Because, according to Hitler's orders, from now on, no indigenous volunteer unit would be permitted to be larger than a battalion. Two weeks before, I had discussed with General Hellmich the formation of a Caucasian Army; obviously, we were moving in opposite directions. One could only assume that the underlying reason for Hitler's order was his mistrust toward the Eastern Volunteer Units. He must have realized that the volunteers were not mercenaries but patriots of their respective countries and his brutal East Policy precluded such a trust.

I knew too well that our friends in the German Army did not share Hitler's views, and if they could not change him, hopefully they would rebel against him, inasmuch as he was losing the war. I met First Lieutenant Wilhelm Reissmüller, to begin with in Kokosi, when he visited us in the line of duty on May 5, 1943.[155] This again coincided with a field exercise of a "Bergmann" company around the Ai-Petri Pass over the Crimean Mountains. Reissmüller went up there with us, so we walked and shared the beauty of nature and our thoughts on a variety of subjects including the problems of our volunteer units. As we got to know each other better, we devoted considerable time to criticism of the dismal German East Policy; he had a keen grasp of reality and we shared many common views. Originally Reissmüller had been an officer in the 1st Mountain Division but because of serious combat injuries, he was transferred to General von Kleist's staff and later to the staff of General for the Eastern Troops.[156]

I visited Reissmüller off and on at headquarters in Simferopol, at times with Professor Oberländer. We always found him helpful and pleasant. Doctor of Philosophy, accomplished artistic painter and sculptor,[157] First Lieutenant Reissmüller,

---

155- Author's "mini diary"; Professor Theodore Oberländer's personal diary.
156- "General der Osttruppen," this name was subsequently altered to "General of the Volunteer Units."
157- His paintings were a great success during major German art exhibits in 1955; for instance, the *Portrait of President Theodore Heuss* was bought by the city of Munich. After the war, he settled in his home city of Ingolstadt/Donau and became the publisher of the newspaper *Donau Kurier* (*The Danube*

in my opinion, was by far above the average young officer. He was a tall, handsome gentleman, a native of the city of Ingolstadt/Donau in Bavaria, with a great sense of humor, regardless of the seriousness of the situation. His features somehow reminded me of a Cossack ataman (chieftain), and it amused him when I told him so. Reissmüller and Herwarth got along splendidly and fate guided the three of us to become lifelong friends. Somewhat later, we were blessed by another mutual friend, Captain Siegfried Ungermann, a wonderful fellow and the head of the personnel department in General Köstring's staff. I will have more to say about this later.

Conditions in the P.O.W. camps in Crimea were quite satisfactory. In Simferopol, while visiting the camp, I became acquainted with a P.O.W. M.D., Dr. Jankhoteli (whose first name I cannot recall). He was a Georgian, native of the province Lower Svaneti—one could say that we were neighbors since I am from the Upper Free Svaneti. Dr. Jankhoteli had dignified manners, appeared confident and was much respected by the German officer in charge and his aides. He was consulted by the Germans, especially concerning the P.O.W.s' health, nutrition, hygiene and etc. The P.O.W.s generally appeared in good health, relaxed and without discernible anxiety. I told Dr. Jankhoteli that a transfer to "Bergmann" could be arranged for him and some other P.O.W.s if they felt it would be the better place for them. None of them voiced such a desire, and I thought that we had come a long way in our quest for the betterment of P.O.W.s status in Army Group A's domain. This was the result of Field Marshal von Kleist's orders in the Caucasus and Crimea and "Bergmann's" monitoring of their realization during daily life. I also felt that even if we did not achieve anything else but this, our coming to the Caucasus still would have been worthwhile.[158]

In Simferopol, life was flourishing during the summer of 1943, thanks to Kleist's reforms.[159] Even the local theater reopened with performances at a professional level. Several local restaurants offered good menus. The owner of one of them was a brother-in-law of Niko Nakashidze, an "old" emigrant from Berlin and a friend of my uncle, whom I had met in the Caucasus and is mentioned in the corresponding chapter ["To the Ukraine and Caucasus"]. He retreated from Caucasus with the staff of the 17th Army, where he served as an interpreter and continued to do so in Simferopol. Nakashidze's brother-in-law was an ethnic Russian but had settled in

---

Courier) and also many excellent books. The city of Ingolstadt declared Dr. Wilhelm Reissmüller an honorary citizen for his many-fold promotions and contributions to cultural life, not only for the city but also at the state and national level and moreover, for his humanitarian and charitable help to the less fortunate.

158- Long after the war, I received happy news that Dr. Jankhoteli was alive and well and working as a physician in Tbilisi.

159- The agricultural productivity was also greatly helped by above average precipitation.

Crimea some time before. His wife, a charming and vivacious Georgian, was very happy to have found her "lost" brother now years after the German occupation of Crimea. Needless to say, I was invited to their restaurant a number of times. We enjoyed the gourmet food as well as toasting each other, but above all we enjoyed being together to share our past experiences and to ponder about the future.

A number of Georgian emigrants in "Bergmann" decided to return to their families in France. Most of them had health problems, others probably felt that "Bergmann's" chance of returning to Caucasus were very slim. There was not enough incentive left for them to stay and therefore petitioned Oberländer to be discharged from "Bergmann." While Oberländer (assisted by a German officer) discussed this matter with them, some linguistic and other difficulties occurred. This being the case, one of the participating emigrants, Themo Taktakishvili, wondered, "why the Georgian Liaison Officer Dr. Givi Gabliani was not present" during what was for them such an important meeting. Oberländer, at once, dispatched a messenger to locate me and the negotiations were resumed after my arrival and were finally concluded to everyone's satisfaction.

Oberländer later explained the reason I had not been notified about the meeting in the first place. Apparently, a German officer made an erroneous assumption that the "old" emigres would resent my presence during the meeting, as I was not one of them but rather a "new comer" from "Sovietland." I was glad, as was Oberländer, that such an assumption turned out to be incorrect. This was more proof of the amalgamation of the "Bergmann" Georgians, in spite of the psychological stress created by the retreat from Caucasus. For me, personally, it confirmed again that my newly found compatriots accepted me as one of them, had confidence in me and felt my affection for them. During the fall of 1943, I experienced more proof of this, as we shall see later.

The psychological stress revealed itself in the Georgian 5th Company. Oberländer told me that he had been informed by a German non-commissioned officer (in charge of the 5th Company) that two soldiers, Jason Alania and Apollon Giorgadze, were considering defection to the Soviet side. Alania had recently returned from a military hospital in Ukraine or Poland. He had been sent there from the Caucasian front because while cleaning his gun, it accidentally discharged, causing considerable damage to one of his hands. While in the hospital, he met a Georgian P.O.W. military pilot who was employed by the Germans somewhere but had a plan to defect back to the Soviet side. He deemed it safe to do so and expected no punishment from the Soviets for having worked for the Germans. He advised Alania to do the same when the first opportunity presented itself, (for instance, when on the front line again). After his arrival in "Bergmann," Alania shared all of this with

Giorgadze and apparently both of them agreed this was the thing to do. Actually, Alania was a likeable and good natured chap; I was sure he would never hurt anyone. He also was talkative, including talk about his "secret plan." Some of his well-wishers, among them Sergeant Shota Dumbadze, bluntly told him that he talked too much, and anyone who really wanted to defect would have carried it out without being so vocal about it. He also warned him that such talk could lead to serious trouble.[160]

Alania had two reasons for defection, one was the fear of hurting his relatives, who could have been mobilized in the Soviet Army and now perhaps would oppose us across the front line.[161] The second reason was the fear that unless he defected, he would never see his country and home again. I personally could not help but have compassion for him although the incidence of killing our compatriots across the front line in the Caucasus, according to all the information we had, was very rare. The main reason for this was that the "Bergmann" Caucasians, through loudspeakers, made their presence known across the front line quite early. The result was mass defection of the Soviet Georgian and Azerbaijani soldiers to our side. Therefore, such indigenous Soviet troops were expeditiously transferred from our region.[162] As far as Alania's returning home was concerned, I had great doubts about this, fearing that instead he would most likely be sentenced to the gulag with an uncertain final outcome because he had been a "Bergmann" soldier.

Having been informed by a German non-commissioned officer about Alania's and Giorgadze's intentions, Oberländer talked with the Georgian sergeant, Shota Dumbadze. He was considered to be an excellent soldier and one of the pillars of the 5th Company. Dumbadze told Oberländer that Alania and Giorgadze could not be taken too seriously and the former was just talking too much. Following this, Oberländer had a meeting with von Kutzschenbach and me, and we sat together on the porch of Yusupov's villa in Kokosi, pondering about what to do. Lieutenant Süss joined us later. Needless to say that none of us wanted these two soldiers to get hurt, but one could hardly afford to ignore such a thing. It was wartime, and if nothing else, it would hardly be a morale booster for other soldiers. Therefore, the three of us felt that it would be best for all concerned to transfer Alania and Giorgadze to some working unit in the rear region. There were two problems with this: first, to find an appropriate unit and second, the military court had to agree to it. Therefore, Oberländer explained the whole situation and its unusual features to the military court investigator. The trial followed during the early part of July 1943,

---

160- Dumbadze told me about it after the war.

161- Some of his comrades suspected that because of that, the bullet injury to his hand in the Caucasus was a self inflicted injury rather than an accident in order to escape the front line.

162- Hans von Herwarth, *Against Two Evils*, p. 232; Professor Theodore Oberländer, *History of the "Bergmann" Unit*, pp. 24–25.

and the court ordered a transfer of both soldiers to a working unit under supervision for the duration of three years.[163]

One day upon my return to Kokosi from a trip, I was informed that two soldiers, Vakhtang ("Botso") Chikvinidze and Tariel Kutateladze had been lodged in an improvised prison near regimental headquarters. Their arrest was linked with Alania's "secret" plan for defection. Because both were considered Alania's friends and his frequent visitors, they now became suspects as potential defectors. Vakhtang and Tariel were the youngest soldiers in "Bergmann," being nineteen to twenty years old. Both had been with us on the Caucasus front and proved to be reliable soldiers. I knew about their background from Tbilisi. Vakhtang's father, Platon Korisheli, had been a well-known stage actor and "The People's Artist" of the Rustaveli Theatre as well as one of the many victims of the 1937 purges of the Soviet intelligentsia. Tariel had been a friend of my sister. His father, Apollon Kutateladze, was a famous artistic painter who also had been assigned as a portraitist to the Kremlin.

I was keeping an eye on Vakhtang and Tariel since they were so young and relatively inexperienced and therefore more vulnerable. I went to see them at once, listened to their story and then I told Oberländer and von Kutzschenbach that I personally would vouch for them and moreover could use them as my helpers. So it was agreed on—they were freed from jail and until the end of the war I tried to keep them "under my wing"; however, it was not because of that but through the mercy of the Lord that those two youngsters survived the war.[164]

Around this time, Giorgi (Jora) Indjia, an old emigrant from Paris whom I have mentioned before, returned to "Bergmann." He had recovered from a wound sustained at the Caucasus front. We found lodging for Jora next to ours since changes in "Bergmann" were pending and Indjia's future assignment had to be clarified. He got along very well with Vakhtang and Tariel, and the bonds of friendship grew even more among us. Misha Kavtaradze, Irakli Djaparidze and other emigrants

---

163- Notes, Professor Theodore Oberländer's personal diary; Notes, author's "mini diary." Shota Dumbadze related to me that shortly before the end of the war in Czechoslovakia, a Georgian poet, Giorgi ("Guguli") Gamkrelidze saw Alania. He, with two other Georgians, was working at manual labor; Giorgadze was not among them. Alania apparently was in good health.

164- After the war, Tariel of his own free will, chose to return to the Soviet Union. It is my understanding that he was sentenced to some remote gulag. But happily he survived and returned to Georgia, thanks to his exceptionally good health and Khrushchev's reforms. At the present time, he is dean of a university faculty of architecture in Tbilisi and also a grandfather. Vakhtang emigrated to the United States and settled in California where he had a relative. He graduated from university, acquired a doctorate in music and subsequently became a professor of music, art and humanities. Encouraged by Giorgi Papashvili (the author of *Anything Can Happen* and a sculptor), Vakhtang also became a sculptor. He and his talented wife, Margaret, had a number of successful exhibits of their works of art here and in Europe. The city of Morro Bay, California, commissioned him to erect a sculpture, "The Family of Pelicans" in their downtown area—a great success. In the United Sates, he assumed his father's pseudonym, Korisheli. They have two adopted children and also are grandparents.

also visited us for a chat or a business matter in the regimental headquarters. Indjia had been in France on a short vacation before rejoining "Bergmann" and brought some presents to many of us—for me, a French pocket calendar, where I commenced making notes. Thanks to it, I have a "mini" diary of the years 1943 and 1944, without which writing my memoirs would have been even more difficult.

One of the first personally significant meetings that I recorded in the diary was when Air Force Major Otto Baumhauer came to see us in Kokosi; we met before in the Caucasus. The "Air Force 4" headquarters had learned about "Bergmann" in the Caucasus during 1942, and decided to have a Georgian company of its own. Therefore, they contacted Oberländer for help and also appointed Major Baumhauer to head the project. The Major visited us in Nalchik and Oberländer introduced us. Baumhauer was an "unusual" German major; during the Georgian independence, he was a teacher in the German school (a gymnasium)[165] in Tbilisi. There he met a lovely, young Georgian lady, Margarita Chikovani, they fell in love and were married. After a truly democratic young Georgian Republic was occupied by the Red Russian troops or in anticipation of that happening, the Baumhauers left for Germany, settled there and had one son.

The Major loved Georgia, and there was instant "chemistry" between him and the "Bergmann" Georgians, which "spilled over" to the soldiers of the newly formed "Air Force 4's" Georgian company. The soldiers loved and trusted their Major and at times affectionately referred to him as "our brother-in-law," because of his marriage to Margarita Chikovani. The company consisted mainly of "Bergmann's" recent recruits. Two of the Bergmann Georgian emigrants, Victor Nozadze and David Vachnadze also were seconded to it in an advisory capacity and also as interpreters. Among the new recruits from the P.O.W. camp in Prokhladnaia[166] was a Georgian doctor, Dr. Mirian Galashvili, who was also attached to Major Baumhauer's company as a physician for his group.[167] After retreat from Caucasus, the "Air Force 4" no longer had need for the Georgian company and it was sent back to "Bergmann" in Crimea, where it was incorporated into the Georgian Battalion, "Bergmann I." (As noted before, two other battalions were the Azerbaijan Battalion, "Bergmann II"; and the North Caucasian Battalion, "Bergmann III.") I was glad to see Mirian and

---

165- In many continental European countries, this is the equivalent of high school and two years of college. It prepares students to enter the university.

166- The city and railroad station in North Caucasus between two cities, Mozdok and Georgievsk.

167- I knew Mirian from our medical school days in Tbilisi. He was not only a conscientious physician and a gentleman but also had a talent for creative writing. This he probably inherited from his mother, whose uncle, Daniel Tchonkadze was a well known writer in Georgia. Mirian was two years my junior in medical school. He was a gymnast and also on the medical school cross country skiing team. I was also on the team, and this is how I met him the first time on our way to training at the Georgian skiing resort, Bakuriani.

Major Baumhauer again, as we had a lot to talk about until time came for the Major to bid us goodbye and rejoin "Air Force 4."

Crimea was not considered to be the rear region. We only had a respite from the major engagement with the Soviet forces, which could change any time. The Soviets could land on several areas of the sea coast and then penetrate deep or occupy the Perekop Isthmus and Sivash to cut us off from the mainland; or do both. Moreover, partisans were being landed in Crimea with increasing frequency and although, as already noted, "Bergmann" was not bothered by them, some other troops were. "Bergmann" was also given the responsibility to defend the long coastal area as well as provide infantry protection for the German coastal artillery. In the event of a Soviet landing, the best "Bergmann" could do was to engage the landed Soviet troops in combat, slow them down and at once inform the reserve troops to rush larger units to the battle area.

I traveled almost daily on horseback to keep a liaison with the Georgian companies, including the cavalry squadron, commanded by Lieutenant Mikheil (Misha) Dadiani, whom I mentioned before. Such trips were also important to me personally; it helped maintain the friendship with other officers. In Dadiani's company, I had many friends, among them Lieutenant Giorgi (Goglik) Vachnadze; non-commissioned officers Archil Dadiani and Aliosha Abashidze; Konstantin (Kote) Vashadze; Irakli Kalandarashvili; Shota Gedevanishvili and others. Among the soldiers from the "new generation" I also became acquainted with Mamia Zakradze, whom I would see off and on after the war.

I had a perfect excuse to stay overnight in the cavalry squadron since it would not be possible to turn around and get back to Kokosi by daylight in one day. During one such visit, after being an excellent host, Lieutenant Misha Dadiani declared that he would like to ride with me in the morning to visit the regimental headquarters and see his friends there. So we rode side by side on two excellent horses and during our conversation covered many topics close to our hearts. Misha was not only an expert on horses and the art of war but had enormous charm and was well read. He could recite medieval as well as other poetry; for instance, a poem by an emigrant poet, Simonika Berejiani. He also recited a short poem written in Georgian by his father, Koki Dadiani, a great patriot who died in France as a political emigrant. It is written on his gravestone in the Georgian cemetery in Leuville, France and freely translated by me:

Pray for me and while telling my country bitter stories...
Say also that you saw the writing on my gravestone.
That even my bones are thinking about Georgia.

Although not as eloquent as Misha, I did my share of talking and reciting. I began to appreciate why some troubadours loved to travel on horseback. Shortly before sundown, Misha and I arrived in Kokosi. I felt that this one day of riding together further contributed toward better understanding of each other.

Usually I traveled alone, especially on long trips. I argued with some friends that should I run into a couple of stray partisans in the wooded areas (which was unlikely) and their hostile intentions were noted, my horse "Nalchik" and I should be able to take care of ourselves. If we did stumble on a larger group, then it would be up to Nalchik to act like Pegasus.

Just how fast Nalchik was, I had found out in an unusual way. One day, I visited the stable to see how Nalchik was doing following an extended trip the day before and I found him to be wet and "foamy." The soldier in the stable responsible for Nalchik's care, Valodia Gabrichidze, explained that he had given Nalchik a bath in the nearby river. "What about this foam, and why is the horse so hot?" I wanted to know. Valodia appeared embarrassed and admitted that every so often the "stable boys" raced the officer's horses. Valodia and Nalchik always won the races and the betting money. "There is no horse around here as fast as Nalchik and I believe he was bred for racing," said Valodia.

His remark failed to soften my heart, and I told Valodia that he, in a way, betrayed my and Nalchik's trust in him. That Nalchik was a hard-working horse since we had to leave our vehicles in the Kuban Peninsula. Moreover, races may cause injuries in both the man and the horse. "As your officer, I have legal authority to restrict your freedom for ten to fourteen days, Soldier Gabrichidze," I said. As usual, my anger did not last that long and after a couple of days, the restrictions were lifted. Valodia promised never again to do such a thing, and other "stable boys" also got the message. Valodia was a good man, he knew a lot about horses, he loved and took excellent care of Nalchik. He was a master blacksmith and taught others the best way of fitting horseshoes. It was an original method of his uncle who trained Valodia in Georgia. Nalchik's shoes never rattled or came off, and he never limped.

During the early seventies, I had a surprise visit in Quincy, Illinois from Valodia, his Austrian wife and their children. The family had settled in Wisconsin. Valodia's skills as a blacksmith were in great demand far beyond his community. One of their children, Haidi, helped her papa in his business. He also had a position in an industry as a skilled worker. At that time, there were four horses running in our pasture in Quincy. Valodia inspected all of them and rode my personal quarter horse, "Rocky." "They don't even come close to Nalchik," he said. He strolled on our land and said, "Doctor, you surely don't know how to care for your trees." I was willing to learn; Valodia went to work and cut almost one fourth of the branches off. Now my wife, Rusudan, and our son, Gregory, who both were speakers for the rights of trees, rebelled against "such a barbaric surgery." I reminded them of Valodia's ultimate expertise since he had also done his "graduate work" in gardening under his father and uncle in Georgia. It was a happy reunion with Valodia after so many turbulent years of the war.

10

LEAVING CRIMEA FOR GERMANY
The Dresden Military School

During early July 1943, the state of affairs in Crimea was stable and satisfactory. However the Battle of Kursk had begun between the massive German and Soviet forces. It was a considerable distance from Crimea, but the outcome would certainly affect all of us. A letter arrived in Kokosi from the general of the Eastern Troops concerning me. I was instructed to visit Professor Gerhard von Mende in the Ministry of Eastern Affairs ("das Ostministerium") in Berlin on my way to the Dresden Military School.

Since Professor Oberländer was also leaving on his vacation, he suggested that first of all I meet his family and spend some time at their home in Greifswald-Pomerania. I accepted this invitation with pleasure although I could only stay there a couple of days due to my appointment with Professor von Mende. Oberländer and his "man-Friday," Ismail, an Azerbaijani soldier and the professor's devoted servant, left by plane on July 12th. I said goodbye to all my friends in Crimea, rode Nalchik one more time and was able to get an airplane seat for the following day. I had to change planes several times with much delay between; therefore, there was plenty of time for me to ponder a number of things.

I was entering military school with mixed feelings. On one hand, I was curious about the prestigious military institution of learning. On the other hand, it was difficult for me to leave "Bergmann" for three and a half months, where I had so many friends. Moreover, being in Crimea was, at least geographically, closer to the Caucasus. And who knew what could develop during this time? Occasionally, my thoughts turned into fantasies, such as "Germany may not win the war, but perhaps neither will the Red Empire, which might collapse as did the Czar's during W.W. I and if so, we the 'Bergmann' soldiers, legionnaires and P.O.W.s would need to get back home quickly and help our people there because ensuing chaos with enormous problems was to be expected" (not unlike ones after W.W. I, which we enumerated before). During the present war, nearly one-half million able-bodied Georgian men apparently were drafted into the Red Army and sent to Russia. If nothing else, that alone rendered Georgia defenseless. Therefore, we may also need to establish a liaison with the western powers and seek their understanding and help. Perhaps the Georgians in General de Gaulle's army would also speak on our behalf.

I arrived in Greifswald at noon, after a two day trip. It was easy to find Professor Oberländer's house in this university city where he had been lecturing. Mrs. Erika Oberländer impressed me as a very kind, thoughtful and intelligent lady, totally devoted to her family. She was a daughter of the Protestant pastor from Northeast Germany. I was privileged to meet her parents after the war, then themselves refugees from East Germany. They settled in Augsburg-Bavaria, joining Oberländer's family. However brief, it was very pleasant to be a guest in Greifswald. I made friends rather quickly with Oberländer's three sons but in this respect one could not compete with Ismail (the professor's Azerbaijani servant), who had already captivated the children's hearts. It was delightful to observe the contrast of totally blond boys playing with Ismail, who had a strikingly dark complexion.

The professor and I strolled in the city and discussed a number of subjects close to our hearts. We were especially concerned about the future of "Bergmann," which was to be separated into three battalions, as noted before. Oberländer suggested that I bring up this problem during the pending meeting with Professor von Mende, in the Ministry of the Eastern Affairs, and perhaps he could be of some help through his connections. "Von Mende," he said, "has been 'one of us', a real friend who from the very beginning shared and supported, without reservation, the Army's view about decent treatment of the people from the East." Many years later I came across a citation in Dallin's and von Herwarth's books, where Mende's name was mentioned and which further supported Oberländer's opinion of him.[168]

When bedtime arrived, surprisingly enough one was able to read without a lamp; in other words, we were experiencing a "white night." I had not realized how

---

168- Alexander Dallin and Hans von Herwarth quote from U.S. National Archives, Document N.G.–1657. This concerns the report of the Inspection Commission consisting of Schulenburg and Pfleiderer (from the foreign Office), Köstring and Herwarth (from the Army). During August 1942, the Commission toured the various camps that housed P.O.W.s bound for slave labor in Germany.

    The Commission reported very bad conditions in those camps at a meeting that was also attended by Nazi officials. The commission stressed the need for a plan for the establishment of the federated and the autonomous Caucasian states (Armenian, Azerbaijani, Georgian, North Caucasian). Although this plan assured German control over the Caucasus, it was deemed too liberal for a Nazi official present. He suspected and reported to his superiors that the military-like Köstring understood "freedom" for the Soviet nationalities "very broadly, namely to mean sovereignty."

    "The worst, however, of what I experienced was a statement by Herr Herwarth von Bittenfeld that some of the gentlemen in the Ostministerium, notably Bräutigam and von Mende, have the same point of view as the Foreign Office." (See Dallin, pp. 237–238; Herwarth, pp. 228, 230.)

far north Greifswald was located until then. I left for Berlin at 8:00 a.m. and arrived there early enough to keep the noon appointment with Professor Gerhard von Mende in the Ostministerium. I was much impressed by the professor; he was a very intelligent, cultured, well informed, capable and dynamic person with a great sense of humor. We basically spoke German but at times he would switch to Russian, especially while quoting some old proverb, such as "Terpi Kosak, Atamanom, budesh." ("Be patient, Cossack and you shall be an ataman"—chieftain.)

Mende needed patience while championing the rights of the Caucasians as the head of the corresponding department of the Ostministerium. It had been an uphill battle and right now, the professor felt the time was overdue for formation of the effective, national representative and working organization for each of the Caucasian nations on a nonpartisan basis. As far as Georgians were concerned, the representative or speaker for those in the armed forces should be included as somehow, they had been notably absent from prior similar organizations, as we shall elucidate later on.

Generally speaking, "the younger generation" of Georgians had to infuse some energy in such an undertaking, since the discussions alone about the political dogmas and the rights would not suffice. If this is not carried out now, Mende envisioned, a potentially dangerous situation for the legionnaires, P.O.W.s, as well as the Georgian civilians would result. Such "missionary" work already had been carried out by the "Bergmann" Georgians and Germans while on the Caucasus front, Mende said. Caucasus had been militarily lost, but in principle, taking care of the people's problem remains more or less the same, albeit very complex, given the present circumstances. Mende indicated that so far he failed to move his "higher ups" to call such organization "The Committee," therefore the name "The Liaison Staff" ("der Verbindungsstab") had been proposed.[169]

Now von Mende wanted my input concerning this matter. Why me? I was interested to know. Apparently, Mende, Kedia and others had done considerable "research and polling" among the "old" as well as the "new" emigres; those who returned from the Caucasus or Crimea, passing through Berlin on their way to France or remaining in Germany; also, of the persons belonging to the "National Alliance" in Paris, representing almost all political parties and groups, including the close circle around the former President Noe Jordania. It would appear that the "National Alliance" in Paris had information about me from the "Bergmann" emigres from France. According to Mende, with a rare exception, they all suggested that I

169- Hitler simply forbade the name "Committee" since this may have implied some political concessions toward the "Eastern People." His obedient Minister of Eastern Affairs, Mr. Rosenberg, complied as usual, apparently contrary to his own personal view.

be the speaker for those in the armed forces. Clearly, I was pleased to hear about this expression of confidence by the people, and I thanked Professor von Mende for his part in it.

On the other hand, I had to tell him that such a thing was not in my plans. As he knew, I was soon entering the Dresden Military School and after graduation (hopefully) during November of 1943, I was committed to rejoin "Bergmann" as soon as possible. Mende said that I probably could help "Bergmann" and other Georgian units better from Berlin than from the front during the difficult times and challenges that lay ahead for them. That, in fact, was one of the reasons for establishing the "Liaison Staff." In any case, he suggested that I meet M. Kedia, Dr. Gogi (Giorgi) Magalow (Magalashvili) and Misha (Mikhail) Alshibaja, all of the "old emigres." It had also been proposed that they be the other members of the "Liaison Staff." It was also suggested that I should take some time to get acquainted with other Georgians in Berlin and get better oriented about the existing situation.

I told Mende that I had already met Kedia, almost two years ago in Berlin. The professor flashed his boyish smile, nodded and said that he knew about it and also about the "impressive" letter I had written at that time to our President in exile, N. Jordania. He added that Kedia, more than anyone else wanted me to serve on the "Liaison Staff." Professor von Mende's office had checked with the Military School in Dresden and found that the course did not begin until August 10th. Since I had better than two weeks to look around Berlin, he asked if I would please see him again during the later part of the next week. As far as keeping the "Bergmann" battalions together, he would see what he could do.

Hans von Herwarth, a friend of mine and the diplomat whom I frequently mention in this work, tells us,

> "Diplomacy is an art about treating human beings, its material is the living human, surely the most precious but at the same time, the most sensitive material. The sculptor, who works on stone or wood, when in error or unhappy with his work can redo his work on new material. But if one hurts a human being, the wounds remain and it could take a long time before they are healed."[170]

This definition applied to Professor Gerhard von Mende, who had the makeup of a diplomat and was swimming upstream in order to be able to function.

Outside the Professor von Mende's office, I had a surprise. There was a remarkably handsome, middle-aged gentleman—a giant waiting for me. He greeted

---

170- Hans von Herwarth, *Von Adenauer Zu Brandt: Erinnerunger, From Adenauer to Brandt: Memoires*, Berlin, Frankfurt: Propyläen, 1990.

and embraced me so vigorously that I thought my ribs would crack; obviously he did not know his own strength. He said in a Svan dialect that he was no one else but Tengiz Dadeshkeliani, a distant relative from my father's side. Tengiz had learned of my meeting in the Ostministerium and felt it was his duty to be my guide in Berlin. For starters, we went to the place he recommended that I stay, Hotel "Leibnitz Eck" (also referred to as "Hollywood") on Kurfürstendamm, owned by a Persian rug dealer—married to a Georgian lady, with the family name Potskverashvili. The two of them had hosted many Georgians who came to Berlin and right now two floors below me, a Georgian couple from Paris, Mrs. Nino and Mr. Kale Salia, had an apartment. Professor Mikhako Tsereteli and I were invited by the Salias for dinner a few days later. I mentioned this informal get-together in the chapter "In the Bergmann Unit and Caucasus," while discussing the Georgian political parties in exile. I shall add more to it a little later in this chapter.

Tengiz and I strolled on Kurfürstendamm, and we had a lot to tell each other. He said that he had volunteered for Thamar II but in the training camp, the German Army could not find a steel helmet large enough to match his head. It was just as difficult to fit this medieval knight with boots and uniform. Finally he had to be honorably discharged from the Army, and thoroughly disgusted, he went back to Paris. He had a sister there, Ekathirine ("Katia"); one daughter, Irina and a cousin, Ilamaz Dadeshkeliani—once a well-known lawyer and talented gentleman but not in the best of health at this time. If my memory serves me right, my mother was one of Ilamaz's godmothers and years later, she spoke with great affection of him. His childhood pictures were to be found in our albums at home.

When Tengiz first heard from some vacationing emigres in Paris that I was in "Bergmann," I received a very warm letter from him in Mittenwald-Bavaria, early summer of 1942. I promptly responded with a long letter in answer to his many questions, and now we could talk and share our thoughts freely. What was he doing in Berlin during the summer of 1943? Well, he became very restless in Paris, feeling that he was idling while other Georgians carried out their patriotic duty. Then Dr. Giorgi ("Gogi") Magalashvili, who worked for the Ostministerium in Berlin, offered Tengiz the opportunity to be his assistant for some projects.

The weather was beautiful, and Tengiz and I spent the day walking in Berlin, which had not as yet revealed the major destructions due to allied air raids. We ended up in a Russian restaurant, "Medved"—"The Bear," and there we met four Georgians at once. Two of them, Sandro Kordzaia and Mose Imnaishvili, worked there; Eretheos Ramishvili and the fourth Georgian (whose name I don't recall) were having a meal. With beaming faces, they all greeted Tengiz, who in turn introduced me to the gentlemen. All three, whose names I mentioned, were well-known members of the Georgian Social Democrat Party and disciples of the President in exile, Noe Jordania. Tengiz did not particularly care for the social democratic theories but this never kept him from having a warm and friendly relationship with them.

On our way back home, he told me of the episode from the past concerning his uncle, Tatarkan Dadeshkeliani, and my father who were close and "inseparable" friends. Tatarkan was many years my father's senior and was also very fond of my mother, Vera, to whom he often referred to as "my little dove." These three frequently visited each other, dined together and engaged in discussions about ethnography, history and literature. Tatarkan whose title would properly translate to be the equivalent of a duke, was the Lord of part of Upper Svaneti, west of the Bali mountain range.[171]

Lord Tatarkan himself was a liberally minded member of the splendid Georgian intelligentsia of the late-nineteenth and early-twentieth century. He was beautifully educated, a scholarly grand seigneur, spoke several languages and was very good looking.[172] Alas, the deep friendship between Tatarkan and my parents came to a screeching stop. At that time, my parents resided in the community of Latali—part of Free Svaneti, bordering Tatarkan's estate. Father was the Administrator of the Upper Svaneti that included the territories east as well as west of Bali. (He had been so appointed by the order, "In the Name of the Czar.") A local farmer of Latali complained to my father that the manager-steward of Lord Tatarkan's estate took several heads of cattle from him because while grazing, the herd stepped over into the Tatarkan's property. The farmer felt that such a severe penalty was unreasonable, inasmuch as there was no damage done and it was a first "offense." Father rode to the scene of conflict at once, without his bodyguards, to mediate between the involved sides before things got out of hand. The farmer pledged to watch his cattle better in the future and to reimburse now for damages if such would be discovered. Father thought that the farmer's plea was reasonable, but the manager-steward was an uncompromising man and wanted to keep the cattle as a penalty for the intrusion. "By whose laws?" asked Father and advised the manager to return the cattle to his lawful owner and settle the grievances, if any, later.

171- Some of his ancestors had tried in vain to also conquer the Free Upper Svaneti—located east of the Bali, but the freedom loving Free Svans were determined to remain so and ready to shed blood for it. Therefore they remained free and offered refuge for many persecuted and displaced, proud people, some of them of noble origin. Even today, impressive looking medieval defense towers owned by each clan are one more testimony to the heroic past of Free Svaneti. West of Bali Svaneti, only the Dadeshkelianis had such towers; therefore, the townships there did not look quite as spectacular, especially from a distance. In a sense, the Free Upper Svaneti reminded me of the frontier countries of the U.S.A.

172- The artistic painter, Zichy in Tbilisi, used Tatarkan as his model for the main hero while illustrating the poem "The Knight in Tiger's Skin" by Rustaveli. I have seen such photos in our family album.

On this, the manager rather rudely replied that he was accountable only to Lord Tatarkan and no one else. Father became infuriated (he did so occasionally) and slapped the manager-steward, shouting, "How dare you," and ordered the return of the cattle to the farmer or "the worst is yet to happen." The frightened manager returned the cattle but complained to his master. Tatarkan was upset and felt that what Father did to his manager also reflected disrespect toward him as the master.

Father took exception to such a view, answering that the man was slapped not because he was his Lordship's manager but in spite of it. He had been rude, unreasonable and he had it coming; he also hurt Tatarkan Dadeshkeliani's image among the townspeople. For the next three weeks or so, there was a "cold war" between the "former friends." But they loved and missed each other and sure enough, the wiser and more experienced grand old man made the first move. He "dropped in" with a bouquet of flowers at a time when he knew Father would not be at home. "Where is your difficult husband?" he asked my mother and both of them broke into laughter—the cold war was over.

Tatarkan's demise must have been very painful to my parents; they often mentioned him to me. They had both lost their fathers as little children and perhaps Tatarkan had been, in a way, a father image for them. He was in ill health for some time, with his feet swollen and too weak to walk. His men would take him outside on a stretcher; he enjoyed seeing the eagles soar over the mountains, the beautiful scenery and to hear the sound of the waterfalls. This was approximately what Tengiz Dadeshkeliani told me about the touching friendship of his uncle and my parents. This was also essentially what I had heard from my parents about it during my formative years. I was moved by this story and remembered that the following day, July 17th, was the sixth anniversary of the arrest and disappearance of my father by the Kremlin henchmen during the 1937 purges.

July 18th was a Sunday. Tengiz stopped by my hotel and suggested that I get acquainted with the number of Georgian personalities in Berlin. We started with Dr. Gogi (Giorgi) Magalow (Magalashvili) with whom Tengiz had a special relationship as noted above. We found Magalow in a spacious apartment, dictating a report to his secretary, Greta Balarjishvili, a lovely young lady of German descent from the Balticum, married to a Georgian, Leo Balarjishvili, who also worked in the "Ostministerium."

Dr. Magalow was a tall, handsome gentleman with excellent manners and very friendly. He graduated from medical school at Munich University a number of years ago. He was married to Monika Witt, daughter of a well-known progressive industrialist from the city of Weiden. Mr. Witt specialized in the production of bed linen and ready-to-wear clothing, applying some American methods in his industry and marketing. The Magalows had three sons, and they all lived happily on their estate, Ising on the Chiemsee in Bavaria. The doctor also had a splendid opportunity for a lucrative medical practice. After the outbreak of the war, he chose to abandon the safety and comfort of his home and went to Berlin. He hoped to be of some help to the Georgian cause from his position in the Ostministerium. In this, he had strong backing from his influential friend, Professor Alexandre Nikuradze. Such support should have been a significant factor since the minister, A. Rosenberg, in charge of the Ostministerium, had been a friend of A. Nikuradze ever since they were students in Munich during the early 1920s. Both were emigrants—Rosenberg an ethnic German from the Balticum and Nikuradze a Georgian, at first a student in Germany from the Sovereign Georgian Republic but after its occupation by the Red Army during February 1921, also turned emigrant. We will have more to say about this later.

Magalow wanted to know firsthand about my experience in "Bergmann," Caucasus and Crimea, as well as about Georgia while I was there. He had been aware of a positive policy by the German military administration in the Caucasus and was glad that my observations further confirmed it. Then he told me briefly about his activities in Berlin. The bottom line of his view was that creation of the Liaison Staff was clearly indicated and the official recognition of Georgian sovereignty was just a matter of time. As during the meeting with Mende, I did not commit myself to participate in the Liaison Staff, as this was far too unclear as far as I was concerned and in addition, I had different objectives in mind. Magalow thanked Tengiz and I for our visit and he told me if there was anything he could do for me to please let him know. I was pleasantly impressed by Dr. Magalashvili.

Tengiz and I next visited the Togonidzes, living in a pleasant house. Valiko ("Huhu") Togonidze was married to Tina Gogelashvili. Both were old emigres. The Oberländers were former neighbors of some of Tina's family, the Gogelashvilis, and thought highly of them. Apparently, Tengiz had warned Tina and Valiko of our pending visit beforehand, so they not only expected us but insisted that we have a "Georgian" lunch with them.

Our hosts and I shared our experiences. I had to answer many questions, but so did they. Valiko Togonidze, like some other Georgians, found employment in the Ostministerium as an interpreter and carrying out other modest functions. Their leitmotif was somehow to help the Georgian cause. For instance, this gave them an opportunity to visit their countrymen in P.O.W. camps in non-combat zones and to comfort and improve their conditions. A number of P.O.W.s were freed and transferred to the Wustrau compound near Berlin, where they had an opportunity to learn the German language and about the western world, which until now was not accessible to them. In Wustrau, a cadre was prepared by the Ostministerium for certain civilian organizational functions in case Georgia would be taken by the German military forces. Some of them took jobs outside the compound; for instance, the group of former Soviet Army nurses or doctors' assistants now worked in a nearby hospital. They seemed to have adjusted well to the new environment.

During my own visit in Wustrau, the former P.O.W.s had been very curious and "hungry" for news. They also wanted to know all about "Bergmann." For instance, was it true that the Georgians there were such good soldiers? I assured them that they were. What about the political party activities? I said that political party activism would not be welcomed in a military unit such as "Bergmann." To be sure, there were some soldiers there who had this or that political party preferences and affiliation but such was not advertised. I further explained that "Bergmann" and other military units would serve any Georgian government which had been elected by the will of the free Georgian people, no matter what party or coalition thereof it may represent. I believe I may have disappointed some people with such an answer—I had noticed a number of men wearing the "Tetri Giorgi ("The White George") Party badge, with the insignia "Georgia First of All" and thought that some Georgian emigres who were organizers and instructors in Wustrau, being themselves members of "Tetri Giorgi," had influenced the newcomers; I found later that some of them were energetic and skillful recruiters. The Georgian singing and dancing ensemble was also organized in Wustrau. It was directed by David Kavsadze, a member of the Georgian family famous for such artistic talent. The ensemble performed at a good level and served the purpose of propagating Georgian art and culture abroad and was quite successful. I remember on a festive occasion, one year later, I had to deliver a speech about Georgia. It was followed by a performance by the ensemble, the high point being the Georgian dance by Miss Mariam Kereselidze and Givi Khandashvili; a thunderous applause followed from the audience.

On July 19th, Misha (Mikheil) Kedia returned to Berlin after a trip and wanted to see me at once. This was the first direct contact between us after an interval of almost two years. Following a cordial greeting, he told me about his unhappiness that the Germans refused his request to let me stay in Berlin with him during October of 1941. "But after the "initial 'blackout'," he said, "ever so often news about you would flash 'like lightning' mostly from the emigres or certain German friends." As he said, he was glad that his instinctive very good first impression of me had been confirmed by the facts on the front. Perhaps now, during 1943, we could do the work together at last that we should have started during 1941.

Kedia was renting an apartment in Mrs. Nino Kazbek-Dadiani's house. He invited me for lunch and introduced me to her. She was a gracious hostess. Our conversation continued after lunch, but before I go into detail about this, some comments about our hostess and her family are in order.

Nino was one of the most captivating persons I have ever met. No longer in her prime age, Nino was feminine and beautiful with expressive, unforgettable eyes. She had a soft and dignified voice with matching manners and intelligence. She certainly was a worthy representative of an old Georgian aristocracy. And all of this, in spite of hardships endured due to the untimely demise of her husband and the insecure life of an emigre with a little daughter, Marina, who grew to be not only beautiful but also a wonderful daughter; mother and daughter adored each other.

As already has been told, when I first came to Berlin in October 1941 (and still in a P.O.W. outfit), as I was led into a building to meet Mikheil Kedia, Grigol Robakidze and some German representatives, I noticed a striking brunette running upstairs, and I was sure she had to be a Georgian—she was no one else but Marina Kazbek, working as a secretary for Dr. Ehrenfried (Teddi) Schütte, Director of the Zentralstelle Osteuropa.[173] Marina was married to a very nice, young Air Force officer, Helmuth (Helo) Oscar von Moltke. Von Moltke is an illustrious Prussian aristocratic name. The famous nineteenth century military leader, Field Marshal Count Helmuth von Moltke was not survived by children but had other relatives. Marina's husband, Helo, was one of his great-grand nephews.[174] It was a great tragedy that Helo was killed in action during the battle for Stalingrad. The only comfort Marina could find was in their daughter, little Nina, who was also referred to affectionately by her grandmother as "Kikibush." It was almost impossible not to fall in love with little "Kikibush."

Our first day of conversation with Kedia lasted until evening and he invited me for dinner in a very good restaurant, probably "Eden." There were two other guests for dinner, Shalva Maglakelidze and his son, Gaios (Caius). I had met the father Maglakelidze in conjunction with the problems in the Legion's Battalion 795 as noted in the chapter about the Caucasus ["Patriots and Defectors"]. Apparently,

---

173- Teddi and I met later in "Bergmann," became friends, and our friendship continued after the war.

174- Another of the Field Marshal's great-grand nephews was Count Helmuth James von Moltke. His opposition to the Nazi regime was known to the authorities for some time. He was arrested on other charges even before the July 20th putsch, but general investigation after the putsch revealed his deep involvement in it. He was tried and hung.

George F. Kennan speaks with great admiration about H.J. von Moltke in his *Memoirs 1925–1950* (Boston, Toronto: Atlantic-Little, Brown & Co., 1967, pp. 119–123). There, Kennan also makes the astute observation, "Actually, Hitler found his main support in the lower middle class and to some extent in the nouveau riche. The older Prussian aristocracy was divided but from its ranks came some of the most enlightened and courageous of all the internal opposition Hitler was ever to face."

meanwhile, Maglakelidze left the Legion's battalion after the retreat from the Caucasus and was now residing in Berlin with his only son. Gaios Maglakelidze wore a military uniform with an insignia of the Georgian Legion and the rank of a lieutenant. He was working for military propaganda ("Wehrmachts Propaganda") in Berlin and had married a German girl of Baltic origin also with the first name Greta. Gaios appeared to be a well-educated and an intelligent young man. I met his wife about one year later in the Bavarian town of Ruhpolding, where she had a position as a manager of a recovery home for the disabled, wounded and sick Georgian legionnaires. Her charges were no longer in need of acute hospital care, but still had some way to go before being rehabilitated. They all loved Greta who was charming, good-natured and a compassionate friend to strangers who had neither relatives nor homes of their own.[175]

M. Kedia characterized Shalva Maglakelidze to me as a person of great ambitions, an adventurer and not always predictable. Having heard him say that, I told Kedia about the circumstances under which I had met S. Maglakelidze in the Caucasus during the fall of 1942. (See the chapter about the Caucasus ["Patriots and Defectors."]) Kedia listened carefully since he apparently had meager information about this, while he knew much more about "Bergmann." Kedia said that Maglakelidze was difficult to judge and while his conduct in the Battalion 795 aroused his concern, the whole situation surrounding the Georgian Legion was too complex for fair evaluation.

I met Kedia almost daily. We visited Professor von Mende together to have a "three-way" discussion. Mende informed me that his efforts to prevent the separation of the "Regiment Bergmann" into three independent battalions failed because the "higher orders" (almost always it meant Hitler), could not be amended. Nevertheless, Mende gave me the phone number of the colonel in the General Staff (perhaps still a lieutenant colonel at that time), Heinz Danko Herre, and suggested I inform him

---

175- Affectionately, the legionnaires referred to her as "Gretiko," a diminutive Georgianized twist to her first name. My future wife, Rusudan Alshibaja, whose parents resided in the nearby town of Reichenhall, accompanied me to Ruhpolding. We spent the day with Greta and her disabled friends and liked them very much. Greta told us of three close girlfriends, also Germans from the Balticum, who decided to marry only Georgian men. One of them, Karen, I met during October; she had married Osik Djavakhi. Karen became my part-time secretary later. She and her husband were both good-natured, pleasant and helpful people. "The Club" of the young ladies from Balticum who were married to Georgians was increased by the fourth "member." Her name is Ilse Barateli, who married a good friend of mine, Sandro Barateli, in Munich after the war. They emigrated to New York and for many years Sandro was one of the most popular, conscientious and hard-working presidents of the Georgian Colony in the U.S.A. He was deeply devoted to his people and at the same time became a successful business man. Fortunately he had at his side a loving, intelligent, capable and supportive wife, Ilse, who also became our friend. As I mentioned in Chapter 4 "Transfer to Germany," a group of Baltic German soldiers prevented my imprisonment in the infamous Dachau concentration camp. This personal experience superimposed on four Baltic German-Georgian marriages made me wonder "Could it be that these two ethnic groups have some special affinity for each other?"

about my views. I did so; Herre was very friendly during the phone conversation and while he could not promise anything at that time, he said that formation of the bigger units should be our goal for the future.

Within the next day or two, Kedia arranged our meeting with Mikheil (Misha) Alshibaja, another prospective member of the Liaison Staff yet to be formed. He had been employed by a German Panzer division as an interpreter on the Eastern Front and wore a "non-combat" officer's uniform with a lieutenant's rank. But this "non-combat" officer was already decorated by his commanding general with the Iron Cross of the Second and then First Class for courage shown during combat. To the best of my knowledge, M. Alshibaja at that time was the first Georgian to receive such recognition. He made friends easily and was popular among the front line officers. They referred to him fondly as "Ali Baba," a nickname they had invented. His parents, Barbara Kiziria Alshibaja and Grigol (Grisha) Alshibaja, M.D. came to Berlin under different circumstances than most other emigres. The government of the Sovereign Georgian Republic sent Dr. Alshibaja to Germany as a replacement for the retiring Georgian Ambassador Vladimir (Lado) Akhmeteli.[176] The ambassador to-be and his family left Georgia during early 1921, when fighting was already going on between the invading Red Army and much weaker Georgian armed forces. Soon after their arrival in Berlin, the Bolshevik Russian troops had completed the occupation of Georgia. Therefore, Dr. Alshibaja never assumed the ambassadorship.[177] So for now, the family settled in a fashionable suburb of Berlin—Wansee.

Misha, then approximately aged twelve, went to German schools and climbed the steps of education with the final result of a Master's degree in economics ("rerum politicarum") from Munich University. He spoke Georgian, Russian, Polish, German and French. He married a charming, lovely, sporty and courageous Georgian emigre from Paris, Ivlit (Ivlita) Mamulashvili.[178] Before Poland's occupation by Hitler and Stalin, Misha Alshibaja was offered work, first in the banking system of Poland and then in the management of an ammunition factory. Misha Alshibaja was one of the representatives of the National Democrats. He also had the support of the Georgian officers, who had previously served in the Polish Army (and fought against the German as well as the Russian troops who attacked Poland during 1939). But as previously mentioned, after the German invasion of Bolshevik Russia, they joined the Georgian Legion in order to better defend Georgian interests.[179] Misha

---

176- Not to be mistaken for his nephew, Prof. Mikheil Akhmeteli.

177- For more on Grigol (Grisha) Alshibaja and these circumstances, please consult the Appendix.

178- Ivlit's education also included an excellent English boarding school. She and Misha had two adorable children, a girl Nino and a boy Theimuraz, both born in France.

179- They were Captains Vano Bakradze, Vaso Indjia, Siko Kobiashvili, Datha Lagidze, and Dima Shalikashvili. Misha Dadiani, who had moved to France, joined "Tamar II" and then "Bergmann" as noted. I am not aware of his support for Misha Alshibaja.

Alshibaja was cordial to me from the very beginning and was helpful to me whenever he could be.

During my "free time," Tengiz Dadeshkeliani and Mrs. Thina Togonidze continued to be my "guides" in Berlin. Soon Niko Nakashidze, whom I left in Crimea, moved back home in Berlin and joined Thina and Tengiz in guiding me. As nice and helpful as the Berlin Georgians were to me and to each other, I recognized some polarization existing between the two larger groups and some divisiveness was discernible within each group proper. For example, I was invited for dinner by my hotel neighbors, Nino and Kale Salia. The guest of honor was one of the original founders of the Tetri Giorgi Party, Professor Mikhako Tsereteli,[180] and the wife of the Persian hotel owner had also been invited. The professor apparently had a great deal of interest in my past experiences. He kept asking many questions. Others also listened to my story. While telling them about the 1937 purges, I mentioned that my father had been arrested by N.K.V.D. (secret police) chief, Napo Kedia, in Svaneti (no kindred of Mikheil Kedia). The professor, rather theatrically, spread his hands and with an anguished tone of voice said, "One Kedia there and another Kedia here" (referring to Mikheil Kedia). "Lord have mercy upon us." This surely was not meant as a compliment for Mikheil Kedia and pointed to a divisiveness, if not outright hostility between these two Georgian patriots. Later, I learned that Professor Mikhako also referred at times to the Georgian Social Democrats as the "cursed ones" ("es tskeulebi").[181]

Kale Salia appeared to be a very active member of the Tetri Giorgi Party. A few days after he had hosted dinner for us, he wanted to see me for a "business talk." As it turned out, he intended to brief me about his party and the situation in general.

180- See chapter "In the Bergmann Unit and Caucasus" concerning Georgian political parties abroad.

181- Somewhat later I found out that Professor Tsereteli did not really dislike his political rivals and at times even had deep affection for them. I had an unusual opportunity to read some of the letters Professor Tsereteli had written to Misha Kedia. It became obvious to me that these two had been good old friends. Moreover, when two prominent leaders of the "cursed" social democrats, Noe Jordania and Evgeni Gegechkori died, Professor Mikhako became depressed each time. And what a moving and highly praising obituary he devoted to Noe Jordania and had it published in a periodical in Paris. Before that, he wrote to Kedia about Evgeni Gegechkori's demise, "No longer have we our Evgeni, not only am I saddened, but also horrified. Who is going to defend the Georgian cause in the international arena now?" I soon learned an important lesson about some of our "old" political leaders, that when in anger they often played "enfants terribles." But in fact, with rare exceptions, deep in their hearts they loved, helped and respected each other. They knew when and where to stop in order not to go too far. Therefore some of their publications, especially written in anger or during a crisis, should be carefully evaluated and at times questioned. They were endowed with outstanding qualities but not free of some human weaknesses and errors. Accept them as they were, and before criticizing them, recall how things are always clearer in hindsight than it is possible to comprehend of an event when it happens.

This is not bad advice for a young historian who chooses to do a "post mortem" of political emigration and supports his preconceived ideas by specially selected items from the prolific publications, without the advantage of being an eyewitness to history.

Salia was eloquent, polished, diplomatic and distinguished looking. He spoke of Tetri Giorgi, not so much about the party but the "movement of Georgian unity"; such a motto also appeared on the party's letterhead. Among the party's accomplishments, he emphasized the contribution toward creation of the Wustrau camp for the freed former Georgian P.O.W.s, now turned civilian, and their importance to the future free Georgia. He was pleased with their rapid progress in Wustrau, including the spirit of unity. He also spoke of good connections with Ostministerium and brought up the name of Professor Alexandre Nikuradze, Director of the Research Institute of Continental Europe and the adviser to Minister Rosenberg. Had I met him yet? "No," I said, "but Niko Nakashidze had suggested I do, and he wanted to be my guide for such a visit."

Salia briefly discussed some "divisiveness among the Georgian emigres," and Kedia was a part of it. I had the feeling that during the existing "divisiveness" he intended to recruit me for Tetri Giorgi but did not feel the time was right. It probably would have been easier to recruit an inexperienced P.O.W. brought to the Wustrau camp. It seemed to me that such a person would have a justified feeling of gratitude toward the "Superman" who had freed him and would be naturally inhibited to refuse such a suggestion.

In order to discourage Salia from future recruitment efforts directed toward me, I asked him the difference between Tetri Giorgi—"The Movement of National Unity"—and Erovnuli Ertoba—"The Georgian National Alliance," located in Paris. He answered that the Parisian "Alliance" was a loosely organized body and situated far away from Berlin, where the real action was taking place. Then I said that as I understood it, Tetri Giorgi was one party bound together by its inner party discipline. The Parisian organization, however, represented a bipartisan coalition of the several existing different parties, (regardless of their divergent political views) to better serve the Georgian cause. I went on to say that the majority of the "Bergmann" Georgians would prefer the alliance regardless of the party affiliation. Later on, should Georgia be liberated, let the parties compete with each other and submit to the will of the free Georgian people concerning who is going to lead the country. We in "Bergmann" do not emphasize party membership at the present time because we are soldiers, but if free elections are held in Georgia one day, we shall participate. My information was that Tetri Giorgi did not participate in the Alliance in Paris but in order to be diplomatic, I stopped short of asking Salia if it were true and if so, why.[182]

182- I thought that for Salia, a former Social Democrat, now turned Tetri Giorgi, ideology was of secondary importance—in other words he was a utilitarian. Both he and his wife Nino had the ability to make themselves indispensable for some important people of mature age, and they were eager to play a role. They also mastered the art of survival; among several stories concerning this matter, one is my favorite and especially amusing. It brings to mind Goethe's German version of the medieval fable,

The time came to see Professor Alexandre Nikuradze; an appointment had been made by Niko Nakashidze, an old friend of our family, as already noted. We visited the professor on the premises of the "Research Institute for Continental Europe," where he had been appointed as a director by the Minister of Eastern Affairs, A. Rosenberg. Professor Nikuradze was a bespectacled gentleman and of rather short stature with excellent posture and a great deal of self-confidence in his voice and emotion. Our audience lasted at least an hour. He listened to my views based on my experience in the Caucasus politely and without interruption. At the end of our meeting, Niko Nakashidze wanted me to tell the professor how I, as a representative of the "'Bergmann Georgians' declared an amnesty for the Georgian communists," in a leaflet printed by German Air Force 4 and dropped over Georgia [in the chapter "Patriots and Defectors"]. Professor Nikuradze did not appear surprised nor disturbed about it—in fact, I had the impression that he approved of it. Then he told us about his research and also his view about the future of Georgia and other Caucasian nations if the Germans won the war—which he thought they would.

Nikuradze stated that there was no question that they would all get their sovereignty with Georgia playing a leading role in the Caucasus because the Georgians by their nature were leaders. But he added that our number one concern should be how to teach our people the western ways of living. He also assured us that he had the complete backing of Minister Rosenberg and other representatives of "The Reich." He had a warm handshake for us at the end of our audience. "He is just a Georgian patriot as we all are," said Niko Nakashidze to me on our way home; "don't let anyone tell you that he is no longer a Georgian but now turned into a German."

When I met Professor Nikuradze a second time during April of 1945, World War II was coming to an end. I left Berlin with a few friends; each of us had a variety of business to attend to as well as one common mission to take care of.[183] We were driving through Oberpfalz, in the direction of South Bavaria. Somehow we learned that Professor A. Nikuradze with a "skeleton staff" of his institute had been moved from Berlin to the nearby town of Schwarzenfeld. We stopped there to see them

---

"Reinard" the fox—"Reineke Fux." This is allegedly what took place: During the Summer of 1944, and shortly before the western allies liberated Paris, Salia, who intermittently lived in Berlin, was now in Paris. A small detachment of armed Georgian men from S. Odisharia's group (who worked for the German police) drove by Salia's residence. They picked him up and left for Germany, doing a favor for Kale Salia, who had to be there on business. Nino Salia soon emerged from the house, apparently in great distress and informed their French neighbors that the "Gestapo" just deported her husband to Germany. This not only aroused sympathy for Salia among the neighbors (who naturally did not care for those who communicated with Germans), but the word also got around and after the war, Nino could safely welcome her husband back to Paris. I was not an eyewitness to this episode and therefore can not vouch for its authenticity. *[See the Appendix for more on Salia and* The Georgian Destiny, *a periodical he started, which later became embroiled in controversy as Soviet propoganda. –Ed.]*
183- This matter will be discussed later.

and he invited us to lunch. While others chose to rest after lunch, the Professor and I took a walk, sharing our thoughts with each other. We tried to evaluate the dangerous situation the Georgians were facing in Germany. This was especially critical for the P.O.W.s, workers and the legionnaires of Soviet origin due to the Yalta Agreement [which would forcibly repatriate them —Ed.]. What could be done to remedy such a state of affairs? Clearly things were in the hands of the Western Allies. The Professor remarked that the time was over when he had the backing of the "German Reich" and he was not in a position now to help the Georgians and other Caucasians. Nevertheless, he was not afraid as a responsible person to account for his past and the work he had done, where and when the need should arise. He was also sure that my friends and I were prepared to do the same. This statement led me to inform the professor briefly that M. Kedia, with other Caucasian representatives Alibekov, Djamalian and Kantemir were already in Switzerland. With the help and mediation by the International Red Cross and some Swiss personalities, they wanted to get assurance from the Western Allies to repatriate only those Caucasians who were willing to return to the Soviet Union voluntarily. His friends also hoped to clarify the Caucasian problems in general and our activities during World War II, as well as our views for the future, to the Americans with whom they had already established preliminary contact (as we shall see later on).

I also told Professor Nikuradze that while this was going on in Switzerland, here in Germany with the help of General Köstring and his staff (now located in Bad Reichenhall—I intended to visit them shortly), other measures had been taken. Some Caucasian units had been transferred to Denmark and also there were a few units in Italy. These were considered to be two relatively safe bases since it was unlikely that the Red Army would ever get there. We were trying to get "Bergmann I" out of the Balkans and direct it to one of the two bases and also some other units from the Eastern Front. The liaison officers had been sent to "Bergmann" to inform them about it and also to deliver a written order from O.K.H. (The Army High Command) concerning this matter, to the commanding general of the corresponding front, the Field Marshal Schörner. I also told Professor Nikuradze that after I made other arrangements in Bad Reichenhall and Salzburg, I would join M. Alshibaja, A. Tsomaia and Professor von Mende at the Swiss border in Austria. From there we would contact Kedia to learn the results of their negotiations and if successful, we should be able to reach our people on their bases for further arrangements. Gogi Magalow decided to remain in Ising, Bavaria, with his family. We bade farewell to Professor Nikuradze, none of us being sure we would survive to the end of the war, but somehow we did.[184]

184- See Appendix for more on Alexandre Nikuradze.

11
THE GEORGIAN LIAISON STAFF—A MISSION

During the spring of 1942, I was introduced to Spiridon Kedia, a main founder in 1917 and leader of the Georgian National Democratic Party.[185] He came from Paris to Berlin on the invitation of Ambassador von Schulenburg, as did some other Caucasian political leaders. This was the part of Schulenburg's early initiative of promoting a rational and humane German policy toward people of the U.S.S.R. after Hitler's invasion of the East. But Schulenburg's attempt was in vain because of Hitler's adamant refusal of change. Spiridon Kedia realized that as long as Hitler and his henchmen led Germany, meaningful negotiation was not feasible. (But Schulenburg never gave up on his efforts, as we shall see.)

On the other hand, Spiridon Kedia knew, as did Professor von Mende, Mikheil Kedia and many others, of the dangers the Georgians were facing in the German occupied territories; especially the P.O.W.s and legionnaires. Therefore, Spiridon Kedia told his followers, Tsomaia and Sindikashvili and others, that they, the "younger generation," should now "carry the ball" and form an organization—a mission to defend Georgian interests and help the people. He also said that he himself was too old to engage in such activities and a man of his age could not afford to make "newer mistakes" since there may be no time left for him to correct them.[186]

My meeting with S. Kedia was very pleasant. He was a soft-spoken, fine gentleman with clear vision and great depth. He conveyed his thoughts to me without dramatic expression; I understood and felt great respect for him. His views about the current situation were shared by the majority of the National Alliance in Paris, regardless of party affiliation, including the Georgian President in exile, Noe Jordania, his Secretary of Foreign Affairs, Evgeni Gegechkori, as well as the social democrats.

185- Not to be mistaken for Mikheil (Misha) Kedia. The introduction was made by A. Asatiani, A. Tsomaia and D. Sindikashvili (whom I had already met in the Caucasus during the fall of 1942).
186- Personal communication with Sindikashvili.

The opinions of some legionnaires had also been reported to Mende. They were wondering why there was no Berlin organization in existence representing their interests? I was under considerable "pressure" to join the Liaison Staff. I was especially urged to do so by A. Asatiani, Tengiz Dadeshkeliani, Victor Nozadze, Jora Indjia, Aliosha Abashidze, Niko Nakashidze, Grigol Lordkipanidze, Misha Kedia, A. Tsomaia, Mikheil Alshibaja, Gogi Magalow, Kale Salia, Valiko Togonidze and many others, especially the "Bergmann" soldiers. From the German side, Professor von Mende tried to persuade me to join the Liaison Staff as "head of the Military Department and the speaker for the Georgians in the German Army." The Professor said that he consulted about the matter with the headquarters of General Hellmich and Köstring, who were in complete agreement.

On August 3rd, 1943, Professor Oberländer phoned and told me that he was passing through Berlin and wanted to see me. I invited him to my hotel where we could talk undisturbed. We were both aware that a very important "tank battle" of Kursk went badly for the German Army. The Soviets now advanced further south in the Kharkov sector and this had a potential for endangering the rest of the southern front, including Crimea, causing our concern for "Bergmann."

During the end of July, Hamburg had been heavily bombed by the R.A.F., resulting in many civilian deaths and injuries. During the beginning of August the U.S. Air Force began and the Royal Air Force continued to attack German targets; this was expected to increase immediately and include Berlin. Oberländer expressed his interest in meeting my new friends and potential associates, and this was arranged for the next day in Adlon. M. Kedia (whom Oberländer already knew), G. Magalow and M. Alshibaja came; I also invited a non-commissioned officer, Jora Indjia, from "Bergmann" who had just arrived in Berlin. For almost four hours, we enjoyed each other's fellowship and shared our views about a variety of subjects important to us.

I then accompanied the Professor to the "Silesia" railroad station. On our way to the station, Oberländer said that in his opinion, I ought to consider joining the Liaison Staff in Berlin. He said that due to changed circumstances, I probably could do more from Berlin to help all the Georgian volunteer military units, including "Bergmann." Oberländer indicated that the General of the Volunteer Troops and his staff would be pleased to see me lead the Military Department of the Georgian Liaison Staff, as most of them were the same people who had already worked with us during the Caucasus military expedition and in Crimea.

"The confidence they have in you could be a distinct advantage for the Georgian troops and also indirectly for other Caucasians," said Oberländer, who then took the train to Loetzen-Prussia for a meeting in the Army headquarters. This is also where he then learned that because of "higher orders," he had been removed from being the commanding officer of "Bergmann," due to his memoranda criticizing the German East Policy as already discussed (see Chapter "In Crimea"). On August 22rd, 1943, Oberländer bade a final farewell to "Bergmann" whose founding fathers were Admiral Canaris and himself. The psychological impact of Oberländer's forced resignation on "Bergmann's" soldiers was bewilderment and disappointment, since he was a trusted and admired leader.[187]

There were several reasons why I still hesitated joining the Liaison Staff. First of all, I felt a bond toward the "Bergmann" soldiers; second, the rights and obligations of a soldier in the combat zone are clearly outlined. Not so in the Liaison Staff, where we would have many obligations and almost no rights; except one, to be speakers on behalf of our people—advocates of a kind. We would, therefore, totally depend on the good will of the German institutions for our proposals to bear positive results. The "selling" points of the Liaison Staff were first, that as long as our German friends—Schulenburg, Canaris, Mende, Bräutigam, Stauffenberg, Köstring, Herwarth, Ungermann, Reissmüller and their associates—led certain institutions, our suggestions would almost always be met to the best of their abilities. All of them were in resistance against Hitler's policies. Second, our German friends had already tried very hard to create politically, fully-approved organizations for us and other Caucasians, as well as other "Easterners," such as committees and official statements of German commitment to our sovereignty but failed because of Nazi leadership's refusal.

So now, at the time of an obviously pending German defeat, we had to put our heads together in order to save what could be saved. (There was remote hope that perhaps after one evil, Hitler, was defeated, the western democracies might have to stop another evil, the Bolshevik dominated Soviet expansion led by Stalin.) I felt somewhat uncomfortable to further refuse the suggestion of the senior Georgian politicians, especially A. Asatiani and V. Nozadze for me to participate in the formation of the Georgian Liaison Staff, and I finally agreed. In so doing, I was mindful that our ability to achieve certain goals may fall short of our hopes and some people's' expectations. Therefore, in the final score it was possible that we may be made the scapegoats by disappointed people even for occurrences beyond our control.

But what about the Dresden Military School, where I was enrolled and which would commence within a couple of days? Professor von Mende said that the Liaison

---

187- On November 11, 1943, the Gestapo searched Oberländer's living quarters and he was placed under house arrest. The following day he was dismissed from the party. He was also discharged from the Army. He was saved from a court martial only through the intervention of some influential benefactors. See Hans von Herwarth, *Against Two Evils* (on Oberländer); Professor Theodore Oberländer's personal diary; author's "mini diary."

Staff could not be formed before the end of October or beginning of November 1943, pending negotiations about approval by several German governmental agencies. These were (in addition to the Eastern Ministry):

1. High Command of the German Armed Forces
2. General of the Eastern Troops in the Army Headquarters
3. Armed forces Propaganda Staff Section (WPr)
4. Of course, the real "watch dog"—SS Main Office for State Security

I left for Dresden, August 10, 1943, arrived during the late afternoon and was received in the school office by the Director's adjutant in a very friendly and courtly manner. The following morning the director of the military school, Colonel Mangold, welcomed me cordially as he said he would do his best to make our time spent in his institution useful and pleasant. I reported to him that three other Caucasian officers—K. Aleskirov, I. Alimbarashvili and S. Okropiridze—should be arriving in Dresden that very evening. The Colonel asked me to show my friends the way to his office so that he and the four of us could have an orientation discussion. We did, and it put all of us at ease; we had the best impression of Colonel Mangold, his adjutant and the officer-instructors. The Colonel ordered that we be shown the Dresden Military School's guest book. To our amazement among other visitor-V.I.P.'s signatures, there was one of the Soviet General Tukhachevski. Apparently he had visited the school a number of years ago when the relationship between the German and the Red Army was good. (Tukhachevski, of course, fell victim of Stalin's purges.) The Colonel suggested that since we also were guests, we should affix our signatures in the book. We did so hoping that our final fate would be different than that of General Tukhachevski's.

While three newly-arrived Caucasian officers organized their belongings in our living quarters, Colonel Mangold invited me to drive with him through Dresden and the surrounding area, probably in a further gesture of making us welcome; we also attended an officer's seminar. Classes teaching military theory and field exercise started the next day with an intensive schedule. The sessions progressed to cover nearly all aspects of modern warfare and were of high quality. On August 16th, the Colonel suggested that I address the class about Georgia, her history, her geography, her goals and her relationship with Germany. My main point and conclusion was that the previous German and Georgian generations left a legacy of friendship and cooperation and both sides should continue in the same spirit. The Colonel led the applause and expressed his appreciation for my presentation.

One day, Tengiz Dadeshkeliani visited us in Dresden for a few days. He paid his respect to Colonel Mangold and once again introduced himself as my uncle. The

Colonel was visibly impressed by this handsome "Georgian giant" with impeccable manners. He extended an invitation to Tengiz to come with us to the officer's party which he accepted. During the party, it was obvious Tengiz was a great success; he proposed a moving toast to German-Georgian friendship—which I translated. The Colonel responded with an appropriate toast and wished the best future for Georgia. The end result of the toasting was the consumption of a considerable quantity of spirits. It became progressively louder and livelier. Finally, the officers decided to organize "a cavalry parade." They turned the chairs backwards, sat on them and slid, one following another, in a big circle. The Colonel, Tengiz, and we (the Caucasian officers) stood on the side lines and received the "parade." Finally Colonel Mangold declared that only the Caucasians and he remained sober and coherent and moved to adjourn.

I received the Colonel's permission to travel to Berlin on weekends in order to keep in touch with my Georgian friends and Professor von Mende. They deemed it necessary for keeping me abreast of new developments and to have my input; it also helped us to become better acquainted. It was of a special interest for me to learn in depth what really took place in Berlin concerning the Georgian question during nearly two years of my absence.

Dresden was one of the most beautiful cities I have ever seen with its remarkable architecture and art treasures. The opera house was an example of this.[188] There were also wonderful churches, including Kreuz Kirche, where one could attend not only church services but also excellent concerts, which we did. Colonel Mangold had a lady secretary, Maria von Finck, who more than anyone else made a special effort to personally guide and help us to see Dresden in its splendor and to enjoy the art that it offered. Somehow she always managed to secure tickets for us. She was the wife of a colonel who served on the southeast front, perhaps in Italy.

Pursuant to my passion for exercise, one day I was walking rather briskly, following the path of the Elbe River shore, when I overtook Mrs. von Finck, walking in the same direction. After saying "hello," she explained that this was her favorite way of going home from work. She was living in her aunt's home and I asked if it was alright for me to walk along; her response was that this would please her. Mrs. von Finck had a great desire to learn more about Georgia and also the Soviet Union in general. For my part, I wanted to know more about the land of Saxony and Germany. And so, deeply involved in conversation, we reached her home. She invited me to meet her aunt but because of it being near supper time, I suggested we

---

188- For the first time I saw and listened to Beethoven's "Fidelio."

do so another time. We also agreed to continue our discussions in the future. Such an opportunity presented itself between curtain calls at the following Sunday's church concert. When I walked her home from the opera house, she introduced me to her delightful aunt, and we had a three-way exchange of views. Some evenings Mrs. Finck and I dined in restaurants. We began addressing each other on a first name basis and gradually a platonic friendship developed, which meant a great deal to me.

Dresden Military School had a good setup for field exercise because of the Elbe River and surrounding terrain. It encompassed the woods of the "Dresden Heide," the ridges on the north and the foothills of the Erzgebirge mountains on the south. The Caucasian officers received good marks in the classrooms but especially during field exercise. They scored well in target-shooting practice with a broad variety of weapons and did well on maneuvers, where usually live ammunition was used. Friendships developed between a number of German officers, non-commissioned officers and us. During the outings we taught them the Georgian song, "Suliko" (as we had in "Bergmann"). Lieutenant Michaelis invited us for supper at his home where we met his very nice wife. Lieutenant Kuhne invited us to a "high tea" and introduced us to his fiancee and her friends. We went with them several times to restaurants and to the movies. We had swimming lessons by a professional teacher; I badly needed them. There were tennis courts, a gym and a running track. We felt we were getting a good officer's training fitness program and also useful orientation about our host country. An example of the latter was our trip to the city of Weimar because of our interest in Goethe and Schiller, which left us both impressed and happy. Another very pleasant excursion was conducted for some German officers and us to see the mountainous town of Alpenberg. We stayed there overnight, and inspired by the beauty of the land we sang with our German friends, "Suliko" and equally beautiful German songs.

During mid-October we learned that the Minister of Eastern Affairs, A. Rosenberg, was to deliver a speech at the Dresden Military School. The Caucasian officers had to be excluded (or "excused"), which made a poor impression not only on the Caucasian officers but on the German officers as well. One of them confided in me that, "you did not miss much." That brought to memory the "Bergmann's" officer's identical impression in Crimea when they attended Rosenberg's speech there.

While in Dresden, I received considerable mail; two letters pleased me most. One from a close friend or my school days in Tbilisi, Dr. Ramaz Gvetadze. He wrote from Crimea, where he was serving as a doctor in one of the legion's battalions. I rejoiced that he was alive and well and wrote a letter at once promising that I would see him there. (I kept that promise.) The second letter was from Mrs. Margarita Chikovani-Baumhauer, the Georgian wife of German aviation officer Major Otto

Baumhauer,[189] informing me that all was well with their family. Needless to say, I was happy about this news.

The next day was Sunday and as usual I went to church, this time in Frauen Kirche. I prayed for my relatives, friends, and Georgia; then stayed in church for a wonderful concert. I walked out of there "with a song in my heart." But the military and political situation was growing worse for Germany. For instance on September 9th, 1943, the Italian surrender to the Western Allies was announced by Colonel Mangold during a specially called meeting for the officers, where he analyzed this new development. It was the consensus of opinion that the German Armed Forces would be able to stop the already landed American and British troops in Salerno and Montecorvino, without Italian help.

On the Eastern Front, during late September, the Red Army took Smolensk and Roslavl; during the second week of October they occupied Kuban (but the elements of the German 17th Army safely evacuated to Crimea). The Soviets also took Melitopol in Ukraine—north of Crimea. On November 3, I was in Berlin to attend a meeting when we learned of the Red Army occupation of the Crimean Isthmus, thus cutting it off from the Ukrainian mainland; however, the German counter-offensive was in progress and the Soviet units were not able to penetrate further south in Crimea so for now the situation was stable. A number of days later, we learned that "Bergmann" distinguished itself during the hard battles for Crimea. This was finally confirmed in the Armed Forces special radio report on November 17.

Meanwhile the Red Army had retaken an important Ukrainian city, Kiev. In Berlin, at a meeting of a not completely organized Liaison Staff, we were told (probably by Professor von Mende) that during October 1943, a number of the Georgian and other Caucasian Legion battalions had been transferred to the West. This was an order by the German Army High Command and obviously the Liaison Staff had nothing to do with it, not even any input.[190] Köstring tried to convince the

---

189- See the Chapters about Caucasus and Crimea. We kept corresponding periodically.

190- Herwarth explains, "While Hitler managed to prevent the formation of an entire army of volunteers, he failed to stop their being added to the regular German fighting forces. In October 1943, a large number of German troops were shifted from the U.S.S.R. to the West. Nearly all German units by now included at least ten to fifteen per cent volunteers, for whom German replacements were no longer readily available, even if the German officers wanted them. In fact they did not, and many refused flatly to leave behind their volunteers, knowing them to be excellent soldiers. It infuriated Hitler that any German officer could prefer untermenshen to good German soldiers.

"Nearly all the generals whom we met were sympathetic to Köstring's message regarding volunteer helpers, though few had any great understanding of foreign peoples. There were exceptions like General Kurt Zeitzler, Chief of the General Staff, who in 1943 proposed to leave all volunteers on the Soviet Front or to send them to work as laborers. Köstring rightly objected to this degrading suggestion. But for all the debates over the usefulness of the volunteers that occurred among people at a distance from the front line, I doubt if there were more than a handful of generals who accepted Hitler's ideas about the so-called untermenshen." *Against Two Evils*, pp. 267–268.

German leadership that the volunteers were useful for Germany. This he did in order to improve the treatment for the volunteer soldiers, Eastern workers and P.O.W.s.[191]

And why did General Köstring agree to the transfer of the volunteer units to the west? He explained to me that given the German retreat on the east, this was the only acceptable alternative to prevent their falling into the hands of the advancing Red Army. Cases had been reported that even some of the Caucasian officers who defected back to the Soviets were shot by them.

General Ralph von Heygendorff, who was closely associated with the volunteer troops, in discussing the same subject states, "When we had been forced on the defensive in the East in 1943 and to retreat, our Supreme Command gave an order to transfer the volunteer battalions to other battlefields to prevent terrible reprisals by the Red Army in case they became war prisoners. Frightened by this possibility, many volunteers no longer fought. It must be stated here that the transfer of the volunteer units to other fronts was not so easy for psychological reasons. They wanted to fight against Bolshevism and felt no enmity against Americans or British people, in whom the National Committees even saw possible allies of tomorrow."[192]

Generals Köstring and Heygendorff were correct inasmuch as for now there was no fighting in France and Holland, where the Caucasians had been stationed on the Atlantic Coast. But this could change if the Western Allies landed troops somewhere on that coast. On the other hand, they (hopefully) would land instead in the Balkans as they recently had in Italy. The Liaison Staff was very worried by the thought that the Caucasians may have to fight the Western Allies one day. This was not why they had joined the Legions, which had been formed by the Germany Army. Also, France had been a host country for the Georgian and other Caucasian refugees, and allowed the Georgian government in exile to keep its embassy open until 1934 for which we felt indebted to her.

Thus the Georgian Liaison Staff (L.S.) inherited two critical situations from the very beginning of its creation. During the L.S. meeting, its military department was charged with the responsibility of visiting all Georgian volunteer military units within the German Army, identifying their problems and trying to correct them, save lives and "prepare the soldiers as a necessary military force, which would serve the Georgian national interests."[193] This was a tall order. Two of us, Mikheil Alshibaja and I, decided to visit the Georgian Legion and its field battalions in France and

---

191- Köstring's letter to Siegfried Ungermann, December, 8, 1952, in the author's archives.

192- General Ralph von Heygendorff, "Experience with volunteers of Soviet-Union Nations Fighting Bolshevism during World War II," Manuscript of lecture (1951), p. 19, Author's archives.

193- This approximately corresponds to the resolution of support for the "Liaison Staff" on a meeting of the "National Alliance" in Paris. November 27, 1943. (The document is included in the Appendix—the original is in the private archives of the author.)

Holland first, then I would immediately fly to Crimea. During the second part of the trip, M. Alshibaja would remain in Berlin in order to "cover for me." The fact that we wanted to travel to France and Holland first, rather than the East Front where the fighting was going on, reflects our special concern due to the transfer of the volunteer units to the west. We intended to stress to the legionnaires the importance of faultless conduct toward the French and Dutch people.

The Caucasian officers graduated from the Dresden Military School with good overall evaluation by our teachers. I was amazed and amused when I read the part of our evaluation concerning our personalities—they were remarkably accurate. Our capable instructors led by Colonel Mangold could not have been more hospitable, we felt that they genuinely liked us. It was a moving experience to bid them farewell on November 17, 1943. It was especially difficult to say good-bye to our helping angel, Maria von Finck; she became a true friend and confidant of mine.[194]

M. Alshibaja and I visited General Hellmich of the "Eastern Troops" and received his permission to visit the Georgian units in the West. Our friend Herwarth supplied us with a map, where the troops and their location were clearly marked. He also made some useful comments with his usual characteristic openness, for our benefit. During the night of November 20, 1943, we arrived in Paris and were warmly received by the Mamulashvilis, the family of M. Alshibaja's wife, Ivlit; it was a heartwarming experience.

Before a description of the trip to France and Holland, it may be useful to review the situation in Berlin as it developed during the period between the outbreak of the German-Soviet War in June of 1941, and formation of the Liaison Staff in October-November 1943. The military conflict in the east took many people by surprise and one could ask with some justification, Why? Didn't they read Hitler's *Mein Kampf*? Yes, probably many did in the free countries, but in the Soviet Union only a highly select group of VIPs (the "nomenklatura") could. And what was the reaction of those who read it? They did not take it seriously. A good example of this was the conversation between General Köstring, then a German military attache in Moscow and the Chief of the Red Army General Staff, General Jegorov, 1935:

Jegorov: "General, furthering a hatred between our two nations cannot go on this way. The state forms may alter, but the nations remain forever."

Köstring: "It has been exactly my duty to restore a good relationship between

---

194- Shortly after the war, while working in West Germany as a surgical resident, I received a letter from Maria's sister who had somehow found my address. She informed me of a horrible tragedy. Maria had fled Dresden because of the approaching Red Army. Somewhere in the adjacent Thuringia she became ill. The correct diagnosis was not made and she succumbed to a ruptured appendicitis. I have no words to measure my sadness.

your country and my country. But you would understand how difficult this is if you read Hitler's *Mein Kampf.*"

Jegorov (laughingly): "Forget about this old well-worn book ('Schmoker'); Hitler wrote it when he was bitter during his incarceration in the Landsberg prison cell. Therefore, we don't take it seriously."[195]

It was equally surprising to many when, after the outbreak of the war, there was no political declaration by Hitler for the Bolshevik enslaved people promising a better future in case of German victory—sort of the new "Bill of Rights." It would have been especially fitting to do so after an incredibly friendly reception of the advancing German troops by the indigenous peoples of the east.[196] But even if Hitler wanted to disregard that, surely he knew from history that Germany did poorly when simultaneously fighting on two fronts. And what about the vast Soviet territory—very cold winters, bad roads and nearly inexhaustible manpower? Surely he would not base crucial decisions according to the theory of the "National Socialist's" paranoid delusions and a folly but on a council of seasoned German experts on the U.S.S.R. and on pragmatism.

Indeed Germany had such experts in the Foreign Service, Armed Forces and even in the Ostministerium, some of whom were considered old friends of the Caucasians. They tried from the very outset to influence and direct the German East Policy in the right direction. A firm bond developed between the Caucasians and such Germans. They made it possible to initiate the first steps on the difficult path for protection of Caucasian interests. Initially, all these institutions had instruction from Hitler not to engage the emigres, and at the beginning such connections existed only unofficially.

One of them was Count Friedrich Werner von der Schulenburg from the Foreign Office,[197] who proposed a plan (later to be referred to as "The Schulenburg Plan") according to which Germany had to declare:

195- Hermann Teske, *General Ernst Köstring: Der militärische Mittler zwischen dem deutschen Reich und der Sowjetunion 1921-1941*, Frankfurt am Main: Mittler, 1966, p. 85.

196- By the account of many eyewitnesses, the overwhelming majority of the people received the German soldiers with a traditional "Bread and Salt," a symbol of welcome and with flowers. Herwarth tells of a Soviet artillery officer who, after being captured by the Germans, directed the German artillery fire against his own (Red Army) troops; reflecting the hatred toward the Soviet regime.

197- Many times mentioned, Schulenburg was a splendid personality and trusted friend of the Georgians and other Caucasians, the former German ambassador to Moscow and the German Foreign Office Representative in Tbilisi, Georgia during its independence 1918–1921. For his services to the Georgian State, he was decorated with a Georgian Order of Queen Tamara. In the German Foreign Office, Schulenburg represented and lead a group of diplomats who had served in Moscow, so called "The Russland-Gremium." They were proponents of political warfare.
    Also see Dallin, pp. 504–505.

1. It had no territorial designs toward the U.S.S.R.

2. The people of the occupied areas to be permitted a self-government.

3. Germany was to recognize such local governments as the allies and help them unify in a common anti-Soviet cause.

4. Each individual nation of the U.S.S.R. should be granted the right for self determination, including ethnic Russia.

5. Germany should help them to set up independent states. Should those sovereign national states decide in the future to form a Federation, Germany should not interfere with it.

To gain a momentum for his plan, Schulenburg invited a number of well-known Caucasian political personalities in exile. They were housed in the Hotel Adlon in Berlin therefore this undertaking was given a nickname, "Adloniada." The conference took place April–May, 1942. Among the Georgian participants were the leader of the Georgian National Democrat Party, Spiridon Kedia; also the National Democrats, Zurab Avalishvili and Datha Vachnadze; the co-founder of the Tetri Giorgi Movement, Leo Kereselidze; and Prince Irakli Bagrationi. Officially absent were the Social Democrats but Mikheil Kedia had their mandate. He represented Jordania and Gegechkori and maintained close contact with Schulenburg.[198] Among Schulenburg's other Caucasian guests were two editors of the periodical *Kavkaz* (the Caucasus), Haidar Bamat and Ali Khan Kantemir; the former president of Azerbaijan; and a member of the organization "Promethe" (Prometheus)—Resulzade, with some of his former ministers. From the North Caucasus, Said Shamil, (the great grandson of the legendary Imam Shamil who in defense of freedom fought Imperial Russia for three decades).[199]

The Adlon Conference did cause the Eastern Affairs Minister Rosenberg's indignation. He felt that the Foreign Ministry was infringing on his zone of competence, and he complained to Hitler about it. Rosenberg's complaint fell on fertile ground. Hitler issued strict instructions that the Foreign Office stay out of the affairs of the German occupied U.S.S.R.[200] So after a face-saving interval, the Foreign Ministry had to introduce and refer its "Adloniada" guests to the Ostministerium.

198- Schulenburg could not officially invite Jordania and his circle since at the outbreak of war between the Western Allies and Hitler in 1940, he openly declared himself on the side of the Western Democracies and against Stalin and his allies. (Meaning Hitler, since at that time a friendship pact existed between Hitler and Stalin.)

199- Patrik von zur Mühlen, *Zwischen Hakenkreuz und Sowjetstern*, Düssdeldorf: Droste Verlag, 1971, pp. 71–72. (He cites Professor von Mende's archives.)

200- Nuremberg document 1420 P.S. in IMT, Bd XXVII S (p. 289 f.), cited by Patrik von zur Muhlen, p. 72. Also see Dallin concerning this matter.

This took place during a special banquet. In fact, it was a defeat for the Schulenburg group of the Foreign Ministry and a setback for the Caucasian cause. However, all was not lost because two important "host" officials of the Ostministerium, Professor Gerhard von Mende and Dr. Otto Bräutigam emerged as protectors of the Caucasians, and they also shared the views of Schulenburg, Stauffenberg, Köstring, Canaris and Herwarth.

Several Caucasian representatives of the Adlon Conference left Berlin. But for those who remained, Mende organized respective national representation, officially referred to as the "National Ausshuss." The Georgian "National Ausshuss" consisted of Spiridon Kedia, Professor Mikhail Tsereteli, Zurab Avalishvili and Dr. Giorgi (Gogi) Magalashvili (Magalow). The dictionary definition of "Ausshuss" is a broad one and includes such words as choice, board, elite, management, commission and general council but it also includes the word committee—the word Mende carefully avoided. The reason? It was generally forbidden by Hitler, in order to prevent political concessions for the nations they represented. This did not figure in Hitler's plans at that time. Preceding the "Ausshusses," Mende had put together, with the participation of the indigenous people, the "Mittlestelle" which subsequently was modified to the "Leitstelle" (meaning to manage, lead or guide.) This he used in order to secure lodging, clothing and food for the P.O.W.s (or the former P.O.W.s) and to facilitate traveling or obtaining necessary information for them.

At the time of organizing the "Ausshusses," the "Leitstelles" were still in place and functioning. Mende was not a party member, making it even more impressive how much autonomy and strength he could gain for his Caucasian Department of the Ostministerium. The reason for this being that he was an outstanding specialist in his field of Turkology and the Caucasus, he spoke the languages and also knew the U.S.S.R. in general very well. Mende related well with the people around him because human interests and values were very much on his mind. He was hard-working, well-organized and difficult to replace. The ineffectual and passive Minister Rosenberg was glad to delegate problems to Mende while he concerned himself with writing memoranda about "big" ideological and philosophical problems without interest in practical details.

We have discussed "Schulenburg's Plan"; what was Rosenberg's plan for the U.S.S.R. and how did it differ from the former? Briefly stated, Rosenberg wanted to separate ethnic Russia from the non-Russian Republics. He would set up the non-Russian ethnic states under German leadership and surround the Russian State by them; the Baltic States (Estonia, Latvia, Lithuania), Belarus, Ukraine—on the west; the Caucasus (Armenia, Azerbaijan, Georgia)—on the south; Kazakhs, Uzbeks, and Turkmen—on the east. "Our Policy," wrote Dr. Otto Bräutigam, the head of the Department or General Politics in the Ostministerium, "[was intended to make] the Ukraine a counterweight against mighty Russia, against Poland and the Balkans and a bridge to Caucasus."[201]

The Georgians I knew felt more comfortable with Schulenburg's Plan rather than Rosenberg's Plan. The adversarial relationship was obviously promoted by Rosenberg because of setting up the "sanitary cordon" between the Great Russians and Europe. Moreover, contrary to Schulenburg, Rosenberg made no mention of individual sovereign states holding a referendum should they decide to form a federation. All in all, Rosenberg's plan conveys the message of total German control over the entire area, as well as humiliation and degradation of the ethnic Russians. Georgians are not Russian haters; our goal was to reestablish our lost sovereignty and to soothe our hurt pride sustained during the two very rough Russian occupations. After reaching our goal we wanted to establish a good, lasting relationship with Russia. Therefore, the overwhelming majority of Georgians did not agree with Rosenberg's plan.

A few weeks after the invasion of the U.S.S.R., Hitler established the Ostministerium civilian administration of occupied Eastern territories headed by Minister Alfred Rosenberg. This was to eliminate the power struggles between institutions with vested interests in the occupied East. However, this did not happen in practice. The Army kept its influence, not only on the front but also in the rear area since its supply lines lay there. The police force was under Himmler's SS jurisdiction. Many organizations concerned with the economy were not under Rosenberg's orders. Recruitment of labor was carried out by a brutal Fritz Sauckel. Ruthless Erich Koch had been appointed a commissar of Ukraine, by direct party connections and in spite of Rosenberg's protest against it. In the inner Nazi circles, Koch was referred to as the "Red Erich"; apparently he would have become a fanatical communist but through Hitler's influence became a Nazi. During the German depression, Koch was the main speaker of the Nazis who advocated a close relationship with the Soviets. A first rate demagogue and the Gauleiter of East Prussia, Koch was also a protege of Göring and Bormann and had direct access to Hitler. Therefore he could afford to ignore his Minister Rosenberg and make fun of his "naive and romantic plans" toward the people of the east and reject them.[202]

Koch completely shared Hitler's following positions:

1. The Germans were a nation of overlords.

201- Alexander Dallin quoting Bräutigam, Document 294-P.S. TMWC. XXV, 340, p. 108; Wallace Carroll, "It Takes a Russian...," *Life*, December 19, 1949.
202- See Dallin and Herwarth concerning E. Koch.

2. The conquered Eastern Nations were destined to serve them.

3. It was a German right and duty to exploit such people.

4. For total control it was necessary to destroy the indigenous intelligentsia and all those who would interfere with such a goal. E. Koch's immediate objective was to squeeze all agriculture and other resources out of the Ukraine for German benefit in spite of A. Rosenberg's protests. This included many Ukrainians rounded up by F. Sauckel and transported to the forced labor camps in Germany.

Due to abominable conditions, some of them were found dead on arrival in railroad cars or totally disabled. Those engaged in the labor force had to wear a degrading sign "Ost" (the East), thus isolating them from the German populace. Their living conditions were substandard. When word got around about these conditions, all able-bodied people took to the forests. Some of them joined the Ukrainian nationalist partisans, ("The Ukrainian Insurgent Army") who fought against the Germans as well as the "Reds." Others joined the partisans parachuted by the Soviets.[203]

Hitler was so convinced he could defeat Stalin and his Red Army within a matter of a few months that the Germans did not even prepare for a winter war in Russia. He discounted any need for political warfare and failed to take advantage of the dissatisfied Soviet people—dissatisfied by their own government and the system and eager to change.[204] Rosenberg, on the other hand, revealed more acumen than most of his colleagues. He argued for political involvement and actions, commensurate with his plans from the very beginning.[205] According to Hitler, the German troops would rapidly advance to the imaginary "AA Line" drawn from Arkhangelsk on the White Sea in the north to Astrakhan on the Caspian Sea in the south. By the time the German troops reached the "AA Line," Hitler assumed the Soviets would no longer be capable of any organized resistance and therefore there would be no need for a peace treaty with the remnants of the Soviet regime. Three German mechanized armies would guard the "AA Line" protecting the "New Europe" from the "Asiatic Hordes." European Russia with its agricultural and industrial centers would then become a German colony and its subhuman (Untermenschen), indigenous people the slaves of the German overlords (Übermenschen). The country's riches

---

203- Wallace Carrol, "It Takes a Russian...," *Life*, December 19, 1949. Dallin, Chapters VII and VIII; Dallin, p. 444, see Bräutigam's note of October 1942 protesting poor treatment of the Eastern workers on behalf of the Ostministerium.

204- Dallin correctly states, "The Germans had made no plans to satisfy popular aspirations in the east," p. 65.

205- Dallin, p. 51.

would belong to Germany, making her independent of imports from overseas. The population of Crimea would be deported to some other parts of Russia and Crimea would be populated by the South Tyroleans and turned into a "German Gibraltar." The conquered territory of Russia would become a "German India."[206]

Count Schulenburg's plan, to convert the military conflict with the Soviets into a civil war against the Soviet system, found many supporters among the German military leaders. They agreed that Stalin's regime could be defeated only by an alliance with the Bolshevik-abused Soviet people, if the Germans would honestly promise the betterment of their life and behave accordingly. Professor von Mende and Dr. Bräutigam from the Ostministerium were of the same conviction. They formed an alliance with like-minded persons from the foreign office and the military, as has been discussed before, and were proven correct by the change of events in late fall and winter.

Red Army soldiers, now aware of the inhumane treatment by the Germans of those who surrendered, began to fight fiercely in defense of Moscow and Leningrad. Disillusioned peasants and the indigenous populace in general turned hostile and partisan activities flourished. By the spring of 1942, the German Army leaders felt that unless there was a radical turnaround of the German East Policy, the war was going to be lost. Out of this was born the successful Army-sponsored Caucasus Policy. It was hoped that this would be extended to other occupied Eastern areas.[207] However, Hitler adamantly refused such an extension and he especially forbade development of General A. Vlasov's movement of the Russian Liberation Army beyond its use for the purpose of propaganda. But opponents of Hitler's East Policy did not give up. For instance, Schulenburg, in spite of the failure of his 1942 "Adloniada" initiative, again reopened the "Caucasian Dossier" during June 1943. He probably felt that given Germany's present unfavorable military situation, Hitler would now be willing to change his infamous East Policy.

To start, it was hoped that the Caucasus question would be less irritating for Hitler with other suggestions to follow. So Schulenburg once again moved Ribbentrop, his mediocre Minister (of Foreign Affairs), to present Schulenburg's Plan to the Führer in his Obersalzberg residence.[208] Schulenburg did not accompany Ribbentrop up in the "Eagle's Nest" but chose to wait for him in the town

---

206- Wallace Carroll, "It Takes a Russian...," *Life*, December 19, 1949; Dallin and Herwarth concerning Hitler's plan.

207- As we have explained earlier in the chapters relating to Bergmann and Caucasus; also refer to Wallace Carroll; Dallin; and Herwarth.

208- Schulenburg did not think much of his Minister Ribbentrop. For instance, during one meeting with M. Kedia and A. Tsomaia, the latter wanted to know if Ribbentrop really had learned some verses from Georgian poetry in order to please Stalin during their 1939 negotiations. "My dear friend," exclaimed Schulenburg in French, "you are overestimating my Minister."

below. Ribbentrop returned with bad news. Having read the plan, Hitler became furious, threw the paper away and shouted, "This does not interest me." Regretfully, Schulenburg informed M. Kedia about his failed attempt in Obersalzberg.

In Berlin, M. Kedia represented the Georgian National Alliance in France and also had a mandate from the Georgian government in exile to defend national Georgian interests in Germany. Therefore he wrote a spirited letter to the president in exile, N. Jordania and Secretary of State E. Gegechkori (Guegechkori) about Schulenburg's information. The conclusion or his letter was "...my presence in Berlin no longer makes any sense, so I am packing and will soon be leaving for Paris."[209] The letters were delivered personally to N. Jordania and E. Gegechkori by M. Kedia's special envoy, Shota Berejiani, who also brought their answers back to Kedia. These were crucial for Kedia and the rest of us for agreeing with a concept of the Liaison Staff and partaking in such a mission; we shall quote from the letters.

E. Gegechkori's letter to M. Kedia. July 6, 1943:

"What you are writing did not surprise me, since I already knew from the Marshal[210] that the Leader's[211] opinion, at least for now remains unchanged. So much worse for all of us. In spite of it, not even for a moment did I regret what we did in order to alter this dangerous path. I know well how dangerous my trip was also.[212]

". . . So the fate of the struggle should be decided by arms only. Also in that case our position remains the same. We will make an effort and act wherever

---

209- M. Kedia's letter to the author, personal archive.

210- Finland's Marshal Mannerheim.

211- Refers to Hitler.

212- E. Gegechkori undertook to visit Marshal Mannerheim, the Finish Commander in Chief and President, in order to have him plead with Hitler for a change of the German East Policy with particular emphasis on Caucasus. Mannerheim did so but to no avail. Gegechkori knew Mannerheim during the "old days" of Imperial Russia in St. Petersburg. Apparently there had been a feeling of solidarity and affinity between the Finns and Georgians, as the history of these two nations shows many parallels.

    Both had been buffeted over centuries by larger invading forces, both had fallen victims of Russia's drive to expansion and had been annexed into the Tsarist Empire by the nineteenth century. With the outbreak of the Russian Revolution, both countries managed to regain their independence. While Georgia became the victim of Red Russian aggression, Finland was spared the Soviet assault in its formative years. However, during 1939, the Red Army invaded Finland, managing only to gain but one tenth of its territory. In 1941, the Fins became German allies and fought the Russians off their land. This did not mean that the Fins shared Hitler's ideology and goals; neither did the Georgians who served in the German Army. They just wanted to regain their lost freedom. Who could understand this better than Mannerheim.

    Perhaps Winston Churchill and Franklin D. Roosevelt could also understand it since they allied their countries with Stalin's Russia in order to win the war against Hitler. This is the "real politik."

an opportunity presents itself. You know that for us the matters concerning the Georgian P.O.W.s is one of paramount national interest. On their survival may well hang a delicate balance for our nation—to be or not to be. The political and military organization is a big problem and here should be spent all our energy.

"Here also, we may not be able to achieve much, or steer things in a necessary direction for us but our efforts should be clearly seen. Since we are lacking political recognition, it will be very difficult for us to influence German military leadership into accepting our views; but it should be the sacred duty of every Georgian to see that the already depleted manpower of our tortured nation would not be further exhausted and spent there, where it would have no bearing on the outcome of the war but may well spell disaster for us.

"Therefore, we consider it obligatory that such an undertaking be headed by a person who is in agreement with the above-expressed view and thus would assure the fulfillment of it.... from what was said it is easy for you to conclude about the Verbindungsstab (The Liaison Staff). Here should remain a reliable and politically responsible person who enjoys the trust of Georgian circles."

From Noe Jordania's letter to Kedia, dated July 10, 1943:

"...you probably have already received the answer to your letter from Evgeni. We shall remain in our old position and continue the work—pursuing the same line. It would have been good if the political side had been revealed from the very beginning but since this is not feasible now, let us wait for a suitable moment."

This was then an opinion of the legal Georgian government in exile which, pursuant of the instructions of the Constituent Assembly, had left for Western Europe to appeal for restoration of the sovereign Georgian state, now occupied by the Red Russian troops, who won the war against much weaker Georgian opposites in a surprise attack during 1921.[213] The annexation of Georgia was against international law and since that time the country had been administered by puppet "governments." Even the first secretary of the Georgian Communist Party had a "watchdog" appointed over him by Moscow—the so called "Second Party Secretary," a Russian who was the real power behind the scene.

213- Constantin Kandelaki, p. 14.

Therefore, as far as we were concerned, the only representative and freely elected Georgian government was in exile in Paris. They alone could speak for the people. It follows then the importance we attached to Jordania's and Gegechkori's opinions. The majority of the Georgian emigres in France, Germany and Poland felt the same way about the Liaison Staff as the government in exile did, with the exception of the small left wing of Georgian Social Democrat Party in France. As soon as the Liaison Staff was established during October–November of 1943, the Georgian National Alliance in Paris declared strong support for it which is clearly seen from the minutes of a special meeting called in Paris on October 27, 1943, where the "resolution introduced by Mr. E. Gegechkori . . . was unanimously adopted." (See Appendix for full text.) The resolution:

> "Having heard Mr. M .Kedia's presentation about the establishment of the Georgian Liaison Staff during the meeting, the Georgian National Alliance expresses the hope that in spite of the existing complex general situation, the above mentioned organization will undertake every effort to give appropriate care to the Georgian P.O.W.s and legionnaires, instilling in them the right spiritual and political attitude. This in turn will convert them into the necessary force for the Georgian National struggle. The meeting urges members of the National Alliance to energetically support the above-mentioned Liaison Staff toward the realization of its goal."

(Signed) P. Sardjveladze, Chairman   (Signed) N. Urushadze, Secretary

M. Kedia, M. Alshibaja, Dr. Magalow, myself and our associates strongly believed that without the support of the Georgian National Alliance, the Liaison Staff would never have been established. It was an assignment during a desperate situation, a job from which none of us expected glory and perhaps not even gratitude. But after the war, it was a consensus of opinion that some worthwhile goals had been achieved and things would have been worse without the Liaison Staff.[214]

214- Therefore, in my opinion, it was less than fair when after World War II, a few men who loved to write and/or make their own ego-boosting statements did so at the expense of the Liaison Staff. They chose to ignore the facts and situations that existed during the tenure of the Liaison Staff from the fall of 1943 until the end of the war in the spring of 1945. Of course, they had every right to express their own opinions; nevertheless, this did not serve the cause of objective history. Those opinions also caused disdain among those who were risking all while trying to assist their countrymen in peril during the war, while the postwar critics had lived in relative safety and comfort.

12

IN FRANCE AND HOLLAND

M. Alshibaja and I arrived in Paris on November 20, 1943, and were very well hosted by his in-laws, the Mamulashvilis. The following day, he and I visited the key members of our government in exile: President Noe Jordania; Minister of Foreign Affairs Evgeni Gegechkori (Gueguetchkori); and the Minister Plenipotentiary in France, Akaki Chkhenkeli. They had distinguished looks and personalities and along with their associates were an integral part of modern Georgian history. I had never met them before but M. Alshibaja had, especially Gegechkori who was an old family friend; I was excited to see them. We briefed them about the current condition of the Georgian P.O.W.s and the civilian workers; considerable improvement had been observed for both. The efforts were made on behalf of the legionnaires by our friends on the staff of the General for the Eastern Volunteer Troops to upgrade their status to the level of the German soldiers. It was also planned to gradually replace the German officers by their qualified Georgian opposites. This was the reason for the experiment of sending four Caucasian officers to Dresden Military School, and it was a success. Many more officers were sure to follow. On the other hand, we were currently experiencing a great deal of resistance from the German political "higher ups" against organizing our troops in larger units, which would be of considerable logistic and other advantages for us. Our supporters in the Army shared our view and were far from giving in on that point. Then we tried to evaluate the transfer of some of our troops to Holland and France, the subject of mutual concern to all of us. We were sure the commanding German officers had already explained to the legionnaires the reasons for the transfer to the west but we felt we ought to also address this issue.

We told Messrs Jordania, Gegechkori and Chkhenkeli what we intended to tell the legionnaires while visiting them for the very first time: The voluntary units had been put together during a different military situation when the Germans were successfully moving forward. Our military and political goal was to get to the Caucasus and we did. But because of the thinned out German forces over vast Russian territory and the heavy losses during the battle of Stalingrad, the Germans had to fall back to conducting a defensive war. Although the Kremlin leaders claim the entire credit for themselves, the Red Army could not have achieved this without help from America and England. We ourselves saw an example of this even on the Caucasus front—south of Mozdok, where among the abandoned tanks, roughly fifty percent were American-Sherman tanks, used by the Red Army. Due to the defensive German war and retreat, an obvious change of the situation developed for us. We lost the Caucasus, and there was greater danger for the legionnaires to fall in Red Army hands, especially those wounded and disabled. As it has been reported in such instances, the legionnaires were accorded horrible treatment—usually a summary execution. This kind of news (although not surprising) had an unnerving effect on some legionnaires. At the same time, during October, a number of German troops had to be transferred to the West and with them the Eastern indigenous units that could not be replaced. The generals of the Eastern Volunteer Troops agreed with the transfer mainly due to the already discussed dangerous situation for the legionnaires on the East Front; it also offered them a respite.

Therefore, this was not a political but a military decision; the legionnaires being part of the German Army were sent where they could be better utilized. Clearly this had not been an ideal choice but the soldiers had to comply. Nevertheless, our goal remained the same: to free Georgia and the Caucasus from Bolshevik-Kremlin tyranny. Possibly the global situation would yet change to our advantage and we would be able to play a role useful to our country.[215] Another message to the legionnaires would be that they should behave as knights toward the indigenous populace and also to please remember that France had been a supporter of the Georgian cause and a good host to the Georgian emigres.

Messrs. N. Jordania, E. Gegechkori and A. Chkhenkeli listened to us approvingly; there were a number of questions for us but no corrections or suggestions for our intended address to the legionnaires. I had the feeling that Kedia had been briefing them on an ongoing basis. I loved these three "Old Men" from the Georgian government in exile and was proud of them. After a warm handshake, we left in good spirits. The following day we visited the opposition party leader, Spiridon Kedia, whom I had met in Berlin a few months before when the formation of the

---

215- We shall not elaborate about this but we had in mind a possible split between the Western Allies and Stalin because of his unchanged aggressive design toward the "Capitalistic World." Stalin only temporarily and partly postponed this goal since he needed the Western Allies' help against Germany. (Over four decades of postwar domination of East Europe and the creation of trouble spots all over the world plus the Cold War are testimony to this.)

Liaison Staff was being considered and he had encouraged us to join it. We briefed him along the same lines and felt that we had his blessing.

After seeing Spiridon Kedia, we visited the former commander in chief of the Georgian Army during its independence, the much respected General Giorgi Kvinitadze and his delightful wife, Mariam, in Chatou, near Paris. They had three daughters; we met one of them, beautiful Nano, with an enchanting smile; the other daughters, if I remember correctly, were married and not at home. We briefed the General along the same lines as we had our politicians. He told us that some of his cadets from the Tbilisi Military School, who later were contract officers in Poland's army, were now serving in the Georgian Legion battalions. We probably would see them during our tour and he asked us to convey to them his regards. We loved our "old" General as much as we did our "old" political leaders we had met before him. The General could not speak Georgian well enough to keep up with the conversation, so we had to carry it out in Russian. He explained that ever since he was a cadet, while in his teens, he had to train and serve in the Russian-speaking world.[216]

In all fairness, the General's views as addressed in his memoirs should be balanced against the memoirs of President Jordania and the existing documents by the nonpartisan historians.[217] I must add that I personally do not question the integrity or sincerity of either of these two historic personalities from Georgia's past. The retrospective evaluation will reveal that the Georgian government probably made a number of mistakes but not more than any other governments of the civilized world. It also is clear that neither the Georgian government nor its armed forces nor the people were to be blamed for the loss of our sovereignty. The real reason was the treaty broken by Bolshevik Russia and the coercion of Georgia by the overwhelming Russian military force into becoming part of the Red Empire.

We need not list other countries similarly annexed by the Bolshevik Kremlin. The difference in the case of Georgia was that the Red Army, after having swallowed the rest of the Caucasus and having engaged in fighting the Georgian troops, received aid from Turkey, who stabbed Georgia in the back and demanded part of Georgian territory. Georgia was then completely surrounded by enemies and had no chance, while the civilized world that had recognized Georgia as an independent sovereign state looked on without being able to help. Georgia, during its modern history, stood up against its conquering major power, with probably more valor than any other small nation with the exception of Finland.

General Kvinitadze never lost hope that someday Georgia would regain its lost sovereignty. When Germany invaded Russia in World War II, General

216- For more on General Giorgi Kvinitadze's background, please see the Appendix.
217- For instance, the Georgian Archives at Harvard University Library.

Kvinitadze thought that such time had arrived. So from his home in Chatou/Seine he wrote to Hitler (with the help of the German military field commandant) thanking him for the "pending liberation of Georgia" and expressing confidence concerning further developments.[218] A short time after that, Lado Akhmeteli (not to be mistaken for Mikheil Akhmeteli) the former Georgian Ambassador in Berlin, wrote to the German Foreign Ministry. He suggested formation of a "Big Caucasian Federation."[219] Two months later L. Akhmeteli suggested to Hitler the formation of the Georgian Legion, from 30,000 to 50,000 P.O.W.s and recommended that his friend General Kvinitadze be appointed as a commander of it.[220] Neither G. Kvinitadze nor L. Akhmeteli had any affection for Hitler and his political doctrine, but they made such appeals in order to gain freedom for their county.

I also had a happy reunion in Paris with former "Bergmann" emigre soldiers who had been discharged after the retreat from Caucasus because of poor health or, in certain instances, difficult domestic problems. We had many things to discuss, especially trying to figure out what lay ahead for our soldiers. At that moment, special concern was felt for "Bergmann," engaged in a bitter fight on the Crimean Isthmus against the Soviet troops, who cut them off from the mainland. I was fairly confident that in due time their evacuation to a less precarious place would be feasible and tried to cheer up our retired comrades with my view. I also promised them to convey their greetings and best wishes to the "Bergmann" Georgians during my pending visit to them in Crimea.

In Paris I made many acquaintances, among them two charming Georgian ladies, Vera Pagava, a talented painter in France, and Maro Gogoberidze, both members of the "Ladies' Committee" for the relief of the Georgian legionnaires and P.O.W.s. This committee did much to alleviate the legionnaires' feeling of homesickness, receiving presents and letters of encouragement from the emigres but also invitations to visit their homes while on vacation. The "Ladies' Committee" felt it would be a more comfortable feeling for all concerned if during such visits the legionnaires were permitted civilian clothes rather than the German uniform. Mikhail Alshibaja and I visited the officer for the Eastern Volunteer Troops in the

---

218- Kvinitadze on Hitler, October 6, 1941 (document BA, R665) in Patrik von zur Mühlen, *Zwishen Hakenkreuz und Sowjeststern*, p. 105.

219- Lado Akhmeteli on F. M., Oct. 23, 1941 (doc. PAAA) Pol XIII, Kaukasus Volker, S247939, in Zur Mühlen, p. 105.

220- L. Akhmeteli on Hitler, Dec. 30, 1941, in Zur Mühlen, p. 105.
   During January 1942, L. Akhmeteli submitted some additional plans to Hitler's "Reichskanzlei" about the Caucasus. It envisioned: Step I—Caucasus to become a German Protectorate temporarily, headed by the German general residing in Tbilisi; from where he would appoint other German generals for each Caucasian nation. Step II—Establishment of the sovereign Caucasian states; Georgia should become an independent monarchy as it had been a thousand years before the Russians ever were. Please see Zur Mühlen, p. 106.

Army headquarters in (or near) Paris, with an agenda in our hands for discussion. Permission for the legionnaires to wear civilian clothes while on leave was on the list. The officer's response was positive and he promised to write an ordinance about it for the Legion battalions. Some other items on the agenda included such requests as making it known to the Georgian units that the Georgian Liaison Staff had established a branch office in Paris in order to address the legionnaires' needs more efficiently, which was already up and running with Durmishkhan Djuruli in charge.

I fell in love with the Georgian emigres in France; such feelings remained with me life-long. I shall always have a special spot in my heart for them. The overwhelming majority of them were hospitable, warm persons—humanitarians, generous and dedicated patriots. Mariam and Levan Mamulashvili's family (in-laws of Mikheil Alshibaja), where we stayed while in Paris, was also an example of this. [221]

Elena Mamulashvili graciously volunteered to be my guide in Paris. I was overwhelmed by this city beautifully located on the Seine riverbanks with memorable bridges, booksellers' stalls along the river, Montmartre, typical sidewalk cafes, view of the Eiffel Tower from across the Seine, the Champs Élysées with the Arc de Triomphe, the Louvre and much more. But the Notre Dame Cathedral, which took one century to complete, left the greatest impression on me. Not only because it was (and still is) considered one of the greatest masterpieces of Gothic architecture but more so due to the deep religious feeling one experiences while inside.

221- My bedroom was on the second floor and the master bedroom was one floor higher. Having slept rather soundly during the first night, I was awakened in the morning by a man's voice saying what sounded like a prayer from the floor above. I got up, did my routine exercise, showered, but the gentleman was still praying. I have been a believer since early childhood probably due to my maternal grandmother Irene's influence but I had never seen even Grandma pray that long. What a true Christian this gentlemen had to be. Much inspired, I went downstairs on the main floor where Thina (one of the three Mamulashvili daughters) was preparing breakfast. I said good morning to Thina and expressed my admiration for the religious gentleman upstairs. Thina broke out in melodious laughter and said that the gentlemen in question was no one else but their father Levan reciting from the book of Rustaveli's poetry—every morning as usual. Small wonder that during the preceding centuries the Georgian clergy was less than happy because allegedly their parishioners spent more time reading Rustaveli than religious books.

Mamulashvili had three captivating daughters—Elena, Thina and Ivlit and two sons, Jason and Givi (Guivi). The young men were in Grenoble—southeast France—during our visit in Paris. I have already spoken of the youngest daughter, Ivlit, in conjunction with her husband Mikheil Alshibaja and their adorable children Niniko and Theimur. Theimur (Theimuraz) was still too small a boy for keen observations but not his sister Niniko (Nino) who immediately made one. She threw her arms up and exclaimed, "Father Mikho took off the Germany"—referring to her daddy who took off the German uniform and was dressed in civilian clothes. I would be glad to do the same and cheer up Niniko and probably other family members as well, but I possessed no civilian garments at that time.

One can indeed understand such feelings of the French civilian population in German-occupied France. The Georgians felt the same way, when during 1921, the Russian Red Army occupied Georgia. I was six years old at that time, when Grandmother Irene and I ran into the detachment of the Red Army troops marching on the street that was parallel to Grandma's property fence. I jumped through the gates shaking my fist and shouting at them. "So you are the Bolsheviks, aren't you? I will show you." I was too little to be taken seriously, but my attitude revealed how the people felt in our household. Grandmother was petrified with fright and dragged me back behind the fence.

Before entering the cathedral, Elena informed me that since it was my first visit to Notre Dame, my prayers would be answered. I had a long list, not unlike the one presented to St. Basilius during New Year's Eve in Georgia. While walking outside the cathedral, Victor Hugo's *Hunchback of Notre Dame* came to mind with Quasimodo defending the life of beautiful Esmeralda. Elena's beautiful face resembled an icon, she was also intelligent, eloquent and well-read. Many eligible bachelors had fallen in love with her, albeit only one of them appealed to Elena. He was unfortunately not a "marrying type" and also became seriously ill, so both remained unwed—what a pity.

The Mamulashvilis' second oldest daughter, Thina, was a striking brunette just as lovely as Elena with soft, warm brown expressive, intelligent eyes. She was a lady of few words. Understandably so, as she too had many admirers (rumor had it that one of them committed suicide). Finally, one of the suitors was lucky, Major Aliosha Kintsurashvili of the French Foreign Legion, a veteran of World War II on General de Gaulle's side, who she married.[222] Mother Mariam Mamulashvili, a wonderful person, was loved not only by her own family but also by everyone who knew her. She was a devoted mother, wife and friend; always placing her own interests last. Father Levan Mamulashvili, in spite of his "mature age" had a sharp mind and keen interest of the world around him. Now retired, in the past he had been connected with the well-known oil industry in Baku, Azerbaijan.[223] It has been mentioned before that the Mamulashvilis had a boardinghouse in Paris for young English ladies who had come to enjoy France and to learn to speak their language. I had not experienced such a warm, homey, family atmosphere as at Mamulashvilis since I left Georgia.

I was very pleased to meet Misha Alshibaja's sister, Kethevan (Kethi) in Paris. She stayed with her sister Thamara Alshibaja-Pataridze.[224] Kethi was well-educated,

---

222- Other officers were Majors Aliosha Djintcharadze and Alexis Chkhenkeli (son of the former Georgian Ambassador-Plenipotentiary in France and cousin of Bagrat Chanturia who served in "Bergmann"). My wife Rusudan and I had the pleasure of meeting Major Aliosha Kintsurashvili and Thina Mamulashvili, a delightful couple, a number of years after the war in France. Major Kintsurashvili, as well as other Georgian officers I met who had served in the French Army on General de Gaulle's side, understood very well that those Georgians who were in the Germany Army (which had a real possibility of occupying Caucasus) did so in defense of Georgian national interests.

223- Baku was a part of Imperial Russia and preceding World War I, a number of serious Georgian businessmen gathered there and under the leadership of Akaki Khoshtaria, formed "Rupento," The Russian-Persian Oil Association. Levan Mamulashvili was part of this. He was a very successful lawyer and shareholder. The business was going well even through the time of the Georgian Independence. But during April of 1920, the Russian Red Army, with overwhelming forces, invaded and occupied Azerbaijan, including Baku. Levan was still able to provide for his family but due to the fall of the Georgian Republic, they had to emigrate to France.

224- Thamara, in fact, was Kethevan's cousin from her father's side, but she and her brother Konstantin (Kako) left Georgia with their uncle Gregory Alshibaja and his family for Germany. As children they were adopted by Doctor Kiziria-Alshibaja and his wife, Barbara. Thamara's and Kako's parents remained in Georgia due to complex circumstances.

spoke many languages and was a Georgian beauty. She certainly contributed to the pleasantness of her brother, Mikho's and my stay in Paris. Kethi even volunteered to type our business correspondence. She told me about her younger sisters, Martha, Rusudan and Thina. They had all studied in Poland and were now continuing their education in Germany. (Martha was in Vienna.) Little did I realize then that eventually I would marry Rusudan.

Kethi introduced me to Thamara and Elise Pataridze and their three darling children, Thina, the oldest one and the twin babies, sister and brother Gulnara (Guliko) and Othar. I loved all of them. Elise was one of the leading members of the Georgian National Democrat Party, (the author also has the honor of belonging to this party) and after the war, founded the periodical *Iveria*. I had much to discuss with Elise. My visit there coincided with that of my friend, Alexandre Asatiani, which made the conversation even livelier. Thamara's and Elise's hospitality was fabulous, their home was the gathering place for many Georgian emigres. They were able to support the family with hard work in their own grocery store.

During the later part of November, Mikho and I commenced visiting the Georgian Legion battalions in the west. The branch office of our Liaison Staff in Paris appeared by now to be functioning well; some obstacles had been cleared. The Georgian (and other Caucasian) field battalions had been attached to the German Army divisions which were part of the Atlantic Coast defense system. The Georgian units were separated from each other by distance, making our trip time-consuming and rather inefficient. Mikho and I suspected the reason for such an arrangement was insufficient confidence by the Army Staff in the fighting spirit of the Eastern Volunteer Units. This was not an unreasonable assumption and indeed the over-whelming majority of "the Easterners" felt no animosity but only admiration for the Western Allies.[225] The approximate disposition of the Georgian battalions in the west at that time was as follows:

Battalion 822 located in Zandvoort, Holland

Battalion 795 in Cherbourg, Normandy, France

Battalion 823 on the English Channel or Guernsey

Battalion 797 near La Haye-du-Puits (Granville, France)

Battalion 798 in St. Nazaire, Normandy, France

Battalion 799 by Périgueux, France

225- This was especially true toward America. A rather amusing example was that during the author's school days in Georgia, at least two incidences of abortive attempts took place by a group of teenagers to run away to America. Among these students were children of ranking Georgian Communists. Probably the American reputation of freedom and equal opportunity was enhanced by Hollywood movies, American autos and the Singer sewing machine.

Battalion II/198 was located in Italy, and we had to travel there later. [226]

This is how our visit was organized: At first we arrived in the city of Le Mans, east of Paris, reported to the Army headquarters where the staff for the Eastern Volunteer Units in France was also located. We wanted to get clearance for visiting the units, general orientation and information about the battalions, especially if there were any problems. The Army staff apparently expected us; they were courteous and helpful in every possible way. They informed every army division to which Georgian battalions were attached, which assured our proper reception, including transportation, lodging, etc. The divisions would then inform the regiments and they in turn the battalions. From the very beginning they told us in Army headquarters that the transportation to Battalion 823 on the island of Guernsey (in the English Channel) was most difficult and had to be reached by airplane. Flights often were off-schedule, and some did not take place at all. We may lose time both ways, going and coming. They expected the transportation to improve and therefore postponement of our trip to 823 was suggested until such time. On the other hand, there would be no problem visiting all other units. The Army staff also shared new information with us, that small Georgian units had been attached to the offshore artillery batteries in the area of Biarritz (a well-known resort on the Bay of Biscay some distance from Bordeaux and not far from the Spanish border) and suggested we also visit them.

During early December, we arrived in La Haye-du-Puits in Normandy to see Battalion 797. The German commander of the battalion personally gave us a tour of his battalion and the fortifications. He introduced us to two Georgian emigre officers, Vano Bakradze and Dimitri Shalikashvili from the third and the "Staff Company" respectively. [227] Mikho knew them well from Poland, but I had never met them before and was very impressed by both. We shall say more about them later on. We not only met officers but nearly every soldier, in small groups at first. Then I was asked by the battalion's commander to address the larger groups. Such "speeches" were conducted along the same lines as discussed with our political leaders in Paris on the preceding pages. The questions most often asked were about their comrades who remained on the Eastern Front, concerning the Liaison Staff

---

226- Georgian Battalions I/8 and II/4 were also transferred from the Eastern Front to the Albi-Castres area (France) later during 1944.

227- Lieutenant V. Bakradze later was in Battalion 799, and during early 1945 was appointed the commanding officer of this battalion. After the retreat, D. Shalikashvili was appointed in the Military Dept. of the Georgian Liaison Staff as a consultant, first in Paris then in Germany. *[Dimitri Shalikashvili's son, General John Shalikashvili emigrated to America with his family, joined The United States Army and had a remarkable military career culminating in being appointed Chairman of the Joint Chiefs of Staff of the United States Armed Forces by President Bill Clinton from 1993 to 1997. General Shali, as he preferred to be called, is the subject of a 2019 book called* Boy on the Bridge: The Story of John Shalikashvili's American Success *by Andrew Marble published by University Press of Kentucky. —Ed.]*

and the Georgian emigrants in France. There was little doubt in Mikho's and my mind that the presence of emigre officers in 797 had been of great positive influence. It helped, to a considerable degree, to eliminate misunderstanding between the German commander, his personnel and the Georgians. This was true in almost all other units we visited who had such emigres and the German commandant was wise enough to listen to council. Moreover, emigres could speak to the legionnaires about Georgia's history, free of Soviet distortions. The emigre officers who had been educated during the time of free Georgia and continued his education in free Europe, could set an example of ethical conduct; different from the one taught by Marxism and Leninism. We enjoyed the hospitality in 797 and parted from them with a mutual pledge to keep in touch on an ongoing basis.

Battalion 795 in Cherbourg was only one of the Georgian Legion battalions I had visited in the Caucasus. At that time it was going through a crisis and General Köstring and his associate, von Herwarth had requested "Bergmann's" assistance.[228] I was very impressed, while in the Caucasus, by a former Soviet Army officer, Lomtatidze, who commanded a heavy machine gun company. I was glad to see him again and we had much to talk about. His conduct as a professional officer and a Georgian patriot remained excellent throughout the war.

Battalion 798,[229] near Saint Nazaire also made a good impression on us. The German commanding officer was very friendly. He felt fortunate, as he said, to have in his unit such excellent emigre helpers as Captain Simon Kobiashvili, First Lieutenant David Lagidze[230] and Sergeant Gaios Berikashvili, whom Kobiashvili later introduced to us. Here again, Mikho Alshibaja knew Kobiashvili and Lagidze very well from Poland, but I had never met them before. Neither of us knew Berikashvili, who had been living in Belgium. They all three impressed me favorably. There was a supper after the usual inspection tour, conversations with the legionnaires and a formal address to the battalion companies. Then the battalion's ensemble performed Georgian songs and dances. Later during the evening, the battalion commander invited all officers for after-dinner drinks. Here First Lieutenant David (Datha) Lagidze delighted us with his solo performance on the piano, at times accompanied by nostalgic songs. He was not only a real gentleman and a good officer but also a talented pianist. The next morning we bade our friends from 798 goodbye

---

228- As discussed in previous chapters. After reorganization, 795 conducted itself well on the Caucasus front. During April of 1943, it was transferred to Radom in the so-called "General Government" for further reorganization and training and during the latter part of the year to France.

229- My "mini diary" fails to reveal the names and the rank of several German officers.

230- Lt. D. Lagidze later served as an "Ordonnanzoffizier" in Battalion 797 (rather than 798). During early 1945, Lagidze was made second in command of the reorganized Georgian Legion and S. Kobiashvili first in command by General Köstring, on our recommendation.

and left by car via the city of Saint Nazaire, which had been severely damaged due to air raid bombings while surrounding areas were spared.

We traveled from Saint Nazaire by train and during the night back to Le Mans. There we visited a lieutenant colonel in the Army Operations Department for briefing. He advised us that there had been no change in the overall military situation—"all was quiet," except for some air raids. Unfortunately there was no improvement of transportation to the English Channel where Battalion 823 was located. Therefore, instead of Guernsey we arrived back in Paris after four hours of train travel. The following morning we had a meeting in the branch office of the Liaison Staff and received a report from Director D. Djuruli. It was clear that many legionnaires and also former P.O.W.s, now free and turned civilians, were helped by his office on an ongoing basis. For instance, they received useful briefings concerning personal matters, as well as periodical publications such as two Georgian newspapers, one of them, published by Dr. Gogi Magalow's Department of the Liaison Staff in Berlin and another by the German military propaganda (Wpr), also in Berlin.[231] Also made available were books such as *Georgia-Europe and the East*; the Georgian-German Dictionary; Akaki Tsereteli's novel, *Bashi Achuki*, etc. Djuruli said that our branch office in Paris was enjoying a great deal of help, cooperation and input from an already mentioned "Ladies Committee" as well as members of the National Alliance, especially Elise Pataridze (National Democrat), Pavel Sardjveladze (Social Democrat) and Niko Urushadze (Federalist).

Mikho and I remained in Paris two days, then boarded the night train for Périgueux and arrived there at 7:00 a.m. We were driven by car to Battalion 799, which was located some distance from the city. Captain Schmidt, the German commanding officer, received us warmly but informed us about a tragedy that had just occurred in his unit. Seven legionnaires drowned during training maneuvers. Mikho and I attended the burial and the Captain delivered a moving eulogy honoring the lost comrades. Touring battalion quarters, fortifications, conversations with legionnaires and my "routine" address were all understandably subdued due to this tragedy. During the evening, we got together for a chat with a small group including the battalion's Dr. Kometiani, legionnaire Gongladze and others whom I knew in Georgia before the war. Captain Schmidt and his adjutant also visited us to share their views about Battalion 799, and to learn our impressions. We all agreed that the situation appeared to be satisfactory but the legionnaires and the non-commissioned officers would fare even better from additional training and

---

231- The editor was Gaios Maglakelidze, son of Shalva Maglakelidze, as noted before.

schooling, which included safety rules and regulations. We parted with a pledge to keep in touch with each other and assurance that the Liaison Staff would help them all it could.

Our next goal was to travel by train via Bordeaux to the famous sea resort city of Biarritz, where a Georgian detachment was serving in a coastal artillery. Someone in Paris gave us an address and suggested to Mikho and me that we visit a Georgian family, Tsitsishvili, in Bordeaux. We found the Tsitsishvilis easily, (I can no longer recall their first names) and could not resist their cordial invitation to stay at least one day with them. I was especially curious about the lady of the house because she was of Basque origin. It is common knowledge that the Basques, who live in the West Pyrenees in Northern Spain, are people of unknown origin—they are neither Spaniards nor French or other ethnics of that region. There exists a not adequately proven theory that they came from Caucasus and are perhaps related to the Georgians. Our charming hostess certainly resembled her Georgian counterparts, but I am afraid this will not solve the ongoing debate that divides linguists and historians. For Mikho's and my part it was an attractive idea to have two sets of Georgians, one of them living in the Caucasian and another in the Pyrenees Mountains.

The next morning in Biarritz, we were cordially received by Captain Ludwigmann. He drove with us in a car to visit the positions of two coastal artillery batteries with fifteen Georgians serving in each of them. The Georgians were treated well and on equal footing with German soldiers. The captain excused the Georgians from duty so they could be with us and have an uninhibited conversation. During lunch, the captain observed that it was the first time that the Georgian volunteers had ever been visited by their representatives (meaning us) in this unit and he was pleased about it. We explained that the Georgian Liaison Staff was the only Georgian representative organization known to us at that time, and we would hope to keep open channels of communication in the future. Our tour was resumed after a delicious lunch; we answered many questions of the soldiers and parted before dark from our newly found friends in good spirits.

We arrived early the next morning in Paris and paid a visit to the headquarters of the General of the Eastern Troops. The General was not in Paris that day but we had a meeting with his adjutant and the heads of other departments. It consisted of a mutual briefing before our trip to Holland to visit Battalion 822, after which I would return to Paris but then soon depart for the East Front—especially Crimea. Although we found things to be quite satisfactory in the battalions we had visited, we had a list of suggestions for further improvements. For instance, in the absence of combat activities we felt additional training of the Georgian officers and non-commissioned officers in the German military schools was feasible and a number one priority. They would then replace a number of German counterparts. Equitable assignment of the emigre officers to the battalions was also suggested, etc.

In the headquarters of the General of the Eastern Troops in Paris we ran into the representatives of other Caucasians: Kantemir—North Caucasus, Alibekov—Azerbaijan and Djamalian—Armenia. They had come there for information about their battalions. They told us about the current situation in Berlin, including the severe air bombings. In friendly circles they were referred to as the "Three Musketeers" and Mikheil Kedia was the fourth one—D'Artagnan. The "Musketeers" were strong promoters of Caucasian unity and visualized existing battalions as an embryo of the future Caucasian Army. We got along very well.[232] During the evening, I visited General Kvinitadze again, this time alone since Mikho had another obligation to meet. I told the General all I knew so far about the Georgian battalions and his former pupils—the Georgian emigre officers now serving there. They sent affectionate regards to their general. Then he wanted me to tell him about my personal experiences during the war. At the end I told the General, in confidence, that in my opinion there was a great deal of difference between the present German government's policy toward us and what I had heard about and he had experienced during 1918–1921. They were much more supportive, courteous and friendly then. The General said that he had already heard about it from others; nevertheless, he added, we had no other choice but to continue our position given existing circumstances. I hastened to reaffirm that I was of the same opinion inasmuch as we had real German friends especially in the Army but also among the civilians, and they were doing their best to help. We parted with a warm handshake.

The next morning Mikho and I again traveled by train to Amsterdam and arrived before midnight. We checked into the Hotel Victoria near the railroad station; got up early, decided to walk into the city and see as much of it as possible. We were the only ones on foot; the bicyclists had taken over the streets. I had never seen so many of them in one city. We were also impressed with the clean and orderly streets and the well-arranged clean canals (artificial waterways). The Georgian Battalion 822's headquarters at that time was located in the town of Zandvoort—only one-half hour's drive from Amsterdam. We arrived there in the early afternoon and received the message that everybody was "in the field" but there would be a special supper for the officers in our honor and would we please attend. Then a non-commissioned officer showed us our quarters.

During supper, we met the battalion's officers, headed by Captain Klaus

---

232- In Berlin, the North Caucasians were also represented by Ahmet Nabi Magoma.

Breitner. Among other officers he introduced to us a Georgian "ordonnanzoffizier," Lieutenant Vassili Indjia,[233] Lieutenant Shalva Loladze, Lieutenant Katamadze and others. The Master Sergeant Konstantin (Kako) Alshibaja, a nephew of Mikheil was also present. During supper, informal discussions took place and we also toasted each other. The following morning the 3rd and the "Staff Company" were lined up and I had to deliver a speech covering the "usual" topics. Then we toured the fortifications or so-called bunkers and had considerable discussions with small groups on a one-to-one basis. They shared their views and lunch with us. That evening, Lieutenant Shalva Loladze hosted supper for us. It went well except it revealed to Mikho and me that the Ordonnanzoffizier Lieutenant Indjia and the Master Sergeant Kako Alshibaja did not get along well and probably never would. It was mostly a personality clash—they both knew it, and the Master Sergeant asked his cousin Mikho to talk to me about it and arrange his transfer. (This was indeed arranged later and we found an opening for the Master Sergeant in the Military Department of the Liaison Staff.)

The following morning we met in conference with Captain Breitner; he was friendly but came across as a bit arrogant and opinionated. A simple difference of opinion which emerged between us was this: We in "Bergmann" firmly believed that all soldiers and officers regardless of their ethnic origin and rank should have the same kitchen and the same kind of food. Captain Breitner felt it was best to have separate kitchens, one for Germans and another for Georgians so, as he said, that the "Easterners" may prepare food of their own choosing. This would at first appear not even worthy of discussion but I felt the same way about it as did Oberländer and von Kutzschenbach in "Bergmann." The reason was most legionnaires were former P.O.W.s and quite often had endured severe food shortage as well as other discriminations and therefore were sensitized. Breitner could have asked the Georgian soldiers about their kitchen preference and acted accordingly, instead he pursued his own preconceived idea. The rest of the day we spent visiting the remaining 4th and 2nd Companies. Lieutenant Tsamalashvili was host at the lunch for us and non-commissioned officer Gongladze was a co-host.

We again stopped to bid goodbye to Captain Breitner and thank him for his hospitality. We all felt that things were moving well in 822. None of us realized then, December 16–18, 1943, that near the conclusion of the war during the spring of 1945, a major tragedy would take place in Battalion 822 as a result of which more

---

233- He was an "old" emigre, who had served in the Polish Army and fought for Poland during 1939, when this brave nation was invaded by Hitler's and Stalin's troops and defeated. After the outbreak of the war between the former allies (Hitler and Stalin), he joined the Georgian Legion like others in order to protect Georgian interests. His brother, Jora Indjia, served in "Bergmann."

than one hundred Dutch civilians, two hundred German soldiers and five hundred Georgian legionnaires would lose their lives, as we shall see in some detail later.

Having visited the Georgian units, our impression was that the legionnaires had so far adjusted rather well to the new environment. I personally felt that they did not really believe the Western Allies would land in France in the near future.[234] Therefore, the legionnaires, at least for now, enjoyed a relatively better life than they would have on the Eastern Front. This mood was likely to change in the case of the Western Allies landing in France, which would surely develop into heavy combat with an unfavorable outcome likely for the German troops. The German soldiers who survived on the battlefield would land in the P.O.W. camps of the Western Allies. Sooner or later they would be discharged and returned to their own homes. But what about the legionnaires? They could only hope for humane treatment by the Western Allies—in accordance with the Geneva Convention. Perhaps it would be possible for them to settle in some countries in need of their working skills.[235] Their return to the Soviet Union would mean torture and an outright death penalty or in the best cases, a slow death in the Siberian gulags.

Mikho and I arrived back in Paris from Holland on December 19th. It was my birthday—I was already twenty-eight years old. Without telling anyone about it, I celebrated "getting old" by spending most of the day with Lieutenant Goglik (Giorgi) Vachnadze from the "Bergmann" Georgian Cavalry Squadron. His two week vacation was coming to an end; he was returning to Crimea the following day. With Misha (Mikhail) Dadiani, Goglik had led the cavalry attack coordinated with other "Bergmann" companies at the Crimean Isthmus in Perekop and in Sivash, approximately five weeks previous. They repelled elements of the Red Army, preventing it from penetrating the Crimean Peninsula but the isthmus further north remained occupied by the "Reds"; the German forces now had access to Crimea only by sea or air.

"As I rode my horse next to Misha's," said Goglik, "I had an exhilarating feeling. Explosions and shooting were all around us but I shouted to Misha Dadiani, would it not be nice if our Parisian-Georgians could see us now? It was just like in

---

234- In retrospect, such an assumption may appear far-fetched and could be referred to as wishful thinking. But during December 1943, the Red Army was pressing forward in a successful offensive. The Germans apparently no longer had the reserves to reinforce most of their thinned out Eastern front lines. On the other hand, in Italy the Western Allies met stubborn German resistance. In order to further strengthen the Italian Front, the Germans sent their reserve force from North Italy, the Balkans and France. This should have further slowed the Western Allies and made them focus on Italy and perhaps on the nearby Balkans rather than open a new front by landing in France—sustaining heavy losses due to well-defended Atlantic coastal fortifications. Moreover, the Western Allies still had to defeat Japan.

235- Such an outlook severely worsened for the legionnaires after the Yalta Agreement on Repatriation was signed by Stalin, Roosevelt and Churchill (February 1945), as we shall discuss in some detail later.

the movies but the casualties were heavy," he added sadly. He informed me how our mutual friend, Lieutenant Martin Schütte, had also been mortally wounded. How did he judge the military situation in Crimea? "I can only tell you that we will hold Perekop," he said. When I told Goglik that I would see him in the Perekop area in about two weeks, he promised to invite me for dinner there and serve a "rabbit ragout"; the Perekop prairie was full of the hares, he explained.

Our mutual friend, Tengiz Dadeshkeliani, joined Goglik and me for dinner in Paris. He had arrived a couple of days before to visit his sister, Kati (Katerina) and his daughter, Irina. The following day we accompanied Goglik Vachnadze to the train with other well wishers. "Do not forget about the Perekop 'rabbit ragout'," I shouted to Goglik as the train began to move. The same day Mikho and I again had a meeting with the staff officers of the Eastern Troops in Paris. There I received the message to phone the Lieutenant Colonel of General Staff, H.D. Herre, the Chief of Staff of the Eastern Volunteer Units in the Army headquarters in Lötzen, Germany. Herre wanted to know our impressions of the Georgian units in France. He also said the two generals and he "were looking forward to meeting" me in Lötzen before my trip to Crimea (and within the region of the Army Group South). So we set the date for January 4, 1944;[236] 1943 was quickly coming to an end.

There were a number of requests in our branch office in Paris for help, transfers, etc., and since Mikho and I were there, Director D. Djuruli frequently consulted us about them. An embarrassing case, and not to be solved easily, was the conflict between the Director and his assistant, Chichiko Mdivani, who was also many years Djuruli's senior. Apparently, Mdivani became so angry that he threatened to slap Djuruli's face—certainly a very unusual situation. Mdivani also happened to be a former classmate and friend of my father in Georgia. He treated me with affection and helped me to learn more about the Georgian emigration during our walks in Paris. Finally, during one of our longest walks, Mdivani and I somehow resolved the unpleasant matter between he and his "boss" amicably. He made it known to Djuruli that what he had said was said in anger and he had not really meant it—sort of an apology to the younger man. After some time, Mdivani quietly resigned from his position in the branch office of the Liaison Staff.

Incidentally, in that office I also met an acquaintance from Georgia, Kako Nijaradze, now in charge of the "cafeteria." He was a confirmed Bolshevik and made no secret of it, being sure that in spite of this the Georgian emigres would protect him. When we first met five or six years previously, he had been appointed as a political commissar of the alpinist group of the sports organization "Spartacus."

236- The dates are taken from my "mini diary."

(The Bolshevik Party had to have its hand in everything.) The "Spartacus" group, jointly with the medical school alpinists, undertook an ascent on Mount Khabarjina, which had to be dedicated to the anniversary of the October Revolution. After the outbreak of the war, Kako apparently was mobilized in the Red Army and was taken as a P.O.W. by the Germans. He then was freed by the Georgian emigres, and since Kako's father had been an old emigre in France, he was discharged in his father's care. Kako found employment as indicated above and because of that, I was his "boss." What I found rather amusing was that during the summer of 1944, and after the German retreat from Normandy, Kako cautiously tried to convert me to the Bolshevik cause, as we shall see later on. I thought at that time that he was a utilitarian with delusions and told him so.

We visited Evgeni Gegechkori (the Georgian Minister of Foreign Affairs in exile) twice after our tour of the Georgian battalions and shared with him our impressions. He said he would inform President Jordania, Ambassador Chkhenkeli and others in their circle about it. We agreed that we would communicate with them again after my trip to the Eastern Front, especially Crimea and bade him goodbye. I unexpectedly met Gegechkori again at a party given by Rezo Gogitidze's aunt, Barbale Gogitidze and her husband, Magilevski, a Russian emigre. The party was attended by the young as well as the not so young guests, but one could not feel a "generation gap" and the people mingled freely from one group to another. I noticed one sedentary group including our secretary of state who was concentrating on a card game, or was he? I would not have been able to concentrate had I been in his place because of a lady of indescribable beauty and grace who sat next to him. Although I never had the good fortune of meeting her before, I knew that she had to be Mary Shervashidze. I understood now why the Russian Emperor told her during one reception, "Princess, it is a sin to be as beautiful as you are." We were introduced and as she asked me to "please sit down." I could feel my heart pounding, probably at twice its normal rate. I was sitting next to her on one side with the secretary of state on the other, and I kept the conversation alive since I was not playing cards. This must have bothered the secretary somewhat. Therefore, with a protective and warm tone he told me, "My son, Givi, do not let us old folks bog you down, why don't you mingle with the young people again and have some fun." I assured him that it was a pleasure to be with them, but I also realized that I must not further overstay my welcome and soon left this card-playing, fascinating group to themselves.[237]

237- I saw Mary Shervashidze in Paris one more time at some gathering but could never forget her and heard about her well-being off and on with great interest. She lived to a very old age, but I was assured by those close to her that her age never affected her beauty.

At last, Tengiz Dadeshkeliani and I got around to visiting his sister, Kati (Katerina) Dadeshkeliani. She met us with warm embraces and asked me to call her Aunt Kati. She was unpretentious, humble, and an unselfish person working hard to make ends meet. During World War I, she had volunteered to serve in the Imperial Russian Army. She joined other brave ladies, from whom a special regiment was formed; they served in the combat zone as an auxiliary unit. She had lost her husband, who, if I remember correctly was a Russian nobleman and there were no children from that marriage. Tengiz's and her older sister died and life in emigration had been very difficult, and it became even worse after the German occupation of France. The only employment she could find was as a cleaning woman in the German soldiers' home in Paris. She never complained, but it obviously was hard work for her as she was now a fragile, elderly lady. Around noon, Kati's close friend, Vera Pagava joined us. As already mentioned, she was a talented artistic painter, a delightful person and an active member of the Ladies Relief Committee for P.O.W.s and the legionnaires. I had many questions to answer about the legionnaires and also requests to "look into my crystal ball to foretell the future." We all agreed that perhaps not in our lifetime but one day Georgia and other subjugated people of the Soviet Empire would be free.

During the few days I had left in Paris, I visited a number of persons. One of them was Victor Homeriki's wife, Colette, and Themo Taktakishvili, a former "Bergmann" soldier and our mutual friend who alerted me about the difficult situation. Victor, who was in "Bergmann" in Crimea which was cut off, could only help his wife and small children by sending his salary to them. But somehow the money did not reach them. Colette confirmed that and also told me to give love to Victor from her and their children. Through the intervention of our branch office this situation was somehow normalized. Kati Dadeshkeliani's unsuitable employment was altered with help from Kako Schavgulidze who was a faithful business associate of Misha Kedia and a Georgian patriot who was always eager to help. I shall discuss him later. I also met Misha Kedia's wife, Valia Kedia, whom we invited to lunch. She was a very energetic and strong person handling well a stressful situation due to her husband's absence and his dangerous occupation.

On Christmas Day, Mikho and I visited Konstantin Gvarjaladze, a former Georgian ambassador to England and his wife Babulia, both very dear, old friends of Mikho's parents. I liked them very much and enjoyed the sagacious words of the ambassador, and we briefed them about the situation. There we also met Lida Nozadze, Mikho's wife. She was Victor Nozadze's sister-in-law and the cousin of his brother Gogi's wife, Ivlita.

For us, the high point of Christmas was being with the Mamulashvili family.

We all gathered around the Christmas tree with Elena disguised as "Père Noël" distributing the presents. These were tranquil and happy moments and it was difficult to believe that the destructive war was not that far from us. At the Mamulashvilis', I also met their family friend, a very interesting gentleman, Noe Tsintsadze. He was a mathematician and physicist and moreover had excellent broad-based knowledge of the world around us. He was considered to be one of the best educated Georgian social democrats and had been a member of the Sovereign Georgian Government as an associate of the Minister of Education (second in command). During 1922, he was among those who were exiled by the Bolshevik government. At first he lived in Germany and then in France. During his youth he had attended the theologian seminary and then turned socialist (as have some other socialists, notably N. Jordania). Being an intellectual and cosmopolitan, he firmly stood on his principles and therefore connected well with the circle of the "Second International." Among them were a number of Russian and Jewish Socialists who respected and appreciated Noe Tsintsadze.[238] I personally liked him very much and did not miss meeting him during my trips to Paris—usually at the Mamulashvilis' family home. I enjoyed exchanging views with him and although we did not always agree, I greatly profited from such discussions.[239]

The day before our departure, Misha Kedia arrived in Paris from Berlin. Mikho and I had a long meeting at his home and we informed him about our experience in France. Most of our time after that was devoted to the organizational matters of the Liaison Staff. Kedia also told us about his views and Gogi Magalow's

---

238- *Iveria* no. 20,1978, Paris, editor in chief, Michel Kavtaradze.

239- After World War II and the demise of the senior members of Jordania's government in exile, N. Tsintsadze was the only representative member left. He felt a great deal of responsibility and in spite of his being an octogenarian and in poor health, because of his love for his country and for justice, he continued to serve the common cause with his last energy. Two remarkable accomplishments to be mentioned here were his momentous contribution to the organization of the Georgian Section of Radio Liberty. The second, just as important, was through negotiations with Harvard's Professor Richard Pipes and with his help, transferring the Archives of the Government of the Sovereign Georgian Republic to the Harvard University Library. Here they were microfilmed, arranged in an orderly fashion and saved from ultimate disintegration due to the precarious state of the original papers. Thus they were saved for history and scholars. Professor Giorgi Nakashidze was in charge of the above procedure and he carried out this Herculean job with assistance from American specialists. Noe Tsintsadze was greatly assisted in such undertakings by an old wartime friend of mine, Victor Homeriki, who after the minister's demise (at the age of ninety, during the fall of 1978), kept these activities alive.

I had the pleasure of visiting Minister N. Tsintsadze several months before his death in a hospital in Paris. He was incredibly alert, brave and in good spirits. After I left, Victor Homeriki remained with him for a while. Victor reported to me how happy Noe was with our visit but expressed his concern about me. He asked Victor, "Do you think I wore Givi out with my lengthy discussions today?" He wondered about this—not a bad attitude for a ninety-year-old gentleman who was also fighting a treacherous disease. I had the honor of being appointed by him as one of many members of the Board of Directors of the Georgian Government Archives.

(Magalashvili's) views about it. In order to better address the existing problems, we agreed to organize four departments within the Liaison Staff: 1. Civilian, 2. Political, 3. Management of Finances and Relief, 4. Military.

Dr. G. Magalow agreed to head the Civilian Department and he chose his personal associate to be Valodia (Vladimer) Tskomelidze.[240] The Political Department was headed by Misha Kedia and his associate was Alexandre (Sasha) Tsomaia. Mikho (Mikhail) Alshibaja was in charge of the Management of Finances and Relief Organization and the author of these memoirs accepted the charge of the Military Department and also to be the "Speaker for the Georgian legionnaires and other Georgians serving in the German Army." My associate and second in command in the Military Department was Mikho Alshibaja, thus he had to wear two hats.

The number of other officers and non-commissioned officers were appointed by us to the Military Department of the Liaison Staff; for instance, Captain Dimitri Shalikashvili and Major Alexandre Bokeria as consultants for purely military matters. Lieutenants Jora Indjia and Mikheil Kavtaradze were to observe and report the situation on an ongoing basis in the non-combat working units and the field battalions respectively.[241] The non-commissioned officers were Aliosha Abashidze, Konstantin (Kako) Alshibaja, Shota Margwelashvili and Irakli Macharashvili for day-to-day special assignments. We also employed a few soldiers for a variety of duties such as guards, accounting, janitorial and dispatch.

On the day Mikho and I were leaving Paris, we had many visitors. Thina Dadiani-Gomarthely, wife of Mikheil Dadiani, knew that I would see her husband soon and had much to tell me. He was commander of the cavalry squadron in "Bergmann." Some of them came to the train station to say goodbye, among them Mikho's sister, Kethi Alshibaja; Misha Kedia; his business associate in Paris, Kako Schavgulidze; Alexandre Asatiani; Themo Taktakishvili and Tengiz Dadeshkeliani.

We arrived by train in Berlin the following noon, on December 28th. The sight of the city was depressing with many parts laying in shambles due to frequent air raids. There were significant human losses. The Liaison Staff office and its workers,

---

240- The Germans (without whose approval the Liaison Staff could not have been established) chose to refer to the Civilian Department also as a Propaganda Department. We did not like such a name and felt the best "propaganda" was good treatment of the people and to be honest with them and explain about our goals and thinking. The name "Propaganda" already caused disbelief among the majority of Georgians because of their experience with the Communists as well as the Nazi propaganda based on deceit.

241- Captain Mikheil Dadiani from "Bergmann" was also assigned to the Military Department of the Liaison Staff during July or August 1944 until March of 1945, at which time he took over the command of the Georgian Battalion II/198 in Italy. During the summer of 1944, Lieutenant Shalva Okropiridze from "Bergmann" was appointed in the Military Department of the Liaison Staff as an adjutant to me. I also requested from the General of the Eastern Troops that Lieutenant Walter von Kutzschenbach from "Bergmann" be transferred to my department and this was granted. I thought he would make a good liaison officer to the German military organizations and I knew him well.

however, had not been hurt so far and therefore "business" was conducted as usual. I had to remain in the Berlin office for several days since certain matters required urgent attention. I also visited daily as many Berlin Georgians as possible in order to inquire about their well-being. First of all, Mikho and I spent one evening with the delightful Nino Kazbek-Dadiani. We invited her and one of her lady-friends to the restaurant "Mazurka" and to cheer them up even more, we went to a movie. This was interrupted by the air raid alarm; the movie was stopped so the four of us walked in the direction of her home. Finally we reached the subway train and accompanied them by subway to her home. We were impressed by the lack of anxiety of our lady companions and the majority of the Berlin Georgians who were exposed to the air raids day and night. This indeed applied to the "real" Berliners who appeared to be a "special breed" of people which probably led to the conclusion of President Kennedy's celebrated address, "Ich bin auch ein Berliner."

I was happy to see Badu Tsulukidze, a lady M.D. who worked in Berlin's Charita Hospital. She was very busy and doing well.[242] I visited my friend, Gigo Jordania, former "Bergmann" soldier now in Berlin. He apparently became a close friend of Liza Margwelashvili, the daughter of Tite Margwelashvili, the President of the Georgian Colony in Berlin.[243] During the evening I visited Jora Indjia who, off and on, had a flare-up of his duodenal ulcer. He was following a diet and taking some medication but I wondered about the adverse effect of the air raids on his ulcer and thought maybe he should move to France. His response was that they did not bother his ulcer at all. As soon as he said it, the air defense alarm went on and we could not help but laugh because of such incredible timing. We decided not to go to the shelter right away, being sure that our house would not be hit. When the alarm was over, Jora said, "You are the doctor, check me and see for yourself; you will agree that my stomach is painless and the alarm did not even increase my pulse rate." He almost convinced me; in any case, he remained on his job in Berlin.

242- As mentioned in the chapter "A German P.O.W. Outside the Prison Camp," Dr. Tsulukidze's associate—a German M.D.—visited the P.O.W. hospital in Ukraine during the summer of 1941. When he learned that I was a German-speaking Georgian doctor, he spoke to me and informed Dr. Tsulukidze about me. She responded and asked the German M.D. to do all he could to assist me. Very likely he spoke on my behalf to the German commandant which at least contributed to the permission I obtained to see Kedia in Berlin.

243- "Liziko" was a vivacious, cheerful, charming person who loved to dance. I wished that she and Gigo would decide to marry. During this time, I also visited Grisha and Margarita Lordkipanidze and their "children," Nanuly, who was married to Niko Nakashidze, and Kichia, a handsome young man. We were able to assist Kichia by coordinating his employment and study. On New Year's Day of 1944, I was invited for lunch by the Tsitsishvili family in Berlin. I had met them through Lulu Kereselidze who had a position in the Georgian Liaison Staff. I enjoyed being with them. I also checked on Mrs. Gertrude Malania, a German lady whose husband, Kuchia Malania, had passed away recently. She never lost interest in the Georgian cause and followed in her husband's footsteps. I found her in good health and spirit.

* * *

The next afternoon, I boarded a train to Lötzen and arrived there at noon, January 4, 1944. A few hours later, I had a meeting with General Hellmich and his chief of Staff, Lieutenant Colonel of the General Staff, H. D. Herre and their aide, an intelligence officer, Lieutenant Michel. The purpose of the meeting was mutual briefing of the current condition of the Georgian military units and how to eliminate possible shortcomings. I previously had such discussions on the phone with Lieutenant Colonel Herre about "Bergmann" first and then about the field battalions which Mikho and I had visited in France and Holland recently.

I was especially interested in the remaining Georgian field battalions on the Eastern Front, most of which were with the Army Group A (southern part of the Eastern Front). I had never seen them and wanted some information. Here, General Köstring and his adjutant Herwarth were especially helpful to me since they were traveling and visiting the units and had firsthand knowledge of them. General Hellmich and Lieutenant Colonel Herre usually remained in the Army headquarters probably according to an informal agreement between Generals Köstring and Hellmich.

The battalions in question were especially 796, I/9 and II/4. Battalion 796 was put together by the Commando of the Eastern Legions in the so-called "General Government" of Poland under identical circumstances as the Georgian Battalion 795.[244] Consequently, it was beleaguered by problems even worse than 795. Briefly stated, 796 had been inadequately "trained" for only an incredibly short time of just three weeks. An even worse shortcoming was that the principle of accepting the soldiers only on a volunteer basis had not been sufficiently followed. Then hastily, beginning in November 1942, Battalion 796 was sent to the front and attached to the 1st Mountain Division—part of the 17th Army. This division was bogged down in a bitter fight against the numerically superior and well supplied Soviet troops in the area not far from Tuapse.[245] The 17th Army High Command had ordered 796 to keep out of battle because of poor training until this had been corrected in the army rear region.

Undoubtedly the division's commandant was experiencing an acute manpower shortage, therefore the higher order was disregarded and 796 was sent into combat. In spite of all said, the Georgian legionnaires of 796 did better than

---

244- In the chapter "In the Bergmann Unit and Caucasus," I have referred to some problems surrounding organization of the Battalion 795.

245- Located in Northwest Caucasus near the Black Sea, with forest-covered hills and also known for its high level of precipitation.

expected—they fought well but sustained heavy casualties. After over a month of heavy Soviet attacks and very bad weather, the supply lines to the division were cut off. Many soldiers were sick with diarrhea, without food or dry clothing and a number of them died of exhaustion in the trenches or in the gathering place for ill soldiers. Not only the poorly trained, inexperienced and exhausted legionnaires but even veteran soldiers could break down mentally as well as physically given such circumstances. Moreover, some of them still had residual weakness from being the inmates of P.O.W. camps during the murderous winter of 1941–42. There was no relief in sight, and communication with the Germans in the unit was difficult at best, mostly because of the language barrier. Consequently during December of 1942, seventy to eighty legionnaires, among them a few officers, defected to the Soviets; they had succumbed to Soviet propaganda. But the overwhelming loyal majority of the legionnaires remained with the 1st Division. Nevertheless, the outraged commanding general chose to disregard this fact and instead of rewarding the remaining good soldiers, he ordered them disarmed and transferred to the rear for building roads and other similar purposes. A great deal of psychological damage had been done and Herwarth explained to me that the dissolution of 796 as a field battalion was finally approved by Army Group A and 796 became a working unit. Then it was transferred to Crimea to repair roads and fortifications, etc.

The Battalions I/9 and II/4 were organized not in Poland but in Myrhorod Ukraine by the 162 Infantry Division. Major General, Professor Doctor Ritter von Niedermayer was in charge of the division as well as of putting together a number of the Eastern Volunteer Units.[246] Battalion I/9 arrived at the front of Taman Peninsula in Kuban during December 1943 and was attached to the German 9th Infantry Division. Herwarth said that the battalion had no winter clothing, was not adequately armed and it did not possess the necessary ancillary technology for satisfactory function as a unit. Apparently its founding "mother," the 162 Infantry Division in Myrhorod was not able to provide such essentials. Therefore, the Georgian Legions Battalion I/9 had to be divided and the individual companies attached to the larger German units in the Kuban-Taman area. Some companies carried out combat duty, others had to work on improvement of the roads and bridges and keeping the supply lines intact. During the middle of March, the major part of Battalion I/9 was evacuated to Crimea by airplanes. Two companies remained with the 9th Division on the Kuban bridgehead until the end of April, at which time they were also airlifted to Crimea. There Battalion I/9 was made a part

---

246- Joachim Hoffmann, *Die Ostlegionen 1941–1943*, pp. 60, 66–70; and see the chapter "In the Bergmann Unit and Caucasus" of this memoir.

of the coastal defense line in Feodosia.[247] Köstring and Herwarth were pleased by the battalion's performance.

One could say that the history of the Battalion II/4 was similar to the one of Battalion I/9, especially as far as its organization and front-line activity was concerned. The difference was that II/4 could not join the German Mountain Division 4 as originally planned, since the Division had already been pulled out of the Kuban. Therefore after various duties in Kuban, Battalion II/4 was also airlifted to Crimea and incorporated in the Feodosia coastal defense line, as recommended by General Köstring and Herwarth to the higher army staff.[248]

I stayed in Lötzen four days and on several occasions met the above-mentioned generals and the heads of all departments of the staff. In addition to regular business meetings, we met daily in the officers' "casino" for lunch and supper, where informal discussions continued in a very friendly and cordial atmosphere. Major Röpke, the head of the Operations Department; Captain Siegfried Ungermann, the Director of the Personnel Department and I had a long exchange of views about the practical measures necessary for gradual replacement of the German officers by the Georgian opposites. In this connection, another military school for preparation of Caucasian officers in Pozen (Poznań) was favorably mentioned. While bidding farewell to my hosts in Lötzen, the Chief of Staff, Lieutenant Colonel Herre told me, "Please get those Georgian units in order."

During the morning of January 8, 1944, I took the flight over Brest-Litovsk,

---

247- Feodosia is located southwest of the Kerch Strait and northeast of Sevastopol, two important areas strategically.

248- The names of some Georgian Legions battalions such as, for example I/9, II/4 or II/198 signified that the 1st Georgian Battalion would be attached to the 9th German Division, the 2nd Georgian Battalion to the 4th German Division and so on.

When my memoir was nearing completion, Dr. Joachim Hoffmann's scholarly book in German appeared, *Kaukasien (Caucasus) 1942/43* devoted to the "German Army and the Oriental Nations of the Soviet Union." In my view it is a great contribution to the history of W.W. II and there are no discrepancies of our views concerning this chapter of my memoir. However, and understandably so, there are certain areas where our interpretation of the events diverge. This applies especially to certain aspects of the Battalions 795 and 823 as well as the description of my occupation in "Bergmann." This has in no way affected my above-expressed positive opinion about this remarkable work. After all, my memoir, even if I wanted to, could not compete with the scientific work of a specialist in military history. But even a specialist may also at times have certain disadvantages when he has not personally been an eyewitness of the events that took place in the past.

He emphasizes in three places that I was an intelligence officer in "Bergmann." As a matter of fact, all officers in "Bergmann" were "intelligence officers" since the unit was organized by Admiral Canaris, the Head of Military Intelligence. I was told in "Bergmann" that I was a Georgian "Ordonanz" Officer or a "Liaison Officer." After "Bergmann" was transferred from the jurisdiction of the German High Military Command to the Army High Command, during the latter part of 1942, the affiliation with Military Intelligence came to an end.

He also lists among the "Bergmann" officers Lt. Mshvenieridze. There was no such lieutenant. I believe Dr. Hoffmann adopted this fictitious name from a Soviet propaganda book, *In the Name of Life*. The same Soviet book depicts me as a "Chief" of "Bergmann" Intelligence Service; I never had such a position.

Lemberg (Lviv) and Odessa to Mykolaiv,[249] where in the staff for the Eastern Volunteer Troops I was glad to see my friend, Lieutenant Dr. Wilhelm Reissmüller. He briefed me about the current status of the Georgian and other Caucasian units in Crimea and elsewhere in the area of the Army Group South, including the hospitals manned by doctors and nurses of "Eastern origin." For the moment, the military situation appeared rather stable and satisfactory. The next day Reissmüller introduced me to Major Kurth, who was headed for his office in the Crimean capital Simferopol, where he represented the staff of the General of the Eastern Volunteer Units. The Major suggested we travel together and I welcomed this, not only for the sake of pleasant companionship but also from the business point of view, since we would have to work together during my presence in Crimea.

Indeed we had more undisturbed time together in order to discuss things of mutual interest during this trip than anticipated, since our car broke down on the way from Mykolaiv to Odessa from where the flight would take us to Crimea. We had to stay overnight in Odessa and we caught another flight the next morning. The Major and I had a head start in learning some of each other's views. For instance, he thought that I had the intention of carrying out a propaganda mission among the legionnaires. He learned from me that I had very little if any intention of doing so. I had been given a task to be the official speaker for the legionnaires and at the same time the Head of the Military Department of the Georgian Liaison Staff. Therefore, my main quest clearly was to defend the legionnaires' rights. In so doing I could act in the advisory capacity only. Nevertheless, due to a very good relationship with the General of the Eastern Troops and based on past Caucasus field experience, mutual trust and respect. I felt my suggestions—if reasonable, would be supported by the General and his staff. I mentioned to Major Kurth that in my view the best "propaganda" for the legionnaires would be just and good treatment.

I shared with him my unpleasant experience with the Georgian Legions— Field Battalion 795 on the Caucasus front during the late summer of 1942, and compared it with entirely different conditions in "Bergmann." I did not have to tell the Major that given the German retreat from Caucasus the situation was even more sensitive now. The Major was a good listener. I also mentioned to him that I would stay in Crimea as long as needed and we promised each other close cooperation and help. After the three hour flight from Odessa, we landed at Karakiyat Airport of the Crimea, north of Simferopol, which we reached by car. The Major introduced me to the officers' quarters of the "soldiers' home" in Simferopol; a clean, comfortable room was assigned to me for the duration of my visit in Crimea. The Major's office

---

249- Mykolaiv is located in Ukraine, northwest of and not far from Crimea.

was within walking distance; I received a map from him with the disposition of Georgian units in Crimea and some useful tips. He said that he would inform them about my pending visit. (In addition, I had a letter of introduction, "TO WHOM IT MAY CONCERN," signed by General Hellmich from Army headquarters.) The Major also graciously loaned me his car for the trips from Simferopol to the various Georgian units. The Major and I dropped in to see Georgian Doctors Kervalidze and Bregvadze who were working in a local hospital and apparently doing well.

Early the following morning, I left for Sarabuz [Hvardiiske], where the 1st Company of the Georgian Infantry Battalion II/4 had its quarters. The battalion's German commander, Captain Bartscht was a friendly gentleman, proud of his legionnaires and introduced me to the Georgian "ordonanz officer" of the Staff Company Pochkhua. The three of us then visited the soldiers and non-commissioned officers of the 1st Company. I spoke to small groups as well as individuals, expressing my opinion about the current situation we were facing and addressed their questions. I stayed overnight with Pochkhua and we had a candid one-to-one talk which contributed a great deal to my knowledge of the battalion. Early the next morning, Captain Bartscht, Pochkhua and I left for Karangut, where the 2nd and 3rd Companies were located. The Georgian company chief of the 2nd Company was Giorgadze and of the 3rd Company was Losaberidze. They joined us while visiting the legionnaires. Again I spoke to them and their non-commissioned officers, listened to their questions and answered them. I stayed overnight and enjoyed their hospitality; this also contributed toward establishing mutual confidence between us. This I thought was especially important because of the less than satisfactory military situation for the German Army.

The following morning I traveled to Otarchik to become acquainted with the 4th Company and its wounded Chief Gugushvili. (If I remember correctly, he had sustained this injury while in Kuban and was recuperating.) At noon I visited the "Staff Company," then bid goodbye to the officers and legionnaires and left for Simferopol late afternoon. Battalion II/4 made a good impression on me; there existed a satisfactory relationship between the German personnel and the Georgians. In my opinion the reason was Captain Bartscht's good leadership. I noticed his broadmindedness, his grasp of reality, understanding and lack of prejudice toward his legionnaires who after all were not "perfect German soldiers." I expressed my appreciation for that and also brought to his attention a few relatively minor matters that needed to be worked out, especially the animosity between Pochkhua and the battalion's German accounting officer, Zahlmeister. I also recommended that some Georgian officers be sent to German military schools to increase their qualifications and gain even more respect from the legionnaires as well as the German officers. It was my wish that after my visit, the legionnaires of II/4 would have the impression that their interests were represented by their own countrymen in Berlin and that they would not be abandoned. This would be the message for all other Georgian units I was to visit in Crimea. Back in Simferopol, I discussed my impression concerning II/4 with Major Kurth and he seemed pleased.

I could hardly wait to see the Georgian battalion "Bergmann I" with so many of my friends there. The battalion was now located in Kurajevka and its cavalry squadron in Kart Kasak, both south of the Perekop Isthmus. Having sustained heavy combat losses of one hundred seventy men killed and wounded, the battalion with the cavalry squadron had been withdrawn to the secondary defense line to regroup and have some respite.

13
REPORT ON THE THREE "BERGMANN" BATTALIONS

After three and one-half hours of driving from Simferopol to "Bergmann I" field headquarters, I was greeted there by Captain (later Major) Edmund Brand, the battalion's commanding officer. There was much to talk about; for instance, he wanted to know when I had last seen Captain Professor Doctor Oberländer, who as already mentioned had been dismissed from "Bergmann" and the Army because of his open criticism of Hitler's "East Policy." Brand considered the Professor a man with clear political vision and great courage. "It was difficult to keep the 'Bergmann' soldiers' spirits up after their very popular commander Oberländer was removed," said Brand. And what were my impressions of France and the Georgian legionnaires there? And of the Dresden Military School? Upon their return from Dresden, Lieutenants Okropiridze and Alimbarashvili had a glowing report, said Brand. What about my activities in the Liaison Staff, etc.?

In turn, I wanted to know from Brand and other friends what took place in "Bergmann" since I left Crimea in the summer of 1943. Brand and I visited the companies together. I had conversations with many friends there and also read *The History of "Bergmann" in Combat*. This is what I learned: During my absence the "Bergmann Regiment" was finally separated into three "independent" battalions. First Lieutenant Brand was made commander of the "Georgian Bergmann I" battalion. It was transferred from the beautiful upper Belbek Valley to the northwest part of the peninsula and charged with defense of the coastal line from Ak Mechet as far as Evpatoria. There were no military activities there as yet, but the possibility of Soviet landing attempts could not have been ruled out. The Georgian Cavalry Squadron remained attached to "Bergmann I." During September 1943, "Bergmann I" was transferred again; this time southeast of Sevastopol in the area of Baydary. It was considered a reserve unit now, to be called on as needed for a combat engagement. The battalion was utilizing "free time" for training maneuvers and scouting missions in the nearby Crimean Mountains.

During the fall, the remaining German troops from the Kuban Bridgehead were evacuated to Crimea. The High Command of the Army Group South was considering further distribution of troops now present in Crimea. The main reason being how they would best meet the challenge if the Soviet troops would quickly advance north of Crimea, aiming at isolating the German troops from the mainland. With this in mind, many military units were shifted from the south to north Crimea. The advanced commandos of such troops were sent ahead in order to prepare future quarters and defense positions. "Bergmann" was no exception, and its representatives along with officers of the 153rd Infantry Division (to which "Bergmann" had been attached) set out to explore the area between Perekop and Kherson during the end of October. It was planned to transfer all three "Bergmann" battalions to an area north of Dnipro.[250] During the third week of October, "Bergmann I" left Baydary. First of all they crossed the mountains on foot to the Belbek Valley in order to bid farewell to the Tatar villagers in the spirit of mutual affection—it was a deeply moving event.

During the following days the battalion continued on foot, via Bakhchysarai to the Simferopol area, where by coincidence it met the "Bergmann II" and "Bergmann III" battalions. From here they continued marching over Sarabuz to Kijak-Strukova, direction north. The sudden onset of cold weather was most unwelcome. By the end of October (1943), "Bergmann I" reached Bezchastnoe, south of Sivash—the "Putrid Sea," which separates the Crimean Peninsula from the land in the north. Sivash has shallow water, therefore an army can cross it on foot which had been readily demonstrated during the Russian Civil War.[251]

In Bezchastnoe, "Bergmann I" learned that the Soviet tanks and infantry units had occupied all northern approaches of Crimea and were now attacking further south over three areas, the towns of Taganash, Perekop and Sivash, in order to penetrate Crimea. On the evening of November 1st, "Bergmann II" was ordered to engage the Soviet forces in the Sivash area and to counterattack them. After heavy and stubborn combat in the lagoons of Urshin, the cavalry squadron and the 3rd Company stormed and took the town Urshin but could not completely eliminate the enemy bridgehead. The Red Army was steadily throwing more and more infantry and heavy weapons, including artillery, in combat. On November 6th and 7th, an especially heavy battle took place with a steadily increasing number of wounded. During the night of November 7th and the following day, after a massive attack by overwhelming numbers, the Soviets succeeded with the invasion of Urshin and the

---

250- *Bergmann Memoirs*, edited by Heinz Beher.
251- "Sarabuz" is the Crimean Tartar name for present day Hvardiiske. The location and present names of "Kijak-Strukova," "Bezchastnoe," "Taganash" and "Urshin" could not be ascertained prior to publication. —Ed.

retreating Georgian 3rd and 4th Companies were temporarily separated from the rest and partially surrounded by the enemy. In order to strengthen the defense line, the Romanian regiment and the German Battalion 370 were thrown into the Urshin combat which stabilized the situation. In spite of the heavy losses, the morale and the fighting spirit of "Bergmann I" remained superb.

Meanwhile the "Bergmann III" Battalion (North Caucasian) fought with great valor for the defense of the Perekop area. On November 17, 1943, the armed forces' broadcast made it known that two Caucasian volunteer battalions especially distinguished themselves in the tough combats for the northern approaches of Crimea. Field Marshal von Kleist also confirmed his appreciation in a special letter to the commanding officer of "Bergmann I," Lieutenant Brand.[252] This was, so far, the combat history of "Bergmann I" in Crimea, when I visited them in Kurajevka and Kart Kasak, south of the Perekop Isthmus during January 1944.

As Captain Brand and I continued our tour of the companies it was a thrill for me to see old friends again, among them Victor Homeriki, Misha Dadiani, Goglik Vachnadze, Aliosha Abashidze, Irakli Alimbarashvili, Shalva Okropiridze and others. Since they all wanted me to be the guest of their company, we made a rotating schedule to proceed in an orderly fashion.

Things went smoothly until I visited the cavalry squadron. The horses there were getting the usual alloted portions of forage, but now because of the positional war they received less than their usual daily exercise so they were "full of oats." In order to please me, Aliosha Abashidze dispatched the most spirited and beautiful horse he could think of for me to ride to the squadron fortifications. This horse had reared, hit and dislocated one of the caretaker's shoulders not long ago when he tried to saddle him. The squadron's young doctor was not able to reduce the shoulder, and he was hoping that perhaps I could, but I had to get there first. When two different caretakers, riding two different horses, led "my" horse by a long bridle to me, one caretaker said, "Sir, be careful, this horse is rather difficult today." Then both of them—one from each side, steadied the horse for me. I barely got my foot in the stirrup and mounted the horse when he took off in a gallop without the slightest sign on his part of obeying the bridle or any other signals to stop. With my right foot still out of the stirrup, I decided to give up the efforts of controlling him and let him run until he had enough. I temporarily lost sight of both caretakers and did not know of either the Soviet positions or possible mine fields. I was hoping that, since horses most often run back to their stables, this horse would do the same. This involuntary race continued for a considerable time. The horse now was steaming

---

252- *Bergmann Memoirs*, edited by Heinz Beher.

wet when I finally managed to slow him down and turn around. I then challenged him to a gallop and joined the two worried caretakers, who explained that they had not wanted to further excite the horse by chasing after me. As it turned out, my mount did not quite follow the correct course to his quarters, which were located further west.

I was able to reduce the dislocated shoulder of the soldier-caretaker in his bunker with considerable difficulty after which we celebrated our reunion with an excellent brandy and the "Perekop rabbit ragout." Lieutenant Goglik Vachnadze obviously remembered his promise to host such a dinner for me in Crimea when we bade each other farewell a few weeks ago at the railroad station in Paris.

The alarm was sounded twice during the night while I stayed with the cavalry squadron. This meant another Soviet attack in our direction. We were ready, but both advances of the Red troops were stopped on the first defense line before they reached us. I remained in "Bergmann I" eight to nine days and spent at least one day and night with each company. I was impressed by the positive attitude of the soldiers in spite of the heavy combat losses and the unenviable general situation of being cut off from the mainland. I wrote my preliminary report about my observations to the Georgian Liaison Staff and also to Generals Hellmich and Köstring; additional reports were to follow after I had visited other units. I sent almost identical letters to Lieutenant Colonel Hessel and Dr. Reissmüller—but already in this first report the bottom line was the urgency of evacuation of our units from Crimea.

I left "Bergmann I" on January 27, 1944, in order to see the other Georgian battalions in Crimea; I told my "Bergmann" friends that I would return as soon as possible. Back in Simferopol, I briefed Major Kurth about "Bergmann." He showed a great deal of interest in the details and suggested that together we see some other units in the near future, to which I agreed. While waiting for Major Kurth, I met a "Bergmann" emigre, Vaso Shalamberidze, in Simferopol. He was one of the "Bergmann" emigre soldiers who had been assigned to P.O.W. camps while in the Caucasus to observe and report about conditions there.[253] After his retreat from the Caucasus, Shalamberidze continued visiting P.O.W. camps in Crimea to ensure their decent treatment. The following morning Vaso and I visited a P.O.W. camp near Simferopol where living conditions and general treatment of the P.O.W.s appeared satisfactory. We met two Georgian doctors in the camp, Kraveishvili and Chikhladze. The former was working as a doctor and as a result of our recommendation to the camp commandant, Dr. Chikhladze was also allowed to exercise his profession.

253- See the chapter "Patriots and Defectors."

From Simferopol Vaso and I traveled to Sevastopol, where we also saw the P.O.W. camps. Dr. Grisha Jankhoteli had been transferred to this area during the interim time.[254] Now as before he enjoyed a great deal of respect from the German personnel as well as from the Georgians. Other Georgians around and close to him were Tabtadze, Darbalseli and Simonishvili. I was glad to see them doing so well under the circumstances.

My next "field outing" from Simferopol was undertaken with Major Kurth. We traveled through Staryi Krym and Islâm-Terek [Kirovske] to Chancha.[255] There we were received by Captain Strack, commander of the Georgian Infantry Battalion I/9 at his quarters. We stayed overnight, and there I had a joyous reunion with my close friend, Dr. Ramaz Gvetadze from the Tbilisi Medical School. Ramaz was working as a physician for the battalion, whose companies were spread over the surrounding area. I had received a letter from Ramaz while in Dresden during the fall of 1943, informing me of his whereabouts. In answering his letter, I promised that I would see him in Crimea. Ramaz introduced to me the battalion's ordnance officer, Kavjaradze, whose preliminary briefing about I/9 was very interesting to me. The next morning, with Captain Strack, we paid a visit to Major Dr. Eismann, the commanding officer of the infantry battalion 796, in the village Barak. He suggested that we all see the 4th Company in its nearby quarters. In the 4th Company we became acquainted with First Lieutenant Wagner, who was Eismann's associate and second in command.[256] During (at that time, Captain) Dr. Eismann's sick leave, Lieutenant Wagner remained with the troubled Battalion 796, on the northwest Caucasus front. He greatly contributed to the investigation and the establishment of the true and honest story about Battalion 796. I had a brief initial discussion with Major Doctor Eismann, Lieutenant Wagner and Captain Strack about the past, present and possible future. It was resolved to meet again after completion of my tour. Then I spoke to the nearby lodged 4th Company of the 796 Battalion and the 5th Company of I/9 Battalion. Such a formal address was always followed by man-to-man informal conversations. I then continued to see other companies of Battalions 796 and I/9. The former was the "working and building" unit with headquarters in Islâm-Terek while the latter was a regular field battalion with headquarters in Parpach. In spite of the sudden onset of poor weather that rendered the motor vehicle useless, I decided to continue the tour on a horse-drawn carriage. This gave my friend, Dr. Ramaz Gvetadze and I an opportunity to spend some time together and talk endlessly.

254- See the chapter "In Crimea."

255- The location of "Chancha" could not be confirmed. —Ed.

256- Dr. Joachim Hoffmann, *Kaukasien 1942–43*, pp. 291–304 for details; and see remarks about 796's Front deployment etc. in the previous chapter.

In addition to Kavjaradze, my friend Ramaz introduced to me two other young Georgian officers, Rukhadze and Turdshaladze; all three were very interested in enrolling in the German military school. I told them I would see what I could do about it but was unable to promise for sure. Later while we were passing through the town of Semikolodez, we learned that a working Battalion 245 had its headquarters nearby. I introduced myself to a major and his adjutant (whose names I can not find in my "mini diary"). There were many Georgians in 245, but there were also many soldiers of other nationalities. The soldiers appeared tired and rather dissatisfied but there were no definite grievances; I decided to find out more about this unit later on.

My friend, Doctor Ramaz had a wife and baby in Tbilisi. His wife was the daughter of a well-known dramaturge, Sandro Shanshiashvili. Ramaz's father, Rajden was a writer in his own right and a gentleman of considerable influence among V.I.P.s. We both knew for sure that after the end of the war, Ramaz had to return home, but how? Would his father's connections help? Ramaz was a fellow who I knew was not capable of doing anything indecent or harming others. He had only taken care of people who were ill while in the Red Army as well as while he was in the Georgian Legion. But neither Ramaz nor I could believe that Stalin and his entourage would even consider the reasoning that the Legion was sponsored not by the Nazis but persons in the German Army like Stauffenberg, who disliked Hitler and his henchmen and their practices. So Ramaz and others like him had to get out of Crimea and as far west as necessary in order not to fall into Soviet hands. After the end of the war, who knows? Perhaps some way would be found for him to be united with his family instead of being shot or sentenced to the gulags.

Ramaz and I remembered our mutual friends Vadim Chkhenkeli, Akaki Topuria and his wife Hachu, Vakhtang Samadashvili and others. With great sadness, I shared with Ramaz the unconfirmed information about Vadim, who had been mobilized in the Soviet Army after graduation from medical school. He was sent to the Moldavian Republic as a military doctor. Soon after the outbreak of the war, Vadim was critically wounded. Realizing the hopelessness of his situation, Vadim put an end to his suffering by his own bullet.

After completion of the tour, I had a meeting with the German commanding officers of the Georgian battalions—Eismann, Bartscht and Strack. They wanted my frank views and suggestions concerning their units. First of all, I complimented them on good leadership during such a challenging and unusual undertaking, which was further complicated by an unfavorable military situation and therefore, to say the least, an uncertain future for the legionnaires. Some reported defections to the partisans reflected just that, with the defectors considering this to be the only way of returning home. In my view (shared by the officers of "Bergmann"), there were other potentiating factors for defection of the legionnaires, such as incredible hardships they endured in the P.O.W. camps, from where they were later recruited. There was another factor which might be within our reach to change; I refer to the German personnel in the Georgian battalions, especially non-commissioned officers and the rank below them. I suspected that the German divisions, while furnishing such people for us, used this opportunity to get rid of the undesirable Germans in their units. Some of them appeared to have personality defects, others were hopelessly arrogant and believed in propaganda according to which the Eastern people, including legionnaires, are subhumans and the "Teutonic" people (including themselves) were "super humans." I then told the German commanding officers that I had a credible list of incidents of rude and at times, unlawful discrimination against the Georgian legionnaires, officers, non-commissioned officers and soldiers by German personnel. It included such cases as:

1. Undermining the authority of Georgian officers and non-commissioned officers among their subordinate soldiers.
2. Verbal and physical abuse of the legionnaires.
3. Taking from the legionnaires (without their consent) belongings such as bicycles and back packs.
4. Unequal distribution of certain foodstuffs, clothes, and lodging— favoring German personnel.

I suggested to the German commanding officers that I would gladly share my list with them should they so desire. They ought to investigate the situation following the list and if the grievances were true, appropriate measures would be needed. I also told them that we only had a few such men among the German personnel in "Bergmann" during its formative time. Professor Doctor Oberländer transferred them expeditiously somewhere else; otherwise there would not be a "Bergmann" as we know it today. I further told the German officers that until October 1943, the Georgian legionnaires did not even have political representation such as the national committee in Berlin with their speaker in it. It would have been much better for the legionnaires' morale if formation of such a committee had proceeded or at least coincided with the creation of the legion. Finally the Georgian Liaison Staff was established in October 1943, and is a substitute for such a committee and is the only recognized Georgian representation in Germany and its occupied territories. I informed the officers that I had been given the unenviable task of being the speaker for the legionnaires in this organization and the head of the military department; therefore, I maintained a close liaison with the general for the Eastern Volunteer

Troops in the Army headquarters. The general was working toward upgrading the status of legionnaires to equal German soldiers. We believed it would be made known in an Army ordinance.

In my address and conversation with the legionnaires, I dwelt on this fact; since it was important for the legionnaires to know not only about their duties but also about their rights. I also mentioned to the German officers that our general and his staff were resolved to gradually replace the German personnel by the indigenous personnel after training them. There will still be a place for dedicated and well-qualified German officers and non-commissioned officers, mostly in an advisory capacity in the Georgian units. For example, I had already been approached by First Lieutenant Kremser, who had been introduced to me by Major Kurth in Simferopol, to speak with General Köstring on his behalf and recommend his appointment to a Georgian battalion. (Kremser, who had served time in a unit with Georgians, apparently lost his position when his unit was fused with another.) Major Dr. Eismann, Captains Bartscht and Strack considered our meeting useful and informative. They thanked me for frank discussions and we decided to meet again.

Back in Simferopol, Major Kurth conveyed a message from General Köstring and from Kedia, both asking that I return to Berlin as soon as possible after my two and one-half months' absence from the Liaison Staff office there. The Major also had another piece of information for me. A former Georgian legionnaire who had defected to the partisans some time ago was now captured by an army patrol near Staryi Krym. Major Kurth thought I might be interested in seeing him and if so, the Major could make such a meeting possible. I was of course interested, so Major Kurth and I traveled to Staryi Krym. The "partisan's" name was Lashkhia; he was approximately a twenty-year-old boy with soft, brown eyes. Outwardly he did not appear frightened but rather depressed and with an air of one who has given up. I shook his hand, asked him to sit down and tell us all about himself, and I would translate it for the Major. The story of how he became first a legionnaire and then a partisan served as an example on the subject of defections which I had discussed a couple of days before with the German officers Eismann, Bartscht, Strack, Wagner and with Major Kurth even before that. Now Lashkhia confirmed that our arguments were on the right track. The prisoner appeared sincere and spontaneous and made a good impression on both Kurth and me.

I told the Major that I decided to stay in Crimea, at least another two to three weeks (contrary to General Köstring's communication) rather than be in Berlin and worry about our people in Crimea. I also said that the attitude toward the legionnaires defecting to the partisans should be radically changed. First of all, we should try to prevent it by changing their conditions; secondly, for those who defected, we should declare an amnesty and make it known to the poor, hungry, frozen and scared devils in the forests by special leaflets.

I wrote a letter of explanation to General Köstring, Alshibaja and M. Kedia about my remaining longer in Crimea. The letter, in fact, was a report about the situation in our units, and it was dispatched by Major Kurth. This was the fourth report from Crimea that I had written, and among other recommendations it again emphasized the importance of the transfer of our units from Crimea to the west as soon as possible. In this last letter, the problem of defection was also referred to and included our suggestions of possible "prevention and treatment." I had two requests of Major Kurth: First, to use his influence and have the officers in charge release Lashkhia in my custody and I, personally would vouch for his future conduct. Lashkhia would remain with me and accompany me during the regular tour of the Georgian units. He would tell the legionnaires his story, including why he joined partisans and how his life was with them; I expected considerable psychological impact from this. Second, for Major Kurth to call a meeting in his office of the Georgian ordnance officers and representatives of all Georgian units in Crimea including "Bergmann I" to attend. I gave the list of such people to the Major. There would be only one agenda: The future of the Georgian legionnaires who defected to partisans in Crimea—we should not forsake them.

During preliminary discussions of this problem with Victor Homeriki, Misha Dadiani and other leading "Bergmann I" Georgians, it was our opinion that former legionnaires now with partisans were in grave danger. First of all, they could be thrown into combat with the retreating regular German or Romanian troops and possibly be killed. Should they survive such combats and report back to the Soviet superiors, it was likely that they would be ruthlessly used for special dangerous assignments (for instance, to be parachuted to the rear of the German front). If they lived through all of this and the war ended with Russian victory, then there would be danger that instead of going back home, they would end up in the Siberian gulags or be shot. The reason for such harsh treatment has already been discussed in preceding chapters and shall only briefly be mentioned here. It started with the declaration by the Kremlin hierarchy after the outbreak of W.W. II that the Red Army soldiers taken prisoners by Germans were traitors. Such "crime" had been compounded by joining the legions; which was dedicated to the overthrow of Kremlin tyranny.[257] Defecting to the partisans later on was unlikely to rehabilitate the legionnaires in the eyes of Stalin and his henchmen. On the other hand, we felt that if a credible amnesty could be arranged for the defected legionnaires and it could made known by

---

257- There were also some P.O.W.s who actually had joined the Legion feeling that since they had already been declared traitors by the Kremlin government, they may as well overthrow it in order to return home safely.

the German military authorities, perhaps they could be convinced to return to us. The defecting legionnaires should be given a choice of joining the working and building units or being admitted to the P.O.W. camps as "regular" P.O.W.s. In any case, they should all then be evacuated from Crimea to the west and thus improve their chance of survival. The Major succeeded in releasing Lashkhia and also arranged a time table for the above-mentioned meeting in Simferopol of the representatives of the Georgian units in Crimea.

Lashkhia and I soon started to travel together on horseback, car or train almost daily and visited all Georgian military units in Crimea. After introducing him as a "Soviet partisan until very recently," Lashkhia would tell his story to the captive audience of the legionnaires. "Repetition makes perfect"—soon he became an eloquent speaker. Major Kurth was concerned at first with such an undertaking, especially for my safety while traveling alone with a "partisan." After a while, however, we were both thrilled by all of this and more particularly with the obvious impact Lashkhia's presentation had on the legionnaires. Now some of them realized more clearly that joining the partisans probably was not the best solution to their problems.

As a young Soviet soldier and then a German P.O.W., Lashkhia probably did not have clear political views. At first he thought that the Germans would win the war, besides they had the name of being a cultured and civilized people. He thought that getting out of the P.O.W. camp and joining the Georgian Legion would improve his living conditions and also help him return home with dignity after the German victory. But at a certain point, especially after the retreat from Caucasus, it appeared that the Germans would lose the war and the prospect of getting back home became dim. Moreover it was difficult for him to adjust to the conditions in his unit. He could not communicate with the German personnel—the non-commissioned officers were rude, calling him names and penalizing him for no apparent reason. His unhappiness grew, and after someone told him about the "glorious deeds and the life of the Soviet partisans," he rather impulsively defected to them. But life with the partisans, as it turned out, was worse in every respect. Food and lodging were miserable, conditions very dangerous, requiring them to be on alert at all times, and their superiors viewed all of them with suspicion. After a while, Lashkhia had second thoughts about his defection from the Legion. When the German military patrol captured him, he thought that all was over and that he would be executed. He could not believe that the Major and I talked to him in such a friendly manner nor the good treatment that followed afterwards—especially the trust we had in him. Lashkhia had many opportunities to escape while he traveled with me, especially during the night; he just did not want to.

Meetings concerning the defected legionnaires commenced in Major Kurth's office. They were attended by representatives of the Georgian units. We had to meet in small groups since it was not feasible to get them all together at one meeting. Victor Homeriki (from "Bergmann") was able to remain with me in Simferopol for several days. All participants agreed on a declaration of amnesty for the defectors, and the proposed text of leaflets was also approved. It was deemed more practical that the leaflets be distributed in the communities not far from the known partisan camps rather than dropped from the air. Major Kurth was sure that the higher military headquarters would approve our proposal. It was also decided that Major Kurth and Homeriki, with the cooperation of other participants, would follow through with a practical application of it in my absence. To my great regret, my departure time could not be put off any longer. I visited all units one more time starting with "Bergmann." On my recommendation, Lashkhia was accepted as a regular legionnaire in one of the battalions. As I said goodbye to Lashkhia, I noticed he was holding back tears. I considered it a privilege to have met this honest and courageous, young man—there are many such men out there, I thought.

Major Kurth and I spent almost an entire day together before my departure, summarizing our work together and trying to visualize the future of our legionnaires. We both had assurance from the General of the Eastern Troops, from the Army headquarters, that our units would be evacuated from Crimea in a timely manner depending on the military situation. Finally we bade each other farewell; I flew the next morning, March 24th, from Simferopol to Tiraspol, via Odessa. In the early afternoon, I shook hands with my friend, Lieutenant Wm. Reissmüller; I had been corresponding with him from Crimea, but we still had much to talk about.

The next morning Lieutenant Reissmüller and I traveled by car to Odessa, where we visited two hospitals, 742-S and 741-S. Both were for ill and injured legionnaires. The physicians, their assistants, the nurses and the orderlies had been recruited from Eastern volunteers. Lieutenant Reissmüller was very popular among all of them, being a gentleman of good manners, soft voice and having a great deal of compassion for the "Easterners."[258] We were the guests of honor for the supper in 742-S and stayed for the night in Odessa. I met a number of Georgian colleagues

---

258- Reissmüller received a number of recognitions from the "Eastern people" because of his humanity—especially while he served as a staff officer in the Army Group A (Southeast Front). It is touching to read a letter written to him while on the front by Major Dudarow, in the name of the North Caucasian National Committee and the volunteers, during December of 1944: "Our Dear Friend! One cannot forget the help you rendered personally to the North Caucasian refugees during their endless trek while retreating away from their homeland. Your help was above the call of duty. We also witnessed the outrage with which you responded to the information about the degradation of the Caucasian persons and their rights and how energetically you acted to eliminate them." The Kuban Cossacks declared Reissmüller a honorary Cossack for his meritorious conduct and help. (The document is in the author's personal archives.)

there, among them Drs. Zurab Gamkrelidze and Bakhtadze—the former became a practicing physician near Springfield, Illinois, many years later. The next morning, we stopped by the 742-S to say farewell to the personnel there and dropped in 741-S, where they insisted we have lunch with them. There, unexpectedly, I met a pleasant gentleman, Lieutenant Semler from "Bergmann" who was also a guest. During the evening, Reissmüller and I returned to his office in the Army headquarters in Tiraspol. I stayed overnight and had a discussion with him and other officers about indigenous units and a desirable way of their reorganization. The next day, on March 28th, I bade farewell to my friend Reissmüller and left for Berlin by plane, arriving there safely. Around this time, Mykolaiv fell to the Soviets.

During my three months' absence from Berlin, further destruction of the city took place due to air raids, and they continued. The office of the Liaison Staff had not been hit but some nearby buildings had. In one of these buildings, the neighbors suspected that a lady had been buried in the ruins. All of us from the office ran to that place and were able to uncover a middle-aged lady from underneath the rubble. Fortunately and to our amazement, she had sustained only minor injuries. The supporting columns of the exit door where she was caught held and protected her. After rendering first aid and an examination with reassurance, I suggested she be checked and observed by her physician as well. The Georgian General Leo Kereselidze was less fortunate, he was killed during a similar air raid while I was out of the city.[259] Other changes had taken place; for instance, Köstring had been appointed the General of the Volunteer Troops in January of 1944. Before that, as the Inspector General of the same troops, Köstring and his adjutant, Herwarth, had captured the hearts of many Eastern volunteers while in the Caucasus.[260] After the retreat from Caucasus and Crimea, General Köstring and his staff, from his new position, made great efforts toward achieving for the volunteers equal status with their German opposites.

The list of such efforts included the withdrawal of a widely circulated despicable, discriminatory SS brochure, "Subhuman" ("Untermensch"), meaning the Eastern people. Improvement of material conditions; establishment of recreation centers; vacations for the legionnaires, some of them spent with German families; special hospitals; military schools for the officers; libraries, etc. Abolishment of the

---

259- L. Kereselidze was one of the leading members of the Georgian Legion, organized in Turkey by Schulenburg during W.W. I and also a co-founder of the "Tetri Giorgi" Party established in 1926 in Paris, along with Mikhako Tsereteli, as discussed earlier.

260- Please note that the name "Eastern Troops" was now changed to the "Volunteer Troops." Since the workers in Germany from the Eastern occupied territories had to wear an identifying badge—"East"— such expression became a discriminatory sign for "second class" people.

discriminatory "Ost" ("East") badges worn by the Russian and Ukrainian civilian workers in Germany as well as improvement of their poor living conditions, which could not help but greatly aggravate the volunteer soldiers who had relatives or friends among these "Eastern workers."[261]

Köstring could achieve such betterment (which was opposed by the Nazis) only because he could prove without a doubt that the Eastern volunteers were essential for the German Army. The Georgian Liaison Staff (and other Caucasian liaison staffs) were furnishing considerable feedback to Köstring and his associates on an ongoing basis concerning such matters and worked very closely with them. It proved to be a beneficial cooperation and the Köstring staff's sensitivity to the existing problems was superb. At the same time the Armenian, Azerbaijan, Georgian and North Caucasian liaison staffs (or committees) were deepening their mutual cooperation dictated by an ever increasing and complex situation. This reached the high point during the fall of 1944, when the coordinating Caucasian Committee and the Caucasian Military Council were formed.

Important reshuffling had taken place concerning the organization and locations of the volunteer ("Eastern") Legions.[262] They had been set up during the spring of 1942 to be reserve and training military units in order to form, train, equip and ready the field battalions for combat duty. To begin with, the legions were formed in two different locations. The first location was in occupied Poland, or so-called "Government General" in Rembertów and then Radom area by the "Staff of the Eastern Legions." Later on, in occupied Ukraine in the Myrhorod area, the staff of the 162 German Infantry Division was converted to a second center to organize, train and equip the Eastern legions. This division had sustained such heavy combat casualties during the winter of 1941–42 that only the staff survived without the soldiers. And now it was converted to the second center for putting together training and equipping of the Eastern legions. This location, being nearer the front line, offered considerable logistic advantage over Poland by eliminating the longer transport distance for the volunteers to and from the Southeast Front—("The Army Group A"), Lt. General Ralph von Heygendorff in command. Creation of the legions in both places was carried out under the overall leadership of Major (later Colonel) Claus von Stauffenberg of the Organization Department of the Army General Staff.

261- Such poor treatment did not directly apply to the Caucasian and Cossack civilian workers in Germany because of earlier intervention on their behalf by the Ostministerium. But for the Caucasians and Cossacks it had been a very uncomfortable and "guilty" feeling to see such unjust treatment of other Easterners while they fared much better for themselves.

262- For a detailed description of this organization of legions, which at times is rather confusing, and for changes of terminology, the reader is referred to the informative book of military historian Dr. Joachim Hoffmann, *Die Ostlegionen 1941–1943*.

It was a Herculean task given the surrounding circumstances, as discussed before in the chapter, "In the Bergmann Unit and Caucasus."

During the summer of 1943, the 162nd Infantry Division was transferred from Ukraine to the military training grounds—Neuhammer in Silesia, East Germany. While there and during the process of its "reforming and renaming" of Field Division 162, it kept Turkestani and Azerbaijan soldiers only and transferred the soldiers of all other nationalities to the "Commando of the Eastern Legions" in Poland. This new "Reserve Volunteer Division" in turn was gradually transferred from Poland to South France. In the beginning of 1944, distribution and composition of this Division was:

The headquarters of the Division in Lyon Area:

1. Reserve Regiment #1 consisted of the Georgian, the North Caucasian and Turkestan Legions with quarters in the Albi-Castres area.

2. Reserve Regiment #2 consisted of Azerbaijan, Armenian and Volga Tatar Legions with quarters in Rodez-Albi-Le Puy.

3. Reserve Regiment #3 Ukrainian in Namur [occupied Belgium].

4. Reserve Regiment #4 Russian in Namur.

5. Reserve Regiment #5 Cossack, south of Dijon.

The size of each legion had shrunk because new manpower was no longer available for replacement of losses. Therefore in reality it represented "a regiment" on paper only. Von Heygendorff was no longer the commanding general of this new "division" due to his transfer to the Staff of the High Command of the Army in Berlin.[263] Colonel Hoste, an experienced combat soldier, was now appointed the commanding officer of the "Volunteer Reserve Division." He remained so until the end of March in 1944, at which time he was transferred to front duty. General van Henning then became the commanding officer of this Volunteer Reserve Division in France. Two months later, General von Heygendorff was transferred from Berlin and appointed the commanding general of the 162 Turkic Infantry Division in Italy (which consisted of Turkestani and Azerbaijan units). I did not know the General personally but having read several reports and presentations by him, I came to appreciate his difficult and complex assignments in connection with the Eastern

---

263- General R. von Heygendorff's report concerning this matter, "Experience with volunteers of Soviet-Union Nations Fighting Bolshevism during World War II" (1951) was essential for the above condensed accounting. (In author's private archives.)

Volunteer Units. I could not help but sympathize with him since such a task would have been difficult for anyone, given Nazi policy.

Dallin judges General R. von Heygendorff in his classic book, perhaps rather harshly, as "politically a nonentity" and his 162 Infantry Division, "appears to have been a singular failure."[264] I do not know enough about the 162 Division to judge it; however, I am aware of von Herwarth's special trip to Italy during July of 1944, because defections occurred from this division.[265] Judging from Heygendorff's report on 4-1-51, he was also well aware of the deleterious effect of the existing Nazi government's East Policy on the Eastern Volunteer Legions. He wrote,

> "For our volunteers, the national committees were equivalent to the governments in exile. As such, they could have carried out a highly beneficial task, if only the German political leadership would create an appropriate setup for it. First of all, it required a declaration for a clear political goal for the Eastern nations who were fighting on our side. Unfortunately, we did not have such a declaration, and what we did have was changed from one day to another.
>
> "If one could make it clear to the committees that Germany had no claim—not even as much as one foot of their soil, and that it would help them achieve national independence and freedom from any oppression as well; it would conclude with them the pact of friendship and commercial relationship. Then the national committees would know their position and clearly would propagate such goals with word and print among our volunteers. Absence of such clarity from our side created a mistrust among the leading brains of the national committees."

During mid April, "Bergmann" Battalions, I/9, II/4, Romanian troops, German troops and other volunteer units—altogether 67,000 men were evacuated from Crimea, mostly by sea via Sevastopol Harbor with minimal loss of lives. The Soviets had great gains not only in the Ukraine north and west of Crimea but they also captured in Crimea proper—Feodosia, Evpatoria, Simferopol, Yalta, and they were menacing Sevastopol. Sevastopol held until the ninth of May at which time it fell to the Soviet Army. German evacuation continued from another seaport, Cape Khersones, and by air, but casualties were heavy, approximately 78,000 were

---

264- Dallin, *German Rule in Russia, 1941–1945*, p. 541.
265- Herwarth, *Against Two Evils*, p. 280.

killed or captured. Moreover, among evacuated men many were wounded.[266] After evacuation from Crimea, "Bergmann" gathered for a short time in Romania and from there it was transported by railroad to Greece, in the Athens area. Captain Brand was wounded during the last battle, and Captain Heintze took over the command temporarily. The Georgian Battalions I/9 and II/4 were directed to join the Georgian Legion in the Albi-Castres area in South France, and I was planning to visit them in the near future.[267] Following this, probably in June or July, I intended to see "Bergmann" in Greece, the country with which Georgia had such a close cultural as well as political relationship since ancient times.

266- *The World Almanac of World War II.*
267- During our December 1943 tour of the Georgian units in France, M. Alshibaja and I did not see the Georgian Legion (a reserve unit) in Albi-Castres which was the component of the Volunteer Reserve Division, as discussed on the preceding pages.

14
MARCH–JULY 1944: SIGNS OF THE COMING CRISIS

During the last days of March and the first week of April in 1944, I participated in many meetings in Berlin. Among them with members of the Georgian Liaison Staff, Professor von Mende, Ludersen and Gaios Maglakelidze both from the WPr (The Armed Forces Propaganda). Nearly all those I met wanted to know about my three-month experience in the Army Group A (South), especially with the Volunteer Units. The WPr people wondered about the effectiveness, or lack thereof, of the military propaganda. In answering this question, I recited one more time my favorite statement, "The best propaganda is improvement of conditions for the legionnaires and the indigenous population in the German occupied territories and to make it known in the WPr periodical. Also stress in your publication that in spite of all other changes around us our goal to help achieve a free Georgia remains the same." It was not an easy task for the WPr propagandists to inspire optimism during the days of the German Army's retreat everywhere.[268]

I visited several Georgian families in Berlin, among them, of course, Nino Kazbek's family. Her daughter, Marina von Moltke, was leaving Berlin for another town to stay with her little daughter, Nina ("Kikibush"). I took Marina to the railroad station and could hardly get a seat for her in the overcrowded train. A number of hours later, on April 8, 1944, I left for Paris in the company of Mikho Alshibaja and Walter von Kutzschenbach. We traveled twenty-four hours and were met at the railroad station by Walter's cousins (who temporarily resided in Paris) and Misha Kedia's business associate, Kako Schavgulidze. Our main objective at this time was to visit the Georgian Legion in South France but we also had some other business to attend to in Paris first. We stayed as before at Mamulashvili's (Mikho's in-law's)

268- WPr published a periodical *Sakartvelo* ("Georgia"). The editor was Gaios Maglakelidze. The Civilian Department of the Liaison Staff under the leadership of Dr. Giorgi (Gogi) Magalow (Magalashvili) published another Georgian periodical, *Kartveli Eri* ("The Georgian Nation") in Berlin as well.

home and enjoyed their great hospitality. Here again I met Noe Tsintsadze and continued an interesting dialogue with him. Misha Kedia had arrived in Paris just a few days before us and invited us for supper in his home. I met his wife, Valia and their delightful daughter Dika and their son Zurab.

The following morning, I stopped at Kedia's and together we went to visit the exiled secretary of state, Evgeni Gegechkori and other Georgian personalities for briefings and discussions. Gegechkori said that he in turn would inform President N. Jordania, (whom M. Kedia also intended to see personally somewhat later) about our report. While in M. Kedia's home, he took me aside and wanted to know about the feelings of my German officer friends, given the bad military situation for the Germans on all fronts. I told him that the best I could figure was that the feelings varied. Only a few of them believed in the existence of a "miracle" of new German weapons in the making which, once available, would turn things around to German advantage. Other officers still hoped it was not too late for achieving a change of heart of the Russian people. If this is to be accomplished, the East Policy should be reversed at once and General A. Vlasov and his anti-Stalin movement honestly promoted by the German government. However, one good friend with excellent connections and who is well informed had told me already during the spring of 1943, (a year previous) that he did not see how Germany could possibly win the war. [Without mentioning his name, this was Hans von Herwarth; see the chapter "In Crimea." —Ed.] He also believed that Vlasov would be used by the "higher-ups" for propaganda only.

Kedia said that some of his German friends felt it was high time to remove their Führer and his henchmen, otherwise they would completely destroy Germany. They also asked Kedia if the Georgians could help, if need be, on some special assignment. Kedia replied that the Georgians could not help in such an undertaking because first of all, it was entirely an internal German affair. Secondly, should such an attempt fail, the SS would massacre every Georgian they could reach. "I am telling this to you," said Kedia, "because some of our good German friends—almost all of them in opposition to Hitler's policy—may have some idea (of removing him) and also may approach you. I urge you to respond the same way as I have." Then he warned me to keep this conversation strictly between us, which perhaps was a redundant suggestion. Kedia then focused my attention on different problems.

One was concerning the Georgian Jewish colony in France. Kedia said that with the help of our German friends, so far we had been able to maintain the safety of our Jews but constant vigilance was necessary. The situation was made worse because the Vichy regime did not agree with the exception made by the Germans for Georgian and some Oriental Jewish groups; according to which, such groups were not defined as Jews and not registered as such, thus offering them safety.[269] The Germans, however, prevailed and the Georgian Jews remained exempt from registration. A few years later, the authorized Vichy government officials were again opposed to the exemption made by the German officials for the Georgian Jews, said Kedia. He had to take special effort in isolated instances in order to save certain persons from deportation. The entire Georgian Colony in France stood together determined to save the Jews, said Kedia. I told Kedia that he should also tell his German friends in charge of such matters in France that if any harm comes to our Jews, it would have a disastrous effect on the morale of our legionnaires in the field battalions, "and I am telling you this as their official speaker." This I probably said with a Georgian Quixotic bearing since Kedia responded to my words with laughter and then a warm hug and eyes wet with appreciation.

Mikho Alshibaja and Gogi Magalow had expressed early their complete support for M. Kedia concerning this matter and at the same time confirming the views of their constituent Georgian emigres in Poland and Germany. During June–July 1944, the Georgian Colony in France would unanimously agree to set up a committee to determine who was a Jewish Georgian and therefore entitled to be reclassified and thus obtain exemption. The committee was authorized to issue identification cards, a process acceptable to the French Police. The prepared list contained 243 Georgian-Jewish families, some one thousand individuals—more by far than the actual number of the Georgian Jews in France. Of course many non-Georgian Jews were included. Family names were changed, documents (including birth certificates) were forged in order to save lives.[270]

M. Kedia also told me about another problem; it concerned a Georgian emigre, one Shalva Odisharia, who at that time worked for the German Secret Police. His activities toward the French persons were odious and embarrassing for the Georgians. He also had denounced M. Kedia to the secret police as an English spy. Although such an allegation was a total falsehood, it could be potentially dangerous for M. Kedia; therefore, all his friends successfully rallied for his support. Odisharia tried to undermine M. Kedia's good standing among the Georgian emigres as well but found very insignificant support for his covetous attempts.

The branch office of our Liaison Staff in Paris under D. Djuruli continued to function well and we had several conferences with him. Then the time came for Mikho Alshibaja, Kutzschenbach and me to visit the Georgian Legion in the

---

269- Warren Green, *The Fate of the Oriental Jews in Vichy France*. See also "Unternehmen Mainz I" in the author's archives.

270- Warren Green, *The Fate of the Oriental Jews in Vichy France*; also Kedia deposition in the author's archives and appendix.

Albi-Castres area. It was easily accessible by train; non-commissioned officer Kako (Konstantin Alshibaja, Mikho's cousin) from the Liaison Staff also joined us. He came to Paris from Berlin several days ahead of us. The German commanding officers of the Georgian Legion had been changed frequently. Colonel Machts was appointed to this position during 1943 and then elevated to the commanding officer of the Volunteer Reserve Regiment #1 in Castres. This regiment consisted of the Georgian, North Caucasian and Turkestani Legions. Colonel Machts was popular among the legionnaires. This easy-going Austrian gentleman, with considerable charm, warmth and diplomacy, apparently also cared very much for his soldiers' well-being. His regiment was a heterogeneous unit and yet he got along equally well with all three ethnic groups. Perhaps in some way he inherited the mental makeup of his ancestors that had emerged in the past because of the multi-national Austro-Hungarian Empire. Being the reserve units, the legions were characterized by a frequent turnover of the soldiers and officers. Some of the field battalions with heavy losses had been absorbed by the Legions. After rest, additional training and receiving weapons, refreshed legionnaires were dispatched to the different field battalions, now in need of manpower. A number of officers and officer aspirants were also directed to the appropriate military schools for an upgrading of their qualifications.

During April of 1944, the Albi-Castres area was peaceful, and the legion-naires enjoyed it. The Georgian Legions had an impressive singing and dancing ensemble under the leadership of Makashvili assisted by Nalbandishvili. We all enjoyed their performance. It was of great interest to us to meet Colonel Vladimer (Lado) Sharabidze, who held the position of a Georgian commanding officer of the Georgian Legion in the Albi-Castres area since 1943. Sharabidze was a graduate of the Frunze Military Academy and the Academy of the General Staff of the Red Army. He had belonged to the operations section of the Red Army General Staff during 1941. During the end of the same year, he was taken as a P.O.W. by the German Army while commanding one of the Soviet infantry regiments; he had high Soviet decorations. Nevertheless, he joined the Georgian Legion. Colonel Sharabidze was a sincere, dignified and intelligent gentleman, trusted by Colonel Machts and loved by the legionnaires who knew him well.[271] Unfortunately, he was ailing. We met him and his Russian wife who was taking very good care of her husband in their apartment. Sharabidze's case is one of the many examples of a Red Army officer's defiance against Stalin and his government.

271- One of them was a non-commissioned officer, Petre Khvedelidze, who was a friend and confidant of the Sharabidze's family and who hopefully will have more to say about Colonel Lado Sharabidze in his memoir. It is my understanding that he is writing his memoir at present, which covers the dramatic developments in the legion pending the western allied occupation. [Khvedelidze's *From Paris to Washington with Thoughts on Georgia* was published in two volumes {2010, 2012} in Georgian.—Ed.]

My address to the Georgian Legion did not significantly defer from the ones I delivered to the field battalion. However, this time I shared with the legionnaires my three months' observation in the Army Group A (Southeast). It was received by the listeners with considerable interest. After the official part was over, we met with small groups for an informal exchange of views. During the last evening, officers of the legion organized a reception with food, drinks and dancing; some ladies had also been invited. Our handsome Baron Walter von Kutzschenbach was not infrequently a dancing partner for the charming ladies. Soon our small group returned to embattled Berlin via Paris.[272]

Getting an apartment in Berlin was a major problem given the severe destruction of buildings but Mikho Alshibaja found one for me, just one story below his. Several apartments next to ours were also located in the same third of the house since the other two-thirds had been destroyed by firebombs. Mikho found this apartment thanks to a school friend of his, Mrs. Inge Siegel (the wife of a well-known contemporary German songwriter). She rented a portion of her rather large apartment to Mikho. The three of us often breakfasted together reasonably well, considering the difficult times. Mikho and I were surprised by the resourcefulness of the Berliners and their ability to function and secure the necessary things seemingly out of nowhere.

I usually arose at 5:30 a.m. to do my exercise and then jog in the nearby park for an hour. The park had many zig-zag trenches dug in case one would get caught in the air raids. The British usually bombed during the night and the Americans during the day. I tried to interest Mikho in the morning exercise but after a few sessions he somehow always "wiggled" out of it. This disappointed his mother Barbara, who was a firm believer in fresh air and in all such good things; she resided in Poland but would occasionally visit Mikho.

272- While back in Berlin, Walter von Kutzschenbach introduced to me his cousin Joachim von Kutzschenbach, who was attached to the Kalmyk Volunteer Unit (if my memory serves me right, it was a cavalry corps) as an interpreter with the rank of an officer. He had deep compassion for the Kalmyks and tried his best to assist them. Joachim was born and raised in South Caucasus and he left there, as did other Kutzschenbachs, because of the Bolshevik Russian takeover. Joachim was married to the daughter of Field Marshal Friedrich Paulus, commander of the 6th Army, who was taken prisoner by the Russians during the Battle of Stalingrad. Later the Field Marshal participated in the "Committee for Free Germany," which was organized by the Soviets and used for propaganda during the war.

The entire situation had been very stressful for the Paulus family, and if this were not enough, a great tragedy struck; Joachim von Kutzschenbach was killed during the end phase of the war. The two cousins had been close, and my friend Walter was devastated. I kept him as busy as I could (he was a liaison officer of our staff) in order to help him get over his grief more easily. Fortunately, Walter met a very nice Russian-speaking lady, Miss Berthels, who worked as a secretary in the Caucasus Department of the Ostministerium. They had much in common and soon fell in love, were married and shortly after the war settled in Bad Reichenhall, Bavaria. They had a beautiful baby daughter whom Walter nicknamed in Georgian "My little Kakali" ("Walnut"), perhaps because of the nice sound of it.

We usually met our neighbors in the air raid shelter; among them was the Kolarz family. Papa Kolarz was of German descent, born in Russia and married to an Armenian; their only child was in his teens. They were polite, intelligent and interesting people and we had a number of discussions on a variety of topics. After the war, in the mid-fifties, the bibliography of several American and German books made reference to Walter Kolarz's articles on Soviet themes. We at once thought he probably was our young friend from the Berlin air raid shelter, a pleasant feeling.

Mikho and I usually made it to the Liaison Staff office at 8:00 a.m. on the subway. The agenda had been prepared in advance but unscheduled business was frequent. People came to us with all kinds of problems. Some of them were just passing through Berlin while others made a special trip to present their case and ask for assistance or to report some significant news. We were eager to see everyone in order to get as much feedback as possible and assist those in need. To the best of my knowledge not many persons left disappointed and without one of us meeting him or her personally. Mikho was especially good-hearted and generous.

One day, Mikho introduced me to his second younger sister, Miss Rusudan Alshibaja. She was studying economics at Munich University and working on her doctorate. The theme of her thesis was nothing less than, "Soviet Agriculture in the Light of Georgian Experience." In Munich, while living in the pension Rothes, she befriended a very nice young German lady, Hertha Pferdmenges. Having earned her masters degree, Rusudan was invited by Hertha to spend some time on her parents' estate ("Rittergut") in Hilprechtshausen, not all that far from Berlin. Rusudan came to the capital not only to see her brother but also to secure some literature for her doctorate from the Berlin Library as well as from some knowledgeable Georgians living there.[273] During the weekend, Mikho asked if I could substitute for him in escorting Rusudan (since he had another commitment) to visit Aunt Nino Kazbek and also see some of the city. I was glad to oblige, inasmuch as she was a very interesting person and for starters she widened my knowledge, especially about her family, as well as the Pferdmenges and the Soviet agronomy.

Having told her about my pending trip to Greece via Vienna, Rusudan thought I surely would enjoy meeting her older sister, Martha, who was studying at the Vienna Medical School. "She is beautiful and also an outstanding personality," she observed. I could hardly wait until I met Martha. About the Pferdmenges family, Rusudan said that they were outstanding people. They had a well-going textile industry. Hertha had four sisters and one brother, all of them were well educated. Both parents had an affinity for America and before the war they arranged an

---

273- Rusudan would rather have entered a university in Poland since her family resided in Warsaw, but unfortunately all universities there had been closed by the civilian Nazi administration.

extended American tour by car for their three daughters (the fourth was still in school). This turned out to be a positive experience, never to be forgotten by the young ladies.

Mr. Pferdmenges, a "capitalist," was deeply concerned about the needs of his workers. One example of this was that rather then erect the large monotonous, depressing, communal dwelling compounds, he chose to build smaller houses with individual attractive features. It was a fitting example of M. Pferdmenges's personality that he presented Rusudan with an unusual book written in German by Karl Kautsky about the agrarian reform of the Sovereign Georgian Republic 1918–1921.[274]

Rusudan enjoyed the perfectly rustic, peaceful environment while working on her doctorate in Hilprechtshausen with Hertha's family. It was not difficult for her to commute by train to Berlin for necessary material for her thesis. Mikho and I saw her often and enjoyed her company. Soon all our friends got to know her better and liked her very much. Later they confessed that they crossed their fingers that the two of us would become engaged. When Rusudan and I went for lunch in the Russian restaurant "Medved," ("The Bear"), the Georgians who were working there such as Mose Imnaishvili, Sandro Cordzaia, and Eretheos Ramishvili greeted us with beaming faces and happy smiles. The Georgian dining guests acted likewise. We both felt we were being observed at all times and did not quite know what to do with our hands and feet while walking out of "Medved." Such an attitude by well-wishers toward young couples is more visible among small nationalities who at times had been on the brink of extinction; for instance, the Jews and Georgians. As far as Rusudan and I are concerned we fell in love very soon (fortunately for me); and after forty seven years are sure that we would do the same if we had to do it all over again.

As often emphasized, our Liaison Staff and General Köstring attached great importance to the build-up of a qualified indigenous officer's corps by sending them to the German military schools. We encouraged the officers, officer aspirants and non-commissioned officers to keep in touch with us as often as possible. Conversely, the officers from the Liaison Staff were doing the same while "dropping in" on the military schools and getting acquainted with them. I personally met, whenever I could, the Georgian officers, for instance, the ones who just graduated from military school in Bitche. Also on my way from Berlin to Greece, I stopped in Poznań to see

---

274- K. Kautsky was an internationally known German Social Democrat, who a few months before the Soviet Russian invasion, had visited Georgia with other leading European Social Democrats such as Ramsay McDonald, E. Vandervelde, Pierre Renaudel, L. De Brouckere and C. Huysmans. They were impressed by the Georgian experiment.

the officers school. Originally this school was to be located near Berlin but because of the frequent air raids it was transferred to Poznań, Poland. I spent a couple of days there, attended some of the classes and a field exercise and I was well satisfied with the quality of training and the high caliber of the German instructors. Among other officer aspirants I met there, Lt. Archil (Achiko) Dadiani, my 'old' friend from "Bergmann," the nephew of Mikheil (Misha) Dadiani, who was the commanding officer of the cavalry squadron. I also met Givi Porakishvili and Leo Metreveli.[275]

From Poznań, I flew to Vienna but could not get a flight from there to Greece, as the waiting time for departure of airplanes was undetermined. Therefore, I took a chance on a 7:00 p.m. train to Athens via Belgrade, Serbia (sort of an "Orient Express"). During the briefing in Army headquarters in Vienna, I was cautioned about the partisan activities on my route and the explosives they were using against the railroads. Sure enough, the partisans had dynamited our railroad track on Yugoslav territory a short time before so that we had to get out and walk in the darkness some distance to another train waiting for us on undamaged tracks. We reached the Yugoslav capital Belgrade at 2:00 p.m., and with the help of the military commandant I got the 9:00 a.m. flight the following morning to Salonika, Greece (on the northern coast of the Aegean Sea). In Belgrade I used the waiting time to stroll the streets, including those around the royal palace. Continuations of the flight from Salonika to Athens was exciting for me as I anticipated seeing "Bergmann" friends and the legendary city itself. I could not resist the urge to walk up the Athenian citadel Acropolis three times to see the Parthenon, the Erechtheum and the Dionysus Theatre on the southern slope of the Acropolis. While dining in a restaurant, I could hear what sounded like a Georgian lullaby song. Not only the melody but even the Georgian words such as, "Nana" and "Nanina" were definitely there. "It is a Cretan song, and the people who sing it are indeed from the Island of Crete," explained the waiter. Everywhere I felt to have much in common with Greece and its people. However, much to my regret, I did not come here as a tourist. It will be recalled that after leaving Crimea by boat, "Bergmann" had landed and assembled in Romania. Then it was transported by railroad to Greece in the Athens area. Two companies were assigned quarters at the periphery of the city in a schoolhouse and other companies in adjacent towns. The companies were often on outside training maneuvers, including in the beautiful hills and mountains.

275- All three of them had graduated as lieutenants and eventually were assigned to the Georgian Battalion II/198, at that time located near Verona, Italy. They, with other officers, Irakli Kontridze and Zurab Abdusheli (Abdushelishvili) had contributed a great deal toward the stability and reliability of the battalion. We shall say more about this later on.

It was a pleasant reunion with friends. Captain Brand was still recuperating after his injury so his replacement Captain Heintze and I visited the "Bergmann" companies. Afterwards with Victor Homeriki, Misha Dadiani, Goglik Vachnadze and Shalva Okropiridze, I mingled with the soldiers. The following day, the commanding general in Athens, General Felmi inspected "Bergman," and I was introduced to him. He appeared to be a warm and pleasant gentleman and well disposed toward "Bergmann." I accompanied the General during his inspection, after which, he invited Homeriki and me to his office and we had a frank discussion. He was well aware of the special problems the volunteer soldiers were facing, and I was sure that he would do his best to help them. Homeriki, whom the General already knew, had an excellent way of communicating with him and his staff. The soldiers of "Bergmann" were still in good spirits and well disciplined, even though the military situation for the Germans was deteriorating everywhere; just six days before (on June 6, 1944) the American and British forces had landed on the beaches of Normandy and were firmly established ashore. Moreover, shortly before, the Western Allied Forces had entered Rome and the Germans were retreating in Italy.

The "Bergmann" soldiers were constantly bombarded with skillful propaganda leaflets, apparently from the leftist Greek partisans. Pointing to all the unfavorable military conditions for the Germans, they promised a good reception and future if only the soldiers would defect to the partisans. There were some intelligence reports however, according to which the defectors once in the partisans hands were promptly disarmed and after a long interrogation by the partisans as well as the Soviet liaison officers, were shot. Thus the partisans were only interested in obtaining weapons and information. Almost every morning the "Bergmann" soldiers found leaflets spread around their quarters and no one, not even a sentry, ever saw when, how and by whom this was done. No one had ever enjoyed reading the exaggerated version of the bad news day in and day out, and "Bergmann" soldiers were no exception. Moreover, everyone was curious about "the invisible" people of the leaflets. That curiosity almost put us in serious trouble.

Lieutenant Okropiridze learned of a Georgian relative living in Athens with his family and was soon invited to visit them. Of course, Okropiridze had told them about other Georgians in "Bergmann," and the family extended a dinner invitation to include Homeriki and me. We accepted, loved it and stayed there past midnight. It was some distance to our quarters but the three of us decided to walk inasmuch as it was a beautiful Mediterranean night with bright moonlight. The streets were deserted; we approached the business district of Athens when an unmarked, black, civilian limousine drove slowly from a side street and continued ahead of us. Then a back door opened halfway and bunches of leaflets were dropped from the moving car. The three of us looked at each other. "Aha, is this how the communist partisans smuggle their leaflets around the 'Bergmann' quarters"?

"Stop!" The three of us shouted clear and very loud but the limo chose to ignore us completely. The next step was that one of us should fire a warning shot in the sky. (Since I had the biggest gun, I did it.) There was an immediate and rather unexpected response. The limo stopped, several men slipped out of it and from a laying-down position opened fire at us with machine guns. I could hear bullets whistling around us. The three of us spread out in order not to provide an easy target for them. At first we directed our return fire to the empty limo, shouting, "Come out with your hands up!" But they continued their undiminished fire at us. We lowered our aim and this got results as they soon stopped shooting. After a few minutes we "stormed" their position with empty guns in our hands as we had run out of ammunition. Soon the captain of the M.P.s (military police) arrived on the scene, as he had heard the gunfire. Thank the Lord, no one was killed—only one of the limo people sustained a soft tissue bullet wound over the mid thigh. He declined first aid, but I gave it to him anyway. And who were the limo people? Our opponents turned out to be from the German military propaganda (four or five people were in the limo).

Just why they chose such an unusual method of nocturnal "secret" distribution of propaganda leaflets in the Greek language for the citizens of Athens? They chose not to answer, nor did they answer the M.P. captain's other questions: Why the unmarked civilian limo? Why had the Military Police not been informed ahead of time of the pending propaganda distribution? And why did they not stop and identify themselves at our request? Then why did they open massive fire from automatic machine guns against us after merely one warning shot in the air? The M.P. captain checked our documents and took our deposition. I told him that I was willing to assume all responsibility on behalf of Homeriki and Okropiridze, who were following my orders. The captain saluted, shook our hands and said not to worry, clearly the military propaganda company was at fault.

During the early morning, I inspected the "battlefield." The bullets had caused considerable damage to the shop windows; the one behind our backs suffered the most damage, mainly in the display of cosmetics. I told the Greek shop owner to send the bill to the military propaganda company, since it was their machine gunfire that caused the damage. General Felmi wanted to see Homeriki and me at noon; he had been informed about the shootings. His "verdict" was the same as of the M.P. captain's. The General expressed some surprise that the three of us could disarm the limo full of people who were armed with superior weapons. "I am tempted" said the General, "to send the 'propagandists' for some field-training to make better soldiers out of them and abolish the propaganda company altogether." I could not agree more. We parted on the best of terms.

Among the "Bergmann" officers, Misha Dadiani was the only one who did not appear to be feeling well. He was coughing more than usual, was rather pale and nervous and wanted to talk to me personally. His main concern was his wife, Thina Gomarteli-Dadiani who resided in Paris. Given the military situation, especially the Western Allied landing in Normandy, it was possible that they would never see each other again. He felt that he had failed her. I was deeply moved to see a veteran, battle-hardened, senior officer who fought so well in such distress. "Do something before it's too late and before I do something irrational." I promised him that I would do my utmost to get Thina and him together. (Fortunately, I was able to keep that promise, as we shall see later.)

While visiting the "Bergmann" 4th Company, I was given a list of chronically ill soldiers, as had been established by the physicians, in order to expedite their transfer to the Legion's reserve. This led to a meeting with the "Bergmann" leadership for discussion of other problems. It was the general feeling that the Balkan Peninsula was a potential trap for the "Bergmann" soldiers given the worsening military situation. Therefore the battalion should remain "fit and trim" and mobile. I told the officers that the Georgian Liaison Staff, in cooperation with the general of the Volunteer Units, would do all it could to transfer "Bergmann" to Germany or another safer zone. I was planning also to visit Georgian unit 843, located in the wooded hills. The only practical way that I could get there was by a small airplane. The flight could not take place on June 15th because of a strong wind. The following day some damage was discovered in the plane's motor that would take some time to repair. Therefore, the trip did not materialize. On June 17th, I left Athens for Berlin on a military transport plane, via Salonika, Sofia (Bulgaria), Belgrade, Vienna and Dresden. I arrived in Berlin the next day.

During the next few days, I had to brief my colleagues and associates in the Liaison Staff and the staff of General Köstring and also write reports about my impressions during this trip. I was anxious to get the report about our troops in France, where the war was picking up momentum. I considered it my duty to go there and render any assistance I could, but first I had to catch up with my obligations in Berlin. Of note, I had been "drafted" to deliver a speech in Potsdam, where the Georgians celebrated Independence Day on the 26th of May. (It was taking place during June instead of May due to some technical problems.) Among many other distinguished guests, Mrs. Charlotte von Siemens, of the well-known German inventor and industrialist's family, was sitting with Rusudan. She was a close friend of Rusudan's family. After a few more speeches, a Georgian singing and dancing ensemble under the direction of David Kavsadze entertained the guests with a very good performance. Rusudan introduced me to Mrs. von Siemens; I liked her immediately. She asked me if I had met Rusudan's parents and other members of her family. I admitted that I only knew her sister, Kethevan and brother, Mikho. That question led to my trip which had a dual nature, business as well as pleasure. I wanted to see Oberländer in Prague to talk to him about "Bergmann," and on my way back I would stop in Bad Reichenhall and Vienna as well to get acquainted with the rest of Rusudan's family.

On June 25th, I visited Rusudan's parents and her youngest sister, Thina (a medical doctor) in Bad Reichenhall, Bavaria, a well-known health spa, located between the beautiful mountains. But I could stay there for only one day due to a tight schedule. Rusudan's father, a doctor of medicine, Grigol Alshibaja, had suffered from several ailments. Initially he went to Vienna for treatment of his bronchial asthma and heart "weakness." While in Vienna he developed jaundice and had to remain there for three months. Because of the jaundice he was finally referred to the municipal hospital in Karlsbad. After recuperation, Dr. Alshibaja was referred to Bad Reichenhall because of lingering bronchial asthma. When the Soviet Army approached Warsaw during the summer of 1944, his wife Barbara Kiziria Alshibaja had fled Poland and joined her husband in Bad Reichenhall. Their youngest daughter, Thina, the Munich Medical School graduate, joined her parents and was able to secure the position of an intern at the local hospital. The Alshibajas were remarkable personalities with an unusual past.[276]

I felt as if I had known Rusudan's parents and Thina for a long time and liked them very much at once. It turned out that our parents had several friends in common from Kutaisi, West Georgia and the conversation soon became lively, warm and interesting. The doctor was bedridden most of the time but in spite of this, he was handsome, distinguished and in retrospect reminded me of "Uncle Sam." Mother Barbara was majestic and well-poised; the only time one could discern a trace of excitement was the appearance of some red spots on her neck. Thina was a young Georgian beauty with characteristic big, brown eyes. Many years later, our children would admiringly comment that such and such a person has "Thina's eyes." Such a compliment was even extended to our German Shepherd, Phari. (Thina did not appear to mind such a comparison at all since she shared our deep affection for "man's best friend.") Being an intern, Thina would often confer with her father about her seriously ill patients, taking advantage of his great medical experience. It was fun

---

276- See the Appendix pp. 363–366 about Grigol Alshibaja.

to see her sitting at his bedside discussing problems at great length. Other family members teased Thina that she was "squeezing Papa like a lemon" for his knowledge. Thina and Rusudan, the youngest in the family had a very close relationship. Thina confessed to me later that she had conceived my appearance on the family scene as a threat to separation from her older sister; therefore, she was not well disposed towards me. I did my best to change Thina's attitude and I even gave her some Judo lessons in self-defense.

During my trip to the Balkan Peninsula, I intended to meet Martha, the second oldest sister of Rusudan, who was enrolled in the Vienna Medical School but this had to be postponed. Having received the blessing of Rusudan's parents on our engagement, I took the night-train to Vienna and arrived there early morning and finally met Martha. She had been able to obtain an apartment in the house of her anatomy professor. She liked Vienna and she was able to save some of her family's Persian carpets[277] by transferring them from Warsaw to the professor's house in Vienna. Martha accompanied me to the railroad station—we had much to talk about. She was thoughtful and intelligent and had concerns about the future of her uprooted family. She was very noble and beautiful; I cannot imagine a young man not being captivated when meeting her. Time was all too short, the train rolled in and out again—direction Prague. Later Rusudan read a laconic statement from Martha's letter to her. "Rusudan, marry Givi at once." I was deeply moved.

I traveled to Prague in order to meet with Professor Oberländer, von Kutzschenbach and Professor H. Raschhofer because of our concern for "Bergmann." As discussed before, Oberländer had been removed as "Bergmann's" commanding officer, dismissed from the army, investigated and placed under house arrest by the Gestapo. Grave, punitive action had been averted only by the interference of the Army and some other influential persons who knew him well. Himmler's rage was caused because, as mentioned, in 1942–43 Oberländer had written several memoranda in which he denounced the German policy in the occupied Eastern territories and

---

277- The carpets had an interesting history. Martha's uncle from her mother's side, Koki (Alvipi) Kiziria was a general in the Imperial Russian Army. During W.W. I, he was dispatched to organize and train the Royal Persian Artillery. The Persian government paid part of his salary in high quality Persian carpets. After the Bolshevik takeover of Russia and later of Georgia, Koki Kiziria had emigrated to Berlin and utilized his knowledge about Persian carpets to open an import business in Germany. Thus the Alshibajas obtained high quality carpets through him. Rusudan told me a great deal about her uncle Koki, whom the whole family adored—he had to be quite a charming man. In addition to being successful in the military and in business, he had been elected President of the Georgian Colony in Germany. He was an expert sportsman as well and a member of the prestigious sports organization, "The Falcon," which originated in Czechoslovakia and spread especially in Eastern Europe. I did not have the good fortune of meeting Uncle Koki because of a tragic airplane accident which claimed his life while on a business trip.

made suggestions about some radical changes. Removal from "Bergmann" did not diminish Oberländer's feeling of responsibility toward the soldiers of the unit. Therefore, when I arrived in Prague the four of us, all formerly from "Bergmann," discussed how one could prevent its falling in Bolshevik hands. I told them about impressions I had gained during my recent trip to the Balkan Peninsula while visiting "Bergmann." Everyone agreed that they were sitting in a potential trap. Therefore, while it was still feasible, "Bergmann" should be transferred to Austria or Germany or at least to Italy or Denmark where they would have a better chance of survival. We were all sure that General Köstring and his staff would do all they could toward this goal but with Oberländer's previous connections with influential persons, General Köstring's efforts would be enhanced.

Our train for Berlin was not scheduled to leave until the following morning, so Oberländer and I took a walk through Prague. One could not help but be fascinated by the ancient capital of Czechoslovakia, even at this time of German occupation. The city is located on elevated terrain along the Moldau [Vlatava] river with many remarkable bridges over it, especially the Charles Bridge with many statues. Among the impressive buildings were the ancient castle of the Bohemian Kings, St. George's Basilica and the St. Nicholas Cathedral to mention only a few. The fourteenth century Prague University was one of the first universities in Europe. At this time Professor Oberländer was allowed to lecture at the Prague University in economics.

Back in the Berlin office, I had requested Lieutenant Shalva Okropiridze's transfer from "Bergmann" to the military department of the Liaison Staff to report to me as my adjutant. He was capable of good office work and had training and experience in this direction. I had to take frequent trips (in fact, one was pending shortly to Normandy-France) and could barely catch up with my paperwork and other relatively minor obligations in the office.[278]

Okropiridze, on his way from Athens to Berlin, passed through Italy and visited the Georgian Legions Battalion II/198. At that time there were two Georgian officers there, Lieutenants Zurab Abdushelishvili and Irakli Kontridze; both officers had a good service record. Okropiridze reported that the conditions in the Battalion

---

278- Another contributory reason for Okropiridze's transfer to Berlin was that while attending the Dresden Military School, he met and fell in love with a German girl, Ursula (whose last maiden name, I no longer remember) and wanted to marry her. In fact, while on my way back from Prague to Berlin, I stopped in Dresden (which is only seventy miles northwest of Prague) to personally inform Ursula that she would soon see her Prince Charming again. The marriage took place in Dresden and Mikho Alshibaja and I accepted the invitation to attend.

were stable. Later, I requested from General Köstring's staff,[279] that additional qualified Georgian officers be assigned to Battalion II/198.

During early July, three newly graduated Lieutenants from the Poznań Military School, Archil Dadiani, Givi Porakishvili and Leo Metreveli, visited me in Berlin. According to the usual ordinance they had to go to the Georgian Legion's headquarters, Castres-France first and from there be assigned to the field battalions as needed. But A. Dadiani was worried and very upset about the prospect of seeing Miss Martha Amilakhvari in Paris, to whom he was engaged. With help from General Köstring's staff we were able to change this; Dadiani was given a vacation and directed to Paris, the other two also went to Paris for a short time and then all three went via Castres to Battalion II/198 in Italy. As already mentioned, their presence there greatly contributed to further the betterment of conditions in this unit.

As already noted, Professor von Mende was in fact independently running the Caucasus Department in the Ostministerium. At this time, for some reason, Mende thought it necessary to underline that the Caucasians not only had his support but Minister Rosenberg's support as well. Therefore, Mende arranged a rather brief reception for the Georgian Liaison staff members by the minister. This took place at noon on July 6, 1944. The minister appeared rather detached and tired with dark circles under his eyes. Among us, Gogi Magalow was the only one who knew him through Professor A. Nikuradze. On Mende's suggestion, Magalow introduced the rest of us to the minister, who after a handshake expressed his appreciation for our efforts and work and soon departed accompanied by Mende and a few other Germans from his staff. The same evening we had a meeting of the Liaison Staff to discuss several matters. Of immediate relevance, I was getting ready for my third trip to France. This was for two main reasons: 1.) To see the Georgian units, especially those in the battle zone; assist them as best I could and document the situation. 2.) To back M. Kedia, which was necessary for the continued success of his ongoing effort of protecting the Georgian civilians in France, regardless of their political affiliation, creed or race. To this end, I could contribute as a recognized speaker of the legionnaires in the German Army; many of them were losing their lives in combat and deserved to have their wishes heard. Thus the Georgian Liaison Staff felt that we had these bargaining chips in our hands.

The least that certain German authorities could do was to respect the wishes of the fighting Georgians that no harm comes to their civilian brothers and sisters. By the same token, the German authorities had to prevail on the responsible Vichy France government officials, who, as discussed earlier, were hostile to the "oriental"

279- Captain Siegfried Ungermann was the head of the personnel department.

Jews in France, requesting their registration as a prelude for their deportation and destruction in Himmler's extermination camps. Kedia was furious about the renewed attempts of such harassment. He said that the "dying fly during the late fall bites worse" and one has to be even more careful. On July 25th, there would be a meeting of the Georgian Colony in Paris and Kedia insisted that in order to underline the importance of the Georgian legionnaires, I as their representative, should be the "featured speaker." Kedia and a non-commissioned officer, Kako Alshibaja (my special aide during this trip) and I arrived in Paris approximately mid July. We had conferences with several leaders of the Georgian emigration, including Evgeni Gegechkori (Secretary of State in exile), Akaki Chkhenkeli (former Ambassador to France), A. Asatiani and E. Pataridze (the leaders of the National Democrat Party). Also included were P. Sardjveladze (one of the leading members of the Social Democrat Party), Niko Urushadze (representative of the Federalist Party), Konstantine Gvarjaladze (former Ambassador to England), D. Djuruli (director of our branch office in Paris), Sasha Korkia (who had been appointed by the Georgian Colony to issue one thousand identification papers to our Jews and some non-Georgian Jews as well.) These papers claimed that they were all Georgians, which was accepted by the French Police and such persons did not need to register as Jews.

Kako Schavgulidze (Chavgoulidze), M. Kedia's faithful business associate who had remained in Paris during the duration of the war, briefed us in detail about the state of affairs in Paris, including S. Odisharia's hostile intentions. Odisharia intended to create a scandalous situation during the pending Georgian Colony meeting on July 25th, with the help of his armed men. Not only verbally but perhaps even physically, he wanted to humiliate Kedia in front of people thus undermining respect and confidence in him in the colony. Who was going to stop his armed men? I made it known to Odisharia that I was the main speaker of that meeting and I intended to be armed and just in case, I would have other armed officers and soldiers with me. Furthermore, any attack on M. Kedia would be considered an attack on me and my men.

The very next day, David Washadze visited me. He was a former "Bergmann" soldier who had been discharged from there after the retreat from Caucasus at his own request, as had other elderly emigres from France. What I did not know was that he had joined Odisharia's group in Paris (much to my regret) on whose behalf he was speaking to me now. Washadze said that Odisharia and his men had nothing against me, Magalow, M. Alshibaja or other members of the Liaison Staff but they loathed M. Kedia. I told Washadze that I would not attempt to analyze the reasons for such strong feelings against Kedia. Kedia himself would surely have something to say about it, if need be, but I would hope this all could somehow be resolved peacefully—causing a scandalous disturbance during the colony meeting is not one of such ways. Then I repeated to Washadze my previous message for Odisharia, that we would not allow such a disturbance to occur. Washadze asked me, as a favor, to be his guest for supper at his home with typical Georgian insistence. "After all, we are former comrades from 'Bergmann'," etc. It was difficult to flatly refuse his gesture of hospitality. I soon discovered his home was in the quarters of Odisharia's group, as I found out myself sharing the dinner table not only with Washadze but with a few of his "new comrades" including Odisharia. I had not met him before but Odisharia impressed me at once as an ambitious man who wanted to play the important role held by Kedia among the emigres but had not succeeded. He then saw an opportunity by joining the German Secret Police, which gave him some material advantage and a feeling of power but not necessarily of self-esteem. Now he wanted to achieve the respectability and approval of the Georgian emigration, and so he set out to downgrade and undermine M. Kedia in an attempt to replace him. Here, in my opinion, the reality-testing ability of his ego was totally off. He was, however, able to "recruit" David Washadze, whom he needed badly because Washadze was better educated than Odisharia and had a stronger (albeit inconsistent) political orientation.

Washadze was eloquent and able to publish articles, spoke German and served on the Caucasus front in "Bergmann." With the help of Washadze and his associates, Odisharia proclaimed a sort of "Committee for Georgia" but could not find more than a few other followers and never gained acceptance from the Georgian Colony. What surprised me most was that he made a definite attempt to influence me against Kedia. Finally during this meeting, he and D. Washadze realized that they could not succeed in this nor in humiliating Kedia during the pending meeting of the Georgian Colony in Paris. Due to the late hour, I had to stay overnight in the room Washadze prepared for me. I left early morning; this was the last time I saw Washadze and Odisharia. They did not show up for the colony meeting but several members of Odisharia's group occupied the back seats; they were outflanked by our military men—just in case.

The meeting was very well attended with M. Kedia sitting in the first row just a few steps from the podium. I spoke about our current position and how it was connected with the Georgian experience following W.W. I when we had regained our lost sovereignty. I also spoke about the Georgian Legion then and now; about the problems the Liaison Staff was encountering and the efforts we were making to overcome them. I emphasized how much the Liaison Staff depended on the support of our friends in Germany but above all of the Georgian colonies in the west. Finally, I made a plea for unity. It was gratifying that after the meeting, many people approached me with a warm handshake, expressing best wishes and thanks for the speech; Misha Kedia's face was beaming.

On July 21st (about four days preceding the meeting) Kedia had visited me in our branch office in Paris to inform me about the failed putsch against Hitler just the day before. Kedia was afraid for the lives of some of our German friends; unfortunately, he was correct. Stauffenberg had been an immediate casualty, Schulenburg and others were to follow. Canaris survived longer.[280] I worried about Herwarth, knowing about his anti-Hitler views and closeness to Stauffenberg and Schulenburg. Fortunately and miraculously, Herwarth survived but several thousand patriots from the best German families lost their lives in connection with the putsch. It was a tragedy for us also, and we feared it would affect the mission of our Liaison Staff. Admiral Canaris had been dealt a blow already before the putsch. During the middle of February 1944, Hitler issued a decree to create a unified German Intelligence Service headed by Himmler. Canaris was no longer Chief of the Military Intelligence. In fact, the actual immediate boss of the intelligence was now Kaltenbrunner, Himmler being the overall chief of the SS.[281]

280- Canaris was arrested early August and remained in prison until shortly before the end of the war. He was executed in the early spring of 1945.

281- Alexander Dallin, *German Rule in Russia*, p. 28; Heinz Höhne, *Canaris: Patriot im Zwielicht*, Munich: Bertelsmann, 1976; Walter Schellenberg, *Hitler's Secret Service*, Moonachie, New Jersey: Pyramid, 1958.

15

SAVING THE GEORGIAN LEGIONNAIRES

Since my arrival in Paris, I had kept in touch with the staff of the Volunteer Units in the headquarters of the Supreme Commander of the West Front. From briefings I received during late July 1944, as I understood it, the war situation was volatile, especially in Normandy because of the forceful advances of the Western Allies there. Therefore the up-to-date locations of the Volunteer Units on the front was rather difficult to determine. Battalion 795, which had been attached to the German units in Cherbourg, came under heavy fire during the end of June. Reportedly, it sustained heavy casualties in dead and wounded and the survivors were taken prisoner; thus Battalion 795 no longer existed. The German commanding general in Cherbourg was also taken as a P.O.W., pointing out the overwhelming force and speed of the Western Allies. The word had spread that the Georgian legionnaires conducted themselves as good and dignified soldiers.

During early July, the Georgian Battalion 797, located further south in La Haye-du-Puits (Normandy) was engaged in battle as well and retreating slowly—direction south with the Germans. Here the German paratroops went on the counter offensive in the nearby Granville area. This considerably slowed the Western Allied Forces; the difficult terrain was probably a contributing factor as well. Nevertheless, the Allies continued further southeast, direction toward Saint-Lô at a slower pace. During the end of July the Allies approached Granville, further southwest; we calculated that the Georgian Battalion 797 may be in this area. I received permission and also a proposal from the Volunteer Units division of the Supreme Command West to find Battalion 797 and assist them as best I could. They were also wondering and wanted me to judge whether the Battalion's ability measured up to the current military situation; knowing this would probably be useful for other battalions, such as 798 in St. Nazaire, 799 in Périgueux and II/4 with the Georgian Legion in the Castres area. Our main goal was, however, to save lives. Non-commissioned officer Kako Alshibaja, a special aide during my trip to France, volunteered now to accompany me to this combat zone as well. He appeared to be well-qualified, being a battle-hardened master sergeant from the French Foreign Legion who spoke fluent French. He also had quite a personality, as seen from the following example: While in the French Legion, the newly appointed commander of his unit inspected the lined-up soldiers and would occasionally ask questions of some of them. He wanted to know Kako's ethnic origin. Kako simply said he was a Georgian. "Where is such a country?" the officer wanted to know. "Major Sir, I am not here to deliver geography lessons," answered Kako loud and clear. Some of his fellow soldiers thought that this was the reason Kako did not receive his commission.

On July 29th, we reported to the 7th Army headquarters in Le Mans and received clearance and briefing for our journey to the front. We arrived by car in Percy, west of Avranches, before sunrise. The headquarters of the 77th Division was near Avranches (southeast of Granville). The regiment which the Georgian Battalion 797 had been part of was expected to be in or near Granville but we did not find it there. Apparently, the Allied troops had recently broken through the German defense line and proceeded further south. We were approaching this area between Granville and Avranches from the southeast, in other words, from the German right flank, where the paratroopers had been on the offensive.

One could move slowly during the night but at 8:00 a.m. the low-flying Allied fighter planes started patrolling and strafing the roads of our area and beyond in all directions, almost continuously, dominating the skies completely. Many military vehicles lay burning on the roads and there were some human losses as well; for all practical purposes, traffic was paralyzed. An Army Corps liaison officer in whose auto we were passengers decided to turn back and advised us to do the same. Alshibaja and I decided to remain on a country road approximately six kilometers from Granville and we continued on foot. Soon we ran into the retreating sixty Georgian legionnaires from the supply service unit of I/253, who did not know much about the Georgian Battalion 797, which we were trying to find. The German Captain Buchreitz was in charge of this unit. The legionnaires reported to us that things were "not too bad," except for the physical abuse of some legionnaires by the German non-commissioned officers and therefore seven legionnaires had defected. The Captain and the Master Sergeant, however, had treated the legionnaires well. We found the Captain and had a short conference with him without witnesses. I told him that his Teutonic personnel, who probably imagined themselves to be supermen, could not treat legionnaires like slaves and expect them to perform like soldiers. If I were an abused legionnaire, I said, and if my commanding officer were unable to protect my rights as a soldier (since physical abuse is "verboten"), I would hit back and if they were stronger than I, then I would use a rifle butt or worse. The Captain was embarrassed and pledged to see to it that such an unlawful incidence would not happen again. However, he also pointed out some difficulties, noting that his unit consisted of other ethnic groups in addition to the Georgians. The Captain and his unit were retreating south; we bade them "God's speed" and we continued in the opposite direction. Alshibaja and I noted how pleased the sixty legionnaires were to hear words of encouragement from us in our native tongue.

Soon we could hear and actually observe the exchange of fire between the Allies and German soldiers. The latter were gradually retreating and by-passing us; the artillery first and the infantry following. We did not see the element of Battalion 797 among them. A retreating German officer told us that the Allies had already occupied the entire region north of us. So Kako and I had to turn around and follow the retreating troops. At 6:00 p.m. we reached the 77th Infantry Division's field headquarters, where the officer from the operations section informed us that according to an available report, the Georgian Battalion 797 had been captured by the Allies. He also said the Allied Forces were maneuvering around us trying to cut us off. Therefore, the Division's field headquarters would be located somewhere else. There was no place for us in their vehicles so Kako and I proceeded on foot. At sunset the retreating troops were directed toward Avranches—further south. The main road was jammed with military vehicles inching their way, but at least the low-flying planes were no longer harassing us due to the onset of darkness. Here we discovered the twelve Georgian legionnaires from Battalion 797 retreating in the same direction as the column. They told us that the battalion had to fight under the most difficult conditions, without the help of the antitank artillery or other auxiliary forces. There were many wounded and dead, others were surrounded by tanks and captured—only small groups were able to escape. We shook the hands of the legionnaires and told them to try to make it to the Legion's reserve headquarters in Castres, southern France and convey this message to others. If, in the meantime, they should find their commanding officers, Captain Petri and the Georgian ordnance officer, Lieutenant Lagidze, they should follow their orders. All twelve legionnaires were riding in retreating trucks and therefore moved gradually ahead of us while we continued on foot.

Kako and I arrived in Avranches by 7:00 a.m. to discover that the exit roads, direction south and east were already occupied by the Allied tanks. Apparently some Germans on vehicles were able to get out of Avranches during the night. Thorough observation of the perimeters revealed there was an area on the southeast where one probably could escape before the Allied "tankists" and low-flying fighters awoke—if one was willing to take a risk. I told Kako that I could not afford to become a P.O.W. since there were a number or obligations toward our people to be carried out, so we had better proceed quickly. As we returned to the center of the town, I noticed a colonel to whom we introduced ourselves. He was Colonel Wittenberg, commander of the former Regiment 1050; I was granted permission for a short conference with him. I reported to the Colonel about our observations concerning the partially occupied perimeters of Avranches by the Allied tanks and about my concern of becoming a prisoner unless we were able to leave before sunrise. He completely agreed and ordered a group of men headed by a non-commissioned officer to explore the possibility of getting out of Avranches from the southeast direction down the hill and simultaneously that the vehicles were to use the only meandering country road available leading to the lowland in the same direction. During this conversation, the only single German artillery gun which was retreating with the Colonel's soldiers fired and damaged one Allied tank that was spotted on the west side of town. (It caused damage to the tank but no human losses since no one happened to be in the tank.)

Kako and I followed the Colonel's men (about sixty of them); we progressed as far as the hill and then got Allied cross-fire from east and west. Here the Master Sergeant and his soldiers hesitated to continue further. We were losing momentum; therefore, I put myself ahead of the soldiers and with Kako following me, I loudly commanded the men to spread and follow us. I noticed several vehicles racing downhill on the country road, and we soon reached lower terrain out of harm's way. We cleared the top of the hill and picked up a more sheltered area and from there returned fire in both directions in order to somewhat protect the vehicles and to assist the Colonel's men in getting over the hill and thus out of the reach of hostile fire. On our way down the road to flat terrain, we crossed a small dried-out bay. Nearby, there was the village of Servon, where Colonel Wittenberg with his group caught up with us. From here we could clearly see the Allied Air Force repeatedly strafing Avranches. In Servon, the Master Sergeant Kako remembered that we had not eaten nor slept for two days. With his fluent French and imposing looks, he charmed the villagers like a sorcerer and received excellent food and drink for all of us (including the Colonel and his group). After such "picnicking," life appeared much more tolerable. Here we ran into a group of retreating paratroopers, a rugged appearing bunch and somewhat wild. They stopped the village priest walking toward a nearby town. We approached them, and Kako immediately assumed the role of a French interpreter. Some paratroopers suspected the "priest" of spying for the Allies or directing artillery fire against the troopers from the church tower. They were told that "such things were happening in Normandy." The "padre" assured them that he had no ill intentions toward them; he was just going to see his parishioners. Some troopers wanted to take the priest along as a prisoner and have him investigated. Kako and I thought this was as an example of wartime paranoid delusion. We informed the paratroopers of this and in the absence of their officer, ordered them to let the padre go. They complied, somewhat reluctantly.

On our way further south to Pontorson, we met a German master sergeant from the Georgian Battalion and he told us, in addition to what we already knew, that Battalion commander Captain Petri and the ordnance officer Lieutenant Lagidze had survived the battle near Bréhal but he did not know their present whereabouts. Needless to say we were happy about such good news. Colonel Wittenberg, Kako and I traveled over Pontorson and Sougeal and found the new field headquarters of the 77th Division's staff. We wanted to know about the current state of affairs in other Georgian units such as Battalions 823, 798 and 799 but the division staff had no such information. Therefore, we proceeded with many detours and other difficulties to the 7th Army headquarters in Le Mans and arrived there on August 3, 1944. I was received by Colonel Ceretti who I believe was the Chief of the Operation Section of the staff. I reported to him about our experience and based on this, made some recommendations. The summary of which was:

1. The Georgian Battalion 797 conducted itself during combat better than expected.

2. A plea was made to send the splinter groups of the legionnaires to Battalion 798, 799 or to the Georgian Legion in Castres (southern France) as feasible.

3. Under no circumstances should they be directed to the mixed units or to combat against the partisans, for many reasons.

It was my impression that Colonel Ceretti understood and agreed with this. He again strongly advised against my attempt of landing on Guernsey Island to see Battalion 823 because it would not be feasible. He also did not recommend our trip to Battalion 798 in St. Nazaire and said that should we manage to get there, the Battalion was unlikely to be there because of the ever-changing military situation.[282]

In Le Mans, a pleasant surprise awaited us; we found Captain Petri, (the German Commanding Officer of Battalion 797) and his Georgian adviser,

---

282- Ceretti explained that parallel to Normandy, the Allies had advanced in Brittany, southeast direction as well. In retrospect, it was General Patton's 3rd Army which progressed further south in Brittany. On August 2nd, he approached Rennes and after taking it, on August 4th advanced on Vannes. Four days later, the XXth Corps advanced toward Angers and Nantes almost immediately cutting off St. Nazaire, where the Georgian Battalion 798 was stationed. The same day, Le Mans, which was Colonel Ceretti's former headquarters, was taken by the Allies as well; see *The World Almanac of World War II.*

Lieutenant David (Datha) Lagidze. Their account of the events further confirmed our impressions. It is my recollection that Datha now wanted to see his wife, Thamar, and their delightful little daughter, Manana, in Paris; and after that, he wanted to travel with Captain Petri to the Georgian Legion headquarters in Castres. Kako and I also left for Paris; we had gained considerable experience during our journey and were impressed by the formidable human resources and war material the Allies had amassed in France, including the Air Force. It was clear to us that the German armed forces would not be able to stop them and France would be taken over by the Western Allies in a relatively short time. We felt reasonably secure about our emigres but what lay ahead for the legionnaires who survived the battle so far and those in Allied hands as P.O.W.s? We could only hope for humane treatment and understanding. As previously discussed, the Liaison Staff had no jurisdiction over creating the Legion and its field battalions nor about their location. We could only advise and ask the German Army High Command, on behalf of the legionnaires, our only conduit being the General of the Volunteer Units, Köstring. In him, Herwarth and their staffs, we had wholehearted support and protection; their doors were open for us, without which the existence of the Military Department of the Georgian Liaison Staff would make no sense at all. But even Köstring's magic hat could not always be effective, especially during such a critical military situation such as the one in France.[283] In Paris, I visited, discussed and also submitted a written report with recommendations to the Volunteer Units Command in the headquarters of the Supreme Commander West, a copy of which I forwarded to Köstring. During verbal discussion in the headquarters, I strongly emphasized the need of getting Battalion 799 out of Périgueux before it was too late and emphasized that they should be kept near the reserve "regiment," the Legion in Castres in south France and then to play by ear about moving them out of France to Germany.

I also had a conference about this matter with Kedia, Alexandre Asatiani and Lieutenant Alimbarashvili from "Bergmann," who happened to be in Paris. A. Asatiani one of the leaders of the Georgian National Democrat Party was a courageous man and dedicated to the Georgian cause. He also knew Prince Irakli

---

283- Two informative examples of the situation are: First, Field Marshal Gunther von Kluge, the German Supreme Commander of the whole Western Front, during mid August was forced to take cover from Allied air attack for most of the day while attempting to visit the front—without success. Second, in Brittany, the German General Fehrenbacher's XXV Corps (unable to connect with other German troops) pulled back to four major ports, among them Lorient and St. Nazaire (he was able to hold these two ports until the end of the war); see *The World Almanac of World War II*. It was in this area that the Georgian Battalion 798 was located before the Allied landing. Presumably those who survived the battle had been taken P.O.W. by the Allies. It is not known if some of the legionnaires were also among the XXV Corps soldiers who retreated to the above-mentioned ports. Battalion 823 remained on the Channel Island Guernsey; one would assume that at some point and with the German garrison they were taken P.O.W. by the Allies, hopefully without many human losses.

Bagrationi, who resided in Spain, was well connected with Spanish aristocracy and had claims on the Georgian throne.[284] I thought A. Asatiani, a civilian, with Lieutenant Alimbarashvili's assistance should travel to the Georgian Legion in Castres and observe the situation there. In case the German leadership no longer had control over the situation and the legionnaires were in danger, Asatiani was to organize help. This would be in close cooperation with Colonel Machts (commander of the 1st Volunteer Reserve Regiment), Colonel Sharabidze (the Georgian commander of the Georgian Legion) and their staffs.

Mountainous southern France harbored many French partisans but the Georgian legionnaires had not fought against them and were nice to the civilian population. Therefore, I did not anticipate serious hostility toward us, especially from General de Gaulle's followers. If need be, Asatiani with the legionnaires would cross the nearby Pyrenees to Spain and would then contact Prince I. Bagrationi for help through his influential friends.[285] This plan did not have a chance, since due to continuous bombing by the Allies it took ten days (instead of the customary ten hours) for Asatiani and Alimbarashvili to get near the targeted area.

During those ten days, significant changes took place in the Georgian Legion. The background of it was that on August 15th, the Allied Forces landed on the Mediterranean coast of Southern France, east of Marseilles. General de Gaulle's French troops[286] also landed from sea and air in the same region. This was not far from Castres, where the Georgian Legion was lodged. The German troops in South France were weak, air support was missing and they were obviously no match against the Allies. The legionnaires knew about this and could not save the German Armed Forces from defeat now, even if they wanted to. The time had come, they felt, to save themselves and go back home to Georgia as soon as possible. Here again some of them felt that the solution would be to organize a Bolshevik cell, "faithful to Stalin" and somehow credibly document it. If so, they hoped all "sins" would be forgiven, such as the fact of becoming a P.O.W. in German hands and (the very "original sin") being a part of the Georgian Legion, which had been fighting the Red Army on the East Front. To fortify such an impression of "faithfulness" one had to engage in the Communist partisan activities and fight against the German Armed Forces.

284- Irakli Bagrationi was one of the Caucasian personalities who had been invited to Berlin by Count Schulenburg from the German Foreign Ministry during April of 1942. Schulenburg intended to form committees for each Caucasian nation, thereby influencing the German East Policy in a positive direction. Schulenburg favored I. Bagrationi who traveled to Berlin to be President of the Georgian Committee. As noted in a preceding chapter, Schulenburg's attempt failed because it did not conform with the Nazi East Policy. Bagrationi left Berlin but nevertheless he demonstrated his concern for the Georgian cause.

285- See Asatiani's personal letter to the author in his personal archives.

286- Under the command of General de Lattre de Tassigny.

Therefore, the Communist French partisan connections would be helpful. But there were other legionnaires in Castres who thought that all of this would lead to nothing good and also would be ethically wrong, especially since Colonel Machts had treated them so well.

Around this time, halfway between Castres and Marseilles, in the coastal city of Montpellier, two Georgian lieutenants met; Irakli Alimbarashvili and Givi Porakishvili. Irakli wanted to reach the Georgian Legion as instructed by us in Paris with A. Asatiani. Givi had just left Castres as ordered to reach the Georgian Battalion II/138 in Verona Italy, where he would serve as an officer. As Givi recalls (A. Asatiani was not with Irakli during that particular meeting), Givi had advised Irakli to abandon the idea of going to Castres, join him and go to Italy because of a very serious military threat to the Castres area. Irakli did not accept such a suggestion and proceeded in the direction of Castres.[287] After the war, I learned from A. Asatiani about the impossibility of fulfillment of their mission as discussed above. Later, I also learned that, thank the Lord, Irakli somehow had survived. He certainly was one of the most kind, friendly and good-natured persons I have ever met.

I had received a very interesting report about the situation in the Georgian Legion covering the same period from an eyewitness, non-commissioned officer, Petre Kvedelidze, who was a helper, friend and confidant of Colonel Lado Sharabidze, the Georgian commander of the Georgian Legion. Petre Khvedelidze and his colleagues from the "Brandenburg" regiment were honorably discharged from there during the process of reorganization of the Eastern Volunteer Units. They were referred to the Georgian Legion in Castres during mid spring of 1944. Some other volunteers who had been separated from their units were also directed to the Legion (a reserve unit), including several soldiers from "Bergmann." Increasing polarization and hostility became obvious between the Bolshevik-oriented legionnaires and those who were anti Bolshevik. It is fair to say that as a rule the anti-Bolshevik soldiers had better military training. They had also been treated on equal terms with the German members (personnel) in their units (for instance, "Bergmann" and "Brandenburg"). Also the principle of volunteerism had been observed more strictly during the recruitment. On Petre's suggestion, Colonel Sharabidze discussed this matter with the regimental commander Colonel Machts and in order to prevent a potential "bloodshed between brothers," the anti-Bolsheviks were transferred to different units. Only Petre and a few newly arrived soldiers from "Bergmann" and "Brandenburg" remained with the Legion in Castres. Recognizing that danger still lay ahead, Colonel Machts apparently at some point wisely and courageously began

---

287- See the personal communication with G. Porakishvili in the author's archives.

negotiations with the French patriots, the non-communist followers of General de Gaulle in the resistance movement, asking for understanding and peace.

Colonel Sharabidze felt it necessary to warn the Bolshevik oriented legionnaires and for this he dispatched Petre Khvedelidze to the nearby town of Albi, where interesting enough, several Georgian legionnaire doctors were also part of the Bolshevik organization. The Colonel's message was clear, "The Germans know what you are up to; you had better stop such activities or they are going to send you to the P.O.W. camps." Petre also added on his own that whatever they were doing, it would not buy them freedom from the Soviet rulers. It was obviously a well-intentioned and fair warning addressed to them from their own benevolent countrymen. The doctors who met Petre kept poker faces and had no comments.

Colonel Machts had a meeting with Colonel Sharabidze, First Lieutenant Machts and a few other officers. He told them approximately as follows, "We will not be able to fight on our way to Spain nor join the German fighting troops in the north or the east of us. Moreover, if we do not disarm our legionnaires soon, the newly 'born again communists' and their anti communist countrymen will shoot each other. After disarmament, those in favor of going back home to the U.S.S.R. may do so. Others may ask for help from the Georgian government in exile in Paris." So the legionnaires were ordered to line up and were then taken to attend a lecture. Upon returning to their quarters, they discovered that their firearms had been collected and taken away. (In fact, on the orders of Colonel Machts, they were handed over to de Gaulle's non communist French resistance movement. This frightened some legionnaires who thought that first they were disarmed and now they were going to be shot. Petre assured them that there was no danger of this; indeed, the legionnaires were bused to a mountainous area two hours away from Castres, where they were given lodging. During the end of August, the "communist-oriented legionnaires" received permission (from the French non-communist authorities) to transfer to the special camp for former Soviet citizens who would be repatriated.

The legionnaires who did not wish to be repatriated were lodged in quarters on the outskirts of Castres. In this group, however, there was a small subgroup (probably of twenty persons) who behaved in a bizarre way. For some reason, they were unable to join the communist group or did not join at first and wanted to join now. Therefore they set out to harass and persecute the leaders of the non-communist group such as Colonel Sharabidze and people around him. This they did presumably to get acceptance by the communist group as a reward for such despicable deeds. Due to the help of benevolent and kind people and having endured much unpleasantness, the final outcome for Colonel Sharabidze's group was good and they were able to remain in the west. They loved their country deeply, hoping one day she would also gain freedom as the western civilized nations had; this was their motive all along. Until then, their return to Georgia would mean torture and death or in the "best case" remote, life-long gulag.[288]

Our friends from the Georgian Colony in Paris realized that some of us would be leaving soon for Germany and perhaps we would never see each other again. There was a touching outpouring of affection for us preceding our departure. The number of daily visitors in our office had increased greatly; some of them even had practical or politically oriented advice for me. For instance, Tengiz Dadeshkeliani's daughter Irina had a plan that she would volunteer in the International Red Cross in order to help us, the "soldier boys." An unusual and bizarre suggestion came from Kako Nijaradze who worked in the "cafeteria" of our branch office, as noted before. He was a convinced "practicing" Bolshevik but nevertheless had been sheltered by the Georgian Colony which had been traditionally tolerant to displaced people. Nijaradze said that since German defeat now was inevitable, I should join "his side." I would be promoted to a major of the Red Army and take part in the historic battle of the Soviet Union against Anglo-American imperialism. When I realized this was not a joke, I told him that he was just being utilitarian, he obviously did not know me well, that I thought Bolshevism would in time be defeated, and that the only hope we had were the Anglo-American "imperialists." After the war, I learned that K. Nijaradze returned to the Soviet Union. From there he wrote to his father (an old emigre) and encouraged him to return to Soviet Georgia; the father followed his son's advice. I only hope that no harm came to the old man and for that matter to his son in spite of Kako's Bolshevik party affiliation—I never again heard about either of them.

I unexpectedly met another convinced Georgian communist in Paris who grew up there in a emigre family, Sergo Tsuladze. This meeting took place during one of several small parties given in our honor. This particular party was hosted by Mr. and Mrs. Tarasashvili, the brother-in-law and the sister of Sergo Tsuladze, who also had been invited—not necessarily because of his political views. Other guests were Tengiz Dadeshkeliani, his sister Kati and their cousin Ilamaz Dadeshkeliani. It was delightful to see Ilamaz, who had been ailing and who therefore I was unable to see during my previous trip to Paris. He now felt much better and was a remarkably intelligent, handsome gentleman and a respected lawyer. Our parents had been

288- See Petre Kvedelidze's written communication in the author's personal archives. I am grateful for his contribution. As I understand it, he has completed his memoir. [See note p. 267 —Ed.] I believe he will better and in much more detail report the drama surrounding the "sundown" of the Georgian Legion in Castres. Later on, I shall say more about Colonel Machts and compare his way of solving a serious crises to one in the Legion Battalion 822.

friends, and I remembered seeing their photos in our family album where Ilamaz appeared to be in his early teens; we had so much to talk about. Afterwards, I turned my attention to Sergo Tsuladze with whom I had an even longer discussion. Of course, he was a convinced communist but without an aggressive tone and was tolerant of my views, which were contrary to his. I based my arguments on personal experience having lived in the communist state, which was more than he could claim. Neither of us convinced the other, nevertheless we parted on friendly terms. [289]

The time then came for leaving Paris. Thina Dadiani-Gomarthely courageously decided to travel with us to Berlin and join her husband, Captain Misha (Mikheil) Dadiani there. I had promised Misha, while on a visit to Athens during the middle of June 1944, to safely deliver Thina to his loving care. She was all packed and waiting and I had better keep that promise. On August 23rd in the early evening, Kako Schavgulidze (Chavgoulidze), M. Kedia's business associate and friend, drove the four of us, Thina Dadiani, M. Kedia, Kako Alshibaja and I to the Gare de l'Est in Paris. [290] There a young man, Theimuraz Tsulukidze was unexpectedly waiting for us, pleading with us to take him to Berlin so he could reunite with his father, Phridon—we could not refuse. Near the railroad station and other streets, the members of the French Resistance were already shooting. In spite of this, the train rolled out of the station—direction east. The train continued after sunrise, but the passengers had to flee into the fields beside the tracks several times because of low-flying Allied planes over us. But for some reason, they chose not to attack our train. We arrived in Berlin without losses or injury.

First Lieutenant (later Captain) Dimitri Shalikashvili had been assigned to the branch office of the Georgian Liaison Staff in Paris as a military advisor. In this capacity he had to work with the director D. Djuruli while keeping in close touch with the Paris Office of the Volunteer Formations, which was attached to the staff of the Army Command West. While there, he met with his opposites from the Armenian, Azerbaijan, North Caucasian and Russian staffs. During our stay in France, M. Kedia and I spent considerable time with Dimitri and became very fond of him. He was a true gentleman with an excellent background, upbringing

---

289- After the war, Sergo went to Georgia with his wife, who happened to be a French communist. He remained in Tbilisi, taught French there. He also translated Rustaveli from Georgian to French—not a small task and certainly a remarkable contribution to the cause of making Georgian culture better known to the French people. When it was our turn to invite people, D. Djuruli organized it in our branch office. This was so well attended that soon there were no vacant seats available. We toasted each other in a typical Georgian manner. The bottom line was that we would remain friends regardless of what was to come.

290- From here on my "mini diary" is very spotty at best, but I am probably correct about the date of our departure from Paris. Incidentally, when K. Schavgulidze returned to his parking place, he discovered that his car had been stolen.

and military training as a cavalry officer in Poland. His older brother, Major David, now deceased, had been a much respected officer in the French Foreign Legion. Dimitri was conscientious and a diplomat by nature. While in Paris, M. Kedia and I once told him "half-jokingly" that the time would come when we would need him as our Ambassador-speaker to explain to the British about our problems and quest. This turned out to be a "prophecy" since Captain Dimitri Shalikashvili had to play such a role during the end of the war while in Italy, where we sent him on a mission, as we shall see later. Dimitri was evacuated from Paris with the staff of the Army headquarters by army automobiles but it took him two or three days longer to reach Berlin than it did us by train. He continued in the same position in the Georgian Liaison Staff in Berlin; it was good to have him there again.

From General Köstring's headquarters in Potsdam, we received very good news that the Georgian Battalion 799 had made its way from France into German territory. The battalion's German commander took ill and therefore, Captain Siko (Simon) Kobiashvili, at that time an ordnance officer, took over the command. He, against all odds, led the battalion out of France, overcoming many difficulties. Battalion 799 was now directed to the German military training quarters in Neuhammer.

Meanwhile, reports reached our office in Berlin that the Polish patriots staged an uprising and the insurgent army was fighting the German forces bitterly in the streets of Warsaw. I immediately went to Potsdam and met Lieutenant Colonel Röpke, the head of the Operations Division in General Köstring's staff. I told him that regardless of what the circumstances were, neither the Georgian Battalion 799 nor any other Georgian unit should be used against the Polish insurgent army and that this is where the buck was going to stop. I told him that we, the Georgians, have had a special relationship with the Poles. The majority of our emigre Georgian officers in the Legion's battalions had served in the Polish Army. Röpke understood immediately and promised firmly that he would take the appropriate steps at once. I also asked him to notify me should he fail in his attempt and he promised to do so. It was not the first nor the last time that I had asked Röpke for his support concerning the Georgian units but he probably seldom saw me so worried.[291] Röpke kept his promise as usual, and later on Battalion 799 was transferred to Denmark and remained there as a coastal defense force. This move at that time also saved that unit from falling into the hands of the advancing Red Army.

291- Neuhammer, where Battalion 799 was now lodged is in Silesia and not all that far from Warsaw. Therefore, it was entirely possible that Battalion 799 would be pulled into the battle by some regional commanding officer because of the shortage of military manpower. I was told that this actually happened to some indigenous units who were just passing by and were originally headed for different assignments.

The Warsaw Uprising created a very dangerous situation for everyone who resided there, including the Georgian families for whom things were further compounded due to the approaching Red Army. The Liaison Staff put forth much effort to help them and their Polish friends as well. I came to know a number of Georgian refugees from Poland in Germany, among them the Generals Koniashvili and Zakariadze and Colonel Kutateladze, who had a beautiful wife of Polish descent; I profited from their counsel. Professor Doctor Giorgi (Gogi) Nakashidze, who at that time was the President of the Georgian Colony in Warsaw, expediently organized evacuation of the Georgians from Poland to Germany, in close cooperation with our Liaison Staff. But for a variety of reasons, not all of them left or could leave Poland. Among them was Dimitri Shalikashvili's family which, needless to say was of great concern for Dimitri. The city of Warsaw had been surrounded and bombed by German forces. The insurgent forces were badly outnumbered and out-gunned, but in spite of this, the gallant Polish patriots fought courageously as usual. The city was without vital utilities, food and adequate medical help. Close to the city, on the east bank of the Vistula River, stood the "Liberating Great Red Army" watching this obviously uneven battle between the Polish patriots and the German armed forces. They never made an attempt to help the Poles, which, of course, fitted well within Stalin's postwar political design to have Poland left in the hands of the "obedient" Polish Communist government. If the non-communist insurgents were wiped out by the Germans, so much the better. The Western Allies, on the other hand, air-lifted and parachuted badly needed supplies, but some of these fell to German hands. The Polish insurgence, in retrospect, was terribly miscalculated by their political leaders. After heavy losses and with a hopeless outlook for the brave Poles, a cease fire was concluded between them and the Germans. At last, Dimitri and other Georgians were able to travel to Poland and search for their families. After overcoming many difficulties and frustrations, the Shalikashvilis were finally reunited. While Dimitri resumed his work in the Georgian Liaison Staff in Berlin, the rest of his family settled down at their relatives' estate in the delightful, historical town of Pappenheim in Bavaria.[292]

The Georgian Liaison Staff also had a medico-sanitary department, the director of which was Doctor David Chataraishvili. His duties were to inspect the

292- Mrs. Missy (Maria) Shalikashvili's mother, herself Countess Rudiger was the older sister of Countess von Pappenheim, whose family owned an estate with castles in the town of Pappenheim in Bavaria. Missy's and Dimitri's family included, in addition to Countess Rudiger, older and younger sons, Othar and John (Malkhaz) respectively and the youngest member was daughter Alexandra. The Pappenheims received their refugee relatives the Shalikashvilis with open arms. The children started in school, and soon they all felt at home. After the war, my wife and I visited them in Pappenheim and were delighted to see how well they had adjusted to their new life. My wife's family and the Shalikashvilis were old friends, and I was a comparatively new one but gradually we became "old friends" as well.

hospitals and assess the quality of medical care received by the Georgian legionnaires and also assist the civilians in securing proper medical care. Due to his duties he had to travel frequently but nevertheless he found time to work in the well-known Charita Hospital in Berlin as a volunteer-assistant physician (a resident—without pay). This way, David kept furthering his qualifications as a physician. Mrs. Badu Tsulukidze, M.D., who had been employed in the Charita for a number of years (and whom we mentioned before) helped him in obtaining such a position. David kept in close contact with the Georgian M.D.s who resided in Germany at that time and periodically sent medical news letters to all of us in order to keep his colleagues up-to-date about modern German pharmaceuticals, etc.

I knew David from Tbilisi, where both of us were medical school students. I graduated one year before him. He had a very good reputation for his scholastic achievements and also for being an honest and dependable fellow. During the Tbilisi days, two events that took place made me feel especially kind toward him. First and most important, his father and mine were both arrested during the 1937 "purges," and we never saw them again. I felt a special solidarity and bond toward such persecuted families. The second was his participation in the outing of the medical school's alpine group which I had organized for the students with the help of the Georgian Alpine Club. The first ascent took place on Mt. Kazbek during early summer; the weather was good, and the students had a great time. David participated in the second expedition on Mt. Khabarjina during late October. The weather turned wretched, creating all kinds of problems for us. The alpine group from the "Spartacus" sports organization had joined us during the ascent under the leadership of the legendary master alpinist, Aliosha Djaparidze. Although the medical group had no losses, two men from the "Spartacus" died of exhaustion and exposure. Such an experience brings people closer, promoting friendships.

Therefore, I was glad to see David in Berlin during December of 1943, where he had come while on vacation from the German military unit in Ukraine. His German commanding officer sent a companion along with him, a German non-commissioned officer whose family lived in Berlin. The doctor and his companion went for lunch at the Russian restaurant, "Medved"—("The Bear") in Berlin. It so happened that the Georgian non-commissioned officer, Aliosha Abashidze, who worked in the Liaison Staff was also having his lunch at the "Medved." Here for the first time, David heard from Aliosha about the Georgian Liaison Staff and the Georgians in Berlin, among them his friends, Dr. Gede Astaiani and me. Within the next couple of days Misha Kedia, Mikho Alshibaja, Gogi Magalow (Magalashvili) and I met David in the Hotel Adlon. We listened to David and told him our story as well. My three above-mentioned friends were all impressed by David (as I was but I had known him previously from Georgia). We decided that he would be an excellent choice to be the head of the medico-sanitary division of the Georgian Liaison Staff and David accepted this position. We proposed to the appropriate German office, and they agreed that Dr. David Chataraishvili be discharged from military service in order for him to be more flexible while pursuing his new duty, which he carried out conscientiously and with dedication, which was so characteristic of him.[293]

293- Dr. Chataraishvili, who served as a military doctor in the Soviet Army had been taken as a P.O.W. by the advancing German Army in the Ukraine during the summer of 1942. Because of the shortness of physicians and of German-speaking P.O.W.s he was employed as an interpreter and also as an auxiliary physician of the German Battalion as of September 21, 1942. While the Germans retreated during late fall and early winter of 1942, and since the German battalion's doctor was on vacation, Dr. Chataraishvili (who also spoke fluently in German) was entrusted to carry out the German military doctor's duties. During the heavy combat conditions that followed, he demonstrated courage and unselfishness, ignoring personal danger while under enemy fire and cared for the wounded soldiers on the battlefield. He was credited by the German battalion's commanding officer with saving several wounded soldiers' lives by delivering early medical care to them. For this he was awarded a special medal for the Eastern volunteers. (See the copies of war-time as well as after-war documents in the author's archives.)

Shortly before the end of the war, during the process of the evacuation of the Liaison Staff, David went to Karlsbad and worked there as a doctor. There were two other Georgian doctors there, Gede Asatiani and Gogi (Giorgi) Vepkhvadze. During the chaotic end of the war, while in the process of their work as M.D.s, they met Russian doctors from the Red Army. In a show of humanity, collegiately and courage, the Russians warned their Georgian colleagues not to fall in Soviet hands or it may be the end of them. It was very easy to convince David, who immediately emphasized this information to other Georgians in Karlsbad, adding his own similar advice. The advice was followed by two others, however, Gogi pursued some additional "research" on his own first.

After the war, David settled in Munich where he started work in university hospitals training in the specialty of obstetrics and gynecology. A few years later, the Bavarian government, in an admirable display of sympathy toward displaced foreign doctors, issued the regulation according to which such doctors were permitted to undergo an examination at Munich University and if successful, a diploma of that university would be issued to the applicants. At that time, I was in the middle of training in the specialty of general surgery in German hospitals in Lauingen and Augsburg (Bavaria). David advised me about the rare opportunity at Munich University and urged me to do it. We both took this exam and were able to pass it.

16

END OF THE WAR

During September of 1944, the military department of the Georgian Liaison Staff and our other Caucasian counterparts were reassessing the situation of the Caucasian military units. By now, almost all of them had sustained prohibitive human losses.[294] We were hoping that, at least, the legionnaires who were taken as P.O.W.s by the Western powers would be treated by them according to the Geneva Convention and thus many lives would be saved. From this time on, the already existing consultation and cooperation between the Caucasian representatives were further deepened. During this time, Captain Misha Dadiani, whose transfer from "Bergmann" to the Liaison Staff had been requested by us, arrived in Berlin from Greece. We enjoyed having Misha with us, but above all we enjoyed observing his reunion with his wife, Thina (whom M. Kedia and I brought with us from Paris, as noted). Their happiness had no bounds; they did not even mind the frequent air raids over Berlin.

In close cooperation with General Köstring's staff in Potsdam, especially with Captain Siegfried Ungermann (the head of the personnel department), we were preparing ground for M. Dadiani to take over the command of the Georgian Battalion II/189 in Italy. This was part of the plan according to which Captain Vano Bakradze would be appointed commanding officer of the Georgian Battalion 799 in Neuhammer; Captain Simon (Siko) Kobiashvili was to be a commander of the Georgian Legion, which was again being put together from the splinter groups of other units, with First Lieutenant David (Datha) Lagidze second in command after Kobiashvili. Our efforts for getting "Bergmann" out of the Balkans and locating it in a safer place continued.

294- "Report about the Caucasian Military Units in the German Armed Forces" was submitted by this author to the Caucasian committee as requested by them and which formed the basis for their memorandum to the appropriate German authorities.

Meanwhile, with the help of General Köstring's staff, we tried to streamline "Bergmann" by assigning its separated soldiers to other units and not returning them to "Bergmann." We also had an ongoing dialogue with our other Caucasian counterparts and General Köstring concerning the possibility of forming the Caucasian Regiment from battalions already in existence, which would later be a nucleus of the "Caucasian Army" with its logistic and many other advantages.

During the middle of September, I visited the Georgian Field Battalion II/198 in Verona, northern Italy. Although I had a number of reports concerning this unit, I personally had never seen it before. In Verona, I was introduced to the acting commanding officer of the battalion, Captain von Müller, since the commanding officer, Major Schulz was ailing and had to enter the hospital. Captain von Müller was a well-mannered, friendly gentleman who also understood his legionnaires, treated them with respect and was dedicated to them. All five Georgian officers liked him, and I could see why. After several conversations with him, it was clear to me that he did not share the Nazi ideology and prejudices, making his job smoother while in Eastern formation.

Lieutenant Archil Dadiani had been appointed to the battalion's staff as the ordnance officer, and in this capacity he was an adviser to the commanding officer of the battalion. He also conducted lectures for the legionnaires in old as well as modern Georgian history with an emphasis on the relationship between Georgia and its neighbors. This had considerable impact on the legionnaires, who had been deprived of the true history while under Soviet rule. Indirectly and cautiously but nevertheless effectively, it also clarified the fallacies of the cannibalistic Nazi propaganda. Other Georgian officers were distributed as follows: Lieutenant Leo Metreveli in the 1st Company with Captain von Müller, Zurab Abdushelishvili in command of the 2nd Company, Lieutenant Givi Porakishvili in the 3rd Company with Lieutenant König, Lieutenant Irakli Kontridze in the 4th Company with Lieutenant Müller. After a brief respite in Verona, the battalion began intensive military training especially for the non-commissioned officers. Moreover A. Dadiani kept up his lectures regularly and the Georgians started taking German lessons while the German personnel concentrated on the Georgian language, for better mutual understanding.

I remained in Verona for three or four days, observed the battalion and spent as much time as feasible with the officers and the legionnaires. I also enjoyed excellent hospitality and its backdrop—the remarkable city of Verona with its old towers, not unlike ones in "my" Svaneti, as if a huge, painted curtain hung some distance from us. I left for Berlin with a relatively comfortable feeling about Battalion II/198, as far as its safety was concerned. Its main activity had been to guard important bridges, roads and railroads from Italian guerrillas. So far the loss of human lives had not been heavy on either side, and we hoped that this would remain so. My visit to Verona convinced me that if the Battalion would be placed completely under Georgian command the legionnaires would do all right. They, of course, would need a German liaison officer, an accountant and a few secretaries for paperwork. The Georgian Field Battalion II/198 had its failures and successes in the past but generally speaking performed satisfactorily.[295]

I next visited the Georgian Battalion 799 in Neuhammer-Silesia (Germany). They were housed in military barracks and were receiving additional training. As already discussed, this battalion had made its way from France to Germany under the most adverse military conditions, holding together well during its meandering retreat between the advancing Western Allied troops. It will be recalled that Battalion 799 was among several other similar Georgian units that M. Alshibaja and I had visited while on our trip to France during December of 1943 and we were favorably impressed by it. General Köstring and his staff were agreeable to our suggestion of placing certain battalions under Georgian command but this took a couple of months to implement. When I informed Bakradze and Kobiashvili concerning this matter, they did not quite believe that the Germans would agree to it. During my second visit to Neuhammer, W. von Kutzschenbach accompanied me. We found Siko Kobiashvili recuperating following major surgery for a perforated duodenal ulcer. He had been discharged from the hospital and was under the loving care of his wife, Khira.[296]

During the fall of 1944, when it was obvious that the German defeat was inevitable, Himmler began to promote Vlasov. In this he apparently was gradually influenced by thoughts of Gunther d'Alquin, who was one of a "new breed" of SS officers. As the head of an SS unit of war correspondents, whose reporting impressed Himmler, d'Alquin came to the conclusion that political warfare was needed now and he made efforts to "convert" Himmler[297]—with success, but it was at least two years too late. Already during late December of 1942, facing German military disaster in Stalingrad, German military propaganda had broadcast about

---

295- See Captain von Müller's report, "The Georgian Field-Battalion II/198," in the author's personal archives and also in the Bundesarchiv in Freiburg, Germany ("Militärgeschichtliches Forschungsamt").

296- Mrs. Khira Kobiashvili, the daughter of General Bakradze was not only beautiful but also intelligent, courageous, an independent thinker and very capable of coping with the critical situations of life, which in spite of her young age, she had already experienced several times and had been able to overcome. I had met Khira in Berlin as a refugee from Poland but Kutzschenbach had not and he appeared to be very impressed by her. She and Siko had two darling children; a daughter, Maiko and a son, Zurab. Being the elder, Maiko was, to a certain extent, "mothering" her brother and had a couple of loving nicknames for him.

297- Alexander Dallin, *Soviet Rule in Russia*, pp. 603–604.

the captured Soviet Army General Vlasov, now a P.O.W., who under German sponsorship formed the Smolensk Committee in order to organize the Russian opposition against Stalin and his Bolshevik oppressive system. Formation of the Russian Liberation Army (ROA) was also lauded, and it found many supporters among the influential Germans, especially among the military. It was clear to them that victory over the Soviet State by German military power alone would not be possible. There was only one solution; to form an honest alliance with the disillusioned Soviet people against Stalin's Bolshevik tyranny—to overthrow it and offer to the people a State with appealing human rights and economic conditions. This, of course, would also entail a radical change of the inhuman Nazi design for the people of the Eastern territories, but Hitler had adamantly refused such suggestions. The last such proposal appeared to have been especially well-coordinated, had broad support and included not only the military but as incredible as it may seem, even Minister Rosenberg. But Hitler again refused, and his refusal was aimed not only at Vlasov but at the non-Russian national committees as well.[298] Consequently, Vlasov's name and his movement only had been used for German propaganda purposes and at times without Vlasov's prior knowledge.

The "Russian Liberation Army" (ROA) in fact did not exist at that time since all volunteer soldiers of Russian and non-Russian origin served in the German Army either on an individual basis or in the small national units, not larger than a battalion, that were attached to the German divisions.[299] But now, when the German defeat was obviously unavoidable, Himmler made up his mind to promote Vlasov, which the SS went about with considerable vigor. In the autumn of 1944, Vlasov was permitted to create the committee for the "Liberation of the Peoples of Russia" and at the founding congress in Prague, he proclaimed a manifesto.[300] Vlasov now was allowed to have the "Russian Liberation Army" (ROA) consisting of two divisions. General Köstring was asked to help in forming those divisions and he in turn, appointed Colonel Heinz Danko Herre (his former chief of staff) to carry out this task.[301]

Meanwhile the SS was pressing the non-Russian representatives to join

---

298- Alexander Dallin, *German Rule in Russia*, pp. 574–576. Among the documents quoted, there is the letter from Keitel to Rosenberg on June 1943, which reads: "(1) The National Committees are not to be used for the recruitment of volunteers. (2) Vlasov is not to appear in the occupied territory. (3) For the continuation of the Vlasov propaganda operation, the Führer has not refused his consent only insofar as none of the points of the Vlasov Program are to be carried out without the Führer's express sanction. No German agency must take seriously the bait (Lockmittel) contained in the thirteen points of the "Vlasov Program."

299- There were few exceptions; for instance, General Pannwitz's Cossack Cavalry Division and Turkestani Division 162.

300- Prague was picked up as a symbol because the Pan-Slavic Congresses had been held there in the past.

301- For details, see Herwarth; Dallin; and Dr. Joachim Hoffmann *Die Geschichte der Wlassow—Armee, POA 2*, unaltered edition, Freiburg im Breisgau: Rombach, 1984.

Vlasov. But from the very beginning, the position of the Caucasians remained clear. They had welcomed General Vlasov's 1942 Smolensk Declaration, considering this to be a potential milestone in overthrowing the Kremlin Bolshevik tyranny. Expecting the German leadership to follow Vlasov's other suggestions at once, the Caucasians were ready to join in discussions with him at the "round table" as equal partners. They also expected him to recognize the sovereignty of their respective countries. Without this, the Caucasians would not be representing the majority views of their people abroad, including the national alliances and the governments in exile and likely the views of the people in the Caucasus. If need be, a plebiscite of the Caucasian people would be held concerning this matter after the war.

The Caucasian coordinating committee was established and M. Kedia elected as their speaker. In this capacity he had to attend the meeting with Vlasov. Before going there, Kedia communicated with other directors of the Georgian Liaison Staff and a select group of our co-workers. He also received input from other Georgian political leaders who were present in Berlin at that time. He told them that the Caucasian committee would not accept the suggestion to join Vlasov's committee, unless the latter first recognize the sovereignty of the Caucasian nations. Kedia also said that according to his information, in the case of such refusal, there was a real possibility of him and his followers being arrested by the SS. Therefore, he left it up to us to choose our own position concerning this matter.[302] Of course, we all assured Kedia of our complete support for him. Victor Homeriki, who was on a short visit to Berlin and now on his way back to the Balkans, also strongly endorsed M. Kedia's policy. He told me, "Let the SS arrest you people; it will be the frosting on the cake for all your deeds."

During the Kedia-Vlasov meeting that took place against the former's wish, a powerful SS representative, Kaltenbrunner, participated. In a threatening voice, he tried to intimidate Kedia and force him into submission to join the committee for the Liberation of the Peoples of Russia under Vlasov. In this, Kaltenbrunner did not succeed. Kedia, angry and without a trace of fear, pointed out to the participants that in the Soviet Union there were not only the "Peoples of Russia" but also the "non-Russian nations" and that the Caucasians would not fight for the replacement of Red Russian domination by a new imperialistic Russia that would not recognize the rights to national self-determination. The Belarus, Ukrainian and Turkestani representatives took the same position as the Caucasians concerning the Vlasov committee. Faced with such definite, unified refusal, General Vlasov himself did not want to have the non-Russians coerced into joining his committee. And apparently

---

302- See Prof. Mikhako Tsereteli's letter of response to Kedia in the author's archives.

SS Kaltenbrunner chose not to arrest Kedia and others after all. Of course, there were some non-Russians found who joined the Vlasov committee, but in reality they represented no one but themselves. To the best of our knowledge there was only one Georgian who joined Vlasov—Colonel Shalva Maglakelidze.[303] Confronted by other Georgians in Berlin, he explained that he did not really join Vlasov as Maglakelidze but as a fictitious "General Morozov." Allegedly, he did this on orders of the German Intelligence Service. Among the unanswered questions that remained, what was to be his function there and just how long would such a disguise remain credible for a "General"? None of us took his "explanation" seriously. We wondered, what was his real motive for joining Vlasov?

During the last phase of the war, the SS tried to take over the functions of the Army more and more. This was especially noticed after the failed 20th of July putsch. They wanted to extend their influence over the Eastern Volunteer Units also. Once totally hostile to such formation they now showed an interest in them. These were "a new breed" of young SS officers who believed in the urgent necessity of converting the war into political warfare in the East, ignoring the fact that the war was already lost for Germany. One of them, d'Alquin, we have discussed previously; others were Dr. Fritz Arlt and Dr. Erhard Kroeger. The former apparently understood the problems of the non-Russian minorities and was against forcing them to join Vlasov; Dr. Kroeger, however, did not share such a view and was "strongly pro Vlasov." There was a senior SS officer, Gottlob Berger, who was made Himmler's liaison man to the Ostministerium as paradoxically requested by Minister Rosenberg himself. Rosenberg did this as a part of a complex, inner-circle power struggle among the Nazi hierarchy in order to have Berger on his side.[304]

Such SS interest in the Eastern Volunteers caused considerable concern within the military departments of the Caucasian Liaison Staffs and General Köstring's headquarters in Potsdam. It appeared that Berger was planning to use both of his offices to promote formation of the "Eastern Volunteer Waffen-SS Units." If not outmaneuvered, he would probably takeover the existing volunteer units already in the German Army as well. Why should we oppose this? First of all, because it was a matter of general principle toward the SS, which was a ruthless establishment. The Army also disapproved of the unfair preferential treatment of the

---

303- See the chapter "Patriots and Defectors," concerning Maglakelidze.

304- While detailed discussion of this matter is outside the scope of this memoir, it should be mentioned that soon Minister Rosenberg made Berger Director of the Political Operations Staff in the Ostministerium. During the summer of 1944, parallel to this, Berger also formed a special agency in his SS main office (SSHA) in order to handle the Eastern Volunteers. The above-mentioned Dr. Arlt and Dr. Kroeger both were assigned to this agency. (Alexander Dallin, *German Rule in Russia 1941–1945*, pp. 28, 611–612.) Berger himself was primarily a Waffen-SS general working in the SS main office under Himmler.

Waffen-SS soldiers and officers. They received better weapons, equipment and faster promotions than their opposites in the Army. The SS was using this as a lure for the Easterners and at times with success. But above all, we considered the SS to be our enemy, based on the observation of their attitude toward us. It was further confirmed by a very recent SS brochure about us, "The Eastern Subhumans," an incredibly discriminatory publication. While Köstring and the Caucasian Liaison Staffs were attacking this brochure, we also had an excellent argument against the formation of the Caucasian Waffen-SS Units. We had a great shortage of manpower, including the officers and non-commissioned officers, and we wanted the consolidation of our already existing resources within the Army to form one Caucasian army under the indigenous leadership there, and General Köstring and his staff supported us.

One day, Köstring informed me that he wanted to see me in Potsdam. I had been a frequent visitor there and enjoyed the General and his staff's support and friendship. I was flattered to be dubbed by them, especially by the head of the personnel department, Captain Siegfried Ungermann, as "unsere nerwen seege," ("the one who is sawing our nerves"). He was obviously referring to my frequent requests to them and my arguments on behalf of the legionnaires. The reason for the present meeting was that Köstring had learned about a Georgian "Waffen-SS Cavalry Regiment" being formed as a part of the "Caucasian Waffen-SS Division." Köstring wanted to know how this came about and why had I permitted such a thing to happen?

I explained that this had been negotiated behind my back and without my prior knowledge. Apparently the Waffen-SS General Berger, who wore two hats, one of the SS and another of the Ostministerium, approached Dr. G. Magalow, (one of the four directors of the Georgian Liaison Staff and who also had a special relationship with Minister Rosenberg through their common friend, Professor A. Nikuradze). At this point, I said I did not really know Magalow's motive that led him to agree with Berger to form such an unit, but there would shortly be a meeting of the four directors of the Liaison Staff and I would oppose the formation of the Georgian "Waffen-SS Cavalry Regiment." I also told Köstring that I should like to have the General's backing concerning this matter and he agreed. We also decided to accelerate, as much as possible, formation of the "Caucasian Army" by consolidating all the Caucasian units now in the German Army. This would be one more way of preventing further meddling by Waffen-SS in the Caucasian Units. I also informed General Köstring that while discussing this matter with other members of the Caucasian Military Council, we all agreed that the commanding general of the future Caucasian Army should be General Lazar Bicherakhov. The proposition about Bicherakhov and some other officers had also been discussed in more detail between

Captain Ungermann and me. I also told General Köstring that there was no way that Waffen-SS would find enough Georgian manpower to put together the planned "Regiment," which was presumed to be made up of at least three thousand soldiers. It was typical for the SS during this period to have some "Divisions," "Regiments" and "Battalions" existing on paper only; of course, this was kept as a "secret."

Indeed, at the next meeting of the Georgian Liaison Staff, Dr. G. Magalow moved that we support formation of the Georgian Waffen-SS Cavalry Unit—eventually to be a "regiment" on which Berger and Magalow had already agreed. He enumerated the advantages of it:

1. Berger promises that such a unit would be placed under the command of the Georgian officers, headed by Colonel Phridon Tsulukidze (Magalow's close friend).
2. They would all be well-trained, equipped and armed.
3. After training they were to be transferred to North Italy.
4. This would, in due time, serve as a vehicle for the transfer of the Georgian civilian emigres as well as former P.O.W.s out of Berlin and other endangered areas to North Italy where they would be helped, if need be, by this cavalry unit.

"This is more than the Army has done for the legionnaires during the number of years of our association with them," said Magalow. In his view, the Waffen-SS appeared to be a more dynamic, imaginative and resourceful organization than the Army.

I took exception to Magalow's views, reminding my colleagues about our desire to consolidate our existing units into a Caucasian Army and not to separate them. I reminded them that we knew where we stood with the Army which had learned from its past mistakes but we had no experience with Berger's outfit. They may or may not be able to work together with the "Easterners," and I pointed to the infamous SS brochure about the "Eastern Subhumans" as a testimony to the original SS creed about us. It was this very attitude that made it impossible for the Army to do a better job to begin with, as they were simply forbidden to follow any different blueprint than the one which was prescribed from above. "I should like the record to show my opposition to such an experiment," I added. I was sure that Kedia and Alshibaja felt the same way I did but were more diplomatic and just kept listening to our arguments. Finally they spoke that they would go along with Magalow's motion concerning formation of this particular unit, inasmuch as it already had been agreed between Berger and Magalow. But the manpower from the existing Legion and its battalions should not be shifted to this cavalry unit. Magalow, Kedia and Alshibaja agreed on this compromised wording, but I could not. Of course, all four of us were friends; moreover, we wanted to keep unity and demonstrate this to the Germans.

Therefore, the minutes of this meeting—written by Alshibaja—had been significantly "edited" by him. When I read them sometime later, I noticed that there was no mention of a number of my statements, for instance that, "I wanted to show my objection to such an experiment," and my criticism of certain quarters where the infamous brochure had been composed about the "Eastern Subhumans." I informed General Köstring about our meeting. He said that at this point he could not block formation of this particular unit but at least our opposites received the message that they cannot repeat such adventures without our resistance. It was also my impression that Dr. Magalow realized that he had made a mistake and in retrospect he would rather discuss such a matter with the military department of the Liaison Staff first, before agreeing with Berger's proposition. Furthermore, I found out rather unexpectedly that Magalow and P. Tsulukidze had opposition in their own Tetri Giorgi Party circle against the formation of the cavalry unit.

The commanding officer of this unit, P. Tsulukidze, addressed a letter of complaint to the Georgian Liaison Staff. According to this letter, certain members of the Tetri Giorgi, notably Kale (Kalistrate) Salia advised the potential recruits against joining his unit.[305] Tsulukidze urged us to take measures against Salia. This matter was referred to Dr. Magalow and his close associate, Valodia Tskomelidze, who were members of the Liaison Staff and at the same time members of the Tetri Giorgi inner circle, together with Salia and Togonidze. Regardless of such a referral, the Military Department could not completely wash its hands concerning the soldiers of this formation.

Among other reasons for my worries was the commanding officer, Phridon Tsulukidze, himself. I personally liked him and his son, Theimuraz, whom Kedia and I brought to Berlin shortly before Paris was taken over by the Western Allies. The Colonel was grateful to us for that and we got along on a personal basis very well. But I was told by many that he was a man of an explosive temperament and too quixotic even by Georgian standards. This opinion was reinforced by a recent incident in my office during some argument he had with two other people. He pulled a gun on them—hardly an appropriate way of resolving differences or an argument. I managed to disarm him quickly and returned his weapon to him after the two others left the room and Tsulukidze promised not to use it. I approached my special consultant for military matters, Captain Dimitri Shalikashvili, and we both felt that it was not safe to have Colonel Tsulukidze command the cavalry unit, especially during the existing complex military as well as political state of affairs. But, what to do? We had no hope of reversing this decision as the Colonel and formation of

---

305- See Tsulukidze's letter, in the author's archives. (In my personal opinion, Salias's advice to the recruits was justified.)

this unit had been approved by the highest political institutions in Germany. The best we could do was to try to build in some safety measures for the Colonel and his military formation.

I knew that Tsulukidze was in dire need of well-trained and experienced cavalry officers while putting his unit together. My military advisor, Dimitri Shalikashvili, surpassed such qualifications. In fact, he was more qualified than anyone in Tsulukidze's formation so far, including Colonel Tsulukidze himself. Even more importantly, Dimitri was a true gentleman, level-headed, cautious, a born diplomat and in spite of all of this, or maybe because of it, he kept a low profile. He also spoke several foreign languages, and I remembered how in Paris, M. Kedia and I half-jokingly told Dimitri that he would be our Ambassador with the Western Allies. Such a time would come very likely during the occupation of Italy by the Western Allies, where not only Tsulukidze's unit but also many Georgian civilian displaced persons as refugees would be relocated. Moreover, it was expected that the Georgian Legion Battalion II/198 would remain in Italy.[306] Some additional Georgian, Caucasian and other Eastern formations, now retreating from the Balkans, were also expected to reach Italy. Therefore, Italy had the potential of becoming an important base for us while at the same time challenging our representatives to be astute negotiators with the Western Allies, Italians and the "Eastern People."

I did not discuss the above in detail with Dimitri at first, since our immediate goal was the creation of a safer environment for Tsulukidze's unit; however, we decided that Dimitri would join the unit for the limited time it was being put together and trained. In fact, he already had been approached by Tsulukidze's officers to help them out, and they were sure that the Colonel would welcome him. For my part, I just had to arrange Dimitri's temporary transfer from the Georgian Liaison Staff to Tsulukidze's unit. I did so, and as a result I worried much less about the safety of the Georgians in that unit, knowing that my friend would be there and would exercise good influence on the Colonel's temperament and judgment. Dimitri and I would keep in close touch. I informed M. Kedia in confidence about our plan, and he was delighted. Dimitri did very well on his new job; in fact, to no one's surprise, he was made second in command.

The military situation was deteriorating for the Germans rather rapidly. General Köstring's headquarters had been evacuated from Potsdam to Bad Reichenhall in the middle of February 1945. M. Kedia, along with the representatives of other Caucasian nations, Alibekov, Djamalian and Kantemir,[307] left Berlin

---

306- Under the command of Captain Misha Dadiani.
307- Azerbaijan, Armenia and North Caucasus, respectively.

for Geneva after the first week of April on a special mission to be discussed later. The remaining part of the Georgian Liaison Staff was evacuated from Berlin approximately in the middle of April. Dr. Gogi Magalashvili remained near Munich. M. Alshibaja, Professor G. von Mende and A. Tsomaia, after a stop in Bad Reichenhall and Salzburg, embarked on a journey to a small Austrian town bordering Switzerland, not far from the city of Bregenz on the Bodensee, where M. Kedia would communicate with them from Switzerland the results of negotiations with the International Red Cross and also with the Western Allies on behalf of our people.

I went to Salzburg for a number of days, where I met Dimitri again and we discussed what to do about the problems we were facing now and the ones we anticipated in the future, especially after the war. I informed him that he was appointed to be the official representative of the Georgian Liaison Staff in Salzburg and in Italy and handed a certificate to him confirming this. One of his duties was to supervise the transfer of the Georgian refugees from Salzburg to North Italy and assist them. I was commuting between Bad Reichenhall and Salzburg, where I was kept busy. The most serious problem facing us was the Yalta Agreement, signed between the Western Allies and Stalin in early February of 1945. According to this agreement, all persons of Soviet origin who had left the Soviet Union after September 1, 1939, and who were found on territory occupied by the Western Allies, whether they were civilians, soldiers who served in the German Army or inmates of the P.O.W. camps, were to be expeditiously repatriated to the Soviets. Stalin was to accord similar treatment to subjects of the Western Allies.

The original document presumed that all former Soviet citizens would want to be repatriated, but obviously this was not the case. Therefore, supplementary instructions by the Western Allies stated, "repatriation by force if necessary," which was clearly designed to please Stalin and not the Soviet repatriates. It is hard to imagine that a former Soviet subject who was a civilian political refugee or who had served in the the non-Russian military units or the Vlasov Army would want to be sent back to Stalin. For that matter, one could hardly imagine an English or American soldier liberated by the Red Army from a German P.O.W. camp in East German territory who would rather remain with the Soviets than go back home. Stalin, having eliminated real, potential or imaginary opposition in bloody purges at home, now had the aid of his temporary Western Allies in eliminating the major part of his remaining opposition that was abroad. Yes, the Western Allies adhered precisely to the Yalta and all other agreements and treaties, but Stalin adhered to practically none of them. Before the Yalta Agreement, during the summer of 1944, General Köstring's office and the Caucasian Liaison Staffs assumed that our and other Eastern legionnaires who had fallen in the hands of the Western Allies in France or Italy would not be turned over to the Soviets, but rather that the principles of the Geneva Convention would be applied to them and they would be treated as German soldiers. For clarification on this point, Köstring and Herwarth worked through the Ministry of Foreign Affairs and especially through Gustav Hilger, former Counselor of the German Embassy in Moscow before the war who worked during the war in the Foreign Ministry. It was amazing how rapidly the bad news about the Yalta Agreement spread among the Caucasian and other Eastern volunteer soldiers. One has to imagine to what extent this would add to their already strained emotions and morale. In my opinion, such a situation substantially contributed to late defections to the partisans and one especially painful mutiny for all of us which took place in Holland. An even stronger motive for joining the partisans was their possible rehabilitation for a safe return home.[308]

The International Red Cross and other agencies had been contacted, "but no firm assurances were forthcoming." Therefore, the Foreign Office used every means available to persuade the Western Allies to treat the legionnaires as German soldiers and not as Soviet subjects. It also was pointed out to them that during W.W. I as well as W.W. II, Czechs, Poles and other foreigners had fought and were fighting on the Allied side and were treated by Germans as prisoners of war in accordance with the Geneva Convention.[309]

All of us in Salzburg and Bad Reichenhall were hoping that the Western Allies would amend the forced repatriation in favor of the Geneva Convention, especially after the mission of M. Kedia and his associates. Meanwhile we continued our efforts to geographically locate our people in the relatively safe zones. Italy appeared to be one of these zones because:

1. It would be occupied by the Western Allies only.

2. The Georgian military units were there.

3. The Italian Civilian Authorities and the people, in a great display of humanity, actually had invited the Georgian displaced persons and offered them refuge. On our side, this was negotiated by Kedia's and Magalow's departments; I don't know the details.

It was reported to us from all sides that the Italians and Georgians got along very well. They were thoughtful, warm and caring toward the Georgians during and

---

308- See the chapter "Patriots and Defectors."
309- Hans von Herwarth, *Against Two Evils*, pp. 295–297.

after the war.[310] Apparently, the Georgian soldiers in Italy were the favorites of the local populace as compared to others. Denmark and the north part of Holland were also considered to be relatively safe areas for our military units. Therefore, in close consultation with General Köstring's staff and especially Colonel Röpke, we all agreed that this would be an appropriate location for putting together the Caucasian Regiment. As part of this plan, Battalion 799 under the command of Captain Vano Bakradze was transferred from Neuhammer-Silesia to Denmark. It arrived there during the later part of February, which saved the 799 from falling in the hands of the advancing Red Army in Silesia. In Denmark, Battalion 799 was charged with coastal defense duty. Other Caucasian units were also sent to Denmark with Captain Siko (Simon) Kobiashvili was put in charge of this newly-formed Caucasian regiment. According to reports I had, the local population of Denmark was friendly to the Caucasians. As far as the northern part of Holland was concerned, we placed the Georgian Legion's Battalion 822 there, first in Zandvoort and later moving it further north to Texel, one of the Frisian Islands in the North Sea. M. Alshibaja and I had visited Battalion 822 during the middle of December 1943 for the first time and were their guests for two days. We gained a good impression of the unit and its commanding officer, Captain Klaus Breitner, although he came across as a bit arrogant and opinionated.[311] Fortunately, the battalion had never been engaged in combat against the Western Allies, and we were hoping and praying that it would remain so until the war was over. I did not make notes during my second visit to 822, perhaps because of the hectic pace. It is likely that it took place during the early part of January 1945.

Heavy Allied air raids accompanied us throughout the trip to Holland, whether we were passing through the industrial areas, the cities or railroad stations. In contrast, a quietude prevailed around Battalion 822, and the German commander, Captain K. Breitner appeared to be enjoying his job and peace while the majority of other German units were engaged in combat. The Georgian officers and

---

310- I became a witness to this during my trip to Italy from Munich after the war in order to assist the group of Georgians. They had been interned on the Italian island of Lipari because of the totally fabricated charges against them by the communists. I was deeply moved by how well the local populace treated the Georgians. The Bishop of Lipari even offered them a plan of hiding on the island in case the Soviets came after them for deportation. The guards of the detention camp in Lipari had a similar attitude as well and allowed their "captives" to walk in the streets freely.

The Vatican was most helpful especially his Eminence Cardinal Eugène Tisserant (in charge of the Vatican's Eastern Affairs). So were Italian officials almost everywhere. His Holiness Pope Pius XII (on February 20, 1946) published his protest against "the repatriation of men against their will and refusal of the right of asylum." The Vatican representative told American reporters that the Yalta Policy was "a betrayal of the morality and ideals for which the Allies fought" and "against humanity and justice." (Nicholas Bethell, *The Last Secret: The Delivery to Stalin of Over Two Million Russians by Britain and the United States*, New York: Basic Books, Inc., 1974.)

311- See the chapter "In France and Holland."

non-commissioned officers appeared at ease and were inviting and entertaining each other at small dinner parties. I was included twice; one of my hosts was Lieutenant Shalva Loladze. He told me he had participated in the Spanish Civil War as a Soviet Air Force officer. On his way to Spain, he had landed in England, where he had met some liaison men who helped him to get to Spain. Loladze had a considerable sense of humor. For example, he greeted his dinner guests as if he were the main character from a novel by Georgian writer Ilia Chavchavadze, a lazy epicurean nobleman by the name of Luarsab Tatkaridze, whose estate was run entirely by a manager steward, Mouravi. Everyone had a good time and we toasted each other according to Georgian custom.

In contrast to my first visit to Battalion 822, this time apparently not a single German had been invited to the party, which was rather unusual for the Georgians. Perhaps this was because it was a small party, but in addition there was very little trust between the Germans and Georgians in this battalion, as I was told in confidence by Lieutenant Vasili Indjia, the Georgian ordnance officer and adviser to Captain Breitner. Indjia was worried, and although he did not put it that way, I understood that the Captain and his German personnel had lost touch with the legionnaires. I heard that Captain Breitner had made a statement to the Georgians that a German private was more intelligent than a Georgian officer. If it was meant to be a joke, no one was amused by it. I was also told about a comment made by a non-commissioned officer in response to Breitner's statement to other Georgians. "If it were true, why is the Georgian, Marshal Stalin leading Russia to victory over Germany?" I attended one field exercise of the battalion and observed especially Lieutenant Loladze's company. Part of the field exercise consisted of a demonstration of how to cross the water with small boats under combat conditions; Loladze and his company did well. Vasili and other Georgians bade me a warm farewell. I said a polite goodbye to Captain Breitner but thought that my personal advice to him about cultivating better human relations with the legionnaires would lead to nothing. I was worried about the battalion but of course, I did not suspect the pending mutiny which would soon take place.

Back in Berlin I conveyed greetings to Lieutenant Jora (Giorgi) Indjia, from his older brother, Lieutenant Vasili in Holland. Jora told me about his serious concerns for the safety of his brother with whom he had been in touch and pleaded with me to transfer him somewhere else. "I have no one else in this world but Vasili and one elderly aunt," he said. I would have liked very much to have done so for my friend, but after long consideration, I made the difficult decision not to, since in my view his brother was an important stabilizing factor in the battalion. A man of good will, modest, patient and with compassion toward the legionnaires as well as the

German personnel, Vasili could have been of inestimable help for both sides. Jora Indjia never forgave me for not transferring Vasili from 822, and he was the only one from the members of my department who, due to anger, completely severed all connections with me after the war. Sadly, in Munich a few years after the war, Jora Indjia succumbed to complications after surgery for his intractable peptic ulcer.

I met with General Köstring's staff members in Potsdam, especially Colonel Röpke and Captain Ungermann. Köstring and Herwarth were on a trip and therefore I did not see them. After considerable discussion with Röpke and Ungermann, I urged them to support my request for Captain Breitner's removal from command of Battalion 822. I did not get a firm promise but they said they would do their best; however, it did not occur. This was the first time I had made such a request concerning the battalion's German commanding officer.

In Breitner's battalion there was a German interpreter, Dr. Hans Kruse, who was fluent in Georgian and well-schooled about the Caucasus. He had a special interest in Georgia and had cultivated a warm relationship with the legionnaires based on mutual respect. Not far from Georgian Battalion 822, there was an Armenian battalion stationed. Dr. Kruse's friend, interpreter Timm, had been attached to this battalion.[312] These two friends were in touch, and they observed several parallel developments in both units. Dr. Kruse was deeply concerned because of the progressively deteriorating mutual relationships and the growing distrust between the Germans and the Georgians in his battalion. This was superimposed on the worsening of the military situation for Germans which made the legionnaires wonder what would happen to them after their return to the Soviets. These Georgians wanted to somehow rehabilitate themselves in order to be able to go back to the Georgia they loved so much.[313] Dr. Kruse also noted that the legionnaires were listening to the Soviet radio propaganda during the winter of 1944, including Stalin's address about the progress of the war. They were also connected with the Dutch underground movement. In Dr. Kruse's opinion, the German personnel of 822 were not only unfit for the task they were facing but were also disproportionately arrogant and called the Georgians by derogatory names. They were also unhappy about the introduction of the ordinance concerning treatment of the Eastern volunteers to be on equal footing with German soldiers. This arrogance and other derogatory statements were well known to the Georgians—adding to the distrust.[314]

312- Probably the Armenian Battalion 812 and Mr. Timm probably was a former adviser to the Ostministerium's Armenian Section, Mr. Wolfgang Timm.

313- Dr. Hans Kruse, *Stellungnahme zu Thorwald Buch, on General Heygendorf*, Göttingen, Institut für Völker. March 14, 1953, and May 27, 1953. In author's archives (the letter and report).

314- Dr. Kruse quotes a German non-commissioned officer, "When the military situation turns serious, I shall order the Georgians to gather in a place that would have been mined before. Then I would

One day, Dr. Kruse received confirmation about an existing plan of mutiny from a simple Georgian soldier whom he had befriended and who had a bit too much to drink. He assured Kruse that no harm would come to him because he was considered a friend, and in addition they would need an English to Georgian interpreter (Kruse spoke English) when the English troops approached. Then the Georgians would furnish rifles to the Dutch, and together they would eliminate the Germans. After some research, Kruse was able to make a list of the organizers of the pending mutiny. When Captain Breitner heard about this, he demanded definite proof from Dr. Kruse, who explained to him that in such matters it would hardly be possible to get such proof. Kruse also suggested to Breitner a practical solution based on the experience of his friend Timm, the interpreter in the nearby Armenian battalion. Apparently the situation there had been quite similar to the one in Georgian Battalion 822. Because of the efforts of Timm, in close cooperation with the commanding officer, the Armenian battalion had been disarmed and converted to a working non-combat unit. Thus the serious threat of bloodshed had been averted. But Captain Breitner rejected this suggestion and the main leaders of the conspiracy, including Lieutenant Loladze, remained in the battalion, which had never converted to a non-combat working unit. Breitner even insinuated to Dr. Kruse that he was a coward.[315]

The mutiny started at 1 a.m. April 6, 1945; as a result, more than one hundred Dutch civilians, two hundred German soldiers and five hundred Georgian legionnaires met their death, including the Georgians who chose not to participate in the

---

ignite the mines and explode Georgians in the sky. Then, at last, no one will shoot me in the back." The Georgians heard about this.

315- I read Captain Breitner's report to General van Heygendorff about the mutiny in his battalion as well as a book by Jurgen Thorwald. There is not a word concerning Dr. Kruse's timely warning to him about the pending disaster and his suggestion to Breitner concerning the prevention of it; as if the mutiny took Breitner by surprise. One would naturally ask why he did not heed Kruse's suggestion?

The answer was, we don't know for sure because Captain Breitner chose not to talk about it, but Dr. Kruse in his report tried to find an answer for us. He describes the complex problems inherent for the Eastern Volunteer Units such as the Georgian Battalion 822, where he had gained some experience. He notes the mentality of the "Easterners" and that their way of verbalizing is different from their German counterparts. Because they are different from us, the Georgians should not be considered to be worse than others, states Kruse but their differences must be taken into account. Otherwise, it would become dangerous if one expects that their big words and gestures are more than a facade, he concludes. Dr. Kruse then, in obvious reference to Breitner, continues, "If the responsible German commander of a Georgian unit is not aware of the above said and declares that his battalion 'would die in the combat line' in order to prevent transformation of that unit into a working battalion, one can only assume that he did not know any better." Then Dr. Kruse elaborates again on what an unusual and difficult task it is for a German to understand and evaluate the Caucasians and other Easterners.

I would take exception to Dr. Kruse's explanation as it applies to Breitner's lack of action for the prevention of mutiny. At this point, Kruse (and Timm) had already "deciphered" the "oriental mentality," knew about the pending disaster and now Kruse, a German, was alerting Breitner and suggesting a reasonable measure for the commander to take—which he did not take. It would appear more likely that the reason was Breitner's lack of experience coupled with his egotistic attitude and poor judgment and not the "Eastern mentality" of his legionnaires.

mutiny, among them the ordnance officer, Lieutenant Vasili Indjia.[316] I shall not dwell on the details of the mutiny since they have been reported by others at an earlier date.[317] Although Breitner had a poor image among the legionnaires, I am not implying here that he caused the Texel mutiny; things were not as simple as that. But we were sorrowful because of the human tragedy and outraged about his lack of response to Dr. Kruse's warning and wise suggestion. Had he done so, the tragedy certainly would have been prevented. Many families on both sides of the postwar "Iron Curtain" had been grieved due to the loss of their loved ones. The war was almost over and more human sacrifices would not in any way change its outcome.

As a contrast to Breitner, one recalls Colonel Machts, the German (Austrian) commander of the 1st Volunteer Reserve Regiment, the Georgian Legion being a part of it, in the Albi-Castres area of South France during the German retreat in 1944. In close cooperation with the non-communist Georgian legionnaires and de Gaulle's Resistance, Machts disarmed the legion and prevented bloodshed between the communist and non-communist legionnaires and the German personnel. (See the chapter "Saving the Georgian Legionnaires.")[318] Clearly every ethnic group has its own national features but in the presence of good will, this should not hinder good human relationships with others, not even due to a language barrier. In fact, many lasting friendships were formed between the Caucasians and the Germans during World War II. In my view, the differences were much less due to the geographical origin than the political system the people had to endure. The Easterners and the Germans were caught between "two evils," Hitler and Stalin. But the Nazis had ruled since 1933 "only," while the Bolsheviks had since 1917; therefore, the Soviet people had suffered longer and changed more. The Germans had some other advantages such as the right to private property and the right of belonging to the church of their choice. The spying on one's own citizens and the "purges" had not reached the proportions in Germany as were carried out by Cheka or NKVD in Russia except for the racially persecuted groups. Postwar East Germany is an example of how

---

316- Dr. Hoffmann, *Kaukasien 1942–1943*, p. 267.

317- Pelham Wright, *Texel's Opstand*; letter and report from Dr. Hans Kruse (from Göttingen) May 27, 1953 and March 14, 1953; Professor von Mende, *von Heygendorff*, June 6, 1950; Breitner, *V. Heygendorff*, April 18, 1950; Thorwald November 21, 1952, author's archive; Vlis, *Tragedie op Texel*.

318- There were other German commanding officers of the Georgian units who also conducted themselves well. Some of them have already been mentioned; among them was Captain von Müller of Battalion II/198. In spite of some inherent problems in such units, his battalion fulfilled its duty. For this, the Captain deserves a great deal of credit because of his understanding of the problems and his measured response to them. He knew about certain shortcomings of his legionnaires, but still he liked and respected them. The legionnaires felt it and in turn responded with respect and affection for their commander.

Captain von Müller, *Report about the Georgian Field—Battalion II/198*; also Captain von Müller's speech delivered at the meeting of the Georgian Field Battalion II/198, in the author's archives.

much people can change in forty-five years compared to their Western counterparts.

I was commuting between Bad Reichenhall and Salzburg rather frequently, keeping in close touch with General Köstring and his staff in Reichenhall and through their assistance with our remaining military units wherever they were. Georgian Battalion "Bergmann I" remained of special concern to us. It was fighting its way out of Yugoslavia, direction of retreat being northwest, hoping to reach German territory. From Reichenhall, I dispatched non-commissioned officer Aliosha Abashidze to Yugoslavia in order to assess the current situation in "Bergmann." Abashidze reported that the soldiers were conducting themselves well. Lieutenant Goglik Vachnadze and the interpreter, Bagrat Chanturia, were with them and helping to keep spirits up, but the military situation was critical. After a conference with Abashidze and me, Köstring sent General von Wartenberg to Yugoslavia to bring about the release of "Bergmann" by the commander of the front and transfer to the German territory, thus preventing its capture by the advancing Russian troops. This, however, did not materialize. The optimal time for such withdrawal would have been a few weeks previous when I dispatched Lieutenant Okropiridze from Berlin to the headquarters of the Army Group South. There he delivered the written order from Army headquarters to release "Bergmann" and transfer it to Germany. The Army Group South agreed the problem appeared solved, and Lieutenant Okropiridze left for Berlin. But according to "Bergmann's" non-commissioned officers, Probst and Gaumann, now "Bergmann's" commander, Major Brand took a stand against it. He argued that the presence of his unit was essential for the stability of the front line. Brand's view was supported by his immediate superior officer and consequently Colonel-General Schörner retracted his previous order and "Bergmann" remained in Yugoslavia.[319] During April, "Bergmann" I had reached Sarajevo and had to take part in heavy combat around it; then proceeded further Northwest toward Agram. Commander of the 181 German Division to which "Bergmann" had been attached praised it for very good conduct.

By now all signs indicated that Germany was on the verge of capitulation. But before this took place, I needed to expeditiously join Tsomaia, Mende and Alshibaja in the small Austrian town of Höchst, bordering Switzerland. Because the end of the war would spell the end of organized transportation and other means of communication for us, I would never be able to reach them or any of our other people without the help of the Western Allies. This problem was already being addressed by the Caucasian representatives in Switzerland: Alibekov, Djamalian, Kantemir and

---

319- From personal communication with Probst and Gaumann.

Kedia. There were negotiating with the International Red Cross and hopefully with the Americans as well. The Red Cross was helping to apply the Geneva Convention to the Caucasian refugees to prevent the forced repatriation stipulated in the Yalta Agreement.[320] With the Americans, they were seeking not only support against Yalta but also to open a dialogue concerning the Caucasian cause before and during World War II as well as in the future.

It was by serendipity that Tsomaia and Kedia established contact with the Americans and explained to them our goals. By chance there was a young man in Germany by the first name of Yuri, probable last name Vinogradov, who somehow was related to the Caucasians, probably from his mother's side. Yuri had wanted to travel to Paris in order to see his relatives and to help them as well. Paris was already occupied by the Western Allies; the first problem Yuri had was to overcome the German and then the Western Allied front lines. He was an intelligent and daring young man but in his quest, he had still needed some help, which came from Sasha Tsomaia, whom Yuri knew from the past and who had connections with the German Intelligence. When Yuri reached France, at some point he connected with American Intelligence—the OSS (Office of the Strategic Service) and was then sent back to Germany on a mission. Whatever that mission may have been, in addition, Yuri, upon his return to Germany, told Tsomaia and Kedia that his American friends would be willing to meet the Caucasian representatives in Switzerland. Yuri had obviously told his American friends positive things about the Caucasians he knew, including that they were not Nazis. He told the Americans of the Caucasians' desire to meet and have a dialogue concerning matters of mutual interest, and they agreed.

320- On May 9th, "Bergmann" learned about the German capitulation that took place the day before and the Georgians were devastated They had hoped to reach Germany and surrender there to the Americans and not to the Russian troops in Yugoslavia. Goglik Vachnadze, Bagrat Chanturia and "Bergmann's" German officers, in agreement with the 181 Division, dissolved "Bergmann" and mixed its soldiers (Caucasians as well as Germans) with the men of other German units. Their identification papers were changed as if they were non-combat auxiliary "helper-soldiers"—hoping it would be of some help to them. On May 14th, they all became P.O.W.s in Communist Yugoslavia's hands.

    Those who were recognized as being of Soviet origin were separated and turned over to the Soviets. The "old" emigres such as Vachnadze and Chanturia and the German personnel were allowed to remain in the West (since the Yalta Agreement did not apply to them) and eventually discharged. The North Caucasian "Bergmann III" had also been deployed in the Balkans and shared the fate of "Bergmann I." Just as difficult was to "pull out" the non-combat, working Caucasian units from East Prussia. They had heavy human losses and many fell in Soviet hands.

    The Georgian Legion, a reserve unit, had been sent to the East Front, near the Oder river to build a defense line. I had visited them during February 1945, at which time the Red Army succeeded in crossing the river in one place and establishing a bridgehead. Eventually due to a massive Russian breakthrough, the Legion had to retreat toward Czechoslovakia first and then was led to Germany by Captain David Lagidze, the commander of the Legion (after S. Kobiashvili had been transferred to Denmark). It was an almost superhuman and heroic effort on Lagidze's part. He was already seriously ill, which led to his demise in Munich. While marching on foot through difficult terrain, being cold and undernourished, he found strength by keeping his mind on his wife and two small daughters in France whom he wanted so much to see.

    (From personal communications with Lagidze and Vachnadze, also see "Bergmann" by Baher.)

So now, Kedia and his friends were waiting at their quarters for the Americans in Geneva's Hotel d'Angleterre.

It had been agreed previously that I would join Tsomaia, Mende and Alshibaja in the Austrian town of Höchst on the Swiss border (Bregenz-Lustenau area). Kedia would establish contact with us there and should his and his associate's negotiations with the Americans and Swiss be positive, we would then contact our people in Austria, Italy, Germany, Denmark and elsewhere and inform them about the possibility of transfer into Allied hands. For this, of course, we would need logistic and other help from the Americans and perhaps from the Swiss as well. All the necessary measures would be taken for the people's security and welfare. Then it had to be determined who would want to be repatriated and who would not and arrangements be made accordingly.

On my way to the Swiss border, I stopped at Gogi Magalow's estate in Ising, not far from Munich. I stayed overnight and enjoyed his and his wife Monika's hospitality. We discussed our important, mutual problems late into the night and again in the early morning. Gogi definitely would stay at his home base in the Ising-Munich area and from there assist our people, trying to keep the channels of communication open. We promised to contact each other as soon as possible. Then Gogi instructed his chauffeur to drive me to a number of railroad stations—as many as necessary until I made a train connection to Innsbruck; we finally succeeded. I had to stay overnight in Innsbruck but was fortunate to get another train in the early morning, direction Bregenz-Lindau. But due to a technical problem and/or military situation, the train could not continue, so I hitchhiked a number of rides to Höchst and was finally united with my friends.

We found satisfactory lodging with a farmer, then had a "business meeting," and since I was the youngest and perhaps a bit faster than my three colleagues, I was "elected" to be the communications man with Kedia and his friends. That entailed walking, at least once a day, to the Austrian-Swiss border and over a bridge to the nearby hotel (a Swiss "gasthaus") to make a telephone call to Kedia in Geneva's Hotel d'Angleterre. For this, I needed permission from the officer of the Swiss Border Guard; soon they knew me and were rather friendly. I also made the acquaintance of Swiss Colonel Baumgartner, who at that time worked for the International Red Cross and traveled back and forth freely from the Swiss Saint Gallen area to Höchst in Austria. In Höchst, there was a transit camp, mostly for French workers in Germany on their way back to France via Switzerland, who were crossing the bridge at Höchst in great numbers after the Armistice. I had a dialogue with Colonel Baumgartner, explaining our problem, and he appeared sympathetic to us. His help was essential for us to obtain permits allowing us to remain in Höchst while waiting for the Americans, as we shall see later.

During our very first phone conversation, Kedia told me that they were negotiating with the International Red Cross. Thanks to Yuri, an American representative, Mr. Jolis, had had a conference with them, following which Kedia submitted a memorandum to him reiterating the most important points. It was Kedia's impression that the problems discussed were completely new for the Americans and therefore rather perplexing. He felt it would take some time before they would understand, but sooner or later they would have to face them because of their wartime Soviet ally becoming ever more aggressive. In this memorandum-exposé, Kedia informed Mr. Jolis of his and other Caucasians' views about the dangers the Western Allies would face during the postwar period. He said,[321]

> "The main problem now is Stalin's determination to be sole beneficiary of World War II; never mind that it was very costly for the Western Allies too. The West cannot afford to entertain erroneous thinking that Stalin is a benevolent statesman and a Russian patriot. Such an assumption could possibly cost them the loss of Europe and more. He is only using the Russian patriotic sentiment for furthering his own power. If he were a patriot, he should have been satisfied with the gains he already achieved; no, he wants more. Intelligent, cunning and a ruthless man of 'steel willpower,' Stalin will not be stopped from reaching his goal. Nazi Germany is already defeated and now he wants to chase the Western Powers out of Europe and Asia.
>
> "To this end he would use military power, blackmail and the fifth column, the range of which increased in proportion to his advancement in Europe. He also posed as a glorious liberator. It is necessary for the democratic powers to act without delay and organize counter-measures if another armed conflict is to be prevented, this time with Stalin. Realizing the crucial importance of Germany, Stalin's immediate goal is to dominate and convert it into an instrument against the Western Democratic Powers. Stalin is not without convinced supporters in Germany, some of them on an ideological basis, while others are alienated due to the Western Allied bombings and still others would like to revive Bismarck's East Policy.[322]

321- A copy of M. Kedia's memorandum in French is in the author's archives. This English translation is not necessarily made verbatim but rather follows what appears to be Kedia's reasoning and arguments.

322- To prevent France from allying itself with either Russia or Austria-Hungary, the collapse of which policy by Bismarck's successors seeded the conflicts that created conditions for World War I. See *The Encyclopedia Britannica,* "Germany: Foreign policy, 1870–90" https://www.britannica.com/place/Germany/Foreign-policy-1890-1914. —Ed.

"Fortunately there are other forces in Germany who were opposed to the Nazi regime and who would like to align themselves with western democracy. They should be encouraged and promoted and with them, the West could gain support of the German people. Such anti-Nazis had supported us while we were in Berlin and with them we opposed the inhuman Nazi East Policy. We have a list of such friends, who in turn would add still more names. Once the West gained Germany for the cause of democracy, the entirety of Western Europe would be gained as well and later on Eastern Europe will follow suit.

"Now about the people of Soviet origin in Germany: We were speakers for the Caucasian peoples in Germany and at times for other non-Russians as well while such was dictated by the common goal, which was the quest for national independence and human rights. This is why there was a mass desertion from the Red Army and its former soldiers wanted to enroll in the German Army as volunteers. But due to cruel treatment by the Nazis and their inhuman policy in the German occupied territories, the same people, now disillusioned, deserted back to the Soviets.

"Yet some of them still remained in the German Army units, harboring not only anti-Soviet but also anti-Nazi feelings. Initially these masses could have been organized against the Soviets if there would not have been a Nazi policy based on the cruel theory of the 'Eastern Subhumans.' The Western Allies should not hand these people over to the Soviets but preserve them, the Caucasians and all other nationalities, whether they are refugees, workers or legionnaires. Naturally part of them, especially those who were impressed by Stalin's triumphs, would want to go back home.

"They will try to get an alibi in order to gain Stalin's pardon and save their lives. But unfortunately, this will not help and as soon as they have served Stalin's purpose, they will be destroyed. Not only because they took up arms against him but because they have been 'contaminated' by exposure to western life. Should the current situation not permit keeping the masses of these people here, then one should at least save the elite who do not want to go back. They should be guarded for the future.

"For that reason, we would like to get permission and help from the Americans to search for our compatriots. With the help of our German friends, we managed to transfer them to places such as

Denmark, Germany, Austria and Italy, since such locations appeared advantageous for them. One also has to find all our German friends. We were in contact with Professor G. von Mende, his help would be of inestimable value for laying the groundwork. He is a great European, anti-Nazi, humanist and scholar and has long been connected with the problems of the non-Russian nations of the Soviet State.

"We would hope that this memorandum would be forwarded to whom it may concern so the Western Allies would not be misled. Stalin can be counteracted by rendering active support to the anti-Bolshevik forces and not by diplomatic moves."[323]

The war came to an end while we were in Höchst; there were no casualties and no destruction of our area. Dynamite charges had been placed under an important bridge over the Rhine river by some German Army detachment but fortunately sanity prevailed and they were never exploded. Höchst was occupied by the French-Moroccan troops. The company chef was a French Lieutenant Dumas, who occasionally rode a beautiful Arabian stallion. A few days before that occupation took place, Kedia had obtained my [riding] costume and other civilian clothes that I had left in Paris during 1944 with Pavla Sardjveladze. It was delivered to me by Mr. Khariton Chavichvili (Shavishvili), who resided in Switzerland. He was a former delegate of the national Georgian government to the League of Nations in Geneva. Mr. Chavichvili had to take a train from Geneva to Saint Gallen and stay overnight in a Swiss hotel not far from the Swiss-Austrian Border. I visited him in the morning; we continued our conversation during lunch and a walk that followed. When the time came for us to part, we felt as if we had known each other for a long time. I was moved that a gentleman of his age went through all the inconveniences in order to deliver my garments to me and I told him so. "Don't mention it," he replied, "we both served our country as best we could and we shall continue to do so."

323- Not long ago I read a book, *Piercing the Reich: The Penetration of Nazi Germany by American Secret Agents during World War II* by Joseph E. Persico (New York: Viking, 1979). He elucidates the personalities of Yuri Vinogradov, Misha Kedia and his other Caucasian colleagues and their meeting with OSS representative Albert ("Bert") Jolis in Geneva. For me it was interesting mainly from the point of view of the documentation, although it is written with considerable humor and in the spirit of adventure. Even of more interest to me was (but I could not obtain it) Jolis's manuscript, *When the Red Army Fought Stalin.* It was mentioned in George Fisher's book in the section of the bibliography, "Soviet Opposition to Stalin." Apparently, Mr. Jolis has developed an interest in Soviet affairs. M. Kedia, as noted, had met Jolis, who thought well of him. Kedia correctly predicted that it was only a matter of time until Jolis and other Americans would do so in return.

17
DISPLACED PERSONS

After the French occupation of Höchst, certain changes took place. More significant for us was that the International Red Cross camp which was essentially managed by the Swiss now was gradually converted to a transit camp for French displaced persons under French management. My friends and I had moved there for temporary lodging since our Austrian landlord needed our apartment for his relatives. An advantage of being in the camp was better information about the general situation and at times a hot lunch. Moreover, it was a good meeting place with other refugees of various nationalities. Also one could listen to the radio announcements. Then one early morning after I had phoned Kedia and returned back to camp, I found that the camp was completely surrounded by French soldiers. No one was allowed to leave the camp, but one could enter it. I found Tsomaia, Mende and Alshibaja at the gate with their suitcases packed but their request to leave the camp had been refused. I did not enter the camp but told my friends (over the fence) that I would immediately phone Kedia again so he would inform "his Americans" about this new development. During our latest conversation, Kedia had told me that "soon" the Americans would visit us in Höchst and "will take us with them."

As I was crossing the bridge from Höchst into Swiss territory, I ran into my acquaintance, Colonel Baumgartner, the Swiss colonel who worked with the International Red Cross. I told the Colonel about our problem, that we were waiting for the Americans, but now as we understood, the Red Cross camp will only be for French transients while other nationalities will be forcefully evacuated to other cities and placed in camps according to their national origins and under guard. The Colonel understood immediately, turned around and told me to go with him to Swiss territory and call Kedia again; and he himself would also like to talk to Kedia and confirm what I had just told him. We did so, and the Colonel quickly returned with me to the Höchst camp. The guards let us in and the Colonel, my friends and I went to the temporary office of Lieutenant Dumas. The Colonel informed him about the situation including the phone confirmation about the Americans who were going to pick us up in Höchst. Lieutenant Dumas, being the commandant of this area, issued the paperwork authorizing the four of us to remain in Höchst.[324] Swiss Colonel Baumgartner saved us from serious complications and perhaps even from danger.

With the blessings of a farmer, we spent several nights in his barn opposite of the Red Cross camp until we eventually found suitable lodging. It was already June; we became more and more worried about our people, and there was no way we could contact them. Kedia's most recent phone message was that his American friends, although they understand our problems, will not be able to render the assistance to our people that we are asking for. But they would pick you up and transfer you to the American zone, where they would like to learn our opinion concerning certain matters." Two American officers arrived after a week or so, each of them with their own Jeep. They were friendly and polite; how long would it take us to get ready?

"We are packed every morning and waiting for you," we said.

"Okay," they said, "but since this is a French zone we have to be diplomatic and ask permission for transferring you to our zone."

The French Commandant of Höchst, Lieutenant Dumas remembered us well and the "diplomacy" was entirely successful. Our little caravan, consisting of two Jeeps, two Americans and four Georgians, (Mende was given an honorary Georgian status and the nickname of Gogi Metreveli), left in the direction of Frankfurt and Wiesbaden. By American standards this distance did not qualify as a "long" one. Nevertheless, on our way there, we were introduced by our benefactors to chewing gum as well as delicious American food. Our American hosts assured us that we were their guests and not their prisoners. Our final stop was in a small city of Oberursel, between Frankfurt and Wiesbaden. We were housed in a rather long one-story building, which we shared with a number of German persons who were of obvious interest to the Americans. We mingled with them freely and had rather stimulating discussions at times. We were comfortable, clean and well-fed from the military kitchen and allowed to walk in the yard but not allowed to leave the compound for the city.

Every day one OSS officer, Mr. Turner, a very pleasant and well-mannered gentleman, would visit us. We had a question and answer period as well as informal conversations essentially concerning our past activities, goals, problems, associates, friends, the Caucasus and the Soviet Union. We noticed how well and easily he was able to pronounce the Caucasian names and how well-informed he already

---

324- In author's archives.

was—certainly an encouraging observation. Following such sessions, he would ask us to do written "homework" relating to World War II, Germany, our country, our people, our German friends and our goals. This went on approximately two and a half months. Our impression was that the American intelligence service was well-informed not only about our problems but also about Stalin and his entire State.

It was also felt that the American government was probably committed to the policy of continued accommodation toward Stalin. One day, due to the aggressiveness of Stalin, the Americans would probably have no choice but to modify their stand, but would this be timely enough to help our people, who were stranded over the entire European continent? We had the feeling that the Americans Kedia had met and the ones we had met were sympathetic to our quest but could do no more than gather correct information about certain aspects of World War II. We were hoping that one day this would be of some help to our people and their Democracy. The time came to part from our hosts. Misha, Sasha and I decided to go to Bad Reichenhall where Misha's family, my in-laws and my wife were residing. Professor von Mende's family hopefully was in northwest Germany (in the city of Bielefeld?). The three of us bade Mende goodbye and he was flown to that area. On August 29th, we landed in Salzburg and we were driven to Bad Reichenhall.

Our escorting American officers introduced us, thoughtfully enough, to the American military government officials of the Bad Reichenhall district. They, in turn, instructed the local (German) City Hall to issue us a permit of residence in this region, without which we simply would have no place to go. After such a real accomplishment, our Americans said farewell and departed. It was a happy reunion with our relatives, who had not known our whereabouts for nearly four months. If this had not been bad enough, they were almost forcibly "repatriated" to the Soviet Union during May or early June. This was prevented thanks to the American Captain Kraus from Texas, in a display of humanity and common sense. Kraus was the local military commandant after the end of the war. The order had been received from headquarters that only persons of German ethnic background should remain in Germany. Non-Germans are displaced persons, and they should be rounded up and repatriated to the countries of their origin. This ordinance was made public and the American Military Police (M.P.) went from house to house to check compliance with this ordinance. When they came to my in-laws' apartment and examined their papers, it became obvious that they were not German but "stateless" people without any citizenship and originally from Georgia. The military police informed them about the ordinance and suggested they ready themselves for a journey in the near future.

It was useless to argue with the M.P.s who were carrying out orders, so the family went to the commanding officer, Captain Kraus. My father-in-law displayed his documents as a former Ambassador of the Sovereign Republic of Georgia in Azerbaijan and also a number of documents in recognition for services he had rendered to the Western powers and the Pope. He told Kraus that the Alshibajas had never been Soviet citizens and they had left the country before Georgia was forcibly occupied by Bolshevik Russia. He then informed Kraus that if his family were deported to the Soviet Union, they would all take lethal injections before that could come to pass.

Kraus knew that Dr. Alshibaja meant what he said; he was visibly moved and said that there was something terribly wrong with those orders from above, there must be some error. He advised the family not to stay in their apartment during the following day since the M.P.s were scheduled to repeat the checking on foreigners one more time. After that, he would see that there would be no further inspections. Captain Kraus reassured the doctor and his family of his continued support. The following morning the family went to church and stayed there the entire day. Captain Kraus kept his word and we all owe him deep gratitude, but he soon left the area and could not be located so that we might express our feelings to him. Actually the Yalta Agreement did not apply to the emigres who left the country prior to September 1, 1939, but such "details" were not always communicated to those who had to carry out the orders and men like Captain Kraus from Texas were not always there.

During September of 1945, it was announced by Americans on German radio that all soldiers who had not yet been formally discharged from the German Army should be discharged now. The regional centers had been designated for such purpose, and I went to one in the nearby city of Rosenheim (if my memory serves me right). There, I found a well-organized camp where, under American supervision, a team of German officers were screening the applicants to be discharged. One had to present the German Army soldiers' booklet, the "Soldbuch" [a form of identification card]. I did so and received a discharge certificate, allowing me to go anywhere in the American Zone of Germany freely; it was an important document.

Meanwhile, a small group of Georgians gathered in the Bad Reichenhall area, some of them had worked for the Georgian Liaison Staff and they knew that Mikho, his parents, Sasha and I would be there. A larger group formed in Munich. Among them were Captain David Lagidze who retreated from Czechoslovakia with the remnants of the Georgian Legion (a reserve unit, as noted previously); the Drs. David Chataraishvili and Gede Asatiani, and somewhat later Gogi Vepkhvadze came from Czechoslovakia (the Karlsbad area), where they had worked in their profession until the Soviets took over. Dr. Gogi Magalow, who communicated with Munich off and on, had sheltered a number of Georgians near his own estate in Ising, including Captain Siko Kobiashvili with his wife and two children and two lieutenants, G.K.

and V.S. All three officers made their way from Denmark via northwest Germany to Munich. Kobiashvili was a commanding officer of the Caucasian Regiment in Denmark and Lieutenants K. and S. had served in Georgian Battalion 799 (under Captain V. Bakradze), which was part of this regiment.

Eventually the Georgians from Italy began to arrive in Munich (or elsewhere in Bavaria), among them Captain Dimitri Shalikashvili, Niko Nakashidze. Gogi Kordzakhia (he settled in Hamburg), Jimsher Akhmeteli, Lieutenants Zurab Abdushelishvili and Givi Porakishvili. From them I learned about the fate of our troops in Denmark and Italy.[325] Captain Misha Dadiani had already arrived in Italy at the end of January in order to familiarize himself with Georgian Battalion II/188, which was located in Verona. After an appropriate interval, Dadiani would take over the command of the battalion from German Major Schulz, as had been agreed between General Köstring and the Georgian Liaison Staff in Berlin. During the latter part of April, there were frequent air raids on Verona, inflicting losses of wounded and dead, and Battalion II/188 had lost all transport vehicles and gasoline reserves. During April, Captain M. Dadiani replaced Major Schulz as commanding officer of II/198 and the German personnel of the battalion was also reduced. Consequently, the former adjutant, Lieutenant Müller, remained as a German liaison officer. Other Germans who remained in the battalion's staff were the officer accountant ("Zahlmeister"), two staff secretaries and a few others for ancillary services. In addition, each company had an accountant and one secretary. The Georgian officers took over the command of the companies. (Captain von Müller remained with the 1st Company a while longer, where Lieutenant Metreveli was a new commander.)

In 1945 the military situation continued to progressively deteriorate for the Germans. They were retreating, direction north, and the Americans were advancing. The end of the war appeared near, and the partisan propagandists further increased their efforts to convince the Georgian non-commissioned officers and the legion-naires to defect and join them, otherwise their future would be hopeless. Captain Dadiani had no choice but to point out to his legionnaires that there was an alter-nate way out of this dilemma. He shared with them his plan to negotiate with the Americans—the Georgians would not fight against them and would surrender to them if the Americans promised not to turn the Georgians over to the Soviets.

325- The following written reports have been of special help to me: Captain von Müller about Georgian Battalion II/198; Lieutenant Givi Porakishvili about Battalion II/188; Captain Dimitri Shalikashvili about the Georgian Cavalry Unit in Comeglians, a small town in Udine Province, northeast Italy; non-commissioned officer Giorgi (Jora) Lolua about the same Georgian unit in Comeglians. Their help is gratefully acknowledged. The writings are kept in the author's archives.

Dadiani also indicated to his legionnaires that the Georgians had some connections with the Western powers and in due time they would again fight with them against the Soviets.

Apparently Captain Dadiani's presence and his address had considerable influence on the legionnaires. Of course, those who had made up their minds to return home had joined the partisans, since they considered this to be the only way to be pardoned by Stalin. The battalion had left Verona and was now in Badia, where Major Schulz and Captain Dadiani parted amicably and the Major commenced to retreat with other Germans, direction north. Dadiani remained in Badia but the 1st Company headed by Lieutenant Metreveli was separated from the rest of the battalion by American tanks and partisans. Captain von Müller and the German personnel had left the 1st Company and joined a German battle group which was retreating further north. During the night, the 1st Company left the position and apparently went over to the partisans. Other Georgian officers, Lieutenants Dadiani, Abdushelishvili and Porakishvili remained with the battalion together with the Commanding Officer, Captain M. Dadiani. It was fortunate that mutiny and bloodshed between the Germans and the Georgians did not take place in spite of communist propaganda. In my view, this was in great measure due to the positive influence of the Georgian officers as well as their German counterparts, especially Captain von Müller. He often had been an acting commanding officer of II/198, since Major Schulz had suffered a number of health problems, including a battle injury.

While in Badia, Captain Dadiani was able to establish contact with the American General and proposed a deal, according to which the Georgian Battalion would peaceably surrender to the Americans if in return they would have the General's promise that the Georgians would not be handed over to the Soviets. The General accepted and gave his word of honor that the Georgians would not be handed over against their will. Therefore the battalion lay down their weapons and surrendered to the Americans.

But contrary to the promise, the Georgian non-commissioned officers and soldiers, together with the P.O.W.s from other Soviet nationalities were readied for repatriation according to the Yalta Agreement. While I very much doubt that the American General deceived the Georgians by a false promise, I think that he did not recognize the situation as it had been created by the Yalta Agreement. Probably higher authorities stepped in to amend his initial orders. Considerable confusion and at times even a controversy was reported to have occurred during the application of the Yalta Agreement.[326]

326- Julius Epstein, *Operation Keelhaul: The Story of Forced Repatriation from 1944 to the Present*, Old Greenwich, Conn: Devin-Adair Company, 1973—concerning the Yalta Agreement.

The Georgian officers remained in the American P.O.W. camp with the German P.O.W. officers. The German P.O.W. officers helped their Georgian colleagues as best they could. For instance, Lieutenant Abdushelishvili was saved from falling into the hands of the Soviet repatriation officer by the German commandant of the camp, who concealed his presence. Lieutenant Porakishvili pretended he was a German citizen; he spoke good German but the Russian repatriation officer observed that he did not look like a German. Immediately, several German P.O.W.s shouted in tandem "What do you mean by that? Lots of people in South Germany look like that." The Russian gave in and left.

Finally, when the time came for the German P.O.W.s to be discharged and were on their way home, the Georgians had no place to go. Here again the Germans helped by furnishing them with the addresses of their relatives or good friends in Germany; obviously, not all Germans had a negative attitude toward the "Easterners." Lieutenant A. Dadiani, being an "old" emigre from France, was able to return there. The French authorities were hostile to him at first since he had served in the German Army. However, after a lengthy interrogation, the French official told him, "I would not say that you conducted yourself as a good Frenchman, on the other hand I cannot say that you are not a good Georgian patriot." The case was closed.[327] [328]

While the Georgian Legion's Battalion II/198 in North Italy—the Verona region, was going through a crisis, another Georgian unit (not affiliated with the Legion), the Cavalry "Regiment" of SS weapons, was experiencing similar difficulties. It was located some distance east of Verona in the town of Comeglians, Udine Province.[329] About fifteen kilometers east of Comeglians in Arta, the Georgian

---

327- Almost without an exception the Georgian emigres in France chose to remain stateless hoping the time would come for them to return to a liberated Georgia. They never became French citizens; Lieutenant A. Dadiani was no exception.

328- Captain M. Dadiani had served in the Polish Army as a contract officer. He was freed by the well-known Polish General Anders, from the American P.O.W. camp in Italy and taken to his staff. The Poles understood very well that after they had lost the war against the Germans and the Russians during 1939, there was not much the Georgian officers could do for Poland. By the same token, the Poles themselves great patriots, understood after Hitler invaded his former ally Stalin's territory, a number of Georgian officers joined the German Army in order to better defend the interests of their own country. Lieutenant General W. Anders was captured by the Soviets during the German-Russian invasion of Poland in 1939. He was lodged in jail but after the German invasion of the U.S.S.R., he was freed. After many negotiations, Stalin finally permitted the thousands of deported Polish families to leave the Soviet territory in 1942 for Palestine, where the Polish Army was trained. One year later, it joined the British 8th Army in Italy. The Poles distinguished themselves as courageous and excellent soldiers. Anders never returned to Poland. After the war, he remained in England where he died in 1970. ("Brigadier Peter Young," *The World Almanac of World War II*.)

329- This unit was formed under considerable controversy, as described earlier in the chapter "End of the War." Its approximate strength during April of 1945 in Comeglians was four hundred men. Therefore it could hardly have been called a "regiment." See non-commissioned officer, Jora (Giorgi) Lolua's report included in the author's archives.

civilian refugees were housed. Five kilometers south of Comeglians in Ovaro, a Cossack cavalry detachment had its quarters. The division headquarters to which the Georgian regiment was attached was fifteen kilometers east of Comeglians in Paluzza. Additional units of Cossack and North Caucasian troops were distributed in other places of north Udine Province. This entire region was heavily infiltrated by Italian partisans and as one studies a map, it becomes clear that the German Army in Italy had carefully planned the relocation of the Cossack, North Caucasian and Georgian troops in order to prevent the partisans[330] from cutting off army supply routes from Germany.

During the latter part of April, the military situation in Italy had further deteriorated for the German Army and in proportion, the combat and propaganda activities of the partisans reached the highest level. The mood and morale of the Georgian soldiers sank to an all time low and the communist partisan propaganda fell on fertile ground. The situation for the Georgian and other "Eastern soldiers" was much more dangerous than for their German comrades, who could retreat to Germany and after the war at some point would be discharged from P.O.W. camps to their families. The "Easterners" had no place to go and moreover they could be handed over to Stalin, according to the Yalta Agreement. For some persons, the solution (however imperfect) appeared to be in joining the partisans as propagated by them. This, in fact, took place when on April 30th, approximately one hundred fifty soldiers (among them, members of Kavsadze's singing and dancing ensemble) defected to the Communist partisans. In spite of the great promises, the lives of these defectors were by no means safe. Unfortunately, already during early May 1945, seven Georgian defectors were killed in combat when the communist partisans attacked the Cossack quarters in Ovaro.

Something drastic had to be done by the leadership of the "Regiment" in order to save human lives. The only bright spot during this general gloom was a warm and good human relationship which had developed between the Italian population and the Georgians. This mutual affinity probably can be explained because they both were Mediterranean. Apparently this had even influenced the attitude of the Italian partisans toward the Georgian soldiers. Once when Colonel Tsulukidze, commander of the regiment, had to travel to Division headquarters in Paluzza, he asked Captain Dimitri Shalikashvili to take over command in his absence. Shortly after he left, Dimitri was informed by Dodik (David) Chavchavadze, a fellow officer,

---

330- There were two major groups of the partisans, the communists or so-called "Garibaldists" and non-communists, representing the National Party of Italy. These two groups competed with each other for postwar political dominance of Italy. It was commonly believed that the Communist partisans were heavily supported by Tito's Yugoslav forces, including with weapons. Therefore, they were considered potential winners of the power struggle.

that the Chief of the North Italian partisans, de Antonio, wanted to see him; Dimitri agreed at once. The meeting between Dimitri and de Antonio took place in his home, Dodik Chavchavadze and de Antonio's adjutant also attended. De Antonio said he and his men, the non-communist partisans, represented the National Party of Italy. They were sure of German defeat but as soon as the war ends there would be a bloody battle for power between the communist partisans and his group, the non-communist National Partisans of Northern Italy. De Antonio then revealed his deep concern that the communist partisans could easily win that struggle, as they would get the support of the Communists in Yugoslavia. The Communist takeover of Italy would be a disaster for all concerned. Therefore, de Antonio offered a proposition to the Georgians as follows: when such a struggle begins, the Georgians should render their support to the national group of Italian partisans against the Communists. After further exchange of views with de Antonio, they decided to have a second meeting as soon as possible. Meanwhile, Dimitri was thoroughly analyzing this newly developed situation with its inherent risks but also great opportunities for saving the lives of his men, which had been his main mission for joining this "Regiment" to begin with.

Dimitri summarized his thoughts concerning de Antonio's proposition which led to an agreement (with minimal edition for abbreviation) as follows:

1. "It was opening certain possibilities for Georgians; the partisans were, to a certain degree, on the side of the Allied Forces . . . and to get in touch with them would be very useful to us.

2. The only reason we were on the side of the Germans was that with their support we had hope of liberating our country from Communist domination. De Antonio asked us to help non-communist partisans to fight against the Communists; in this matter they had our full support.

3. Now the war was nearing an end, Germany was defeated—they did not need us anymore. Therefore, we were not betraying the Germans. Now we should help our men to escape a tragic fate.

4. Despite the great risks we are taking, it is justified as this could save hundreds of human lives."

During the second meeting, Dimitri made it clear to de Antonio that the Georgians would not fight the Germans. "So an agreement was signed to support the North Italian Partisans against the Communists when the war was over."[331]

331- See D. Shalikashvili's written account in the author's archives.

When the Regimental Commander Tsulukidze on his arrival was informed of the agreement, he was reluctant and at one point even furious; finally, he agreed with it. But before he would formally sign this agreement, he had to discuss the matter with the German Division Commander Colonel Tennerman and get his approval. The German Commander said that the general situation was so grave that he would permit Colonel Tsulukidze to decide the matter of signing himself. But he took from Tsulukidze a promise not to mention the Division commander's name in the document. So Tsulukidze signed the document, and at a special meeting of the Georgian officers it was discussed and unanimously approved. The Georgian "Regiment" received secret orders from the National Partisans of Northern Italy that they were accepted as members of the partisan division whose task it was to liberate the region. They also received the partisans' insignia to wear.[332] As a result of all of the above, the local populace even became friendly toward the Georgians.

There was very little doubt that thanks to this agreement with the non-Communist partisans, many lives were saved, including the Georgians, who could remain in North Italy. The Cossacks and North Caucasians who had to retreat with the Germans to Austria were forcibly handed over to the Soviets by the English with well-documented tragic consequences. It would appear that having received a glowing report from the local populace, the English officers were better disposed toward the Georgian soldiers than they would otherwise have been. It was further enhanced by the friendliness with which the English troops were received by the Georgians. Dimitri Shalikashvili and Dodik (David) Chavchavadze deserved the most credit for initiating the agreement with the non-communist Italian partisans.

During early May, the Georgian "regiment" had been moved to Forni Avoltri, twenty kilometers north of Comeglians. Following this, the British Infantry Battalion occupied Comeglians and on May 7th the British rolled into Forni Avoltri. Colonel Tsulukidze met them with his soldiers lined up; he introduced himself and Dimitri Shalikashvili to the British battalion's commander (also a colonel) and welcomed him with a well-prepared speech. Following the ceremony, he invited the commander and all officers for dinner. Champagne, the best French and Italian wines flowed, and a very good meal was served. There was a friendly atmosphere and Georgian hospitality at its best with Georgian songs and music. The British were delighted by our warm welcome.[333]

332- See D. Shalikashvili's and G. Lolua's reports in the author's archives.

333- Dimitri mentions two English lady tourists who loved Italy and somehow had managed to live in a nearby town while the war was going on. They had befriended the Georgians and were included by them for the dinner party given for the English officers. They were happy to be with their fellow Englishmen and told them how well the Georgian soldiers, who were true gentlemen, had been to

Soon the Georgian "Regiment" received orders to be ready for transfer to some unspecified area. The transport vehicles arrived and the Georgian officers were separated from the soldiers, who were taken to a camp which was surrounded by barbed wire. The officers were driven to a small town occupied by the British and were lodged in nice living quarters. The British officers turned out to be very good hosts, inviting the Georgian officers to excellent meals with matching drinks. The spirit of friendship was genuine and when the time came for the Georgians to leave their new British friends, it was a moving moment. The Georgian officers were transported to the city of Udine, where in a P.O.W. camp they were united with their soldiers from the "Regiment." The Georgians had to turn over their weapons to the P.O.W. camp officials. From Udine, the Georgians were transferred to Forlì and from there the civilians, including women and children, were directed to Rome but the soldiers to the camp of Chivovala. Three hundred and fifty men who had defected to the Italian communist partisans were transported to the Soviet repatriation camp. Others, including G. Lolua and his group of thirty-seven men remained in the English P.O.W. camp since they had refused to go to the Soviet camp.[334] Then began what appeared to be an endless transfer of the Georgians from one P.O.W. camp to another. Conditions in some of them appeared to be "satisfactory" or "good," some less so and outright "bad" in others. Apparently, a great deal depended on the English officer commandant's disposition and/or the resources that were made available to him. It took Dimitri Shalikashvili about one year before he was discharged and reunited with his family in Pappenheim, Bavaria. He did everything humanly possible to fulfill his mission of helping the Georgians in Italy.

There were no hard feelings between the Georgian soldiers who decided to be repatriated and those who chose not to; in fact, warm, emotional feelings had been expressed for each other. If there were any exceptions to this, they must have been

---

them. A good introduction would not harm the Georgians—theirs was a very unusual and confusing past and probably difficult for the English officers to fully understand. It was certain, however, that the Georgians were friendly toward the English. At one point the English commander rose and proposed a toast to the Georgians' future. He said it was impossible for him to know what was going to happen to his hosts. However, he believed that everything would be alright and if the need arose he would speak in their defense. The commander added that it was not up to him to decide his hosts' future and suggested that Tsulukidze and Dimitri see the British brigade commander, but apparently he had gone and could not be found. Upon their return to Forni Avoltri, they found that the British battalion had gone as well. But the English battalion's commander left for Colonel Tsulukidze an important letter of recommendation where he spoke well of the Georgian soldiers. He emphasized their anti-communist feelings but at the same time their friendliness toward the Western Allies. Dimitri felt that due to this letter and with the paper from the Italian National Partisans, the Georgians fared better than they would have without them.

334- See J. Lolua's written communication, including his map, in the author's archives.

very uncommon.[335] It was an individual and complex decision for those who went back. The only durable reaction I personally had concerning those who returned was that I prayed for them, and they needed it. I prayed as well for those who remained in the west as emigrants; they also had to face many dangers and difficulties ahead.

And while this was going on in Italy, what was happening in Denmark? Reports I received from there were mainly about the Georgian Legion's Battalion 799, which was to form a nucleus of the Caucasian regiment that was just being organized in Denmark under the command of Captain S. Kobiashvili. Captain V. Bakradze was the commanding officer of 799 and his battalion had arrived in Denmark during the second part of February 1945, as previously noted. The elements of the regiment were separated and displayed as a coastal defense force. Fortunately, they were never involved in combat against the Western Allies. Moreover, they got along well with the local population and, to the best of the author's knowledge, the Danish Resistance and the Caucasians had not clashed. All of the above was very gratifying for us. After the end of the war, the English military authorities of Denmark transferred the Caucasian units to Schleswig-Holstein in North Germany by foot.

Battalion 799 was assigned quarters near the small city of Meldorf. Here, the English allowed the Soviet repatriation officers to visit the legionnaires. Soviet propagandists assured the legionnaires that no harm would come to them if they returned to the Soviet State, and they also assured them of a bright future. The Motherland was impatiently waiting to embrace her prodigal children. Two Georgian officers and one non-commissioned officer of 799 did their best to help the Soviet propagandists succeed. Indeed, the majority of legionnaires of 799 opted for repatriation. One hundred twenty men chose to remain in the West, among them two medical doctors and several officers. I was told by some who remained in the West that many who agreed to be repatriated felt that the repatriation was inevitable anyway and perhaps they would fare better if they went voluntarily.

Then the English commander approached the "no returners" and in a congratulatory manner informed them of their pending transfer to another place in Germany where they would find work. He also very politely said that they had

---

335- See D. Shalikashvili's and J. Lolua's written reports in the author's archives. All Georgians in Dimitri's English P.O.W. camp were released the same day. They traveled to Rome by train. On arrival, they were greeted by several members of the Georgian Colony in Rome. Then they were taken to the I.R.O. (International Relief Organization). Here, they were "processed," part of which was filling out forms for "Displaced Persons." A long and tedious process was started in order to find a host country who would accept them. Some of the Georgians who shared the P.O.W. camp and tent with Dimitri were Tsulukidze and his son, Theimur; Mrelashvili; Mamaladze; Tumanishvili and his son, Kote; Chavchavadze; Andronikashvili; Djavakhi; Menteshashvili; Shervashidze; Dr. Kordzakhia; N. Nakashidze; Lordkipanidze and his son, Eric.

only one day to prepare for the journey. Some Georgians became suspicious about the commandant's sincerity, among them Captain Bakradze, the Lieutenants K.; S.; and Ko. They left the quarters and mingled with the Germans. Bakradze sent his aide B. to the commanding officer of the nearby Baltic Volunteer Unit to see if they had received a similar order as well from the English commanding officer. They had not, therefore, Bakradze had good reason not to trust the commander. Bakradze realized that since the Baltic displaced persons had been excluded from the Yalta Agreement on forced repatriation, the English commander did not have to transport them to "another part of Germany" (meaning the Soviet Zone), while according to the Agreement, the Caucasians had to be transported.

Other legionnaires could not imagine that the English officer would make an untrue statement to them. Lieutenant K. did not trust the English commander but nevertheless, he accompanied the transport train. The train was under heavy control by English guards with automatic weapons. Lieutenant K. noticed that after a while the train turned east in the direction of Lübeck, a city one-half of which had been occupied by the Soviets. He jumped off the train which was going full speed. The English guards opened heavy fire at him, but he was not even wounded. It was Lieutenant K.'s feeling that the guards had not really wanted to kill him and missed him on purpose. Lieutenant K. hurt his leg badly but limped his way back. He found several friends who managed to remain in the West, among them a German officer, who helped to get identification papers for K. as a German officer which he, in fact, had been. K. finally reached Bavaria to join other Georgians and stayed at first near Dr. Magalow's estate and moved later to Munich—so did Lieutenant S. A significant number of legionnaires who chose to stay in the West managed to do so. It was not very difficult to get out of loosely guarded English or American P.O.W. camps. Besides, there were many English and American military and civilian persons, even in the higher echelons, who were opposed to the forced repatriation. They helped those wretched, displaced people as best they could. They had to obey higher orders but because of feelings for humanity they were willing to "bend" orders. They would give useful "hints" to P.O.W.s or "did not notice" their escape, etc. Some had officially protested against not applying the principles of the Geneva Accord to former Soviet citizens and were finally instrumental in altering the situation.[336] Those former legionnaires or civilian displaced persons joined the political

---

336- Nikolai Tolstoy, *The Secret Betrayal 1944-1947*, New York: Scribner, 1978, p. 24.

    Count Nikolai Tolstoy in his documentary book mentions some of such personalities: Lord Selborne, Sir James Grigg, Field-Marshal Alexander and General Montgomery—on the British side. Among the Americans, the objection was almost universal; the opposition being led by diplomats such as Joseph C. Grew, Robert Murphy, Alexander Kirk, and Generals Dwight D. Eisenhower and Walter Bedell Smith.

emigration, settled down gradually and formed families and lasting friendships with each other.

The Westerners gradually learned about Stalin's unchanged hostile designs toward them and cruelty toward their own people. The momentous warning came in Winston Churchill's celebrated speech at Westminster College in Fulton, Missouri. Churchill, of course, had known about it all along, but the great statesman had to win a war first. Having defeated one evil, Hitler, Western Democracy was now resolved to defend itself and its freedom from the aggression of another evil. The Marshal Plan, Truman Doctrine and N.A.T.O. were the instruments of such defense. It was too late to help the repatriated Easterners who had been caught between two evils, Hitler and Stalin. But perhaps their death and suffering in the gulags was not totally in vain since this human tragedy may have contributed toward the understanding in the free world about the Soviet State and the need for it to change. Since it could not be done by voting at the polls, armed rebellion was the only way left. One of the great Soviet Russian dissidents in exile, Aleksandr Solzhenitsyn, further helped the world to focus on this better.[337]

After the war, Kedia and I corresponded with each other while he resided in Switzerland and I was in Bavaria. It was our mutual belief that the much feared war between the Western powers and Stalin's empire would never happen because of deterrent atomic weapons. We also believed that empires are like human beings: they are born, grow, get old and eventually die; and the Red Empire would not be an exception. We were totally convinced that this would not happen in our lifetimes. However, when it does happen, it may turn into a cataclysm. In order for the Caucasian nations to survive such political, economical and ethnic tremors, they should be unified. "Caucasian Togetherness" would be very difficult to achieve but not impossible, and it should be nourished at all times and given a chance to succeed. Such unity in no way presumes to be against our neighbors or anyone else. Patriotism is not a cannibalistic chauvinism which leads to destruction only. Caucasians need a liberal-democratic Russia and Ukraine to replace Imperial Russia, not only as a marketplace and as trading partners but for vital political and military stability and

---

337- Gabriel Garcia Marquez said, "I am not serving my government but my people." I would add, especially one that has not been elected by the people. Many people in the Western world gradually understood that the Soviet Russian and non-Russian people who during World War II took arms against the Stalinist-Leninist ruthless and tyrannical government were not traitors to their people.

Lord Nicholas Bethel in *The Last Secret*, quotes Rebecca West, from her book *The Meaning of Treason*, "A citizen owes loyalty to the country which gives him protection and consequently a citizen cannot commit treason if his country has given him no protection by its laws." Lord Bethel then comments that Mrs. West's idea is now supported by many lawyers and "by this standard there would certainly be many millions of Soviet citizens who owed no loyalty at all to the Soviet Union under Stalin." Lord Bethel goes on to mention the "massive repressions, confiscations and deportations under Stalin." (*The Last Secret,* p. 205.)

security. The Caucasus is very important to Russia and Ukraine for the same reasons, and if Russia would respect the sovereignty of the Caucasian nations, she would gain in them faithful lifelong friends and partners. History has demonstrated such readiness for friendship. The Georgian Kings, during the eighteenth century, were on good terms with Russia, as was the government of the sovereign Democratic Georgian Republic during 1918–1921. Both sincere attempts at friendship were buried by the imperialistic designs of the Russian State; they should be resurrected and protected.

Belief in the need for Caucasian unity had been kept alive among the Caucasian political emigration before and during W.W. II. It is fitting to quote here Resulzade, the President of Azerbaijan in exile:

> "The Allies of Azerbaijan are the Georgians—this politically mature country with its old culture, which greatly enriched world literature by Rustaveli's writings. North Caucasus, whose national hero, Imam Shamil, resisted and held the Russian armed forces at bay for more than thirty years. These three great Caucasian nations are sworn together in the fight for their sovereignty and are allies according to the Pact of Confederation which was signed by them in Brussels during 1934. The fourth Caucasian nation is Armenia, who for the time being still has not joined us. Their place is kept open, and they may join anytime they so desire. The above-mentioned Caucasian nations are convinced that their good future is contingent on the fulfillment of the idea of confederation."[338]

During W.W. II, the Caucasians demonstrated remarkable unity in protecting the interests of their nations with active Armenian participation, having very good results. We would hope that such an attitude will prevail in the future, not only abroad but more importantly in the Caucasus.

338- M. E. Resulzade, *Das Problem Azerbaijan*, Berlin-Charlottenburg: Verlag der Zeitschrift "Kurtulosch," 1938.

18

FROM GERMANY TO AMERICA

The intended "cut off point" of my memoirs was the end of World War II. I am very grateful to the Lord for surviving the war, although at first life seemed almost unbearable to me. The reason was a painful realization that many legionnaires I had known were killed in battle or doomed because of repatriation to the Bolshevik empire. I had been elected to be the Speaker for the legionnaires, and I did my best to serve them. Even after the war, I tried to establish contact with those who remained in the West and visited a number of them. I also kept in touch with persons who served, as I did, in the Georgian Liaison Staff. Ours was not a glorious job; it was a mission that by the consensus of opinion achieved some worthwhile goals. Many P.O.W.s, civilian workers, emigres as well as legionnaires had been helped, and human lives were saved. Examples of this included the Georgians who survived in Italy and Denmark and before that in France and Crimea. Most of all, we were proud of the letters of appreciation from several Jewish organizations in France and a personal letter from Israel.[339] The realization of all the above made life emotionally less difficult for us and helped us cope with the grief.

I was able to get the position of an assistant surgeon (surgical resident) in the county hospital in the city of Lauingen on the Danube river. At first, I did not receive a salary as I was receiving approved training for the specialty board certification and postwar Germany was poor. Unfortunately, I was even poorer than the country. When the war ended, my possessions consisted of five hundred German marks, two civilian and a matching number of military attire, my medical education and quixotic pride. My wife, Rusudan, was an economy student in Munich and could not find employment.

Meanwhile, Johnnie von Herwarth was working for the Bavarian government,

---

339- Copies are included in the author's archive and the Appendix. [See pp. 398–401—Ed.]

helping to rebuild the country. When he learned from our mutual friends, Reissmüller and Ungermann, about my state of affairs, he immediately went into action, as was so characteristic of him, and wrote an official letter concerning me to the chairman of our municipality. After a month or two, I was notified that my status had changed to an assistant surgeon with pay. It could not have happened at a better time since it coincided with Minister Ludwig Erhard's new monetary policy, which did wonders for the West German economy and the Gabliani household. The Russians have a true saying, "You don't need one hundred rubles if you have one hundred friends."

My chief surgeon, Dr. K. von Hoesslin was not only an excellent surgeon and teacher but a true gentleman as well. He was a general surgeon with a broad spectrum of knowledge and treated me with kindness and consideration. I profited from this during my three and a half years of surgical residency there. After the initial period of adjustment and orientation, I felt at ease. I took great comfort in the discovery I had made that the general basic education I had received in the Tbilisi Medical School had been very good. This was due to our excellent professors, who in spite of the meddling political system, had managed to transmit their knowledge and medical ethics to their students. After my surgical residency training in Lauingen, I was accepted by Professor O. Hennig as an assistant in the Surgical and Urological Department of the Deaconess Hospital (Diakonissenanstalt) in Augsburg-Bavaria. I did this to add another dimension to my surgical training. Because he already had two assistants, he said that he would pay my salary directly from his income.

Not far from the hospital, Hennig had a private clinic, chiefly for outpatient examinations and treatment. Before moving to Augsburg, Hennig had worked with the well-known surgeon, Professor Völkel in Halle University (not far from Leipzig), as a senior assistant for ten years. But his political views did not conform with those of the local Nazis and thus he actually had no chance to be appointed as a professor at Halle University. Therefore, he moved to Augsburg and established a lucrative surgical and urological practice there, receiving referrals from the many surrounding regions. After the war, he received his professorship and became a visiting lecturer at Munich University. He was also instrumental in founding the Museum of Natural Science of Augsburg. He especially enjoyed ornithology and could imitate birds—and his assistants had better recognize the particular bird species which the professor chose to imitate that particular day! He sponsored and promoted the art of music as well. He was a humanitarian and a master surgeon. The following is an example: one early morning while making his way to work he picked up and brought to the hospital a "hobo" who was sitting on a pile of dirt and bleeding to death from a cut of the main artery near his groin. Within minutes the Professor operated on this poor man saving not only his life but his leg as well. This took place at a time when, as yet, the art of vascular surgery was not well developed.

Augsburg is a beautiful, historical city and was founded by the Romans as their colony in 15 B.C. It is only forty miles northwest of Munich, and in spite of some damages incurred during W.W. II, it retained its functional ability and looks. It is a cultural and industrial center in its own right. The business houses were founded by the Fugger and Welsen families in the sixteenth century. As early humanitarians, their concerns for their fellow men is clearly seen in the establishment of the Fugger Home, a shelter for the needy. The shelter was free, but nominal pay from those who could afford it was accepted. During Professor Hennig's absence, I had the pleasure of caring for one of his patients who was a descendant of the Fuggers. An orthopedic surgeon himself, he was an unassuming and humble gentleman, who kept a low profile. Happily he got along well while in our hospital.

Hennig's secretary, Sister Lotte, was an important person and had many duties. She arranged the Professor's schedule, business and social appointments, and saw to it that he did not forget his meals. She took the Professor's dictation and kept the patient's flow sheet, etc. Small wonder then that she was on the run most of the time. One day at noon, she simply told me that, "Professor and Mrs. Hennig invite you and your wife to their home for trout at 7:00 p.m. today." As it turned out, it was not an invitation for a trout dinner but to a chamber music concert featuring Schubert's masterpiece "die Forelle"—"the trouts." So my wife and I sat there, hungry, but still enjoying the high quality performance. Fortunately, after the concert there was a reception to honor the performers during which refreshments were served.

Among the patients referred to Professor Hennig, there were some Americans, including Hugo Becker, doctor of theology, originally from New York, now one of the directors of the War Relief Organization for Europe. In this worthy organization, Dr. Becker represented the Church World Service. He had a health problem for which the regional American hospital did not have an expert of Professor Hennig's caliber, which was the reason for his referral.[340] Dr. Becker, while recuperating nicely after his operation, was encouraged to walk in the hospital garden. Professor Hennig and his assistants would, at times, walk along with Dr. Becker just to keep him company. Dr. Becker mistook me for an Italian because of my name and wondered what I was doing in Augsburg, leaving me no choice but to deliver a lecture about Georgia and the Georgian people. He appeared to have understood my problem and was pondering a bit about it. The next time I met him in the garden he brought up

340- Another V.I.P. referred to Hennig was the wife of Robert Jackson, the chief American prosecutor in Nuremberg. As an expression of gratitude, Mrs. Hennig got Mrs. Jackson's beautiful horse "Johnny" as a present. Mrs. Hennig was an enthusiastic equestrian, as was I, but Professor Hennig was not. I had the pleasure of riding occasionally with Mrs. Hennig's equestrian group in Augsburg. It was fun to observe a spirited beautiful animal; skillfully ridden by Mrs. Hennig.

the subject again and advised me to emigrate to the United States. He said that there were many opportunities in the United States for skilled doctors who were willing to work hard. He said Professor Hennig had told him that I was "more than that"; then he went on to say that the situation in Germany, which was divided into four zones, appeared to be rather uncertain especially for refugees such as my wife and I.

Dr. Becker said he would be happy to initiate some steps toward emigration to the United States, if we so desired. My wife and I had thought about this before, but it was not an easy decision for a number of reasons. First of all, we were doing well in Augsburg; we loved the city and had made friends with a number of nice people. Association with Hennig was a rewarding and interesting experience in more than one way. I learned much from him. He had already assigned me to a rather easy but interesting research project and treated me every bit as well as his German associates. He had introduced me to the regional medical community. Munich, where a considerable number of Caucasian refugees had assembled, was a short distance from Augsburg. Many friends from there visited us and vice versa. Moreover, our German friends such as Herwarth, Ungermann, Reissmüller, General Köstring, Professor Dr. Theodor Oberländer and others were in Bavaria. Oberländer had been instrumental in moving us to Augsburg, where he and his family had settled after the war. He had been appointed by the Bavarian government as the "Secretary of State for the Affairs of Displaced Persons from their Home Lands." A refugee from East Germany himself, Oberländer had organized the building of small but comfortable and affordable houses in suburban Augsburg, basically for German refugees. My wife and I were permitted to occupy one of these houses after we moved to Augsburg so long as Hennig accepted me as his assistant. As mentioned, Oberländer knew Hennig and introduced me to him, which may have helped my acceptance.

The enjoyable small settlement was in lovely suburban Augsburg. Our immediate neighbors were Professor Dr. Oberländer with his family, including his in-laws; Professor Dr. Hans Raupach with his family and a few others.[341] Our families got along very well and it was my pleasure to have been the physician and surgeon to our friends in Augsburg. I had completed training in the specialty of surgery and my wife had earned her Ph.D. in Economics at Munich University. All of the above argued against our leaving Europe for the "new world" that we had never seen. On the other hand, America offered a more stable political climate for political refugees like us. This was true especially when compared to Germany, where one out of four of the occupation zones was under Soviet domain, posing a potential threat for the other zones. We knew very little of freedom and wanted our children to enjoy the freedom that could be found in America.

341- See the chapter "Plot in Bergmann" about Raupach and also Raupach about Kedia in the appendix.

We informed Dr. Becker of our decision to emigrate to America, if America would accept us. So he initiated a number of necessary steps, which included examinations for our health status, security clearance and to have a sponsor in the United States who would find work and shelter for us and get us started in the new country. Dr. Becker found that there was a small town in Illinois that had lost their only doctor and was rather urgently looking for a replacement. Apparently, there was a considerable shortage of doctors in rural America, since the majority of them preferred to practice in large urban areas. Dr. Becker said that American medicine was becoming more and more specialty oriented. In fact, many already established general practitioners were leaving their practice for specialty training. He also said that in America, a doctor who practices in a town that is within driving distance of a nearby city hospital could admit and remain as attending physician of his patients if he was qualified and his credentials were in order. This was completely different from the European system. Dr. Becker did not expect any serious problem for me in America, since I was "a well-trained physician and could speak English." Rusudan and I had been taking English lessons since the end of the war, which we continued in Augsburg under a capable teacher, Mrs. Stelzenmüller, an American who had married a German some time before W.W. II and had remained in Germany. She was quite a personality, very outspoken and loved both America and Germany.

She taught us not only the language but also how to visualize America as it really was. For instance, she would say, "Americans are a gadget-loving nation" or "Americans say that time is money." Also: "If they tell you in America to come and see them, don't ask them when because they usually do not mean it; they are just being polite," and then she would usually elaborate.

During the latter part of March in 1950, we were informed by the emigration authorities that we had passed all required examinations and security screening and had sponsors from the State of Illinois in the community of Bowen. With mixed feelings we bade farewell to our relatives and friends, some of whom remained in Germany and others in France. We boarded the American military transport ship "General Blatchford" in the Bremen seaport, bound for New York. The Atlantic Ocean turned furious; the waves were of incredible size and they battered our ship during most of the journey. The majority of passengers were seasick as were many sailors; rumor had it that the Captain was not feeling well, neither was the ship surgeon. Rusudan braved her misery; she kept walking on the upper deck and taking Dramamine. All doctors who were among the passengers were asked to help. Several passengers had to be given intravenous feeding in the ship hospital. Fortunately, I did not get sick and kept an excellent appetite; I tried to work around the clock. For this, I received a citation from the U.S. Armed Forces.

While disembarking the ship in New York, I must have had an unsmiling face. So a number of sailors who had become my buddies, shouted from the upper deck, "Hey, Doc, do not worry—make money and go to Europe." Having survived customs (they were after narcotics and I had a home first-aid kit) we were met and driven to the airport by very friendly people from the Church World Service. We had only two hours left until the T.W.A. flight to Chicago, therefore we did not see any of New York. We did however have a long look at the unforgettable Statue of Liberty. During our flight to Chicago we were glued to the window; what we saw below us was an overwhelmingly huge country with hills, forests and meadows. The farm houses with silos and the towns far, far from each other; it was an incredible experience for newcomers from an overcrowded Europe and our first important lesson about America. And how considerate, helpful and friendly the captain and stewardesses were.

In Chicago, we changed to another T.W.A. flight to Quincy, Illinois, where upon arrival, we were met by a reception committee of the Bowen people waiting for their "future doctor" and his wife. We greeted each other warmly; the reception committee members present were Mr. and Mrs. Harry and Ethel Sherrick and Anita, their daughter-in-law (who took pictures), Harry Corse and Rollie Dittmer. We were told that the "Doctor's Committee" had broad-based support in Bowen and nearby towns as well. They had tried for three years to get a doctor, but in vain. Other organizations such as the Lions Club; American Legion, as represented by Keith Mecum, and the Methodist Church were enthusiastic about the project of getting an M.D.

From the airport, we were taken on a forty-five minute ride to the Sherricks' home, which was a well-built two-story comfortable house, where Ethel and Harry resided. Not far from them in a similar home lived their only son, Neal, a college graduate with his wife Anita, two teenage daughters, Sandra and Jane, and their son Johnny, who was probably three or four years old. The Sherrick home was to be our temporary residence until the problem of establishing the medical practice had been solved. There was a heavenly peace at their home, which was surrounded by their huge farmland with a new silo, barn and cattle enclosure. Rusudan and I slept twenty-fours straight after our arrival in our upstairs bedroom. After a couple of days we were invited to attend a service in the Bowen Methodist Church. There, we met Reverend Albert Sonius and his wife; very warm and supportive people. During prayer, Reverend Sonius included us by saying, "We thank you Lord for the Gablianis," which made us feel like we were already a part of this wonderful community. Following the service, Reverend Sonius and the Sherricks introduced us to the parishioners. They had many questions about war-torn Europe, which we tried to answer to the best of our ability. It became clear to Rusudan and I that in America, church was not only the place for worshiping but it also had deep influence on the life of the entire community. This was apparently in keeping with the tradition of the early American settlers, who depended on God and each other.

Establishing a medical practice in Bowen did not turn out to be as easy as we had anticipated. Soon several important points became clear. First, one had to obtain a license as a "physician and surgeon" from the State of Illinois; for this, one had to declare the intention of becoming a citizen of the United States. One year of a rotating internship in an approved Illinois hospital was also needed. After completion of this internship, it was necessary to apply for the state medical board examination. If accepted for the examination, one would hope to pass. In order to be accepted for the above examination, one had to be a graduate of a medical school, the name of which appeared on the list of the approved schools, acceptable by the board. One cannot blame the licensing authorities for the above precautions. It was necessary in order to protect the public from unqualified physicians.

Nevertheless, the "Doctor's Committee of Bowen" was disappointed, realizing that it would be at least one year or longer until I would have a chance to open practice as a doctor; that is, if everything went well. But they were as determined as I to work toward meeting the regulations. I immediately made the declaration of my intention of becoming a United States citizen.

Quincy, Illinois had two very good hospitals; one of them, St. Mary, was approved for the rotating internship. After presenting credentials and appropriate interviews with the administration, the chief of the medical staff, heads of the departments and the internship committee, I was accepted as an intern for the required year in St. Mary Hospital. We went to the capital of Illinois, Springfield, to the Department of Registration and Education for an interview and met a very capable supervisor of the Medical Division, Mrs. Louise Hatcher. She told us that the board had made an observation that my credentials were impressive, but no one had ever heard of the Medical School of Tbilisi, Georgia and it did not appear on the list of approved schools acceptable to the Board of Examiners here. After a number of negotiations, we were finally told that if a dean of one of the American medical schools would write to them that in his opinion Tbilisi Medical School was on the level of American medical schools then the board would look more favorably on my admission to the examination. So my wife and I wrote many letters to the A.M.A. as well as to the American medical schools for advice but were unable to locate a dean who knew much about Tbilisi.

Meanwhile, my internship of one year at St. Mary Hospital was coming to an end. It had been a very busy year and physically as well as mentally demanding because of long hours and frequent emergency night calls with hardly any time to get enough sleep. On the other hand, it also had been a rewarding year of mutual cooperation with the medical and nursing staff. I enjoyed their confidence and apparently became popular with them. The medical staff of St. Mary was upset that the State Board of Medical Examiners would not even give me a chance to take the examination and prove my knowledge. Therefore, they elected Dr. Arthur Bitter, who was at that time Chairman of the Intern Committee, to represent the hospital medical staff and introduce me to a special interview with the Board of Examiners. Dr. A. Bitter said that he would be delighted and made arrangements. Then we boarded the night train and reported early morning to the board meeting in Chicago.

The meeting was chaired by Dr. Ed Hamilton from Kankakee, Illinois, one of the well-known leaders of organized medicine. After introducing himself as Chairman of the Intern Committee and the speaker of the medical staff, Dr. A. Bitter made a very strong plea on my behalf, that I be admitted to the licensing medical state board examination based on their observation by the medical staff of my performance in St. Mary Hospital. He elaborated on this in some detail and then added that it was the unanimous opinion that I was a well-trained, experienced and capable physician and surgeon and my ethics were beyond reproach. (I felt rather uncomfortable during this discussion in my presence.) The gentlemen on the board were polite to us but at this point noncommittal, and we wondered if we had convinced them in a positive direction or not. After completion of the internship, St. Mary Hospital's administration and medical staff proposed that I should stay as a resident physician in the hospital while my admission to the licensing examination was being decided; I agreed.

Back in Springfield, I checked with Mrs. L. Hatcher to see if there had been any improvement in the Board's attitude toward my admission to the exams after our meeting with them. She said that there was none. She must have noticed the disappointment written on my face, for her rather unusual show of compassion told me that the board had been positively impressed but they still had to follow existing rules and regulations. My chance of admission was therefore dismal; I needed better documentation about my university. I asked her if she would please go over my credentials in her files with me and she agreed.

Among my documents, there was a physician's diploma which had been issued to me by Munich University. I pointed out to Mrs. Hatcher that if Tbilisi University were not on equal footing with Munich University, they would not have admitted me to their examination and then issue a diploma with the mark of "Very good" ("Magna Cum Laude"), which they had done. Mrs. Hatcher thought awhile and then said something to the effect of, but this is a license to practice and not a diploma. My answer was that it was a diploma and usually the universities do not issue a license but a diploma. The copy of my diploma had also been certified as being an authentic document by the German Consulate in New York as one could see. I had the feeling that Mrs. Hatcher began to understand this complex situation a bit better, but this was a far cry from being admitted to the exams. Therefore, I told the Doctor Committee of Bowen to start looking for another doctor, which they so badly needed. Their first reaction was that they did not want to "abandon" me, but finally common sense and the community's need prevailed. Soon they secured a doctor-emigrant from East Germany. But for the people of Bowen, Rusudan and I always kept a special spot in our heart, and we remained lifelong friends. A number of years later, after I became an established general surgeon in Quincy, some of them came to me for professional advice or help, and it was with great pleasure that I took care of them.

After my last meeting with Mrs. L. Hatcher, I wrote to some friends in various European countries asking them to get opinions about the Tbilisi School of Medicine from European deans and other appropriate organizations. It took some time to get answers but finally positive opinions did arrive; one from England pleased me the most. Mr. Soumbatoff (Sumbatashvili), an old friend of our family who had been residing in England for a long time, had connections with Oxford University. His request for evaluation of the Tbilisi School of Medicine was answered by the Oxford University Registry. The letter stated that Dr. John F. Fulton, Professor of Physiology and the History of Medicine from Yale University in Connecticut, was considered an expert on Tbilisi and other Soviet schools of medicine. In his reply to Oxford, Professor Fulton gave very high marks to Tbilisi University School of Medicine.[342] Another very good and rather in depth analysis about Tbilisi University was from Dr. Walter Wienert, Main Office for Foreign Educational Systems, Göttingen, September 22, 1951, Wilhelmsplatz 1, Journal #2347/51/WI.[343] I wrote to Professor Fulton, who unfortunately had some health problems at that time, but as soon as he recuperated he wrote me a warm letter and we continued corresponding.[344] In Fulton's opinion, Tbilisi University School of Medicine had been among the top three in the Soviet Union. Professor Fulton, a physiologist himself who had published a remarkable textbook of physiology, knew the Georgian professor of neurophysiology, Beritoff (Beritashvili), considered the Dean of Soviet Physiologists after Professor Pavlov's demise, and was internationally recognized.

342- Oxford Registry letter on Soumbatoff, Esq., Ref. Gen./ 51S. 28 Sept. 1951, in author's archives.
343- In author's archives, in German with English translation.
344- See Fulton's letters in author's archives; one of them is presented here.

Yale University School of Medicine
333 Cedar Street
New Haven, Connecticut
Historical Library

TO WHOM IT MAY CONCERN

June 23, 1952

This is to certify that in my opinion graduates of the School of Medicine of Tiflis (Tbilisi) in Georgia, U.S.S.R. should qualify for licensing in the United States. The standards of Tiflis have always been high and while I am not aware of what has happened since the war, Dr. Gabliani, who is applying to the Illinois State Boards, was there when Professor Beritoff, the distinguished neurophysiologist was at the height of his reputation and there were other men on the Tiflis faculty of international repute. I would think that Tiflis would rank with the first two or three medical schools in the Soviet Union. Before the recent suppression of activities in the Russian universities, Tiflis was certainly outstanding among the universities of the world.

Yours very truly,

(signature) John F. Fulton, M.D.
Sterling Professor of the History of Medicine

Original letter and copy in the author's archives.

Needless to say, I referred Professor Fulton's and the other evaluation letters to the Illinois Department of Registration and Education. I also mailed copies of them to the other Tbilisi Medical School graduates who resided in the United States at that time, hoping it would help them too. After a few weeks, I was notified by the Department that my application for admittance to the examination had now been approved and the next examination would take place in Chicago during April of 1953. It was a victory for the Tbilisi University School of Medicine.

I continued working in the hospital as usual and prepared as best I could for the pending examination. I hoped that should I fail during the examination, it would not be considered a bad mark against Tbilisi University. The examination turned out to be difficult but fair. Mrs. Louise Hatcher supervised us, making sure no one was cheating; she disqualified two doctors on the spot. They apparently "consulted" with each other while answering questions. However, she did not notice a gentleman with a strong Hungarian accent who repeatedly wanted me to tell him the dosage of nitrogen mustard. (I did not understand what he was asking for at first since the Hungarians pronounce Budapest as "Budapesht" and Mustard as "Muushtard.") At that time, there were no multiple choice questions but written examinations in all subjects. During the middle of the examination, I developed "writer's cramp." I prayed that I would make it to the end. Thank the Lord, Mrs. Hatcher called for a recess; I rushed to the bathroom to massage my hand under hot, running water.[345] After the written examination, we were led to the Cook County Hospital where we had to examine a patient, make the diagnosis and suggest treatment. It was a "piece of cake" when compared to the written part. A couple of weeks after I returned to Quincy, I was notified that I passed the examination and was licensed to practice medicine as a "physician and surgeon"; this lifted our spirits.

Soon after, the Local Board #1 of the Selective Service System wrote to inform me that I was classified as Class I-A, which meant that I could be drafted into the Army at any time. In order to put this behind me and meet my obligation now, I decided to volunteer for service. I filled out some forms, and with other recruits from the Quincy area, was taken to St. Louis, Missouri for a rather extensive physical examination. I received an official letter from Army headquarters that I had been accepted as a medical specialist and to wait for further notification. This notification, which took considerable time to arrive, said that due to peace negotiations with North Korea, there was now a reduced need for medical specialists and suggested that I apply again in August. The letter also thanked me for my willingness to serve. I informed the medical staff of St. Mary's, who already had given me a very nice present as "bon voyage" to Korea, that the Army did not need me after all. They told me that there would always be a place for me in Quincy, and sure enough, the very next day while scrubbing for surgery, one of the senior surgeons and practitioners asked if I would be interested in joining him in his practice. I agreed, as I had helped him rather frequently with his surgeries before and we got along well. His name was Dr. M. E. Bitter of Quincy, whose father had been a doctor in Quincy and his brother, Arthur was a member of the surgical departments of both Quincy hospitals. In this way, I gradually established a surgical practice in Quincy, Illinois, where people had been so nice to us.

345- Mrs. Hatcher came across as a strict disciplinarian and a cold person who did not care for people. A number of years later, I was in a local bank and as I was leaving, an attractive young lady tried to catch up with me. I stopped and waited for her to see what the problem was. She apologized for imposing on my time and said that she had wanted to tell me about this for a long time but did not have the opportunity. Her aunt, Mrs. Louise Hatcher from Springfield had some health problems now but she had been a great admirer of my wife and mine and kept her fingers crossed hoping that I would succeed in my efforts to be admitted to the Medical State Board Examination. It made her very happy that I achieved this and also that I passed the examination. I could not have been more surprised; there was a good-hearted person hiding behind the mask.

Our three children were born here; we lost one prematurely born baby, Alexander. Our family feels that America is a wonderful country and the overwhelming majority of people here are compassionate, helpful and generous. We have no doubt about its good future and its continued importance to the world. There is more to say about the Gablianis in America but I think our children, Gregory, Eteri and Vera are eminently qualified to write about this; hopefully they will so desire.

George F. Kennan in his book, *Russia and the West,* in closing quotes Bismarck as follows, "Let us leave a few problems for our children to solve; otherwise they might be so bored." I share such a feeling.

Givi C. Gabliani
Quincy, Illinois 1993

Afterword
by Gregory Gabliani

My father Givi Gabliani seldom spoke in any detail about his life before his immigration to America in 1950. At the age of thirty-five years, his past life was filled with disturbing memories. The execution of his father Egnate Gabliani. The tragic death of his younger sister Eteri. The cruel imprisonment of his mother Vera. The forced reparation, under the Yalta Agreement, of countless Georgian refugees to Stalin's brutal, distant gulags, where so many died. The Cold War subjugation and isolation of the Georgian people behind the Iron Curtain.

These tragedies were seldom mentioned but never forgotten. My sisters Eteri and Vera and I grew up sensing our father's unspoken losses.

My father retired from medicine in 1987. For many years he had been collecting materials related to his life before he came to America; now he had the time to read, think and write about the events from his past. Over time, my father organized these writings into a manuscript, which he wrote in English, his fourth language. He chose English because these writings were principally for his American children; to help us understand the past he had largely left unspoken.

With the help of my mother Rusudan Gabliani and his loyal secretary Vivian Andrews, he recorded his memories into a typed manuscript. In 1993, he gave me the manuscript to make copies, which were given to Eteri, Vera and myself and to a few close friends. One of these friends, Guivi Zaldastani (son of the Colonel Soliko Zaldastanishvili mentioned in this book), took the English manuscript to Georgia where it was translated into Georgian and published in two volumes in 1998 and

2000. My father passed from this world in 2001. His manuscript, books and papers lay undisturbed for years.

In early 2020, my sisters and I began discussing what to do with the books and papers that my father had collected. We contacted our family friend Elizabeth (Lizzy) Zaldastani, daughter of Othar and Elizabeth (Ibby) Zaldastani and niece of Guivi Zaldastani. Lizzy put us in contact with two Georgian scholars, Alexander (Aliko) Kartozia and his wife Rusudan (Rusiko) Gorgiladze, with whom we discussed the possibility of donating these items to the Georgian National Library in Tbilisi. We also discussed republishing my father's manuscript in a professionally edited book form, which Aliko and Rusiko encouraged us to do.

So how then did my father's untitled manuscript become the book *Allies Against Two Evils* published by DoppleHouse Press? I am sure that my father would say that this unlikely occurrence was "by the Grace of God."

Over the years with hard work, the loving support of his wife, my mother Rusudan and, truly, the grace of God, Givi Gabliani became a very successful surgeon in the town of Quincy, Illinois. In the late 1950s, my parents purchased a home on ten acres of land at the outskirts of town. In 1965, they built a new home on the hill overlooking their property. Soon after, our family began taking skiing vacations in Aspen, Colorado, staying at the Boomerang Lodge, "where you are certain to return" and to which we did return both in the winter and summer. My parents became friends with the architect, owner and operator of the Boomerang Lodge, Charles Paterson and his equally remarkable father, Steve Schanzer. In 1969, Charlie had the great good fortune to meet and marry Fonda Dehne and they were blessed with two children, Carrie and Jenny. In 1972 my parents bought a home in Aspen that they named Villa Svaneti. By that time a family friendship had formed between the Gablianis and the Patersons that continues to this day.

In August 2013, Charlie gave gift copies of his family memoir *Escape Home: Rebuilding a Life After the Anschluss* to myself and my sisters. Over time, we read and discussed this book with great interest, noting the similarities our families shared. The founders of both the Gabliani and Paterson families had come in hope to the new world after many tragedies. Both families had ultimately done well. Both families still carried heavy memories from their pasts.

Charlie, who was of Jewish heritage, was born in 1929 in Vienna, Austria as Karl Schanzer. In his memoir, he tells the fascinating life story of his travails getting from Vienna to Australia in 1940, to America in 1947, and then, in 1949, to Aspen. His older daughter, Carrie, among many other things, founded and is the editor of DoppleHouse Press, which published *Escape Home*.

When the time came in 2020 for my sisters and I to explore the possibility of turning my father's manuscript into a book, we knew whom we could rely on for an honest opinion about whether this was possible and, if so, who we could trust to undertake the task of editing and publishing Givi Gabliani's manuscript. After some discussion with Carrie, it was decided that some reorganization and editing would be required. This editing, done by Carrie and myself, was a delicate and lengthy task. This prolonged labor of love was made no easier by the Covid epidemic and then, in February 2022, by Putin's invasion of the Ukraine. For us, that war has called up many historical echoes and their collective traumas.

Our goal, in which I think we succeeded, was to make my father's writings more accessible to the reader while preserving his unique voice. We were blessed by the generosity of Alexander Kartozia, who agreed to write the historical preface. Givi Gabliani's typescript manuscript, titled "The Second World War and the Georgians: People Caught Between Two Evils," has thus been miraculously transformed into the book *Allies Against Two Evils* that you now hold in your hands.

I think my father would be pleased.

Gregory Irakli Ignatius Gabliani MD, FACC, FACP
St. Louis, Missouri, February 2023

APPENDICES

Introduction to Dr. Givi Gabliani's Memoirs
by Hans von Herwarth

"The Second World War and the Georgians" documents the relationship between the Germans and the Georgians. During that period there were Georgian volunteers on the German side against the Soviet Union. This was the time Givi and I became friends. This took place in the military unit "Bergmann." While Givi, at first, did belong to "Bergmann," I was a captain in the cavalry and adjutant attached to General Köstring, who also had busy activities with volunteer military units. So together we lived through the stress and strain of the Second World War. The subtitle, "People Caught Between Two Evils" describes very well the actual situation.

Before the war, I knew the Georgians from history and from personal experience as well. During World War I, in 1918, German troops occupied Georgia. Before 1914, my ambassador in Moscow, Count von der Schulenburg, was a German Council in Tbilisi (Tiflis). Therefore, he had been a representative of the German Foreign Service. Jointly with Colonels von Lossow and Kress von Kressenstein, they lifted a new state, Georgia, from its baptism. In 1918, Turkish troops invaded Georgia from Azerbaijan. There were dead and wounded. Together Georgian and German troops successfully repelled the attack on Georgia; one should remember that Turkey and Azerbaijan were allies during the First World War.

The State of Georgia, despite all efforts, did not last long. It eventually succumbed in February 1921 to a treacherous invasion, without provocation and without warning, by Red Russian troops. The last constitutional Assembly of the Georgian Republic ordered its representatives to emigrate to the countries of the free world and from there make strong effort to gain necessary support to reestablish freedom for Georgia. However, all efforts were in vain.

On the other hand, there were several Georgians who had played a leading role among the Soviet leaders, such as Ordzhonikidze, Yenukidze, Beria and last but not least, Stalin himself. In the years of 1933 until 1939, I had traveled in Georgia several times. I learned to love the country and its people. Especially impressive to me were the ancient churches of Georgia, erected long before our Romanesque churches. The German settlers arrived and put down roots as they settled in Georgia.

The climate was excellent for vineyards and they established themselves in villages, where their vineyards flourished until the onset of the revolution.

The following describes very well the mood of the population against Soviet rule. During 1934, while the Congress of the "Comintern" in Moscow was postponed for one month, the Russian delegates as well as delegates from other countries who had already arrived, used this opportunity to travel throughout the Soviet Union. I went to a Tbilisi restaurant and ordered a meal. The waiter took me for a German Communist Delegate and scolded me for being fooled by the "Potemkin Villages." He simmered down only when I showed him my diplomatic papers.

The military unit of "Bergmann" was created in 1941. It was composed of Georgian emigrants to the West as well as those who had stayed in their home country. This rekindled the German-Georgian friendship that had begun during World War I.

Givi Gabliani, in the frame of the "Bergmann" unit, and later as a member of the Georgian National Committee, had an important role in this period of the German-Georgian relationship. His memoirs will offer a rich source pertaining to German-Georgian history. After the war, Dr. Gabliani practiced medicine in Germany and later in the United States.

When German Chancellor Conrad Adenauer made his first official visit to the United States in 1953, Dr. Gabliani approached me to be introduced to him as a former Georgian captain in the German Army. After the introduction, we two old comrades, truly touched, fell into each other's arms.

Today there is an independent state of Georgia with a German diplomatic representative. We Germans will not forget the role that President Shevardnadze of Georgia played as a Soviet Foreign Minister, an important and positive role in the reunification of Germany.

The state of Georgia acquired a national flag—possibly under German influence—similar to the present German flag: black, white and red with the insertion of an emblem of black and white.[346]

346- The Georgian black, red and white flag referred to here, with similarities to the Prussian flag, was flown from 1918–1921 and again adopted after the collapse of the Soviet Union, from 1991–2004. After the bloodless Rose Revolution in November 2003, the five-cross flag in red and white, a national patriotic symbol dating back to the medieval Kingdom of Georgia, was adopted by Georgian Parliament and has become part of the Georgian national revival. —Ed.

HANS VON HERWARTH
Staatssekretär a. D.

✓   8643 KUPS   18ᵗʰ Jan.1988
SCHLOSS
TEL. 09264/7174

A F F I D A V I T

I herewith declare in lieu of an oath:

I know Dr.Giwi G a b l i a n i since 1942.
I was then serving as an officer (captain) under Colonel
Stauffenberg,who tried to kill Hitler in July 1944 and
under Count von der Schulenburg who was also executed
in 1944. I belonged to the German Resistance since 1938,
see Charles Bohlen "Whitness to History".

Dr.med.Giwi Gabliani is a Georgian patriot. His
father and many of his professors and friends were murdere
by Stalin. Georgia had been conquered by Zarist Russia
in the 19th century and had regained its independance
from 1917 to 1921. The independance of Georgia in this
period was protected by German troops. Count von der
Schulenburg was representing the German Ministery of
Foreign Affairs in Georgia. (Tiflis). In 1921 the
Soviets occupied Georgia by force.

Giwi Gabliani naturally opposed to Soviet
imperialistic and criminal rule. The German Resistance
wanted - after the overthrow of Hitler - to liberate
the different nations in the Soviet Union from Soviet
dictatorship. Therefore Giwi Gabliani as a prisoner of
war in 1941 decided to cooperate with the German
Resistance. In 1942 he joined a Caucasian volunteer
unit which was formed by Admiral Canaris, a leading
member of the German Resistance, executed in 1945.

In 1943 Gabliani became a member of the
Georgian liaison-mission, which represented also the
Georgian exile-government in Paris. The Georgian
liaison-mission worked closely together with the
German Resistance, e.pecially with Colonel Count
Stauffenberg and Ambassador von der Schulenburg, who
both were the fathers of the Soviet Volonteers in the
German Army.

In January 1945 Giwi Gabliani married a georgian
emigrant in Bavaria. In order to avoid repatriation
to the Soviet Union he had to change his identity by
pretending to be also an emigrant and not a prisoner
of war. I was then director in the Bavarian States-
chancellery in Munich and helped him to stay in Germany.

After 1949 I worked under the Federal President
Heuss and Chancellor Adenauer. Later on I was Ambassador
in London and Rome (Quirinale) and Undersecretary of
State and Head of the Office of the President of the
Federal Republic of Germany. I ended my career as
Undersecretary of State in the Ministery of Foreign
Affairs.

Hans von Herwarth

Hans von Herwarth

Circumstances Surrounding the Brest-Litovsk Treaty

In 1949, I was working in the Deaconess Hospital of Augsburg, West Germany, where I had the pleasure of taking care of the ailing Isaak Mazepa. He had been the leading member of the Ukrainian "Rada" (council of representatives). He and his associate Professor Panas Fedenko were both eye witnesses to the circumstances surrounding the Brest-Litovsk Treaty.

Their account grossly correlates with the presentation by George F. Kennan's in his scholarly book, *Russia and the West Under Lenin and Stalin.*[347]

After the February 1917 Democratic (not the Bolshevik) Revolution in Russia, Mr. Kerensky, "a Socialist revolutionary," became the head of the provisional government. He was under constant pressure from the Western Allies to continue the Russian war effort against Germany and her allies. Kerensky's government reluctantly agreed to it. Apparently, the English and the French did not realize that Russia was no longer in condition to further carry out such a task. The separate peace treaty with Germany therefore would have been the wisest choice for Russia to follow. This would then strengthen the cause of democracy and not of Bolshevism. The danger of it was real and more so since the German Intelligence Service had smuggled Lenin to Petrograd, then St. Petersburg and financed the Bolshevik activity there. While so doing, the Germans were not motivated by a special affinity for the Bolsheviks but by a "Realpolitik." Lenin's party was the only force in Russia firmly committed to the immediate cease fire. Needless to say, the peace with Russia would be of the greatest help for Germany, as she was fighting on two fronts.

Lenin, for his part, saw an opportunity to seize the power in Russia for himself. Therefore, his propaganda slogan was then "War against War" and immediate peace. His agitators, sent to the Russian Army, spared no effort to thoroughly undermine the fighting spirit of the soldiers and sailors. For instance, they told the soldiers that now the farmland had been taken away from the big landowners, they should therefore hurry home and claim their share before it was too late.

347- George F. Kennan, *Russia and the West Under Lenin and Stalin,* New York and Toronto: Mentor Book/The New American Library, 1961; also see *Encyclopedia Britannica* (Brest-Litovsk Treaty) and Marshall Lang, *A Modern History of Soviet Georgia,* pp. 198, 202–204.

The summer offensive by Kerensky's troops against the Germans resulted in a disastrous defeat for the Russians. This gave an additional propaganda advantage to the Bolsheviks.

Some units of Petrograd Garrison together with workers staged a spontaneous uprising which was easily put down by the Kerensky government. Lenin, who considered such an ill prepared revolt premature, had to go underground temporarily in order to escape arrest.

But now General Kornilow of the Russian Right threatened to march on Petrograd in order to overthrow Kerensky's government and save "Mother Russia." Actually, the General did not have enough troops available to do that. Nevertheless, Kerensky overreacted and allowed the Bolshevik-dominated soldiers and workers to rearm against the common enemy from the Right. This turned out to be a fatal mistake. Now the well armed Bolsheviks staged a successful coup-d'etat during November 1917.

They also surrounded the constitutional assembly "The Duma" while in session and prevented it by force from discharging its duty. Lenin did this because the majority of representatives in "The Duma" had been elected by the people not from the Bolshevik Party but from other political parties.

Thus, this early real Russian democracy was "nipped in the bud" by the Bolsheviks, who usurped the power and now became the self-appointed rulers of Russia.

The Bolshevik government made its peace declaration known at once in a form of a direct address to the people of the allied countries of Russia. They chose not to use the normal diplomatic channels as is customary. The Bolsheviks did so, as they believed that the workers, soldiers, socialists and other fellow sympathizers in the western democratic countries would also spontaneously raise in revolution against their own governments, following the Bolshevik example in Russia and in support of it.

After all, they reasoned, Karl Marx predicted that the communist revolution was going to take place in the highly industrialized capitalist countries. (Russia did not belong to these countries.) Capitalism, he said, is breeding the class of proletariat which has nothing to lose. Reconciliation between these two classes is not feasible, and therefore the proletariat will rise and overthrow the capitalistic system by violent means. Having established the dictatorship of the proletariat, it will then achieve the ultimate goal of the classless communist society where everyone will produce according to his ability and consume according to his need and the State itself shall eventually be abolished.

The agricultural country such as Russia, with a strong peasant population and a weaker class of proletariat, was of course the last place that Marx would ever consider a potential place for the communistic revolution.

Lenin's explanation stated that since capitalism in agricultural Russia represented "the weakest link" in the world capitalistic chain, that is where the chain broke and the revolution therefore did succeed. Such a view has been considered by many other Marxist Socialists as absurd and contradictory to Marxist theory.

Bolshevik negotiators at Brest-Litovsk did not agree at first to the stiff German terms of the peace treaty and withdrew from the meeting. However, on one hand, Bolshevik expectation of a spontaneous revolution in the western world did not materialize and on the other hand, the German High Command did resume the military offensive gaining more and more of the Russian territory.

And why not? Who would stop them? The Russian troops already were thoroughly demoralized by the Bolshevik antiwar propaganda and now had no desire to fight.

Therefore, on Lenin's personal insistence, the peace negotiations were resumed. (Trotsky and a few others were opposed to it at first.) When concluded, they were on even more unfavorable terms for the Russians than before.

German-Georgian Friendship Speech
upon German Withdrawal in W.W. I

"But in those last gloomy days, the friendship of the gallant Georgians for the Germans was once again shown in a heartrending way. They could no longer expect anything from us. Neither militarily nor diplomatically, neither financially nor commercially, the Germans could do nothing for their Georgian friends. England's army occupied the Georgian capital, and the Georgians depended on England's Grace for protection against Russians in the north, Tartars in the east, and Armenians in the south. Their emphatic friendship for Germany could no longer bring them the slightest benefit, but every harm. And yet the Georgians were loyal to us. The Minister of War insisted on giving the delegation a splendid party on the eve of their forced departure, at which heartfelt words reaffirmed the German-Georgian friendship. Representatives of the government, the parties and many personal friends of the Germans had gathered at the station, and the delegation left Tbilisi with cheers for Germany. The stay in Kutaisi was a series of banquets and testimonies of friends; all the inhabitants of the city, which had housed a German garrison for months, endeavored in every way to show their sympathy and friendship to the Germans. If the Germans had come to Georgia then as victors and liberators, instead of leaving it broken down as prisoners, the noble Georgian people could not have greeted them more heartily and splendidly. Even upon departure from Kutaisi, when the railway station was already glaring with the Gurkhas' bayonets, the waiting room was festively decorated, a farewell drink was prepared, once more the joint work, joint victories and loyal friendship were commemorated in enthusiastic words, and as the last minute came, the last cup emptied, the last handshake exchanged, a Georgian military band played 'Deutschland über alles!' Adjutant of the Minister of War, the young Prince Abchasi, accompanied the German delegation until shortly before Batumi, where an English officer boarded the train with a few soldiers and the Germans finally left the country of their Georgian friends.

"Such chivalry cannot and will not be forgotten in Germany; it is a comforting realization that even in these difficult times there can still be true friendship between peoples, and every German who has his heart in the right place will always be loyal to the brave Georgians who have remained loyal to their friends in times of need.

"Georgians will also never forget that Germany brought them national freedom, and this great deed of Germans is engraved in Georgian history with golden letters.

"The collapse of Germany came as a surprise to Georgia. The fledgling friendly relations between Germany and Georgia—both in the political and economic spheres—suddenly suffered a rupture, and Georgia found itself suddenly on its own. Now the English were in Georgia. They viewed the Georgians as traitors to the Entente and tried to treat them as such. The Georgian government sent a delegation to Paris in order to regulate relations with the Entente powers and to obtain recognition of Georgia."

"Aber in jenen letzten trüben Tagen zeigte sich noch einmal die Freundschaft der ritterlichen Georgier für die Deutschen in herzerreißender Weise. Sie hatten nichts mehr von uns zu erwarten, weder militärisch noch diplomatisch, weder finanziell noch kommerziell konnten die Deutschen nur das Geringste für ihre georgischen Freunde tun. England saß mit Heeresmacht in der georgischen Hauptstadt, von Englands Gnaden waren die Georgier abhängig, wenn es um Schutz gegen Russen im Norden, Tartaren im Osten, Armenier im Süden ging. Ihre betonte Freundschaft für Deutschland konnte ihnen nicht den mindesten Nutzen mehr bringen, aber jeden Schaden. Und trotzdem hielten die Georgier treu zu uns. Der Kriegsminister ließ es sich nicht nehmen, der Delegation noch am Vorabend ihrer erzwungenen Abreise ein prächtiges Fest zu geben, bei dem die deutsch-georgische Freundschaft in herzlichen Worten bekräftigt wurde. Auf dem Bahnhof hatten sich Vertreter der Regierung, der Parteien und viele persönliche Freunde der Deutschen eingefunden und unter Hochrufen auf Deutschland verließ die Delegation Tiflis. Der Aufenthalt in Kutais war eine Reihe von Banketten und Freundschaftsbezeugungen; alle Bewohner der Stadt, die monatelang eine deutsche Garnison beherbergt hatte, bestrebten sich, den Deutschen in jeder Weise ihre Sympathie und Freundschaft zu beweisen; wären die Deutschen damals als Sieger und Befreier nach Georgien gekommen, statt dass sie es zusammengebrochen als Gefangene verließen, das georgische Volk in seinem Edelsinn hätte sie nicht herzlicher und glänzender begrüßen können. Noch bei der Abfahrt aus Kutais, als schon der Bahnhof von den Bajonetten der Gurkhas starrte, war der Wartesaal festlich geschmückt, ein Abschiedstrunk bereitgestellt, noch einmal wurde in begeisterten Worten der gemeinsamen Arbeit, der gemeinsamen Siege und der treuen Freundschaft gedacht, und als die letzte Minute kam, und der letzte Becher geleert, der letzte Händedruck getauscht war, spielte eine georgische Militärkapelle

'Deutschland über alles!' Adjutant des Kriegsministers, der junge Fürst Abchasi, begleitete die deutsche Delegation bis zu dem Augenblick, in dem kurz vor Batum ein englischer Offizier mit einigen Soldaten den Zug bestieg und die Deutschen endgültig das Land ihrer georgischen Freunde verließen.

"Solche Ritterlichkeit kann und wird in Deutschland nicht vergessen werden; sie ist eine trostreiche Gewähr dafür, dass es auch in diesen schweren Zeiten noch wahre Freundschaft zwischen Völkern geben kann und jeder Deutsche, der das Herz auf dem rechten Fleck hat, wird immerdar in Treue den tapferen Georgiern Freundschaft halten, ihnen, die dem Freund Treue in der Not gehalten haben.

"Die Georgier werden auch niemals vergessen, dass Deutschland ihnen die nationale Freiheit brachte und diese große Tat der Deutschen ist mit goldenen Lettern in die georgische Geschichte eingemeißelt.

"Der Zusammenbruch Deutschlands kam für Georgien überraschend. Die jungen freundschaftlichen Beziehungen zwischen Deutschland und Georgien—sowohl auf politischem als auch auf wirtschaftlichem Gebiete—erlitten eine plötzliche Unterbrechung und Georgien sah sich plötzlich sich selbst angewiesen. Nun waren die Engländer in Georgien. Sie betrachteten die Georgier als Verräter an der Entente und versuchten, sie in diesem Sinne zu behandeln. Die georgische Regierung hat, um mit den Ententemächten die Beziehungen zu regeln und die Anerkennung Georgiens zu erlangen, nach Paris eine Delegation entsandt."

The Red Army Offensive
in November 1942

The Red Army winter offensive began during the second part of November 1942, with one-half million infantrymen, supported by new T-34 tanks, artillery and airplanes along the river Don. Simultaneously, the German 6th Army of General Paulus in Stalingrad was gradually cut off. The German military forces opposing the Soviet offensive were over extended and "thinned out." Paulus wanted to break out of Stalingrad and link with other German forces, but Hitler ordered Paulus to hold Stalingrad. Goering's promise that his air force could adequately supply Paulus in Stalingrad failed. Meanwhile, General Manstein was maintaining an important position at Elista (between the rivers Don and Volga) as a link with Kleist's Army Group A in the Caucasus.

During the second part of December, Manstein appealed to Hitler to allow Paulus to break out of Stalingrad but by now Paulus was too short of fuel to be able to do so. At the same time, General Hoth had been fighting his way toward Stalingrad to link with and rescue Paulus with initial success. But shortly before Christmas, his attack was brought to a halt by the Soviets on the river Myshkova, not all that far from Stalingrad. Shortly after Christmas, Manstein also had to retreat south of the river Don. Now the six Soviet armies began to attack around Nalchik, "our" area. Kliest was defending his position very well against the overwhelming Soviet force but felt endangered to be cut off further north at Rostov on the river Don. Therefore, he sent his 1st Panzer Army through Rostov before it was cut off, under Manstein's command to strengthen him.

Then with the 17th Army remaining with him and already cut off from other German forces, von Kleist began to retreat from Caucasus toward the Kuban Peninsula. Kliest had, under his command, 400,000 men. The Soviets finally committed eight armies against Kleist but were repelled by him. He held Kuban until the time came to evacuate his men to Crimea in an orderly fashion. "Bergmann," as noted, was part of the 17th Army.

The World Almanac of World War II, edited by Brigadier Peter Young, has been of great help in compiling some of the above listed data.

Grigol (Grisha) Alshibaja

Dr. Grigol Alshibaja was born in the city of Kutaisi in 1880. Kutaisi was then considered the cultural and administrative center of West Georgia. He graduated from the humanistic gymnasium there and continued his studies at the Faculty for Natural Science of Kiev University since the Czar forbade universities in Georgia. In Kiev, Grigol Alshibaja participated in student demonstrations against the Czar's regime. One particular protest was because of the Jewish pogroms, staged by the czarist authorities. Alshibaja was arrested, removed from the university and sentenced to two years of military duty as a simple soldier. Fortunately, after eight months the students were granted amnesty, whereupon Alshibaja entered Berlin University in 1903, graduating five years later as an M.D. after passing the state examination. The following four years he worked as a volunteer physician at Berlin University Hospital. He had passed the state examination at the Medical Military Academy in St. Petersburg as well. During 1912, the doctor returned to his native Kutaisi and opened a lucrative private practice. Four years later, he was drafted and transferred to Baku (Azerbaijan) as a military doctor. It was permissible to have a private practice on the side and with his medical background and imposing personality, his practice flourished. In Baku, as recommended by his friends, he acquired shares of the Russian-Persian oil company, "RUPENTO" and was later elected to its board of directors. Many lasting friendships were formed among those "Baku Georgians," e.g. with Khoshtarias, Kvitaishvilis and Mamulashvilis, extending over two generations. Meanwhile, Georgia declared herself to be a sovereign, independent, democratic republic. It was the rebirth of the Georgian state after years of occupation. It was recognized "de jure" by Great Britain, Belgium, France, Italy, Japan, Germany, Turkey, Poland, Bolshevik Russia, Argentina, etc.

Bolshevik Russia and Georgia had also concluded the Treaty of Moscow on May 7, 1920, according to which, "Russia agrees to refrain from all intervention in the internal affairs of Georgia," (Articles I and II). In 1919, Dr. Grigol Alshibaja was appointed as the Georgian Ambassador in Baku (Azerbaijan) by the Georgian government. In April of 1919, when Bolshevik Russia occupied Baku, they arrested all foreign diplomatic representatives there, among them Dr. Alshibaja. But after the conclusion of the May 7th treaty with Georgia, the Georgian ambassador was freed by Soviet Russia while other foreign diplomats remained in Bolshevik custody, among them the British, French, Polish ambassadors and the Papal Nuncio. Their respective governments entrusted Alshibaja with representation of their interests. For a "job well done" he was rewarded with the "Legion d' Honneur" by France, the "Golden Cross of Merit" by Poland and a "Special Blessing" from His Holiness, the Pope, as well as a note of appreciation from England.

As discussed before, in February of 1921, the Bolshevik Russian Army, without a declaration of war, invaded and occupied Georgia, despite stiff resistance. Dr. Alshibaja donated one million rubles to the "defense fund of Georgia." Finally, militarily defeated, the Georgian government had to go into exile. Dr. Alshibaja was sent to Germany where he was supposed to assume the position of the retiring Georgian ambassador in Berlin—Lado Akhmeteli. Due to the Bolshevik takeover of Georgia, this did not occur. Nevertheless, the Alshibaja family settled in Berlin, where Dr. Alshibaja again took up his work at the university clinic. At that time he sold the "RUPENTO" shares in London to British admiralty and received a substantial sum in English currency. With the help of Ramsay McDonald (whom Alshibaja had known before), he received permission to open an account in the Bank of England where he deposited this money. Subsequently, he transferred it to a German bank since he resided in Berlin, but due to German inflation and the currency reform of 1922–1923 in Germany, he suffered great losses. Dr. Alshibaja, who had donated a considerable number of scholarships for Georgian students studying abroad, could no longer support his own family of nine. For years to come, the Germans could not afford to pay salaries to foreigners.

At that point, the Polish Foreign Service Secretary of State, an old friend from his ambassadorial times, offered Dr. Alshibaja a position in the military hospital in Grodno in east Poland, where he was also permitted to open a private practice on the side. Grodno was chosen because it had a Russian speaking population, as in the past this had been a part of imperial Russia, with the Alshibajas fluent in Russian but unable to speak Polish. As in other places, Dr. Alshibaja's medical practice flourished in Grodno because he was a very well-trained, experienced and caring doctor. Soon among his patients were many V.I.P.s. In 1937, he was transferred to Warsaw and was appointed as a director of internal medicine of the outpatient clinic of the Military Academy. His patients included the Military District Commanding General A. Litwinowicz, Minister Kościałkowski, Metropolitan Dionysius of the Polish Orthodox Church, Colonel Dr. M. Woyczyński, who was the personal physician and friend of Marshal Piłsudski.

After the German occupation of Warsaw during the end of September in 1939, the Georgian Colony appealed to Dr. Alshibaja to accept the Presidency of the Colony, which he accepted, although it meant an additional heavy burden for him. Later, he had to take care of the entire Caucasian Colony (Armenian, Azerbaijan, North Caucasian and Georgian). At that time there existed four committees: Russian, Belorussian, Ukrainian and Caucasian. It was his task to represent and defend the interests of his countrymen in front of the German authorities. Because of the firm stance of his positions, he was dismissed by the occupational "Government General" in Poland. He was informed that his dismissal was on the following grounds: he had been "making depreciating utterances, criticizing the measures taken by the 'Government General' and not executing nor following the orders of the 'Government General'."

The German ambassador, Count von Schulenburg, an old friend of Grigol Alshibaja, came to his rescue and advised him to leave Warsaw in order to avert the punitive action of the Gestapo. Schulenburg made it possible for Dr. Alshibaja to travel to Germany, in a manner that would favor the treatment of his threatening aforementioned health problems. [See p. 275 —Ed.]

During the end of World War II, Dr. Grigol Alshibaja, his wife, Barbara and daughters Kethevan, Martha, Rusudan and Thina resided in Bad Reichenhall, with the family eventually moving to Munich. Barbara Kiziria Alshibaja was a very well educated, beautiful lady and an outstanding person. She was a totally devoted wife and mother and an excellent example for her daughters to follow. She was also a suffragette and had studied at St. Petersburg University. When the universities were temporarily closed because of the student revolutionary turbulences against the Czar's regime, Barbara persuaded the other Georgian lady-students in St. Petersburg to join her and continue studies in Berlin. This was at the beginning of the twentieth century and one can imagine the concern of parents back home in Georgia who felt that St. Petersburg was already far enough away from home for their daughters. But for Barbara and her friends, there was no turning back. In all fairness, one has to mention a bit of amusing teasing that Barbara was suffering from her children asking if it was it really only science she was after in Berlin, or whether "a handsome young gentleman, 'Grisha' Alshibaja" had anything to do with it.

Barbara studied psychology and after the completion of her studies and training, married Grisha and then the two of them returned to Georgia. As already noted, they moved to Baku, later to Berlin again, then to Grodno, Warsaw, Bad Reichenhall and Munich. All of their five children had post graduate university educations. It was a very good marriage, they deeply loved and respected each other. The Doctor was a straight-forward, honest and outspoken person; a "very undiplomatic diplomat" as his close friend, Georgian foreign minister E. Gegechkori once told him.

Consequently, Grigol Alshibaja had many devoted friends but made some enemies as well. His total devotion to duty on whatever assignment was extraordinary and earned him the respect of his associates. His diplomatic and beautiful wife, Barbara was of immeasurable help to him not only managing domestic matters but as a gracious hostess for the multitude of constant guests. At times, when needed, she would intervene with her soothing feminine voice, charm and humor to defuse the tension and "heal wounds." During World War II, Barbara Alshibaja was a leading member and organizer on behalf of the Georgian Red Cross with other persons, notably Mrs. Maria Shalikashvili [mother of General John Shalikashvili, Chairman of the United States Joint Chiefs of Staff —Ed.], and Razo Gabashvili. They supplied food, clothing and medicine to Georgian P.O.W.s who lived under abominable conditions.

Toward the end of 1951, an anonymous letter, printed in Russian, was distributed in Munich where a small post World War II emigration center had formed. It was directed against "Dr. Grigol Alshibaja and his son, Mikheil." It was defamatory and repugnant with incredible distortions and outright vicious lies. The author of the letter was finally recognized to have been A. Demetra and he was taken before the district court in Munich by the Alshibajas and proven guilty. Copies of the proceedings and of some documents enclosed here are self-explanatory [pp. 404–408].

Dr. Rudolf Aschenauer, attorney-at-law clarifies the matter from the very beginning until the end of the process and should be read first. (Some depositions and documents listed by Dr. R. Aschenauer are not included here for the sake of brevity but they shall remain in my archives.)

In his declaration for court [pp. 409–411], Professor von Mende mentions Shalva Maglakelidze, who is also mentioned elsewhere in this memoir.

Kale Salia and *The Georgian Destiny*

During the years of 1943 and 1944, I would occasionally run into Kale Salia or hear about him from other emigres. We were both polite and friendly to each other and got along well. According to German documents, Kale Salia was among the Georgians to whom the Germans had a connection since the occupation of Paris (1940).[348] He participated until the end of the war, and yet I was much less impressed by his political endeavor during the period of the war when I knew him in 1943–1945 than his postwar effort as an editor of a periodical in Paris. During the late forties or early fifties, he started *The Georgian Destiny* (*Bedi Kartlisa*), written in the Georgian language. It was composed of historical, literary and scientific material pertaining to Georgia, and was "modest" in its form and size but in fact, from the very outset, some outstanding Georgian men of letters such as Grigol Robakidze and Professor Mikhako Tsereteli contributed their articles to it. The journal kept a dignified tone and was free of political infighting, thus keeping true to its scientific commitment.

Nino and Kale Salia for many years not only published the journal but converted it into a larger and beautiful publication with pictures and diagrams. Internationally known scientists in the fields of Georgian (and Caucasian) history, literature, philology, architecture and art in general were published in English, French, German and in Georgian. Some Soviet, as well as emigre Georgian scientists also participated. In my and many others' view, it served the purpose well to better acquaint the Georgian (and at times, Caucasian in general) culture to the western world. Most likely, in times to come this publication will remain in the libraries of the world as a reference for those who are interested in Georgia.

Alas, during 1972–1973, an unpleasant conflict developed in Paris between K. Salia and Levan Zurabishvili, one of the dynamic and influential postwar leaders of the Georgian Colony in France who had many followers. Zurabishvili had been favorably impressed by Salia's periodical, but now was very unhappy with it. The

---

348- *Unternehmen Mainz* I. p. 1. The document refers to Salia as one of the "Nationalists—Salia, in Paris." It also mentions that from the point of view of news and politics, there was more value in the close circle around M. Kedia, Tsomaia, Korkia, Kobakhidze and the Social Democrats, Jordania, Gegechkori, Menagarashvili. Interestingly, concerning this matter, I formed the same opinion as the German who wrote the above-mentioned document.

reason was the 1972 issue of *The Georgian Destiny* where K. Salia authored a brief Georgian history in French. Zurabishvili wrote sharp criticism in his bulletin and in the newsletter about Salia's "explanation" or lack thereof as to exactly how Georgia had lost her sovereignty. It was in fact due to Bolshevik Russia's unilateral breech of the treaty with Georgia against international law and coercion by military invasion with overwhelming armed forces. Instead, Salia depicted this part of history using the official Moscow line "Georgia became Soviet." The overwhelming majority of the emigres in France apparently agreed with Zurabishvili, but Salia's friends from the scientific field took strong exception to it. Among them was David M. Lang, a noted British scholar, reader of Caucasian Studies in the University of London and the author of many books including *A Modern History of Soviet Georgia*. It was their opinion that in this connection Salia's phraseology, "Georgia became Soviet" was just a "diplomatic" move, but the critics were not convinced. Additional forceful criticism was voiced by Niko Urushadze in his letter to Salia, also concerning some Soviet Georgian contributors to Salia's recent publications. As an example, he mentioned Professor Tabagua, whose two articles represented falsification of nineteenth century Georgian history. Such was only serving the well known Moscow policy of Russification of captive nations.

Incidentally, Professor Tabagua was an assistant to the "Georgian Soviet Socialist Republics, Secretary of State," Mr. Kuchava. This was the same Kuchava who was used by Khrushchev, during the United Nations debate in New York, to deliver the speech against the "colonial governments" (meaning the Western democracies, of course). Kuchava's speech displeased the French Foreign Minister Schuman so much that he wrote a letter to Kuchava, reminding him that he—a Georgian and the son of the enslaved nation—had no right to speak about western colonialism. Schuman also briefly reminded him under what circumstances independent Georgia had been conquered.

The bottom line for criticism of Salia's issue of *The Georgian Destiny* was that it was trying to earn the reputation of an "acceptable" publication in the eyes of the Soviets; hardly an appropriate goal for any political emigre. Two years later, in a special English edition of the same journal, the controversial sentence had been altered to: "In February 1921, Georgia was Sovietized by the Red Army" (p. 64). It seems some criticism helped Salia to improve.

After his demise, Professor Kale Salia was buried in one of the two pantheons of Tbilisi; his burial took place long before "perestroika" and therefore was unprecedented treatment by the Soviets for a political emigre. May the Lord grant him peace and forgive his sins. If he had no sins, then, I would say, he did better than most of us.

Alexandre Manvelishvili

One active Tetri Giorgi member (and, I was told, the "party ideologist") who I was introduced to in Berlin was Alexandre Manvelishvili, a prolific and gifted writer and the author of some interesting publications. Most of his publications were devoted to Georgian history and literature. But curious enough, by his own admission, this was to be the means for fulfillment of his ambition to play a political role.

But such was frustrated by others, first of all from his own party (M. Tsereteli and L. Kereselidze, G. Magalashvili, K. Salia. V. Togonidze and Valodia Tskomelidze), secondly from the member parties of the "National Alliance in Paris" who had their representatives in Berlin, notably M. Kedia, A. Tsomaia and others. This probably prompted Manvelishvili to publish during the late 1980s an unfair and incorrect judgment about M. Kedia and others who had risked everything, including their lives to help many Georgians in dire situations. It did appear that he was holding back publishing such writing until after many of the persons he was attacking had died, but not all of them. For instance, the Messrs. Mikhail Kavtaradze and Levan Pagava, themselves old emigres and editors of periodicals and contemporaries of Manvelishvili whom they also knew well, took strong exceptions to his views.

First one has to review the background of this polemic. It all started because of a book, *On the History of the Georgian Emigration*, by a Bolshevik "historian," Pharnaoz Lomashvili, published in Tbilisi during 1965. It was a typical Brezhnev-era defamation campaign against the Georgian Emigration including all the political parties, the government in exile and those who fought against the Bolshevik occupation of Georgia, including the period of World War II. The main reason for this propaganda onslaught was to influence the young Georgian generation abroad as well as in Georgia.

This being the case, the Georgian National Council and the National Political Center in Paris responded with a sixty-three page booklet revealing the Bolshevik propaganda falsehoods.[349] A. Manvelishvili, on the other hand, apparently chose his

---

349- Georgian National Council and National Political Center in Paris, *On Judgment Before the Georgian People*, Arpajon: Imprimerie Cooperative Arpajonnaise, 1966, with the declaration of the Georgian Colony in France included at the end.

own "private" and curious selective response to the Bolshevik historian's book. He more or less ignored other chapters but chose to strongly comment on the W.W. II period. Here, he essentially agreed with the Soviet with relatively minor exceptions and where slander was not directed toward Manvelishvili, his party and his friends.

As noted before, Manvelishvili did not publish his response until approximately twenty-three years later and on top of this without additional comments. Needless to say that Manvelishvili's strange behavior outraged many Georgian emigres. I had met Manvelishvili only a couple of times during the war and not since; therefore, I could not honestly say that I knew him, but I was also angered by his unfairness and obvious malice. It was with interest that I heard and read of the opinion of those who knew him better.

Mikheil Kavtaradze, the editor in chief of *Iveria*, a journal of "the National Democratic Party direction" and an eyewitness to the history, wrote an extensive and well-documented essay about the disagreeable matter and proved A. Manvelishvili wrong on all counts. Kavtaradze's conclusion was that Manvelishvili had been frustrated by the lack of personal achievement and not playing an important political role during W.W. II, and therefore, being envious, he attacked those who (he thought) stood in his way.[350]

Another eyewitness to this history, Levan Pagava, a prominent social democrat and the son-in-law of the deceased Georgian president in exile, N. Jordania, also published a sharp answer to Manvelishvili, again proving him wrong. The article states,

> "Although A. Manvelishvili is a gifted writer, he also has been pathologically obsessed since his youth about playing an important political role. When, as a very young man he left Georgia, he went first to Turkey and there with his cronies formed a 'New Georgian Government' and he assumed the portfolio of the 'foreign minister'. He declared the already existing Georgian Government in exile to be invalid. He arrived in Paris with his fantasy 'cabinet' but shortly thereafter, and predictably so, it dissolved.

> "M. Kedia, a great Georgian patriot, who in the service of his country with the valor of a knight, carried out many humanitarian deeds of extreme importance in close cooperation with the Georgian government in exile. For instance, M. Kedia saved many Georgian P.O.W.s from certain death by freeing them from the P.O.W. camps. He did so regardless of their political affiliation. (This included active

---

350- *Iveria*, April 1990, Paris. pp. 72–79.

card-carrying communists.) He saved many Georgian Jews and with them Russian and French Jews from certain death and from being herded to the Nazi crematoriums. From his position, M. Kedia could have easily amassed a fortune but in this respect he also remained spotless."

The journal also elucidates M. Kedia's tragic death and further rejects as false other "lesser" accusations against M. Kedia by Manvelishvili.[351]

I had read some of A. Manvelishvili's books, which he had autographed and sold to me after World War II, and I thought them to be well written. I especially enjoyed one, *The Golden Age of the History of Georgia*. In response, I wrote to the author expressing my appreciation of his excellent work, adding that I wished I possessed his ability to author such books, that I could use this while struggling with my memoirs. He responded with an encouraging letter stating that I should have no problem at all because of my background and gave me some technical tips. He also added that some time ago he had read my essay, "The Georgians and World War II" in the journal *Iveria*, 1981 No. 24, and pointed out two data in it that he did not agree with but observed that apparently I had been misinformed by others. More recently I read A. Manvelishvili's thirteenth (and presumably last) publication containing a disagreeable article, "some remarks" pp. 17-22, about which we just discussed. I could hardly believe it and wrote a polite but a firm letter reproaching him for an unwarranted attack on our good compatriots who were already dead and therefore unable to defend themselves. I also mentioned the total lack of documentation for his accusations. He chose not to answer my last letter.

One cannot take away from A. Manvelishvili his accomplishment of writing some valuable works about Georgian history. His political views, however, are something else. The Georgians fought a long battle (that is still not over) to regain national sovereignty and other human rights. It is true that the Georgian question is not one of political parties but of national freedom. Nevertheless, they did not fight for replacing one dictatorship—communism—for another one, fascism. I wish (and so do others) that A. Manvelishvili would have confined himself to what he did best, writing on the pure historical themes.

351- See "Our Flag"—May 1990, Paris, pp. 38–44 in Georgian. Editor L. Pagava. (The journal was originally founded by Noe Jordania, the Georgian President in exile.)

Alexandre Nikuradze

After the war, I was to see Professor Nikuradze again several times in Munich. Being a physicist, he was doing research in his field. He had more time to see the members of a small Georgian Colony in Munich, including my in-laws. He entertained them with short pieces of his poetry—stories from the past about his work and his predictions of the future. They all became fond of him. The professor married his German secretary, and they had a darling little daughter. During one of our visits in Munich (we did not live there), he invited my wife and I for a dinner and insisted we spend the night at their home. Needless to say, we talked late into the night. He told me that after the war the American intelligence service had detained him for a few months, mainly because he had been researching the atom. After a thorough investigation, he was freed.

During the war, a certain mystery surrounded Professor A. Nikuradze. In postwar literature, opinions were divided about him—was he a "good doer" or a villain? For instance, Professor David M. Lang writes about him, "The Georgians under Nazi domination were saved only by the intervention of Alexandre Nikuradze, a Georgian scientist, held in high esteem in the German official world." Professor Lang also states, "Rosenberg and other exponents of Nazi racism wanted all Georgians to be exterminated along with the Jews and Gypsies on a racial basis." With all due respect to Professor Lang, his second statement is not correct and probably represents a fantasy of his informant. As already noted, the Georgians did not feel racially threatened and were secure enough to protect not only the Georgian Jews but also a number of the Russian and French Jews. Moreover, concerning Caucasus in the Nazi mind, "Only three things were spelled out in advance: German need for Caucasian oil; Nazi 'knowledge' that the population of Caucasus was largely non-Slavic and 'Aryan' and the absence of German designs for resettlement in the Caucasus."[352]

As stated before, Professor Nikuradze's influence on Rosenberg was great, but I was curious if he used it for personal gain only? Was he really a Nazi at heart

---

352- Alexander Dallin, *German Rule in Russia*. [No page number given –Ed.]

or was he a utilitarian? I did not know him long enough or well enough to be able to answer such questions, (although I had a "gut feeling" about it). Therefore, I needed help and got it from another Georgian, Professor Wachtang Djobadze, who knew Professor Nikuradze rather well. Professor Djobadze's observations were that Professor Nikuradze was an exceptionally talented and capable scientist, a prolific writer and publisher, capable of carrying out serious research projects. He was also an ambitious person. It would probably be impossible for him to advance in the competitive and especially Nazi dominated Germany, inasmuch as he was a foreigner (and not exactly a "Nordic-Germanic" type). Therefore, he took German citizenship and joined the Nazi Party, very much like many of his colleague-scientists did in Germany and just as the Soviet scientists had to join the Communist Party in the U.S.S.R.

Nikuradze took advantage of an old friendship with Rosenberg (both were emigres and students in Munich, as noted). After Rosenberg became the Reich's Minister for the Eastern Occupied Territories, Nikuradze became his main adviser and the Director of the Research Institute of Continental Europe. But whatever Nikuradze researched or wrote, the Georgian question was always included in it. In other words, "Georgia was on his mind."[353] I need to add to Professor Djobadze's statement that Nikuradze remained alert during the cataclysm of World War II, where potential dangers were ever present, especially for the people of small nations. For instance, I know from M. Kedia that while he was undertaking the mission of saving the Jews, he had support not only from Professor G. von Mende of the Ostministerium but also from Professor A. Nikuradze.[354]

Another example of Nikuradze's influence is as follows: During the fall of 1941, General Ali Fuad Erden, former commandant of the Turkish General Staff Academy and a member of Parliament, and Hussein Erkilet, a prominent pan-Turkist and pro-German general of Tatar origin, arrived for an official visit in the Reich, which included a reception by the Führer. The Germans sought to revive memories of German-Turkish "brotherhood in arms" during the First World War and to impress their guests by a tour of the Eastern Front. Upon their return, the generals reported at length to the Turkish President, foreign minister and chief of the General Staff.[355]

According to Dallin, "The guests also urged upon the Germans better treatment of Turkic P.O.W.s and suggested the formation of 'volunteer' legions among

---

353- Professor Nikuradze (nom de plume—A. Sanders), especially *Kaukasien*, Munich: Verlag Hoheneichen, 1942 and 1944, and *Osteuropa in kontinentaleuropaeischer Schau*, publisher as above, 1942 and 1944.

354- See document in the author's archives.

355- Alexander Dallin, *German Rule in Russia*, p. 234.

them." The other factor influencing Hitler likely was a letter written to him by an Azerbaijani major of the Soviet General Staff, now a P.O.W. in German hands, who wrote that, "...he had always had pro-Nazi, anti-Bolshevik leaning and only sought an opportunity to fight for his homeland." It appears that these two factors changed Hitler's mind. Whereas at first he forbade military service by all the Eastern people, regardless of their national origin, Hitler now felt that "the pure Moslems," that is to say "the real Turkic peoples," were reliable and therefore authorized the formation of a Turkic legion during mid-November 1941.[356]

Dallin notes, "...unlike some of the diplomats, the top officials of the Ostministerium were decidedly hostile to the pro Turkish orientation. The evil genius once again appears to have been Nikuradze. The two imperialistic conceptions of a 'Turkish-led Caucasian Grossraum' and of a 'Georgian-led Caucasus' were bound to clash fiercely."[357] I cite this example here in order to demonstrate Nikuradze's readiness and effectiveness to move Minister Rosenberg when he felt, rightly or wrongly, that the concessions to Turkey may be forthcoming at the expense of Georgia.

Incidentally, in spite of Hitler's authorization only to form the Turkic legion, O.K.W. (the Supreme Command of the Military Forces), with the "enthusiastic" support of the Ostministerium, soon ordered formation also of two separate non Muslim legions for Armenians and Georgians. How did this come about? In explanation, Dallin quotes a document, according to which, "Apparently, Rosenberg convinced Hitler that the creation of separate national legions for each ethnic group would permit simultaneously the inculcation of anti-Russian ideas and neutralizing the danger of a pan Turkanic movement."[358] Consequently four separate legions were formed—Turkastani, Caucasian Muslims (the North Caucasians and Azerbaijani), Armenian and Georgian.

Although not mentioned in the document, I favor the thought that Professor A. Nikuradze also in this instance moved his minister to go to Hitler with such a proposal. This is, however, not an indirect expression of approval for the institution of the Ostministerium nor of its Minister Rosenberg. The Caucasians and the other "Easterners" did not ask for such a ministry and would rather deal with the Germans on the basis of Schulenburg's plan. However, this plan was forbidden by a ruthless dictator who in its place had already established the Ostministerium. This being the case, from a practical point of view, while solving the problems on a day-to-day basis, it was essential for us that two important workers of the Ostministerium, Professor von Mende and Bräutigam promoted the Caucasian cause. As it turned out, from

---

356- All quotes from Alexander Dallin, *German Rule in Russia*, p. 540.
357- A. Dallin, *German Rule in Russia*, p. 236.
358- A. Dallin, *German Rule in Russia*, p. 540; Document 1517—P.S, TMWC, XXVII, 272.

a somewhat different position, Professor A. Nikuradze also thought to protect the Caucasian cause.

As far as the Foreign Office was concerned, "some of the diplomats who were espousing pro Turkish policy" were von Papen, Henting and Woermann but not von Schulenburg, with whom we would be all be too happy to deal and who was planning to rely on the Caucasian refugees. Our general feelings toward the Ostministerium are made clear by examples, such as referring to it as a "colonial ministry" as well as at one Caucasian meeting in Berlin (which was also attended by Professor von Mende), when M. Kedia exclaimed, "If the Ostministerium will send Mr. Schikedanz to Caucasus as a Reich's Commissar, we the Caucasians are going to take to the hills as partisan fighters."

General Giorgi Kvinitadze

General Giorgi Kvinitadze's roots originated in the West Georgian family of Chikovani. His grandfather, Simon Chikovani, was a courtier to King Solomon of the Imereti (West Georgia). During 1830, Russian troops occupied Imereti. King Solomon and his faithful went into exile in Turkey, among them Simon. Simon's son, Ivan (the father of our general), was left in the care of a noble family of Tsitsishvili in East Georgia. The Kingdom of East Georgia had been occupied twenty-nine years earlier by the Imperial Russian troops which constituted a breach of the 1783 treaty between the Empress Cathrine of Russia and King Irakli of East Georgia. Although their national pride had been hurt because of this occupation, many Georgians (mostly nobility) still entered the Russian Army and served there with distinction. Among them was the father of our general, then thirteen-year-old Ivan who had changed his name Chikovani to Kvinitadze and made an excellent carrier in the Russian Army. He spoke many languages, and when a well-known French author, Alexandre Dumas embarked on the Caucasus journey, Ivan Kvinitadze was appointed to accompany and guide him.

Our general, Giorgi Kvinitadze, following his father's footsteps, also as a teenager entered and progressed through excellent military schools of the Russian Empire. During the Russian-Japanese War, 1904, G. Kvinitadze volunteered for front duty where he gained his first combat experience and distinguished himself. Five years later, then a Captain, G. Kvinitadze graduated from the General Staff Academy and was appointed to the staff of the Caucasus Military District. During World War I, Colonel G. Kvinitadze had the position of Chief of Staff of the 4th Caucasian Infantry Division, which fought on the Turkish Front and took the Fortress of Erzurum. There he was awarded the coveted St. George's Medal for bravery and "St. George's Weapon."

At the time of the October 1917 Russian Bolshevik Revolution, Major General of the General Staff, G. Kvinitadze was a much respected military leader. During the Independent Georgian Republic 1918–1921, the Georgian patriot General G. Kvinitadze devoted all his energy and know-how to the creation of the Georgian Military School, which played a very positive role during the Republic and thereafter (also during World War II). The government of the Georgian Republic appointed General G. Kvinitadze as a commanding general of the Armed Forces more than once; but then would relieve him of his duties. Obviously, the government and the Commander in Chief had major differences of opinion about the ways of solving the manifold difficult problems. Briefly stated, General Kvinitadze felt that the government was agreeing, compromising and yielding to the Armenians, Turks and Soviets, instead of showing more initiative and power to govern and decisiveness aiming at victory. At times, in his view, the government appointees to supervise the armed forces were not made according to their ability and credentials but because of partisan political considerations. The General also felt that creation of the National Guard with its ideological orientation to the Social Democrat Party doctrine and their preferential treatment was weakening the armed forces. He considered them inadequately trained and disciplined and prone to act independently instead of in coordination with the regular army units. They, in fact, resembled the "praetorian guards" and undermined the Georgian defense.

The above information is based mainly on General G. I. Kvinitadze's memoirs, *My Recollection of the Years of the Georgian Independence 1917–1921.*

The General and his family of six endured much deprivation after his emigration from Georgia. But true to his nature he was far from being discouraged. He and his family organized a small family-based yogurt production business in Chatou/Seine, where each of them worked hard and it went well. A great Georgian patriot, Giorgi Kvinitadze maintained a keen interest in the political activities of the Caucasian emigration. He belonged to the Georgian National Democrat Party as well as Haidar Bamat's "Kavkaz" ("Caucasus") circle. His former pupils—graduates of the Georgian Military School who, after annexation of Georgia, served in the armies of several European countries, loved and revered their General and kept in touch with him.

The Plot in "Bergmann":
Court Documents and Soviet Propaganda

I had no idea until I read F. L. Carsten's publication that one of the suspects, Vaso Jugeli [spelled Dschugeli in German], had found in his wardrobe the diary of a non-commissioned officer, Shara Tsutskiridze [spelled Zuzkiridze in German] and handed it over to the battalion's chief. This diary apparently had served as important evidence against the accused in court. The diary commences on November 1, 1941, and ends on May 17, 1942.

It discussed the goal of the conspiracy, its strategy, methods, meetings, recruiting of members, some of the names of participants and Tsutskiridze's confidence in them or lack thereof. For instance on page sixteen of this diary, it reads, "... Vaso Jugeli disturbs the comradeship. We shall see how he will do in the end. I think that regardless of whatever place he may be occupying, he should be removed (eliminated)." In describing alleged individual participants in the conspiracy, the main document states about Captain Tsiklauri, "The accused contests issue of his being a member of the leader of the conspiracy. He also denies knowledge of a plan to turn over the battalion, 'Bergmann' to the Russians. Tsiklauri maintains that "those accused and/or the witnesses who had incriminated him are telling lies and are themselves the greatest enemies of the German Armed Forces. They intend to undermine Tsiklauri's authority in the battalion's staff and thus destroy his proposed plans for military action."

It was also new to me that Captain Tsiklauri, in self defense, chose to counterattack, as a group, all those who in their deposition incriminated him. At the same time he emphasized the importance of his military plan submitted to the Germans some time ago. Yet he never pointed an accusing finger at any individual. The document enumerated the number of various accusations alleged against Captain Tsiklauri, some of them less serious than others. For instance, the witnesses Alimbarashvili, Dschanelidze and Okropiridze stated how the Captain castigated a soldier named Simsive after the soldier ridiculed Stalin in a song. The Captain had said that Stalin was a great man, "our Georgian" and we don't want to give reason for other nations to ridicule us because we don't respect our own Georgian.

I think the three witnesses mentioned above had been asked by the court investigator to confirm this incident which had been known to almost everyone in "Bergmann" and in itself, it was not proof of an existing conspiracy. Rather, it could have been a feeling of one Georgian, Tsiklauri, for another Georgian, Stalin, who achieved great fame. I personally hated Stalin but would not have enjoyed such a silly song about him. This great ruthless tyrant had to be defeated and removed; a far too serious matter to be joked about. The traditional Georgian chivalry that has been one of the foundations in the upbringing of its youth also accorded certain respect to the enemy.

There were more serious allegations by Okropiridze and Tabidze about the ideological creed of Captain Tsiklauri, which could have led him to the conspiracy. Okropiridze quoted Tsiklauri as telling him, "I can only tell you that I am already on the side of the Bolsheviks, you should not fault them because your father was arrested. The shootings (executions) in the Soviet Union are maneuvered by Nazi agents in Tokyo. Your enemies are not the Bolsheviks but those under whose leadership you are now." And then, "Without Bolshevik victory, life will make no sense to me at all." In court, Tabidze also quoted the Captain, telling him, "Should the Germans be victorious, I will shoot myself."

Tsutskiridze's diary in February and March also records Captain Tsiklauri's attitude as well as his active coordinated activity with Tsutskiridze. Tsiklauri recruited persons in the companies for participation in the plot and was holding "pep talks" for such a purpose. The court document also states that Tsiklauri had been a leader of the conspiracy as told by the witnesses, Ossipashvili and Zurgashvili and by the accused Arabuli, Bakhtadze and Tabidze.[359]

Of considerable interest to me in the court document was the report about Jimuhadze and Khmelidze.[360] The former denied taking part in the plot as well as knowledge of its goal. However, Jimuhadze admitted writing a letter that had been dictated to him by Tabidze. This letter was then signed by Jimuhadze, Tsiklauri, Tabidze and Ossipashvili. As Tabidze informed the court, the purpose of this letter was to tell of the existence of a battalion in German uniforms which nevertheless, in a patriotic spirit, was dedicated to the cause of the Soviet home country. The letter had been hidden in a house and in good time when the "Reds" arrived, they would see the letter and it would prove to them the loyalty of these men, now in their hands again.

The witness, Pogosov, said that Jimuhadze was spreading false news about the strength and the new weapons the Soviets possess and like Kharkov had been retaken by the Bolsheviks. The accused Khmelidze, in self-defense stated in court

---

359- See page 498 of the document.
360- The German spelling in the document is Dschimuchadze and Chmelidze. See page 503 therein.

that the way he acted was due to his stupidity and the influence of the radio news which he heard from Tabidze and Jimuhadze. This statement is interesting to me, as I often felt that Soviet propaganda reached the German occupied territories better than was generally appreciated.

The court's opinion about the accused, while testifying against each other in self-defense, was such as to view them with considerable caution. They note this applies especially to Tabidze and Tsutskiridze, since these two would use any means to escape punishment. In this entire document, where my name, Givi Gabliani, is mentioned as a witness, there is not a single quotation from my deposition used against Tsiklauri or anyone else. Quite the opposite, where the document quotes my statements, they are on behalf of Lieutenant Albert Andreasjan, who was freed by the court, and Lieutenant Fedor Tadeev, whom the court found guilty in spite of my statement in his favor. (I have no recollection of such an occurrence at all.)

Tsiklauri appeared to be a lonely man in court without a visible friend. His associates in the plot testified against him in order to save their own skins. This is why, during our only encounter in court, he returned my handshake and greeting with a warm handshake. He also reminded me of his unusual dream he had told me about when we were roommates. He considered this dream a bad omen as I indicated above. (I was not the only one who expressed human compassion and respect for Captain Tsiklauri. A member of the military court, Colonel Dr. Grobholz, in an unusual move, also approached Tsiklauri, shook his hand and complimented the Captain for his dignified conduct in court, as the "Bergmann" interpreters told me.)

In the final analysis, why and how did Captain Tsiklauri's conspiracy come about? The Georgians in "Bergmann" had often pondered about it and we had to admit to ourselves that most likely we would never know the exact answer to the question. Nevertheless, some consensus of opinion had emerged, according to which Tsiklauri was not a Soviet spy, nor was Tabidze. The senate of the court investigated this possibility through the witness Okropiridze's deposition concerning this matter. Allegedly, Tabidze had told the witness, Okropiridze, earlier that he (Tabidze) and Tsiklauri defected to the German side in order to embark on a spy mission for the Soviets. Moreover, Tabidze also told the court that allegedly Tsiklauri informed him that he was a Soviet spy. But both of the accused, during a heated argument, insisted that this had never been their intention when they became German P.O.W.s and introduced counter evidence. After due investigation, the senate of the court came to the conclusion that the previous statement by the accused had been of rather boisterous design for the purpose of appearing in front of other P.O.W.s as representatives of the Soviet Union.

Tsiklauri was a product of Bolshevik education, including military school. He was grateful to the Soviet system for his rank in the Army and all the privileges and prestige that came along with it. But somewhere deep in his heart, he could not have approved of the mass execution of the leading Red Army officers, the "watch dog" commissars constantly breathing down his neck and the abolishment of the Georgian Red Army units which first had been allowed by Bolshevik Russia but disbanded after the Georgian conquest. Thus Georgian military men were dispersed over vast Soviet territory, as already noted.

Tsiklauri had also been aware of some shortcomings of the Red Army and other negative aspects of Soviet reality but absolutely could not bring himself to blame Stalin and Bolshevik rule for it. While on the Ukrainian front during early July, he must have been devastated when he recognized that the Soviet Army was no match for the Germans. His career and the world he belonged to were crumbling, but instinctively he felt that life had to go on. He was encouraged by German propaganda leaflets that promised good treatment for defectors, a positive prospect for him. So he defected with the soldiers under his command to the Germans. This he told to his recruiting person, Professor Dr. Raupach. On November 28, 1941, he joined "Bergmann" and while in Neuhammer-Silesia, he carried out duties as an officer.

On March 26, 1942, he was transferred to Luttensee in Bavaria with "Bergmann," where I first met him during April and he revealed to me that he had shot a commissar. Between early July 1941 (the time of his defection from the Soviets) and the winter of 1941–1942, several important developments and changes took place which had to influence his thinking. One, the German "blitzkrieg" came to a halt and it was not able to mortally wound the Soviet Army—not even to take Moscow and Leningrad. In fact, the Soviet counter offensive near Moscow inflicted considerable losses on the Germans, including their tanks.

During December 1941 and the beginning of January 1942, the Soviets launched a major successful offensive west and northwest of Moscow along the five hundred mile sector. At that time, while in Silesia, Tsiklauri and his friends listened to Soviet broadcasts and knew of the important developments. To them this was a turning point of the war, favoring Soviet victory.

Another major event was when England and the United States extended a helping hand to the U.S.S.R. and even entered an alliance with Stalin's government. For the Soviets, it meant tremendous relief from the critical shortage of military and other supplies. Almost as important was that it boosted the prestige, in the eyes of the Soviet populace, of their own government—as if Stalin and his henchmen's monstrous deeds had all been forgiven and now they became equal partners of western democracy. Moreover, contrary to earlier fear among many of the rank and file Red Army soldiers, Japan did not attack the Soviet Union but chose to remain neutral. Thus the danger of a second front for the Soviets had been eliminated—a substantial "morale booster" for them.

Last but not the least reason for the creation of the conspiracy was Tsiklauri's five-month long exposure to the P.O.W. camp in Ukraine with the well documented poor treatment of the inmates and where he also learned about the misdeeds of the civilian Nazi administration in the German-occupied territories. His thought had to be, "They may behave the same way in Georgia." This was not what the German propaganda leaflets had promised and what Tsiklauri expected to see on the German side in the first place. He had a change of heart and decided to defect back to the Soviet side, but how?

As already noted, according to the Kremlin declaration, any P.O.W. in German hands was a traitor. The degree of Tsiklauri's guilt had soared to astronomical proportions after shooting the commissar,[361] his self-proclaimed defection to the Germans and joining "Bergmann." Perhaps carrying out an extraordinary pro Soviet deed would sufficiently rehabilitate him to be welcomed back "home" again? Tsiklauri met groups of men with similar ideas while in Neuhammer-Silesia and the conspiracy was born.

After the court investigation, there was no doubt that had the plotters carried out their final plan undisturbed, much more bloodshed and human sacrifice would have resulted than the twelve soldiers who were found guilty and sentenced to death.[362] (Although we would rather have seen their lives spared by transferring them to P.O.W. labor camps.)

It would also have ruined "Bergmann's" mission on behalf of the Caucasian people. Zurgashvili, who took on the very unpleasant task of informing about the conspiracy, first to Bagrat Chanturia and subsequently Oberländer, deserved credit, which he never received to the best of my knowledge. How did Soviet propaganda react to the Tsiklauri plot in "Bergmann"? During the immediate postwar Stalin era, there was total silence about it. Apparently, the whole thing was too embarrassing for the "monolithic" regime to talk about and further propagate. Whenever they could, however, persecute the partakers in the voluntary units, they did so, even if they had plotted against the Germans as Tsiklauri did. Often their relatives in Georgia were also sentenced to exile in remote areas of the U.S.S.R. Generally speaking, everyone who for whatever reason had been beyond the "Iron Curtain" was viewed as an agent of the "Western imperialist world" and treated accordingly.

361- Shooting the commissar may not have been politically motivated but rather on a personal basis.
362- Professor F. L. Carsten, *The Slavonic and East European Review*, Vol. XL 52 #109, 1969 London, pp. 483-509.

Khrushchev, during his early "liberalization" and "de-Stalinization" policy, chose a somewhat "milder" course to follow toward the dissidents, their families and emigres. Some "amnesties" were declared and propaganda also reflected such an attitude. But it was short-lived, and Khrushchev actually had to reverse his "liberalism" in several areas during the following years and remained ambivalent in others. When Brezhnev replaced Khrushchev, he "re-Stalinized" everything again. The "amnesties" were revoked and the press, literature and art were ordered to start defamation campaigns against those who had opposed Kremlin tyranny. Great emphasis was placed on promotion of "Soviet patriotism" again, especially among the young people.

As an example, the "Soviet patriot" during W.W. II was put on a pedestal; he was endowed with superhuman qualities, as opposed to emigres and generally all of those who were against the Soviet system. Those people were depicted as traitors of their own country, agents of foreign imperialistic powers devoid of ethics, moral conscience, courage, wisdom and intelligence. Captain Tsiklauri's "Bergmann" plot was also utilized as a suitable example of it all.

Several books have been published in the Soviet Republic of Georgia about it. I read two of them, allegedly authored by M. Nemirova and E. Kalandadze, one of them in Russian, *In the Name of Life* and another in Georgian, *The Secret Deeds of the Wehrmacht*. They are not accurate presentations but rather fictional stories full of incredible distortions of the truth, half-truths and outright false statements made with intent to deceive the reader. In response, I had no choice but to publish articles in *The Georgian Opinion* (an emigre newspaper in New York), with the title "About Some Books Published in Georgia." They were well received by emigres in the U.S.A. and Western Europe.

But what was the use of it? The majority of emigres, many of them by personal experience already knew the true story. Therefore, the publisher, Dimitri Sindikeli, mailed a number of copies to every library in Georgia, hoping that someone there would read it and pass it on to the next person. All we wanted was for the people in Georgia to learn the truth.

Anyone seriously interested in the true story could easily obtain F. L. Carsten's published document listed here in the bibliography. It is quite informative about the plot, the individual participants in it, their conduct, witnesses and their depositions. Therefore, my presentation can be checked and compared to the one by Carsten. I have one more remark: In Bolshevik propaganda books, the main hero, Captain Tsiklauri and his co-plotters were not acceptable as they really were. A fictitious legend had to surround them first before they would be presented to the Soviet reader. For instance, according to the legend, Captain Tsiklauri became a P.O.W. in

German hands only because he had sustained a chest wound and was unconscious. Apparently, the Bolshevik heroes had to be dead or near death before they dared to be captured. Why not die then? Lenin's and Stalin's "Valhalla" awaits the Red heroes. Nor was it possible for them to follow honestly the document published by Carsten, which by their own admission had been in their possession as early as the Spring of 1968. By the same token, I could not be accepted in these books as a political opponent who had also tried to be fair, because Lenin's and Stalin's legacy did not allow them to do so.[363] It was necessary to defame those who stood up against the persecuting system. So as a "villain" who opposed the hero, Tsiklauri, I had to be the chief of military intelligence of "Bergmann." If there was such a position, I have never heard of it. However, all "Bergmann" officers were considered to be intelligence officers since "Bergmann" was established by Admiral Canaris's Military Intelligence.

Being Tsiklauri's roommate, "I had discovered" that he had a safety box, which was opened in secrecy and with the help of a German specialist. There it was, a document that revealed the existence of the conspiracy and the participants of it in "Bergmann." Never mind the fact that there was not such a box, with or without documents in Tsiklauri's room and that I had never suspected the existence of a conspiracy.

And why would I be so interested in getting rid of the Captain? The Soviet book gives a very clear reason: I wanted to take away from Tsiklauri the position of Commander of "Bergmann." Again, never mind that the Commander of "Bergmann" was to begin with and remained Captain Theodor Oberländer until the summer of 1943, at which time we both left "Bergmann," but this is another story which we have previously addressed.

Why was I singled out with some other Georgians and Germans by Soviet propaganda literature? It does not even mention the real names of those who really reported the existence of the conspiracy and discovered the documents.[364] Perhaps because the names of some of us were better known in Georgia and had been identified with Georgian opposition to Bolshevik oppression. Therefore, our defamation was more important and justified, pursuant to the Lenin (and Stalin) line, which is so clearly explained by Viktor Chernov.

363- Viktor Chernov, "Lenin: A Contemporary Portrait," *Foreign Affair*, March 1924. Viktor Chernov, Lenin's contemporary revolutionary and political rival, characterized him in an article published a few days after Lenin's death. The concept of a fair (honest) opponent was alien to Lenin, writes Chernov, and to him such an idea was absurd. The protector of the proletariat, in Lenin's opinion, has an obligation to put aside the ethical considerations toward his opponent. Therefore to betray, belittle and defame an opponent was considered normal by Lenin, who admitted this with matchless cynical rudeness, remarks Chernov.

364- See Professor F. L. Carsten, *The Slavonic and East European Review*, Vol. XL 52 #109 1969, London, pp.483–509 for the real names.

DOCUMENTS FROM THE AUTHOR'S ARCHIVE

and

MAPS

Letter from E. Gegechkori, Secretary of State of Georgia (in exile)
to M. Kedia on July 6, 1943

For an abbreviated English translation of this letter, see pages 219 through 220.

For an abbreviated English translation of this letter, see pages 219 through 220.

Verbindung.

**Letter of Noe Jordania, the Georgian President in exile
to M. Kedia on July 7, 1943**

For an abbreviated English translation of this letter see page 220.

10. X. 43

There was a resolution during the meeting of the Georgian National Alliance in Paris on the 27th of October 1943. Because of this letter, and Gegechkori's and Jordania's letters, Kedia remained in Berlin and the Georgian Liaison Staff—a mission—was formed.

For the abbreviated English translation of this letter see page 221.

Augsburg, 10/01/49
Arnulf Str. 40

Professor Dr. Hans Raupach
DECLARATION;

My acquaintance with Michael Kedia dates back to the fall of 1940. At that time I was charged with the care of the social well-being of the emigration from Russia—as far as it would be within the competence of the Army. Mr. Kedia came forward as a trusted representative of the Georgian Colony in France. Like all other emigrations the Georgians were also divided in several opposing groups. M. Kedia acted in a splendid nonpartisan way, for the good of all these groups. He intervened with success before the German Security organs for the benefit of his countrymen who had been arrested because of their affiliation with the social democratic organizations. While working with the German Armed Forces, Kedia was thus hoping to liberate his country which did belong, as he emphasized, with the Western Christian world. He was hoping that the German Armed Forces would ensure a morally superior program. However, later he observed with growing concern the exploitation by the Nazi Civilian Administration of the occupied land. With great courage Kedia verbalized his criticism to the higher party functionaries, which was, at that time, extraordinary. Kedia maintained such an attitude especially on behalf of his host country, France, at a time when it was of a disadvantage for him personally. Such behavior was born out of his feeling of moral responsibility and of humanism.

of Dr. Hans Raupach   Augsburg, den 1 .10.49
                                                        Arnulstr. 40

E r k l a r u n g .
=====================

Meine Bekanntschaft mit Herrn Michael K e d i a datiert seit dem Herbst 1940. Im Auftrage der deutschen Besatzungsmacht hatte ich in Paris die Aufgabe, mich um die sozialen Belange der Emigration aus Russland zu kümmern, solange die Zuständigkeit der Wehrmacht hiefür gegeben war. Herr K. trat dabei als Vertrauensmann der georgischen Kolonie in Frankreich in Erscheinung. Wie alle Emigrantengruppen waren auch die Georgier in gegensätzliche Gruppen gespalten. Herr K. hat jedoch in hervorragend unparteiischer Weise das Wohl aller Notleidenden aus diesen Gruppen wahrgenommen. So intervenierte er auch mit Erfolg zu Gunsten von deutschen Sicherheitsorganen wegen Zugehörigkeit zu sozialdemokratischen Organisationen verhafteter Landsleute. In Zusammenarbeit mit der Wehrmacht hoffte Herr K. auf die Befreiung der Heimat, deren Zugehörigkeit zum christlichen Abendland er betonte. Er hoffte dabei auf ein moralisch überlegenes Programm, dessen Garant die Wehrmacht sein sollte. Mit grosser Sorge und seine Meinung frei zum Ausdruck bringend, verfolgte er später die Ausbeutungsmassnahmen, die von der NS-Zivilverwaltung in den besetzten Gebieten ergriffen wurden. Der Freimut mit dem Herr K.seine Ansicht auch gegenüber hochgestellten Funktionären der Partei vertrat, war in jener Zeit aussergewöhnlich. Er entsprang persönlichem Verantwortungsgefühl und humaner Grundgesinnung. Diese Haltung bewahrte Herr K. insbesondere auch seinem Gastlande Frankreich gegenüber, auch in Situationen, wo ein anderes Verhalten ihm hätte persönliche Vorteile bringen können.

DRaupach

Geneva

May 3, 1946

Affidavit

During the German occupation of France, I was able to save a large number of Georgian Jews and those of other nationalities from persecution by certain German functionaries. For this undertaking, I received letters of appreciation from the Grand Rabbi Weil of Paris, from the Association Culturelle Sepharadite de Paris and from the President du Groupement Georgien de confession mosaique, which are included here.

I declare emphatically that such action was possible for me only because of the other three gentlemen of the Georgian Committee, Dr. Georg Magalow, Michael von Alschibaya [Mikheil Alshibaja] and Dr. Givi Gabliani, who were of the same opinion and helped me in this matter.

Signature and seals.

Notary seal validating signature of M. KEDIA
by Henri Fontaine, Chef de bureau

(second notary seal from August 21, 1946)

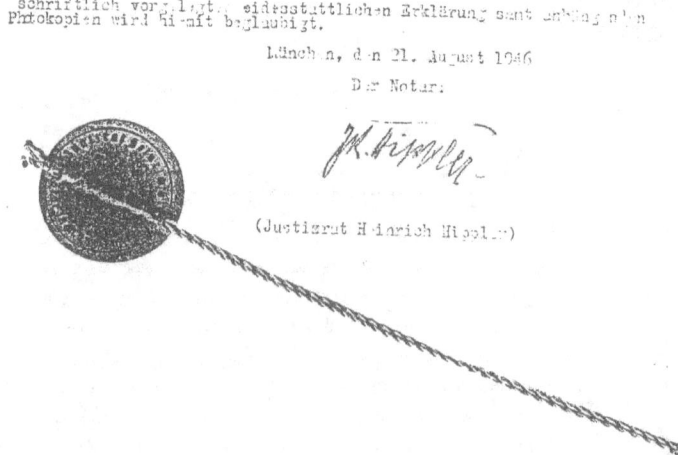

schriftlich vorgelegt, eidesstattlichen Erklärung samt anliegenden
Photokopien wird hiemit beglaubigt.

München, den 21. August 1946

Der Notar:

JR. Tissler

(Justizrat Heinrich Tissler)

698

Beglaubigt Photokopien.

Genf, den 3. Mai 1946

Eidesstattliche Erklärung

In der Zeit der deutschen Besetzung Frankreichs konnte ich eine grosse Zahl georgischer Juden und solche anderer Nationalität vor dem Zugriff der deutschen Behörden retten.

Für dieses Verhalten habe ich ein Dankschreiben des Oberrabiners Weil von Paris, von der Association Culturelle Sepharadite de Paris und vom Präsidenten du Groupement georgien de confession mosaïque bekommen, welche ich dieser Erklärung beilege.

Ich erkläre ausdrücklich, dass mir diese Aktion nur möglich war, weil in diesem Punkte die drei anderen Herren des georgischen Komitees Dr. Georg Magalow, Michael von Alschibaya und Dr. Givi Gabliani der gleichen Auffassung mit mir waren und mitgeholfen haben.

C. Kedia

pour la légalisation de la signature de
Mr. **Michael KEDIA**
apposée ci-dessus
Genève, le 4 mai 1946
pr. la Chancellerie:

Henri FONTAINE
Chef de bureau

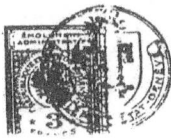

Israelite Central Consistory of France
Consistory of Paris
General Secretariat
17 Rue Saint-George
Paris IX

October 16, 1944
Mr. Michael Kedia

Sir:

Having been informed by Mr. Eligoulachvili of the great services which you have rendered to your countrymen of Jewish faith by generously aiding to save them from the consequences of racial laws, I associate myself with the sentiments of gratitude which they feel for you.

Please be assured of my personal thanks for your kind solicitude for their welfare and accept the expression of my respect.

The Grand Rabbi of Paris

Julius Weiss

Association Consistoriale Israélite de Paris

CONSISTOIRE DE PARIS

SECRÉTARIAT GÉNÉRAL :
17, Rue Saint-Georges
PARIS-IXe

PARIS, LE 16 octobre 1941

à Monsieur
Michel KEDIA

Monsieur,

Mis au courant par Monsieur
J. ELIGOULACHVILI des services signalés
que vous avez rendus à vos compatriotes
de religion israélite, en aidant, par
votre généreuse entremise, à les mettre
à l'abri des conséquences de l'application des lois raciales, je viens m'associer
aux sentiments de reconnaissance qu'ils
éprouvent pour vous.

Soyez assuré de ma personnelle
gratitude pour votre bienfaisante solli-
citude à leur égard, et veuillez agréer,
Monsieur, je vous prie, l'assurance de
mes sentiments les plus distingués.

Le Grand Rabbin de Paris

Association Culturelle
Sepharadite de Paris
18 Rue Saint-Lazare
Paris IX

Paris, October 18, 1944

Mr. Michael Kedia

Paris

Sir,

We had the honor of expressing to Minister E. Gueguetchkori our deep gratitude to him and his friends for their efficacious intervention before the authorities of the German occupation in favor of our Georgian coreligionists. We would like to tell you how happy we have been to also know of your courageous and heartfelt actions undertaken toward the same goal.

Thanks to your tenacity and your keen feeling of justice, so much in keeping with the traditions of the noble Georgian Nation, you have not only contributed to the repeal on behalf of your Jewish nationals of the humiliating racial laws which we had to endure for four years, but over and above that you succeeded in freeing numerous inmates of concentration camps.

We consider it to be our duty to thank you cordially and to express to you our genuine gratitude and our deep feeling of moral satisfaction.

Yours very sincerely,

Honorary President,

J. Mossery

Association Cultuelle
Sepharadite de Paris

18, RUE SAINT-LAZARE
PARIS-IXE
(LOI DU 8 DÉCEMBRE 1905 - N° 155-909)

CONSEIL COMMUNAL

CABINET DU PRÉSIDENT

Le Président reçoit tous les
Mercredis de 10 h. à 12 h.
au Siège de la Cultuelle.

TÉLÉPH. : TRUDAINE 46.32

703

PARIS, LE **18 Octobre** 19 **44**

Monsieur Michel KEDIA

P A R I S

Monsieur,

Nous avons eu l'honneur d'adresser à Monsieur le Ministre E. GUEGUETCHKORI, le témoignage de notre profonde reconnaissance, aussi bien à son égard qu'à celui de mes amis, pour leurs efficaces interventions auprès des Autorités d'Occupation en faveur de mes Coreligionnaires Georgiens.

Parallèlement à cette lettre, nous nous permettons, Monsieur, de vous exprimer par la présente, à quel point, nous avons été heureux de connaître également vos courageuses et chaleureuses démarches dans le même but.

Grâce à votre ténacité et votre ardente soif de Droit et de Justice, tellement conformes aux traditions de la noble Nation Georgienne, vous avez non seulement contribué à rapporter, en faveur de vos compatriotes Israélites, les humiliantes lois d'exception que nous eûmes à subir durant ces quatre années, mais encore, vous réussîtes à faire élargir de nombreux internés.

Aussi considérons-nous de notre devoir de vous en remercier chaleureusement et vous prions de vouloir bien croire, en notre gratitude émue et nos profonds sentiments de réconfort moral.

Veuillez bien agréer, Monsieur l'assurance de notre parfaite considération .

Le Président d'Honneur,

J. MOSSERI.

President of the Union of Georgians of the Jewish Faith
4, Villa Eugéne Manuel
Paris 16°

Paris, August 15, 1944

Mr. Michael Kedia

Dear Sir,

At the moment of the near liberation, please permit me in the name of my coreligionists and my own name to express to you our gratitude and deep appreciation for all you have done for us. We were not deceived in our faith when we looked to you as a Georgian patriot for the defense of our lives and interests in the time of occupation.

Thanks to your courage, your tenacity and your energy you have fully succeeded in exempting your Jewish nationals from anti-Jewish legislation. Besides that when our coreligionists were seized, you immediately did whatever was necessary in order to free them.

Your conduct has not surprised us because it conformed with the noble tradition of your nation. I took the liberty of informing the Grand Rabbi of Paris and the Religious Union of Jews in France who express their homage to you and wish to thank you personally.

Once again we thank you from the bottom of our heart and we wish to assure you that your action will remain indelible in our memory and that of our fellow Jews.

Signed
J. Eligoulachvili
President of the Union of Georgians of the Jewish Faith

Joseph ELIGOULACHVILI
Président du Groupement Georgien
de Confession Mosaïque
4, villa Eugène Manuel
    PARIS 16°

Paris, le 15 Aout 1944

Monsieur Michel KEDIA

Cher Monsieur,

    Au moment, quand l'heure de la libération approche, permettez-moi
au nom de mes coréligionnaires et en mon propre nom de vous exprimer
notre gratitude et profonde reconnaissance pour tout ce, que vous avez
fait pour nous.

    Nous ne nous sommes pas trompés en nous adressant à vous, comme à
un patriote Georgien pour défendre notre vie et nos intérêts en temps
d'occupation. Grace à votre courrage, votre tenacité et votre énergie
vous avez pleinement réussi que les mésures anti-juives ne soient pas
appliquées à nos compatriotes. En plus, quant il y avait des cas d'ar-
restations de nos coréligionnaires, vous faisiez immédiatement le néc-
ssaire pour les faire relacher.

    Votre conduite ne nous a pas étonnée, car elle était conforme aux
nobles traditions de notre peuple.

    Je me suis permis de faire savoir ces faits à Monsieur le Grand
Rabbin de Paris et à l'Union Cultuelle des Israëlites en France, qui
vous rendent hommage et qui tiennent à vous remercier personnellement.

    Encore une fois, nous vous remercions de tout notre coeur et croye
bien que ce fait restera inoubliable pour nous et nos coréligionnaires

                          Président
       du GROUPEMENT GEORGIEN de
          CONFESSION MOSAIQUE

Dr. Rudolf Aschenauer Attorney-at-Law

Munich, December 12, 1951

To The District Court Munich

Criminal Court : libel case

Dr. Rudolf Aschenauer
Attorney-at-Law

To:
The District Court Munich
Criminal Court

Munich
Palace of Justice

Munich, December 12, 1951
Auenstr. 86

SUBJECT: Legal notice against A. Demetra, Munich, Muellerstrass 45/I, for libel in accordance with par. 187, Criminal Law Code.

I herewith notify the Court that I represent Dr. Gregor and Michael von Alchibaya. On their request and as their attorney I bring legal notice against A. Demetra for livel (Par. 187, CIC). Contrary to his better knowledge the defendant put false facts into circulation, which are apt to bring my mandators into contempt and degrade him in public opinion. He perpetrated this by sending out the inclosed writ of accusation on my mandators.

The defendant was an active member and functionary of the Russian Social Revolutionary Party. When the archives of the Czarist political police, called "Ochranka" were opened after the Revolution in 1917, it was found that Alexander Demetra had been an informer for the Ochranka. As this fact became known and there were grave reasons for the suspicion that he had betrayed a number of persons, acknowledgement of his Georgian citizenship was refused him in 1918. It is characteristic for him that after 1921 he again was suspected to work for the NKWD. These suspicions were confirmed. Demetra himself was unable to deny the fact. In 1936 he published a pamphlet with which he wanted to conceal the fact of his collaboration with the NKWD and their channels of communication. Since the French authorities distrusted him, he was interned by the French in 1939 as a suspected Soviet agent.

Towards the end of the war, in February 1945, Demetra fled to Italy and immediately took up contact with the Communist partisans with whom he closely collaborated also after the German capitulation. He moved to Rome and lived permanently in the house of the Communist partisans. He worked for the Soviet Intelligence Service and carried on a lively propaganda among the Russians and Caucasians with the aim to induce them to return to Russia. He informed the Soviet intelligence people of the exact residences of former Soviet citizens whose extradition was due in accordance with the Yalta Treaty. Because of his collaboration with the Soviet intelligence service a warrant of arrest was issued on him by the Italian police.
Proof: Commissary Riccardo Giancarlo, Messina, Italia, Casella Postale 428;
Statement of Ing.Sergio Gabunia,Campo IRO Mereatello, Salerno, dated 15 February 1951.

He succeeded, however, to escape to Germany. Evidently on orders of the above-named agencies the defendant endeavors to prevent the emigration of my mandators to the USA by calumnious assertions. The reason behind this is that my mandators have taken an active stand against the Soviets.

- 2 -

Dr. Gregor von Alchibaya, Munich 23, Destouchesstr.18, was
born at Kutais on 25 December 1880 and studied medicine. In
1919 he was appointed ambassador in Azerbeidjan by the
Georgian Government.

As references on the character of Dr. von Alchibaya I inclose
the following:
    Letter of A. Delpuch,former Apostolic Visitator in Tiflis;
    Letter, 25 June 1920, of the British Representative in
    Transcaucasia, St. Luke;
    Letter, 1 July 1920, of the French Representative in
    Tiflis;
    Letter, 4 July, 1920, of Consul Bialoprozeski, Polish
    Representative in Tiflis.

For the services rendered by him, Dr. Gregor von Alchibaya
was made a member of the "Legion D'Honneur" by the French
and was given the Golden Service Cross by the Polish.

It tells in the favor of my mandator Dr. Gregor von Alchibaya that he subscribed one million Rubles for relief when
the Soviets attacked and occupied Georgia in February 1921
without any declaration of war. There exists a receipt for
this amount, bearing the signature of the Second President
of the Georgian Parliament.

When the Georgian Government was forced to leave the country,
Dr. Alchibaya went into exile together with his family.
Via Constantinople and Vienna he came to Berlin in 1921.
Before the inflation he donated 7000 US Dollars for scholarships in Berlin.
In the libelous publication it is asserted that the Polish
general Litsch made it possible for Gregor von Alchibaya
to go to Poland. The truth, however, is that Gregor von
Alchibaya saved the life of minister Filipowicz in Baku
and later met him again in Berlin. Through his intervention
and after a ministerial decree had been issued to this effect
Dr. Gregor von Alchibaya took over a position in the military
hospital of Grodno. It was only there that he made the
acquaintance of the Commanding General A. Litwinowicz who
later became vice-minister. It is not true that a scandal
occurred at Grodno. This assertion in the libelous publication is refuted by the inclosed testimonial on Dr. von Alchibaya's medical work at Grodno and also by the fact that
Dr. von Alchibaya was appointed Chief Internist at the
Policlinic of the Military Medical Academy in 1937. It
tells in Dr. von Alchibaya's favor that he acted as family
doctor for the following persons:
    Minister Kostialkowski
    Vice-Minister General Litwinowicz
    Dionisius, Metropolitan of the Orthodox Church
    Colonel Dr. M. Woyczinski(a personal friend of Marshal
    Pilsudzki)
After the occupation of Warsaw by the Germans Dr. Gregor von
Alchibaya was elected president of the Georgian Colony in
Warsaw; later he was appointed president of the entire
Caucasian Colony. It was his task to protect the interests
of the Caucasians before the authorities. Owing to his
strict opposition against the then existing conditions he was
removed from his post by the Germans.

Last line: "he was removed from his post by the Germans."
—Ed.

Proof: Letter, 12 November 1943, of the Reich Minister for
    the Occupied Eastern Territories.
In this letter it is said that this removal took place "bec...
you made defeatist remarks, opposed the measures of the
General Government and did not comply immediately with
orders of the General Government". Ambassador Graf von der
Schulenburg, who had been Chief of the Diplomatic Commission
in Georgia during the independence of Georgia, advised Dr.
von Alchibaya to leave Warsaw in order to escape reprisals
by the German Secret State Police. This is what happened.
At the end of July 1944, when the Soviet armies approached
Warsaw, his family also fled from Warsaw and came to Reiche
hall, Germany, where Dr. von Alchibaya was then already
living. Since October 1949 Dr. von Alchibaya has been
living in Munich.
It cannot be Dr. von Alchibaya's or his son's task to prove
that the so-called writ of accusation contains only false
charges but it is up to Demetra to prove their correctness.

Nevertheless I will go into some details in order to
illustrate the falseness of these charges.

In his libelous publication Demetra mentions a protocol
drawn up by the commission which was allegedly appointed by
the Georgian Colony in Warsaw for the purpose of investigat-
ing into the abuses of the Alchibayas. The protocols in
question will be presented to the court. In the meeting of
the Georgian Colony, held on 15 February 1942, it is clearly
said that great appreciation is owed the Chief of the
Georgian Representation for his successful and devoted work.
In this protocol it is also said that Michael Alchibaya
left his home in order to fight against the Bolsheviks and
for the sake of his Georgian homeland. A letter of the
Commanding Officer of the 52nd Rifle Regiment was also
read in this meeting, in which it was stated that Michael
Alchibaya had been awarded the Iron Cross Second Class for
his achievements.
The protocol of the General Assembly of the Georgian Colony,
held on 9 May 1943, shows how great the gratefulness was
that the Goergian Colony owed Dr. von Alchibaya. The
assembly protocol states that Michael Alchibaya had been
two years at the front and that he was then appointed liaiso
officer between the Supreme Command of the Army and the
Georgian National Committee. This proves that Michael
Alchibaya had nothing to do with the Secret State Police
and did not visit any Russian prisoner of war camps. That
this was so can be witnessed by:
    Ahmed-Nabi Magoma, Munich, Jugendstr. 2
    General Jolasse, Ising near Seebruck.

Michael von Alchibaya's attitude towards the Jews is shown
by the inclosed affidavit of Kedia, dated 3 May 1946, with
attachments. It proves that Michael von Alchibaya saved
a great number of Georgian Jews and of other nationalities
from the German authorities. The untrustworthiness of the
assertions in the accusation in this connection is evident.

As for the activities of Gregor von Alchibaya in Warsaw
I name the following witness:
Professor Georg von Mende, Duesseldorf, Caecilienallee 52,
and also the present Chief of Protocol, Herr von Herwath.
Further witnesses are:
Professor Dr. M. Tseretheli, Munich 23, Hermann Vogel-Str. 25
Prince Nakaschidse, Munich, Ungererstr. 86/III,
Prince Schalikaschwili Dimitri, Pappenheim, Altes Schloss.
Inclosed is also a letter, dated 4 December 1951, of Serge
Woyciechowski.
Prince Nakaschidse can also prove that the statement on
the denunciation of General Makaschwili is libelous.

In connection with the assertions on Makaschwili reference
is made to the deposition of E. Gueguetschkori, Georgian
State Minister of Foreign Affairs, ret. The testimonial
given by Dr. C. Gvardjaladse, Under-State-Secretary, ret.,
may also serve as proof.

The fact that Gregor von Alchibaya tried to free Georgian
officers and also succeeded in liberating them, is proved by
the witnesses:
Professor Michael Achmeteli, Unterweilbach near Dachau,
Hebertshausen, with Count Spretti.

Frivolously it is stressed in the so-called writ of accusation that Gregor von Alchibaya stole sugar. The late Finance
Minister Jourouli, who is mentioned in the writ of accusation, had a deputy who later became Finance Minister. He is
now living in Paris. If such a theft had happened, this
Minister, whose name is Kandelaki, ought to know something
about it. And then also the gentlemen of the Foreign Service,
who have given their testimonials, ought to know about it.

Gregor von Alchibaya never had German citizenship. This is
proved by his identity papers which can be presented.

One of the main points of the writ of accusation is the
following assertion:
"In the surroundings of Warsaw there disappear at one time
six Georgians owing to a denunciation by Alchibaya. The
request of a representative of the Colony to take the men
who were arrested by the Gestapo, under his protection, is
refused by Alchibaya cold-bloodedly. Alchibaya's sadistic
vindictiveness because of his failure with the officers who
are hindering him in his abuses, does never end and he continues his calumnious denunciations against all who do not
obey him or will not assist him in his robberies, his thefts
and the misappropriation of other people's property. After
being denounced by Alchibaya the following people disappear:
N. Bagration
W. Atabegischwili
Macharadse
Archimandrite Gregor Peradse, etc.
The number of the Jews missing cannot be determined."

These assertions can easily be refuted. Bagration died
simply of pneumonia, which can be witnesses by Prince Schal-
kaschwili, Pappenhim, address given above. Macharadse went
to Kiew to do business there.

It is interesting to note how Peradse is treated by the
author. In reality Peradse was working with the Soviets.
The following witnesses are named for the case Peradse:
Professor Mende, address given above,
Mr. Engelhaupt, address will be submitted later,
Prince Schalikaschwili, address given above,
Mr. Bagradse, Paris
Prince Nakaschidse, address given above,
Professor Tseretheli, address given above,
Professor Dr. Nikuradse, Institution for Electronic and
Ionic Research, Schwarzenfeld, Upper Palatinate.
Professor Mende is also acquainted with the affair which
the writ of accusation circumscribes as: "In the surroundings
of Warsaw there disappear at one time six Georgians owing
to a denunciation by Alchibaya".

In connection with the entire complex the following evidence
is presented:
Letter, 18 November 1951, of Professor Dr. Tseretheli,
Statement, 18 November 1951, of Professor Nikuradse,
Statement, 23 November 1951, of Prince Nikolaus Nakaschidse.

Finally, as to the case Tsiklauri at Mittenwald the following
can be stated:
In order to clarify the facts I name Secretary of State
Dr. Oberländer, Munich, State Secretary for Refugee Matters,
as witness.
There was a trial by court-martial which lies underneath
this libelous assertion. At that time Dr. Gregor von Alchibaya, and Michael von Alchibaya were not even acquainted
with G. Gabliani.

s/ Dr. Rudolf Aschenauer
Attorney-at-Law

Translation from the German
Prof. Dr. Gerhard von Mende
Düsseldorf ·
Cecilienallee 52
December 10, 1951
D e c l a r a t i o n

From my intimate knowledge of the situation of the emigration groups in Poland after the occupation of this country by the German troups [sic.] and, above all, from my very intimate acquaintance with the activity and personality of Dr. G. Alchibaya [Alshibaja], with whom I came into frequent contact as Section Chief in the Eastern Ministry during the war, I can give the following declaration in matters of Dr. G. Alchibaya.

After Warsaw had been occupied by the German troups and the president of the Georgian Colony there, Imnadse, had fled, Dr. Alchibaya was asked by the Georgian Colony because of his personal reputation, his knowledge of languages and his former capacity as Georgian ambassador in Berlin to take over the representation of the Georgian interests in the so-called General-Government. This request was supported by the Azerbeisjanians [sic.], Armenians and North Caucasians then living in Warsaw. Therefore Dr. Alchibaya represented the interests of all Caucasian emigrants for the entire territory of the General Government. Dr. Alchibaya did his work in close connection with the Caucasian representation in Berlin, headed by W. Achmeteli, and always without receiving any remuneration.

Dr. Alchibaya succeeded by a continuous and energetic representation of the Caucasians with all offices in the General Government and by frequent visits to Berlin, to advance the economic and legal security of his compatriots so far that they were spared starvation and misery. In doing so, Dr. Alchibaya often used a very outspoken language with the competent authorities and never kept back his opinion on grievances and political abuses. He always reached his aims in favor of his compatriots, but exposed himself so much that the German authorities endeavored to get rid more and more of this inconvenient critic and declared champion of equal rights for all. In June 1943, he was suspended effective immediately from his post as president of the Caucasian Colony in Warsaw by the authorities of the General Government, because he was alleged to have made defeatist utterances, criticized measures of the General Government and did not carry out orders of these authorities.

During the time of his activity as president of the Caucasian Colony in Warsaw happened the affair of the Archimandrite Peradse. Peradse was a priest at the Russian Church in Warsaw, and had been in Berlin before and during the war allegedly in order to further his project of an Russian Orthodox University in Berlin. At this occasion I made his acquaintance. Accidentally the German counter- intelligence captured a woman on the Russian border, with whom coded information was found the origin of which was Peradse. Peradse was then arrested by the German authorities. In his apartment two diaries with records in Georgian language of his activities in the service of the Soviets and amounts in Dollars and Pounds were found, which [line cut off]

...a representative of the Soviet Embassy in Berlin. Peradse was tried by a German court martial and sentenced to death because of espionage for the Soviets.

I may point out that the Peradse case caused quite a sensation not only among the Georgian emigrant but also in other circles, since Peradse was widely known as priest with ambitions. His spying activities for the Soviets was quite unexpected and caused many authorities, which were involved in the Peradse case, to conduct the investigation about him as carefully and correctly as possible.

Dr. Alchibaya had nothing to do either with the disclosure of the case Peradse or with his arrest. This arrest was just as unexpected for Dr. Alchibaya as it had been for all who had known Peradse. After Peradse's arrest Dr. Alchibaya in his capacity as president of the Caucasian Colony applied to the German Secret State Police (Gestapo) in order to learn for what reasons the arrest was made and what could possibly be done for the arrested man.

On the request of the competent German authorities Dr. Alchibaya was made to name several Georgians who could translate Peradse's diaries. As far as I can remember, a committee of three Georgians, among them Captain Bakradse, was formed, which were requested to go through and translate Peradse's diaries. From the part of the Germans a second review of the diaries was made by Prof. Meckelein, Berlin. From his own records and his later statements it became quite evident that Peradse had been spying for the Russians for many years and kept close contact with the Soviet authorities in Berlin. I can say this on the grounds of my own intimate knowledge of the Peradse case. From the part of the Georgians, and much less by Dr. Alchibaya, not the least had been undertaken against Peradse. In the contrary they tried every possible means in order to get an irreproachable, objective trial and find alleviating circumstances for Peradse.

Immediately after the occupation of Warsaw by the German troops the Georgians Engineer Berischwili, Atabegaschwili and Katschachmadze were shot in Warsaw. As the shootings caused a justifiable stir among the Georgian Colony, I tried to assist in the examination of the circumstances. I was then told by the German Counter-Intelligence the shootings happened in the course of the military actions in capturing Warsaw and without preliminary examination and that they have to be considered as probable acts of personal revenge of the Georgian Maglakelidze who worked with the German Counter-Intelligence. At the time of the shootings Dr. Alchibaya had no contact at all with any German authority. One of the victims was his closest colleague and partisan. It is entirely absurd to bring Dr. Alchibaya in any connection whatsoever with these shootings.

The reason why false accusations are raised today against Dr. Alchibaya is probably that Dr. Alchibaya as a man of pure character and strong will was used to always speak his mind openly. He did not always make friends that way. The authority, however, which he possesses among his compatriots at home and in exile, and the reputation which he acquired as politician and physician in Poland and German as well as with allied authorities, show clearly that he possesses a personality which stands high above the things which are now imputed to him out of jealousy and ill will.

I am ready at any time to repeat my statements under oath.

signed Dr. Gerhard von Mende
University Professor,

Former Chief of the Sections
"Caucasus and Foreign Nations"
in the Reich Ministry for the Occupied
Eastern Territories

Author's note: See original documents in author's archives. For an abbreviated translation in English of Gegechkori, Jordania, and minutes of the National Unity, see pages 219–221.

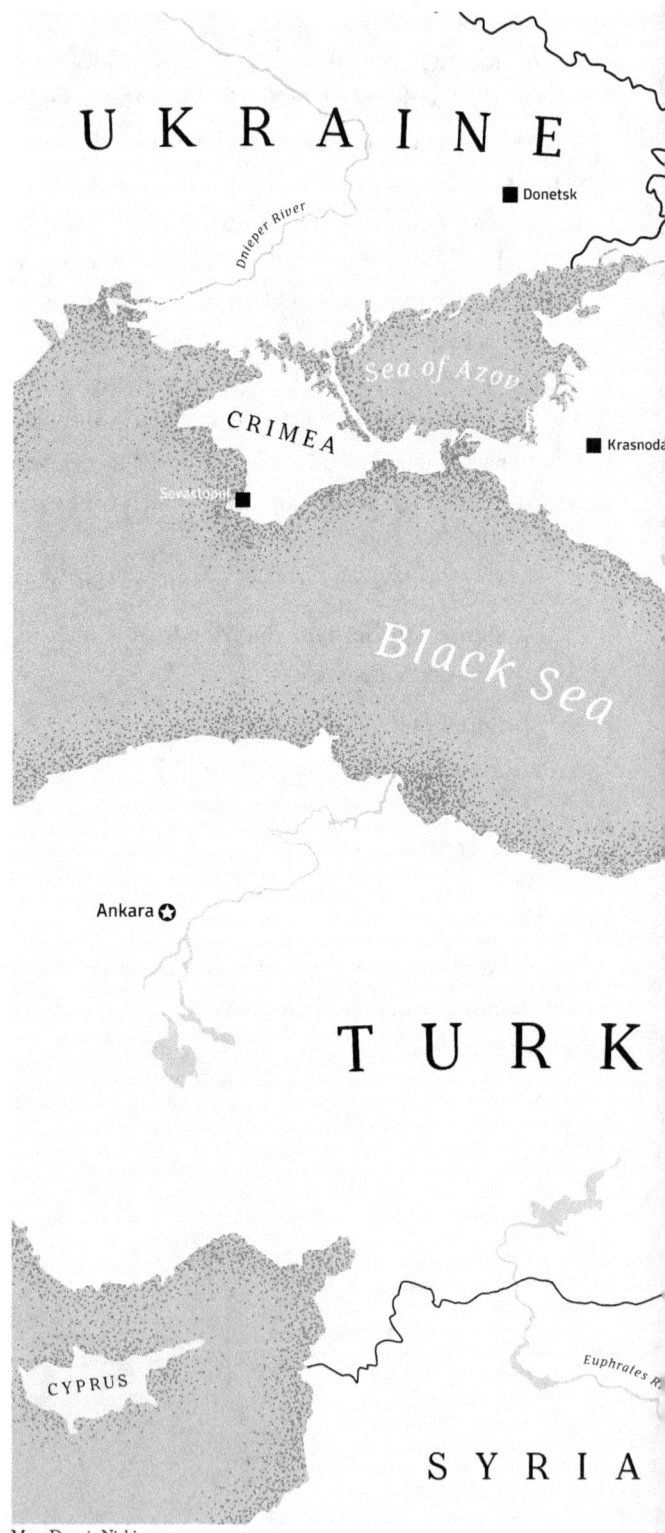

Map: Dennis Nishi

Map: Dennis Nishi

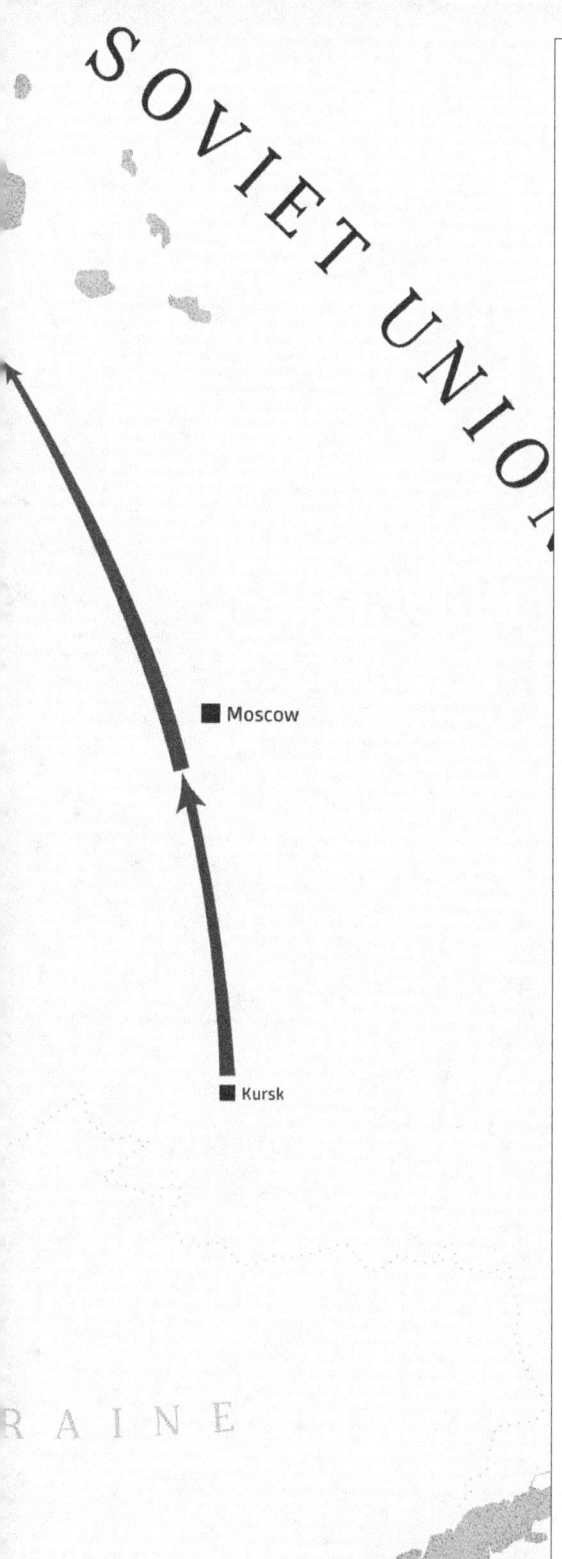

Timeline for Givi Gabliani's days
as a conscript in the Russian Army

September 1939:
Givi Gabliani is sent from Tbilisi as
a conscript to Kursk, where he
becomes a military doctor for the
Russian Army's 55th Division.

Early March 1940:
Soviet invasion of Finland. The 55th
Division is dispatched to the front.

June 1940:
Soviet invasion of the Baltic states.
Givi Gabliani is in Ukmerge,
Lithuania.

September 1940:
At the military base in Brest-Litovsk,
Givi Gabliani is a military doctor.
This is a historically important city
due to the treaty signed here at the
end of WWI, whereby Russia cedes
Poland, the Baltic States, and parts
of Turkey and recognizes the
independence of Ukraine, Finland
and Georgia.

December 1940–June 1941:
Givi Gabliani is a military doctor at
the base in Slutzk.
He briefly returns to Tbilisi to see
his ailing sister, Eteri, attend her
memorial services and comfort his
mother, Vera.

June 22, 1941: Operation Barbarossa
Germany invades Russia, prompting
a retreat of the Russian Army's 55th
Division toward Smolensk. They are
captured near Propoisk, Belorussia
in early July 1941 and transferred
through Ukraine to Berlin.

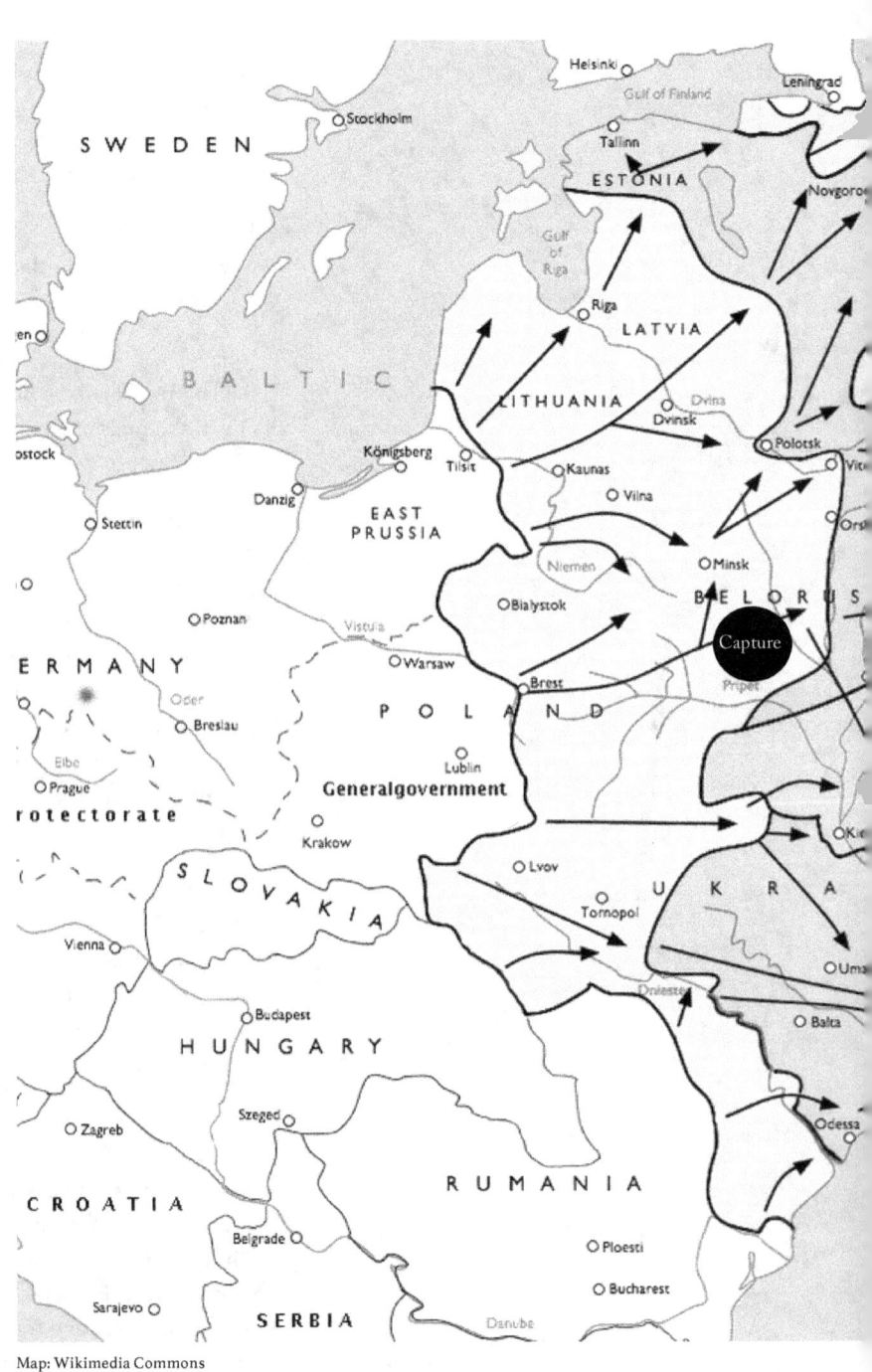

Map: Wikimedia Commons

Eastern Front

22 June 1941 – 5 December 1941

- ☐ to 9 July 1941
- ☐ to 1 September 1941
- ☐ to 9 September 1941
- ☐ to 5 December 1941

0   200   400
km

Kalinin   Volga

Rzhev

Mozhaisk

○ Moscow

Kalomna ○ Oka

Tula

R   U   S   S   I   A

Bryansk

○ Orel

○ Livny

Kursk ○

○ Voronezh

○

Belgorod

Kharkov

Don

Krasnograd

○ Izyum

Donets

○ Stalingrad

Volga

○ Voroshilovgrad

Dnepropetrovsk

○ Kotelnikov

Rostov

○ Elista

Sea of
Azov

Kerch

○ Maikop

Novorossisk

○ Grozny

Yalta

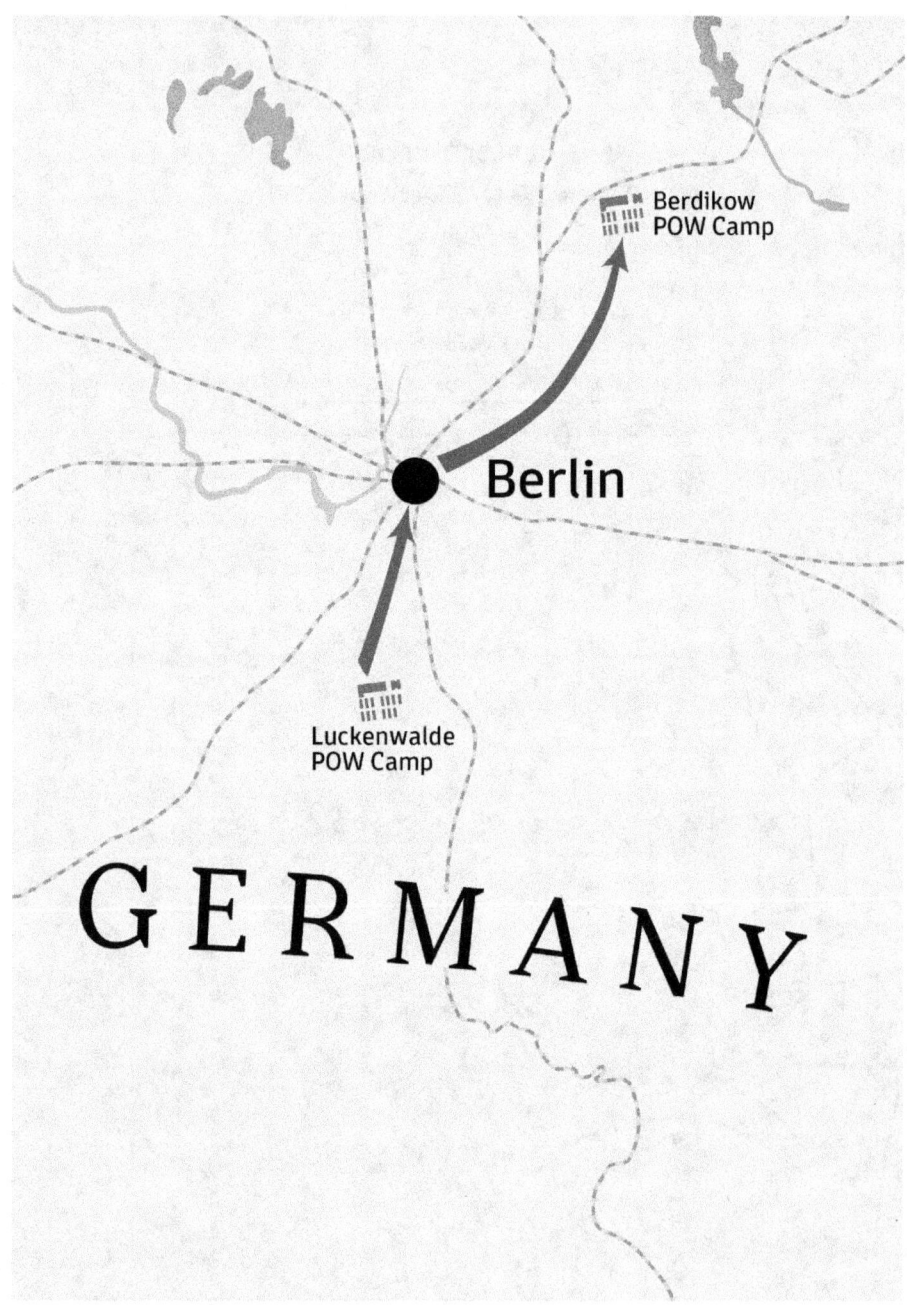

Map: Dennis Nishi

Interned first at the Luckenwalde P.O.W. Camp with other Soviet prisoners, Givi Gabliani is soon transferred back through Berlin to the Berdikow P.O.W. Camp, where he begins training with other Caucasian P.O.W.s for a "special mission," at that time kept secret.

The Military Days and Travels of Givi Gabliani

September 1939–June 22, 1941
Days in the Red Army
Kursk -> Border of Finland (Soviet
invasion) -> Ukmerge, Lithuania ->
Brest-Litovsk -> Slutzk, then <- retreat to
Smolensk. The author is captured by the
German Army near Propoisk, Belorussia.

July 1941–April 1942
Days as a P.O.W.
Krestitelevo, Cherkasy Region, Ukraine ->
Alexandria, Ukraine -> Berlin ->
Luckenwalde and Berdikow P.O.W. camps
-> Mittenwald, Garmisch-Partenkirchen
(hospitalizations for injury) -> Steinau
(punitive work camp)

Mid-April 1942– August 1942
Becoming part of the Georgian Legion
Mittenwald and Luttensee -> Berlin ->
Garmisch-Partenkirchen -> Luttensee ->
Neuhammer-Silesia

Mid-August 1942–July 1943
"Bergmann" Fights in Ukraine
Mariupol on the Sea of Azov -> Donetsk
-> fighting in and around Mozdok (Terek
River) and Georgievsk -> Mozdok and
Terek (taken by the Russian Army)
<- retreat to Malgobek then Nalchik.
Nalchik becomes "Bergmann" HQ.
Alagir on river Ardon is taken back from
Russian Army. The Battle for Stalingrad
ends in resounding German defeat.

Retreat from the Caucasus
Pyatigorsk (near Stavropol) -> Krasnodar
-> Taman Peninsula (cities of Taman and
Temryuk) -> Stavropol ->
Grigoripolnskaia. Entire "Bergmann"
evacuated from Crimea: Simferopol/
Bakhchysarai/Kokosi/Belbek Valley;
Germans retreat through Crimea

July 1943–December 1943
Dresden Military School and Liaison Staff
Berlin -> Dresden -> Paris
Paris -> Le Mans -> La Haye-du-Puits (in
Normandy) -> Cherbourg -> around/near
Saint Nazaire -> Le Mans -> Paris
Paris -> Périgueux -> Biarritz -> Paris
Paris -> Amsterdam -> Zandvoort -> Paris
Paris -> Berlin

January 1944–March 1944
Back to the Eastern Front/Ukraine
Berlin -> Lotzen -> Mykolaiv -> Odessa ->
Simferopol -> Sarabuz (Hvardiiske) ->
Karangut -> Otarchik -> Kurajevka and
Kart Kasak
Simferopol -> Sevastopol P.O.W. camps ->
Staryi Krym and Islam-Tertek (Kirovske)
-> Chancha -> Barak -> Semikolodez ->
Simferopol -> Tiraspol -> Odessa -> Berlin

April 1944–June 1944
Liaison Staff duties
Berlin -> Paris -> Albi-Castres area -> Berlin
to Greece via Poznan, Poland, Vienna and
Belgrade:
Salonika, Greece -> Athens -> Salonika ->
Sofia, Bulgaria -> Belgrade and back to
Berlin via Vienna and Dresden
Berlin -> Bad Reichenhall -> Vienna ->
Prague -> Berlin

July 1944–April 1945
End of the war
Paris -> Le Mans -> Percy (west of
Avranches) -> Granville -> Avranches
(almost caught by Allied troops) -> Servon
(village) -> Pontorson -> Sougeal -> Le
Mans -> Paris -> Berlin -> Verona, Italy ->
Neuhammer-Silesia -> Salzburg / Bad
Reichenhall -> Ising (not far from Munich)
-> Innsbruck, ending up in Höchst,
Austria in displaced persons camp

Map: Wikimedia Commons

December 30, 1942: From Nalchik, 50 or so miles north of Georgia's mountainous border, "Bergmann" is ordered to retreat, with devastating psychological impact for the Caucasians.

January 31, 1943: General Paulus commanding the German 6th Army capitulates after the Battle of Stalingrad. His forces are cut off from the rest of the German Army.

February 1943: Field Marshal von Kleist orders the retreat of the 17th Army, approximately 400,000 men. "Bergmann" is part of the 17th Army. They hold the line at the Kuban Bridgehead (from Novorossik to the Sea of Azov); allowing troop evacuation to Crimea.

February 12, 1943: "Bergmann's" cavalry squadrons cross part of the Sea of Azov at Kerch Straight, from the Taman Peninsula to Crimea. Gabliani writes, "Fortunately, this part of the sea was solidly frozen. The ice broke only once or twice under the horse-driven wagon."

February 22, 1943: All Caucasian forces are evacuated to Crimea to defend the coastline, Kerch, and the Perekop Isthmus.

July 13, 1943: With the situation stabilized in Crimea that summer, Gabliani leaves for Dresden Military School. By October/November 1943, the Soviets are poised to take Crimea and force a full withdrawal of the German Army.   [See pages 165–173; 362.]

PHOTOGRAPHS

Givi Gabliani (left) and fellow Georgian mountaineers.
Svaneti, Georgia. Circa mid 1930s.
Courtesy Georgian National Library.

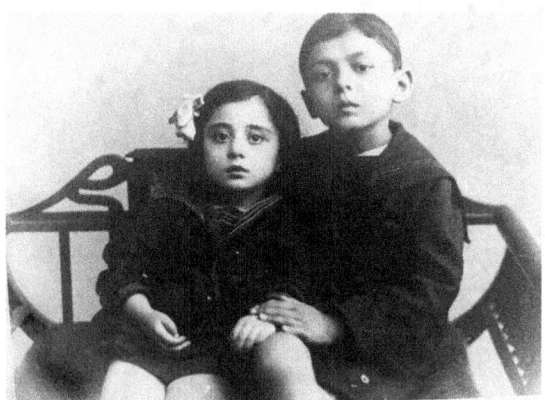

above left and right: Vera and Egnate
Gabliani; Egnate and Givi Gabliani.
Svaneti, Georgia.
Circa early 1900s and 1916.

center: Eteri and Givi Gabliani.
Svaneti, Georgia. Circa mid 1920s.

below: Eteri Gabliani. Circa late 1930s.
All courtesy Georgian National Library.

left: Egnate Gabliani. Svaneti, Georgia. No date.
right: Fellow Svan with Egnate Gabliani (on right). Svaneti, Georgia. No date.

below: Egnate Gabliani (center) and fellow Svans.
Svaneti, Georgia. No date.
All courtesy Georgian National Library.

above: Georgian priest with Egnate Gabliani. No date.

center: Egnate Gabliani (3rd row, left) and schoolchildren. Presumed Svaneti, Georgia. No date.

below: Vera Gabliani (front, middle) and schoolchildren. Presumed Svaneti, Georgia. No date.

All courtesy Georgian National Library.

above: Givi Gabliani (2nd from left) and fellow mountaineers. Presumed Svaneti, Georgia. Circa 1930s.

below left: Givi Gabliani; *right*: Rusudan Gabliani.

All courtesy Georgian Nationan Library.

top row, left to right Solomon Zaldastanishvili, Evgeni Gegechkori, Grigol Alshibaja:
Georgian National Library.

center row, left to right Ilia Chavchavadze, Mikhako Tsereteli: Wikimedia; Grigol
Robakidze: Georgian National Library.

bottom row, left to right Spiridon Kedia, Dimitri Shalikashvili, Alexander Nikuradze:
Georgian National Library.

top row, left to right Georgian President in exile Noe Jordania, Georgian Liaison Staff Misha Kedia: Georgian National Library; German Ambassador to Moscow Hans von Herwarth: Bundesarchiv.

center row, left to right Colonel Claus von Stauffenberg; Admiral Wilhelm Canaris; Friedrich-Werner von der Schulenburg, Ambassador to the Soviet Union prior to Operation Barbarossa. All members of the German Resistance executed for their role in the plot to assassinate Adolf Hitler: Wikimedia.

bottom row, left to right Professor Gerhard von Mende of the Ostministerium, Professor Theodor Oberländer, head of "Bergmann": Wikimedia.

above:
Ushguli community, Svaneti, Georgia.
Photo by Florian Pinel, CC BY-SA 3.0.

left:
Ushguli towers in Svaneti, Georgia.
Photo by Dito 1993, CC BY-SA 4.0.

below: Shatili stone houses.
© Vyacheslav Argenberg / http://www.
vascoplanet.com/ CC BY-SA 4.0.

above:
Ushguli, Svaneti.
Photo by Andrzej Wójtowicz,
CC BY-SA 2.0.

left and below:
Mulakhi, Svaneti, ancestral
home of the Gablianis.
Photos by Jim Irwin.

Eteri Gabliani Irwin on a horse in Mulakhi, Svaneti,
ancestral home of the Gablianis.
Photo by Jim Irwin.

Shota Rustaveli, Georgia's national poet. His epic, *The Knight in Tiger's Skin*
was composed in the 12th or 13th century during Georgia's Golden Age.
Georgian National Library.

left: Egnate Gabliani. Presumed Svaneti, Georgia. No date.
Courtesy Georgian National Library.
right: Givi Gabliani at his home in Quincy, Illinois. Circa 1990s.
Courtesy Gabliani Family Archive.

Gabliani Museum.
Mestia, Svaneti,
Georgia.
Photo by Jim Irwin.

above: Givi Gabliani and his daughter, Vera at "Villa Svaneti,"
the Gabliani's vacation home in Aspen, Colorado.
Circa late 1970s.

below: "Villa Svaneti." Aspen, Colorado. No date.

Both courtesy Gabliani Family Archive.

above: Rusudan and Givi Gabliani. Quincy, Illinois. Circa late 1950s/early 1960s.

center: Givi and Rusudan Gabliani with their daughters, Vera (left) and Eteri (right). Aspen, Colorado. Circa late 1970s/early 1980s.

below: Greg Gabliani, Vera (back) and Eteri (front) with their father, Givi. Aspen, Colorado. Circa late 1970s/early 1980s.

right: Greg, Vera, and Eteri Gabliani. St. Louis, Missouri. Circa late 1970s/early 1980s.

All courtesy Gabliani Family Archive.

LITERATURE

Alexsiev, Alexander. *Soviet Nationalities in German Wartime Strategy, 1941–1946*. Santa Monica, Calif.: Rand Corporation. 1982.

Allen, W. E. D. *A History of the Georgian People*, introduced by Sir Denison Ross. London: Kegan Paul, Trench, Trubner and Co. 1932.

Asatiani, Alexandre. *The Old and New Inheritance* (in Georgian). France. 1928.

Bergmann Memoirs. Various authors, edited by Heinz Beher. Munich: Josef M. Greska. 1983.

Bethell, Nicholas. *The Last Secret: The Delivery to Stalin of Over Two Million Russians by Britain and the United States*. New York: Basic Books. 1974.

Bohlen, Charles. *Witness to History 1929–1969*. New York: W.W. Norton & Company. 1973.

Carroll, Wallace. "It Takes a Russian to Beat a Russian." *Life*. December 19, 1949.

Carsten, F. L. *The Slavonic and East European Review*, Vol. XL 52 #109, 1969.

Chernov, Viktor. "Lenin: A Contemporary Portrait." *Foreign Affair*. March 1924.

Conquest, Robert. *The Harvest of Sorrow: Soviet Collectivization and the Terror-Famine*. New York: Oxford University Press. 1986.

Dallin, Alexander. *German Rule in Russia, 1941-1945: A Study in Occupation Policies*. New York: MacMillan. 1957.

Epstein, Julius. *Operation Keelhaul: The Story of Forced Repatriation from 1944 to the Present*, introduced by Bertram D. Wolfe. Old Greenwich, Conn.: The Devin-Adair Company. 1973.

Georgian National Council and National Political Center, Paris. *On Judgment Before the Georgian People* (booklet). Arpajon: Imprimerie Cooperative Arpajonnaise. 1966.

Green, Warren. *The Fate of Oriental Jews in Vichy France*. Wiener Library Bulletin (Great Britain) vol. 32, no. 49, 1979.

Herwarth, Hans von (with S. Frederick Starr). *Against Two Evils*. New York: Rawson Wade Publishers, Inc. 1981.

———. *Von Adenauer Zu Brandt: Erinnerunger, From Adenauer to Brandt: Memoires*. Berlin and Frankfurt: Propyläen. 1990.

Heygendorff, Ralph von. "Experience with volunteers of Soviet-Union Nations Fighting Bolshevism during World War II" (manuscript of lecture given in Uelzen, Germany, 4/1/1951).

Höhne, Heinz. *Canaris: Patriot im Zwielicht*. Munich: Bertelsmann, 1976.

Hoffmann, Joachim. *Die Geschichte der Wlassow—Armee, POA 2*, unaltered edition. Freiburg im Breisgau: Rombach. 1984.

———. *Kaukasien 1942/43: Das deutsche Heer und die Orientvölker der Sowjetunion*. Freiburg: Rombach Verlag. 1991.

———. *Die Ostlegionen. 1941–1943*. Freiburg: Rombach. 1986.

Iveria (journal). Various years, including No. 20 1978; November 1981; and April 1990. Editor in Chief, Mikhail Kavtaradze.

Jordania, Noe. *My Past*. Paris. 1953.

Kandelaki, Constantin. *The Georgian Question Before the Free World* (Acts – Documents – Evidence). Paris: Impr. de Navarre. 1953

Kennan, George F. *Memoirs 1925–1950*. Boston, Toronto: Atlantic-Little, Brown & Co. 1967.

———. *Russia and the West Under Lenin and Stalin*. New York and Toronto: Mentor Book/ The New American Library. 1961.

Kramarz, Joachim. *Stauffenberg, the Architect of the Famous July 20th Conspiracy to Assassinate Hitler*, translated from German by R. H. Barry. New York: MacMillan. 1967.

Kruse, Dr. Hans. *Stellungnahme zu Thorwald Buch, on General Heygendorf*, report. Göttingen: Institut für Völker. March 14, 1953, and May 27, 1953.

Lang, David Marshall. *A Modern History of Soviet Georgia*, New York: Grove Press, Inc. 1962.

Lomashvili, Pharnaoz. *On the History of the Georgian Emigration* (Soviet propaganda book, in Georgian). Tbilisi: publisher unknown. 1965.

Mamull (Georgian journal) No. 6. January 1953.

Nemirova, M. and E. Kalandadze. *In the Name of Life* (Soviet propaganda book, in Russian).

———. *The Secret Deeds of the Wehrmacht* (Soviet propaganda book, in Georgian).

Oberländer, Theodore. *Denkschriften aus dem Zweiten Weltkrieg: über die Behandlung der Sowjetvolkes.* Quellenstudien Der Zeitgeschichlichen Forschungsstelle Ingolstadt, Volume 2.

— — —. *History of the "Bergmann" Unit, Geschichte der Einheit "Bergmann"* (report). Munich: Josef M. Greska.1983.

— — —. Personal diary.

Persico, Joseph E. *Piercing the Reich: The Penetration of Nazi Germany by American Secret Agents during World War II.* New York: Viking. 1979.

Raschhofer, Hermann. *Political Assassination: The Legal Background of the Oberländer and Stashinsky Cases.* Tubingen, West Germany: F. Schlichtenmayer. 1964.

Raupach, Dr. Hans. "The Impact of the Great Depression on Eastern Europe." *Journal of Contemporary History.* London, 1963.

Resulzade, M. E. *Das Problem Azerbaijan.* Berlin-Charlottenburg: Verlag der Zeitschrift "Kurtulosch." 1938.

Rustaveli, Shota. "The Knight in Tiger's Skin." Various editions.

Sanders, A. (pseudonym for Alexander Nikuradze). *Kaukasien: Nordkaukasien, Aserbeidschan, Armenien, Georgien — Geschichtlicher Umriss.* München: Hoheneichen-Verlag. 1944.

— — —. *Osteuropa in kontinentaleuropaeischer Schau.* München: Hoheneichen-Verlag. 1942.

Schellenberg, Walter. *Hitler's Secret Service.* Moonachie, New Jersey: Pyramid. 1958.

Teske, Hermann. *General Ernst Köstring: Der militärische Mittler zwischen dem deutschen Reich und der Sowjetunion 1921-1941.* Frankfurt am Main: Mittler. 1966.

Tolstoy, Leo. *War and* Peace. Various editions.

Tolstoy, Nikolai. *The Secret Betrayal 1944-1947.* New York: Scribner. 1978.

Tsereteli, Mikhako von. *Das Neue Georgien. Eine Denkschrift, Nebsteinem Anhang* (presentation to the German Reichstag). June 24–25, 1918.

Weinberg, Gerhard L. "Munich After 50 Years." *Foreign Affairs.* Fall 1988.

Werth, Alexander. *Russia at War 1941–1946.* New York: E.P. Dutton. 1964.

Wheeler-Bennett, John. *The Nemesis of Power: The German Army in Politics 1918–1945,* New York: St. Martin's Press, 1954.

Young, Peter, ed. *The World Almanac of World War II.* New York: Pharos Books. 1981.

Zur Mühlen, Patrik von. *Zwischen Hakenkreuz und Sowjetstern.* Düssdeldorf: Droste Verlag. 1971.

Additional Literature from the Preface and Editors

Carrere d'Encausse, Helene. *L'empire éclaté. La révolte des nations en U.R.S.S.* Paris: Flammarion. 1978. (In German: *Risse im roten Imperium. Das Nationalitätenproblem in der Sowjetunion.* Wien-München-Zürich-Innsbruck: Verlag Fritz Molden. 1979.)

Eimermacher, Karl. *Die sowjetische Literaturpolitik 1917-1932. Von der Vielfalt zur Bolschewisierung der Literatur. Analyse und Dokumentation.* Bochum: Universitätsverlag Dr. N. Brockmeyer. 1994.

Gabliani, Egnate. *The Old and New Svaneti* (in Georgian). Tbilisi: S.S.S.R. Sakhelmtsipo Gamomtsemloba. 1925.

— — —. *Free Svaneti* (in Georgian). Tbilisi: Sakhelgami. 1927.

— — —. *Ibex in the Mountains of Svaneti* (in Georgian). Tbilisi: Sakhelgami. 1930.

Herwarth, Hans von (with S. Frederick Starr). *Against Two Evils.* New York: Rawson, Wade Publishers, Inc. 1981.

Jeloschek, Albert/Richter, Friedrich/Schütte, Ehrenfried/Semmler, Johannes. *Freiwillige vom Kaukasus. Georgier, Armenier, Aserbaidschaner, Tschetschenen u. a. auf deutscher Seite. Der "Sonderverband" Bergmann und sein Gründer Theodor Oberländer.* Graz und Stuttgart: Leopold Stocker Verlag. 2003.

Marshall, Alex. *The Caucasus under Soviet Rule.* London and New York: Routledge. 2010.

Oberländer, Theodor. *Der Osten und die Deutsche Wehrmacht. Sechs Denkschriften aus den Jahren 1941-43 gegen die NS-Kolonialthese.* Asendorf: MUT-Verlag.

Peter-Schwarz, Hans. *Konrad Adenauer: A German Politician and Statesman in a Period of War, Revolution and Reconstruction — The Statesman: 1952–1967.* New York: Berghahn Books. 1997.

Prishvin, Mikhail. *Diaries. 1932–1935* (in Russian). Saint Petersburg: Rostoc. 2009.

Robakidse, Grigol. *Das Schlangenhemd. Ein Roman des georgischen Volkes (Mit einem Geleitwort von Stefan Zweig).* Jena: Eugen Diederichs. 1928.

Robakidse, Grigol. "The Artistic Tbilisi" (in Russian). *Novy den.* No. 6, June 2, 1919.

Silling, Victor. *Die Hintergründe des Falles Oberländer.* Germany: Grenzland Verlag. 1960.

Stalin, Joseph. *Marxism and the National Question* (in Russian). Saint Petersburg: Priboy. 1914.

Struve, Kai. "Theodor Oberländer and the Nachtigall Battalion in 1959/60—an Entangled History of Propaganda, Politics, and Memory in East and West." *Slavic Review* 81 (3), February 2023: 677–700. DOI: 10.1017/slr.2022.228.

INDEX

GG refers to Givi Gabliani. Surnames starting with "von" are entered under the final surname. Many people are identified only by surname; where possible their rank or title is given. L.S. refers to "Liaison Staff."

www.ingramcontent.com/pod-product-compliance
Lightning Source LLC
Chambersburg PA
CBHW061130120626
46546CB00005B/1731